Knowledge & Information

Knowledge & Information
Studies in Information Science

Edited by

Wolfgang G. Stock (Düsseldorf, Germany)
and
Ronald E. Day (Bloomington, Indiana, U.S.A.)
Sonja Gust von Loh (Düsseldorf, Germany) – Associate Editor
Richard J. Hartley (Manchester, U.K.)
Robert M. Hayes (Los Angeles, California, U.S.A.)
Peter Ingwersen (Copenhagen, Denmark)
Michel J. Menou (Les Rosiers sur Loire, France, and London, U.K.)
Stefano Mizzaro (Udine, Italy)
Christian Schlögl (Graz, Austria)
Sirje Virkus (Tallinn, Estonia)

Knowledge and Information (K&I) is a peer-reviewed information science book series. The scope of information science comprehends representing, providing, searching and finding of relevant knowledge including all activities of information professionals (e.g., indexing and abstracting) and users (e.g., their information behavior). An important research area is information retrieval, the science of search engines and their users. Topics of knowledge representation include metadata as well as methods and tools of knowledge organization systems (folksonomies, nomenclatures, classification systems, thesauri, and ontologies). Informetrics is empirical information science and consists, among others, of the domain-specific metrics (e.g., scientometrics, webometrics), user and usage research, and evaluation of information systems. The sharing and the distribution of internal and external information in organizations are research topics of knowledge management. The information market can be defined as the exchange of digital information on networks, especially the World Wide Web. Further important research areas of information science are information ethics, information law, and information sociology.

De Gruyter Saur

Frank Linde, Wolfgang G. Stock

Information Markets

A Strategic Guideline
for the I-Commerce

De Gruyter Saur

ISBN 978-3-11-023609-5
e-ISBN 978-3-11-023610-1
ISSN 1868-842X

Bibliographic information published by the Deutsche Nationalbibliothek
The Deutsche Nationalbibliothek lists this publication in the Deutsche
Nationalbibliografie; detailed bibliographic data are available in the Internet
at http://dnb.d-nb.de.

Printing: Hubert & Co. GmbH & Co. KG, Göttingen
∞ Printed on acid-free paper

Printed in Germany

www.degruyter.com

Contents

Part B
Information Society

Preface

The markets for digital information–this means both software applications and all sorts of content (from blogs via images, films and games up to scientific articles and patents)–are different than markets for non-digital goods. When a non-digital good is purchased, it physically changes hands from the seller to the buyer. On the other hand, goods on information markets stay with the seller, buyers merely receiving a copy. Trade with digital information, which we call "I-Commerce" (in the sense of E-Commerce with information), mainly occurs with the aid of networks, particularly the internet. The products are thus characterizable as network goods. Here, too, there are particularities: network goods may have their basic value (for an operating system, this value might be, for instance, that it allows applications to run on a computer), but they receive an additional value via the number of their users (the more the better for the network) and via the number of complementary products (in our example: application programs that run on the operating system). A further particularity of these markets is the technically illegal "swapping" of digital information. To put it provocatively: there is theft on a scale that puts most other markets to shame. In light of the network effects (the more users the better), though, this does not have to be detrimental to the market in question–to the contrary, sometimes it can be useful.

Markets for digital information are the prototypical markets of the information and the knowledge societies or–following Manuel Castells (1996)–the network society. Many an author thinks we are on the threshold of an entirely new culture, the "multimedia culture" (Rauch, 1998). Such a transition to a new form of society or even culture goes hand in hand with a change in social values, a new sense of legal boundaries and a modified code of ethics. It is in front of this background that information markets develop the economic goods proper to them.

This book mainly deals with five research questions:

A. What particularities are displayed by pieces of digital information as economic goods?
B. In what environment (society, law, ethics) are information markets located?
C. What digital goods are traded on information markets?
D. What competitive strategies are pursued by providers on information markets?
E. Which role is played by piracy and the illegal information market?

The Spectrum of Digital Information Goods

In the early days of scientific endeavors toward the information market (from the nineteen-sixties onward), led by Peter F. Drucker (1959), Fritz Machlup (1962) and Marc Uri Porat (1977), among others, this concept is defined very broadly, encompassing all non-manual work. The delineation of the "knowledge worker" from all others was a rather arbitrary one (Webster, 1995). We consider to be more realistic. The approach of demarcating information markets works with two salient characteristics: on information markets, *digital* (or at the very least: generally digitizable) *information* is traded via the usage of *networks* (such as the internet).

Information markets are embedded in societal structures. This is why it is necessary to consider the conceptions and manifestations of the information, knowledge or network society. We will also lead an intensive expedition through the territories of information law. Considering the importance to information markets of free access to knowledge, of privacy and of dealing with intellectual property, it is unavoidable to take a look at information ethics.

Our book extensively analyzes the products and submarkets of I-Commerce. We look at products, the steps taken toward their production, their buyers as well as their providers' business strategies. An initial overview exemplifies the multitude of digital products:

- Business, market and press information,
- Legal information: norms, cases, annotations, citation services,
- STM information (scientific, technical and medical information): STM literature, bibliographical information services, facts,
- Search engines and content aggregators,
- Web 2.0 Services: sharing services, social bookmarking, knowledge bases, social networks,
- Commercial online music services,
- Internet TV,
- Digital games: "classical games", gambling, videos games, Massively Multiplayer Online Role Playing Games (MMORPGs), social games, games with a purpose,
- Software: products: system software, middleware, application software (each either as individual or as standard software), services: consulting and implementation services, software as a service.

Many goods–such as search engines and Web 2.0 services–are offered for free. The providers generate revenue by selling their customers' attention to advertisers. This is why internet advertising is an important subject to us. We are dealing with banner advertising, target-group-specific and personalized advertising, in-game advertising, permission-based marketing, context-specific advertising (such as "sponsored links" in search engines) and viral marketing.

I-Commerce: Mechanisms, Value Net, Strategic Variables

Competitive advantages are of great importance for information providers who want to be successful on information markets, in "I-Commerce", just as they are important to all providers on all markets. It is, however, necessary to account for the special characteristics of information goods in order to represent information providers' strategic positioning and courses of action. Three aspects are of central importance:

- the economic particularities (mechanisms) that occur in relation to information goods,
- the value net (stakeholder configuration), as well as
- the specific strategic variables that information providers can apply to gain competitive advantages.

From an economic perspective, is there anything special to be detected in information goods? Four *mechanisms* play a central role:

- dominant fixed costs,
- distinct information asymmetries,
- pronounced network effects and
- the tendency toward mutating into a public good.

In information goods, the production of the *first copy* is extremely expensive, compared to the cost of its reproduction. If we consider the sums expended upon a music title or movie, we will soon arrive at sums of several tens of thousands, or even millions, of Dollars. Once the software, the album or the film are finished, however, they can be reproduced nigh-on perfectly for a few Cents only. Furthermore, the transmission costs are very low for digital information goods. If a fast internet connection on a flat-rate basis is a given, data can be sent and received with no additional cost. This relation between very high fixed costs to very low variable costs leads to a pronounced unit cost reduction. This means that average costs per unit decrease very quickly when production numbers rise–boosted by the rapidly decreasing average fixed costs.

It can often be observed in information goods that one side of the market is better informed about the quality of its products than the other. A software provider knows his product, whereas the layman cannot assess its quality prior to a purchase and only partially afterward. Even an information professional should run into problems rating the quality of a search engine's sorting algorithms to any degree of exactitude, since providers of such search tools (let's say: Google and Yahoo!) may disclose a lot about patent writs, while keeping the details of their practical application tightly wrapped. Such unbalanced distributions of quality information is what we call *information asymmetries*. The value of an information good, e.g. the blueprint of a new production method or a chemical formula, can only be judged for good once the information has been received and processed (experienced). Once the information is in one's possession, however, the question becomes how high one's willingness to pay still is. In contrast to a new pair of shoes, information cannot be fully inspected prior to a purchase. Every kind of closer inspection leads to a disclosure of (parts of) the information, which runs counter to the provider's interests. Kenneth J. Arrow (1962, 615) has described this problem as an *information paradox*: "[...] there is a fundamental paradox in the determination of demand for information; its value for the purchaser is not known until he has the information, but then he has in effect acquired it without cost."

When buying an information good, it is often of great importance how many other users this good already has. If you want to buy a word processing or spreadsheet application, you will think long and hard about whether to buy the product of a small provider, which is not very widely used, or to whether to turn to the market standard. Before buying an operating system, it is important to know what application software it supports. Buying the program that is most prevalent offers distinct advantages, e.g. in the possibilities for swapping files or helping one another solve any problems that might arise. The case is similar for films, books or music. A provider like Amazon is successful because a lot of customers cooperate (partly without being aware of it), generating basic information for recommendations via their clicking and buying behavior or consciously submitting ratings and comments. Facebook is mainly used because many others also use it, and because the individual can maintain many friendships or other contacts in this way, even internationally. Perhaps one or the other user also uses Facebook because of its neat additional offers, such as the games. Hence, in information goods the decisive factors are how many users the product is able to bind (*direct network effect*) and how many related products are available on the market (*indirect network effect*).

Whether goods are to be classed as *private* or *public* is decided, according to standard economics textbooks, via the two criteria of user rivalry and the principle of exclusion. User rivalry or user competition is what we call when usage of a good deprives others of the option of using it as well. Information goods can be used by many people without being used up, or consumed. An information good does not decrease with usage. When a person acquires a certain knowledge via processing information, this does not decrease the odds of another person acquiring the same knowledge. As opposed to many other goods, one need only think of a pair of trousers or a chocolate bar, the same information can be used by a multitude of people at the same time. There is thus generally no user rivalry in the traditional sense. It is more appropriate for the characterization of information goods to focus on changes to the benefits enjoyed by user (in terms of software) and informed party (in terms of content), respectively, when an information good is widely distributed. These changes can be very aptly described via network effects. They can be positive when the existing network becomes more valuable due to its increased usership, i.e. when its participants are increasingly better off. This is the case, for example, when one is able to communicate with a growing number of people about certain events or in a certain language. The network effects can also be negative, however, when the growth is to the participants' detriment. An undesired communication of a private or business secret would be a fitting example for this scenario. The principle of exclusion is not applicable to public goods as it is to private ones. This means that people who are unwilling to pay for usage of a good cannot be excluded from using it anyway. This is a grave problem for information providers in particular, since information goods are easily distributed without the provider being able to control it. This goes both for information that started out being known in a small circle (e.g. plans concerning a new research result in the R&D department) and, particularly, information that has already been widely released (e.g. in the company bulletin or even as a specialist publication via open access). The further usage of such information goods can hardly be controlled by the provider anymore. Information goods thus display the strong *tendency to become public goods*.

Each of the four economic mechanisms of information goods described bears a great potential for *market failure*. Market failure is what the economist talks about when the market results are less than ideal when compared to a reference model. Following microeconomic standard textbooks, we would even have to suppose that no market can be created for information goods at all. Several examples illustrate this problem.

What company will offer goods that cost large sums to produce but for which it is unclear whether they will ever reach the high unit sales required in order to recoup these costs? Big providers with a large market share have a distinct advantage in this scenario. What's more, the copy costs are not only very low for legal users, but also for all illegal ones, which means that one must always expect the distribution of pirated copies to impair legal sales.

What provider wants to be active on a market where he will have to disclose his product to the customer for processing prior to a sale? Potential customers want to be as certain as possible that they will like the music, film, book etc. or that the software will suit their purposes.

Who wants to enter a market as provider where the customers will tend to settle for a product that is widely used rather than a high-quality product? Established providers enjoy immense advantages.

Who is prepared to offer goods on a market where one cannot, only with great difficulty, make sure that the buyers will actually pay for their usage? And what customer pays for a product that he could also have for free?

The starting point to *Competitive Strategies of Information Providers* occurs via the introduction of the instrument of industry analysis. In order to systematically comprehend an industry, there is the so-called "Five Forces" model developed by Porter (1980). According to this model, there are five fundamental forces that, put together, make up the attractiveness of an industry. Individually, they are the rivalry between the competitors extant in the industry, the market power of suppliers and buyers as well as the threat posed by replacement products and potential competitors.

The Value Net model by Nalebuff and Brandenburger (1996) is much better suited to describe the stakeholders active on an information market, however. This model stresses that there are not only competitive but also cooperative relationships in a market, and that they are of great importance to business success. This combination of competition and cooperation–co-opetition–ends, in contrast to Porter's Five Forces model, in a slightly modified model of market analysis. Nalebuff and Brandenburger speak not only of forces that threaten profitability, but also of a *Value Net*, in which different agents are able to create values collaboratively. Apart from the usual stakeholders, like customers, competitors and suppliers, which Porter also talks about, the Value Net explicitly makes allowances for co-operative relationships.

Complements play a hugely important role on information markets, since it is always necessary to have some form of end device in order to be able to use digital information goods. Music files cannot be used without a player, eBooks cannot be read without a reader and application software is useless without a computer. How then, taking into account the particularities of information goods, can value nets be designed in such a way that they can lead to competitive advantages? In every textbook, strategic considerations end with the question "What is the basis on which companies develop their competitive advantages?" Here, too, the doyen of strategy, Michael Porter, has wielded enormous influence. He shaped strategic management by stating that companies generally have two strategic alternatives for gaining competitive advantages: the differentiation strategy and the cost/price leadership strategy. Porter's fundamental thoughts on positioning are directed at traditional markets, however. Since information goods are clearly different from traditional goods, they also require different competitive strategies. Porter's strategy alternatives do not become obsolete, but they have to be used in new variants on information markets. In their fundamental work "Information Rules–A Strategic Guide to the Network Economy", Carl Shapiro and Hal R. Varian (1998) offer multifarious starting points that are of great importance for information providers' strategy development. Their work has strongly influenced the debate about strategy, particularly from the perspective of the software industry. We worked out a total of seven strategic variables that are of towering importance for information goods:

- Timing of Market Entry,
- Pricing,
- Compatibility Management (Standardization),
- Complement Management,
- Copy Protection Management,
- Signaling,
- Lock-In Management.

These seven aspects are *strategic variables* due to being "manageable", i.e. subject to entrepreneurial influence. Such decision variables, or action parameters, can be used by companies in such a way that certain goals can be reached, relating for instance to market share, brand recognition or revenue.

The three aspects introduced above (mechanisms of the information market, value net and strategic variables) are summarized in a model, complemented by the technological (e.g. provision of broadband connections) and the institutional environment (e.g. the configuration of copyright). With the help of this model (see p. 358), information markets can be analyzed and design recommendations deduced.

It is possible, for example, to use the strategic variable *timing of market entry* to influence the different stakeholder groupings. Thus the timing of the market entry affects customers' willingness to pay, suppliers' readiness to collaborate, complementors' interest in creating complementary products as well as the competition's endeavors toward creating competing offers. The stakeholders' actions, in turn, influence the degree to which economic mechanisms take effect on information goods. If many customers decide to buy a new product, this will attract followers who also want to have the product. Such direct network effects can be observed quite clearly in the case of the recently released iPad. At the same time, expectations for a large number of customers affects the offer of complements. Indirect network effects arise, such as publishers' eBook offers for the iPad.

The mechanisms can also be addressed directly via some strategic variables, such as *copy protection management*. A software, for instance, which is brought on the market early in a beta version without copy protection–a fairly common practice, by the way, in release changes by Microsoft–can spread very quickly but also uncontrollably and is thus pretty much to be regarded as a public good. So here too, network effects begin to work. Direct network effects arise via exchange of data in new formats or early communication about the software, indirect ones via complementary product developments, as can be very nicely observed in the number of apps, which were developed with great speed at the time of the iPhone's release.

Another example for a direct influence on the mechanisms can be seen in *signaling*, which is when preannouncements are made concerning a product release, for example. This can be used to reduce information asymmetries by giving customers early information about a new product and its release date. At the same time, though, this can increase information asymmetries, if for example the competitors' hand is forced because they are unable to accurately estimate what features the new product will have.

Feedback may act from mechanisms to stakeholders. A broad offer of *complements* (e.g. movies in the HD format) boosts further sales of HD TVs. A greater demand in turn gives the provider pricing latitude. This serves as an example for the reaction of a stakeholder grouping to the strategic variables, in this case *pricing*.

There are also, however, direct reactions of mechanisms to strategic variables. Thus network effects play a crucial role for a successful *market entry*. The stronger they are, the harder it will be for a pioneer to survive, since neither customers nor complementors want to make an early commitment.

Piracy on Information Markets

Piracy occurs massively in information and knowledge societies. The production of illegal copies with no loss in quality challenges–thus the industry associations–many of the traditional business models for information goods. The music industry in particular complains of massive losses in revenue due to the multitude of illegal access paths to the information good music. Why do people bootleg? There is a variety of reasons, such as gender, age, income, technical know-how, available bandwidth or legal alternative offers. To put it very simplistically, male students can be termed the core group of pirates.

The question as to what concrete damage piracy causes, however, must be deemed an open one from a scientific point of view. A large number of studies from the music industry have arrived at differing results. They run the gamut from extremely strong negative effects, where every illegal copy substitutes a purchase, to positive effects, where illegal downloads even boost legal sales. If we take into consideration the studies' quality, we can see that negative effects cannot yet be cleanly proven.

What are information providers' scopes for design in the face of piracy? Educational work is to be preferred to criminalization, and a further tightening of copyright appears counterproductive. The central factor is the offer of attractive (legal) commercial offers in connection with innovative pricing models and new, creative usage options of the information goods for sale.

Remarks on Citations

A short note on the literature cited: Since the chapters each represent a unit, the sources are listed at the end of a chapter. For reasons of space, there is no summary of all cited sources at the end of the book. Sources from the internet are always marked "online". Due to the length of many URLs, we decided not to state the exact Web address. The interested reader will locate such sources via his or her search engine of choice. These websites are up to date as of early 2011.

Some of our quotations are in their original version in German language. All those quotations were translated by us.

Target Groups

This book is the result of the cooperation between an economist and an information scientist. We thus aim to address fellow scholars and all students of both disciplines. *Information Markets* is a comprehensive overview of the state of the art of economic and information-scientific endeavors on the markets of digital information–software as well as content. We address the following groups in particular:

- Economists (economics and business administration),
- Library and Information Scientists,
- Computer Scientists,
- Students of these disciplines,
- Professionals on the markets for information.

Acknowledgements

This book has resulted from the effort of many. The following persons contributed intensively toward the fruition of this work: *Anneliese Volkmar* obtained literature (frequently hard to access) and created a lot of the graphics. *Lisa Beutelspacher* compiled the index. *Paul Becker* translated the original German text into English. Many thanks to all! Without their help, this book might not have been.

Köln and Düsseldorf, Germany
Spring 2011

Bibliography

Arrow, K.J. (1962). Economic welfare and the allocation of resources for invention. In The Rate and Direction of Inventive Activity. Economic and Social Factors. A Report by the National Bureau of Economic Research, New York (pp. 609-626). Princeton, NJ: Princeton University Press.

Castells, M. (1996). The Rise of the Network Society. Malden, MA: Blackwell.

Drucker, P.F. (1959). The Landmarks of Tomorrow. London: Heinemann.

Machlup, F. (1962). The Production and Distribution of Knowledge in the United States. Princeton, NJ: Princeton University Press.

Nalebuff, B.J., & Brandenburger, A.M. (1996). Co-opetition. New York, NY: Doubleday.

Porat, M.U. (1977). Information Economy. 9 Vols. Washington, DC: Office of Telecommunications. (OT Special Publication 77-12[1]–77-12[9]).

Porter, M.E. (1980). Competitive Strategy. Techniques for Analyzing Industries and Competitors. 62th printing. New York, NY: Free Press.

Rauch, W. (1998). Informationsethik. Die Fragestellung aus der Sicht der Informationswissenschaft. In Kolb, A., Esterbauer, R., & Ruckenbauer, H.W. (eds.): Cyberethik. Verantwortung in der digital vernetzten Welt (pp. 51-57). Stuttgart, Berlin, Köln: Kohlhammer.

Shapiro, C., & Varian, H.R. (1998). Information Rules. A Strategic Guide to the Network Economy. Boston, MA: Harvard Business School.

Webster, F. (1995). Theories of the Information Society. London, New York, NY: Routledge.

Part A

Propedeutics of Dealing with the Information Market

Chapter 1

History of Exploring the Information Market

1.1 Knowledge Workers in the Knowledge Economy

Information–understood as knowledge set in motion (as in a patent document, for instance)–and knowledge itself (e.g. the concrete content of the patented invention) first became the focus of economic studies around 1960. However, this does not mean that information had become an economic good all of a sudden. From the beginning of the modern era, especially pointedly in Francis Bacon's "knowledge is power" at the beginning of the 17th century (Stock, 2007, 26 et seq.), through Enlightenment and particularly in the course of the industrial revolution, the significance of information has been steadily on the rise (Ortner, 2006). Peter F. Drucker (1959) and Fritz Machlup (1962) in the U.S.A., as well as Tadao Umesao (1963) and Yujiro Hayashi (1969) in Japan (Duff et al., 1996) were the first to have pointed out this significance of knowledge for society and economics. In the period following, the terms

- Knowledge Industry / Information Industry,
- Knowledge Economy / Information Economy,
- Knowledge Society / Information Society

were coined, which are, respectively, viewed as more or less quasi-synonymous or as part-whole relations. Added to them were the terms

- Knowledge Worker / Information Worker.

With the advent of services and the foreseeable loss of jobs in the industry, Peter F. Drucker (1959, 91) "discovered" the **"knowledge workers"**, who do little manual but a lot of intellectual work:

> Productive work, in today's society and economy, is work that applies vision, knowledge and concepts–work that is based on the mind rather than the hand.

This was accompanied with a new form of organizing enterprises (Drucker, 1959, 50 et seq.):

> The principles and concepts which automation applies to mechanical production-work have earlier been developed for non-mechanical work in the business enterprise. They are fast becoming the rule for the work of all those who are not 'workers' in the traditional usage of the word, but who work productively as technicians, professionals and managers.

Drucker was less concerned with knowledge itself than with the management of the companies that employ knowledge workers. Knowledge work is accomplished in teams, and knowledge workers are either (as a rule) directly integrated into the company or at the very least closely tied to it. Joseph (2005, 249) observes that

> knowledge is not treated explicitly and it is the organization that is in control. Knowledge workers do not have a real definition if they are not associated with an organization.

The publication "The Production and Distribution of Knowledge in the United States" (1962) by the Austrian-born Fritz Machlup was seminal for the economic exploration of the information market. Machlup was one of the first to formulate knowledge as static and information as dynamic. Knowledge is not transmitted; only information is subject to being sent and received (Stock, 2007, Ch. 3). Machlup (1962, 15) defines:

> to *inform* is an activity by which knowledge is conveyed; to *know* may be the result of having been informed. „Information" as the act of informing is designed to produce a state of knowing in someone's mind. „Information" as that which is being communicated becomes identical with „knowledge" in the sense of which is known. Thus, the difference lies not in the nouns when they refer to *what* one knows or is informed about; it lies in the nouns only when they are to refer to the *act* of informing and the *state* of knowing, respectively.

Knowledge–as in knowledge representation (Stock & Stock, 2008, 20 et seq.)–is defined very broadly, comprising "knowing how" and "knowing that", implicit and explicit, subjective and objective as well as scientific and every-day knowledge. Machlup (1962, 19) inclines to agree with Hayek (1945), who introduced knowledge in terms of a critique of Neoclassical Theory. While this theory (falsely, according to Hayek) assumes the prevalence of perfective information (consumers about prices, companies about production technologies etc.), Hayek stresses that information is never simply "a given" for an entire economy, but are distributed entirely unevenly, depending on the economic agent. Benoît Godin (2008a, 9-10) emphasizes:

> In Hayek's hands, the concept of knowledge was used as a criticism of perfect information in economic theory. ... In real life, no one has perfect information, but they have the capacity and skill to find information.

Machlup (1962, 21 et seq.) classifies knowledge into five types:
- practical knowledge,
  - professional knowledge,
  - business knowledge,
  - knowledge of the worker,
  - political knowledge,
  - knowledge in the household,
  - other practical knowledge,
- intellectual knowledge,
- small-talk knowledge,
- spiritual knowledge,
- unwanted, superfluous knowledge.

It is a matter of both the production of said knowledge and its distribution via information. Godin (2008a, 12) summarizes Machlup's conception of knowledge:

> Defining knowledge as composed of all kinds of knowledge ... was the first aspect of Machlup's definition of knowledge. The second was defining knowledge as both its production and distribution. To Machlup, information is knowledge only if it is communicated and used.

Machlup also regards the labor market of knowledge producers (1962, 393), but centre stage is taken by the knowledge economy's contribution toward the total valuation of a national economy (Webster, 1995, 11). According to Machlup, the following industries come under Knowledge Economy in the total economic account:
- education (domestic education, schools, universities, job training, education in church and the military, libraries),
- research and development (basic research, applied research and development),
- communication media (print products, photography, stage and cinema, broadcast and television, advertising, telecommunication media such as telephony and mail),
- "information machines" (printing machines, music instruments, film projectors, telephones, signaling systems, measuring instruments, typewriters, electronic computers, other office machines and their parts),

- "information services" (professional services: law, engineering, accounts, medicine, financial services, wholesalers, other business services, government).

In data acquisition, Machlup uses diverse sources outside official statistics, such as figures by the National Science Foundation, and also makes informed estimates. Machlup presents figures for every single industry of the Knowledge Economy, as well as aggregates for the industry level, which at the very least come close to measuring its valuation. Godin (2008a, 20) regards this as the essentials of Machlup's approach:

> Machlup then arrived at his famous estimate: the knowledge economy was worth $136.4 million, or 29% of GNP in 1958, had grown at a rate of 8.8% per year over the period 1947-58, and occupied people representing 26.9% of the national income.

In summary, Machlup discusses the effects of the further development of the Knowledge Industry on the labor market. His result points into two directions: (1.) The labor market for knowledge workers is getting larger (Machlup, 1962, 396-397):

> (W)hile the ascendary of knowledge-producing occupations has been an uninterrupted process, there has been a succession of occupations leading this movement, first clerical, then administrative and managerial, and now professional and technical personnel. Thus, the changing employment pattern indicates a continuing movement from manual to mental, and from less to more highly trained labor.

The last sentence of this quote already hints at the second trend. (2.) The labor market for untrained labor shrinks (Machlup, 1962, 397):

> If employment opportunities continue to improve for high-level-knowledge-producing labor and to worsen for unskilled manual labor, the danger of increasing unemployment among the latter becomes more serious.

Roughly ten years after Machlup's "Knowledge Economy", Daniel Bell (1973) called the goal of this development the "postindustrial society" and, a further six years later, the "information society" (Bell, 1979). The characteristics of such a postindustrial society are the prevalence of services on the labor market, at which point we have to critically parenthesize that not all services are automatically information services (Webster, 1995, 40). Alvin Toffler's "Third Wave" (1980) also describes–after agriculture (first wave) and industry (second wave)–his third wave as a postindustrial society.

1.2   Information Economy as Fourth Sector

A nine-volume work by Marc Uri Porat, dating from 1977, refines Machlup's approach and provides detailed statistical data of the United States' Information Economy. He thus lays the foundation for regarding information as an independent fourth economic sector, and acknowledging that this sector dominates the economy as a whole. Porat (1977, 2) defines "information" very broadly:

> Information is not a homogeneous good or service such as milk or iron ore. It is a collection or a bundle of many heterogeneous goods and services that together comprise an *activity* in the U.S. economy. For example, the informational requirements of organizing a firm include such diverse activities as research and development, managerial decision making, writing letters, filing invoices, data processing, telephone communication, and producing a host of memos, forms, reports, and control mechanisms. ...
>
> Information is data that have been organized and communicated. The information activity includes all the resources consumed in producing, processing and distributing information goods and services.

Mainly, there are two fundamental differences to Machlup's approach (Porat, 1977, 44). Porat draws data and definitions for economic branches from official statistics and divides the Information Economy into two areas, the primary and the secondary information market. The **primary information sector** summarizes all branches that produce information machines or sell information services on (established) markets (Porat, 1977, 15). Information services have two central aspects: they are sold on markets and their utilization installs knowledge in the buyer (Porat, 1977, 22).

> The end product of all information service markets is knowledge. An information market enables the consumer to know something that was not known beforehand.

The **secondary information sector** comprises all sorts of bureaucracy, company administration as well as government agencies (Porat, 1977, 15 et seq.):

> It includes the costs of organizing firms, maintaining markets, developing and transmitting prices, regulating markets, monitoring the firm's behavior and making and enforcing rules.

These services of the secondary information sector are not offered on the market but performed internally in companies or the apparatus of state.

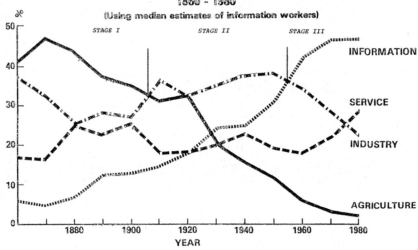

Figure 1.1: Development of the U.S. work force in the four sectors after Porat. Source: Porat, 1977, 121.

Porat, too, calculates figures that express the information market's contribution to the overall economy, but most influential were his estimates concerning the labor market. The "information workers" (Porat, 1977, 105) are employed in three areas (Porat, 1977, 107):

- in organizations that offer their products on information markets ("markets for information"); among them knowledge producers (scientists, lawyers, architects etc.) as well as knowledge distributors (mainly teachers and librarians),
- in organizations corresponding to the secondary information market ("information in markets"); among them accountants, insurance agents, salesmen as well as managers,
- in organizations that produce or operate information infrastructure, i.e. those that work with computers, telecommunication and non-electronic information machines (e.g. printing presses).

Porat translates the manpower into the sum of information workers' income and arrives at the following figures for the year 1967 (Porat, 1977, 107):

Markets for Information	
Knowledge Producers	$47m
Knowledge Distributers	$28m

Information in Markets

Market Search & Coordination Specialists	$93m
Information Processors	$61m

Information Infrastructure

Information Machine Workers	$13m

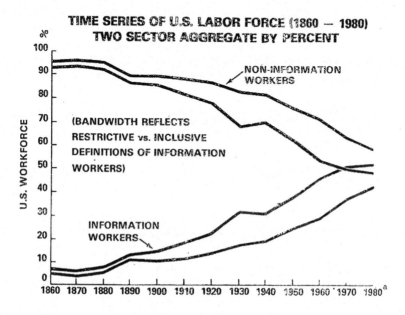

a 1980 projections supplied by the Bureau of Labor Statistics (unpublished).

Figure 1.2: Development of the U.S. work force by information workers and non-information workers. Source: Porat, 1977, 120.

This corresponds to an overall volume of $242m for the information market, or 53.2% of the United States' entire earned income. The rest of the labor market is made up by agriculture, industry and other services (Porat, 1977, 117 et seq.). The first phase ("Stage I") is dominated by agriculture, whereas the labor market in Stage II belongs mainly to industry. Today, in Stage III, information work is dominant. In an aggregation of this data into only two sectors (information workers / others), we see a convergence, starting approx. in the middle of the 1960s, of both labor markets' volumes to around 50%. In the face of such a description, it seems natural to believe in the existence of an information society (at least in the U.S.A.). Frank Webster (1995, 12) comments on this:

> The quantification of the economic significance of information is an impressive achievement. It is not surprising that those convinced of the emergence of an 'information society' have routinely returned to Machlup and especially Porat as authoritative demonstrations of a rising curve of information activity, one set to lead the way to a new age.

However, diverse problems hide in Machlup's and Porat's deliberations (Robinson, 1986; Schement, 1990). Delimiting information activities from all others is highly arbitrary. Neither theory gives appropriate space to all the services not belonging to the information market. All people who do not obviously and exclusively work "with their hands", are information workers per definitionem. A clear distinction between "thinking" and "doing" is impossible, particularly for the secondary information sector, which means that all secretarial and accounting activities are not regarded as services but as information work. Webster (1995, 16) is very skeptical:

> Librarian, for example, can encompass someone spending much of the day issuing books for loan and reshelving, as well as someone routinely involved in advising academics on the best sources of information for progressing state-of-the-art research. Is it really sensible to lump together such diversity?

1.3   "Information Superhighways"

From the late 1970s through to the 1990s, the information society has become the subject of national and international political programs. The point is the *creation* of the information society—with a view also to strengthening national economies and labor markets via political measures, as there is a continuing discussion on the effects of technological progress on the job situation. One side holds that the rationalizing component of technological progress will lead to redundancies, and as a consequence, to underemployment and technological unemployment. The other side sees technological progress as the precondition for economic growth, with production growth, in turn, the precondition for employment (Stock, 1997).

With regard to the information society, there is a fundamental difference to the earlier discussion (Stock, 1997). There has always been technological progress locally, in the sense that it has led to innovations in a particular technology or economic sector. If there have been redundancies, in the end progress still led to new jobs being created elsewhere, and all in all the job situation more or less stayed the same. **Information-technical progress**, however, works on a global scale; it has consequences for all economic sectors and industries. This could lead to a loss of jobs in agriculture, industry and services. The opposite could also happen: the information society will manage, despite all rationalization effects, to achieve positive labor market aspects.

The negative scenario is invoked by Jeremy Rifkin (1995), for example, who sees us heading for "The End of Work". The positive scenario is mainly the product of the political programs for building the information society. Jobs in the information society are created by the providers of information (e.g. in the industry for computer manufacturing or entertainment electronics as well as by service providers in software and content production) as well as its users (e.g. in public administration or management). In the sense of a "Big Bang" (Pelton, 1994, 182), the new jobs of the information society clash, creating entirely new employment structures.

An early expert testimony on the government's role in creating the information society was submitted by Simon Nora and Alain Minc (1978). They coined the neologism "**telematics**", in the sense of a connection between telecommunication and informatics, thus endorsing the coalescence of both areas. Nora and Minc observe that the government cannot effect the change toward the information society by itself; however, it can so shape the underlying conditions that the hoped-for development is allowed to occur in the first place. The advancing computerization is proving to be one of the driving forces (Weygand, 2004).

The greatest influence on the development of the information society is wielded by the American programs for creating the information infrastructure, toward the implementation of which then-U.S. Vice President Al Gore contributed significantly. In one of the first programs (Information Infrastructure Task Force, 1993), relating exclusively to the **U.S.A.**, the **National Information Infrastructure** (NII) is sketched, which would later find its popular appellation in "Information Superhighways". The NII is

> a seamless web of communications' networks, computers, databases, and consumer electronics that will put vast amounts of information at users' fingertips.

The international expansion of the NII is the **Global Information Infrastructure** (GII) (Information Infrastructure Task Force, 1995). Al Gore (1996, 2) motivated the GII by stressing the international component, which is vital for the information society:

> We will not enjoy all of the benefits of the National Information Infrastructure ("NII") unless it is linked to a global network of networks, a GII, linking every country, every town, every village, providing not just telephone service, but high-speed data and video as well. Such a global network would enable Americans to communicate across national boundaries and continental distances as easily as we communicate across state separations today. Time zones, not cost, will be the biggest barrier to keeping in touch with family, friends, and co-workers, no matter where they are.

According to Gore (1996, 3), five principles governed the construction of the NII and the GII: private investment, competition, universal service, free market access and flexible regulations.

Also at the beginning of the 1990s, the **European Union** discussed its path toward the information society (Stock, 1995; Stock, 1996a; Stock, 1996b). The fundamental planning paper is the "White Paper" from 1993, written under Jacques Delors' guidance, which introduces the information society as "the centrepiece of the twenty-first century's development model"–"Europe hinges upon it" (European Commission, 1993, 14). Expectations in the information society are very high (European Commission, 1993, 110):

> The community's policy for creating a common information area intensifies competition and increases Europe's competitiveness. It creates new jobs and should go hand in hand with special measures facilitating change in both economy and society, allowing every citizen to gain employment according to his or her qualifications.

The White Paper's statements are made more concrete by a working group led by Martin Bangemann (1994). As in the White Paper, the **Bangemann Group's report** puts the building blocks of the information society on top of each other, in a layer model. The bottom layer is made up of the networks and the technical facilities of data compression. The second layer contains the basic services (such as e-mail). In the last layer are the applications; paradigmatically, ten layers are worked out in which pioneer work is meant to be accomplished for the creation of the information society. Rather neglected in the White Paper as in the Bangemann Report, information contents are given due consideration in the European Commission's action plan "Europe's Way to the Information Society". The layer model is thus complemented by another layer and closed. For the EU Commission, there are two large groups of content; firstly audiovisual programs (films, TV productions and other multimedia applications), and secondly "high-quality information resources" (European Commission, 1994, 18). In the program "Info 2000" (European Commission, 1995), information contents take center stage. Here the market for content is split into three segments: print publications (newspapers, books, magazines etc.), electronic publications (online databases, teletext services etc.) as well as audiovisual content (television, video, radio, audio and cinema).

The programs for creating Information Superhighways prove successful, as long as the underlying technological infrastructure of the information market is being tackled. Around the same time (early 1990s), the World Wide Web appeared as the basic internet service; first search engines like Yahoo! and AltaVista counteract the chaos of the non-trawlable mass of digital content.

1.4 "New Economy"

With the advent and quick success of the WWW, several authors asked themselves whether the new "internet age" would also give rise to a "new economy", formed in such a way that it would override the previously known economic regularities and replace them with new ones. Looking back, we have to state, for business formations–and, particularly, the valuations of these businesses–that the history of the "New Economy" is the story of an error.

Picot and Scheuble (2000, 22) use the term "intellectual capital" to denote the knowledge of a company, and they (negatively) define this term as follows:

> Highly simplified, and abstracting from valuation problems as well as from market psychology, intellectual capital in listed companies corresponds to the difference between the market and the book value of an enterprise.

The market value is calculated via the product, consisting of market rate and number of shares, and the book value is noted in the balance sheet, representing the company's assets. In New Economy enterprises, this difference between market and book value proved to be gigantic. Following Picot and Scheuble, these companies thus had to have a fortune in intellectual capital. However, as investors had to find out when the New Economy collapsed, the difference turned out not to be "intellectual capital" but merely a bubble of "hot air", caused by feelings of euphoria; they were thus not the expression of new economic regularities, but instead of market-psychological circumstances (from which our authors abstracted–falsely, as we know today). Such market-psychological effects, observed in the New Economy, are in no way a new phenomenon. Such behaviors could already be seen during the Netherlands' "tulip mania" of 1636/37 (Baddeley & McCombie, 2001). The price for tulip bulbs rose sky-high (one single bulb commanded prices that rose to several times the annual income of a craftsman), only to take a drastic fall shortly after, alighting on a more realistic price range. This cost some tulip dealers their livelihood; the flowers themselves, however, are still blooming in Holland.

What, then, is the realistic economic core of this economy, previously deemed new by some? Kevin Kelly (1997; 1998) goes the furthest; he is actually convinced that the New Economy has features not even hinted at until today. Far more cautious are J. Bradford DeLong and A. Michael Froomkin with their "Next Economics" (2000), as well as probably the New Economy's most influential theoreticians, Carl Shapiro and Hal R. Varian (1998; 2003) with their conception of the "Network Economy", or "Information Economy", respectively. The authors agree that the information market displays all features of a **Network Economy**. Networks have, in fact, always existed (we need only think of railways or electricity grids), yet they command a dominant position in the information society in two respects: real networks are the information society's central infrastructures. The (information) goods traded on information markets may themselves represent networks, of the virtual kind. Such networks display so-called **network effects**, meaning that their value increases the more participants they have (direct network effect) and the larger the offer of complementary products is (indirect network effects). The consequence of this "the-bigger-the-better" phenomenon is that standards often take shape which dominate a market. Users–end customers and companies both–are "trapped" within a standard, as the costs of switching (from one office software to another within a company, for example) may get very high; no network is possible without standards, and if a standard has reached critical mass, positive feedback will create a situation where the "winning" standard generally asserts itself. This last aspect quickly clashes with conventional antitrust legislation (Shapiro & Varian, 2003, 61). These laws protect the market by requiring several competing companies within any one industry, whereas network economy prognosticates the market dominance of a single standard (which may even be coupled with a single company). The second particularity of the information market is in the **business good of "digital information"** (Shapiro & Varian, 2003, 49 et seq.). Such goods are costly to produce but extremely cheap to reproduce; the legal protection of these goods is very difficult to survey and implement, so that some providers distribute certain information products for free ("follow the free!"; Kelly, 1997), generating their profits elsewhere. Commercially distributed information is never a search good, as its quality can under no circumstances be adequately assessed prior to purchasing them; lastly, information markets (as ad-financed television did before) use attention as their currency, which also generates profit. Hence, the "core" of the New Economy turns out to be the meeting of networks and digital content, where economic particularities can definitely be encountered.

1.5   Digital Information Services

What kinds of information are offered digitally, via networks? Whereas the "broad" approach of the information market, originating from Machlup and Porat, declares all non-bodily activities to be information work, the "narrow" approach starts with digital information goods. Some early market surveys were published by the **"Information Market Observatory"** (IMO) of the European Union's Commission. The IMO analyses the submarkets of online databases (IMO, 1989a), CD-ROM (IMO, 1991), teletext services (IMO, 1989c) and audiotext services (IMO, 1991). Even summarizing studies–e.g. on the European market (Casey, 1991; Schwuchow & Stroetmann, 1991; Bredemeier & Stock, 2000) hardly go beyond this small area of focus. Commercially distributed content is at the center of attention (Bredemeier & Stock, 2000, 228):

> We define "electronic information services" as electronic products that
> are distributed either online, via specific data nets (such as X.25 or the
> internet, or via teletext), or offline (as CD-ROM or Floppy Disks), and

in which the information content (knowledge) takes center stage; in other words, they are the totality of products offered by the information economy's industry... on the market, with commercial purposes.

With the success of the internet and of the information offered for free on the World Wide Web, the IMO broadened its observation radius to include the internet (IMO, 1994). The restricted perspective on priced content is opened up, and content is now understood to comprise all sorts of knowledge (IMO, 1995, 9 et seq.):

> Originally, the IMO... concentrated on the relatively restricted area of electronic information services–the co-called traditional online ASCII database services, teletext and CD-ROM services as well as audiotext and fax-based services. In 1993/94, the perspective was broadened with regard to the now more extensive environment of the information service industry. This is meant to accommodate the phenomenon of convergence, which can be observed in a whole series of information-based sectors. The hardware and software industry, the telecommunication industry, the cable and satellite industry, all areas dealing with information content, such as film, television, music and print media, and of course the area of electronic information services display a tendency to converge in their striving toward markets and their technological development.

Relating to content, two approaches exist side by side. The goal of the "narrow" information market is to sell content, the goal of the New Economy's broad information market is to distribute information contents for free and charging customers' attention. For Rainer Kuhlen (1995), there is an additional third market, which is strictly non-profit-oriented and which he calls the "information forum". Here, predominantly scientific information is exchanged.

The **OECD** has developed a "guide" for recording indicators for the information society (OECD, 2005; Godin, 2008b, 54-61). As in the IMO (1995), here too the overall focus is on information and communication technology *and* information contents. Information contents become the subject of the information society in their digital online form exclusively (OECD, 2005, 58):

> According to this definition, digitised products include both:
>
> Products (such as reports, movies, music and software) which can be delivered over the Internet in digitised form and have a physical analogue (such as CD or DVD). For those products, the analogy with the physically delivered product is direct (*e.g.* a downloaded movie file and a DVD of that movie, an MP3 file and a CD); and other digitised products where the analogy with a physical product is less direct, for in-

> stance, new kinds of Web-based products which are accessed on line. They include online news, information or financial services and online games (…).

Why does the OECD thus place digital online content at the center of its considerations (OECD, 2005, 60)?

> It is clear that digital content–and digital delivery of content–are increasing in significance, driven by enhanced technological capabilities, a rapid uptake of broadband technologies and improved performance of hardware and software.

In the North American industry classification **NAICS** (2002), the information industry is at the first hierarchy level of the system–i.e. on the same level as, for instance, wholesaling, education or industry (Stock & Stock, 2008, 218). Sector 51 (Information) is classified into seven groups:

511   Publishing industries (except Internet), containing 5112: Software publishers,
512   Motion picture and sound recording industries,
515   Broadcasting (except Internet),
516   Internet publishing and broadcasting,
517   Telecommunications,
518   Internet service providers, Web search portals, and data processing services,
519   Other information services.

Manuel **Castells** (1996) devises a layer model of the internet industry, which is provider-oriented and considers four layers:
- Layer 1: Companies providing internet infrastructures (telecommunication companies, internet providers, manufacturers of network supplies etc.),
- Layer 2: Companies providing applications for internet infrastructures (particularly internet software and related consulting services),
- Layer 3: Companies providing free internet services and generating their income via advertising or commissions (content providers such as news portals, search engines, auction sites and the like),
- Layer 4: Companies transacting their business (exclusively or in addition to more common distribution paths) on a Web basis (E-Commerce).

1.6   M-Commerce

A new line of research comes about via the connection of the online world with mobile telephony: "mobile trade", or M-Commerce. Not the entire spectrum of M-Commerce (which, after all, additionally comprises the distribution of physical goods or electronic payment options) is relevant for our context, but exclusively the M-Commerce of digital information goods. M-Commerce is distinguished by the fact that at least one of the participants is not location-bound in his actions, being mobile. Balasubramanian, Peterson and Jarvenpaa (2002, 353) distinguish between three scenarios:

- Applications are dependent on location,
- Applications are dependent on time,
- Applications are dependent on the technology being used (by the sender or the receiver, e.g. when using a cell phone).

The precondition for this sector of the information market is broad usage of internet-capable mobile telephones or small computers with corresponding software for the operating system on the customer side. Another central concern should be the offer of application software and content tailored to the needs of M-Commerce (so-called "Apps"). On the one hand, we can observe application scenarios that are already known–so far, in respectively different contexts (telephony, SMS, e-mail, search engines, playback of music or navigation)–and can now be accessed mobilely from a single device, and on the other hand new services are created that presuppose a genuinely mobile application. Information to be requested mobilely by the receiver are, for instance, location-dependent navigation questions ("How do I get from here to X?"), time-dependent aspects for the observation of stock portfolios ("How are my shares currently doing?") or location and time-dependent requests such as information on traffic jams or delay messages for public transportation. Messages to be registered mobilely by the provider are, for example, location and time-critical problem reports by customers and their forwarding (the message "Car by Manufacturer X is stuck at location L" is sent to the nearest possible service point run by X), the offer of mobilely compiled (e.g. via satellite) data (e.g. for use in agriculture) or a service allowing the virtual participation in an auction (in which the provider acts via a mobile end device) (all examples taken from Balasubramanian et al., 2002). A sweeping success of M-Commerce is yet to make itself be felt (Godoe & Hansen, 2009).

1.7   Information Market–Today: Digital Online Information *and* Network Economy

At this point, the information market's demarcation as posited in this book has been located. Our subject matter concerns the digital information goods from NAICS 51, which are distributed via networks (chiefly the internet) and thus display significant network effects. It should be emphasized that the entire internet economy (Layers 2 through 4 in Castells) belongs to the information market, but only insofar as information (in Machlup's broad sense) is offered there, either for sale or for free. Formulated negatively: we are not dealing with the E-Commerce of non-digital goods, but exclusively with I-Commerce, i.e. trade with information itself. M-Commerce with information goods is subsumed within this definition.

	Information	**Network**
Machlup, Porat	broad definition: "no manual labor"	---
IMO	digital information	---
Information Superhighways	not specified further	build-up of infrastructure
New Economy	digital information (misleading: "intellectual capital")	Network Ecomony
OECD	digital online information	Internet
NAICS	digital information	Internet
Information Market	digital online information	Network Ecomony (Internet)

Table 1.1: Approaches to Capturing the Information Market (I-Commerce).

In Table 1.1, the development toward the information market as we find it in to-day's scientific debate (and delimit it in this book) is sketched in a very simplified manner.

1.8 Conclusion

- Early economic discussions of the information market in Drucker, Machlup and Porat "discover" knowledge as an industry (or sector) of a national economy, in which "knowledge workers" are employed.
- Fritz Machlup (1962) "defines" knowledge very broadly, including in it all activities that are not accomplished manually. According to him, the United States' information market generates 29% of the Gross National Product and employs 27% of all manpower (both estimates applying to the year 1958).
- Marc Uri Porat (1977) distinguishes a primary information sector, in which companies offer information (again in Machlup's very broad sense) on markets, and a secondary information sector comprising all sorts of information processing activities by institutions. Both information sectors put together yield a volume of more than 50% of the U.S. labor market (for the year 1967).

- For many governments, the information society represents the salvation of ailing national economies and labor markets. The new jobs are hoped to provide decisive impulses for positive labor market developments.
- Programs from the early 1990s, like the National Information Infrastructure (NII) and the Global Information Infrastructure (GII) in the U.S.A. as well as the European programs for encouraging the Information Society (White Paper of 1993, Bangemann Report and actions by the European Commussion) provide the stimulus for building and expanding the information infrastructure, respectively.
- In the New Economy, the networks (particularly the internet), now well-developed, coincide with the economic good "digital information". In the economy, it is recognized (particularly by Shapiro and Varian) that remarkable particularities, but no new economic "laws", dominate. Valuations of New Economy enterprises show vast overestimations, which are not–as had falsely been assumed–due to mere "intellectual capital", but particularly to market-psychological effects.
- Apart from information and communication technology, information contents prove crucial for information markets. Early studies on content, e.g. by the Information Market Observatory, restrict themselves to online databases, CD-ROMs and video/audiotext services.
- The North American industry classification NAICS (2002) expands the perspective to all information; the OECD indicators for the information society (2005) exclusively consider such digital information as is distributed via the internet.
- On the information market in the sense of I-Commerce–as we understand it today–digital online information is exchanged, where all particularities of the information and network economies are to be taken into consideration.

1.9   Bibliography

Baddeley, M., & McCombie, J. (2001). An historical perspective on speculative bubbles and financial crisis. Tulipmania and the South Sea Bubble. In Arestis, P., Baddeley, M., & McCombie, J. (eds.), What Global Economic Crisis? (pp. 219-243). Basingstoke. Palgrave.

Balasubramanian, S., Peterson, R.A., & Jarvenpaa, S.L. (2002). Exploring the implications of m-commerce for markets and marketing. Journal of the Academy of Marketing Science, 30(4), 348-361.

Bangemann, M. et al. (1994). Europe and the Global Information Society. Recommendations to the European Council. Brüssel.

Bell, D. (1973). The Coming of the Post-Industrial Society. A Venture in Social Forecasting. New York, NY: Basic Books.

Bell, D. (1979). The social framework of the information society. In Dertouzos, M.L., & Moss, J. (eds.), The Computer Age: A Twenty-Year View (pp. 163-211). Cambridge, MA: Harvard University Press.

Bredemeier, W. (1993). Herausforderungen und Chancen für eine Wachstums-branche in der Rezession. 2. Jahresbericht zur Lage der deutschen Informationswirtschaft 1992/1993. Hattingen: Institute for Information Economics.

Bredemeier, W., & Stock, W.G. (2000). Informationskompetenz europäischer Volkswirtschaften. In Knorz, G., & Kuhlen, R. (eds.), Informationskompetenz–Basiskompetenz in der Informationsgesellschaft (pp. 227-242). Konstanz: UVK.

Casey, M. (1991). The electronic information industry in Europe. Journal of Librarianship and Information Science, 23(1), 21-36.

Castells, M. (1996). Rise of the Network Society. Oxford: Blackwell.

Debons, A., King, D.W., Mansfield, U., & Shirley, D.L. (1981). The Information Profession: Survey of an Emerging Field. New York, NY: Marcel Dekker.

DeLong, J.B., & Froomkin, A.M. (2000). Speculative microeconomics for tomorrow's economy. First Monday, 5(2).

Drucker, P.F. (1959). The Landmarks of Tomorrow. London: Heinemann.

Duff, A.S., Craig, D., & McNeill, D.A. (1996). A note on the origins of the 'information society'. Journal of Information Science, 22(2), 117-122.

European Commission (1993). White Paper on Growth, Competitiveness and Employment: The Challenges and Ways forward into the 21st Century. Luxembourg. (Bulletin of the European Communities, Supplement 6/93).

European Commission (1994). Europe's Way to the Information Society - an Action Plan. Communication from the Commission to the Council and the European Parliament and to the Economic and Social Committee and the Committee of Regions, COM (94) 347.

European Commission (1995). Proposal for a COUNCIL DECISION adopting a multi-annual Community programme to stimulate the development of a European multimedia content industry and to encourage the use of multimedia content in the emerging information society (INFO 2000), COM/95/149 final - CNS 95/0156. (Official Journal C 250, 26/09/1995, 0004).

Godin, B. (2008a). The Knowledge Economy: Fritz Machlup's Construction of a Synthetic Concept. Montreal, Quebec: Project on the History and Sociology of S&T Statistics. (Working Paper; 37).

Godin, B. (2008b). The Information Economy: The History of a Concept Through its Measurements, 1949-2005. Montreal, Quebec: Project on the History and Sociology of S&T Statistics. (Working Paper; 38).

Godoe, H., & Hansen, T.B. (2009). Technological regimes in m-commerce: Convergence as a barrier to diffusion and entrepreneurship? Telecommunications Policy, 33, 19-28.

Gore, A. (1995). Bringing information to the world: The global information infrastructure. Harvard Journal of Law & Technology, 9(1), 1-9.

Hayashi, Y. (1969). Johoka Shakai [The Information Society; in Japanese]. Tokyo: Kodansha Gendai Shinso.

Hayek, F.A. (1945). The use of knowledge in society. American Economic Review, 35(4), 519-530.

IMO (1989a). Production and Availability of Online Databases in 1987. Luxembourg: Information Market Observatory. (IMO Report 89/3).

IMO (1989b). Production of Databases on CD-ROM in 1988. Luxembourg: Information Market Observatory. (IMO Report 89/4).

IMO (1989c). The Impact of Videotex on the Online Market. Luxembourg: Information Market Observatory. (IMO Report 89/7).

IMO (1991). Overview of the Audiotex Market in 1989 and 1990. Luxembourg: Information Market Observatory. (IMO Working Paper 91/1).

IMO (1994). The Internet and the European Information Industry. Luxembourg: Information Market Observatory. (IMO Working Paper 94/3).

IMO (1995). Report on the Main Events and Developments in the Information Market in 1993/1994. Luxembourg: Information Market Observatory.

Information Infrastructure Task Force (1993). National Information Infrastructure: Agenda for Action. Washington, DC.

Information Infrastructure Task Force (1995). Global Information Infrastructure: Agenda for Cooperation. Washington, DC.

Joseph, R. (2005). The knowledge worker: A metaphor in search of a meaning? In Rooney, D., Hearn, G., & Ninan, A. (eds.), Handbook on the Knowledge Economy (pp. 245-254). Cheltenham, Northampton, MA: Edward Elgar.

Kelly, K. (1997). New rules for the New Economy. Wired, 5(9), 140-144, 186, 188, 190, 192, 194, 196-197.

Kelly, K. (1998). New Rules for the New Economy. Ten Ways the Network Economy is Changing Everything. London: Fourth Estate.

Kuhlen, R. (1995). Informationsmarkt. Chancen und Risiken der Kommerzialisierung von Wissen. Konstanz: UVK.

Machlup, F. (1962). The Production and Distribution of Knowledge in the United States. Princeton, NJ: Princeton University Press.

NAICS (2002). North American Industry Classification System. United States. Washington, DC: U.S. Census Bureau.

Nora, S., & Minc, A. (1978). L'Informatisation de la Société. La Documentation Française.

OECD (2005). Guide to Measuring the Information Society / Working Party on Indicators for the Information Society (DSTI/ICCP/IIS(2005)6/FINAL). Paris: Organisation for Economic Co-operation and Development.

Ortner, H. (2006). The origin of the „Knowledge Economy". Journal of European Economic History, 35(2), 427-461.

Pelton, J.N. (1994). The public versus private objectives for the US National Information Infrastructure initiative. Telematics and Informatics, 11, 179-191.

Picot, A., Scheuble, S. (2000). Die Rolle des Wissensmanagements in erfolgreichen Unternehmen. In Mandl, H., & Reinmann-Rothmeier, G. (eds.), Wissensmanagement. Informationszuwachs–Wissensschwund? Die strategische Bedeutung des Wissensmanagements (pp. 19-37). München, Wien: Oldenbourg.

Porat, M.U. (1977). Information Economy. Vol. 1: Definition and Measurement. Washington, DC: Office of Telecommunications. (OT Special Publication 77-12[1]).

Rifkin, J. (1995). The End of Work. New York, NY: G. P. Putnam's Sons.

Robinson, S. (1986). Analyzing the information economy: Tools and techniques. Information Processing & Management, 22(3), 183-202.

Schement, J.R. (1990). Porat, Bell, and the information society reconsidered: The growth of information work in the early twentieth century. Information Processing & Management, 26(4), 449-465.

Schwuchow, W., & Stroetmann, K.A. (1991). Der Europäische Markt für elektronische Informationdienste. Entwicklungstrends und Perspektiven. In Killenberg, H., Kuhlen, R., & Manecke, H.J. (eds.), Wissensbasierte Informationssysteme und Informationsmanagement (pp. 450-471). Konstanz: Universitätsverlag.

Shapiro, C., & Varian, H.R. (1998). Information Rules. A Strategic Guide to the Network Economy. Cambridge, MA: Harvard Business School.

Shapiro, C., & Varian, H.R. (2003). The information economy. In Hand, J.R.M. (ed.), Intangible Assets. Values, Measures, and Risks (pp. 48-62). Oxford: Oxford Univ. Press.

Stock, W.G. (1993). Der Markt für elektronische Informationsdienstleistungen. ifo Schnelldienst, N° 14, 22-31.

Stock, W.G. (1995). Europas Weg in die Informationsgesellschaft. ifo Schnelldienst, N° 6, 15-28.

Stock, W.G. (1996a). Die Informationspolitik der Europäischen Union. ABI-Technik, 16(2), 111-132.

Stock, W.G. (1996b). Informationsgesellschaft und Telekommunikationsnetze in der europäischen Informationspolitik. In Zippel, W. (ed.), Transeuropäische Netze (pp. 77-105). Baden-Baden: Nomos.

Stock, W.G. (1997). Die Informationsgesellschaft: Neue Berufe, mehr Beschäftigung? In Mantwill, G.J. (ed.), Informationswirtschaft und Standort Deutschland (pp. 141-171). Baden-Baden: Nomos.

Stock, W.G. (2007). Information Retrieval. Informationen suchen und finden. München; Wien: Oldenbourg.

Stock, W.G., & Stock, M. (2008). Wissensrepräsentation. Informationen auswerten und bereitstellen. München: Oldenbourg.

Toffler, A. (1980). The Third Wave. New York, NY: Morrow.

Umesao, T. (1963). Joho sangyo ron [On the Information Industry; in Japanese]. Hoso Asahi, (January), 4-17.

Webster, F. (1995). Theories of the Information Society. London, New York, NY: Routledge.

Weygand, F. (2004). The state and "the Information Society": 25 years of experts' reports. Communications & Strategies, 53(1), 147-157.

Chapter 2

Information as Economic Good

2.1   Economic Goods

What are goods? According to established definitions, goods are material or immaterial means suited for satisfying human needs (Gabler, 2011; Hopf, 1983, 68 et seq.). In other words, goods serve people. Now, not all goods are also economic goods. Economic actions are only registered when there is an insufficient amount of goods in relation to human requirements. A good such as air, which satisfies the human requirement to breathe, is normally available in sufficient amounts. Such goods, immediately available to everyone, are called **free goods**. At first glance, one might be tempted to describe water as such. However, it soon becomes clear that if one means fresh, drinkable water, it will not be necessary to imagine life in the desert in order to recognize that water is not freely available. In no country are there unlimited amounts of drinking water. Opposed to free goods are thus **scarce goods**.

The scarcity of goods coerces man into acting economically. He must decide how best to use his means of acquiring goods for satisfying his needs. Insofar, it can be assumed that there is a positive willingness to pay for scarce goods, i.e. people are prepared to pay for the value they represent. The acquisition of goods for money is usually conducted on markets. Suppliers and demanders of goods meet there and swap goods for money. The precondition for an exchange of goods coordinated via markets is the goods' marketability. To get back to the example of water: water is–today–a marketable good. Via its connection to the water supply, a household can use measurable quantities of water that will later be brought to account. The case is somewhat different for air–here, marketability has not been a given so far. Only recently have companies started to be required to buy so-called emission certificates if they want to use air as an emission carrier in Europe (Endres et al., 2004). For private individuals, air still remains a free good. In the following, we will focus exclusively on economic goods.

2.2   Information Goods

Let us turn to the specific form of the information good. What do we mean by it? A very broad definition is provided by Shapiro and Varian (2003, 49), who define an information good as everything that can be digitized. We can thus include sports results, books, films, music, stock prices or even conversations. As plausible as this definition may appear initially, it still has its flaws, as one might–at first glance–hold physical objects, say a banana or a tennis racquet, to be subject to digitization. According to this definition, they, too, are information goods. Apparently, Shapiro and Varian do not mean the object that can be digitized but the product of the digitization, the digital copy. In the case of physical objects, logically, information goods can only ever be their digitized reproductions. Expressed a little more precisely, the definition is thus:

> An information good is everything that is or can be available in digital form, and which is regarded as useful by economic agents.

In order to stress that we are talking about a good, we additionally emphasize the aspect of usefulness assumed by the potential consumer. It is doubly significant: the receiver hopes that he will be cognitively capable of processing the information, and that, furthermore, the information will be useful for satisfying his demands. If, for instance, someone were to buy enterprise data about a Chinese company, only to find out that he cannot process them because they are written in the local language, and also to find out–after a translation has been provided–that he had actually previously received the same data from another source, the assumption of usefulness would be disappointed twice.

A "bad" in this sense would be unwanted TV advertisements, for example. It can be digitized, but it does not serve the receiver, it merely annoys him. Another viewer might see it differently and actively enjoy the ads. What we can glean from this is that information goods have different values for different consumers. From a positive valuation, we can derive a willingness to pay.

The chosen definition for information goods is admittedly extremely pragmatic, but it will do for our purposes. A more detailed information-scientific discussion of the information concept can be found in Stock, 2007, 17 et seq.

The business with information goods is full of preconditions. It is not self-evident at all that the supply and demand of information goods will come together and create information markets. In order to be marketable, information must be not only useful, definable and available to an economic agent, but also transmittable (Bode, 1993, 61). The offer, i.e. the transmission of information goods, is always media-specific. These can be, according to Pross (1972, 127 et seq.), **primary** (carrier) **media**, which facilitate direct interpersonal contact via language, facial expressions or gestures, **secondary media** (e.g. devices such as flags, smoke signals or also letterpress printing), which are necessary for producing information, **tertiary media**, which require technology not only for production but also transmission and reception (e.g. telephone, CD-ROMs, DVDs) as well as **quaternary media** (Faßler, 2002, 147), such as the internet or video-conferencing systems, which are information-technology-based means of telecommunication.

When information is saved, this occurs via storage media such as central servers, CDs or printed books or magazines. Such data carriers are copies of an information good containing the good's entire content in encoded and decodable form. The same good can–if with different degrees of effort–be reproduced in any number. Usage of a saved information good generally occurs via the decoding of a copy by the user himself (e.g. reading an e-mail) or via the participation of a third party in the decoding of a copy that is not in his possession (e.g. video night) (Pethig, 1997, 2 et seq.).

Information goods thus always have a dual character, since they are always a combination of **content** (e.g. a sports bulletin) and **carrier medium** (Schumann & Hess, 2006, 34). They are then offered as articles in a magazine, radio segments or a sports show on TV. Digitization allows for a simpler separation of content and medium than was possible in the past. Content can now be offered multiple times via different media with no great effort. Electronic information goods always require, next to the carrier medium, an **end device** (e.g. DVD-player, MP3-player) in order to be played. In the following, we will see how important this aspect is, particularly when dealing with network effects. A fourth aspect with regard to information goods is the **law** that applies to them. Ownership of an information good always resides with the original owner or creator, who in selling copies only grants the buyer certain usage or processing rights (Wetzel, 2004, 101). This aspect, in turn, has a great significance for the passing on and usage of information goods, and we will deal with it when discussing bootleg copies.

Apart from the criteria mentioned above, information is further to be regarded as a (marketable) economic good only if it is relatively scarce (Bode, 1993, 62). Scarcity in information goods, however, can assume an entirely different form than the one hitherto accepted. For relative scarcity, it is generally assumed that (unlimited) human needs are facing a limited amount of goods to satisfy them. Now, information is generally available in abundance, so that scarcity occurs elsewhere, namely in the recipient's subjective processing options. Searching for a particular information good, one is simply unable to look at or listen to everything on offer, because the human capacity for processing information is limited. Hence scarcity can be the result, for instance, of the restricting factor of concentration (Franck, 2007).

Economically speaking, the concept of goods encompasses both **products** and **services**. Analogously, we can distinguish between information products and information services (Kuhlen, 1996, 83 et seq.). The constitutive feature for this distinction is the use of an external factor, such as a company's disclosures for the benefit of the auditor (Bode, 1997, 462 et seq.). If an external factor is involved, one would thus have to speak of an information service. This, however, is not wholly correct, insofar as any information service process always results in an information product, e.g. the finished audit report. Thus an online database can be regarded as an information product

that emerged from out of other knowledge or information products as
the result of various forms of information work, e.g. referencing, indexing and the database-appropriate structuring of publications (Kuhlen,
1996, 84).

Information services, on the other hand, we would have to call researching in a database, for example. The results of those services which would then be compiled
into an information product for a client. A live concert, which at first glance one
would regard as a pure information service, becomes an information product in the
end, i.e. something digitizable.

It soon becomes clear that the distinction of products and services, so clear in
economics, becomes blurred when considering information goods. When discussing information goods in the following, we will do so aware of the fact that there
may be pure information products, but no pure information services. A service is
always being rendered if an external factor applies to the creation of an information product. Under this viewpoint, information goods and information services
may be regarded as virtually identical.

More important for or further deliberations are two other distinctions between
different kinds of goods common in economics. Depending on the position in the
value chain in which they are used, there is a distinction between consumer goods
and investment goods, and the method of their application allows us to distinguish
between durables and consumables. **Consumer goods** are used by (end) consumers. **Durable goods**, on the other hand, are used by non-consumers (enterprises,
administrations etc.) in order to create services. **Durables** provide a lasting, or at
least long-term value, whereas **consumables** are used up either immediately or
have a very limited scope of action (e.g. Olfert & Rahn, 2008, 736). If we combine
these two distinctions, we get the following matrix:

Value chain \ Kind of Usage	Production (durable goods)	Consumption (consumer goods)
Durables	Technological potentials, which can become productive in combination with other goods and/or manpower (e.g. facilities, machines, office equipment)	Have a longer lifespan and, generally, various uses (e.g. clothes, furniture)
Consumables	Go into other products or contribute to the process (e.g. fuels, lubricants)	Have only one or very few uses (e.g. food, articles of hygiene)

Figure 2.1: Classification of Goods.

Let us now turn to information goods. At first glance, it appears obvious that they can be used by both consumers and enterprises etc. The same information, e.g. concerning the price of a good, can serve as an important decision input for a consumer as well as a company. When discussing information content, information tendentially has the status of a **consumable**. Strictly speaking, information cannot be consumed, yet there are many information goods that are used only once or in a limited scope; thus a newspaper, for instance, is bought in order to read the articles once only. The information relevant to the reader is processed, after which the newspaper is usually discarded. Company, market and press information is generally to be regarded as a consumable. It is subject to high rates of change (e.g. due to fluctuating exchange rates, quotes, consumer preferences, product offers) and thus has to be produced permanently and consumed anew, respectively (Ernst & Köberlein, 1994, 6). Sjurts (2002, 11) speaks of "time elasticity" as a fluent distinguishing characteristic. Time-elastic (consumable) goods lose a significant part of their value after being consumed, whereas durables do not, or much more slowly. Among consumables are thus also music, films or literature, if they are subject to strong falls in value and are only consumed once or very few times. If this form of content is used repeatedly, however–which may very well be the case for a favorite piece of music, which one listens to again and again over a long period of time–it will come closer to having the characteristics of a durable. However–and this is in opposition to market information–use or consumption are not coupled with the primary goal of increasing the consumer's knowledge. The main value is in the actual consumption itself. Apart from the purely cognitive aspect of information reception, the consumption of such goods is mainly motivated by affective (aesthetic, emotional etc.) aspects.

Information goods can also be **durables**. Software is such a kind of information good, being installed once and used repeatedly. This is the case for simple office communication software right up to complex enterprise-resource-planning (ERP) applications. Content is created or processed with the help of software, and is then sold or used for other, e.g. in-house, purposes. The case is analogous for software used for telephony or video conferences, for example. These, too, are durables, as they facilitate communication and cooperation with others (Messerschmitt, 1999, 163).

In the following, we will separate information goods into software and content (Messerschmitt, 1999, 139 et seq., 159), primarily regarding the former as durables and the latter as consumables.

Value chain / Kind of Usage	Production (durable goods)	Consumption (consumer goods)
Durables (software)	• Operating systems • Software applications (e.g. for office communication, enterprise resource planning, management information, databases)	• Operating systems • Software applications (e.g. for office communication, audio/video playback, databases, games)
Consumables (content)	• Business information (e.g. acquisition costs, market rates, market and communication analyses)	• Technological information, e.g. about production methods • Business information (e.g. market prices, market rates, product tests) • News • Music, images, videos, literature

Figure 2.2: Classification of Information Goods.

2.3   Digital Information on the Information Market

We will separate the totality of digital information goods in two: software (applications, mainly used as durables) and content (information content, used primarily as consumables). Software can be roughly subdivided into either standard or individual software. For content, we will draw a somewhat blurred line between e-content (serving mainly entertainment purposes) and p-content (tailoring to professional needs) (Spinner, 2000, 179; see also Stock & Stock, 2008, 28 et seq.). In e-content, we find digital versions of images, pieces of music and videos, and online games. The Web 2.0 services are also filed into this category. P-content comprises business and market information and news, legal information as well as scientific, technical and medical information (STM information).

Apart from products with content (such as a piece of music on iTunes or a research article in a professional journal on Elsevier), there are services that help locate such products in the first place: online search engines. Search tools either provide a broad coverage with no depth of content (like the search engine Google) or a technically restricted coverage that aims at depth (such as the information services STN, LexisNexis or DIALOG). The latter are almost exclusively situated on p -content markets and offer their services for a fee, while online search engines are free of charge for information seekers, recovering their investment via online advertising instead, effectively selling publicity. Figure 2.3 will provide a quick representation of our little classification of digital goods on the information market.

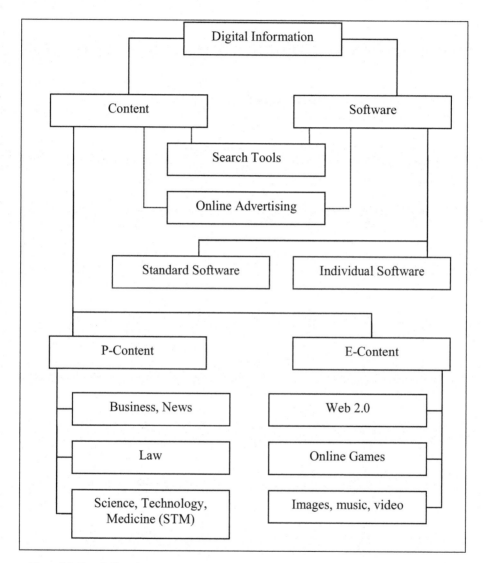

Figure 2.3: Rough Classification of Digital Goods on the Information Market.

In Chapters 7 through 15, we will take a closer look at the information goods addressed above. Here we can describe a select few typical products exemplarily, one at a time; we do not aim to comprehensively represent all product groups or products, as there are thousands of relevant offers on the World Wide Web and particularly the Deep Web, but restrict our focus on a more analytically oriented overview.

2.4   The Economic Significance of the Information Market

The significance of the information markets, of its products and services, must be considered under two aspects. On the one hand, there is its direct significance, expressed in numbers of employees or sales figures. On the other hand–and this may even be the more important aspect–we will regard its indirect significance.

The **indirect economic significance** of the information market is expressed in the customers of this market having made economically significant decisions, or optimized business processes, on the basis of information products acquired. Thus for example a scientific article (acquired for around €25) can inspire an R&D staffer to come up with an idea that results in a completely new production method, netting the company several million Euros. Or a company dossier produced by the in-house information service was at the basis of the decision to acquire that company, allowing the buyer to achieve high profits. In the reverse case, a failure to perform research can lead to notable losses, even leading up to insolvency, e.g. if one misses technological developments about to happen (information which could have been acquired from content aggregators for a few hundred Euros), or if one is thrown into dire straits oneself via the insolvency of a supplier or client, only because one has neglected to acquire documentation regarding the former business partner's solvency. A further example: if a company makes insufficient use of software, this can very well lead to competitive disadvantages. The disadvantage of this indirect economic significance of information is that it cannot be expressed quantitatively.

This is–at least principally–different for the **direct economic significance**, as estimates regarding the market volume are available in this case. Lacking global statistics, we will here present our own informed estimate, compiled on the basis of diverse sources from market research institutes. The following values apply for the totality of digital goods (worldwide, 2009):

Software	€164bn
P-Content	€15bn
E-Content	€6bn
Online Advertising	€50bn
Total Market	*€235bn.*

For software, a huge portion of the entire market volume is a single company's (Microsoft; €43bn in the business year 2008/2009); the situation for online advertising is similar (Google; €17.5bn in 2009). The market for p-content is dominated by the submarket of STM information. For e-content, online games in particular generate significant profits; other submarkets such as Web 2.0 services or Web-

TV do not show any sizeable profits at the time. Web 2.0 services e.g. Facebook, make money with online advertising.

2.5   Conclusion

> • Goods are material or immaterial means that provide use. Their scarcity–in relation to requirements–coerces man into acting economically.
> • Information goods are (potential) digital copies with a presumed usage value.
> • Scarcity in information goods may result from a limited offer as well as from the demanders' limited capacity for processing information.
> • In order to be marketable economic goods, information must be not only useful, definable and available to an economic agent, but also transmittable and–relatively speaking–scarce.
> • Scarcity in information goods can result from excessive demand and insufficient means of satisfying needs, or from oversupply combined with insufficient processing capacities.
> • By and large, information products and services can be regarded as identical.
> • The fundamental manifestations of information goods are content and software. The former generally serves to be consumed, the latter to be used.
> • The direct significance of the information market, expressed quantitatively, is €235bn (total market, worldwide).
> • The indirect significance is qualitative in nature and is expressed in the informational improvement of entrepreneurial decisions as well as productivity gains.

2.6   Bibliography

Bode, J. (1993). Betriebliche Produktion von Information. Wiesbaden: DUV Dt. Univ.-Verl.

Bode, J. (1997). Der Informationsbegriff in der Betriebswirtschaftslehre. Zeitschrift für betriebswirtschaftliche Forschung (zfbf), 49(5), 449–468.

Endres, A., Schröder, M., Kloepfer, M., Marburger, P., Endres, A., & Marburger, P. (2004). Emissionszertifikate und Umweltrecht. 19. Trier-Kolloqium zum Umwelt- und Technikrecht vom 28. bis 30. September 2003. Berlin: Schmidt.

Ernst, M., & Köberlein, C. (1994). Bedarf und Unsicherheit. Eine ökonomische Betrachtung von Information und Qualität auf Informationsmärkten. cogito, 10(1), 6–10.

Faßler, M. (2002). Was ist Kommunikation. 2nd ed. München: Fink.

Franck, G. (2007). Ökonomie der Aufmerksamkeit. Ein Entwurf. München: Dt. Taschenbuch-Verlag.

Gabler Wirtschaftslexikon - Online Editon (2011). Keyword: Gut. Published by Gabler Verlag.

Hopf, M. (1983). Informationen für Märkte und Märkte für Informationen. Frankfurt/M.: Gabler.

Kuhlen, R. (1996). Informationsmarkt. Chancen und Risiken der Kommerzialisierung von Wissen. 2nd ed. Konstanz: UVK.

Messerschmitt, D.G. (1999). Networked Applications. A Guide to the New Computing Infrastructure. San Francisco, CA: Kaufmann.

Olfert, K., & Rahn, H.J. (eds.) (2008). Lexikon der Betriebswirtschaftslehre. 6th ed. Ludwigshafen am Rhein: Kiehl.

Pethig, R. (1997). Information als Wirtschaftsgut in wirtschaftswissenschaftlicher Sicht. In Fiedler, H. (ed.), Information als Wirtschaftsgut. Management und Rechtsgestaltung (pp. 1-28). Köln: Schmidt.

Pross, H. (1972). Medienforschung. Film, Funk, Presse, Fernsehen. Darmstadt: Habel.

Schumann, M., & Hess, T. (2006). Grundfragen der Medienwirtschaft. 3rd ed. Berlin, Heidelberg: Springer. (Springer-11775 /Dig. Serial]).

Shapiro, C., & Varian, H.R. (2003). The Information Economy. In Hand, J.R.M. (ed.), Intangible Assets. Values, Measures, and Risks (pp. 48-62). Oxford: Oxford University Press.

Sjurts, I. (2002). Strategien in der Medienbranche. Grundlagen und Fallbeispiele. 2nd ed. Wiesbaden: Gabler.

Spinner, H.F. (2000). Ordnungen des Wissens: Wissensorganisation, Wissensrepräsentation, Wissensordnung. In Proceedings der 6. Tagung der Deutschen Sektion der Internationalen Gesellschaft für Wissensorganisation (pp. 3-23). Würzburg: Ergon.

Stock, W.G. (2007). Information Retrieval. Informationen suchen und finden. München; Wien: Oldenbourg.

Stock, W.G., & Stock, M. (2008). Wissensrepräsentation. Informationen auswerten und bereitstellen. München: Oldenbourg.

Wetzel, A. (2004). Geschäftsmodelle für immaterielle Wirtschaftsgüter. Auswirkungen der Digitalisierung. Erweiterung von Geschäftsmodellen durch die neue Institutionenökonomik als ein Ansatz zur Theorie der Unternehmung. Hamburg: Kovač.

Chapter 3

Economic Particularities of Information Goods

3.1 Market Failure for Information Goods

Information goods are goods that display particular economic characteristics, which can easily lead to market failure. Market failure occurs when

> the result of marketary coordination deviates from the economically ideal allocation of goods and resources in the model of complete competition (Gabler 2010a).

If we followed the micro-economic standard textbooks, we would even have to assume that no market for information goods could develop at all. Some examples to make this problem clearer:

For information goods, the creation of the first copy is extremely expensive when compared to its reproduction. If we consider the production costs for a piece of music or a film, we will quickly run up several hundreds of thousands, even millions, of Euros. Once the album or the films are finished, however, more or less perfect copies can be made for a few cents each. Furthermore, the transmission costs of digital information goods are extremely low. If there is a fast internet connection, run on a flat rate, files can be received and sent with no additional cost, no matter what their size is.

- From this sort of cost structure, problems arise for the working of information markets: which company is going to offer goods that require large sums in order to be produced, but for which it is unclear whether enough units will eventually be sold in order to recoup those costs? Big providers with a large market share are clearly in advantage here. What makes things worse is that the copying costs are low not only for the legal, but also for the illegal user, and that one must always account for the dissemination of bootlegs hurting one's legal business.

The value of an information good, e.g. of the blueprint for a new production method or of a chemical formula, can only be conclusively assessed after the information has been received and processed (learned). If one then possesses the information, it remains to be seen how high one's willingness to pay still is. Unlike a pair of shoes, information cannot be inspected in their entirety prior to purchase. Each kind of precise inspection means a divulgence of (parts of) the information, and this is frequently against the provider's interests.

- This again leads to problems for a functioning information market: which provider wants to be active on a market where you have to surrender your product to be processed by the receiver prior to purchasing? On the other hand, which customer wants to buy a product without being able to see it, and thus precisely assess its value?

It is often of great importance in buying an information good to note how many other users the good already has. Whoever wants to buy a text processing or spreadsheet application will consider carefully whether he settles on the product of a small provider, which is not very prevalent, or on the market standard. To buy the most widely used program has clear advantages for file-sharing and provides options for mutual assistance in case of any problems in operating it. The case for films, books or music is similar, i.e. many buyers settle on content known by many others in order to have a say.

- Problems that arise for a functioning information market here are: what provider wants to enter a new market in which customers, in case of doubt, will rather buy a highly popular than a high-quality product? Established providers have significant advantages.

Information goods can be used by many people without being used up, i.e. consumed. An information good is not reduced by usage. If a person acquires a certain knowledge by processing information, this will not reduce another person's chances of acquiring the same knowledge. In contrast to many other goods, say a pair of shoes or a chocolate bar, the same information can be used by a multitude of people at the same time. Wear-out effects only occur for information that derives its value from not everybody having it. The insider's tip for the small Caribbean island quickly loses its value if everyone knows about it. For many pieces of information, however, there is no competition in terms of their usage, from the provider's perspective: for him, it makes no difference whether 6,000 or 600,000 people read a magazine or watch a TV show, e.g. the Academy Awards ceremony.

However, restrictions can be imposed via the information's packaging: a book can only be read by one reader at a time as a matter of principle, and the number of viewers of a TV show in one household is limited. However–compared to traditional goods–it is disproportionately harder to exclude customers who are not prepared to pay for the information from its usage: a book can be borrowed at little to no expense from a friend or the library, a TV show can be seen at someone else's house or recorded by a friend for later playback.

- For lack of exclusion options, the following problems apply for a functioning information market: who is prepared to offer goods on a market where it can be ascertained only with difficulty, if at all, that the buyers actually pay for their usage? And what customer will pay for a product that he could also have practically for free?

Economically speaking, the following particularities apply for information goods (Varian, 1998; Hutter, 2000; Gerpott, 2006, 318 et seq., Linde, 2008, 14 et seq., similarly Klodt, 2003, 111 or Buxmann & Pohl, 2004, 507.):

- Information goods have strongly **decreasing average unit costs** (First-Copy-Cost effect), because the attributable costs of production dominate the variable costs of reproduction.
- Information goods have few pronounced search qualities, but the more heavily pronounced **experience and credence qualities**, respectively.
- Information goods have the characteristics of **network effect goods**.
- Information goods have a strong tendency toward so-called **public goods**. Consumer rivalry, per definitionem, is absent and the principle of exclusion can be applied only with difficulty, if at all.

Information goods thus display characteristics that make the occurrence of a market difficult, or at least lead to the market results being suboptimal. The economist here speaks of market failure. What this means in particular–analyzed economically–will be discussed in the following sections in more detail.

3.2   First-Copy-Cost Effect

For many traditional goods, particularly industrially manufactured ones, there are both fixed and notable variable costs (e.g. Meffert, 2005, 508). As opposed to the costs for production and facilities, those are, in the example of the manufacturing of a new laptop computer, all costs that occur in direct relation to the manufacturing of a single product: e.g. drive, chassis, processors. For information goods, on the other hand, there is a strong shift to fixed costs. In publishing houses, the costs of producing the first copy (incl. author's fee, cover design, typeface etc.) eclipse the costs for the following copies (incl. paper, printing, binding etc.) by a large margin. The use of different data carriers during reproduction also results in different costs. Thus for Microsoft's Encarta, the reproduction and distribution costs for the book version were $250, as opposed to $1.50 for the CD-ROM version (Downes & Mui, 1998, 51). Another example: where the production of a music CD can easily cost tens of thousands of Dollars, the variable costs of making copies are entirely negligible. The traditional distribution of music, via audio CDs, presents the music industry with variable costs of around €0.50 per copy (Buxmann & Pohl, 2004, 507; Wetzel, 2004, 205). In comparison, digital goods may even be offered more cheaply than that, particularly when the receiver shoulders the costs for distribution, or downloading, himself. The difference between the costs for the first and the last unit depends on how immaterial the product is (Stewart, 1998, 170). The first copy of Netscape Navigator, for instance, generated around $30m in development costs. The variable costs of the second copy, on the other hand, were only around $1 (Kelly, 2001, 85).

This relation between very high fixed costs and very low variable costs leads to a pronounced fixed cost degression. This means that the fixed costs per unit sink very fast as production numbers increase. On the example of Netscape, the development costs of $30m for the first copy, spread out over all units produced, would already be halved into $15m apiece for two copies. For four copies, they would only be $7.5m, and for 100,000 copies only $300 apiece. This extremely pronounced degression effect is called the First-Copy-Cost effect (FCCE) in media economics (Grau & Hess 2007, 26 et seq.; (Beck, 2006, 2224; Kiefer, 2005, 169).

There is no notable fixed cost degression for information goods with high development costs that cannot be reduced via high production numbers. This is the case for individual software, for example.

Usually, any consideration of the costs includes not only fixed but also variable costs. If fixed and variable costs are related to a produced unit, we speak of average costs.

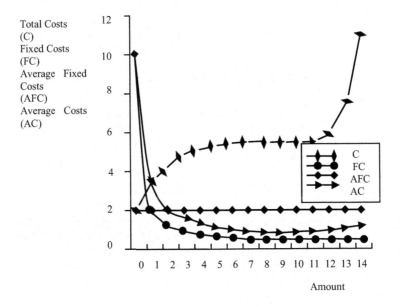

Figure 3.1: Typical Cost Behavior Pattern for Standard Goods.

As a rule, it is assumed for standard goods that average costs show a more or less pronounced u-pattern for companies with increasing levels of output (cf. fundamentally Mankiw et al., 2008, 297 et seq., with empirical data on cost behavior patterns in companies cf. Diller, 2008, 87 et seq., Kiefer, 2005, 173 et seq. and Simon, 1998, 14 et seq.). The total (fixed and variable) costs of production are divided by the amount produced, which results in said average costs. For the fixed costs, the degression effect described above applies, as they are spread over more and more units. The decreasing average fixed costs result in a relatively fast decrease in total average costs. If the variable costs of every additionally produced unit are constant, or even decreasing, this will work in the same direction as decreasing average costs. If variable costs increase over the course of production, which is sooner or later to be expected for standard goods the degression effect of the fixed costs will be overcompensated for from a certain point on and average costs will rise.

The more strongly the average variable costs fade into the background behind fixed costs, the closer the course of the (total) average costs will come to that of the average fixed costs. In the extreme case scenario of $0 of variable costs, both curves will even be coextensive.

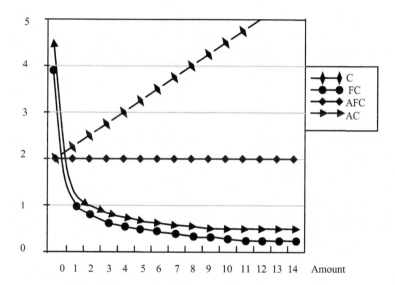

Figure 3.2: Cost Behavior Pattern for Information Goods with Constant Variable Costs.

If average costs decrease continually even as production numbers increase, this is called, in economics, (increasing) economies of scale. Economies of scale (e.g. Woll, 2008, 690) refer to changes in the output (production yield) due to proportional variations to all factor inputs for a given production technology. If the production amount increases proportionally/disproportionally/subproportionally to the additional factor input, we speak of constant/increasing/decreasing economies of scale. The causes for increasing/decreasing economies of scale are decreasing/increasing marginal products. In this case, it is desirable for the individual provider to expand his production amount as far as possible. Precisely these economies of scale occur for information goods, due to the high fixed costs for the first copy and the very low variable costs for all subsequent ones (Kulenkampff, 2000, 60). The very pronounced cost degression is reinforced significantly by the new information technologies. Transmission costs in particular decrease dramatically, as the provisioning and downloading of an .mp3 file, for example, are much cheaper for the provider than the production and distribution of a CD. Very little changes in the development and production costs, though (Klodt & Buch, 2003, 79 et seq.). These two cost aspects–provisioning costs and transmission costs–which are near zero, also represent the basis for the existence of online filesharing sites (Buxmann & Pohl, 2004, 507, 514 et seq.).

3.3   Information Asymmetries

In a traditional transaction of goods, e.g. of clothes, food or electronic devices, the customer has the option of inspecting the object in question. He will observe it, take it into his hands and perhaps even try it, or test its functions. All of this is difficult for information goods. In order to really be able to estimate their full value, one must first process the information. If we draw an analogy to a visit to a restaurant, one would first have to eat the food and then announce one's willingness to pay, i.e. one would determine oneself how much the already eaten food was worth. It is obvious that this can always be misunderstood as an invitation to a free, or at least very cheap, meal. The providers of information goods face a similar problem: if they surrender the information they offer, there will be insecurity as to the value their recipient will ascribe to it, and how his willingness to pay for the already consumed good will develop. If, on the other hand, the provider does not allow the consumer to test the information, that latter has to buy the pig in the poke and will probably either completely forego the purchase or–in view of his insecurity about the information's quality–have a lower willingness to pay than if he had been able to safely assess the quality. In such situations, we speak of asymmetric information distribution: there is a gulf between the information distributed to the suppliers' and to the demanders' side. When one side of the market is better informed than the other, this opens up vistas for exploiting this gradient strategically, e.g. by offering low-quality goods. This phenomenon of asymmetric information distribution mainly relates to the quality of the product on sale (Kulenkampff, 2000, 127). Asymmetric information distribution can also, however, relate to the allocation of product prices on the market, demanders' preferences (Klodt & Buch, 2003, 92 et seq.) or–as we will explain in more detail in Chapter 22–strategic market communication.

3.3.1   *Information Asymmetries on Markets: The Market for Lemons*

The analyses of George A. Akerlof (1970) have been fundamental for all further works on the subject of asymmetric information distribution. He was the first to exemplify the phenomenon of asymmetrically distributed information, on the example of the used-car market. The seller of a used car is very well informed about the state of his vehicle on the basis of having driven it in the past. The buyer, on the other hand, merely knows that there are cars of various qualities on the market. He can thus only make an estimate concerning the average quality. If a symmetric information distribution were at hand, i.e. if both sides of the market had the same amount of information about the product on offer, one could easily set a price for each car based on its quality. As this is not the case, the seller has the option of exploiting this, by taking his low-quality car, advertising it as a good car and selling it at a higher price than would be adequate. Akerlof (1970, 489) calls these vehicles "lemons". The demanders, who are unable to assess the quality on offer on this market, will only be prepared to pay a price that meets their expectations. This can be illustrated via a simple numerical example (Varian, 2007, 827 et seq.).

Let us assume the following for a used-car market: there are 100 buyers and 100 sellers of used vehicles, and everyone knows that 50% of the cars on offer are of low quality (lemons). The quality of each individual car is only known to the sellers, i.e. this is a case of an asymmetric distribution of quality information. The sellers of the lemons are prepared to sell them for €1,000. The sellers of the good cars want at least €2,000. The buyers would pay €1,200 for lemons and €2,400 for good cars. If the quality could be easily assessed, we would get prices between €1,000 and 1,200 for lemons and between €2,000 and 2,400 for good cars. If the quality cannot be assessed, however, the buyers must try to estimate the value of the car in question. If the consumers generally derive the quality from the price, this will result in a uniform price that is oriented on the average quality (Graumann, 1993, 1337). In order to determine this price, the economist will calculate a so-called expectancy value, which is an estimate concerning a chance result to be expected. For the same probability of one of the two quality levels posited above, the rational buyer will be prepared to pay the expectancy value of the cars: ½ * €1,200 + ½ * €2,400 = €1,800. Which leaves us with the question: who would sell his car at that price? The lemon-sellers would be prepared to sell for €1,800, but not the sellers of the good cars, as they are aiming for at least €2,000. The consequence: at this price, only lemons would be sold. The situation becomes even more dramatic when the buyers can see that the price they are willing to pay is only met by lemons. Why? They would have to lower their expectancy value again, which in the extreme case would mean: 1 * €1,200 + 0 * €2,400 = €1,200. The buyers would then only be prepared to pay €1,200 at most. The consequence is that no good cars would be offered on this market. This result is particularly remarkable as there is definitely a willingness to pay for good cars (namely €2,400); it just does not take effect, because the necessary information for assessing the quality is missing. We are looking at an acute case of market failure, i.e. the result of marketary coordination deviates from the ideal result derived with the help of a reference model. The ideal result would be that all cars, good and bad, are sold at their respective prices.

What is so special in this case is that we have to expect not just a few mispurchases, where the buyer is disappointed to find out that the car he has acquired is a lemon, but that it is to be feared that not a single higher-quality vehicle will be sold. Why is that? If a person tries to sell a bad car, and this is discovered after the transaction, this will influence the buyers' perception of the average quality of cars available on the market. They will lower their expectancy values, and thus the price they are willing to pay for the average car. This in turn puts the sellers of good cars at a disadvantage. The cars that will most probably be sold are the ones that their owners most want to get rid of. In summation, it can be said that when too many units of low quality are on the market, it will become difficult for providers of quality to sell their products at a reasonable price (Varian, 2007, 829).

What can we derive from this model? What we have here is the phenomenon called Adverse Selection in economics. The terms "Adverse Selection" and "Moral Hazard", which we will consider at a later stage, spring from insurance economics (Molho, 2001, 9 and 46 et seq. with further "lemon" examples in the context of experimental studies). The so-called Principal-Agent theory deals extensively with this problem (e.g. Richter et al., 2003 or, with a specifically economical perspective, Jost, 2001). The fact that one side of the market, in this case demand, is inadequately informed about the quality of the goods on offer (Hidden Characteristics (Göbel, 2002, 98 et seq.)), and that this information deficit cannot be made up for via search activities, the result is–due to the quality estimates that were made–Adverse Selection. The good offers are ousted by the bad. A general consequence of existing information asymmetries is thus that good quality is superseded by bad quality.

In the extreme case, it can come to the wholesale destruction of the market, namely if the providers–other than in Akerlof's fixed-quality model–can determine the quality they offer themselves (Varian, 2007, 829 et seq.). In this scenario, the (dishonest) providers of low quality–they are dishonest because they demand premium prices for poor quality–will not only drive the (honest) providers of good quality from the market, but in the end break the market itself, when it becomes clear that the (low) quality on offer is linked to too high a price. The downward spiral of the step-by-step withdrawal of quality providers will lead not to partial but to complete market failure.

3.3.2   *Information Asymmetries on Information Markets*

Let us now turn to information goods. Analogously to the above considerations, it will also be the case for information goods that there will be providers of good quality and providers of poor quality on a market. High-quality offers will be those that meet demanders' expectations. Hence, poor offers lead to disappointed expectations. If the demanders are not able to determine the quality of the offer from the outset, providers will feel the impetus to sell "lemons", advertising poor quality as good and thus increasing their profits.

If, furthermore, the manufacturing costs for poor quality are lower than they are for high quality and the provider can assume that the demander will not be able to assess it–at least prior to purchasing–it makes economic sense under profit maximization conditions to produce poorer quality at lower cost and offering it as high quality. It is also evident, though, that that this only makes sense as long as the demanders allow themselves to be deceived, which can only be assumed, permanently, if either the buyer is unable to assess the quality–even post-purchase–or if the product is a one-off buy and there is no exchange of consumer experiences between the demanders. However, the buyer does have the opportunity for a quality experience, particularly if it is his first buy, i.e. if future buys from the same provider are still an option. As long as he is able to assess the quality, this will lead to his willingness to pay for future products being lowered and even–should he share his experiences with others–influence that of other demanders into the same direction. If this occurs, it will lead to the same downward spiral that Akerlof already described for the used-car market. Due to information deficits on the part of the demanders, Adverse Selection occurs, as a consequence of which the poor-quality offers increase at the expense of high quality.

Such an information-deficit-induced market failure occurs on markets for information goods, when the demanders are unable to acquire the necessary quality information (Hopf, 1983, 76). If we disregard the generally undesirable variant of having to make these unpleasant experiences oneself, they can only be avoided by searching for decision-relevant information. Economically speaking, this information gathering is pursued until the marginal cost of acquisition is equal to the marginal utility of the information acquired (fundamentally Stigler, 1961). Put simply, one puts up time and money for the information search–e.g. by buying consumer magazines or talking to other buyers–as long as the result is beneficial. This benefit can be a discount for the product, or the ability to better assess the quality of different offers, allowing the buyer to choose the better quality. It is evident that the benefit (marginal utility) is significantly higher with the first consumer magazine bought than it is with the twelfth.

Information goods display the peculiar characteristic that the acquisition of further information about an information good is principally to be deemed equal to the successive acquisition of the good itself (Kulenkampff, 2000, 129). The more intensively one informs oneself about a specific information good, the more one comes to know about its content. For software, one must differentiate between the application level and the source code level. On the level of the application, the common user can comprehensively inform himself without owning the software. If the user acquires access to the source code, however, he will be in possession of the entire good. If he is then fully informed, this would mean, as a last consequence, that he no longer needs the original information since he already has it. This phenomenon occurring with information goods is called the "information paradox" after Kenneth J. Arrow (1962, 615):

> [...] there is a fundamental paradox in the determination of demand for
> information; its value for the purchaser is not known until he has the information, but then he has in effect acquired it without cost.

The occurrence of asymmetrically distributed information is particularly pronounced for information offers. Hopf (1983, 76), following Akerlof, describes information as a typical "lemon" good. The providers have a strong head start in information compared with the demanders. On the other hand, the demanders can only really inform themselves about the information good if the provider makes it available–at least partially–prior to purchase. If he doesn't, the buyer will only be able to assess the quality post-purchase, by processing the information.

A very apt example for such a situation can be found on the markets for technical knowledge (Klodt, 2001a, 41 et seq.). The existence of the information paradox is the cause, here, of the subordinate role played by industrial contract research (i.e. awarding R&D assignments externally). The majority of (large) companies prefer to produce their technical knowledge internally, because they have insufficient control over the quality of the execution and the results. It is almost exclusively smaller businesses who use the possibilities of external contract research, as they shy away from the high fixed costs of having one's own R&D department.

3.3.3   *Search, Experience and Credence Qualities of Information Goods*

Information, following Arrow, is subject to a paradox: the value of an information good cannot be assessed prior to purchasing without getting to know at least parts of the good itself. Having complete information about an information good, though, would mean having the good, which was meant to be bought, for free. The transmission of information before the transaction creates the problem that as a provider, one can no longer know how high the buyer's payments will be, or if he will pay at all. Contrary to Arrow's allegation, the demanders–if not all of them–definitely have a willingness to pay, even after they have already acquired a(n information) good. In Chapter 18, on Pricing, we will address this under the keyword Reverse Pricing.

As the quality of information goods generally reveals itself only after the purchase, they are often labeled experience goods (Shapiro & Varian, 1999, 5 et seq., 2003, 117 et seq.). **Experience goods** are, according to Phillip Nelson, all manner of goods whose quality characteristics are only revealed after having been bought. For **search goods**, on the other hand, the quality can be ascertained before, via a simple inspection (Nelson, 1970). A third feature that goods can have, according to Darby and Karni (1973), are so-called **credence qualities**. Some examples for this are the services rendered by a doctor or a mechanic, which the consumer cannot entirely assess with regard to their quality even after they have been completed. He can only trust that cost and benefit were adequate.

Now many goods display all three of the above-named characteristics. Even if we are tempted to spontaneously label a daily-needs good, such as a loaf of bread, as a search good, i.e. a good whose quality we can assess in its entirety prior to purchasing via a simple looking-over, a closer look will soon show that here too, experience and credence qualities can be found. Where the color of the crust and the smell may still be search qualities, the bread's taste is already an experience quality that only transpires after the purchase, by taking a bite. Whether the bread has in actuality been biologically produced, as advertised, is not really something the consumer can readily infer; hence, we have a credence quality. If, on the other hand, we consider a consulting offer, e.g. legal consulting, experience and credence qualities will be highly emphasized. Whether the help that was needed has been received is something that can still be ascertained, but the investigative scope of the customer is not wide enough to determine whether the services rendered were of the highest possible quality.

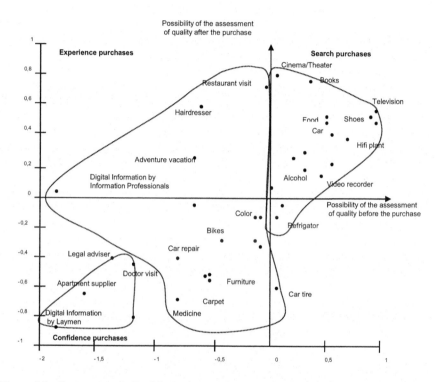

Figure 3.3: Positioning of Goods' Qualities in the Purchasing Process. Source: following Weiber/Adler 1995, 107.

Darby and Karni thus explicitly speak of credence qualities, and not of credence goods. Since goods generally unite several qualities at the same time, we will thus speak, in the following, not of search, experience and credence goods but, more precisely, of goods with search, experience and credence **qualities**. The classification according to goods is thus to be understood as a reference to the respective dominant qualities (Mengen, 1993, 130).

Generally, it can be said that the majority of material goods display search and experience qualities, whereas most services are heavy on experience and credence qualities (Zeithaml, 1981, 187). Empirical analyses show that although there are blurry areas, we can still form product groups in which one or two of the qualities predominate (Weiber & Adler, 1995; Bayón, 1997, 19 and 55 et seq. with a detailed discussion and references to further studies).

The positioning of the information good "book" among search buys in Figure 3.3 is the result of the unilateral suspension of the information asymmetry on the part of the provider. Since he lets the buyer inspect the book, disclosing its content, the buyer can acquire the information even without purchasing the product. Hence what is actually being sold is the information carrier, its advantages including storability, reading comfort and the option for repeated usage. The same goes for music that one can listen to before buying it.

Interestingly, it depends less on the object of purchase than on the buyer himself whether experience or credence qualities dominate. In the absence of sufficient expert knowledge in the relevant area, credence qualities always dominate for the buyer of an information good (Talkenberg, 1992, 74, 172-173). If we define expert knowledge very broadly, we can also include social information (sports, royal houses etc.), which can only be assessed by "experts", in this category. Considering the example of electronic information services (technical databases, credit rating databases, library catalogs etc.), we can soon see that there are no search qualities at play, since the product cannot be inspected prior to the search. An information expert will be able to assess the quality of the result of an online research, as he will concentrate mainly on experience qualities, but an online layman has to accept the fact that, lacking expert skills, he has no option other than trust in the quality he seeks (Stock, 1995, 150 et seq.). Providers of goods with pronounced experience and, even more pertinently, credence qualities, are presented with many options for strategic behavior, as they needn't fear that decreases in their service's quality will be quickly recognized and thus lead to lower profits (Hauser, 1979, 751). For electronic information services, such as online databases, this means that low-quality products can be sold at very low risk, particularly to buyers with no expertise in the relevant subject (Stock, 1995, 153-154). However, even experts, who are able to make accurate assessments of the service they receive, must trust the provider that every detail of the service rendered is as advertised (Ernst & Giesler, 2000, 198).

> E.g. the number and precision of the interviews conducted by a market research institute cannot be controlled by the client, either before or after paying for the service. A steady presence of the client during the interviewing process is possible, in principle, but the costs would be prohibitive for him (the sheer time required). Even if the client were prepared to sacrifice his time, his presence, e.g. during the evaluation of the results via multivariate procedures would still make no sense, due to his (probable) lack of expert knowledge. As the appropriation of the necessary knowledge is, again, prohibitively expensive for the client, he must finally trust in the quality of the market research study (Mengen, 1993, 130).

In summation, we can state that information goods only display a few search qualities if they have already been produced. Generally, though, credence and–depending on the demander's knowledge–experience qualities are dominant.

3.3.4 On the Functionality of Information Markets

We will now list some examples for information markets that typically give rise to information asymmetries, in order to derive from them what the conditions are that make them function in spite of the permanent threat of market failure.

As an example for a functioning information market, let us consider the market for stock information. Information on current market rates are extremely valuable for the business of banks, brokers and financial service providers in general. Independently of whether we assume a supply of stock information in real time or with a delay, it must be assumed that this information good is subject to the information paradox. It would lose its value if it were disclosed prior to purchase. Nevertheless, trade with such information is well-developed and extremely lucrative (Ernst & Köberlein, 1994, 8). Why is that?

On the one hand, we are dealing with so-called price information. With this sort of information, quality insecurities are generally very low, because (Ernst & Köberlein, 1994):

- the form of the information is fixed precisely: as a demander, one expects a price statement with two decimal places in a particular currency. Even if the content, i.e. the actual price, is only released after the purchase, one knows beforehand exactly what the information will look like.
- the value of an information can be very easily gauged despite an ignorance of the specific content. If, for example, one must make a selling decision about a share that has been bought for €37.50, the profit or loss to be expected can quickly be calculated as being the difference to the current rate.
- the costs of the information are known in advance, even if it is generally not single pieces of stock information but an ongoing stream of information that is being sold. To wit, the permanent changes of the rates represent a regularly recurring buying impetus.
- doubts concerning the quality of the information received can quickly be removed post-purchase via comparison with other providers or the often freely available time-delayed share price information.

The case is quite similar for information offers by price agencies, whose service consists of collecting information about the price of goods, analyzing it and selling it in connection with traders' licenses. The information product they offer is practically devoid of quality insecurities, because the form of the offer is precisely outlined, its value known via the calculable price range and even the costs generated by the commission are already set prior to the purchase (Ernst et al., 1995, 72).

Generally, it can be observed that on markets for price information, which are marked by a high degree of transparency and standardization, quality insecurities are few and far between (Ernst et al., 1995, 71).

Let us now turn to some examples, where pronounced information asymmetries are in place, which would have to lead to market failure. As addressed above, we have to assume that (information) goods are always bundles of search, experience and credence qualities, of which one or two are more pronounced than the other(s). Checking for the market failure of information goods must thus be done in two steps: first, it has to be seen whether the product in question is actually an information good. In order to judge, in the second step, whether market failure is to be expected for the good in question, one must analyze its qualities. If search qualities dominate, quality insecurities due to Adverse Selection or Moral Hazard, and hence market failure, are not to be expected **prior to purchase, or completion of the contract**. If experience and credence qualities dominate, respectively, significant quality insecurities are to be expected prior to purchase. For the situation **post-purchase, or completion of the contract**, it holds that: if the information good has pronounced experience and/or credence qualities, Moral Hazard will lead to credence insecurities for follow-up buys or lasting business relationships. Existing quality insecurities can be discovered–as addressed above–either with a delay (experience qualities) or even never (credence qualities). In these cases, market failure would occur. A reminder: market failure refers to deviations of the result of marketary coordination from an ideal result derived with the help of a reference model. A viable yardstick would be a market with symmetric information, i.e. in which suppliers and demanders are equally well-informed. If the market delivers inferior results, due to one side of the market having to suffer disadvantages in the cost-benefit ratio vis-à-vis the reference model of symmetric information, market failure is at hand. Disadvantages can be exorbitant prices for any given service, or inadequate services, particularly in terms of quality, at a given price.

If we consider the (first) purchase of an information good, such as a computer software, we will find typical information asymmetries. In order to be able to gather as comprehensive an impression as possible of the quality of the offer, the buyer would have to be given the information good for free. Only in this way can he test its functionalities and check whether they satisfy his demands.

Hence if one had to buy a project management software purely on the basis of product description and price, it would be impossible to distinguish good offers from bad ones. For precisely this reason, it is common practice for software to make trial versions, restricted either in terms of available time or content, available to the customers. The providers thus make experience qualities, which can only be checked post-purchase, to search qualities that can be inspected before the transaction. However, this is only valid for the qualities that can be inspected during the trial period. For those that only transpire after a prolonged period of usage, such as stability, dealing with larger amounts of data, performance during multiple access, the quality insecurity will prevail. Furthermore, performance insecurities will arise if the software is not subject to a one-off buy, but is planned to be repurchased in all of its subsequent versions. Whereas it could still be stipulated during the transaction how often and at what price updates would be offered, their quality can only be trusted in. However, for all further buys of the same product from the same provider, the information asymmetries will be less severe, as the user can now assess the experience qualities much more easily due to his previous exposure to the product. A trade-off comes to pass: the customer can rate the product more quickly and accurately after follow-up buys than after first buys, but has to accept the risk of his trust being abused by the provider to deliver worse quality than expected (Moral Hazard).

Examples for other information goods are market, industry, product or competition analyses. Here we must distinguish, however, whether the analyses are yet to be conducted or whether results are already available. If we only consider the latter aspect, we need merely consider the situation prior to purchase. Without any access to the result, an information asymmetry will be at play. The demander must make his purchasing decision in the face of insecurity regarding the product's quality. To make matters more complicated, insecurity concerning the quality of production is added to the mix as a further credence quality. The buyer cannot check what level of care went into each single step of the production process. Has the survey sample size actually been reached and completely processed? How carefully have the statistical test procedures been selected? Even if some of this quality information may be documented, its closer analysis and assessment is impossible or too complex for someone without sufficient expert knowledge.

If the desired analysis has yet to be made, insecurities rise. Where an advance payment is required, great quality insecurities have to be accepted prior to signing the contract: information that could be disclosed to alleviate the buyer's doubts does not exist yet. At best, the buyer can determine a service package up front. After the contract has been signed, Moral Hazard comes into play. The customer cannot assess the actual quality of the analysis' implementation, which leads to pronounced performance insecurities.

Despite this problematic assessment, there is still a well-functioning market for such analyses. Certain mechanisms can be recognized that prevent the failure of an information market. Thus renowned companies are favored for market research contracts, as it is clear that they have already made many good analyses and have a comprehensive stock of customer references. These initial considerations already show what behaviors a company can use in order to make viable offers on an information market despite the presence of economic adversity. Such measures on the part of companies to pointedly offer quality information is called Signaling. The whole of Chapter 22 is devoted to this subject.

3.3.5 Information Asymmetries Before and After Completion of a Contract: Adverse Selection and Moral Hazard

For the question of whether information asymmetries occur before or after the signing of a contract, we can distinguish between two kinds of contracts: those that are completed as purchasing agreements according to §§ 433 et seq. of the

German Civil Code (Bürgerliches Gesetzbuch, BGB), or–and this will be of significance in the following–as contracts for services according to §§ 631 et seq. BGB, in which the provider performs a service (e.g. a survey or a Web design with animations) for a fee.

Due to the relatively unpronounced search qualities, information asymmetries **prior to the signing of a contract** give rise to the problem of Adverse Selection. Customers can only really comprehensively inform themselves about the quality of an information product if they have actually received the information (information paradox). The providers, in turn, have no interest in reducing this information asymmetry by comprehensively disclosing the information. Even if the information provider is prepared to disclose parts of the information prior to purchase, the problem still remains that the demander cannot necessarily assess the quality. Depending on his level of knowledge, he may be able to assess the experience qualities, e.g. whether information about a company's business performance is plausible. Assessing the credence qualities, however, is–as has been seen on the example of the market research study–impossible even to the expert, or at the very least connected to prohibitive costs.

From this fact springs Moral Hazard, as the provider has the option of offering lower quality without any risk of the customer easily discovering it. In information goods, Moral Hazard mainly occurs when they are entirely uninspectable prior to purchase, having yet to be produced. In a research contract, disclosing the information is impossible before the (information) work has been begun. Here the buyer even has to act entirely on the basis of credence.

Generally, inadequate search qualities lead to quality insecurity for the demander looking to buy information goods (Bayón, 1997, 19). His information activities prior to (the initial) purchase can merely serve to inform him about the search qualities. Experience and credence qualities only transpire after the purchase, via experience from using the product, or never. The negative economic consequence here is Adverse Selection, where lower-quality offers displace higher-quality ones, and a market even collapses entirely (total market failure), due to information costs that are too high or because it is impossible to inform oneself beforehand at all.

Investigations of the question of what leads a provider to offer high or low quality, see the quality as a decision variable. It is at its lowest when casual customers make one-off buys. This is the case with restaurants in tourist areas, for example (Tirole, 1995, 234). The case is different when there are well-informed customers, e.g. due to product reviews. Here it is shown that as the number of informed demanders rises, so will the probability of a positive correlation between price and quality. This is a positive external effect which spreads from the informed consumers to the uninformed ones (Tirole, 1995, 235 et seq.). The case is somewhat different if repeat purchases are made. Here the reputation of a provider (e.g. his brand image) plays a significant role. It is to be assumed that the provider will offer high quality for as long as the (discounted) quality premium he achieves on the basis of his reputation is higher than the cost savings via quality reduction would be (Tirole, 1995, 245 et seq.). Quality insecurities thus only lead to Adverse

Selection if no mechanisms are being establish on the market that give the provider reasons to offer high quality.

Information asymmetries **after the signing of a contract** bear the danger of Moral Hazard. Moral Hazard occurs in two scenarios: on the one hand, when information goods are entirely uninspectable prior to purchase, as they have yet to be produced. In a research contract, disclosing the information is impossible, after all, before the (information) work has begun. Here the buyer has to act entirely on the basis of credence. On the other hand, Moral Hazard is to be expected when it is not merely a one-off (purchasing) contract, but the demander either plans on making follow-up buys or–which is very common, particularly for information goods–enters a longer-term business relationship with the provider by having information goods (daily newspapers, magazines, stock information etc.) delivered in the context of a contract for services. The provider then has the option of lowering the quality of his service from one purchase, or delivery, to the next, as his behavior can at best be partially observed by the customer. This latter does not know about the care that went into the making of an information product, as one generally only gets to know the result. Yet Moral Hazard can also occur for pronounced experience qualities–we only have to think of the credit of trust accorded to the publisher on the part of the subscriber. He consumes his newspaper, expecting a consistent level of quality. Should the quality decrease, he would only notice after quite some time, before making the decision to cancel–which might only be possible at the end of the subscription period.

The case is similar with follow-up buys. If a demander has obtained a high-quality result from an information search, he will assume the same level of quality to result from his next commission. The provider thus at least has the opportunity of providing an inferior service.

Information asymmetries after the signing of a contract thus lead to performance insecurities and subsequently, due to Moral Hazard, to a potentially decreasing service offer if the provider decides to exploit the information asymmetry. We say "potentially", because–analogously to the example described above–these consequences only take effect if there are no mechanisms on the market that give the provider the motivation to produce high quality anyway.

Independently of whether information asymmetries occur prior to the signing of a (purchasing) contract or after the signing of a contract (for services), there are two critical factors: the **subjective** critical factor is based on the buyer's expertise. Only as an expert can he adequately assess the quality of an information good himself, be it prior to purchase or with regard to a service stipulated in the contract.

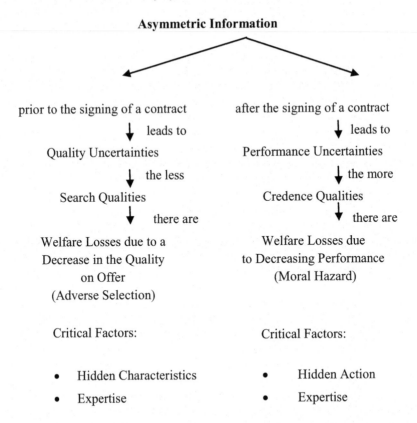

Figure 3.4: Effects of Asymmetric Information.

Objectively problematic is the lack of availability of quality information. Due to the information paradox, a full inspection of the quality of information goods is often impossible, and there remain "Hidden Characteristics" (Göbel, 2002, 101). Also, due to the contractor's services being extremely difficult to supervise ("Hidden Action", Göbel 2002, 102), it is impossible after signing a contract to adequately assess the quality of the performance process (Picot et al., 2003, 57 et seq.).

3.4 Network Effects for Information Goods

Another particularity to be investigated in information goods are the occurring network effects. To begin with a few examples: if a company considers acquiring a software that is meant to be used not only internally, but also jointly with other companies–consider if you will Electronic Data Interchange (EDI) software, for instance–it will consider very carefully whether it wants to buy a software that is also used by other companies or not. For example, if it wants to exchange order data with its customer and/or suppliers, or perform accounting operations undisturbed, it will be of great advantage if both parties use the same standard. Given the right level of prevalence, the information good "EDI software" can thus provide the user with an additional value, which stems from the total number of its users, to the value arising from the product itself (Buxmann, 2002). Economically, this is called a network effect, or network externality. Analogous effects can be observed for the different forms of content, or in the social networks of Web 2.0. Facebook and co. are the more valuable for their existing customers the more widely they are being used. It is easier to find interesting contacts and one's own contributions will reach a greater audience. Content also gains publicity when people talk about it. The positive effects of bestseller lists on sales figures bears this out. If content, e.g. films, is being talked about in a specific form, e.g. on Twitter, one can even predict, prior to the release date, how big its initial profits will be with some accuracy (Peer, 2010).

A net, or network, is, abstractly speaking, similarly to a system, an amount of objects with connections (Economides, 1996, 674; in relation to systems in general Willke, 1991, 194) or the possibility of connections between them (Flechtner, 1966, 353). An information-economic reading will define a network as a summary of the users of a certain good or compatible technologies (Dietl & Royer, 2000, 324).

If the users are physically connected, we speak of **real** networks. This is traditionally the case with fixed telephone networks, in which the individual telephone owners are durably connected with each other via the installed cables.

If the users are not physically but merely logically connected, we speak of **virtual** networks (Shapiro & Varian, 1999, 174, 183; Dietl & Royer, 2000, 324). They are virtual because the relationships between the participants are primarily potential in nature (for a more comprehensive discussion of the concept of virtuality Linde, 1997, 13 et seq.). It is not the case, as it is in real networks, that one is only a participant if one is physically connected with the others. Everyone who buys a virtual network good derives value from the fact that he has the option of establishing a connection with the other network participants. Virtual networks are, for example, all users of DVD players or video recorders, or all users of a certain operating system or gaming console.

Another, more abstract example of a virtual network are languages, e.g. the network of all Anglophone people (Friedrich, 2003, 4). Everyone who speaks this language has the option of communicating with every other English-speaker worldwide. English is not so widely used, and regarded as a world language, because it is so easy to learn, but because it is used by the majority of people as a means of communication. Everyone who wants to make himself understood internationally is thus forced to join the network, i.e. learn English. The value of this network lies in its multiple ways of communicating, and it is increased by every further "user" of the language. It would be imaginable to use another language for international communication–e.g. the artificial, very easily learnable world language Esperanto–but the adjustment costs of establishing it as a valid standard for everyone would be extremely high.

In contrast with many daily-needs consumables (e.g. food, articles of hygiene, medication) or durables such as clothes or furniture, which are traditionally used very individually or by a very restricted number of people, network goods provide value not only through their features (basic value, original value), but further provide each individual consumer an additional value that goes beyond, via the total number of other users, the Network Effect Value (Buxmann, 2002, 443), also called derivative value. The more users, the greater this Network Effect Value will be for the individual. This will be immediately understandable for a real network, if we imagine the value of a telephone network with only three participants as opposed to a network with connections worldwide. But in a virtual network, too, the advantages are obvious, because one can use the same word processing application to effortlessly exchange data with others, or discuss the software's functionalities. For network goods, the value derived from their prevalence is dominant vis-à-vis the value that stems purely from the good's qualities.

According to Weiber (1992, 15 et seq.), network effect or network goods distinguish themselves from singular goods, the value of which stems purely from the product itself (e.g. fuel), and system goods, whose value can only properly unfold when there are sufficient options for interaction with others. Video telephones, fax machines, e-mail applications etc. are examples for such system goods with no basic value. They absolutely require the existence of at least a second user.

	Positive	Negative
Production	• Usage of unpatented inventions via third parties • Investment in human capital	• Environmental pollution • Noise pollution of the residents
Consumption	• Education • Restoration of a historical building	• Exhaust fumes • Barbecue evening • Dogs barking • Excess Consumption of Alcohol

Figure 3.5: Positive and Negative Externalities in Production and Consumption.

External effects (externalities) are present whenever economic activities (buying and selling decisions by economic agents) affect the welfare of uninvolved third parties, and nobody is remunerated/compensated for it (Mankiw et al., 2008, 229). External effects can occur during production as well as consumption, and be of a beneficent (positive) or maleficent (negative) nature. Generally, they lead to the private and social costs/values of economic activities to come apart.

In negative external effects, the social costs outweigh the private. If a company settles on a production method that is very noise-intensive, residents will suffer without being compensated for it. The consumer, who is smoking his cigarette produces smoke, affects his environment but does not face punishment. The private value of smoking outweighs the social. In both cases, the social (additional) costs and (reduced) values play no decision-making role, respectively. From a social point of view we have market failure, as it would be better if companies and individuals produced less noise and smoke, respectively, for others to bear without recompense.

The opposite is the case for positive external effects. If companies invest in their employees, making them more versatile and thus, generally, more attractive for the labor market, the companies' private costs will be higher than their social costs. The case is analogous for a private individual investing in his or her education–here the social value, i.e. more opportunities on the labor market, outweighs the individual one. From a societal perspective, it would be better if companies and individuals invested more in education. Where externalities, both positive and negative, occur, market failure will habitually follow. The socially desirable supply and demand figures do not match the amounts privately supplied and demanded, respectively (Mankiw et al., 2008, 229 et seq.).

3.4.1   Direct Network Effects

Network goods also give rise to consumer externalities: so-called network externalities. These, too, are external effects. They occur because–abstractly speaking–networks provide values via the interlinking of their elements. The number of elements linked in a network thus influences the total value. A new network participant increases the value of the pre-existing ones, and simultaneously makes the network more interesting overall for further participants. Network effects are also called "Increasing Returns to Adoption" (Arthur, 1989, 2004) or "Demand Side Economies of Scale" (Farrell and Saloner, 1986). Also regarded as network effects are the so-called Information Economies of Scale (Habermeier, 1989), which occur when the quality of a good can better be assessed due to its prevalence.

Direct network effects can be described a little more formally in the following way: the value U derived by an individual i from a network good (U_i) depends not only on the (technical) characteristics E but also on the number of individuals Z who also use the same good (Blankart & Knieps, 1994, 451 et seq.). To wit:

$$U_i = U_i(Z, E) \text{ with } U_i(Z, E) < U_i(Z^*, E) \text{ for } Z < Z^*$$

Two network goods with the same characteristics (E) thus provide different values if they have different amounts of participants (Z). The good with the greater number of participants provides the greater value. Put even a little more generally, we can say that the greater the number of a network good's participants, the greater its value for all, both those that are new to the network as well as those who are already members. The more users join a telephone network or buy and use a spreadsheet application software, the greater the value for the existing users. Conversely, the more existing users there are, the greater the value for newcomers will be. Economically speaking, the new users generate positive network externalities for all those who are already a part of the network. If these increased benefits are free of charge, or at the very least extremely cheap, positive network externalities are at play (Steyer, 1997, 206). An example of compensation would be if each new network participant was remunerated by the existing and/or the yet-to-come participants for the increased benefit he caused.

These positive externalities only occur for as long as the network is not crowded, however. If we imagine a cell phone network, for instance, too many registered participants can also cause negative network externalities. Hang-ups or longer waiting periods before registration in the network caused by new participants cause additional costs for the existing customers. At the same time, the entire network becomes less attractive for new customers. Thus–and again, with no (financial) compensation–negative external effects are at play (Liebowitz & Margolis, undated).

Network externalities thus represent a special for an consequence externality, in which the value, marketarily uncompensated, which a person derives form a good depends on how large the **number** of the good's other consumers is (Varian, 2007, 782 et seq.). The occurrence of positive externalities in real network goods has been known for a long time (Rohlfs, 1974), and is largely regarded as a given (Liebowitz & Margolis, undated). But negative external effects in real networks–called congestion costs–have also been observed for some time (Blankart & Knieps, 1994, 452; MacKie-Mason & Varian,1994a, 84 et seq.).

Positive external effects in virtual networks have only become the focus of research at a later date, but they too can be found here (Blankart & Knieps, 1992, 78). If we first regard **software**, we can, for example, make out positive externalities due to decreasing coordination costs. They decrease when a standard is being used. If the same standards are being used, this will make the exchange of data between the single network participants significantly easier. This may be a reason for the dominance of the "Wintel" standard for PCs. This acronym is made up of the operating system **Win**dows and the frequently used chips by **Intel**. Around 90% of the PC market is based on the Wintel standard, which builds on the architecture of the PC as introduced by IBM in the early 1980s. This is why there is often talk of IBM-compatible PCs (Ehrhardt, 2001, 26). Such a standard increases the value for the network participants, respectively lowers the costs connected to network growth, leading to lower data exchange costs or user training, for example (Steyer, 1997, 207). When user numbers are high, software errors will be found more quickly and the number of expert users of a software rises, so that companies who use a prevalent technology will find qualified employees more easily. Such non-marketary services result from the learning effects brought about by the prevalence of a software. The greater the number of users, the more comprehensive the exchange of knowledge and thus the learning effects with regard to the application and troubleshooting (Xie & Sirbu, 1995; Cowan, 1992).

Virtual (software) networks can also give rise to negative externalities, however. Negative network externalities, which have the character of a "congestion", as more and more people clog the network, have so far been given short shrift, though. Among the few exceptions are the analyses of MacKie-Mason & Varian (1994b) as well as Westland (1992). For the users, such phenomena can be experienced as unavailable websites, for example.

Now what is the situation for **content**? Are there direct network effects here, too? An unequivocal confirmation is provided by media economics, which very generally assumes that network effects apply to media (Gerpott, 2006, 332 with many further references; Hutter, 2003, 266 et seq, explicitly for music Haller, 2005, 226). They occur when content of an informative or entertaining character becomes the object of social communication. If people can exchange views on songs, political news or sports results, the contents have a conversation value (Blind, 1997, 156) or a "Synchronization Value" (Liebowitz & Margolis, undated), which springs from the interaction with others. These positive social network effects occur when content (Gerpott, 2006, 332)

- is rated more positively [by economic agents], or demanded more intensively, the greater the number of other people is with whom they can (or could) exchange views on these contents, because social communication, or conversation with like-minded people, thus facilitated is regarded as satisfying (e.g. during a soccer World Cup),

- is demanded [by economic agents] because they want to be able, due to the large number of other people who have (presumably) already taken note of these contents, to eventually develop their own stance ("have a say") on these facts and circumstances (e.g. in the case of bestselling books, such as the Harry Potter series).

These two facets of network effects are often described as Total Effect and Marginal Effect (e.g. Farrell & Klemperer, 2008, 2007). For the former, the value is increased because the existing network participants profit from the inclusion of another user:

One agent's adoption of a good benefits other adopters of the good (Farrell & Klemperer, 2008, 2007).

The latter describes the growing impetus for a potential participant to join the network, the bigger it already is:

> One agent's adoption [...] increases other's incentives to adopt it (Farrell & Klemperer, 2008, 2007).

The Marginal Network Effect thus displays a certain similarity to the bandwagon effect long known in economics (fundamentally Leibenstein, 1950). In the bandwagon effect, demand for a good is increased due to its being consumed by others. The psychological basis of this behavior is regarded as the desire to ape the behavior of a peer group. This effect may be–slightly differently to the social-communicative network effects described above–a more psychologically motivated need for conformity (Stobbe, 1991, 141 et seq.), but it has the same effect on the prevalence of a good.

Content offers can–and this is often neglected–also be subject to negative effects, however, in which case they are

> rated more negatively [...] The greater the number of other persons who already know the content, as a decreasing degree of exclusivity (and the correlative up-to-dateness or novelty reduction, respectively) of the content will lower its subjective value for the single recipient (for example in stock analysts' recommendations to buy/sell) (Gerpott, 2006, 333).

One of the few studies of negative network effects is by Asvanund et al. (2002). They determine, empirically, that in P2P networks

> additional users contribute value in terms of additional network content at a diminishing rate, while they impose costs in terms of congestion on shared resources at an increasing rate.

This example relates a combination of decreasing positive network effects as concerns additional content and negative ones to the emerging scarcity of resources.

Within the direct network effects we just discussed, we can additionally distinguish local and global effects (Sundararajan, 2005). **Global network effects** apply to all participants of a network, **local network effects** occur in "neighborhoods", e.g. Instant Messaging.

> A typical user of communication software like AOL's Instant Messenger (IM) is generally interested communicating with a very small fraction of the potential set of users of the product (his or her friends and family, colleagues, or more generally, members of an immediate 'social network'). This user benefits when more members of their immediate social network adopt IM; they get no direct benefits from the adoption

of IM by other users who they have no desire to communicate with (Sundararajan, 2005, 1).

The increased benefit depends not on the total number of participants in such cases, but on the number of participants in one's personal environment. Such an environment is no longer to be regarded as necessarily geographically determined these days, according to Van Alstyne and Brynjolfsson (2004), since the modern communication channels give rise to communities that generate local network effects location-independently. As opposed to their global counterparts, such local network effects can facilitate diversification due to smaller networks with a larger number of participants from one's personal environment providing greater value than larger networks that have participants who are, socially speaking, further away (Jonard & Yildizoglu, 1998).

3.4.2   Indirect Network Effects

The direct network effects described above always deal with the immediate reciprocal advantages or disadvantages occasioned by an increasing number of users. Apart from these, though, there are also indirect network effects. They describe an increase in a network good's attractiveness due to increased benefits that result not from direct communication, i.e. that are only mediate. Often called indirect network externalities, they mainly refer to the range of offers complementing a network good (Katz & Shapiro, 1985). Indirect network effects thus deal with relationships to the opposite side of the market, whereas direct network effects regard interaction with one's own side of the market, i.e. one's peers (Farrell & Klemperer, 2008, 1974).

In real as in virtual networks, indirect network effects consist of additional offers of complementary products and services. In a real network good, such as a telephone, these can be the different end devices, accessories and information services. In virtual network goods, the primary good–such as an operating system–gives rise to further complementary application (text processing, spreadsheet) and service programs (virus scanners, tuning software). The greater the network, the more complementary offers are to be expected on the market (Economides, 1996, 678 et seq.). A network good's attractiveness, in turn, increases in proportion to the comprehensiveness and variety of the complementary offer of products and services.

Katz and Shapiro here speak of a "Hardware-Software" paradigm (Katz & Shapiro, 1985, 424), which, broadly defined, can be applied to many other goods. If someone plans to buy a PC, it is of no small importance for the individual how many other people have decided to buy a similar hardware, as the number of units sold directly influences the variety of the range of software on offer. In credit card networks, the card would be the hardware and its acceptance by retailers the software. The same goes for durables (hardware) and their complementary repair services (software), or video/DVD players (hardware) and the corresponding films (software), or gaming consoles and their games. Often, there are entire packages of complementary and intra-compatible goods (e.g. operating system, hardware and application software) that are in a utilization context and are factored in during the purchasing decision. In that case, it is not only the individual products which are in competition with each other, but entire systems of goods (Stelzer, 2000, 838; Heindl, 2004, 112 et seq. with further references). Common to all examples is that apart from the primary (basic) product, complementary products and services are of vital consequence for the generation of customer value.

Apart from the aforementioned additional products, complementary services can also be purchasable services such as hotlines or other forms of after sale support. However, in a growing network non-marketary services are increasingly available. Support from other users can be had via Frequently Asked Questions (FAQ) or in newsgroups.

Just like **software**, which requires appropriate complementary products in order to be used, digital **content** can also only be used when the necessary technical complements are available. For example, the more users of online music offers there are, the more providers will bring playback devices such as the iPod onto the market or integrate playback tools into other products, like cell phones or handhelds. For every topic that has a conversation value, i.e. that is subject to direct network effects, electronic communication complements can turn up at any time. The incalculable amount of newsgroups, message boards, blogs, wikis etc. attests the existence of such complements. For physical content, indirect network effects always occur when the electronic or physical complements mentioned just now are available. A physical complement could be a dictionary or a thesaurus, used to complement one's reading of a book. What can also be observed is that the release of a film, for instance, is frequently accompanied by the market launch of related music, books, games or other merchandising products such as mugs or T-shirts. In the case of music, complementary (digital) products are increasingly being created apart from the original song, e.g. ringtones or screensavers. Here we are dealing not with (indirect) network effects as such, though, because no associated form of usage is being created. One first consumes the film and then, possibly, reads the book or listens to the soundtrack. Even if the goods are consumed multiple times, this is done neither simultaneously nor in a direct qualitative relation: in other words, there is no "Hardware-Software" relationship in the precise meaning of the term. Still, it can be observed that film or music hits engender a large palette of merchandising products, the distribution of which is often highly lucrative for the provider (Kiani-Kress & Steinkirchner, 2007, 68). Their sales are boosted by a large network and strong direct network effects. However, a strong distribution of these thematically aligned goods, conversely, positively affects the network of those who have already seen a film or heard a piece of music. Insofar, merchandising offers can be labeled **quasi-complements**.

In our previous representations of indirect network effects, we have not cleanly distinguished between effects and externalities; we will catch up on this now. The aforementioned indirect **network externalities** represent reciprocal influencings, which are partly depicted as prices. When the prices of the complementary products decrease due to an increased demand of the primary product, so-called pecuniary (monetary) external effects are at play. In such cases, market failure is rather improbable. The case is different for the variety of offers as an indirect network effect. Here externalities may well arise, i.e. increased benefits for network participants that are not compensated marketarily. Existing network participants, e.g. Mac users, profit more from additional hardware buyers than the latter do, as each additional buyer increases the impetus on the part of the software industry to provide a more comprehensive offer of applications. The new buyer is not remunerated for the value he provides the existing customers (Church et al., 2002).

Since indirect network externalities are thus not always real externalities, it seems appropriate to speak not of indirect network externalities but, more precisely, of indirect network effects (Gröhn, 1999, 28 et seq., Katz & Shapiro, 1994, particularly 112; Liebowitz & Margolis, undated).

Kind of: Network Effect / Information Good	Direct Network Effects (Interaction Effects) (always network externalities)	Indirect Network Effects (Complementary Offer) (partially network externalities)
Software	• Positive: Data transfer, cooperation, troubleshooting • Possibly negative: Congestion	• Positive: e.g. hardware, additional programs • Possibly negative: viruses, spyware etc.
Content	• Positive: Communication advantages (having common topics of conversation, being able "to have one's say") • Negative: undesirable distribution of exclusive information	• Positive: e.g. end devices, complementary content online, quasi-complements • Negative: e.g. advertising, fraudulent websites

Figure 3.6: Positive and Negative Network Effects for Information Goods.

Indirect network effects are of an overwhelmingly positive nature, because they reinforce the basic product's value. However, they can also be negative. This is the case if the complementary offers provide no value but harm instead. Very large networks often have a downside, e.g. operating systems (MS Windows) or browsers (MS Internet Explorer) are heavily susceptible to attacks via viruses, spyware etc. The costs resulting for the user, for security measures and possibly the rebooting of their systems, must be shouldered by themselves, there is no marketary compensation.

To summarize for network effects: if direct network effects occur, they will always are (positive or negative) network externalities. When it comes to indirect network effects, on the other hand, externalities will only be a part of them, specifically when there is no monetary compensation for the additionally generated value or damage.

There is by now a whole series of empirical studies on the occurrence of network effects. Linde (2008, 54 et seq.) introduces some of them–separated into direct and indirect network effects–in detail. In a broadly conceived analysis of magazines, Clement & Schollmeyer (2009) investigate many empirical studies that deal explicitly with the measuring of network effects. The studies mentioned prove the existence of network effects in the areas of audio/video, Elctronic Payment Systems, IT, communication and gaming consoles.

3.4.3   Two-Sided Network Effects

More recent analyses of network effects show that there is not always–as had previously been suggested–a firm "primary" basic good. Considering once more the traditional complementary goods, it is pretty obvious, for one, in which order the consumer buys: first the car and then the gas, first the razor and then the blades. On the other hand, primary and complementary goods are habitually used in direct connection: the motorist fuels and drives, the bearded man takes up razor and blade.

For complementary network goods, the case is slightly different: depending on one's vantage point, network goods can reciprocally act as complements for each other. Thus in general, the usage of a good by a circle of users can increase the value of a complementary product for another circle of users and vice versa.

> Network effects can also be two-sided: increases in usage by one set of
> users increases the value of a complementary product to another distinct
> set of users, and vice versa (Sundararajan, 2006).

If we regard the users of operating systems (e.g. Windows, Macintosh, Pal OS) as a network and the software developers as another, we will soon recognize that the user of an operating system profits from additional software developers who bring new (compatible) programs onto the market. The developer in turn profits from new users, who boost the sales of his programs. Which is the basic good and which the complement here depends on the perspective one takes.

Goods for which such two-sided (indirect) network effects occur are also called **platforms** (Armstrong, 2004; Rochet & Tirole, 2003). Some examples for this are gaming consoles (console users and game developers), browsers (users and web servers), portals (users and advertisers) (Rochet & Tirole, 2003; Evans, 2003). Platform products can only be successful on the market if both participating networks develop momentum. Thus Rochet and Tirole (2003, 991) report of a scientific journal, the *Bell Journal of Economics* which had been distributed to interested readers for free during its first years of publication in order to let the networks of readers and authors grow as quickly as possible.

In many cases, indirect network effects, as we discussed in the previous section, thus only represent a fraction of two-sided network effects.

In many cases, one may think of indirect network effects as a one-directional version of two-sided network effects (Sundararajan, 2006).

So far, there are only a few empirical analyses, most of them with a rather narrow focus (e.g. Evans, 2003). More broadly defined studies are lacking as of yet (Roson, 2005, 156).

In summation, we can say that network effects are omnipresent in the context of information goods. However, it is also notable that they are not always of equal intensity (Jing, 2000, 3). A very specific textbook will create fewer communicative effects than a new Harry Potter novel. With software, too, there are gradual differences, which can also be confirmed empirically: standard business software emphasizes the basic value for the users over the network effect value, other than is the case with standard office of data exchange software (Buxmann, 2002).

3.5   Information as Public Good

Besides the differentiation into free and scarce goods made above, another distinction common in economics is of significance here, namely the one between public and private goods (e.g. Mankiw et al., 2008, 253 et seq.). **Private goods** we call goods whose ownership rights are allocated to one owner exclusively. We need only think of food, for example, such as a (legally acquired) piece of bread, the consumption of which its owner can be denied by no-one, and the value derived from its consumption belongs to that person alone. Abstractly speaking, we are talking about the principles of excludability (the bread belongs to oneself) and the rivalry of using goods (if one eats the bread oneself, nobody else can eat it). **Public goods**, on the other hand, are goods for which none of these two principles are applicable. We will investigate this in the following.

In the first case, **excludability**, the question is whether others can be excluded from the usage of a good if they are not willing to pay for it. Let us consider, as an example for a public good, the lighting of public streets (Varian, 1998). Here it would be–albeit only with a considerable technological effort–possible to enforce the exclusion of non-paying persons, e.g. by only using infrared light, and only providing those who have paid for it with (only individually usable) infrared goggles. All non-payers would be deprived of the service and have to grope in the dark. This example, as many others, shows that an exclusion could very well be enforced technologically. Generally though, such measures are undesirable, be it for social reasons, because an equal right to lighted streets is regarded as a value for all citizens, or for purely economic reasons, as the costs of changing the lamps and the administration costs are regarded as too high.

	Rivalry Principle	
	Yes	No
Principle of Exclusion Yes	**Private Goods** • Food • Clothes	**Natural Monopolies** • Private security services • Toll streets
No	**Societal Common Goods** • Fish in the sea • Environment	**Public Goods** • National defence • Public streets

Figure 3.7: Consumer Rivalry and the Principle of Exclusion for Goods. Source: following Mankiw et al., 2008, 255.

The second case, the **principle of rivalry**, concerns the question of whether a good's valuation depends upon exclusive usage, i.e. if there is consumer rivalry or if others can use the good without restricting its value for an individual user. A piece of meat can–as long as it is not shared–only be eaten by its owner; in that case, there is consumer rivalry. On the other hand, there is the value from the legal system or inner security, where each citizen derives the same advantage from using the good, independently in principle of the number of other users. If we combine both dimensions in a matrix, we get the four cases in Figure 3.7.

If both principles apply, the good is private, if they both do not apply, it is public. If only one of the principles–either the exclusion or the rivalry principle–is applicable, we are dealing with so-called mixed goods (Mankiw et al., 2008, 254 et seq., Musgrave et al., 1994, 71 et seq.). If, for example, resources are scarce but nobody can be excluded from their usage, we speak of **societal resources**. These are subject to the danger of exploitation. The single user's interest is directed toward as extensive a utilization as possible, as he does not need to pay directly for it. There is no owner who sells the good for a price. In sum, this regularly needs to overuse of the resources, as can be clearly seen in the fishing disputes and the increasing environmental pollution. In the reverse case, the **natural monopolies**, users can be excluded, but there is no consumer rivalry. As long as the provider's capacities are not exhausted, the single users will not impede each other. One more house to be protected by a private security service does not represent a significant decrease of the other contractors' protection. At the same time, it is possible for the provider to exclude some demanders, by not accepting new contracts or canceling existing ones.

Where can we place information goods, then? Are they–as is frequently contested (e.g. Kiefer, 2005, 149 et seq., Beck, 2002, 6 et seq., Klodt, 2001b, 84; Kulenkampff, 2000, 69)–always public goods? In order to answer this question, we have to consult the two principles of exclusion and (consumer) rivalry introduced above.

As regards the **exclusion** of potential customers of an information good, both cases apply–that the exclusion of consumers not willing to pay is possible, and that it is not. The following examples bear this out: if an information is the exclusive property of an economic agent (e.g. an invention in the mind of a scientist), or if it is subject to legal protection, others can very well be excluded from using it legally. Illegally, there is of course still the possibility of information being transmitted, perhaps for a price. In cases where moral and ethical tenets do not form a sufficient basis for securing the principle of exclusion ex ante, it will have to be enforced ex post, after it reaches public consciousness. A particularly radical enforcement of the principle of exclusion is found in the transmission of information relevant to capital markets. It is generally prohibited by the laws regulating financial markets in Germany. In order to secure shareholders' trust in functioning capital markets, it is forbidden to exploit precise, not publicly known information about the emitter, which is of considerable importance for the price of commercial papers, particularly shares ("insider information"), for one's own benefit, transmit it to third parties or use it as the basis of recommendations (Gabler, 2010b). Another form of legal protection applies to patents. Patent-protected knowledge may only be used with the consent of the right holder. In return, the patent's content is made publicly accessible. The principle of exclusion may also be used if the distribution of information is coupled to a private good, as the transmission medium, for which the provider can charge prices.

> The rôle of the information carrier is to transform pure information into an excludable good via coding (Pethig, 1983, 386).

Information, such as the ones that are transmitted via Pay-TV, can only be received in one's household if one owns a decoder and has paid the applicable fees.

For information that is not protected legally or via a medium, the principle of exclusion can only be applied by keeping the information secret. A corporate or trade secret is, for example, a

> not apparently operational procedure, which the proprietor is interested in keeping secret, and which is based on an economic interest worthy of being protected. Confidentiality may apply to technical services not protected under separate rights (construction drawings, calculation sheets, contract documents etc.). They are not conspicuous if kept to a limited and secretive (perhaps even sworn to secrecy) group of people, and if they can be determined only by an expert after arduous study (Gabler, 2010c).

The danger here is still that information can be distributed unwantedly: this goes for information that was first revealed to a small circle (e.g. knowledge of a new research result in the research department), but particularly for such information that are made public (e.g. in the company newspaper, or even as a professional publication via open access; cf. e.g. www.doaj.org). In such cases, its further use can only be controlled incompletely at best. For the codified transmission of information on data carriers (e.g. the reprint of an article, or the copy of a CD), a control may still be possible. However, the mouth-to-mouth spreading of information cannot be prevented.

In this context, it makes sense to distinguish two phases which an information good passes through: production and distribution (Hopf, 1983, 81 et seq.). In the **production** phase, an information good initially remains the exclusive property of an individual, or of a specific group of people, e.g. the team of researchers. In this phase, accordingly, information goods are always private goods for as long as it is either perfectly secured that uncontrolled transmission is impossible or when secure property rights are in place, in the form of patents or licences, by means of which the usage of information can be made dependent upon payment–albeit if, frequently, only with great effort (Hopf, 1983, 81). However, both of these are only seeming certainties–as soon as knowledge is shared by a number of individuals, the principle of exclusion can no longer be safely enforced. If internals from companies leak to the outside, this point stands. A company cannot make the processing of such information contingent upon payment of a fee. The same goes for legal protection, which is not really able to prevent unauthorized usage and frequently cannot even be fully restored retroactively. The multitude of infringement suits filed by companies, and which lead to no clear result, prove this further.

In the phase of (marketary) **distribution**, an information good is always accessible to a multitude of users. The rights holder must expect that the information good will be distributed via illegal channels, resulting in no payments being made.

In using the **principle of exclusion** as a characteristic of the classification of products, a problem arises for information goods, as the principle holds that the usage of goods by one person takes the possibility of its usage away from others (Mankiw et al., 2008, 254). Since information goods–other than physical goods–can be passed on and copied at leisure, though, and–at least electronically–be consumed by an open number of individuals at the same time, no consumer rivalry in the traditional sense applies:

> The usage of information does not wear the product out or use it up, but the information keeps being available to other users, unchanged in scope and quality (Klodt, 2001b, 84).

The entire left-hand side of the matrix in Figure 3.7 would thus be blanked out, since information goods could then, per definitionem, have neither the status of private goods nor that of societal resources. It would be more appropriate for the characterization of information goods to focus on changes experienced by the group of users (of software), or the group of initiates (of content) as a consequence of the respective information good's distribution. As a suitable distinguishing characteristic, we suggest concentrating not on the principle of exclusion, but instead on the emerging **network effects**. They can be positive if the existing network becomes more valuable as it grows larger, i.e. if its participants are increasingly better off. This is the case, for example, if one is able to communicate with a growing number of people about certain events, or in a certain language. The network effects can also be negative, though, if the growth represents a disadvantage for the participants. The unwanted transmission of a private or business secret is a suitable example. If we adjust the goods matrix accordingly, we will find the following four variants:

	Network Effects	
	Negative	Positive
Yes **Principle of Exclusion**	**Private Information** • Secret • Inventor's product idea • Insider information (ideal)	**Market Information** • TV show via Pay-TV • Film in the cinema
No	**System Information** • Stock advice • Insider information (real)	**Public Information** • Radio transmission • Free internet publication

Figure 3.8: Network Effects and the Principle of Exclusion for Information Goods.

For **private information**, others can be excluded from usage by not being allowed to share it, or via effective legal protection. If information is available to a certain group of people (e.g. company employees or subscribers of a stock market journal), and if that group would be at a disadvantage if the information were to be distributed further, we speak of **system information**. Information whose acquisition can be made contingent upon payment of a fee is called **market information**. If, on the other hand, the distribution is free and unfettered, it is **public information**.

In summary, we can say that information goods can be private goods only in their production phase, and even then only if they can either be kept secret or enjoy effective legal protection. If we take into account that even private information goods that are legally protected can only be partly protected from unlawful usage, we can see that information goods are not public goods per se, but display a clear tendency over the course of their distribution to become public goods via an intermediary mixed-good stage (Hopf, 1983, 87).

3.6   Interdependence of Economic Particularities

Information goods thus display four economic particularities that can lead to potential market failure. We introduced these particularities individually in the preceding sections, and it has become clear each time that they noticeably tighten the conditions for a successful market offer on the part of information providers. But this is not the end of it, as these four particularities additionally interact with each other. They thus become elements of a system with relations between each other. For this reason, we will refer to them as mechanisms from now on. How do those four mechanisms work together? This can be made quite clear via the example of four smaller cycles.

When a network is built, and it reaches a growing number of participants, direct network effects will occur from a certain point on. These positive interaction effects cause the occurrence of a network effect value for a network good apart from its basic value. If the number of participants reaches the so-called critical mass (Rohlfs, 1974, 29; Linde, 2008, 125 et seq.), the network effect value will be so strong from that point on that further participants join the network on the sole basis of the existing, or expected, network size (positive feedback). The growing installed base in turn leads to the providers of complements developing an increased interest in producing attractive offers for the network. At the moment, this can be observed for the proliferation of iPhone apps, which grow at breakneck speed. Other providers, like Palm/HP or Nokia, have difficulties building a similar offer. An attractive complementary offer reinforces the cycle, as it draws ever more participants. Chapter 20 of this book will discuss these aspects.

The installed base, i.e. the number of users of a product or a technology, here represents the key variable connecting the mechanisms. The provider experiences a pronounced cost degression as the result of economies of scale, scope and experience (Linde, 2008, 120 et seq.). This improves their cost position vis-à-vis slower-growing competitors and opens up latitudes for lowering prices, which in turn makes it easier for them to increase their market share.

Quality information about a widely prevalent product is easily available. They are found on the web, in testing journals or, increasingly, first-hand from one's social circle. Information asymmetries are thus reduced more quickly and also benefit the increase of one's customer base.

The last of the four mechanisms refers to the tendency of information goods to become public goods, i.e. goods that have (positive) network effects and from the usage of which third parties cannot be effectively excluded. Illegal distribution paths may establish themselves next to the legal distribution. This may have a negative effect on sales, but definitely favors the establishment of a standard, and thus complete market domination. For more on this subject, see Chapter 19 of this book.

Information providers thus face some tough challenges. What kinds of information goods they apply to, how one analyzes one's industry accordingly and how to meet them strategically will be among the questions addressed throughout this book.

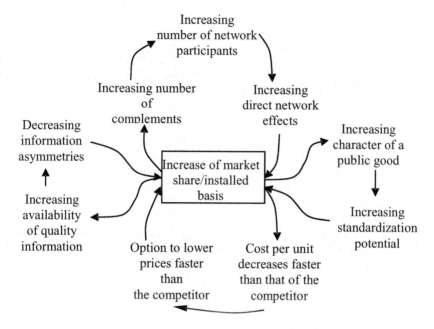

Figure 3.9: Interaction Mechanisms for Information Goods.

3.7   Conclusion

- Information goods have four particular economic characteristics, which can easily lead to market failure: First-Copy-Cost effects, pronounced experience and credence qualities, network effects, the hard-to-implement principle of exclusion.
- First-Copy-Costs are the manufacturing costs of the first unit of an information good. The First-Copy-Cost effect (FCCE) refers to the very pronounced fixed-cost degression that comes about due to the relation between very high fixed costs and very low variable costs.
- The more average variable costs fade into the background behind fixed costs, the more the course of (total) average costs will approach that of average fixed costs. If we assume the extreme case scenario of zero variable cost, both curves will even be congruent with each other.

- Information asymmetry occurs when one side of the market is better informed than the other. This opens up space for exploiting this differential strategically, e.g. by offering lower quality. A general consequence of existing information asymmetries is that good quality is displaced by bad.
- Following Arrow, information is subject to a paradox: the value of an information good cannot be accurately assessed prior to purchase without personally getting to know at least parts of the good beforehand.
- For information goods, experience and credence qualities dominate the search qualities. Sellers have the option of transforming experience qualities into search qualities.
- Whether it is the experience or the credence qualities that dominate in an information good depends upon the buyers' expert knowledge.
- Information-economically, a network is a summary of the users of a certain good or compatible technologies. If the users are physically connected, we speak of real networks. If the users are only logically connected, the networks are virtual.
- Network goods do not only provide a value that stems from their inherent qualities (basic value, original value) but additionally provide their individual consumers with a further value derived from the total number of other users (network effect value, derivative value).
- Information goods are network goods with direct and indirect network effects.
- Direct network effects occur because networks provide value via their linking of their elements (participants). The number of linked elements in a network thus influences its total value. A new network participant increases the value of those that are already members (total effect) and at the same time makes the network more attractive for further, new participants (marginal effect). Direct network effects can occur globally, affecting all participants of the network, or locally, in one's neighborhood.
- Indirect network effects describe an increase of a network's attractiveness due to benefit increases that result not from direct communication but are mediate. They are the result of a good's complementary offer.
- Complementary offers can be additional products for a basic good or services. Merchandising offers are quasi-complements.
- Direct network effects are always (positive or negative) network externalities. Indirect network effects are no externalities, most of the time. They are so only if there is no pecuniary compensation for the additionally generated value or damage.
- If network goods are complements for each other reciprocally, we speak of two-sided (indirect) network effects and platform products.
- For information that is not entirely protected, either legally or via the medium, the principle of exclusion can only be enforced via complete secrecy.

- The rivalry principle cannot be purposefully applied as a feature of the goods classification of information goods. It is far more pertinent to focus on the occurring positive and negative network effects.
- Due to the limited applicability of the principle of exclusion and mostly positive network effects, information has the tendency to become a public good.

3.8   Bibliography

Akerlof, G.A. (1970). The market for "lemons". Quality, uncertainty, and the market mechanism. Quarterly Journal of Economics, 84, 488-500.

Armstrong, M. (2004). Competition in Two-Sided Markets. Department of Economics, University College London.

Arrow, K.J. (1962). Economic welfare and the allocation of resources for invention. In National Bureau of Economic Research (ed.), The Rate and Direction of Inventive Activity. Economic and Social Factors (pp. 609-626). Princeton.

Arthur, W.B. (1989). Competing technologies, increasing returns, and lock-in by bistorical events. Economic Journal, 99, 116-131.

Arthur, W. B. (2004 [1994]). Increasing Returns and Path Dependence in the Economy. [repr.]. Ann Arbor: University of Michigan Press.

Asvanund, A., Clay, K., Krishnan, R., & Smith, M.D. (2002). An Empirical Analysis of Network Externalities in P2P Music-Sharing Networks. Published by H. John Heinz III School of Public Policy and Management. Carnegie Mellon University.

Bayón, T. (1997). Neuere Mikroökonomie und Marketing. Eine wissenschaftstheoretisch geleitete Analyse. Wiesbaden: Gabler.

Beck, H. (2002). Medienökonomie. Print, Fernsehen und Multimedia. Berlin: Springer.

Beck, H. (2006). Medienökonomie - Märkte, Besonderheiten und Wettbewerb. In Scholz, C. (ed.), Handbuch Medienmanagement (pp. 221-237). Berlin, Heidelberg: Springer-Verlag (Springer-11775 /Dig. Serial]).

Blankart, C. B., Knieps, G. (1992). Netzökonomik. In Boettcher, E. (ed.), Jahrbuch für Neue Politische Ökonomie. Ökonomische Systeme und ihre Dynamik (pp. 73-87). Tübingen: Mohr.

Blankart, C.B., & Knieps, G. (1994). Kommunikationsgüter ökonomisch betrachtet. Homo oeconomicus, 9(3), 449-463.

Blind, S. (1997). Fernsehen und neue Medien–eine ökonomische Einschätzung. In Schanze, H. (ed.), Qualitative Perspektiven des Medienwandels. Positionen der Medienwissenschaft im Kontext "Neuer Medien" (pp. 150-159). Opladen: Westdt. Verlag.

Buxmann, P. (2002). Strategien von Standardsoftware-Anbietern. Eine Analyse auf der Basis von Netzeffekten. Zeitschrift für betriebswirtschaftliche Forschung (zfbf), 54, 442-457.

Buxmann, P., & Pohl, G. (2004). Musik online. Herausforderungen und Strategien für die Musikindustrie. WISU, 4, 507-520.

Church, J., Gandal, N., & Krause D. (2002). Indirect Network Effects and Adoption Externalities. Working Paper N°. 02-30. Foerder Institute for Economic Research.

Clement, M., & Schollmeyer, T. (2009). Messung und Wirkung von Netzeffekten in der ökonomischen Forschung - Eine kritische Analyse der empirischen Literatur. Journal für Betriebswirtschaft, 58, 173-207.

Cowan, R. (1992). High technology and the economics of standardization. In Dierkes, M., & Hoffmann, U. (eds.), New Technology at the Outset. Social Forces in the Shaping of Technological Innovations (pp. 279-300). Frankfurt a.M.: Campus Verlag.

Darby, M. R., & Karni, E. (1973). Free competition and the optimal amount of fraud. Journal of Law and Economics, 16, 67-88.

Dietl, H., & Royer, S. (2000). Management virtueller Netzwerkeffekte in der Informationsökonomie. Zeitschrift Führung + Organisation (zfo), 69(6), 324-331.

Diller, H. (2008). Preispolitik. 4th ed. Stuttgart: Kohlhammer.

Donnelly, J.H. (ed.) (1981). Marketing of Services. Chicago, Ill.

Downes, L., & Mui, C. (1998). Unleashing the Killer App. Digital Strategies for Market Dominance. Boston, Mass: Harvard Business School Press.

Economides, N. (1996). The economics of networks. International Journal of Industrial Organization, 14, 673-699.

Ehrhardt, M. (2001). Netzwerkeffekte, Standardisierung und Wettbewerbsstrategie. Wiesbaden: Dt. Univ.-Verlag.

Ernst, M., & Giesler, V. (2000). Erhöhter Preiswettbewerb durch das Internet. Theoretische Analyse und empirischer Befund im Vergleich mit traditionellen Vertriebsformen. In GfK-Nürnberg, Gesellschaft für Konsum- Markt- und Absatzforschung e. V. (ed.), GfK Jahrbuch der Absatz- und Verbrauchsforschung, 46, 191-210.

Ernst, M., Hofmann, W., & Walpulski, D. (1995): Erhöhter Preiswettbewerb durch Informationsmärkte. Theoretische Analyse und empirischer Befund. GfK-Nürnberg, Gesellschaft für Konsum- Markt-und Absatzforschung e. V. (ed.), GfK Jahrbuch der Absatz- und Verbrauchsforschung, 1, 65-84. Berlin.

Ernst, M., & Köberlein C. (1994). Eine ökonomische Betrachtung von Information und Qualität auf Informationsmärkten. cogito, 10(1), 6-10.

Evans, D.S. (2003). Some empirical aspects of multi-sided platform industries. Review of Network Economics, 2(3), 191-209.

Farrell, J., & Klemperer, P. (2008). Coordination and lock-in: Competition with switching costs and network effects. In Armstrong, M., & Porter, R. H. (eds.), Handbook of Industrial Organization. Reprint, 3 (pp. 1967-2072). Amsterdam: Elsevier North-Holland.

Farrell, J., & Saloner, G. (1986). Installed base and compatibility. Innovation, product preannouncements, and predation. American Economic Review, 76, 940-955.

Flechtner, H. J. (1966). Grundbegriffe der Kybernetik. Stuttgart: Wiss. Verl.-Ges.

Friedrich, B.C. (2003). Internet-Ökonomie. Ökonomische Konsequenzen der Informations und Kommunikationstechnologien (IuK). Eine industrieökonomische Fallstudie. Dresden. (Dresden Discussion Papers in Economics, 8/03).

Gabler Wirtschaftslexikon - Online Ausgabe (2010a). Stichwort: Marktversagen. Gabler Verlag (ed).

Gabler Wirtschaftslexikon - Online Ausgabe (2010b). Stichwort: Insiderinformationen. Gabler Verlag (ed).

Gabler Wirtschaftslexikon - Online Ausgabe (2010c). Stichwort: Betriebs- und Geschäftsgeheimnis. Gabler Verlag (ed).

Gerpott, T.J. (2006). Wettbewerbsstrategien–Überblick, Systematik und Perspektiven. In Scholz, C. (ed.), Handbuch Medienmanagement (pp. 305-355). Berlin, Heidelberg: Springer-Verlag Berlin Heidelberg (Springer-11775 /Dig. Serial]).

GfK-Nürnberg, Gesellschaft für Konsum- Markt-und Absatzforschung e. V. (ed.), GfK Jahrbuch der Absatz- und Verbrauchsforschung. Berlin.

Göbel, E. (2002). Neue Institutionenökonomik. Konzeption und betriebswirtschaftliche Anwendungen. Stuttgart: Lucius & Lucius.

Grau, C., & Hess, T. (2007). Kostendegression in der digitalen Medienproduktion. Klassischer First-Copy-Cost-Effekt oder doch mehr. MedienWirtschaft, Sonderheft, 26-37.

Graumann, M. (1993). Die Ökonomie von Netzprodukten. Zeitschrift für Betriebswirtschaft (ZfB), 63(12), 1331-1355.

Gröhn, A. (1999). Netzwerkeffekte und Wettbewerbspolitik. Eine ökonomische Analyse des Softwaremarktes. Tübingen: Mohr Siebeck.

Habermeier, K.F. (1989). Competing Technologies, the Learning curve, and Rational Expectations. European Economic Review, 33(7), 1293-1311.

Haller, J. (2005). Urheberrechtsschutz in der Musikindustrie. Eine ökonomische Analyse. Lohmar: Eul-Verlag.

Hauser, H. (1979). Qualitätsinformationen und Marktstrukturen. Kyklos, 32, 739-736.

Heindl, H. (2004). Der First Mover Advantage in der Internetökonomie. Hamburg: Kovač.

Hopf, M. (1983). Informationen für Märkte und Märkte für Informationen. Frankfurt/M.: Gabler.

Hutter, M. (2000). Besonderheiten der digitalen Wirtschaft–Herausforderungen an die Theorie. WISU, 12, 1659-1665.

Hutter, M. (2003). Information goods. In Towse, R. (ed.), A Handbook of Cultural Economics (pp. 263-268). Cheltenham: Elgar.

Jing, B. (2000). Versioning information goods with network externalities. In Association for Information Systems (ed.), International Conference on Information Systems. Proceedings of the Twenty First International Conference on Information Systems (pp. 1-12). Brisbane, Queensland, Australia.

Jonard, N., & Yildizoglu, M. (1998). Technological diversity in an evolutionary industry model with localized learning and network externalities. Structural Change and Economic Dynamics, 9, 35-53.

Jost, P.J. (ed.) (2001). Die Prinzipal-Agenten-Theorie in der Betriebswirtschaftslehre. Stuttgart: Schäffer-Poeschel.

Kaas, K.P. (1995). Informationsökonomik. In Tietz, B. (ed.), Handwörterbuch des Marketing (pp. 971-981). 2nd ed. Stuttgart: Schäffer-Poeschel (Enzyklopädie der Betriebswirtschaftslehre, IV).

Katz, M.L., & Shapiro, C. (1985). Network externalities, competition, and compatibility. American Economic Review, 75(3), 424-440.

Katz, M. L., & Shapiro, C. (1994). Systems competition and network effects. Journal of Economic Perspectives, 8(2), 93-115.

Kelly, K. (2001). NetEconomy. Zehn radikale Strategien für die Wirtschaft der Zukunft. München: Ullstein-Taschenbuchverlag.

Kiani-Kress, R., & Steinkirchner, P. (2007). Melodien für Millionen. Wirtschaftswoche, 59, 66-75.

Kiefer, M.L. (2005). Medienökonomik. Einführung in eine ökonomische Theorie der Medien. 2nd ed. München: Oldenbourg.

Klodt, H. (2001a). Und sie fliegen doch. Wettbewerbsstrategien für die Neue Ökonomie. In Donges, J. B., Mai, S., & Buttermann, A. (eds.), E-Commerce und Wirtschaftspolitik (pp. 971-981). Stuttgart: Lucius & Lucius.

Klodt, H. (2001b). Die Neue Ökonomie: Aufbruch und Umbruch. Die Weltwirtschaft, 1, 78-98.

Klodt, H. (2003). Wettbewerbsstrategien für Informationsgüter. In Schäfer, W., & Berg, H. (eds.), Konjunktur, Wachstum und Wirtschaftspolitik im Zeichen der New Economy (pp. 107-123). Berlin: Duncker & Humblot (Schriften des Vereins für Socialpolitik, NF293).

Klodt, H., & Buch, C.M. (2003). Die neue Ökonomie. Erscheinungsformen, Ursachen und Auswirkungen. Berlin: Springer.

Kulenkampff, G. (2000). Zur Effizienz von Informationsmärkten. Berlin: Vistas-Verlag.

Leibenstein, H. (1950). Bandwagon, snob, and veblen effects in the theory of consumers' demand. The Quarterly Journal of Economics, 64, 193-207.

Liebowitz, S.J., & Margolis, S.E. (undated). Network Externalities (Effects). (Online)

Linde, F. (1997). Virtualisierung von Unternehmen. Wettbewerbspolitische Implikationen. Wiesbaden: Dt. Univ.-Verlag.

Linde, F. (2008). Ökonomie der Information. 2nd ed. Göttingen: Univ.-Verlag. Göttingen.

MacKie-Mason, J.K., & Varian, H.R. (1994a). Economic FAQs about the Internet. Journal of Economic Perspectives, 8(3), 75-96.

MacKie-Mason, J.K., & Varian, H.R. (1994b). Pricing Congestible Network Resources. University of Michigan. (Online)

Mankiw, N.G., Taylor, M.P., Wagner, A., & Herrmann, M. (2008). Grundzüge der Volkswirtschaftslehre. 4th ed. Stuttgart: Schäffer-Poeschel.

Meffert, H. (2005). Marketing. Grundlagen marktorientierter Unternehmensführung. Konzepte, Instrumente, Praxisbeispiele. 9th ed. Wiesbaden: Gabler.

Mengen, A. (1993). Konzeptgestaltung von Dienstleistungsprodukten. Eine Conjoint-Analyse im Luftfrachtmarkt unter Berücksichtigung der Qualitätsunsicherheit beim Dienstleistungskauf. Stuttgart: Schäffer-Poeschel.

Molho, I. (2001). The Economics of Information. Lying and Eheating in Markets and Organizations. Reprinted. Oxford: Blackwell.

Musgrave, R.A., Musgrave, P.B., & Kullmer, L. (1994). Die öffentlichen Finanzen in Theorie und Praxis. 6th ed. Tübingen: Mohr.

Nelson, P. (1970). Information and consumer behavior. Journal of Political Economy, 78, 311-329.

Peer, M. (2010). Twitter sagt den Erfolg von Filmen voraus. Handelsblatt, 67, 04/08/2010, 61.

Pethig, R. (1983). On the production and distribution of information. Zeitschrift für Nationalökonomie, 43, 383-403.

Picot, A., Reichwald, R., & Wigand, R.T. (2003). Die grenzenlose Unternehmung. Information, Organisation und Management. Lehrbuch zur Unternehmensführung im Informationszeitalter. 5th ed. Wiesbaden: Gabler.

Richter, R., Furubotn, E.G., & Streissler, M. (2003). Neue Institutionenökonomik. Eine Einführung und kritische Würdigung. 3rd ed. Tübingen: Mohr Siebeck.

Rochet, J.C., & Tirole, J. (2003). Platform competition in two-sided markets. Journal of the European Economic Association, 1(4), 990-1029.

Rohlfs, J. (1974). A theory of interdependent demand for a communications service. Bell Journal of Economics and Management Science, 5, 16-37.

Roson, R. (2005). Two-sided markets: A tentative survey. Review of Network Economics, 4(2), 142-160.

Shapiro, C., & Varian, H.R. (1999). Information Rules. A Strategic Guide to the Network Economy. [repr.]. Boston, MA: Harvard Business School Press.

Simon, H. (1998). Preismanagement kompakt. Probleme und Methoden des modernen Pricing. Repr. Wiesbaden: Gabler.

Stelzer, D. (2000). Digitale Güter und ihre Bedeutung in der Internet-Ökonomie. Das Wirtschaftsstudium (WISU), 6, 835-842.

Stewart, T.A. (1998). Der vierte Produktionsfaktor. Wachstum und Wettbewerbsvorteile durch Wissensmanagement. München: Hanser.

Steyer, R. (1997). Netzexternalitäten. Wirtschaftswissenschaftliches Studium (WiSt), 26(4), 206-210.

Stigler, G.J. (1961). The economics of information. Journal of Political Economy, 69, 213-225.

Stobbe, A. (1991). Mikroökonomik. 2nd ed. Berlin: Springer.

Stock, W.G. (1995). Elektronische Informationsdienstleistungen und ihre Bedeutung für Wirtschaft und Wissenschaft. München: ifo Institut für Wirtschaftsforschung.

Sundararajan, A. (2005). Local Network Effects and Network Structure. Center for Digital Economy Research Leonard N. Stern School of Business (ed). New York University.

Sundararajan, A. (2006). Network Effects. (Online)

Talkenberg, A. (1992). Die Ökonomie des Bildermarktes. Eine informationsökonomische Analyse. Göttingen: Vandenhoeck & Ruprecht.

Tietz, B. (ed.) (1995). Handwörterbuch des Marketing. 2nd ed. Stuttgart: Schäffer-Poeschel (Enzyklopädie der Betriebswirtschaftslehre, IV).

Tirole, J. (1995). Industrieökonomik. München: Oldenbourg.

van Alstyne, M., & Brynjolfsson, E. (2004). Global Village or Cyber-Balkans. Modeling and Measuring the Integration of Electronic Communities. (Online).

Varian, H.R. (1998). Markets for Information Goods. (Online).

Varian, H.R. (2007). Grundzüge der Mikroökonomik. Studienausgabe. 7th ed. München: Oldenbourg.

Weiber, R. (1992). Diffusion von Telekommunikation. Problem der kritischen Masse. Wiesbaden: Gabler.

Weiber, R., & Adler, J. (1995). Positionierung von Kaufprozessen im informationsökonomischen Dreieck. Zeitschrift für betriebswirtschaftliche Forschung (zfbf), 47(2), 99-123.

Westland, J.C. (1992). Congestion and network externalities in the short run pricing of information system services. Management Science, 38(7), 992-1009.

Wetzel, A. (2004). Geschäftsmodelle für immaterielle Wirtschaftsgüter: Auswirkungen der Digitalisierung. Erweiterung von Geschäftsmodellen durch die neue Institutionenökonomik als ein Ansatz zur Theorie der Unternehmung. Hamburg: Kovač.

Willke, H. (1991). Systemtheorie. Eine Einführung in die Grundprobleme der Theorie sozialer Systeme. 3rd ed. Stuttgart: Fischer.

Woll, A. (ed.) (2008). Wirtschaftslexikon. 10th ed. München: Oldenbourg.

Xie, J., & Sirbu, M. (1995). Price competition and compatibility in the presence of positive demand externalities. Management Science, 41(5), 909-926.

Zeithaml, V.A. (1981). How consumer evaluation processes differ between goods and services. In Donnelly, J. H. (ed.), Marketing of Services (pp. 186-190). Chicago, Ill.

Part B

Information Society

Chapter 4

Information Sociology

4.1. "Information Society" and "Knowledge Society"

The focus of this and the following two chapters is the environment of the information market, which we will regard from what is a mixture of an information-scientific and a sociological/politological (Chapter 4), legal (Chapter 5) and ethical perspective (Chapter 6), respectively.

Initially, we will turn to the specifics of the information and knowledge society, which leads us to the area of information sociology and politology. Publications on information sociology are particularly numerous, as this area has been researched for decades (the standard German-language work, Gernot Wersig's "Informationssoziologie", is from the year 1973). Today, information has assumed a predominant position in our globalized and networked world, and is thus at the center of political life (Lyon, 2005, 233). According to David Lyon (2005, 233), information sociology deals both with the social effects of the streams of digital information and with the information itself:

> Reference to the internet ... serves as a reminder that today information cannot be conceived separately from communication. The social repercussions of flows of information through networks–the internet, cell phones and so on–present one of sociology's most stimulating challenges (...). But information itself requires sociological analysis if we are to grasp its connection with crucial issues from identity and inequality to matter and meaning.

Information and knowledge have become pillars of our society (and of its subsystems, such as economy, education and culture), so it is with good reason that we speak of an information society and a knowledge society. At this point, we would like to distinguish between these two forms of society: an information society is grounded by information and communication *technology* (ICT) (Sassen, 2002); a knowledge society has information *content*, i.e. knowledge itself, as an additional basis. Knowledge societies of today are invariably also information societies, as the transmission of the information contents is generally performed with ICT. Such an emphasis on knowledge has the advantage that a society is not defined by its technological basis alone (Heidenreich, 2003, 25), in which it remains an open question what exactly to do with this basis. We can thus avoid "tunnel vision", a short-sighted, purely information-technology-centric point of view (Brown & Duguid, 2002).

In order to clarify the two terms "information society" and "knowledge society", we would like to draw on the theory of the **fifth Kondratieff** (Stock, 2000, 1 et seq.). The underlying theory is that of long waves, which goes back to Nikolai D. Kondratieff (1926). Via empirical material, Kondratieff shows evidence of the existence of long cycles in capitalist economy, spanning around fifty years. In these cycles, economic and technological innovations play a central role (Kondratieff, 1926, 591):

> While the long waves decrease, a significant numbers of important discoveries and inventions are being made in production and transport technology, which are, however, generally only applied to economic practice at the beginning of the new long rise.

Changes in science and technology indisputably have a great influence on the course of the capitalist dynamic, but they are not an external effect for economic development (Kondratieff, 1926, 593):

> However, from the scientific aspect it would be a... mistake to think that the direction and intensity of these discoveries and inventions are entirely up to chance; it is far more probable that this direction and this intensity are a function of the requirements of practical reality and the previous development of science and technology.

Kondratieff's conclusion is (Kondratieff, 1926, 594 and 599):

> (It is not enough) for really changing production technology to have scientific-technological inventions; these can stay ineffective, as long as the economic preconditions for their use are lacking... In claiming the existence of long waves and denying that their emergence is due to chance, we claim at the same time that the long waves are due to causes that are in the nature of capitalist economy.

Joseph A. Schumpeter (1961) modifies Kondratieff's approach. Here the technological innovations become driving forces of economic development (Schumpeter, 1961, 181 and 176):

All cyclical movements can be explained via terms from the process of economic development. Innovations, their immediate and more remote effects as well as the system's reaction are the common root of all ...

Innovations (are) the actual source of cyclical fluctuation.

Leo A. Nefiodow (1991) follows Schumpeter and interprets innovations as the cause of capitalist economy's long waves (Nefiodow, 1991, 47):

> Innovations that break extensive new economic ground and cause a swarm of follow-up innovations ('bandwagon effect') are called basic innovations. They have been and are the fundamental innovations for long phases of the economy. The steam engine, the train, electrification and the automobile are some examples for basic innovations. Each of these inventions has generated a long period of prosperity and led to a far-reaching reorganization of society.

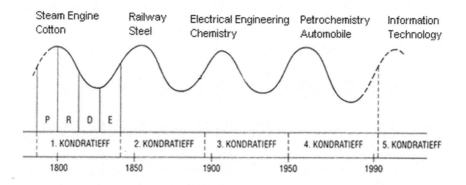

Figure 4.1: Kondratieff Cycles According to Nefiodow. Source: Nefiodow, 1994. P: Prosperity, R: Recession, D: Depression, R: Recovery. Typical Networks of the Single Cycles: 1. Shipping, 2. Rails, 3: Lines (Electricity, Gas), 4. Roads, 5. Internet.

From the beginning of capitalism, four long waves can be observed: a first cycle with the steam engine as its basic innovation, a second cycle based on the train, the third on chemistry and electricity and finally the fourth cycle, based on petro-chemistry and automatization. The fifth Kondratieff wave is already emerging (Nefiodow, 1991, 39):

It is being carried by the innovation potential of the resource information, and it will bring about the conclusive establishment of the information society.

Each Kondratieff cycle gives rise to typical networks, such as railway lines in the second cycle, gas and electricity networks in the third and road networks/freeways in the fourth cycle. The networks of the fifth Kondratieff wave are telecommunication networks, led by the internet.

If we heavily simplify Kondratieff's and Nefiodow's (and Schumpeter's) positions, then Kondratieff sees the economy as the cause of change; the effect is, among others, the respective basic innovation. Nefiodow and Schumpeter regard the basic innovation as the cause, and a typically long economic wave as its effect. In one scenario, the economy of the information society is the cause of innovations in the area of information, communication and telematics, in the other, the named innovations are the causes of the information society. A mediating position between the two seemingly opposed cause-and-effect chains is posited by Gerhard Mensch's Metamorphosis model (1975, 15):

> Schumpeter's concession: 'innovations carry economies' and cause economic upturns, we will elaborate here. We ask where the innovations come from–after all, they don't just fall from the sky ('exogeneous variable'). Rather, they come about within the evolutionary interplay of stagnation and innovation.

According to this, the basic innovation is the cause of the upturn phase of a Kondratieff cycle, whereas the cause of the previous cycle's downturn is the economic system (Mensch, 1975, 85):

> The entire evolutionary goings-on in the socioeconomic whole are tied into a regulatory circuit: stagnation in parts of the system and in the system as a whole facilitates single innovations in structurally suitable spots, and the innovation lets many an established part look like dead wood. Innovation and stagnation induce each other.

Mensch's Regulatory Circuit model thus claims the existence of reciprocal dependencies between the economic system and its respective underlying basic innovations.

So, for the record: according to the theory of the fifth Kondratieff, the resource information is the cause and the bearer of a long economic wave, where the economy of the fifth Kondratieff is closely tied to research and development in the area of information.

What distinguishes the technology of the fifth Kondratieff? The resource information, which carries the information society, requires corresponding information and communication-technological, i.e. **telematic devices and services**: computers, networks, software etc. Additionally, companies, administrations and citizens must be willing to and capable of adequately using these devices. This leads to massive usage of telematic devices, of information and communication technology, in public as in private.

What regularities are inherent to the resource information? The movement of information rests, according to Manfred Bonitz (1986a, 1986b), on the basis of two simple underlying principles: the holography principle and the tempo principle. The **Holography Principle** describes the area of information (Bonitz, 1986b, 192):

> The entirety of human knowledge is one gigantic hologram, which consists of all the stores, databases etc. that mankind has.

The entirety of information is virtually available everywhere (Bonitz, 1986a, 7):

> Any given... information is retrievable from any given location.

The information society–and as its consequence, the information economy–is thus globally defined as a matter of principle.

The **Tempo Principle** contains the movement of information in time (Bonitz 1986b, 192):

> Accordingly, every information has the tendency to move so as to reach its addressee in the shortest possible time.

The tempo principle holds for the entire history of human communication, but the speed has increased from every stage to the next. Every introduction of a new communication channel (e.g. books, magazines, abstracts, professional online databases, internet) has saved society time. Electronic information transmission in international networks such as the internet has reached the tempo limit. Information can be sent at the moment of its inception and received in real time. The object of both principles is knowledge stored and set in motion, so that a society that has realized both the holography and the tempo principle is the first that can be called a "knowledge society". This also means that members of the society collaborate in communicating and creating new knowledge, as David and Foray (2002, 14) emphasize:

> Knowledge-based economies emerge when people, with the help of information and communication technologies, group together in an intense effort to co-produce (i.e., produce and exchange) new knowledge.

This boils down to three main components: a significant number of a community's members combine to produce and reproduce new knowledge (diffuse sources of innovation); the community creates a "public" space for exchanging and circulating the knowledge; new information and communication technologies are intensively used to codify and transmit the new knowledge.

The knowledge society is concerned with all kinds of knowledge, but scientific and technical knowledge reaches a particular significance (Böhme, 1997), as production is heavily driven by scientific-technological results (we need only think of biotechnological or environmentally friendly products, which would be nearly impossible to produce without a scientific basis) and the population's opportunities in life are dependent on the levels of science and technology reached by society (directly–measured by age–on medicine and the health services and indirectly–measured by status and income–on the level of education, which can at least partly be traced back to scientific and technological experiences).

This leads us to another aspect of the discussion, to learning. For Martin Heidenreich (2002, 338), the significance of knowledge-based activity increases in a knowledge society, leading to a change in the status of education, and thus of learning. For every member of a knowledge society, life-long learning becomes essential. Also, a knowledge society as a whole must produce the right institutions to foster this learning. According to Joseph Stiglitz (2000), an infrastructure can only ever be built locally and never imported, as the local institutions have to learn to successfully implement "their" knowledge in "their" country. "Environmental aids" toward building a knowledge society can only work–according to Stiglitz–if the country receiving this aid learns to adequately use its own knowledge capacities and is aware of the fact that a knowledge society, with the continually dynamic stores of knowledge on which it is built, is always changing as a matter of principle. The goal of every knowledge society is thus to learn how to learn in order to become a **learning society**. Stiglitz (2000, 38) stresses:

> Thus if a global knowledge-based institution wants a country to learn a 'truth' about development, then it should help the local knowledge institutes and policy makers to carry out the requisite research, experimentation and social dialogue to learn it themselves–to make it a 'local social discovery'. Creating this local knowledge infrastructure and practice entails 'learning how to learn', that is, creating the capacity to close the knowledge gap, an essential part of a successful strategy.

We can now put together our working definitions of "information society" and "knowledge society". "Information society" refers to a society

- whose basic innovations are carried by the resource information (theory of the fifth Kondratieff) and

- whose members preferably use telematic devices for information and communication purposes.

A "knowledge society", on the other hand, is a society

- that has all the aspects of an information society,
- in which information content of all kinds is available everywhere and anytime in its entirety (holography and tempo principle), and is also used intensively,
- in which lifelong learning (and consequently, learning how to learn) becomes necessary.

No widely prevalent definitions of "information" and "knowledge society" have emerged in the literature, so that both terms are often used synonymously.

Frank Webster (1995, 6) describes the knowledge society (he calls it the "information society") via five criteria:

- technological: the knowledge society uses information and communication technology to process, store and transmit information,
- economic: in the knowledge society, there is an expanding information market (as described by Machlup and Porat),
- occupational: information work (in accord with Bell and Porat) is predominant in the knowledge society,
- spatial: information networks and information streams ("space of flows" in the sense of Castells, see below!) create a second space apart from the one that is geographically defined,
- cultural: due to the ever-present information streams, the knowledge society is dependent on media, so that Webster (1995, 21) characterizes it as a "media-laden society".

It is definitely possible to represent the knowledge society as an "era" of human development. In this sense, the knowledge society replaces the industrial society (Stehr, 1994).

4.2 Information and Knowledge Infrastructure

In statistics on the information society (e.g. of the International Telecommunications Union ITU), we mostly find (reasonably) well-measurable indicators being used, which essentially rest on telephony, broadband networking and internet and the usage of these technologies in private households as well as governmental institutions. Many of these indicators display the number of technological devices or services (e.g. the number of computers or cell phone contracts) in a certain area (mainly per country) as well as the penetration of these devices and services (designated as relative values per resident, sometimes per household) in the regional unit. **Telephony** is described via landline (indicator: telephone lines per 100 residents), cellular network and VoIP (Voice over Internet Protocol). In **broadband networking**, the object is fast data networks such as the currently dominant DSL (Digital Subscriber Line with data rates of up to 2 Mbit/s) or the VDSL (very high speed DSL with data rates of 10 Mbit/s and more). The indicator bundle of the **in-**

ternet registers internet hosts, computer density (number and penetration of computers, respectively), internet connections (households and companies with internet access, respectively) as well as internet users (persons who have used the internet over the last three months–no matter where: at home, at work, in an internet café).

Much harder to operationalize are the parameters of the knowledge society; here we are called upon to demarcate the levels of education, research and development and librarianship of a country as indicators. **Education** can be roughly packed into parameters via the rate of alphabetization and the ratio of high school or university graduates per year group, among other factors. The level of **scientific research** can to some extent be expressed via publication and citation numbers of scientific articles in large multidisciplinary databases (such as Web of Science or Scopus), the level of **technological research and development** via the number of granted patents. (Little suited, but frequently used are the numbers of patent applications. An invention submitted for a patent can be deemed not new and thus rejected as irrelevant. Often, patent applicants do not even apply for an examination of its content.) For **librarianship**, we can think of parameters such as the Library Index developed for German Libraries (BIX), which expresses the offer, use, efficiency and development potential of public and scientific libraries quantitatively (Xalter, 2006).

There exist several established indicators on the country level, which cover the level of development of the country in question. A complete overview of the societal development is available in form of the **Human Development Index** (HDI) (Anand & Sen, 1992), which is calculated by the United Nations' Development Program (UNDP, 2007). The HDI has a value range from 0 (worst value) to 1 (best value) and takes into account four indicators:

- Residents' expected lifespan at time of birth,
- Adults' rate of alphabetization,
- Ratio of pupils and students in their respective age groups,
- Gross Domestic Product per person (in PPP Dollars).

Compound indicators such as the HDI have the methodical problem that they have no clearly delineated real object that can be registered (Kelly, 1991; McGillivray, 1991; Sagar & Najam, 1998). In spite of this, the HDI has asserted itself–at least as a vague parameter–for the registering of the level of development of entire nations. In 2005, the best-developed countries, according to the HDI, were Iceland and Norway (with a value of 0.968), followed by Australia, Canada and Ireland (Germany is in 22nd place with an HDI of 0.935).

The **ICT Development Index** (IDI) of the International Telecommunications Union (ITU) covers the influence of information and communication technologies on a country's development (Figure 4.2). It is made up of three partial indicators:

- ICT Infrastructure and Access: Landline telephony, mobile telephony, internet bandwidth per internet user, number of households with computer and those with internet access,
- ICT Use: Internet users per residents, broadband users via landline and mobile accesses,

- ICT Capability: Rate of alphabetization in adults, number of pupils and students in their age group (only secondary and tertiary education here, as opposed to the HDI).

The countries with the highest ICT influence are–according to the IDI for the year 2007–Sweden, in front of Korea, Denmark, the Netherlands, Iceland, Norway and Luxemburg (all countries with an IDI greater than 7); Germany follows in 13th place at some distance (IDI = 6.61) (ITU, 2009, 22).

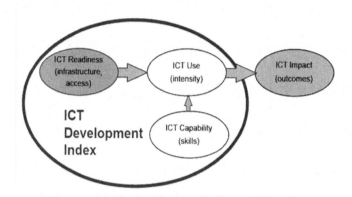

Figure 4.2: Partial Indicators of the ICT Development Index (IDI). Source: ITU, 2009, 14.

The HDI and the IDI have a few aspects in common (alphabetization and number of students), but the high correlation of R = +0.90 (Pearson) of both sets of parameters still surprises: the higher a country's level of development (according to the HDI), the higher the level of development of its information and communication technology (Figure 4.3)–and vice versa.

The (according to Pearson: two-sided) correlation between the Human Development Index and the Network Readiness Index for the year 2005 is +0.75 for all countries for which both values are available. This is, as in the HDI-IDI comparison, a relatively large value, which states: the more developed a country (operationalized according to the HDI), the higher the level of development of its information society (operationalized according to the NRI)–and vice versa (Peña-López, 2006). A similar conclusion is drawn by Graumann and Speich (2009, 41):

> For almost all of these countries (the top countries according to the NRI, A/N), a high level of education, particular technological performance and adjustment capabilities as well as a significant power of innovation are typical.

The two indicators of the information society, the IDI and the NRI (recorded via the value sets of the HDI for 2005 and the IDI for 2007), are strongly correlative with a value of +0.89. Which of the aspects (HDI, IDI, NRI) is the cause of the respective other cannot be gleaned from the correlation; it is to be assumed, however, that the level of development of a country and the level of development of its information society influence and fertilize each other.

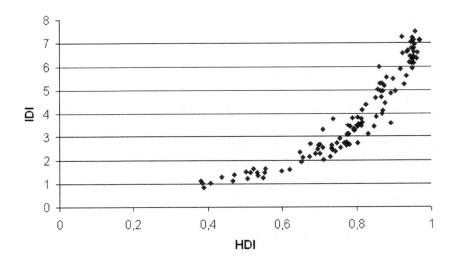

Figure 4.3: Correlation Between the Human Development Index (HDI) and the ICT Development Index (IDI) for 112 Countries. Raw Data: HDI: UNDP, 2007 (Year Under Review: 2005); IDI: ITU, 2009 (Year Under Review: 2007); the Calculations Are Our Own.

Apart from the NRI and the IDI, there are other parameters that attempt to record the level of development of countries' respective information and knowledge infrastructure; the "ICT Diffusion Index" of the United Nations (United Nations, 2006) and the "Knowledge Economy Index" of the World Bank (World Bank, 2009) are worth being mentioned.

As yet unsolved is the open problem of how to explain why some countries get good results in all indicators and others bad ones, respectively. Scandinavian countries are always represented at the top, alongside the large Anglophone countries Canada, Australia and the U.S.A. as well as city-states like Singapore or Hong Kong. It is remarkable that in most of the top countries the catholic church plays only a minor role at best (Bredemeier & Stock, 2000, 238). Does the tendency toward knowledge monopolies of the powerful (including the church) in catholic-dominated countries, observed throughout previous centuries, which simultaneously sought to prevent the spreading of information to all "lower" members of society, really have an influence on the distribution of the information and knowledge society? The most developed information societies are coastal states with a centuries-old maritime tradition, or with important seaports (Henrichs, personal communication 2009). Does such a culture provoke an openness toward foreign countries and economic forms and–connected to this–to a variety of information, which finds expression in today's level of development of these countries' knowledge society?

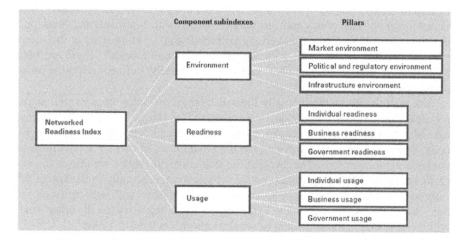

Figure 4.4: Partial Indicators of the Networked Readiness Index (NRI). Source: Mia, Dutta, & Geiger, 2009, 6.

4.3   The Informational City and "Glocality"

The information economy acts in two spaces simultaneously: in geographical space and in digital space. That being said, it strongly affects not only digital, but also geographical space. At this point, we want to discuss two aspects of the meeting of digitalization and geographical spaces: the position of the technological centers of the information market and the role of cities in the age of information (Castells; 1996, 1997, 1998). The informational city, being aligned to streams of information, capital and power ("space of flow"), fundamentally changes the character of the city, previously aligned to spaces ("space of place"). Manuel Castells (1993, 136) thus defines the information city:

> The new spatial logic, characteristic of the Informational City, is determined by the preeminence of the space of flows over the space of places. By space of flow I refer to the system of exchanges of information, capital, and power that structures the basic processes of societies, economies and states between different localities, regardless of localization.

Technological centers of the internet do not occur randomly in space, but are distinguished by two fundamental characteristics:

- dense spatial concentration (often at the periphery of agglomerations),
- digital connectedness with other centers (Castells, 2001, 227).

Examples for technological centers are Silicon Valley outside San Francisco (with Google, Yahoo! and eBay) and Seattle's environs (with Microsoft and Amazon). For Castells (1996), the spatial and digital interlinking of companies in the information economy corresponds with the theory of "small worlds". There are both locally linked companies and short paths (either literally, defined by spatial proximity, or via digital connections).

Although the internet potentially links all regions on earth–cities as well as rural areas–the world's population is concentrated in (large) cities in the internet age. Manuel Castells (1996) explains this via the spatial concentration of jobs, income-generating activities, services and the possibilities of human development in the large agglomerations. The fact that the technological centers are also in the agglomerations reinforces the trend toward urbanization, especially in the age of the information economy. Telework, company-independent and accomplished on one's home PC, is rare, according to Castells. **Mobile telework**, on the other hand, will increase due to the spreading of wireless internet (Castells, 1996):

Informatization is accompanied by the automatization of large economic sectors. This has massive repercussions on jobs, termed **job polarization** (Goos & Manning 2007; Spitz-Oener, 2006). Routine tasks are increasingly accomplished by (information) machines; the corresponding jobs (e.g. accounting or machine operation) become redundant. The working population is left with the non-routine tasks. These are, in turn, split up into the more manual jobs (e.g. domestic aid or pizza delivery) and the more analytic (e.g. research and development) and interactive tasks (e.g. management). The labor market in developed information societies is thus split into well-paid (and trained) workers and (very) badly paid workers with few qualifications–workers in the average education and income bracket tend to disappear due to the increasing automatization of their previous tasks.

The digital connectedness creates a second space besides geographical space. Companies in agglomerations interlink with each other, but also with the rest of the world, via digital networks. According to Castells (1996), such "global knots" are specific areas, all over the planet, that are connected with equivalent areas in any given location, but are only loosely connected to the area directly surrounding it, if at all.

Glocality connects–in language as in the world–globality with locality.

The **informational city** (or "information city") is the ideal-typical city of the fifth Kondratieff cycle (Hall, 1985), and of Machlup and Porat's information economy and Bell's post-industrial society, respectively. Such cities are metropoles and fixate on "spaces of flow" and the information and communication technologies facilitating these (Hepworth, 1987, 253):

Metropolitan cities are the principal loci of the 'information revolution'. In order to differentiate the urban development process by the life span of new information and communication technologies, I propose to use the term 'information city'. For definitional purposes, this type of city has a two-dimensional characterization: it is a metropolitan economy which specializes mainly in the production, processing and distribution of information, *and*, its dominant infrastructure is comprised of the converging technologies of computers and telecommunications.

Glocal cities are found both in former industrial countries (as for example in the City of London–with branches in the West End and the Docklands) and in (former) newly industrialized countries (e.g. in Singapore or Dubai). From the perspective of infrastructure, such cities have two faces: as dual cities, they have an infrastructure for geographical space (such as traffic, power or water), and secondly, an infrastructure for digital space (telecommunication). Dual cities also embody the meeting of informational and non-information professions (following Machlup and Porat, see Chapter 1), Castells (1989, 225-226) describes it:

> The new dual city can also be seen as the urban expression of the process of increasing differentiation of labor in two equally dynamic sectors within the growing economy: the information-based formal economy, and the down-graded labor-based informal economy. ... (T)wo equally dynamic sectors, interconnected by a number of symbiotic relationships, define specific labor markets and labor processes in such a way that the majority of workers are unlikely to move upwardly between them. The economy, and thus society, becomes functionally articulated but organizationally and socially segmented.

Two areas are characteristic of the information city (Gospodini, 2005, 1472):
1. they are the seat of internationally active financial service providers as well as technology and knowledge-intensive companies and institutions, and thus also house their employees–many information cities are thus also "world cities" in Friedmann's (1995) definition;
2. they have extensive cultural establishments, a great offer of leisure activities and enticing shopping facilities.

For Frank Webster (1995, 210), the informational city as Castells sees it (Susser, 2002) has an interesting social (and not necessarily positive) component with regard to the employees of the informationally oriented companies and institutions. In urban areas that either house these companies' seats or their employees, the poor cannot go and the rich are protected by security services. Webster's example is London's Docklands. The former port facilities in East London have been demolished and replaced by modern apartment and office buildings (Webster, 1995, 209 et seq.):

> The Canary Wharf project, aiming to provide 71 acres and 50,000 jobs, was the most ambitious attempt to use the former docks for offices, expensive accommodation (close to the office, but unsuitable for children, hence ideal for yuppies), state-of-the-art rail links to the City, high-class restaurants, and an appealing ambience designed with the informational professionals uppermost in mind. ... Those living and working in the area beforehand, the London working class, had been pushed aside ... Moreover, changes taking place increasingly *exclude the poor* by, for example, a marked expansion of housing and specialist estates which are gated and guarded to keep out the 'dangerous classes'.

The more globally a city acts, the more dependent it will be on international streams of information, capital and power and the less it will depend on national politics and its power dynamics. John Friedmann (1995, 25) emphasizes:

> The more the economy becomes interdependent on the global scale, the less can regional and local government, as they exist today, act upon the basic mechanisms that condition the daily life of their citizens. The traditional structures of social and political control over development, work and distribution have been subverted by the placeless logic of an internationalized economy enacted by means of information flows among powerful actors beyond the sphere of state regulations.

World cities are always "information-rich localities" (Flint &Taylor, 2007, 270). With the advent of informational world cities, accordingly, comes a continual denationalization (Brenner, 1998, 12). Both world cities and the multinational enterprises that inhabit them increasingly act uninfluenced by governments. Flint and Taylor (2007, 270) emphasize, however:

> This is not to say that territorial states are about to disappear; rather, world cities are becoming new loci of power, which will interact with states in new ways.

Formerly industrially-oriented cities that have not managed to make the transition toward the informational city and cities on the periphery of the global economy, including nearly all cities in developing countries, fall by the wayside (as "economic deadlands") (Brenner, 1998, 7). The impulse behind these developments, according to Neil Brenner (1998, 29), is probably globalized capitalism.

Another characteristic of information cities is their development toward a "consumer landscape". Apart from the mixing of cultural forms (in an information city like London, one can be an Arsenal fan while regularly visiting the British Library, go to the opera one week and a rock concert the next) and the emphasis on leisure and pleasure, the central aspect of consumership is "shopping", according to Webster (1995, 212):

> At the heart of all this is consumption, and perhaps most notable, *shopping*, which in the postmodern city takes on a primary cultural role. ... Here we are referring to shopping as *an end in itself*, as a pleasurable experience ... There is a slogan which captures this well (and in appropriate parodic form). 'I shop therefore I am'.

Both the number and the offer of shopping malls in advanced information and knowledge societies, such as Singapore or Dubai, confirm this hypothesis. Please note: we are talking about physical "event shopping", and not online shopping.

The leisure and entertainment offer of glocal cities reminds one of an urban amusement park–as the giant wheels at the center of London or Singapore symbolize–and lets Swyngedouw and Kaïka (2003, 11) speak of a "staged archaeological theme park".

The status of **science parks** is redefined in the informational city. Science parks in the information society comprise the entire process, from basic research via applied research up to product and process innovation, and not–as before–merely the latter stages of the innovation process. It is necessary for the early phases of innovations in particular that universities be integrated into the science parks (Hansson, Husted, & Vestergaard, 2005, 1048):

> A first step in this direction would be to place future science park initiatives firmly within the institutional framework of existing higher education institutions. More generally, when it comes to promoting the commercialisation of research it is highly recommendable to make a clear and consistent choice of base models. In this respect, the present study strongly indicates, that a model without intermediary institutions is preferable to a model in which intermediary institutions play a key role.

If one wants to model the significance of a city, trade or industrial production parameters will be of no avail for glocal informational cities. Rather, one must work out their position in the global information economy. Here, too, one cannot orient oneself on administrative borders, as important companies often do not settle in the city itself but shift their activities (or at least some of them) to the periphery. For New York, it can be observed that central services have been shifted from Manhattan into the direction of suburban areas in Connecticut and New Jersey (Hall, 1997, 319). Peter Hall proposes access to information (both face-to-face and via ICT) as key indicators for the informational city, to be joined by values representing labor costs or rent. The goal is to find alternative ways of measuring the attractiveness of different kinds of information activities in the city (Hall, 1997, 320):

The outcome should be a new urban hierarchy of centres and sub-centres, based on position within a set of global information flows.

Figure 4.5: Start Page of the Digital City of Singapore. Source: www.sg.

Purely **virtual cities** (sometimes called "information cities" in the literature) are strictly to be differentiated from information cities. These former represent either a virtual counterpart of a real city (e.g. www.sg for tourist information and www.gov.sg for government information on Singapore) or a location-independent "city" (e.g. Facebook or eBay, with millions of users that come and go, buy and sell, or socialize by giving other "citizens" ratings, for instance). Virtual cities are characterized by strong interactive and collaborative components that invite one to stay. Sairamash, Lee and Anania (2004, 31) write:

> All this means we can expect a new kind of virtual urbanization, where people spend more and more of their lives socializing and engaging in economic and political activities. We expect them to take many flavors, forms, and specializations, while offering services involving social interaction, business transaction, municipal services, and daily commerce.

4.4 The Digital Divide

Social inequality is a fundamental characteristic of human societies, material (e.g. income and wealth) and immaterial resources (e.g. education and health service) are unequally distributed–single groups in society have more (sometimes much more) resources than other. Social inequality is also a feature of the resource information, so that we can roughly distinguish, at this point, between the information-rich and the information-poor (Warschauer, 2003). What separates these groups is the "**digital divide**" (Britz, 2004; Britz, 2008). On the one side are those that have access to information and communication technology (particularly to the internet; Guillén & Suárez, 2005), who use ICT or the internet and also know how to adequately apply the knowledge acquired there (privately and professionally) (OECD, 2005, 69 et seq.). On the other side are those people

- with (a) no access to ICT, or the internet,
- who (b) have physical access to the networks but cannot use them (e.g. because they do not understand the language of the WWW documents, which are mostly in English),
- who (c) use the networks but are unable to usefully apply the knowledge (e.g. because they are totally fixated on online games).

Aspects (a) to (c) are the expression of "information poverty" (Lumiérs & Schimmel, 2002, 51):

> Information-poor people do not possess sufficient information or they lack opportunities to apply the right information. Therefore they are disabled in their personal development and don't have enough support in their process of decision making.

Chen and Kidd (2008, 130) provide the following handy definition of the digital divide:

> The "digital divide" is the phrase commonly used to describe the gap between those who benefit from new technologies and those who do not–or the digital "haves" and the digital "have-nots".

In the first few years of the internet, the digital divide had been predominantly defined via ICT access, whereas the question today is whether someone has access to knowledge and uses it. According to Vehovar et al. (2006, 281), these two aspects of the digital divide should be kept separate at all times:

> The first digital divide–which refers to differences in access and usage–will inevitably disappear when the Internet becomes universally accessible. However, the digital divide relating to experience and advanced usage will exist after this takes place.

Factors that play a role in deciding on what side of the divide a person is situated are the presence of ICT in the region and the entire country, the motivation to deal with ICT, the internet as well as the services and documents available there in the first place, social status, degree of education, information literacy (dealing with the internet, its services, its tools etc.), age and place of residence (in the country or in agglomerations). Without the realization of important factors–first and foremost information literacy (Hunt & Birks, 2008)–the process of lifelong learning inherent to the information society would hardly be possible. Jan van Dijk (1999; van Dijk & Hacker 2003, 315 et seq.) systematizes the gaps that together make up the digital divide:

- "mental access": the lack of elementary experiences in dealing with digital media,
- "material access": no access to computers and network connections,
- "skills access": the lack of information literacy, caused by inadequate-systems or a lack of experience on the users' side,
- "usage access": the lack of significant usage possibilities.

If we disregard material access, all other gaps named by van Dijk are to do with an inadequate state of knowledge on the part of the information-poor. It thus makes sense to transfer the **knowledge gap hypothesis** to the digital divide. This hypothesis has generally been formulated with regard to the relation of social groups toward mass media usage (Tichenor, Donohue, & Olien, 1970, 159-160):

> As the infusion of mass media information into a social system increases, segments of the population with higher socioeconomic status tend to acquire this information at a faster rate than the lower status segments, so that the gap in knowledge between these segments tends to increase rather than decrease.

When the stream of information increases–more diverse television channels, but also more varied web offers–social groups with a higher status and thus, tendentially, higher education, profit more from the information on offer than lower-status and less-educated groups. Hence, as information grows and grows, so will the knowledge gap between the social groups. The knowledge gap hypothesis is an example for the success-breeds-success principle, which has been formulated by as early a thinker as Matthew (13.12)–with explicit reference to knowledge:

> For whosoever hath, to him shall be given, and he shall have more abundance: but whosoever hath not, from him shall be taken away even that he hath.

The reference point in Matthew 13.10 through 13 is perception, i.e. knowledge. He who knows, will be given even more knowledge; he who knows little will lose that little in time. This lesson from the Bible appears to apply to the knowledge society as well. One of the decisive factors for participating in the knowledge society is one's respective knowledge base; it must be large enough to find further relevant knowledge, process it and thus usefully apply it to one's professional and private activities.

The original knowledge gap hypothesis, which obviously could not refer to the internet and its services, as these did not exist then, can also be observed in the digital divide, as an "internet gap" (Bonfadelli, 2002, 73 et seq.). Heinz Bonfadelli (2002, 75 and 79) reports on the results of his empirical studies:

> (E)ducation seems to be the crucial factor (when accessing the internet, A/N), followed by income; differences based on age and sex are less strong.

> People with higher education use the Internet for informational and service-oriented purposes; people with lower education use the Internet significantly more for entertainment reasons.

The following remark by Bonfadelli (2002, 81) strikes us as extremely important:

> Internet access alone obviously does not automatically guarantee an informed and knowledgeable public.

Participation in the knowledge society does not hinge on education alone. To put it very simplistically: one has to *want* to participate. Motivation changes the tendencies of the knowledge gap. Individuals and groups with a high motivation for using media but a low level of education are similar to better-educated groups in their media behavior–they thus surmount the knowledge gap at least partly. Nojin Kwak (1999, 403) analyzed empirical data on two motivation variables (interest and participation in an election campaign, respectively) and found out that education and motivation influence the knowledge acquisition process independently of each other.

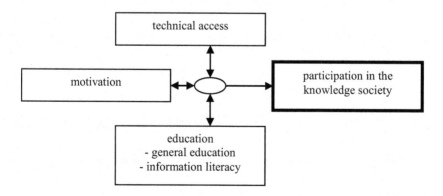

Figure 4.6: Participation Factors of the Knowledge Society.

Figure 4.6 summarizes the main aspects that decide on participation or non-participation in the knowledge society. Access to ICT and the internet (as well as the possibility of financing this in the first place) is a necessary condition, but it only becomes a sufficient condition when it is joined by the motivation for dealing with the particularities of the knowledge society, and when a level of education is reached that facilitates an adequate usage of digital media.

4.5   Deviant Information Behavior

In sociology, psychology and pedagogy, deviant behavior is understood as behavior that does not conform to socially accepted values, or that breaches norms regarded as valid. If someone breaches a moral norm, we speak of "deviance"; if someone breaches codified legal norms, this turns into "delinquency". "Deviant information behavior" refers to deviance and delinquency in dealing with digital information, particularly on the internet (Phillips, 2006). Here we would like to highlight some important forms of deviant information behavior.

4.5.1   Problematic Internet Usage

The first area summarizes problematic internet usage (PIU). This refers to internet use that affects one's mental, emotional and physical health right up to internet addiction. As such a dependence can at best be classified as "behavioral addiction" (Shapira et al., 2003, 209), and is thus an example of pathological conditioning, which is why several authors (such as Shapiro et al.) reject the term "addiction" and speak instead of PIU. It is not clear yet whether PIU is a new psychiatric cluster of symptoms, or whether symptoms previously in existence have merely resulted in a new behavioral pattern in connection with the internet (Yellowlees & Marks, 2007). We can distinguish the following forms of PIU:

- communication-oriented PIU (excessive use of chat, e-mail, message boards, blogs, social networks),
- knowledge-oriented PIU (excessive participation in Wikis or science-oriented blogs),
- game-oriented PIU (excessive use of online games; particularly MMOGs ("massively multiplayer online games") like WoW ("World of Warcraft")),
- sex-oriented PIU (excessive consumption of pornography on the internet).

Common to all forms is that the patients spend a significant amount of time performing non-professional internet activities and, correspondingly, neglect other social relationships (Liu & Potenza, 2007). In surveys of users with PIU it turned out that many suffer from a feeling of loneliness, where cause and effect, however, are not yet clearly distinguishable (Ceyhan & Ceyhan, 2008, 700):

(I)t is difficult to determine whether loneliness is a symptom of excessive Internet use or whether heavy Internet use is a symptom of loneliness.

Even in online games this loneliness can be found, particularly in newcomers ("alone together"; Ducheneault et al., 2006), but it is reduced the longer one plays (and participates in "guilds" in WoW). The common social activities predominantly take place in digital space, but they have effects on the offline world, epitomised by WoW guild members often meeting in person (Nardi & Harris, 2006).

4.5.2   Online Harassment

In online or cyber harassment, we distinguish between "cyberstalking" and "cyberbullying", either in the workplace or (as "dissing") at school (Miller, 2006; Shanmuganathan, 2010). **Cyberstalking** means using the internet and its services to stalk other people, thus massively disturbing them (Hoffmann, 2006, 197). Cyberstalking may occur on its own, but can also happen in addition to traditional behaviors (telephone calls, physical approaches). Frequently, e-mail, Instant Messenger and chat are used to build up a sort of "hyper-intimacy" (sending of "love" mails); these cyber-approaches are then transferred into the real world (after online contact come physical threats or approaches) and threats are made (Spitzberg & Hoobler, 2002, 80).

In **cyberbullying**, the offender intends to harm his victim via internet (Kowalski, Limber, & Agatston, 2008). Online mobbing gained great attention when the media reported the suicide of a thirteen-year-old MySpace user in consequence of receiving malicious posts. Megan, plagued by depression from the start, had befriended a certain Josh on MySpace (Ruedy, 2008). "His" tone, friendly at first, took a turn for the worse when he started saying things like "the world would be a better place without you", which led Megan to kill herself. "Josh" was actually the mother of one of Megan's friends from school, who wanted to use this ploy to find out what Megan thought of her daughter. Josh's account was also being used by the daughter and one of her mother's colleagues, with the latter writing the fatal comment. None of the parties involved has been convicted of a crime. Cyberbullying primarily takes place via e-mail and chat, but it can also manifest itself in the publishing of discriminating reports, videos or photos (possibly even malicious photo montages) in social networks (e.g. Facebook), filesharing services (e.g. YouTube and Flickr) or on the WWW. Cyberbullying seems to have established itself firmly among adolescents. Li (2007) reports that around 15% of those surveyed stated that they had digitally terrorized others, and 25% admitted to having been the victims of such attacks. While there are no gender-specific differences to be observed among the victims, the perpetrators are more commonly male than female. 22.3% of all male junior high school students surveyed have experience in active cyberbullying, compared to 11.6% of girls (Li, 2006, 163).

Figure 4. 7: Seller Profile on eBay. Source: www.ebay.de.

4.5.3   Online Fraud

The internet gives fraudsters many new ways to play their trade. **Fraud on auction portals** (such as eBay), for instance, is widely spread (Gavish & Lucci, 2008). This form of fraud has several manifestations (Gregg & Scott, 2006, 98):

- the product is paid for by the customer but not delivered by the seller,
- the seller deceives the customer about the product's value (and thus exploits the known information asymmetries in the information economy with criminal intent),
- the seller demands additional "fees" after the auction ends,
- black-market products (e.g. illegally copied CDs or DVDs) are offered,
- the seller bids on his own products (under several aliases) in order to increase their prices.

In order to counteract auction fraud, one may use the reputation systems that evaluate buyers and sellers via a simple and self-evident star scale (calculated via the number of ratings and the share of positive ratings) (Figure 4.7) or bills processed by a trustee.

Nigerian Letter Fraud (or "419 fraud", after the relevant paragraph in Nigerian law) plays on the gullibility of mail recipients. The fraudster addresses his victim under some pretext and promises great financial gain (see Figure 4.8). If the victim agrees, certain "fees" will fall due, then others, and so on (Cukier, Nesselroth, & Cody, 2007, 2)

> For the funds to be released, the victim must provide further fees and payments, usually by wire transfer, for various taxes and expenses to consummate the transaction. The victim must pay these fees (attorney fees, duty, taxes, etc.) to process the transaction, and the sender claims

that "just one more" fee/stamp/duty/form, etc. must be processed before the millions can be released.

The more a victim has already gotten involved with the "business", the smaller the probability that he will back out.

Providers of context-sensitive online ads for search engines (e.g. Google with the products AdWords–ads on the Google search page–and AdSense–ads on Google's partner websites) are doubly vulnerable to fraud. **Click fraud** occurs both as competitor click fraud (in AdWords) and as publisher click fraud (in AdSense) (Soubusta, 2008). Competitor Click Fraud regards the multiple clicking of a competitor's ad in order to financially damage him or (after reaching the maximum daily budget) remove his ad from the list of ads on Google. Publisher Click Fraud sees the advertising partner massively click on ads for his website in order to increase his revenue. Click fraud is either done manually or with the help of botnets (see below!).

Phishing ("Password Fishing") means the fraudulent spying of user names, passwords etc. in order to use the information thus acquired for online banking fraud or the unlawful usage of credit cards (Jakobsson & Myers, 2007). The fraudsters create a (more or less exact) copy of a trustworthy website, to which they point via e-mail, or send an equally trustworthy e-mail. The victim is then asked to surrender secret information about accounts, passwords etc. In a variation on this procedure, the fraudster works with malware that enters the communication lines between the customer and his bank, for example, thus "redirecting" the victim's access data. The goal of phishing is always identity theft leading to financial losses for the victims.

Dear Friend,

FROM THE DESK

OF MR IBRAHIM MOUSTAPHA

My name is mr Ibrahim Moustapha. I am a banker with the Bank of africa, Burkina Faso.I am still working with the Bank , but am about to retire from active Bank service to start a new life but I am sceptical to reveal this particular secret to a stranger .You must assure me that everything will be handled confidentially because we are not going to suffer again in life.

It has been 10 years now that most of the greedy African Politicians used our bank to Launder money to overseas through the help of their Political advisers. Most of the funds which they transferred out of the shores of Africa was gold and oil money that was supposed to have been used to develop the continent. Their Political advisers always inflated the amounts before transfer to foreign accounts so I also used the opportunity to divert part of the money hence I am aware that there is no official trace of how much was transferred as all the accounts used for such transfers were being closed after transfer.

I acted as the Bank Officer to most of the politicians and when I discovered that they were using me to succeed in their greedy act, I also cleaned some of their banking records from the Bank files and no one cared to ask me because the money was too much for them to control. They laundered over $150m dollars, during the process .As I am sending this message to you, I was able to divert more than ($20m) to an escrow account belonging to no one in the bank. The bank is anxious now to know who is the beneficiary to the funds because they have made a lot of profits with the funds.It is more than ten years now and most of the politicians are no longer using our bank to transfer funds overseas.

The $20M has been lying waste but I don't want to retire from the bank without transferring the funds to a foreign account to enable me share the proceeds with the receiver. The money will be shared 60% for me and 40% for you .

There is no one coming to ask you about the funds because I secured everything.I only want you to assist me by providing available bank account where the funds can be transferred. You are not to face any difficulties or legal implications as I am going to handle the transfer personally. If you are capable of receiving the funds, do let me know by replying me immediately to enable me give you detailed information on what to do.

For me, I have not stolen the money from anyone because the other people that took the whole money did not face any problems. This is my chance also to grab my own but you must keep the details of the funds secret to avoid leakages as no one in the bank knows about the funds.

Please supply me the following:

Your current contact address and Telephone Numbers. Whether you will be able to come down to my country to meet me before the commencement of the transfer.

I shall intimate you on what to do when I get your confirmation and acceptance. If you are capable of being my trusted associate, do declare your consent to me. Waiting for your urgent response.

Yours Faithfully,

Mr Ibrahim

Figure 4.8: Preliminaries to Nigerian Letter Fraud. Source: E-Mail by "Mr Ibrahim".

4.5.4   *Criminal Internet Usage*

In computer criminality, the computer plays a special role; it can be the target of an attack, the instrument of a criminal act or a piece of evidence (Vacca, 2005, 6). It is evidence insofar as information about criminal acts is stored on it (e.g. if a hacker stores a file illegally copied from another computer on his own computer). If a third party copies unwanted programs that cannot be controlled by the user on a computer, these are termed "malicious software", or malware (Kaspersky, 2008). Malware refers to either viruses (self-replicating program components that attach themselves to other programs, are transmitted alongside them and cause changes in the target computer that cannot be controlled by the user), Trojan horses (independent, non-self-replicating programs) or computer worms (independent programs that self-distribute via networks, e.g. via "infected" e-mails). The motivation for creating and distributing malware lies in the perpetrators' need for self-affirmation or for belonging to an information subculture and in general criminal designs. Thus malware can be used to store keystrokes or copy data from the target computer.

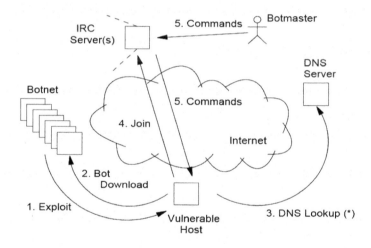

Figure 4.9: Functionality of a Botnet. Source: Abu Rajab et al., 2006, 42. IRC: Internet Relay Chat; DNS: Domain Name System (Optional for Botnets).

A particular type of computer criminality is the running of a **botnet**. A "botmaster" uses malware to "take over" a computer (as "bot") without its user's knowledge, and then interconnects it with other bots to form a network via the Internet Relay Chat protocol. The botmaster can use "Command and Control" (C&C)

channels to exploit the entire network to serve his purposes (Figure 4.9). Cases of application include:

- sending spam mails,
- performing click fraud,
- falsifying online surveys,
- performing diversified Denial of Service (DoS) attacks in order to cause a system crash by overloading the target system (Freiling, Holz, & Wicherski, 2005).

What **motives** lead information specialists to commit "cybercrime"? Neufeld (2010) found out that around two thirds of all internet crimes are committed with the motivation to gain financial advantages, be it via identity theft or fraud. Revenge plays a role in roughly 16% of all cases. Here it is mainly laid-off IT specialists who attack the system of their former employer. In 10% of cases, the hacker seeks to build a reputation in the relevant subculture. 8% are committed with a view to gaining one's own company economic advantages, e.g. via finding out competitors' business secrets. In another 8% of cases, the "thrill" of committing the deed is a leading motive.

4.6   Information Subcultures: Hackers, Crackers, Crashers

Defined by common interests, hackers have formed their own subculture, which has its own set of values and its own style (Thomas, 2002, 141):

> As a subculture, hackers have developed a particular sense of style that has been transformed over time and has been structured as an increasingly fluid and powerful form of resistance. As a youth culture, hackers are continually looking for ways to perturb or disrupt authority and challenge any understanding or representation of who they are.

The typical (American) hacker is white, lives in the suburbs, is a male member of the middle classes and probably goes to High School. As a rule, he is self-motivated, is a great technology enthusiast and has acquired a high level of technical (programming) knowledge (Thomas, 2002, XIII). In a more precise analysis, we can distinguish three separate groups:

- Hackers (defined by the goal of entering other computer systems without altering them–the impetus lies solely in the clearing of access barriers),
- Crackers (defined by the goal of removing copy protection for software or content, e.g. films),
- Crashers (defined by the goal of infecting other computers with malware and eventually running a botnet).

The hacking subculture has its own ethics, which is expressed as follows by the Chaos Computer Club (CCC; motto: "cable salad is good for your health") (CCC, 1998):

Access to computers and everything that can show you how this world works should be unlimited and exhaustive.

All information must be free.

Mistrust authorities–promote decentralization.

Judge a hacker by what he does, and not by common criteria such as looks, age, race, sex or social status.

A computer can be used to create art and beauty.

Computers can change your life for the better.

Do not corrupt other people's data.

Use public data, protect private data.

The cracking subculture was a result of the advent of copy protection. Depending on the way it deals with copy protection and warez (the pirated copies of the cracked documents), we distinguish between three different groupings (Krömer & Sen, 2006):

- Release scene (defined by the goal of using one's own computer to remove copy protection and provide warez),
- FXP scene (defined by the goal of using other computers–i.e. by using server piracy–to acquire and distribute warez),
- Filesharer scene (defined by the goal of acquiring and distributing warez, particularly music and videos; this encompasses all occasional copiers, who acquire documents cheaply).

With Wikipedia, another groups of hackers entered the game: "Wikipedia trolls" try to falsify information or destroy documents. Additionally, they try to spread dissension in discussions about articles, thus sabotaging the development of Wikipedia. Their behavior is similar to that of hackers (Shachaf & Hara, 2010).

These information subcultures partially venture into criminal terrain. While hackers (in our narrow definition) hardly commit criminal acts, crashers definitely infringe on computer penal law. Crackers are in conflict with copyright law, the FXP scene additionally being subject to criminal law by using server piracy.

4.7   Dark Web: Information Behavior of Terrorist Groups

We use the term "Dark Web" to summarize all activities of terrorist groups (or, from an alternative perspective, of "freedom fighters") on the internet. This includes websites on the surface web (i.e. accessible by search engines; Chen et al., 2005), sites on the Deep Web (not accessible via common search tools), entries on message boards, postings on weblogs (including podcasts and vodcasts), video and audio files distributed online, e-mails and discussions in chatrooms. We understand "terrorism" to mean (U.S. State Dept., 2002):

Premediated, politically motivated violence perpetrated against non-combatant targets by subnational groups or clandestine agents, usually to influence an audience.

Figure 4.10: Public Relations via the WWW by the Qassam Brigades. Source: www.alqassam.ps/English (Version Dating from 06/15/2006); Researched via the Wayback Machine (www.archive.org).

A terrorist group is a unit (or subunit of a larger organization) that practises terrorism. The Dark Web encompasses all internet-related activities of terrorist groups and their members. Terrorist groups primarily use the Dark Web to accomplish the following tasks (Thomas, 2003; Weinmann, 2004; Qin et al., 2007, 72):

- psychological warfare,
- public relations,
- fundraising,
- recruiting new members,
- mobilizing existing members,
- networking, exchange of information,
- planning and coordinating activities, "cyberplanning",
- "normal" Web searches (information about possible targets, e-mailing lists etc.).

To do so, they sometimes use methods of steganography (a masked correspondence in cipher in the example below):

The semester begins in three more weeks. We've obtained 19 confirmations for studies in the faculty of law, the faculty of urban planning, the faculty of fine arts, and the faculty of engineering,

ran the code for the operating time, number of assassins and targets of the activities carried out on September 11, 2001 (Thomas, 2003, 119). For Timothy L. Thomas (2003, 112), it is clear that

we can say with some certainty, al Qaeda loves the Internet.

Figure 4.10 shows the start page of the web presence of the Qassam Brigades, which form the military arm of Palestine's Hamas and are regarded as a terrorist organization. Some groups (like the Hamas) aim to create international websites in addition to those in their respective native language. Paul Piper (2008, 38) observes:

These sites are rich in propaganda, alternative scenarios, arguments, philosophies, and often feature donation and/or recruitment options.

4.8 Political Science

The internet has opened up a new communication channel between government institutions and citizens. This becomes particularly clear in elections. However, media have always been crucial elements in **election campaigns**, as Castells, (1997) emphasizes:

In the context of democratic politics, access to government institutions is dependent on gaining the majority of votes. In current societies, people mainly acquire information via media, television first and foremost, and thus form their opinions.

Although television is still a strong medium in the information society, the internet–particularly the WWW and, in it, the collaborative Web 2.0–is steadily gaining in influence. According to Kuhlen and Bendel (1998), the first German political election campaign conducted on the internet was the Bundestag election of 1998, as it was here that both parties and candidates created Web presences, the population could participate in "trial elections" and message boards discussing the election were used intensively. During the 2008 U.S. presidential election, the successful candidate Barack Obama made massive use of his own websites, but also of campaigns on a social network (Facebook) and a microblogging service (Twitter) (Glenn, 2009). For politically interested citizens, internet services are sometimes very trustworthy, as Johnson and Kaye (2009) have already described for the 2004 U.S. presidential election. According to their study, the people they surveyed took weblogs for the most credible online source, followed by so-called "problem-oriented" websites. Websites by candidates as well as mailing lists and bulletin boards are deemed moderately credible, whereas chats achieve hardly and credibility at all. Does a politicized internet give way to another way of doing politics? For Philip E. Agre (2002), political activities on the Web are incorporated into more comprehensive social processes, where the Web merely represents a single element of media usage. The Web has, however, the character of an amplifier (Agre, 2002, 317):

> The Internet changes nothing on its own, but it can amplify existing
> forces, and those amplified forces might change something.

Especially in the example of Obama, it becomes clear that web-related "real-time" politics (Agre, 2002) does not start and end with election campaigns, but also enters every-day politics as "amplifier" (Greengard, 2009, 17):

> While new media has enormous power to help a candidate get elected, it
> also yields influence as a tool for operating a more efficient and trans-
> parent government.

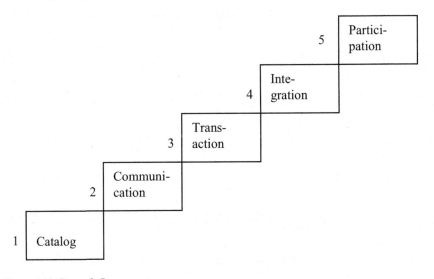

Figure 4.11: Steps of eGovernment.

This leads us to **eGovernment**. Public administrations on all levels work online with the citizens as well as collaborating among each other. The former can be understood in the variants A-to-C (Administration–Consumer/Citizen) and A-to-B (Administration–Business) as a counterpart to Customer Relationship Management, the latter in the form A-to-A as the public adversary of Supply Chain Management. Lee, Tan and Trimi (2005, 99-100) describe the tasks of eGovernment:

> E-government is mainly concerned with providing quality public services and value-added information to citizens. It has the potential to build better relationships between government and the public by making interactions between citizens and government agencies smoother, easier, and more efficient.

We can separate the activities of eGovernment into fives steps (Figure 4.11), according to increasing technological and organizational complexity. Our model is a unification of the approaches by Layne and Lee (2001, 124) and Moon (2002, 426). Step 1, called Catalog, shows the interested citizens documents (e.g. minutes of meetings) and offers printable forms (which must be returned in person, however). From Step 2 onward, a direct digital communication between the participants becomes possible. Forms are now filled out by citizens and transmitted to the institution online. Contact persons (administrative staff and politicians) have a mailing address and process their mail. Step 3 admits transactions; taxes and fees are transferred digitally, and in the other direction, citizens receive grants they have applied for. The integration in Step 4 means both vertical integration (the connection of identical or similar administrations on different levels of the governmental administration pyramid: municipality, district, state, nation) as well as horizontal integration (the connection of all administrations within a municipality, district etc.). This allows citizens to orient themselves as to who they can turn to with their concerns where jurisdictions are not clearly defined. If several administrations are working on the solution of a problem, one motion will suffice, as it will be passed on within and among the administrations. The highest step concerns citizens' political participation. Here we can think of formal participation (e.g. in referendums carried out online) as well as informal actions (operating politically motivated blogs, microblogs, message boards or websites). eGovernment can only work when three conditions are met (Layne & Lee, 2001, 134 et seq.):

- internet access for all involved citizens,
- secure privacy and discretion,
- citizen-oriented administrative action (as opposed to savings-oriented action and the like).

In a comparison of several different countries, it can be shown that the internet's prevalence in a region correlates strongly with the respective degree of democratization, leading Groshek (2009, 133) to speak of a great "democratic potential of the internet". As we have learned from the discussion about the knowledge gap hypothesis, internet access requires not only the technology, but also education and the motivation for using the internet and its services adequately. Thompson (2008, 96) emphasizes this in his study of the information infrastructure and democracy:

> In democratic nations, it is believed such an infrastructure (telephone, postal, and broadcast services, libraries, schools, and other facilities, and electric and telecommunication installations ...) contributes to the realization of the democratic ideals of effective participation and enlightened understanding.

We have seen, in the section on the digital divide, that internet access for all is not nearly a given. Introducing the uninitiated to the new media and simultaneously bridging the digital divide is called **eInclusion** (Kaplan, 2005).

How far will a government go to introduce its citizens to the knowledge society? What services are available to all, either for free or at the very least indiscriminately cheap? Services offered to the public in this way are called **universal services** (Raber, 2004; Stock, 1997). The borders of these services are drawn differently in each respective national information politics. The spectrum goes from voice telephony (Germany) via broadband connection (Switzerland), information services with regard to education, health and public security (U.S.A.) up to unlimited access to scientific-technical databases and magazines (Iceland, van de Stadt, & Thorsteinsdóttir, 2007). If a government merely supports the (purely technologically oriented) information society, a universal service of broadband access should be sufficient; if, however, it wants to advance the knowledge society (defined by content), it will also have to promote the distribution of important content and hence implement the Icelandic model.

What options does a government have in supporting the information and knowledge society? Following Norbert Henrichs (1983), we distinguish between three methods of **information politics**:

- Regulatory Politics: politics restricts itself to drawing up the legal framework for the information and knowledge society, respectively. Some relevant laws are copyright law and industrial property protection, or laws for fighting computer criminality.
- Structural Politics: here politics sets itself targets for developing an information and knowledge society. Two variants can be made out.
  - The government sees it as its duty to expedite certain desired developments by its own actions and financing ("government paradigm"). Thus in Germany in the 1970s, the Information and Documentation (IuD) program was initiated, which was designed to create a comprehensive infrastructure for acquiring scientific-technical information (which however could not be wholly realized due to a lack of coordination and the immense costs of the project).
  - The government sees the market as able to reach the goals ("market paradigm"). It may intervene in order to minimize investment and risk barriers, or to step into the breach in case of temporary market failure in order to compensate for any looming losses (principle of subsidiarity).

- Subsidy Politics: the government subsidizes certain projects either on the institutional level (e.g. financing certain libraries or information providers) or on the project level (by financing individual projects to be applied for and surveyed).

4.9　Conclusion

- An information society is technically defined. Information and communication technology as a basic innovation (in the sense of Kondratieff) consolidates a long economic wave; the members of this society preferably use telematic devices for communication.
- A knowledge society is an information society in which the focus is on information content. Knowledge is wholly available everywhere, all the time. As knowledge changes over time, the members of the knowledge society must be aware of these changes. This leads to lifelong learning.
- The information society's infrastructure is made up of telephony (landline, cellular, VoIP), broadband networking and internet (hosts, computer density, internet connections, internet users).
- In a knowledge society, the technical infrastructure is joined by education, an adequate system of science and technology as well as a fully developed librarianship.
- A country's state of development can be gauged by the Human Development Index (HDI). The HDI correlates heavily with the indicators of the information and knowledge society: the ICT Development Index (IDI) with a value of +0.90, and the Networked Readiness Index (NRI) with a value of +0.75. The level of human development and the level of development of the information and knowledge society are thus strongly connected.
- Technological centers of the information markets are distinguished by dense spatial concentration, being situated mostly at the edges of agglomerations; they are also digitally connected with other internet centers.
- The labor market in the knowledge society is marked by mobile telework (with its "office on the road") and job polarization (well-paid analytic or interactive tasks versus badly-paid manual labor) with a simultaneous tendency toward reducing routine tasks (which are increasingly being performed by machines).

- The informational city is the ideal-typical city of the knowledge society, distinguishing itself through its "space of flows", besides the conventional "space of places". Informational cities are glocally (i.e. locally and globally) aligned cities; they are the seat of internationally active financial service providers and of technology and knowledge-intensive companies. They are capable of acting independently of national politics and power. Some features of such cities are a comprehensive cultural offer, high recreational value and enticing shopping districts.
- Even in an information or knowledge society, there is social inequality. The possibility of participating in this society is what separates the information-rich from the information-poor–between them gapes the digital divide.
- The knowledge gap hypothesis states that as an information stream increases, the educated social groups will profit more from it, whereas the less educated will lose their orientation. Participation in the knowledge society depends on various factors. Technological access to computers and the internet is important, as are the financial means of paying for the former, a high degree of general education and information literacy, as well as the motivation for grappling with the achievements of the knowledge society in the first place.
- Deviant information behavior means both deviance (infringing on social norms) and delinquency (infringing on legal norms) when dealing with digital information.
- Problematic internet usage can be defined as consisting of excessive and time-consuming internet consumption which correlates with the loneliness of the "patient". Harassment via internet can assume the form of either cyberstalking or cyberbullying.
- Online fraud and other criminal ways of using the internet must be ascribed to delinquency. Online fraud can take the form of auction fraud, Nigerian Letter Fraud, Click Fraud for search engines and phishing. Computer criminality further encompasses malware (viruses, Trojan Horses, worms) and botnets.
- Hackers, Crackers and Crashers form subcultures that orient themselves by their own sets of values.
- The internet is also used intensively by terrorist groups. Websites, message boards and other Web services run by these organizations form the Dark Web.
- The relation of internet and politics becomes particularly clear in elections (and their preceding campaigns run on the WWW, Web 2.0 or microblogging services). The internet itself does not change the substance of the politics, but it serves to amplify certain actions.
- eGovernment consists of five steps that each build on each other: Catalog, Communication, Transaction, Integration and Participation.

> • For governmental institutions, there are three options for dealing with the information and knowledge society (in order, for example, to take part in designing it): Regulatory Politics, Structural Politics (with the variants market and government paradigm) and Subsidy Politics.

4.10   Bibliography

Abu Rajab, M., Zarfoss, J., Monrose, F., & Terzis, A. (2006). A multifaceted approach to understanding the botnet phenomenon. Proceedings of the 6th ACM SIGCOMM Conference on Internet Measurement (pp. 41-52). New York, NY: ACM.

Agre, P.E. (2002). Real-time politics: The internet and the political process. The Information Society, 18, 311-331.

Anand, S., & Sen, A. (1992). Human Development Index: Methodology and Measurement. New York, NY: United Nations Development Programme.–(Human Development Report Office Occasional Paper; 12).

Böhme, G. (1997). The structure and prospects of knowledge society. Social Science Information, 36(3), 447-468.

Bonfadelli, H. (2002). The internet and knowledge gaps. A theoretical and empirical investigation. European Journal of Communication, 17(1), 65-84.

Bonitz, M. (1986a). Wissenschaftliche Information und wissenschaftliches Verhalten. Berlin: ZIID.

Bonitz, M. (1986b). Holographie- und Tempoprinzip: Verhaltensprinzipien im System der wissenschaftlichen Kommunikation. Informatik, 33, 191-193.

Bredemeier, W., & Stock, W.G. (2000). Informationskompetenz europäischer Volkswirtschaften. Knorz, G., & Kuhlen, R. (eds.), Informationskompetenz–Basiskompetenz in der Informationsgesellschaft. Proceedings des 7. Internationalen Symposiums für Informationswissenschaft (pp. 227-243). Konstanz: UVK Universitätsverlag Konstanz.

Brown, J.S., & Duguid, P. (2002). The Social Life of Information. Boston, MA: Harvard Business School Press. 2nd ed.

Brenner, N. (1998). Global cities, glocal states: Global city formation and state territorial restructuring in contemporary Europe. Review of International Political Economy, 5(1), 1-37.

Britz, J.J. (2004). To know or not to know: A moral reflection on information poverty. Journal of Information Science, 30(1), 192-204.

Britz, J.J. (2008). Making the global information society good: A social justice perspective on the ethical dimensions of the global information society. Journal of the American Society for Information Science and Technology, 59(7), 1171-1183.

Castells, M. (1989). The Informational City. Information Technology, Economic Restructuring, and the Urban-Regional Process. Oxford; Cambridge, MA: Basil Blackwell.

Castells, M. (1996). The Rise of the Network Society. Malden, MA: Blackwell.

Castell, M. (1997). The Power of Identity. Malden, MA: Blackwell.

Castells, M. (1998). End of Millenium. Malden, MA: Blackwell.

Castells, M. (2001). The Internet Galaxy. Oxford: Oxford Univ. Pres.

Castells, M. (2006[1993]). Cities, the information society and the global economy. Brenner, N. ; & Keil, R. (eds.). The Global Cities Reader (pp. 135-136). London, New York, NY: Routledge. (Original: 1993).

CCC (1998). Hackerethik / Chaos Computer Club. Online: www.ccc.de/hackerethics.

Ceyhan, A.A., Ceyhan, E. (2008). Loneliness, depression, and computer efficacy as predictors of problematic internet use. CyberPsychology & Behavior, 11(6), 699-701.

Chen, H., Qin, J., Reid, E., Chung, W., Zhou, Y., Xi, W., Lai, G., Bonillas, A.A., & Sagemann, M. (2005). The dark web portal: Collecting and analyzing the presence of domestic and international terrorists groups on the web. Lecture Notes in Computer Science, 3495, 623-624.

Chen, I., & Kidd, T.T. (2008). Digital divide implications and trends. In Quigley, M. (ed.), Encyclopedia of Information Ethics and Security (pp. 130-135). Hershey, PA: Information Science Reference.

Cukier, W.L., Nesselroth, E.J., & Cody, S. (2007). Genre, narrative and the „Nigerian Letter" in electronic mail. In Proceedings of the 40th Annual Hawaii International Conference on System Sciences.

David, P.A., & Foray, D. (2002). An introduction to the economy of the knowledge society. International Social Science Journal, 54(171), 9-23.

Ducheneault, N., Yee, N., Nickell, E., & Moore, R.J. (2006). "Alone together?": Exploring the social dynamics of massively multiplayer online games. In Proceedings of the SIGHCI Conference on Human Factors in Computing Systems (pp. 407-416). New York, NY: ACM.

Dutta, S., & Mia, I. (2009). The Global Information Technology Report 2008-2009. Cologny: World Economic Forum, Fontainebleau: INSEAD.

Flint, C., & Taylor, P. (2007). Political Geography. World-Economy, Nation-State and Locality. 5th ed., Harlow: Pearson / Prentice Hall.

Freiling, F.C., Holz, T., & Wicherski, G. (2005). Botnet tracking: Exploring a root-cause methodology to prevent distributed denial-of-service attacks. Lecture Notes in Computer Science 3679, 319-335.

Friedmann, J. (1995). Where we stand: A decade of world city research. In Knox, P., & Taylor, P. (eds.), World Cities in a World-System (pp. 21-47). New York, NY: Cambridge University Press.

Gavish, B., & Lucci, C.L. (2008). Reducing internet auction fraud. Communications of the ACM, 51(5), 89-97.

Glenn, V.D. (2009). Government and Web 2.0. DttP: A Quarterly Journal of Government Information Practice & Perspective, 37(2), 13-17.

Goos, M., & Manning, A. (2007). Lousy and lovely jobs: The rising polarization of work in Britain. Review of Economics and Statistics, 89(1), 118-133.

Gospodini, A. (2005). Landscape transformations in the postmodern inner city: Clustering flourishing economic activities and 'glocalising' morphologies. WIT Transactions on Ecology and the Environment, 84 (pp. 1469-1485) (Sustainable Development and Planning II, Vol. 2).

Graumann, S., & Speich, A. (2009). Innovationspolitik, Informationsgesellschaft, Telekommunikation. Berlin: Bundesministerium für Wirtschaft und Technologie; München: TNS Infratest.

Greengard, S. (2009). The first internet president. Communications of the ACM, 52(2), 16-18.

Gregg, D.G., & Scott, J.E. (2006). The role of reputation systems in reducing online auction fraud. International Journal of Electronic Commerce, 10(3), 95-120.

Groshek, J. (2009). The democratic effects of the internet, 1994-2003. A cross-national inquiry of 152 countries. The International Communication Gazette, 71(3), 115-136.

Guillén, M.F., & Suárez, S.L. (2005). Explaining the global digital divide: Economic, political and sociological drivers of cross-national internet use. Social Forces, 84(2), 681-708.

Hall, P. (1985). The geography of the fifth Kondratieff. In Hall, P., & Markusen, A. (eds.), Silicon Landscapes (pp. 1-19). Boston, MA, London, Sidney: Allen and Unwin.

Hall, P. (1997). Modelling the post-industrial city. Futures, 29(4/5), 311-322.

Hansson, F., Husted, K., & Vestergaard, J. (2005). Second generation science parks: From structural holes jockeys to social capital catalysts of the knowledge society. Technovation, 25, 1039-1049.

Heidenreich, M. (2002). Merkmale der Wissensgesellschaft. Lernen in der Wissensgesellschaft. Innsbruck: StudienVerlag.

Heidenreich, M. (2003). Die Debatte um die Wissensgesellschaft. Böschen, S., & Schulz-Schaeffer, I. (eds.), Wissenschaft in der Wissensgesellschaft (pp. 25-51). Wiesbaden: Westdeutscher Verlag.

Henrichs, N. (1983). Informationspolitik. Stichworte zu einer Podiumsdiskussion. In Kuhlen, R. (ed.), Koordination von Informationen. Die Bedeutung von Informations- und Kommunikationstechnologien in privaten und öffentlichen Verwaltungen (pp. 348-355). Berlin; Heidelberg: Springer.

Hepworth, M.E. (1987). The information city. Cities, 4(3), 253-262.

Hoffmann, J. (2006). Stalking. Heidelberg: Springer.

Hunt, F., Birks, J. (2008). More Hands-on Information Literacy Activities. New York, NY: Neal-Schuman.

ITU (2009). Measuring the Information Society. The ICT Development Index. Geneva: International Telecommunication Union.

Jakobsson, M., & Myers, S., eds. (2007). Phishing and Countermeasures. Understanding the Increasing Problem of Electronic Identity Theft. Hoboken, NJ: Wiley.

Johnson, T.J., & Kaye, B.K. (2009). In blogs we trust? Deciphering credibility of components of the internet among politically interested internet users. Computers in Human Behavior, 25, 175-182.

Kaplan, D. (2005). e-Inclusion: New Challenges and Policy Recommendations. eEurope Advisory Group.

Kaspersky, E. (2008). Malware. Von Viren, Würmern, Hackern und Trojanern und wie man sich vor ihnen schützt. München: Hanser.

Kelley, A.C. (1991). The human development index: "Handle with care". Population and Development Review, 17(2), 315-324.

Kondratieff, N.D. (1926). Die langen Wellen der Konjunktur. Archiv für Sozialwissenschaft und Sozialpolitik, 56, 573-609.

Kowalski, R.M., Limber, S.P., & Agatston, P.W. (2008). Cyber Bullying: Bullying in the Digital Age. Malden, MA: Wiley-Blackwell.

Krömer, J., & Sen, E. (2006). No Copy–Die Welt der digitalen Raubkopie. Berlin: Tropen.

Kuhlen, R., & Bendel, O. (1998). Die Mondlandung des Internet. Die Bundestagswahl 1998 in den elektronischen Kommunikationsforen. Konstanz: Universitätsverlag.

Kwak, N. (1999). Revisiting the knowledge gap hypothesis. Education, motivation, and media use. Communication Research, 26(4), 385-413.

Layne, K., & Lee, J. (2001). Developing fully functional e-government: A four stage model. Government Information Quarterly, 18, 122-136.

Lee, S.M., Tan, X., & Trimi, S. (2005). Current practices of leading e-government countries. Communications of the ACM, 48(10), 99-104.

Li, Q. (2006). Cyberbullying in schools. School Psychology International, 27(2), 157-170.

Li, Q. (2007). New bottle but old wine: A research of cyberbullying in schools. Computers in Human Behavior, 23(4), 1777-1791.

Liu, T., & Potenza, M.N. (2007). Problematic internet use: Clinical implications. CNS Spectrums, 12(6), 453-466.

Lyon, D. (2005). A sociology of information. In Turner, B.S., Rojek, C., & Calhoun, C. (eds.), The Sage Handbook of Sociology (pp. 223-235). London: Sage.

Lumiérs, E.M., & Schimmel, M. (2004). Information poverty. A measurable concept? In Mendina, T., & Britz, J.J. (eds.), Information Ethics in the Electronic Age (pp. 47-61). Jefferson, NC; London: McFarland.

McGillivray, M. (1991). The human development index: Yet another redundant composite development indicator? World Development, 19(10), 1461-1468.

Mensch, G. (1975). Das technologische Patt. Innovationen überwinden die Depression. Frankfurt: Umschau.

Mia, I., Dutta, S., & Geiger, T. (2009). Gauging the networked readiness of nations: Findings from the Networked Readiness Index 2008-2009. In Dutta, S., & Mia, I. (eds.), The Global Information Technology Report 2008-2009 (pp. 3-26). Cologny: World Economic Forum; Fontainebleau: INSEAD.

Miller, C. (2006). Cyber harassment: Its forms and perpetrators. Law Enforcement Technology, 33(4), 26-30.

Moon, M.J. (2002). The evolution of e-government among municipalities: Rhetoric or reality? Public Administration Review, 62(4), 424-433.

Nardy, B., Harris, J. (2006). Strangers and friends: Collaborative play in World of Warcraft. In Proceedings of the 20th Anniversary Conference on Computer Supported Cooperative Work (pp. 149-158). New York, NY: ACM.

Nefiodow, L. (1991). Der Fünfte Kondratieff. Frankfurt: FAZ; Wiesbaden: Gabler.

Nefiodow, L. (1994). Informationsgesellschaft. Arbeitsplatzvernichtung oder Arbeitsplatzgewinne? ifo Schnelldienst, 12, 11-19.

Neufeld, D.J. (2010). Understanding cybercrime. Proceedings of the 43rd Hawaii International Conference on System Sciences. IEEE Computer Society Press.

OECD (2005). Guide to Measuring the Information Society / Working Party on Indicators for the Information Society (DSTI/ICCP/IIS(2005)6/FINAL). Paris: Organisation for Economic Co-operation and Development.

Peña-López, I. (2006). Networked readiness index vs. human development index. ICTlogy, 30.

Phillips, J.G. (2006). The psychology of internet use and misuse. In Anandarajan, M., Teo, T.S.H., & Simmers, C.A. (eds.), The Internet and Workplace Transformations (pp. 41-62). Armonk, NY: Sharpe.

Piper, P. (2008). Nets of terror. Terrorist activity on the internet. Searcher, 16(10), 29-38.

Qin, J., Zhou, Y., Reid, E., Lai, G., & Chen, H. (2007). Analyzing terror campaigns on the internet: Technical sophistication, content richness, and Web interactivity. International Journal of Human-Computer Studies, 65, 71-84.

Raber, D. (2004). Is universal service a universal right? A Rawlsian approach to universal services. In Mendina, T., & Britz, J.J. (eds.), Information Ethics in the Electronic Age (pp. 114-122). Jefferson, NC; London: McFarland.

Ruedy, M.C. (2008). Repercussions of a MySpace teen Suicide: Should anti-cyberbullying law be created? North Carolina Journal of Law & Technology, 9(2), 323-346.

Sagar, A.D., & Najam, A. (1998). The human development index: A critical review. Ecological Economics, 25, 249-264.

Sairamesh, J., Lee, A., & Anania, L. (2004). Information cities. Communications of the ACM, 47(2), 29-31.

Sassen, S. (2002). Towards a sociology of information technology. Current Sociology, 50(3), 365-388.

Schumpeter, J.A. (1961). Konjunkturzyklen. Eine theoretische, historische und statistische Analyse des kapitalistischen Prozesses. Göttingen: Vandenhoek & Ruprecht.

Shachaf, P., & Hara, N. (2010). Beyond vandalism. Wikipedia trolls. Journal of Information Science, 36(3), 357-370.

Shanmuganathan, N. (2010). Cyberstalking: Psychoterror im Web 2.0. Information–Wissenschaft und Praxis, 61(2), 91-95.

Shapira, N.A., Lessig, M.C., Goldsmith, T.D., Szabo, S.T., Lazoritz, M., Gold, M.S., & Stein, D.J. (2003). Problematic internet use: Proposed classification and diagnostic criteria. Depression and Anxiety, 17, 207-216.

Soubusta, S. (2008). On click fraud. Information–Wissenschaft und Praxis, 59(2), 136-141.

Spitz-Oener, A. (2006). Technical change, job tasks, and rising educational demands: Looking outside the wage structure. Journal of Labor Economics, 24(2), 235-270.

Spitzberg, B.H., & Hoobler, G. (2002). Cyberstalking and the technologies of interpersonal terrorism. New Media & Society, 4(1), 71-92.

Stehr, N. (1994). Knowledge Societies. London: Sage.

Stiglitz, J. (2000). Scan globally, reinvent locally. Knowledge infrastructure and the localisation of knowledge. In Stone, D. (ed.), Banking on Knowledge. The Genesis of the Global Development Network (pp. 25-44). London: Routledge.

Stock, W.G. (1997). Universaldienste. Köln: Fachhochschule Köln / Fachbereich Bibliotheks- und Informationswesen. (Kölner Arbeitspapiere zur Bibliotheks- und Informationswissenschaft; 4).

Stock, W.G. (2000). Informationswirtschaft. Management externen Wissens. München, Wien: Oldenbourg.

Susser, I. (2002). Manuel Castells: Conceptualizing the city in the information age. In Susser, I. (ed.), The Castells Reader on Cities and Social Theory (pp. 1-12). Malden, Mass., Oxford: Blackwell.

Swyngedouw, E., & Kaïka, M. (2003). The making of 'glocal' urban modernities. City, 7(1), 5-21.

Thomas, D. (2002). Hacker Culture. Minneapolis: Univ. of Minnesota Press.

Thomas, T.L. (2003). Al Qaeda and the Internet: The danger of „cyberplanning". Parameters, 33(1), 112-123.

Thompson, K.M. (2008). The US information infrastructure and libraries: A case study in democracy. Library Review, 57(2), 96-106.

Tichenor, P.J., Donohue, G.A., & Olien, C.N. (1970). Mass media flow and differential growth in knowledge. Public Opinion Quarterly, 34, 159-170.

UNDP (2007). Human Development Report 2007/2008. New York, NY: United Nations Development Programme.

United Nations (2006). The Digital Divide Report: ICT Diffusion Index 2005. New York; Geneva: United Nations Conference on Trade and Development.

U.S. State Dept. (2002). Patterns of Global Terrorism.

Vacca, J.R. (2005). Computer Forensics. Computer Crime Scene Investigations. 2nd ed. Hingham, MA: Charles River Media.

van de Stadt, I., Solveig Thorsteinsdóttir (2007). Going E-only: All Icelandic citizens are hooked. Library Connect, 5(1), 2.

van Dijk, J. (1999). The Network Society. Social Aspects of New Media. Thousand Oaks, CA: Sage.

van Dijk, J., & Hacker, K. (2003). The digital divide as a complex and dynamic phenomenon. The Information Society, 19, 315-326.

Vehovar, V., Sicherl, P., Hüsing, T., & Dolnicar, V. (2006). Methodological challenges of digital divide measurements. The Information Society, 22, 279-290.

Warschauer, M. (2003). Technology and Social Inclusion. Rethinking the Digital Divide. Cambridge, MA: MIT Press.

Webster, F. (1995). Theories of the Information Society. London, New York, NY: Routlegde.

Weinmann, G. (2004). www.terror.net–How Modern Terrorism Uses the Internet. Washington, DC: United States Institute of Peace. (Special Report; 116).

Wersig, G. (1973). Informationssoziologie. Hinweise zu einem informationswissenschaftlichen Teilbereich. Frankfurt am Main: Fischer Athenäum.

World Bank (2009). Measuring Knowledge in the World's Economies. Washington, DC: World Bank Institute.

Xalter S. (2006). Der „Bibliotheksindex" (BIX) für wissenschaftliche Bibliotheken–eine kritische Auseinandersetzung (Hausarbeit). München: Bayerische Bibliotheksschule.

Yellowlees, P.M., & Marks, S. (2007). Problematic internet use or internet addiction? Computers in Human Behavior, 23(3), 1447-1453.

Chapter 5

Information Law

5.1   Legal Protection of Information

Documents and the content contained therein are not exempt from the law but are protected in various ways. One of the fundaments of an information society is its "mental constructs"–content and software–and thus requires a particular degree of intellectual property protection, as Drahos (2005, 140) emphasizes:

> Intellectual property rights have a fundamental and catalysing role in a knowledge economy.

There is no all-encompassing "information law" (Kloepfner, 2002) at the moment, but there is "traditional" law that is applied to digital information (e.g. commercial property rights and copyright), as well as, sporadically, new laws that directly regulate dealings with digital information (as for example telemedia law). Different laws apply depending on the kind of information being discussed:

- Intellectual Property
  - Commercial Property Rights
    - Technical Information   Patent Law and Utility Model Law
    - Aesthetic-Commercial   Registered Design Law
      Information
    - Promotional Information   Trademark Law
  - "Works"   Copyright Law
- Person-Related Information   Data Protection Law
- Teleservices   Telemedia Law
- Accompanying Aspects
  - Sincerity   Competition Law
  - Public Information   Information Processing Law
  - Obligatory Copy   National Library Law
- Punishable Acts   Criminal Law

If an information society protects intellectual property not enough or not at all, it will be harmed by plagiarized and pirated software and content (Marron & Steel, 2000), but if it protects it too vigorously, the innovative competition in science, research and product development can suffer. The legal protection of information thus faces the task of finding the ideal middle way for a knowledge society to walk the line between protective rights and free availability.

Current law must be noted particularly in problematic instances of dealing with digital content and software, as the verdicts do not cover all details of information law (such as search engine law). Accompanying aspects for all areas of digital information are competition law and criminal law. In this chapter, we will observe some important aspects of information law from an information-scientific perspective; there will be no extensive legal treatment; for such an analysis, we must point to further literature (for "internet law" in general, Haug, 2005 and Hoeren, 2008, among others).

Commercial Property Right Law (Götting, 2007) regulates–together with copyright law–how to deal with intellectual property (Busche, 2008).

The principle of territorial limitation applies to the entirety of commercial copyright law, i.e. the protective laws only apply in the respective country (and, in an exception, in supranational constructs like the European Union) (Götting, 2007). Here, too, the priority principle applies everywhere: to receive protective rights, you have to be the first to perform (or register) a service. Internationally, the TRIPs agreement ("Trade-Related Aspects of Intellectual Property Rights") applies, particularly because it contains regulations for the enforcement of the protective rights abroad (e.g. in case of product piracy).

In commercial copyright law, the subject of protection is the intellectual-commercial service, whereas copyright law protects a "work" as a personal intellectual creation (Götting, 2007, 40). The positive content of commercial legal protection is the rights holder's usage authorization, its negative content the authorization for repelling copies of and attempts at exploiting the article of protection (Götting, 2007, 49). Protective rights can be traded, and the holder is able to license their usage. In commercial legal protection, there is a distinction between the two technical protective rights Patents and Utility Models and the two non-technical rights Registered Design and Trademark; for works, the (legally binding) copyright and Creative Commons must be distinguished, where the latter consists of the holders voluntarily ceding several rights (e.g. of reproduction). All documents in commercial legal protection, but not in copyright law, are recorded content-wise by the respective national bureaus as well as, additionally, by database producers via classification systems (Stock & Stock, 2008, 214 et seq.) and are available in digital form.

5.2   Technical Information: Patents and Utility Models

Inventions are protected wither by patents or utility models (Adam, Gruber & Haberl, 2008; Jestaedt, 2008a; Kraßer & Bernhardt 2008; Osterrieth 2007). Patents must prove "level of invention" that goes beyond the respective state of technology, whereas utility models ("little patents") only require an "inventive step". The inventions must offend neither "morals nor public order" (§2 German Patent Law; §2 German Utility Model Law). We will begin our discussion of technical information with **patent law**. §1 Section 1 of German patent law defines the subject area of patent law as follows:

Patents are granted for inventions on all levels of technology, as long as they are new, based on an act of invention and commercially applicable.

Innovation is deemed absolute: in no way may the invention have been made publicly accessible prior to its registration (including by the inventor himself). In contrast to German patent law, the American version has a grace period of one year, starting at the time of invention. In this period, the inventor may publicly discuss his technical idea without incurring disadvantages. Knowledge is always deemed publicly inaccessible if only few people have access to it and keep it secret. If an invention is disclosed in an obvious case of abuse (i.e. if it is "betrayed" by an unauthorized person), or if it is presented in an international exhibition, a grace period of six months applies in Germany.

The novelty of an invention is negatively affected, with regard to its being granted a patent, by everything relating to the level of technology. The knowledge that is taken as the basis for judging its novelty may already have been published in other patents, in scientific literature, in company fonts etc. In one known case of a patent office rejecting an invention (by Karl Krøyer, Application N° NL6514306), the technical idea had already been similarly described in a Walt Disney comic book (its "true" inventor thus being Donald Duck, or his creator, Carl Barks). Whether Krøyer had been aware of this or not is of no consequence to the judgment of the invention's novelty. If similar inventions are submitted within a short time of each other, the date of application or invention makes the difference. Whereas many countries (including Germany) prefer the date of submission ("first to file"), others (like the U.S.A.) use the date of invention ("first to invent") as the decisive criterion. The date of priority is always the date of submission.

An **inventive act** is always in evidence if the service cannot be readily inferred, by an expert, from the level of technology. The service thus has–measured against the state of the art–a certain level of invention. No inventions are discoveries and scientific theories, which means that the entire area of scientific results is non-patentable. In §1 Sections 3 and 4 of German Patent Law, we read:

(3) Not regarded as inventions in the sense of Section 1 are, in particular: 1. Discoveries, as well as scientific theories and mathematical methods; 2. Aesthetic forms; 3. Plans, regulations and procedures for intellectual activities, games or business activities, as well as programs for data processing equipment; 4. The rendition of information.

(4) Section 3 only forms an obstacle to patentability in so far as the objects or activities in themselves require legal protection.

The formulation "in themselves" in Section 4 is important, as the areas mentioned may very well be subject to patent law in combination with other technical specifications (we will come back to this point in our discussion of software patents). Whereas in Germany, patents on technology are fixed with regard to a mastery over nature, technicality in the U.S.A. is defined more broadly, finally encompassing "anything under the sun that is made by men" (Götting, 2007, 108). Patentable intellectual services have the following characteristics, according to the German legal conception:

- They are technical rules for mastering nature, i.e.
  - procedures (e.g. melting processes) or
  - things: devices (e.g. machines), systems (e.g. electrical circuits) or materials (e.g. metal alloys);
- they are realizable (practically implementable);
- they are repeatable;
- they represent finished solutions;
- they "work". The causal relationship between a technical task and its solution is established, whereas a scientific explanation is of little consequence ("the inventor must know how, not why his invention works", Götting, 2007, 114).

The third patent criterion is the invention's **commercial applicability**. This is given if the invention can be principally used in any given commercial area (including agriculture). Whether it is actually used makes no difference.

If the invention meets these three criteria and does not trigger any of the other reasons for exclusion (e.g. offending morals), the patent request will be granted. The patent holder thus acquires the following **privileges** as per §9 of German patent law:

The patent thus grants the holder a temporary monopoly–with a "service in return", however: the content of the invention is to be made entirely public ("unveiled"), so that other inventors are encouraged to enter into an innovative competition with the published invention by solving the technical problems in other ways.

Patent specifications have not only a legal, but also a technical character. Furthermore, they are carriers of economic information, as they report on the technical achievements of companies and industries.

Patent protection becomes void no later than 20 years after the priority data, i.e. the date the invention was first submitted to a patent office. It can become void earlier, if the holder fails to pay his yearly fees or chooses to forego patent protection.

Patent submission is done at a patent office; at the "Deutsches Patent- und Markenamt" (DPMA, undated) in Germany and the "European Patent Office" (EPO, undated) in Europe. Additionally, there is an option for worldwide submission via the "World Intellectual Property Organization" (WIPO, undated), on the basis of the "Patent Cooperation Treaty" (PCT). An individual request must be submitted for every country (in that country's language) in which patent protection is sought (in a simplified procedure for all member states; in a PCT application, the first phase encompasses all desired countries, the second, national phase being run separately). All (more or less) content-identical applications form a **patent family**, where the (chronologically) first patent is called the "basic patent".

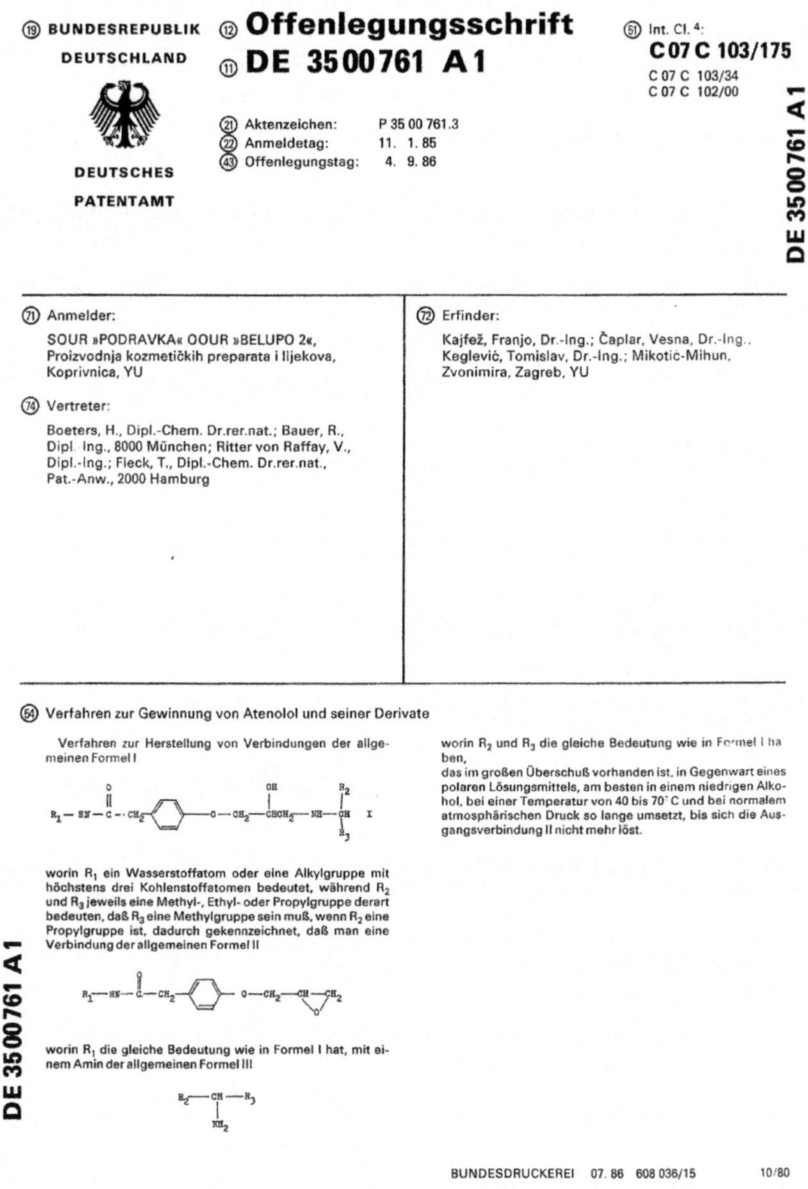

(19) BUNDESREPUBLIK DEUTSCHLAND

DEUTSCHES PATENTAMT

(12) **Offenlegungsschrift**

(11) **DE 3500761 A1**

(51) Int. Cl. 4:
C07C 103/175
C 07 C 103/34
C 07 C 102/00

(21) Aktenzeichen: P 35 00 761.3
(22) Anmeldetag: 11. 1. 85
(43) Offenlegungstag: 4. 9. 86

DE 3500761 A1

(71) Anmelder:
SOUR »PODRAVKA« OOUR »BELUPO 2«, Proizvodnja kozmetičkih preparata i lijekova, Koprivnica, YU

(74) Vertreter:
Boeters, H., Dipl.-Chem. Dr.rer.nat.; Bauer, R., Dipl. Ing., 8000 München; Ritter von Raffay, V., Dipl.-Ing.; Fleck, T., Dipl.-Chem. Dr.rer.nat., Pat.-Anw., 2000 Hamburg

(72) Erfinder:
Kajfež, Franjo, Dr.-Ing.; Čaplar, Vesna, Dr.-Ing.; Keglević, Tomislav, Dr.-Ing.; Mikotić-Mihun, Zvonimira, Zagreb, YU

(54) Verfahren zur Gewinnung von Atenolol und seiner Derivate

Verfahren zur Herstellung von Verbindungen der allgemeinen Formel I

I

worin R_1 ein Wasserstoffatom oder eine Alkylgruppe mit höchstens drei Kohlenstoffatomen bedeutet, während R_2 und R_3 jeweils eine Methyl-, Ethyl- oder Propylgruppe derart bedeuten, daß R_3 eine Methylgruppe sein muß, wenn R_2 eine Propylgruppe ist, dadurch gekennzeichnet, daß man eine Verbindung der allgemeinen Formel II

worin R_1 die gleiche Bedeutung wie in Formel I hat, mit einem Amin der allgemeinen Formel III

worin R_2 und R_3 die gleiche Bedeutung wie in Formel I haben,
das im großen Überschuß vorhanden ist, in Gegenwart eines polaren Lösungsmittels, am besten in einem niedrigen Alkohol, bei einer Temperatur von 40 bis 70° C und bei normalem atmosphärischen Druck so lange umsetzt, bis sich die Ausgangsverbindung II nicht mehr löst.

DE 3500761 A1

BUNDESDRUCKEREI 07. 86 608 036/15 10/80

Figure 5.1: Example of a German Patent Application (Title Page). Source: DPMA.

In an application, the invention must be described in such a way that an expert would be able to operate it. This part can also discuss literature known to the inventor in order to emphasize the invention's originality vis-à-vis the current state of science. Apart from this technical part, the application contains a legal part in which patent claims are made. The main claim (stated at the beginning) describes a common version of the claim of invention, whereas supplementary claims represent solution variants for the main claim and subclaims represent particular emanations of the claims. The application must contain drawings and a summary.

---

(19)		Europäisches Patentamt European Patent Office Office européen des brevets	 (11) **EP 1 273 508 B1**

(12)   **EUROPEAN PATENT SPECIFICATION**

(45) Date of publication and mention
of the grant of the patent:
29.09.2004 Bulletin 2004/40

(51) Int Cl.7: **B62K 25/28**

(21) Application number: **01202618.3**

(22) Date of filing: **06.07.2001**

---

(54) **Rear shock absorbing assembly for a bicycle**

Hinterradfederung für ein Fahrrad

Suspension de la roue arrière d'une bicyclette

---

(84) Designated Contracting States:
DE ES FR GB IT NL

(43) Date of publication of application:
08.01.2003 Bulletin 2003/02

(73) Proprietor: **MERIDA INDUSTRY CO., LTD.**
Meikang Village, Tatsun Hsiang,
Changhua Hsien (TW)

(72) Inventor: **Tseng, Diing-Huang**
Tatsun Hsiang, Changhua Hsien (TW)

(74) Representative:
Prins, Adrianus Willem, Mr. Ir. et al
Vereenigde,
Nieuwe Parklaan 97
2587 BN Den Haag (NL)

(56) References cited:
FR-A- 923 235   **US-A- 4 457 393**
US-A- 5 403 028   **US-A- 5 678 837**

Figure 5.2: Example of a European Patent Application (Title Page). Source: EPO.

An application can be filed by the inventor himself or the company that employs him. In the first phase, the DPMA only performs a preliminary examination (for obvious formal or material defects). No later than 18 months after, the application is published (for an example, see Figure 5.1), recognizable by the "A" in the number. The patent office has only added notations of the International Patent Classification (IPC; top right; the basic claim's notation in bold type), the paper's content has not been checked yet. In the first 18 months after filing the application, the invention's content is thus inaccessible, which makes the situation very difficult in information practice.

The second phase of the examination of the content only begins after another application has been made (either by the original claimant or any other party), which has to happen within seven years. Only now are innovation, technicality and commercial applicability checked for. In case of a positive result, the patent office will publish the granted patent as a B-paper. The title page now contains citations, which are references to all the literature consulted by the examiner over the course of the procedure. Sound claims against the patent may be brought forward by anyone within three months of its being granted.

C.	DOCUMENTS CONSIDERED TO BE RELEVANT	
Category*	Citation of document, with indication, where appropriate, of the relevant passages	Relevant to claim No.
X	US 5630117 A (OREN et al.) 13 May 1997 Whole document.	16
X	US 5848410 A (WALLS et al.) 8 December 1998 Whole document.	16
X	US 5878423 A (ANDERSON et al.) 2 March 1999 Whole document.	16
A	US 5913215 A (RUBINSTEIN et al.) 15 June 1999 Whole document.	1-16
A	US 6012055 A (CAMPBELL et al.) 4 January 2000 Whole document.	1-16

☐ Further documents are listed in the continuation of Box C |X| See patent family annex

*	Special categories of cited documents:	"T"	later document published after the international filing date or priority date and not in conflict with the application but cited to understand the principle or theory underlying the invention
"A"	document defining the general state of the art which is not considered to be of particular relevance		
"E"	earlier application or patent but published on or after the international filing date	"X"	document of particular relevance; the claimed invention cannot be considered novel or cannot be considered to involve an inventive step when the document is taken alone
"L"	document which may throw doubts on priority claim(s) or which is cited to establish the publication date of another citation or other special reason (as specified)	"Y"	document of particular relevance; the claimed invention cannot be considered to involve an inventive step when the document is combined with one or more other such documents, such combination being obvious to a person skilled in the art
"O"	document referring to an oral disclosure, use, exhibition or other means		
"P"	document published prior to the international filing date but later than the priority date claimed	"&"	document member of the same patent family

Figure 5.3: Example of a Search Report from a PCT Application. Source: WIPO.

Applications with the **European Patent Office** (EPO, undated) proceed similarly to their German counterparts. Some differences concern the amount of countries for which legal protection is sought in a single application (one, several or all member states) as well as the languages of the documents to be submitted (initially in one of the three official languages, German, English and French). Before a patent can come into effect in one of the member states, however, it must be translated into one of that country's official languages. In contrast to German law, only the claimant himself can begin the second phase in the EPO. The objection period here is nine months. Figure 5.2 shows the title page of a European patent with the list of countries (N° 84) and citations (N° 56).

A **PCT Application** (WIPO, undated) only has a first phase. In contrast to the practices of the DPMA and the EPO, in international (worldwide) applications citations (in the "International Search Report") are immediately viewed and added to the application (with comments like L, X, Y–notes on problems concerning innovation) (see Figure 5.3). The national (or–when defining the EPO as the designated office–regional) phase occurs in the respective national patent offices (or the EPO). After the (usually customary) submission of the invention in his own country, the inventor has twelve months to submit the application via PCT in his own language and via his national patent office. After 18 months, the WIPO publishes the application (with a WO number) in one of its official languages (English, German, French, Japanese, Russian, Spanish, Chinese). If the paper is not available in one of these languages, it must be translated (usually English is chosen). No later than 30 months after this (in EPO applications: 31 months), the transition into the respective national phases begins (if unavailable in a language of the target country, with another translation). If a claimant foregoes the PCT, he will only have one year (and not the 30/31 months if he chooses the PCT) to submit the patent abroad.

It is possible to request an "International Preliminary Examination Report" in order to assess one's chances for being granted the patent once the application is available. In contrast to the procedure without Examination Report (named after Chapter I of the PCT, or, in short, PCT I), this variant is called PCT II (thus named after Chapter II of the PCT). PCT II procedures are the most commonly used variant of international applications (Sternizke 2009).

Since the WIPO charges independently of the number of target countries, many claimants cannot resist the temptation to check all countries available on the PCT contract instead of only the ones they want. Thus many countries on Earth "enjoy" the privilege of receiving many patent applications. If we research the actual granted patents, however (the ones that require a transition into each respective national phase), the number of inventions in some countries becomes noticeably smaller. For the purposes of internationally comparing patent statistics, this issue must absolutely be taken into consideration, as it can lead to a heavy distortion of the results.

Utility Models (see Figure 5.4) do not have to meet specifications as tough as patents'. In §1 of the German Utility Model Law, the preconditions for protection are laid out:

> Inventions that are new, that are the result of an inventive step and are commercially applicable are protected as utility models.

The difference to patents is in the "inventive step", which suggests a level of invention that does not have to be terribly high. Procedures cannot be protected by utility models. The application is heavily simplified in comparison with patents, as there is no official examination of the content with regard to innovation, inventive step and applicability. Patents are granted explicitly, utility models merely "registered". Third parties can challenge the conditions of protection, so that a utility model provides far less legal security than a patent. Furthermore, the legal protection is limited to a maximum of ten years. As utility models are usually processed more quickly than patents, they can be applied for in addition to patents ("junction").

(19)
Bundesrepublik Deutschland
Deutsches Patent- und Markenamt

(10) **DE 20 2008 001 470 U1** 2008.06.12

(12)   **Gebrauchsmusterschrift**

(21) Aktenzeichen: **20 2008 001 470.0**
(22) Anmeldetag: **01.02.2008**
(47) Eintragungstag: **08.05.2008**
(43) Bekanntmachung im Patentblatt: **12.06.2008**

(51) Int Cl.⁸: ***B62K 21/26*** (2006.01)

(73) Name und Wohnsitz des Inhabers:
  Praetorius, Martin, 29355 Beedenbostel, DE

Die folgenden Angaben sind den vom Anmelder eingereichten Unterlagen entnommen

(54) Bezeichnung: **Lenkergriff für Fahrrad**

(57) Hauptanspruch: Lenkergriff aus relativ festem Material, z.B. Holz, Kohlefaser-Kunststoff, andere Kunststoffe, Aluminium, oder ähnliches, dadurch gekennzeichnet, dass der Griff in der Länge deutlich über das Lenkerende hinausgeht und im Durchmesser viel kleiner als das Lenkerrohr wird.

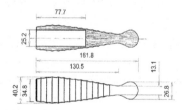

Figure 5.4: Example of a Utility Model Document (Title Page). Source: DPMA.

If granted patents or utility models are sold or licensed, they are (on application) entered into the patent register of the patent office that has granted the protection. With **licenses** (Pahlow, 2006), we distinguish between simple licenses (the rights holder foregoes protection so that the licensee can rightfully use the invention) and exclusive licenses, in which the licensee has the exclusive right for using the invention within the license's area of validity, or can pass it on via sublicenses.

What are the **motives** that lead companies or inventors to have their innovations protected as patents or utility models (Blind et al., 2006)? Are there motives for going without patent protection? Some of the accepted motives leading to a patent application are:

- exclusive commercial usage,
- income via licenses,
- binding knowledge to the company,
- signaling (reputation, bargaining power, incentives for new recruits, performance indicator),
- strategic blockade of competitors ("blocking patents"),
- "smoke bombs".

The main motive is the exclusive commercial exploitation of the invention by oneself. Over the period of 20 years maximum, the holder–and nobody else–has the right to use the items or procedures described in the invention and manufacture or distribute them as marketable products. However, it is also possible to generate income by licensing the patents. Institutes of higher education and freelance inventors in particular aim toward licenses instead of self-marketing. On the other hand, employees–and thus inventors–might leave their company. In order for their technical knowledge to stay on, their innovative know-how is tightly bound to the company via protective rights. The signaling power of granted patents is not to be underestimated. If a company has innovative ideas that are patent-protected, this will get provide them a good reputation, but also advantages in bargaining with suppliers and customers as well as investors. Additionally, patents provide the option of creating stimuli for one's own personnel, e.g. to be named in the patent document. A good patent portfolio also serves as an indicator for the technological capacity of an institution.

However, the goal is not always to actually implement the invention thus protected. Patents can also serve to strategically impede competitors. Koppel (2008, 779) describes such "blocking patents":

> In the framework of a ... blockade strategy, directed toward competing firms from the same or a neighboring technology field in particular, patents are submitted with the goal of making it harder for other enterprises to either find access to complementary technologies, and thus market segments, or–in the reverse–to prevent a limitation of one's own technological leeway in consequence of patents submitted by other companies.

The former case is termed the "offensive blockade strategy", the latter "defensive blockade strategy" (Blind et al., 2006). A defensive blockade strategy can also be pursued via relevant scientific (or other) publications. To wit: once a publication is available, no competitor can apply for a patent for the invention expressed therein–but neither can one's own company. "Smoke bombs" serve only to confuse the competition. They suggest that one is pursuing a certain line of research (which is true) and that one wants to supply the respective markets (which, on the other hand, is untrue). The result is that the competition can no longer merely consult patent statistics in order to see what products are planned for the near future.

Oliver Koppel (2008, 779) stresses the economic necessity of registering an invention in all countries in which the products or services tied to this innovation can be produced or traded. If patent protection is not active, there can be no infringement on the inventor's rights.

> In consequence, if a Chinese company produces goods for the American market, using know-how that is protected in Europe only, it does not break any patent law.

What motives lead companies to refrain from patenting their inventions? A disadvantage of any patent application is regarded by many to be the mandatory disclosure. The competition is thus informed pretty precisely about what a company is capable of. In order to prevent this, one uses the strategy of secrecy (Koppel, 2008, 779):

> The secrecy strategy is of particular advantage in industries with ... short product life cycles. Here the company only has a few years to redeem its research investments; in comparison, the time-consuming application of a patent loses its appeal.

Secrecy presupposes that the company has loyal (and discreet) staff, who intend to remain at the company. In case of coincidental parallel developments that lead a competitor to apply for a patent, one's own work on invention and product must cease. In a study comparing the patenting and secrecy strategy, Katrin Hussinger (2004, 22) shows, firstly, that German industrial companies pursue both strategies, but that, secondly, only the patenting strategy correlates positively with the sale of new products:

> Focusing on product innovating firms in German manufacturing in 2000, ... a strong positive correlation between patents and sales with new products turns out, whereas there is no effect for secrecy. ... (P)atents turn out to be the more effective tool to protect inventions in the market phase as opposed to secrecy, which is also applied by a large fraction of the sampled firms.

5.3   Aesthetic-Commercial Information: Registered Design

The legal protection of Designs is regulated by its own law in Germany (Bulling, Langöhrig, & Hellwig, 2006). It occupies an intermediate position between patent law (in the U.S.A., Designs are regarded as "design patents") and copyright law (in France, an "unité de l'art" belongs to copyright law). Subject of protection are two- or three-dimensional products, or parts thereof, which are both new and have a certain "uniqueness". Registered Design encompasses automobiles, furniture, machines (e.g. washing machines or motors) as well as (according to German law) repair parts, e.g. for use in the auto industry. Since Registered Design law is a pure registered right (for which neither novelty nor uniqueness are examined at the time of application), an examination of content only takes place in case of infringement proceedings. In Registered Design law, there is a grace period of twelve months. One can register a single design, but also apply for legal protection for up to 1,000 designs in a multiple application. The designs are structured into classes of goods, which are recorded in the Locarno Classification (Stock & Stock, 2008, 214 et seq.). They are made available to the public via the Design Bulletin (Figure 5.5) and are valid for a maximum of 25 years. Similarly to patents, it is possible to submit designs throughout the EU (via the "Office of Harmonization for the Internal Market") or (via the WIPO) internationally, in those countries that have joined the "Hague Design Agreement").

001.2   (11) 405 05 219

(11) **405 05 219**   (21) 405 05 219.7
(22) 17.05.2006   (15) 22.07.2008   (45) 14.08.2008
(73) Scharfenberg, Tobias, 44866 Bochum
(74) Scharfenberg, K., Vertreter ohne vereinfachte
  Zustellung, 44869 Bochum
  Zustellungsanschrift:
  Cartronix Europe e.K., Inh. Tobias Scharfenberg,
  Voedestr. 53, 44866 Bochum,
(28) Sammelanmeldung von 8 Geschmacksmustern,
  S 5 Jahre, B
(57) Funk Handsender mit 1,8" TFT Display im Hosenta-
  schenformat (2,4" x 1,5"). 4 seitlich angebrachte gum-
  mierte Tasten in den 3 teigigen Kunststoffen Gehäuse
  mit Carboon Design. Aufschrift Page Guard Cartronix,
  Audio und visuelle Funktionen. Handsender bestehend
  aus Antenne, Gehäuse Vorderseite, Gehäuse Rücksei-
  te, Batteriedeckel und 2 teigige innenliegende Platine
  mit TFT Monitor, Speicherchip und Funk-Signal Emp-
  fänger.

Figure 5.5: Example of a Registered Design. Source: DPMA.

5.4   Advertising Information: Trademark Law

Trademark law protects brands, business terms and indications of geographical sources–in other words, information representing crucial elements for marketing and sales (Berlit, 2008; Campos Nave, 2008; Hacker, 2007; Hildebrand, 2008). Brands are protected by being registered, or by acquiring a reputation through usage (known or "notoriously known" brands, such as *Coca-Cola*), terms and source indications via usage. Terms are either company labels (business names or descriptions of a business process) that appear and disappear alongside "their" company, or work titles (of print products, films, pieces of music and stage productions) that are the result of publication. Essential for brands is their distinctiveness with regard to a product's, or service's, provenance. We distinguish between the following kinds of brands:

- word marks (including numbers and single letters, e.g. *Milka*),
- picture marks (e.g. the symbol of Deutsche Bank),

- word/picture marks (combination of word and picture, such as *Milka Lila Pause* in Figure 5.6),
- three-dimensional marks (e.g. packaging, like the typical Coca-Cola bottle design),

- color marks (e.g. the color *purple* of the company Kraft Foods for Milka),
- sound marks (e.g. the jingles *Wette gewonnen* and *Wette verloren* on the TV show "Wetten, dass…?"),
- cable identification thread mark (e.g. the golden thread of the company *ADO Gardinenwerke*),
- other marks (e.g. color arrangements, e.g. the colors red and green on the packaging of the coffee filter manufacturer *Melitta*).

The graphical components of picture and picture/word marks, respectively, are searchable via notations of the Vienna Classification; the classes of goods for which legal protection is sought are taken from the Nice Classification (Stock & Stock, 2008, 215 et seq.).

We distinguish between **individual marks** (with regard to a particular provenance) from **collective marks** used by several companies, e.g. certification marks (*Fairtrade*).

Brands cannot be registered if there are **absolute grounds for refusal**. These apply to brands that cannot be differentiated. Thus for instance, the work mark *HP* is indistinguishable in the Nice Classification Class 12 (which comprises all automobiles)–after all, every car has horsepower–but it can be distinguished in Class 25 (items of clothing, footwear, headpieces). Neither can brand names that correspond to a "need to keep a trademark free" be registered. This need excludes, as brands, generic terms (*Diesel* as a brand of fuel), places of manufacture (*Park Avenue*), usage instructions (*cough syrup*), insignia (real or faked national emblems or flags) or misleading statements.

(111)	Registernummer	RN	1125335
(210)	Altes Aktenzeichen	AKZ	C37149
(540)	Wiedergabe der Marke	WM	Milka Lila Pause
(540)		Wiedergabe der Marke	
(550)	Markenform	MF	Wort-/Bildmarke
	Verfahrensstand		Marke eingetragen
(220)	Anmeldetag	AT	08.12.1987
(442)	Bekanntmachungstag	BT	31.03.1988
(151)	Tag der Eintragung in das Register	ET	26.07.1988
(450)	Tag der Veröffentlichung der Eintragung	VT	31.08.1988
(732)	Inhaber	INH	Kraft Foods Schweiz AG, Zürich, CH
(740)	Vertreter	VTR	Preu Bohlig & Partner, 20354 Hamburg
(750)	Zustellungsanschrift / -empfänger	ZUE	Rechtsanwalte Preu Bohlig & Partner Warburgstr. 35 Postfach 130789 20107 Hamburg
(511)	Leitklasse	LK	30
(511)	Klassen	KL	30
(510)	Waren- / Dienstleistungsverzeichnis	WDV	Klasse 30: Schokolade, Schokoladewaren, Pralinen, feine Backwaren, Zuckerwaren
(531)	Wiener Bildklassifikation	WBK	27.01.01; 27.05.09; 27.05.10

Figure 5.6: Example of a Trademark Registration. Source: DPMA.

During the **trademark application**, there is an inspection for formal and absolute protection requirements before the trademark is published (Figure 5.6). Formal requirements are, for example, the payment of fees and the certitude that the applicant is even able to hold a trademark. Within three months, the holder of an endangered trademark with an older priority date can challenge the new brand. The protection is valid for ten years, but can always be prolonged. There is an **obligation to use**. Within five years the brand must have been used for the registered product or service.

Claims for cancellation by holders of older trademarks result from cases where brand and product are identical or similar (here oriented by registered Nice Class). The following schema exemplifies the justified claims:

Brands	*Products/Services*	*In Addition*
identical	identical	---
identical	similar	danger of confusion
similar	identical	danger of confusion
similar	similar	danger of confusion
identical	not similar	brand's publicity is used illegally

If the old and new brands are identical *and* both are registered in the same Nice Class, the new brand must be deleted. If the Nice Classes of similar brands are also merely similar, there must be a danger of confusion between the two in order for the new brand to be rejected. This danger can be of an aural (*Zentis–Säntis*), pictorial (in picture marks, but also in similarly-looking words like *Mentor–Meteor*) or conceptual nature (*Sonne–Sun*) (Götting, 2007, 316). In independence of a similarity within a Nice Class, a new brand is denied legal protection if the (large) degree of name recognition of an existing brand is exploited unlawfully (thus the use of the brand name *Dimple*, a Whisky, was deemed inadmissible for a cosmetics product).

As in the case of Registered Designs, brands can be applied for EU-wide, via the "Office of Harmonization for the Internal Market" (OHIP). The **community trademark** thus acquired is legally protected in all member states of the European Union. The application can be submitted directly to the OHIP (in Alicante) or at the respective national patent and trademark office. On the basis of the "Madrid Contract", it is possible to submit an application for the international registration of the brand to the WIPO via one's national trademark office. The "Madrid Union" comprises more than 80 countries worldwide, among them all the most important industrial countries.

The legal protection of **domain names** is regulated by diverse laws. The following German norms may apply:

- personal names (German Civil Code: §12 BGB),
- company names (German Commercial Code: §17 HGB),
- brand names (German Trademark Act: §§14, 15 MarkenG),
- competition (German Act Against Unfair Competition: §1 UWG: Protection of Competitors and Consumers, §3 UWG: Prohibition of Unfair Competition)

Generally speaking, a domain name is given to whoever first applies for it. In contrast to trademark law, the awarding of domain names knows no need for keeping domains free, which can easily lead to generic terms like "sex.com" being used. In disputes about domains, a brand name, work title or company label is a good argument for being granted the pertinent domain name, but only if the brand is singular (which does not have to be the case, as wares from different Nice Classes can have the same word mark). However, this holds exclusively for business use. If a private individual (who wants to protect his or her own name) and a company (with a similar-sounding registered trade mark) are in dispute, name protection is pitted against trademark law (according to the BGB). The case is analog in a dispute between two private individuals who can both invoke §12 BGB. In this case, it seems possible that a famous bearer of a well-known name could enforce their claim against another bearer who is completely unknown (thus in the proceedings of Krupp AG against a Mr. Krupp, which was ruled in favor of the company). Legally dubious are instances of **domain grabbing**, i.e. of registering a domain name before the holder of a trade mark or name or the owner of a company can do so.

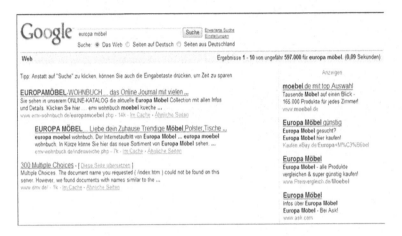

Figure 5.7: Trademark Law Problem: AdWord, which Partially Clashed with a Brand. Source: Google (Search Argument: "Europa Möbel"; registered brand: Europa Möbel; none of the hits in AdWord lead to the brand holder).

Since more and more users do not type URLs into the browser window, but use search engines in order to get to websites, the search arguments and their counterparts in the websites and–in case of context-specific advertising–the auctioned advertising terms are increasingly significant. **Keyword grabbing**–i.e. the use of registered terms either on one's own website (sometimes also hidden in the metatags, or, as "word stuffing", written in white on white background, invisible on browsers) or as search arguments for "sponsored links" (as in Google's AdWords) is another practice that poses problems for trademark law. Grabbing terms protected by trademark law falls, if there is a danger of confusion–at least if intent can be proven–under unfair competition and is thus illegal. The case becomes a little problematic if the AdWord does not match the word mark exactly but only partially. *Europa Möbel* is a registered trade mark; a competitor uses *Möbel* as a keyword on Google AdWords. In this case, the competitor's ad will appear among the "sponsored links" if someone searches for *Europa Möbel* (not via phrase search) (Figure 5.7). Here, according to German law, it is possible that the trademark holder can move the competitor to change this (e.g. by adding the excluding search argument *Europa Möbel*) (Ott, 2008). However, there is no clear and comprehensible line of judgment in this area.

5.5   Works: Copyright Law

Copyright law grants works legal protection as individual intellectual creations (Hertin, 2008; Lettl, 2008; Rehbinder, 2008). Copyright applies automatically, i.e. legal protection does not have to be explicitly applied for as in the case of commercial protective rights. Among the protected works from literature, science and art are literary works (compositions and speeches, but also computer programs), music, dance, visual art, photography, film and scientific-technical images (e.g. pictures or charts). When someone publishes a **work on the internet** (e.g. as a website or blog entry), copyright applies, as it does for all works. Computer programs are also (as "literary works", though not including the ideas and principles underlying them) subject to copyright. The author, as "creator" of the work, is granted a monopoly on his own intellectual property, particularly the right to determine if and how his work is to be published. Additionally, he has the right for his authorship to be recognized, meaning that the user of a work is obligated to always clearly state the source he uses (in a scientific work, for instance, in the form of a reference).

In Germany, copyright law has been adjusted–at least officially–to the demands of the information society via "Basket 1" (2003) and "Basket 2" (2007).

According to §15 of German Copyright Law, the author has three rights of exploiting his work "physically", being

- reproduction rights (§16 UrhG),
- distribution rights (§17 UrhG),
- exhibition rights (§ 18 UrhG)

as well as fourthly–but in "non-physical" form–public communication rights (§19 UrhG), in the form of lectures, presentations, performances, (broadcast) transmissions and making it available on websites.

This positive content of copyright law corresponds to its negative content of denying other parties these rights. Not only the work as such is protected, but also its revised or otherwise rearranged versions. However, once adaptations (e.g. translations or "liberal adaptations" of the original) that are intellectual creations of the persons responsible for them are available, these are protected in the same way as the original work. Outside of these rights, a work can be freely used. In science, accordingly, thoughts or even word-for-word passages can be taken from a work and put into a new one, as long as author and source are named. Otherwise, there is "intellectual theft", i.e. plagiarism.

Copyrights are always limited rights, after the expiration of which–in Germany (according to §64 UrhG), this happens 70 years after the creator's death–the work enters the public domain, and can thus be used by anyone. These terms have been and are constantly being drawn out: where they used to stipulate 30 years, they were prolonged to 50 and finally 70, securing a generation of the author's descendants the rights to his work. For databases (Derclaye, 2008), the protection expires (according to §87 UrhG) as early as 15 years after their publication.

Copyright has **limitations**. Private and scientific usage are regulated by §53 UrhG, according to which single reproductions for private consumption are permitted, on any medium, as long as they serve no commercial purpose. §53 Section 2 defines further limitations in detail:

> It is permitted to produce or have produced single reproductions of a work
>
> for one's own scientific usage, if and as far as reproduction is justified for this purpose and serves no commercial ends,
>
> for adding it into one's personal archive, if and as far as reproduction is justified for this purpose and one's own copy of the work is being used as the basis of the reproduction,
>
> for one's personal edification concerning daily news, if the work is being broadcast,
>
> for any other personal usage
>
> if it concerns small parts of a published work, or single contributions, appearing in newspapers or magazines,
>
> if it concerns a work that has been commercially unavailable for more than two years.

Scientific as well as archival purposes are clearly the beneficiaries. Small parts of works (e.g. journal articles) can also be copied for one's own professional and commercial usage. If a work has been unavailable for more than two years, it can be copied. The freedom to make copies for one's private or commercial usage must not be confused with freedom of charge; customers do have to pay for any copies they make.

The reproduction and distribution of articles from the press is acceptable. This regulation, which is important for the compilation of **press reviews**, is codified in §49 Section 1 UrhG:

> The reproduction and distribution of single broadcast comments and articles as well as images published alongside them, from newspapers and other information organs that merely serve topical interests, in other newspapers and information organs of this kind as well as the public rendition of such comments, articles and images is acceptable if they

address political, economic or religious daily concerns and if they are not subject to protective rights. The author is to be adequately compensated for the reproduction, distribution and public rendition of his work, unless it is a case of reproduction, distribution or public rendition of short excerpts from several comments or articles in the form of an overview.

This claim can only be averred by a collecting society. This regulation also holds for electronic press reviews (Glas, 2008). Copyright also applies to **libraries**. For publicly accessible libraries (such as school, city or university libraries), certain privileges exist, but not for libraries of private enterprises (e.g. company libraries) (Knaf & Gillitzer, 2008). According to §52b UrhG, **electronic reading areas** are permitted, which are used exclusively in the premises of the institution for the purposes of research and private study. Simultaneous access to works is only possible in the amount stipulated by the library's stock. Although not specifically mentioned in the law, it may be assumed that scanned books (which are in fact physically available in the library) can also be viewed in the reading areas. Consumer rivalry in the digital usage of scientific works is artificially created here via the restricted simultaneous access (Kuhlen, 2008, 368 et seq.).

Electronic key texts, i.e. the digital availability of single contributions or smaller works for a limited circle of users for scientific research, are in accordance with §52a UrhG. If entire books are to be made available as electronic key texts, the library must be in possession of each respective book and make the digital version available via their electronic reading areas only.

If a work requested by a user not present in the library, it can be procured from other libraries via interlibrary loan or document delivery. §53a Section 1 regulates **copy dispatch** on request:

> For individual orders, the reproduction and transmission of single contributions published in newspapers and magazines, as well as small parts of a published work via mail or fax by public libraries is acceptable, as long as usage by the orderer is permitted as per §53. The reproduction and transmission in any other electronic form is only acceptable as a graphic file and by way of illustrating lessons or for purposes of scientific research, as long as it is justifiable in the pursuit of non-commercial activities. The reproduction and transmission in any other electronic form is further only acceptable if access to the contributions or small parts of a work is not made obviously available to the public from places and at times of their choosing via a contractual agreement at acceptable conditions.

The formulation becomes somewhat cryptic at the end. The sending of copies via mail or fax, always available for all customer groups, is clear. Electronic delivery to commercial customers is out of the question. For research or teaching purposes, electronic copy is permitted (with graphic files), but only if the publisher does not formulate an "obvious" and "acceptable" pay-per-view offer. The obviousness is operationalized by highlighting the work in databases (e.g. the attestation of the journal "Information Processing & Management" in the database "ScienceDirect" by the publishing house Reed Elsevier), the acceptability via "the usual price". It looks as though publishers are being granted a distribution monopoly over their digital products (Kuhlen, 2008, 396 et seq.). Libraries and document delivery services are on the safe side, legally speaking, if they negotiate contracts with the publishers that regulate the digital delivery of single articles from journals, magazines or anthologies.

Technical measures, such as copy protection mechanisms on a CD or DVD may not be circumvented following §95a UrhG, but §95b allows for limitations on copyright (like the permitted reproductions for research). The software in use for Digital Rights Management would thus have to be able to recognize whether an acceptable limitation is in place in each individual case. The question of how far this can be implemented technically seems to be totally open. §§95a-d cannot be applied to computer programs (§69a, Section 4). Software cannot be copied at all, unless it is to create a backup copy for securing further usage (§69d).

An author must accept these limitations, but there is a **duty for remuneration**. Operators of copying machines or institutions with a high copying volume, i.e. libraries (Schmitt, 2008), performing artists, commercial enterprises etc. pay a fee to the respective **collecting society** (Hertin, 2008, 208 et seq.), e.g. in Germany the collecting society (VG) WORT for authors of literary works, the Society for Musical Performance and Mechanical Reproduction Rights (GEMA) for composers, songwriters and music publishers, and the Society for the Assertion of Film and Television Rights (GWFF) for filmmakers. The respective society then distributes the proceeds proportionately to its members. The Presse-Monitor GmbH (PMG), an establishment of German publishers and publishers' associations is responsible for the distribution of articles from the press. It licenses articles for further use in electronic press reviews and serves as VG Wort's collecting agency.

Insignificant in terms of copyright are **links** to homepages of external websites. This goes for any website and also for search engines (which give out links in their hit lists) (Ott, 2008). However, it is impossible to integrate foreign content as a file on one's own website (e.g. via frames) without the author's permission, as the users would not notice that the content is from another site. "Deep Links", i.e. links that do not lead to a homepage but to a certain site "deep" within the web presence could cause problems. As the homepage is being circumvented (perhaps containing ads or other information that are of importance for the owner of the website) a legal problem will–in exceptional cases–arise (Oppenheim, 2008, 946).

A borderline case of permissible usage of content protected by copyright is in the adoption of **titles and sentences** or sentence fragments, as well as of thumbnails of images in news search engines (Figure 5.8). The admissibility of **thumbnails** in image search engines is deemed to be resolved at the moment, while the adoption of texts is open and depends on each individual case. Google has agreed a licensing contract for its "Google News" with the French news agency "Agence

France Presse" (AFP) and other agencies, which regulates the use of titles and sentence fragments (Ott, 2008).

Une femme de 59 ans accouche de triplés à **Paris**
AFP - Il y a 17 minutes
PARIS (AFP) — Une femme de 59 ans a donné naissance à trois bébés en bonne santé dans la nuit de samedi à dimanche à la maternité parisienne de Port-Royal ...

Aubry lance un appel à Delanoë, favori des sympathisants PS
AFP - 7 sep 2008
PARIS (AFP) — Martine Aubry a estimé qu'elle-même et Bertrand Delanoë avaient "l'essentiel en commun", assurant "attendre" le maire de **Paris** en vue du ...
PS: Mauroy demande aux dirigeants de "faire attention" à l'éclatement AFP
Université d'été de La Rochelle: brouillard persistant au PS AFP
Les socialistes englués dans une inquiétante guerre des chefs AFP
AFP - AFP
973 autres articles >>

Figure 5.8: Copyright on Headlines, Single Sentences and Thumbnails of Images from News Agencies and Newspapers. Source: Google News.

Are infringements on copyright "theft"? Is there even such a thing as **pirate copies**? Jan Krömer and Evrim Sen (2006) argue for the decriminalization of copyright infringements. They are not instances of theft at all; a more fitting appellation would be "bootleg copies". Let us just take a look into the German Criminal Code. In §249, "theft" is defined as follows:

> Whoever uses violence against an individual, or threats that represent a current danger for that person's life or health, in order to take away from that person a foreign physical object with the intention of unlawfully appropriating said object for himself or a third party will be punished with a prison term of no less than one year.

Thus, firstly, theft has to do with violence, and secondly, a third party is deprived of a product–neither of which is given in instances of piracy. Violence against a person is no an issue at all, and the owner is not deprived of anything, since a copy is made and nothing else. Infringements on copyright, however, cannot be ruled out.

If someone infringes on copyright, the rights holder has a claim for **compensation** (§97 UrhG). The following claims are stated:

- removing the infringement,
- (in case of a danger of repetition) forbearance,
- in case of intent or negligence on the part of the offender:
  - compensation or
  - forfeiture of profits,

and additionally (also in case of intent or negligence) compensation for immaterial damage (to provide "satisfaction").

5.6   Creative Commons and Copyleft

While copyright law protects the rights holder and only grants users certain rights in exceptional cases (which become less and less over time), "Creative Commons" (CC) and "Copyleft" place the focus on the user without providing the author with any material recompense (unless stating his name count as such). Creative Commons and Copyleft have no legal status, but are understood as a contract between author and user (Mantz, 2006, 57 et seq.). If the user breaks this contract, the still active copyright is asserted. Creative Commons were established in 2001 by Lawrence Lessig in particular (see e.g. Lessig, 2003), and are regarded as an excellent basis for the free distribution of digital content on the internet. Role models, in a way, were the free software licenses, such as GNU General Public License–often described "copyleft" as they complement copyright.

Let us make a quick sketch of the conception of **Copyleft!** This concerns the conditions of free usage of software Stallman (2004[1996], 91) defines:

> Copyleft is a general method for making a program free software and requiring all modified and extended versions of the program to be free software as well.

If a software is under a Copyleft license, it may be used freely (even commercially), copies may be distributed for free or for a fee, the source code being always included. Programs derived from the original software must also be Copyleft-licensed. If this "inheritance" of free usage is not given, we speak of **Open Source**.

As information provider, one uses **Creative Commons** to define the (legal) degree of content protection oneself (O'Sullivan 2008). The tiered licensing contracts enable content providers to no longer have to choose between full protection ("all rights reserved") and none at all but instead make a sophisticated decision in what form their product should be protected. If next to the obligatory naming (BY), a processing of the work (No Derivative Works) should be allowed but no commercial usage (Non-Commercial: NC), a specific licensing variant is available. Another variant would be to allow transmission under identical conditions (Share Alike: SA).

These licenses can principally be applied to all works and all content that are the result of creative processes, be it texts, photos, images, audio and video files, multimedial content, websites, blogs or other advertising and information materials.

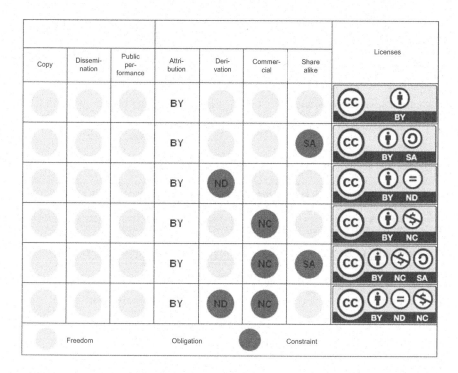

Figure 5.9: Creative Commons Licenses and Their Usage Conditions. Source: Linde & Ebber 2007, 49. Abbr.: BY = Naming of Author, SA = Transmission Under the Same Conditions, ND = No Processing, NC = No Commercial Usage.

5.7 Legal Protection of Software

At first glance, the situation in German law seems clear: computer programs are subject to copyright law (§§69a-g UrhG), programs for data processing systems are excluded from patents "as such" (§1 PatG). In the European Union, this is handled analogously; in the U.S.A., the case is different entirely: here, software can be patented without any restrictions (as long as it serves a useful and technical purpose). According to the German and European conception of the law, software lacks the criterion of technicality, as the code (written in a programming language) makes it a "literary work". Thus, in Europe, it is not possible to protect the idea underlying the software, as copyright forbids the copying of CD-ROMs, but not the usage of the procedure described on them (Stock, 2001).

Europäisches Patentamt

(19) European Patent Office

Office européen des brevets

(11) **EP 0 771 280 B1**

(12) **EUROPEAN PATENT SPECIFICATION**

(45) Date of publication and mention
of the grant of the patent:
16.02.2000 Bulletin 2000/07

(21) Application number: 95926306.2

(22) Date of filing: **18.07.1995**

(51) Int. Cl.[7]: **B60T 8/88**

(86) International application number:
PCT/US95/09001

(87) International publication number:
WO 96/02411 (01.02.1996 Gazette 1996/06)

(54) **METHOD AND SYSTEM FOR DETECTING THE PROPER FUNCTIONING OF AN ABS CONTROL UNIT UTILIZING DUAL PROGRAMMED MICROPROCESSORS**

VERFAHREN UND SYSTEM ZUM FESTSTELLEN DES KORREKTEN FUNKTIONIERENS EINER ABS-STEUEREINHEIT UNTER BENUTZUNG VON ZWEI PROGRAMMIERTEN MIKROPROZESSOREN

PROCEDE ET SYSTEME DE DETECTION DU BON FONCTIONNEMENT D'UN ORGANE DE COMMANDE D'ABS A L'AIDE DE DEUX MICROPROCESSEURS PROGRAMMES

(84) Designated Contracting States:
DE FR GB

(30) Priority: **18.07.1994 US 276344**

(43) Date of publication of application:
07.05.1997 Bulletin 1997/19

(73) Proprietor: **KELSEY-HAYES COMPANY**
Livonia, MI 48150 (US)

(72) Inventor: HORNBACK, Edward, R.
Dexter, MI 48130 (US)

(74) Representative:
Avery, Stephen John et al
Hoffmann Eitle,
Patent- und Rechtsanwälte,
Arabellastrasse 4
81925 München (DE)

(56) References cited:
EP-A- 0 322 141   EP-A- 0 496 509
DE-A- 4 137 124   GB-A- 2 019 622
US-A- 5 243 607

• ATZ, vol.93, no.7/8, August 1991, STUTTGART ,
DE pages 406 - 414, XP267526 STÖCKER ET AL.
'ZUVERLÄSSIGKEIT VON ELEKTRONISCHEN
BAUTEILEN IM AUTOMOBIL'

Figure 5.10: Example of a Patent on a Computer-Implemented Invention. Source: EPO.

In legal practice, the situation is far more relaxed. Pure source code cannot be patented, in accordance with the law; however, if software makes a technical contribution, a patent is usually granted. The European Patent Office (EPO, 2008, 16) observes:

> (T)he EPO grants patents for many inventions in which software makes a technical contribution, such as a novel and inventive computer-controlled process operating a robot arm, enhancing a graphic display, controlling data storage between memories or routing diverse calls through a telephone exchange in respond to demand.

Other processes, such as Internet retailing, though involving the use of a computer, are not patentable in Europe, whereas such processes are often patented in the USA.

Hence, computer-implemented inventions can be patented in Europe (and in Germany),

- if they have a technical character and solve a technical problem
- and if they represent a new inventive contribution to the current state of technology (for an example, see Figure 5.10).

Hence, if computer-implemented inventions solve an economic (and not simultaneously technical) problem, no patent will be granted.

The legal protection of software thus knows several co-existing mechanisms in practice:

- patent (on a computer-implemented invention): Idea is protected; duration: at most 20 years,
- literary work (copyright): Reproduction and distribution rights, among others; duration: up to 70 years after the author's death,
- Copyleft (and related Open Source licensing models): Free usage.

5.8   Person-Related Information: Data Protection Law

"Data Protection" does not protect data, it protects people from an abuse of their person-related information (Kühling & Sivridis, 2008; Wohlgemuth & Gerloff, 2005). In Germany, the significance of person-related information has been recognized early; there has been a state law in Hessia since 1970, which the Federal Republic emulated in 1977. The purpose of the Federal Data Protection Law is defined in §1 BDSG:

> The purpose of this law is to protect the individual from being impaired
> in his personality right by use of his person-related information.

The law applies to all public areas of the Republic and of the states (if they do not have their own data protection laws), as well as to all non-public institutions, if these manage information electronically. There is a specific pointer (in §3a BDSG), in the sense of "data economy", to compile as little information as needed, or none at all, about persons, and, if necessary, to use anonymity. Every person has the following rights with regard to their person-related information:

- disclosure (on application),
- correction of incorrect information,
- deletion (if the information is saved unlawfully),
- blocking (if the deletion is subject to retention periods).

The compilation of person-related information is always admissible if the person in question has agreed to it. §13 BDSG names a series of further kinds of admissible compilation, including when legal regulations demand it or the data in question is obviously of a public nature. For purposes of address trade, **advertising** or market research, the compilation, processing and (in case of a justified interest on the part of the buyer) the transmission of specific data (such as name, age, profession, address) is also possible. In §29 Section 1 BDSG, we read:

> The commercial compilation, storage or editing of person-related data for the purposes of transmission, particularly where it serves advertising, the operation of credit agencies, address trade or market and opinion research, is admissible if
>
> there is no reason to suppose that the individual in question has an interest worthy of protection in the exclusion of compilation, storage or editing, or if
>
> the data can be drawn from publicly accessible sources, or if the responsible authority is permitted to publish it, unless the individual's interest worthy of protection in the exclusion of compilation, storage or editing obviously outweighs these concerns.

Subject to particular protection are further person-related information, e.g. concerning political opinions, religious beliefs, criminal acts or sex life. Here the respective authority must be able to prove the veracity of the knowledge concerning the person in question.

Data preservation in the context of the so-called "telecommunication surveillance" is regarded as problematic, since in this case, public bodies are granted access to certain person-related information with no particular reason to seek them. This concerns the recording of traffic data from any telecommunication (e-mail, internet, telephone) over a period of six months. Not among the saved data is the content, transmitted and received; neither are the URLs of visited websites (Gitter & Schnabel, 2007).

The **right to one's own image** is regulated by §§22-24 of the German Law on the Protection of Copyright in Works of Art and Photographs (KunstUrhG) (Lettl, 2008, 308 et seq.). Apart from the paragraphs concerning portrait rights, this law was repealed in 1965. Accordingly, images may only be distributed with the express consent of the person portrayed, allowing said person to control how they are being represented in public. The law states the following exceptions (in §23 KunstUrhG):

> Without the express consent required after §22, the following may still be distributed and exhibited:
>
> images from the area of contemporary history;
>
> images depicting a person as accessory to a landscape or other locality;

images of assemblies, demonstrations or other procedures that the portrayed individuals participated in;

images that have not been made on commission, as long as their distribution or exhibition serves a higher artistic interest.

The Federal Republic's (and several states') **Law for Information Transparency** goes beyond person-related information (Schoch, 2008). According to this law, everybody has the right to access to any kind of official information from each respective regional authority–but not, without their consent, to files containing person-related information about third parties. In many countries worldwide, there exists such an information freedom. The U.S.A. established its "Freedom of Information Act" as early as 1966.

For the content of a **Web document**, person-related information of others must be taken into consideration, as here, too, of course, data protection applies (Czink, 2006). This regards all manner of Web documents, starting from one's own website and going via blog and message board entries to the uploading of images and videos on collaborative Web services, including any comments made on them. The right to one's own image also applies on the WWW, and is applicable in photosharing services (e.g. Flickr), videosharing services (e.g. YouTube) and social networking services (e.g. Facebook), for example.

5.9   Content on the Internet: Telemedia Law

The Telemedia Law (Heckmann, ed., 2007) regulates the handling of information content provided via "telemedia" (i.e. the internet). This regards private websites as well as commercial web offers; access providers, service providers and search engine providers are also bound by this law. All "business-like" telemedia are subject to an unrestricted **imprint duty** (stating of name, address, e-mail, entry in the commercial register, register of associations or the like, sales tax identification number; §5 Section 1 TMG). For commercial communication via e-mail, the commercial character of the message and the sender must be clearly recognizable, which would–provided a correct application of the telemedia law–largely prevent the occurrence of **spam**.

The **liability for content** lies primarily with the respective provider, and secondarily with providers of
- information transmission according to §8 TMG (access providers),
- intermediate storage for faster information transmission according to §9 TMG (Proxy Cache Providers), information storage according to §10 TMG (Host Providers, Search Engines, among others).

The responsibilities are defined in §7 TMG:

Service providers are responsible for their own information, which they keep ready for usage, according to the general laws.

Service providers in the sense of §§8 through 10 are not required to monitor the information transmitted or stored by them, or to investigate circumstances that point to unlawful conduct. Requirements for the removal or blocking of the information according to the general laws will stay untouched following §§8 through 10, even in the case of the service provider's unliability. The telecommunications secrecy according to §88 of telecommunication law is to be preserved.

As long as service providers have no knowledge of unlawful information in the sense of §§8-10, they are not responsible for said information. The situation changes, however, at the moment that they are informed about such content. For services following §§9-10 TMG, the providers must immediately remove the information in question or block access to them. For algorithmic search engines (such as Google), Sieber and Liesching (2007, 22) observe:

The search engine provider must–and he is able to–remove the information stored by himself, particularly in the case of judicial or administrative decree.

According to §86 of the Criminal Code, the distribution of propaganda materials for anti-constitutional organizations is prohibited in Germany. If a website contains such material, and Google has been notified of it, for instance, access to it must be blocked in the German version of Google (Figure 5.11: Google.de removes two, technically appropriate, documents from the hit list).

This holds, analogously, for sponsored links (e.g. AdWords). If the advertising texts and search arguments are being checked by the search engine provider, the providers are co-responsible for any unlawful information (such as trademark abuse); if the ads are not checked, the responsibility is cancelled and the search engine provider only has to act once he is informed of any violations.

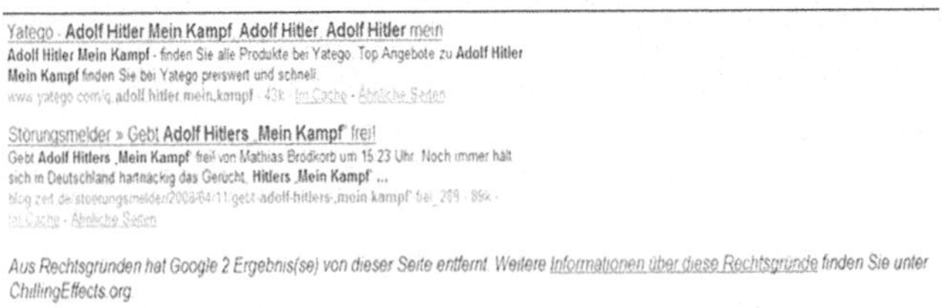

Figure 5.11: Censorship on Google.de. Source: Google (Search Query: Adolf Hitler "Mein Kampf").

Various service providers dispose of person-related information. As long as it is technically possible and reasonable, a provider must facilitate usage of telemedia and payment for them in an anonymous, or pseudonymous, fashion (§13 Section 6 TMG). Person-related inventory data (which are necessary for the specification of contracts) and usage data (features for identifying the user, statements concerning beginning and end of usage as well as its extent, statements concerning telemedia made use of) may be employed for access and billing purposes as well as advertising, market research or the customized design of the services (but only while using pseudonyms). As previously mentioned for telecommunication surveillance, law enforcement agencies can request this data. The telemedia law extends the circle of "competent authorities" for inventory data (but not for usage data) in §14 Section 2, however:

> The service provider may disclose information about inventory data in individual cases if ordered to do so by authorized bodies, as long as it is required for purposes of criminal prosecution, the averting of dangers by the states' police forces, fulfilling the legal obligations of the federal and state constitution protection agencies, federal intelligence services or the military counter-intelligence service, or for the assertion of intellectual property rights.

What is interesting here are the claims of private individuals or of companies to assert their copyright or their entitlement to commercial legal protection. If there is a suspicion of trademark or copyright infringements, for instance, service providers must pass on the inventory data of their customers to the respective claimant.

5.10   Adjacent Fields of Law

The **competition law** (Jestaedt, 2008b; Köhler & Bornkamm, 2007) regulates the **fairness** of markets. The Law Against Unfair Competition (UWG) serves the following purpose (§1 UWG):

> This law serves to protect competitors, consumers and any other market participants from unfair competition. At the same time, it protects the general public's interest in an unadulterated competition.

All acts that influence the competition to the competitors', consumers' or any other market participants' disadvantage are inadmissible according to §3 UWG. Unfair are, for instance, misleading advertising and unacceptable nuisances.

The uncalled-for sending of **e-mails** for competitive purposes after §7 UWG is one such "unacceptable nuisance" and thus anti-competitive (Altermann, 2006). If the recipient has given his explicit consent to being thus addressed, we speak of a "request". There is one single exception: e-mail advertising is admissible if the advertising company has received the e-mailing address via selling a product or service, the ad regards similar products, the customer has not vetoed this usage of his mailing address but can still do at any time.

In search engine advertising, such as Google AdWords, advertising clients purchase search arguments by auction, which by being clicked result in costs for the advertiser. It is possible to settle on a maximum daily budget, which after being exceeded will result in the ad being pulled from the site. If a competitor instigates massive amounts of clicks on a company's ads, that company will be harmed via increased costs (which result in no gains) and—once the maximum daily budget has been reached–the pulling of the ad. Such a **click fraud** at the expense of a competitor collides with §4 N° 10 UWG, which stipulates that a person acts unfairly if they impede competitors (Kaufmann, 2005).

If a user acquires content or software from a commercial provider online, he is granted no **right of objection** (§312d Section 4 BGB)–in contrast with the right to return products in distance contracts usually contained in the Civil Code (§312 Section 1 BGB). This means that bough information goods cannot be returned. From time to time, hosts will protect themselves with additional coverage by defining "general terms and conditions" (GTC). Thus we can read, in the GTC of GENIOS:

> As far as there is a right of revocation according to §§312b et seq., this
> will expire as soon as the user has begun downloading files.

The **Reuse of Information Law** (IWG) is supposed to motivate providers (particularly commercial ones) to develop digital information services on the basis of information compiled and stored by public bodies (Hopf, 2007). **Public institutions** are indeed significant information producers, we need only consider official statistics, commercial protective rights, legal texts or geological data. IWG §2 Section 3 defines this "reuse":

> Reuse (is) any kind of information that goes beyond the accomplishment of a public task and generally aims at generating a fee ...

Hence, it does not involve the one-to-one marketing of public information by the corporate sector; rather, commercial information providers are encouraged to create new, "enriched" information products. Thus, for example, legal texts (compiled in public institutions) can be submitted to an online host (let's say: Juris, or LexisNexis), which will then link these texts to any relevant verdicts they concern. Or, it is possible, that the DPMA leaves the full texts of its patent documents to a commercial database provider (such as Derwent or Questel), which will then furnish it with a specific added value via elaborate retrieval systems (e.g. the offer of a patent-informetric functionality).

It is safeguarded, via laws concerning the **German National Library**, that media works published in Germany will be collected in the German National Library (DNB) in their entirety. "Media Works" are representations in writing, image and sound, which are made accessible either in "physical" (i.e. on paper, electronic or other data carriers) or in "non-physical form" (in public networks) (DNBG §3). There is, according to §14 DNBG, a duty to disclose all media works, excepting films (in which music is not the most important ingredient) and works available via broadcast only. The duty to disclose concerns whoever has the right to distribute the media work in question (e.g. publishing houses) and a business location, production units or main residence in Germany. The Decree for the Obligatory Surrender of Data (PflAV) makes it clear that the **obligatory copies** to be submitted to the DNB include both physical and non-physical works–thus including all publications on the World Wide Web. Excluded from the duty to disclose are, among others, private websites, communication and discussion instruments with no technical or personal aspects as well as e-mail newsletters without archival function (PflAV §9). As the decree does not state clearly which Web works specifically fall under the PflAV and which do not (for instance, it remains unanswered whether and how many posts on weblogs must be disclosed), any practical dealings with the PflAV will require an arrangement with the DNB.

5.11   Information Criminal Law

Work accomplished on the computer as well as the publishing of content on websites can result in criminal prosecution. We would like to separate the pertinent paragraphs of the Criminal Code into the two areas of Computer Criminal Law (Hilgendorf, ed., 2004) and Content Criminal Law.

Computer Criminal Law regulates, in §§202a through c StGB, the **scouting for** and **interception of** data (computer espionage), penalizing both these activities and the production of pertinent computer programs. Hacking into foreign computer systems (including "phishing" for passwords), and generally using information not intended for third parties and furnished with particular protection against unauthorized access, is illegal. **Forgery of evidential data** (such as certificates) via data processing is deemed just as deceptive as non-digital falsification (§270 StGB). In **computer fraud** (§263a StGB), not a human being but a computer system is being "scammed". This can involve the usage of an ATM with a fake debit card. §263a StGB particularly involves all cases of economic crime, which provide the perpetrator with an "illegal pecuniary advantage" via

> incorrect program design, usage of incorrect or incomplete data, unauthorized usage of data or any other unauthorized action to influence the running (of a data processing program).

Computer fraud is thus closely linked to theft, embezzlement or misappropriation of funds. **Data changes** (§303a StGB) and **computer sabotage** (§303b StGB) are criminal acts. Data changes refer to the deletion, suppression, rendering unusable or changing of content, thus extending the concept of property damage to information. The central paragraph is §303b on computer sabotage:

> Whoever substantially obstructs a data process that is of substantial importance to another person, by
>
> committing an act following §303a Section 1,
>
> entering or transmitting data (§202a Section 2) with the intention of causing another person a disadvantage or
>
> destroying, damaging, rendering unusable, removing or changing data processing equipment or data carriers,
>
> will be punished with a jail term of up to three years, or by having to pay a fine.
>
> If it is a data process of substantial importance for a foreign company, a foreign enterprise or an administration, the penalty will be a jail term of up to five years or a fine.

In particularly grave scenarios, a jail term of up to ten years may even be applied. Computer sabotage involves not only the destruction of hardware, but also of software and content, thus including all manner of viruses, Trojans or bots that harm the working of foreign computers.

Depending on **content**, it is possible that aspects of criminal law will be touched upon. Thus according to §86 StGB, it is forbidden to distribute content by **anti-constitutional organizations** that "go against the liberal-democratic constitution". Likewise, "simple" pornographic texts and performances may not be transmitted via telemedia, according to §184c StGB, unless "this pornographic performance is inaccessible to persons under the age of 18 years", i.e. if some effective age verification system is in place to safeguard youth protection. Always prohibited is the distribution of **porn** that contains depictions of violence, sexual acts of humans and animals (§184a StGB) as well as depictions of sexual abuse of children (§184b StGB)–in the case of the latter, even purchase and ownership are illegal. Children are defined as any persons under the age of 14 years. Content on websites, in blog entries, message boards, comments for images, videos etc. that represents **insults**, defamation, libel or slandering the memory of deceased persons is illegal under §§185 et seq. StGB.

5.12   International Information Law?

How are cases to be regarded if they touch upon several countries' legal conceptions? A classical example of a conflict between different letters of the law regards
Yahoo!. According to French law Yahoo! acts illegally if its search engine (ya-
hoo.com) offers fascist literature, while according to U.S. law, and a current court
decision, the company can ignore the French ruling (Oppenheim, 2008, 951). Michael Saadat (2005) reports:

> The French Court held that blocking French access to www.yahoo.com
> was technically possible, and that because www.yahoo.com could be
> viewed by French citizens, it came within the jurisdiction of France. It
> ordered Yahoo! to comply, or face penalties. Yahoo! sought a declara-
> tory judgement that the "French Court's orders are neither cognizable
> nor enforceable under the laws of the United States." On 7 November
> 2001, Judge Fogel granted Yahoo!'s request for declaratory judgement.
> Substantively, this was to be expected. U.S. courts have previously de-
> nied enforcement of foreign judgements that have been deemed incom-
> patible with the U.S. Constitution, including enforcement of foreign
> defamation judgements.

The law, and thus also information law, is national; providers in the information
economy thus often act internationally. Outside of international agreements (such
as TRIPs), conflicts regarding the definition of what makes "good law" can in no
way be excluded.

5.13   Conclusion

- Especially in the information society, the legal protection of intellectual
  property plays a particular role. There is no information law as such; rather, there is a cross-section of "traditional" areas of the law (such as
  commercial legal protection and copyright) as well as the relevant specific laws (e.g. data protection law and telemedia law). Additionally, competition and criminal law are to be regarded.
- The right to one's intellectual property consists of commercial legal protection (technical protective rights: patents and utility models; non-
  technical protective rights: registered designs and trade marks) as well as
  copyright. The object of commercial legal protection is an intellectual-
  commercial service, the object of copyright is a work as a personal intellectual creation.

- In commercial legal protection, the principle of territorial restriction and the priority principle always apply.
- Technical information (inventions) is protected via patents or utility models ("little patents"). The criteria for receiving this protection are novelty, inventive act (or, for utility models, inventive step) and commercial applicability. Patents have a maximum validity of 20 years, utility models 10 years at most. The application is filed with the respective national patent office (the German Patent and Trademark Office DPMA, for instance), regional patent office (e.g. the European Patent Office) or, on the basis of the Patent Cooperation Treaty (PCT), as an international application with the World Intellectual Property Organization (WIPO).
- Phase 1 of the application process checks exclusively for formal or material defects and ends in a patent application (A-document); only in phase 2 are the criteria for granting the patent examined for content, after which, in the positive scenario, the patent document (B-document) is published.
- The legal protection of designs is a register right, i.e. neither the novelty required nor the uniqueness are checked when a design is registered. Designs can be protected for up to 25 years.
- Trademark law protects brands, indications of sources and terms (company labels and work titles). Protection is not only the result of registration, but also of usage and notoriety. Trademarks can be prolonged for ten years at a time (with no upper limit); an obligation to use applies.
- Claims for cancellation filed by owners of older trade marks arise from identity or similarity of brand and product/service.
- Claims for domain names can be backed up by various norms (such as person, company or brand names, work titles or company labels). Domain grabbing (analogously: keyword grabbing) is very problematic from the perspective of trademark and competition law.
- Works are protected by copyright, which expires 70 years after the author's death (exception: databases, for which the protection expires as early as 15 years after their publication). The author holds the rights for the reproduction, distribution, exhibition and rendition of his creation. If a third party uses his work, the author's name must categorically be stated. The author has to accept certain limitations (such as reproductions for private or scientific usage, incorporation in press reviews, the building of electronic reading areas as well as key texts in libraries or copy dispatch on request), but will receive adequate compensation. These fees are collected by collecting societies (like VG WORT or GEMA).
- In licensing contracts for Copyleft (for software) or Creative Commons (for content), the author willingly waives certain authorship rights.

- Software falls under copyright, according to European and German law, since programs for data processing equipment are excluded from patents as such. However, computer-implemented inventions can be patented if they have a technical character and solve a technical problem.
- The data protection law protects people from any abuse of their person-related data. A specific law (on the protection of copyright in works of art and photographs) regulates the individual's rights to his own image.
- The telemedia law formulates norms for dealing with content on the internet, among which the imprint duty for commercial providers as well as liability for content. Every content provider is liable for the information he publishes. Service providers, search engines etc. only have to act after they are informed of illegal information in their systems.
- According to the law against unfair competition, the unrequested sending of e-mails for advertising purposes is anti-competitive. Click fraud for sponsored links, which benefits a competitor, also break the competition law.
- The right to return wares bought online, which normally applies, does not apply to software or content.
- Information from public institutions can be enhanced with informational added value by private providers and distributed commercially, following the reuse of information law.
- A mandatory copy of every media work that appears in Germany must be submitted to the German National Library. This also goes for online publications.
- Subject to prosecution by criminal law are offenses such as computer espionage, computer fraud, data change and computer sabotage (computer criminal law) as well as the publication of certain contents from anti-constitutional organizations, (hardcore) pornographic representations as well as insults (content criminal law).
- The law (and thus information law) is primarily nationally oriented. Conflicts between different national legal systems are thus a definite possibility on the international information market.

5.14   Bibliography

Adam, T., Gruber, S., & Haberl, A. (2008). Europäisches und Internationales Patentrecht. Einführung zum EPÜ und PCT. 6th ed. Basel: Helbing & Lichtenhahn.

Altermann, K. (2006). Die Zulässigkeit unverlangter E-Mail-Werbung nach der UWG-Novelle. Hamburg: Kovač.

Berlit, W. (2008). Markenrecht. 7th ed. München: Beck.

Blind, K., Edler, J., Frietsch, R., & Schmoch, U. (2006). Motives to patent: Empirical evidence from Germany. Research Policy, 35(5), 655-672.

Bulling, A., Langöhrig, A., & Hellwig, T. (2006). Geschmacksmuster: Design-schutz in Deutschland und Europa. 2nd ed. Köln: Heymanns.

Busche, J. (2008). Gewerblicher Rechtsschutz und Urheberrecht. Frankfurt/M.: UTB.

Campos Nave, J. (2008). Praxishandbuch Markenrecht. Deutsche, europäische und internationale Markenrechte. 2nd ed. Frankfurt/M.: Verl. Recht und Wirtschaft.

Czink, M. (2006). Datenschutz und WWW. In Gamer, T. et al. (eds.), Datenschutz in Kommunikationsnetzen (pp. 85-101). Karlsruhe: Institut für Telematik.

Derclaye, E. (2008). The Legal Protection of Databases. Cheltenham: Edward Elger.

DPMA (undated). Deutsches Patent- und Markenamt. Homepage: www.dpma.de.

Drahos, P. (2005). Intellectual property rights in the knowledge economy. Rooney, D., Hearn, G., & Ninan, A. (eds.), Handbook on the Knowledge Economy (pp. 139-151). Cheltenham, Northamption, MA: Edward Elgar.

EPO (2008). Patents for Software? European Law and Practice. München: European Patent Office.

EPO (undated). Europäisches Patentamt–European Patent Office–Office européen des brevets. Homepage: www.epo.org.

Gitter, R., & Schnabel, C. (2007). Die Richtlinie zur Vorratsdatenspeicherung und ihre Umsetzung in nationales Recht. Multimedia und Recht, 10(7), 411-417.

Glas, V. (2008). Die urheberrechtliche Zulässigkeit elektronischer Pressespiegel. Tübingen: Mohr Siebeck.

Götting, H.P. (2007). Gewerblicher Rechtsschutz. Patent-, Gebrauchsmuster-, Geschmacksmuster- und Markenrecht. 8th ed. München: Beck.

Hacker, F. (2007). Markenrecht. Das deutsche Markensystem. Köln, München: Heymann.

Hardege, S. (2006). Informationstechnologische Entwicklungen und der Schutz von Verfügungsrechten für Informationsgüter. Eine ökonomische Analyse zur Ausgestaltung des Urheberrechts. Frankfurt/Main: Lang. (Schriften zur Wirtschaftstheorie und Wirtschaftspolitik, 34).

Haug, V. (2005). Grundwissen Internetrecht. Stuttgart: Kohlhammer.

Heckmann, D. (ed.) (2007). Juris PraxisKommentar Internetrecht. Saarbrücken: Juris.

Hertin, P.W. (2008). Urheberrecht. 2nd ed. München: Beck.

Hildebrand, U. (2008). Harmonisiertes Markenrecht in Europa. Rechtssprechung des EuGH. 2nd ed. Köln, München: Heymann.

Hilgendorf, E., ed. (2004). Informationsstrafrecht und Rechtsinformatik. Berlin: Logos.

Hoeren, T. (2008). Internetrecht (Stand: März 2008). Münster: Institut für Informations-, Telekommunikations- und Medienrecht.

Hopf, H. (2007). Das Informationsweiterverwendungsgesetz. Das Recht im Amt. Zeitschrift für den öffentlichen Dienst, 54(2), 53-59 (part 1), and 54(3), 109-115 (part 2).

Hussinger, K. (2004). Is Silence Golden? Patents versus Secrecy at the Firm Level. Mannheim: ZEW / Zentrum für Europäische Wirtschaftsforschung. (ZEW Discussion Paper; 04-78).

Jestaedt, B. (2008a). Patentrecht. Ein fallbezogenes Lehrbuch. 2nd ed. Köln, München: Heymann.

Jestaedt, B. (2008b). Wettbewerbsrecht. Ein fallbezogenes Lehrbuch. Köln, München: Heymann.

Kaufmann, N.C. (2005). Click-Spamming–ein Fall für das reformierte UWG. Multimedia und Recht, (8)2, XV-XVI.

Kloepfer, M. (2002). Informationsrecht. München: Beck.

Knaf, K., & Gillitzer, B. (2008). Das neue Urheberrecht–wichtige Aspekte für die Benutzung. Bibliotheksforum Bayern, 2, 146-152.

Köhler, H., & Bornkamm, J. (2007). Wettbewerbsrecht. Gesetz gegen den unlauteren Wettbewerb, Preisangabenverordnung, Unterlassungsklagengesetz. 25th ed. München: Beck.

Koppel, O. (2008). Patente–unverzichtbarer Schutz geistigen Eigentums. Wirtschaftsdienst, 88(12), 775-780.

Kraßer, R., & Bernhard, W. (2008). Patentrecht. Ein Lehr- und Handbuch zum deutschen Patent- und Gebrauchsmusterrecht, Europäischen und Internationalen Patentrecht. 6th ed. München: Beck.

Krömer, J., & Sen, E. (2006). No Copy: Die Welt der digitalen Raubkopie. Berlin: Tropen.

Kühling, J., & Sivridis, A. (2008). Datenschutzrecht. Frankfurt am Main: UTB.

Kuhlen, R. (2008). Erfolgreiches Scheitern–eine Götterdämmerung des Urheberrechts? Boizenburg: Hülsbusch.

Lessig, L. (2003). The Creative Commons. Florida Law Review, 55, 763-777.

Lettl, T. (2008). Urheberrecht. München: Beck.

Linde, F., & Ebber, N. (2007). Creative Commons Lizenzen: Urheberrecht im digitalen Zeitalter. Wissensmanagement, 9(3), 48-50.

Mantz, R. (2006). Open Access-Lizenzen und Rechtsübertragung bei Open Access-Werken. Spindler, G. (ed.), Rechtliche Rahmenbedingungen von Open Access-Publikationen (pp. 55-103). Göttingen: Universitätsverlag.

Marron, D.B., & Steel, D.G. (2000). Which countries protect intellectual property? The case of software piracy. Economic Inquiry, 38(2), 159-174.

O'Sullivan, M. (2008). Creative Commons and contemporary copyright: A fitting shoe or "a load of old cobblers"? First Monday, 13(1).

Oppenheim, C. (2008). Legal issues for information professionals IX. An overview of recent developments in the law, in relation to the internet. Journal of Documentation, 64(6), 938-955.

Osterrieth, C. (2007). Patentrecht. 3rd ed. München: Beck.

Ott, S. (2008). Die Entwicklung des Suchmaschinen- und Hyperlink-Rechts im Jahr 2007. Wettbewerb in Recht und Praxis, 4, 393-414.

Pahlow, L. (2006). Lizenz und Lizenzvertrag im Recht des Geistigen Eigentums. Tübingen: Mohr-Siebeck.

Rehbinder, M. (2008). Urheberrecht. 15th ed. München: Beck.

Saadat, M. (2005). Jurisdiction and the Internet after Gutnik and Yahoo! Journal of Information Law and Technology, 1.

Schoch, F. (2008). Informationsfreiheitsgesetz. München: Beck.

Schmitt, I. (2008). Öffentliche Bibliotheken und Bibliothekstantieme in Deutschland. Bibliotheksforum Bayern, 2, 153-157.

Sieber, U., & Liesching, M. (2007). Die Verantwortlichkeit der Suchmaschinenbetreiber nach dem Telemediengesetz. Multimedia und Recht, 10(8), Beilage, 1-30.

Stallman, R.M. (2004[1996]). What is Copyleft? In Gay, J. (ed.), Free Software, Free Society: Selected Essays of Richard M. Stallman (pp. 91-92). 2nd ed. (Original: 1996). Boston, MA: Free Software Foundation.

Sternitzke, C. (2009). The international preliminary examination of patent applications filed under the Patent Cooperation Treaty–a proxy for patent value? Scientometrics, 78(2), 189-202.

Stock, W.G., & Stock, M. (2008). Wissensrepräsentation. Informationen auswerten und bereitstellen. München: Oldenbourg.

Stock, M. (2001). Rechtsschutz für Software: Urheberrecht oder Patentrecht?–Ein Schutz mit sieben Siegeln?! Password, N° 7+8, 20-28.

WIPO (undated). World Intellectual Property Organization. Homepage: www.wipo.int.

Wohlgemuth, H.H., & Gerloff, J. (2005). Datenschutzrecht. Eine Einführung mit praktischen Fällen. 3rd ed. Neuwied: Luchterhand.

German Laws

Bürgerliches Gesetzbuch (BGB). Bürgerliches Gesetzbuch in der Fassung der Bekanntmachung vom 2. Januar 2002 (BGBl. I 2002 pp. 42, 2909; 2003 p. 738). Last amended on July 4th 2008.

Bundesdatenschutzgesetz (BDSG). Bundesdatenschutzgesetz in der Fassung der Bekanntmachung vom 14. Januar 2003 (BGBl. I 2003 p. 66). Last amended on August 22nd 2006.

Gebrauchsmustergesetz (GebrMG). Gebrauchsmustergesetz in der Fassung der Bekanntmachung vom 28. August 1986 (BGBl. I 1986 p. 1455). Last amended on 12/13/2007.

Geschmacksmustergesetz (GeschmMG). Geschmacksmustergesetz vom 12. März 2004 (BGBl. I 2004 p. 390). Last amended on December 13th 2007.

Informationsfreiheitsgesetz (IFG). Informationsfreiheitsgesetz vom 5. September 2005 (BGBl. I 2005 p. 2722).

Informationsweiterverwendungsgesetz (IWG). Gesetz über die Weiterverwendung von Informationen öffentlicher Stellen vom 13. Dezember 2006 (BGBl. I 2006 2913).

Kunsturhebergesetz (KunstUrhG). Gesetz betreffend das Urheberrecht an Werken der bildenden Künste und der Photographie vom 9.1.1907. Last amended on February 16th 2001.

Markengesetz (MarkenG). Markengesetz vom 25. Oktober 1994 (BGBl. I 1994 p.
3082; 1995 p. 156; 1996 p. 682). Last amended on December 13th 2007.

Nationalbibliothek (DNBG). Gesetz über die Deutsche Nationalbibliothek vom
22. Juni 2006 (BGBl. I 2006 p. 1338).

Patentgesetz (PatG). Patentgesetz in der Fassung der Bekanntmachung vom 16.
Dezember 1980 (BGBl. I 1981 p. 1). Last amended on December 13th 2007.

Pflichtablieferungsverordnung (PflAV). Verordnung über die Pflichtablieferung
von Medienwerken an die Deutsche Nationalbibliothek vom 17. Oktober 2008
(BGBl. I 2008 p. 2013).

Telemediengesetz (TMG). Telemediengesetz vom 26. Februar 2007 (BGBl. I
2007 p. 179).

Strafgesetzbuch (StGB). Strafgesetzbuch in der Fassung der Bekanntmachung
vom 13. November 1998 (BGBl. I 1998 p. 3322). Last amended on August
13th 2008.

Urheberrechtsgesetz (UrhG). Urheberrechtsgesetz vom 9. September 1965 (BGBl.
I 1965 p. 1273). Last amended on July 7th 2008.

Wettbewerbsgesetz (UWG). Gesetz gegen den unlauteren Wettbewerb vom 3. Juli
2004 (BGBl. I 2004 p. 1414).

Chapter 6

Information Ethics

6.1   Ethics of a New Culture

The knowledge society forms an entirely new culture. Knowledge is delinearized in and between hyperdocuments, graphic input devices (like the mouse) require less ability to write, while output links alphabetical signs with icons and graphics, thus changing the way we read. Computer and telecommunication are becoming uncircumventable tools. Knowledge is available everywhere, all the time. If this is indeed the case, then we are standing on the threshold from the culture of writing to the culture of multimedia. In taking this step, we would be entering the third phase of the informatization of human society, after the cultures of spoken language and of writing. Wolf Rauch (1998, 52) compares the current transition period with the move from spoken language to writing:

> A comparable cultural upheaval took place around 500 BC, in ancient
> Greece. Prior to this time, a culture of spoken language dominated in
> the Mediterranean region. ... After that, only two generations, i.e. 50 to
> 60 years, were necessary in order to go from a predominantly speaking
> culture to a wide prevalence of writing culture.

A new culture requires new thinking about the values and norms that accompany such a "cultural earthquake" (Rauch, 1998, 55), and about which of the previous tenets should be adopted and which changed. Information ethics takes up this challenge: on the one hand, its objective is to think ahead to codified values (i.e. legal norms) (in places where no laws exist, as technical development moves a lot faster than legal) and to scrutinize existing regulations (in order to justify, but also to discard, where needed), and on the other hand, to work in areas beyond governmental standardization, which concern general ethical and moral subjects.

If we compare information ethics with (general) ethics, we can make the blanket statement that without information (no matter in what medial form), no ethics is possible in the first place, as moral action absolutely requires information streams. This is not the object, though. Rather, information ethics is a specific area of ethics mainly concerning information. Luciano Floridi (1999, 43) describes this as follows:

> Without information there is no moral action, but information now moves from being necessary prerequisite for any morally responsible action to being its primary object.

Ethics–and thus information ethics–is purely descriptive on the one hand (observing how something *is*) as well as, on the other hand, normative (prescribing how something *should be*), as Rafael Capurro (2004, 6) observes:

> Information ethics can thus be conceived as a descriptive *and* emancipatory or normative theory, from a historical and systematic perspective, respectively:
>
> As a descriptive theory, it describes the different structures and power relations that determine information behavior in different cultures and eras.
>
> As an emancipatory or normative theory, it deals with the critique of the development of moral behavior in the area of information. It comprises individual, collective and human aspects.

Alongside the knowledge society, **power factors** arise, which must then be paid particular attention. Norbert Henrichs (1995, 34 et seq.) names the following examples:

> the power of chip manufacturers, from which all hardware producers depend (…);
>
> the power of the market leaders in the areas of hardware and software (…);
>
> the power of the providers of large (service) computer centers (…);
>
> the power of network providers and the providers of telecommunication services (…);
>
> the power of maintenance technicians (…);
>
> the power of database producers, providers and distributors (…);
>
> the power of those who are educated and authorized to use the systems.

Power always has to do with the possible abuse of or careless conduct with power. The position of power becomes particularly obvious if a company has a monopoly in a specific area (or is at least the predominant force), as is the case for Microsoft and PC operating systems, or Google and search engines. What virtues, which behaviors are morally justifiable in the information society, and which are not? We are in "virgin territory", in which "the condition of being human in itself is affected by the advances in informatization" (Henrichs, 1995, 36), and in which networking is regarded as "an art of living" (Capurro, 2003, 50). The information society demands its own information ethics. One of the tenets of an emancipatory information ethics could be, following Floridi (1999, 47):

> (I)nformation welfare ought to be promoted by extending (information quantity), improving (information quality) and enriching (information variety) the infosphere.

The subject areas of **ethics and law** are separated: in law, the central messages are "you may not / you must", whereas (normative) ethics states that "you should not / you should". Gerhard Reichmann (1998, 135) draws a clear line between law and ethics:

> Ethics ... deals with socially desirable behavior, and from this, it derives–apart from those norms of behavior that are already subject of law–many behavioral guidelines which to obey is dictated by custom, reason and morals, but which to disregard entails no clearly defined negative consequences. In contrast to this, the law will ideally define required and forbidden behavior in a clear and binding fashion.

The goal of ethics can be to create justice (Rawls, 1971); the goal of information ethics would thus be, analogously, to establish "information justice" as the "utopian horizon" (Capurro, 2003, 84). The philosophical conceptions of morals and ethics (diverse as they are) try to justify human behavior in such a way that it is to be regarded as "good". One of the best-known formulations of moral law is by Immanuel Kant (1973[1788], 53):

> Act only according to that maxim whereby you can at the same time will that it should become a universal law.

Actions that follow this principle are morally good. Related to Kant's dictum is the "golden rule": do unto others as you would have others do unto you. If we were to relate Kant's "Categorical Imperative" to informational action, this would mean that one's own informational behavior is to be conducted in such a way that it should be–or, at the very least, could be–done in the same way, by everyone, always. One always has to ask oneself what the effects–on oneself, too–would be if one were to perform the action under consideration. If one detects problems for oneself, one must refrain from doing whatever one plans to do. An example from everyday life: if I do not want other people to "sniff around" on my site–let us say: on Facebook–without detection, I will not do so on other people's sites either.

What is the subject area of information ethics? According to John Weckert and Douglas Adeney (1997, IX), all areas of information processing are addressed:

> The domain of information ethics comprises all of the ethical issues related to the production, storage, access, and dissemination of information.

Information ethics is thus closely related to computer ethics. However, there are subjects in computer ethics–we need only think of the role of computers as "social agents" (Moore & Unsworth, 2005, 11)–that play no role in information ethics. On the other hand, subjects like fair knowledge representation, or access to public libraries for all members of society, are hardly of interest for computer ethics.

Information ethics is thus exclusively distinguished from ethics in general via its reference to information activity as restricted above. Although information ethics is as a professional ethics (i.e. an ethics regarding a certain profession–information scientists and related jobs), most of its questions are of such a universal nature that they regard everybody living in an information society.

Apart from professional information ethics, the following three subject areas are relevant for an ethics of the knowledge society (for a comprehensive bibliography, cf. Carbo & Smith, 2008): Free access to information, protection of privacy and the question of who own knowledge (Figure 6.1). These subjects are interlinked and may even work in opposite directions. Thus, free access to knowledge will find its limits in the definition of privacy. Or, in other words: if a certain information represents intellectual property, they cannot be used freely.

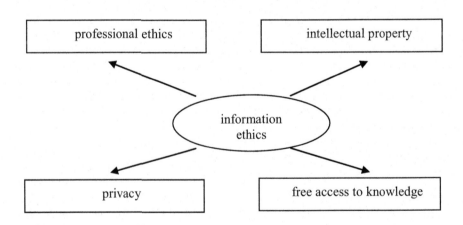

Figure 6.1: Subject Areas of Information Ethics.

6.2 Professional Behavior

The aspect of professional information ethics (Weckert & Adeney, 1997, 17 et seq.) becomes particularly clear in the case of "professional guidelines", or "codes of ethics", as brought forward by many information-professional associations, e.g. the Association for Computing Machinery (ACM, 1992), the American Library Association (ALA, 2008) and the American Society for Information Science & Technology (ASIS&T, 1992). They regulate the professional behavior of computer scientists, librarians and information scientists by stipulating norms that their members should adhere to.

According to Froehlich (1992), the professional is in an eternal triangle between his self, his organization and the respective context; he avoids unethical behavior and acts courageously in the sense of his moral guidelines (Hauptman, 2002).

A professional information ethics can include, for example, the maxims of a fair knowledge representation to not exclude any relevant sources in digital information services or index or refer to topics in a malicious manner. Likewise, information professional are required to keep secret any information pertaining to their employers (including the enquiry topics) in the context of conducting a research or creating information profiles. Scientific authors, for instance, are asked to cite, according to their best knowledge, everything they have read and used in the preparation or completion of a publication, and furthermore, only to appear as author if they have actively contributed to the publication of a text (avoiding "ghostwriting" and "honorary authorships") (Fröhlich, 2006).

6.3 Free Access to Knowledge

There is a lot of demand for free access to knowledge. The ethical question in this context is: what knowledge should be freely available to whom? Not all information should be freely available, evidently: trade secrets should stay in the business, delicate, person-related information with their carrier and false information that would humiliate and insult certain people should not even be created in the first place. Also, "free" cannot always be taken to mean "free of charge". Commercial information–let us say: market research reports–are free in the sense that anybody can acquire them in principle, but they are not free of charge; generally, they are sold in the high-price range.

Private knowledge goods (such as the content of a patent-protected invention) or mixed goods (such as the content in digital databases) are protected via laws (copyright and commercial legal protection). The rights holder thus has a large influence on the kind of access that is possible to such information. (The ethical problems of intellectual property will be discussed further below)

If free access to information is guaranteed by the constitution, as it is in Germany (in Section 5 of German Basic Law), the onus is on the government. Free access to public **libraries** is clear. The American Library Association's "code of ethics" (ALA, 2008, I) has the following perspective:

> We [the librarians] provide the highest level of service to all library us-
> ers through appropriate and usefully organized resources; equitable ser-
> vice policies; equitable access; and accurate, unbiased, and courteous
> responses to all requests.

This goes for all actual library visits, but also for any availment of library information services via digital channels, such as e-mail, chat or forms on the WWW (Hill
& Johnson, 2004).

The question of whether it is the government's duty to digitally compile information (at least for important areas of life, such as health, education or law) and
distribute it is still under debate (Capurro, 1988). For the public sector, this means
financing the production of **electronic spezialized information** as well as its distribution via search engines or online archives. Several countries (such as the
U.S.A.) assume this burden and finance the corresponding information services in
the context of universal services (even going so far as to distribute the results for
free), many others (including Germany) keep a low profile and only subsidize information providers if they compile information for federal ministries (as in the
case of the DIMDI) or if they manage important STM information in the context
of the principle of subsidiarity (as in the case of the FIZ Karlsruhe).

The norm of **communication freedom** (the right for free communication) can
be separated into two subnorms: the right to read and the right to write. According
to Rainer Kuhlen (2004, 262), information ethics specifies a regulative idea

> of keeping communicative spaces as open and permissive as possible,
> so as not to restrict any developmental freedoms via containment strate-
> gies.

Censorship is the active prevention of the distribution of content, independently of
the respective carrier. Censorship can thus apply to books, newspaper articles,
films or content on the World Wide Web. Censorship is the counterpart to freedom of expression and to free access to information. An indisputable limit of freedom of expression is its interference with other people, e.g. when person-related
information is published or people are defamed or slandered. Weckert and Adeney
(1997, 47) emphasize:

> The freedom of expression of one person can cause harm or offence or
> both to another, so some restrictions need to be placed on how and to
> what extent a person can be allowed free expression.

While not taking into account this (very weak form of) "censorship", there are five subject areas for which censorship is under serious discussion (the first four after Weckert & Adeney 1997, 51 et seq.):

- pornography (e.g. sex with animals, sex with minors),
- hateful content (e.g. racism),
- information supporting criminal or terrorist activities (e.g. instructions for building a suitcase bomb),
- "virtual violence" (e.g. the gruesome execution of a character in a digital world),
- contents that are in opposition to an (accepted) opinion (e.g. anti-Islamic representations, anti-semitism, content attacking China).

Censorship occurs in all five forms, all of which are protected by corresponding laws in certain countries. Censorship is expressed (as is the case in Germany, for pornographic documents displaying sex with minors) by penalizing the possession of censored documents, blocking certain websites with hateful content from being registered by search engines (again, in Germany, the deletion of indexed information about fascist literature on Google.de) or blocking undesirable content via large-scale national firewalls (as is currently the case in China).

It may be possible to find justification for single forms of censorship, but it is very difficult by principle to draw a clear, unarbitrary line between permissible and inadmissible content. Due to the "side effects", it seems ethically reasonable to generally reject censorship on the internet (with the sole exception of damage to specific persons, including representations of sex with children). Weckert and Adeney (1997, 55) arrive at the following result for the assessment of the pros and cons of censorship:

> Effectively censoring activity on the Internet will not be easy to do without limiting its usefulness. While it may not be good that certain sorts of things are communicated, ... it may well be worse overall if this form of communication is restricted in ways that would limit the effectiveness of the Internet. It is difficult to see how it would be possible, given current technology, not to throw out too many babies with the bath water.

Free access to information and communication freedom are fundamental rights of every person, and not merely of an intellectual or economic elite. Jack Balkin (2005, 331 et seq.) expresses this very pointedly on the subject of digital communication in a democratic culture:

> Freedom of speech is more than the freedom of elites and concentrated economic enterprises to funnel media products for passive reception by a docile audience. Freedom of speech is more than the choice of which media products to consume. Freedom of speech means giving everyone–not just a small number of people who own dominant modes of

mass communication, but ordinary people, too–the chance to use technology to participate in their culture, to interact, to create, to build, to
route around and glom on, to take from the old and produce the new,
and to talk about whatever they want to talk about, whether it be politics, public issues, or popular culture.

For all those who have access to the internet and know how to use the technical
means that can be found there, its services (we need only think of weblogs and
search engines) provide new possibilities for optimizing both freedom of communication and free access to information. However, the new information services also carry problems with them (Balking, 2005, 341):

However, these same technological changes also create new forms of
social conflicts, as business interests try to protect new forms of capital
investment.

Thus it is definitely rational economic behavior if a search engine that generates
profits via advertising also wants to do business in a country that censors certain
information. Correspondingly, this business–in order to take up the above example
of Google once more–will adjust to the respective government guidelines and
make parts of its database inaccessible for users from that country. The index for
both the German and Chinese versions of Google is censored at the time. These
conflicting goals between economic and ethical interests should continue to exist
in the knowledge society.

6.4   Privacy

Respect of privacy is mentioned explicitly in all of the professional information
ethics we cited (ACM, 1992, 1.7; ALA, 2008, III; ASIS&T, 1992). The subject of
privacy touches on many problems that people deal with in their attitude toward
information technology (Weckert & Adeney, 1997, 75).

People are worried about the ease of the collection of personal data, its
large-scale storage and easy retrieval, and about who can get access to
it. They are also worried about the surveillance made easy by computer
systems.

Privacy is one of the counterweights to free access to information. If people were
at a disadvantage due to free access to "their" information, that information should
not be freely available. Above, we called this a "weak form" of censorship. However, privacy can definitely be regarded as a human right (Kerr & Gilbert, 2004,
171):

> Our right to privacy is a fundamental human right, one that allows us to define our individuality free from interference by the state and its agents.

We would like to distinguish between ongoing person-related information and traces that an individual leaves behind in digital spaces. Among the first group of privacy information are demographic statements (age, gender, job, income etc.), health information (from the digital patient file), bank connections (including PIN code) etc.

The second group of privacy information is made up of **digital traces** (Kuhlen, 2004, 186 et seq.), which may consist of an Internet Service Provider (ISP) or search engine collecting data and allocating it unequivocally to a person (or an internet address, or a password). If a public authority gains access to these traces, ISPs act "as agents of the state" (Kerr & Gilbert, 2004, 166). The data provided others–let us say: prosecuting authorities–by Internet Service Providers as well as other internet agencies concern four levels:

- customer names and their addresses,
- "traffic" data: e-mail (sender, recipient, subject, extent) or Web (URLs visited),
- content (e.g. e-mail text, search arguments in search engines),
- transactions (products bought, financial transactions).

A particular technique of securing digital traces is epitomized by **spyware** (Stafford, 2008, 619):

> Spyware is a class of remote monitoring applications designed to survey and report across the Internet to third parties about computer user behavior.

Spyware is not always ethically problematic. The URLs accessed by users of a toolbar provided by a Web service, for instance, are transmitted to the service provider and then–in anonymous form–generate data for Relevance Ranking. However, if a user has not given his consent to such actions, if the statements are not anonymous or if the spyware takes over the computer's capacity for criminal purposes (as in the creation of a botnet), massive legal and moral concerns arise.

If we take seriously the human right to privacy, data from all levels fall under privacy and may not be transmitted for private, commercial or public purposes due to ethical reasons. However, if ISPs are only required by law to save data, and copy it by request, they will not be able to say not. Especially the more elaborate tools of information science–such as retrieval systems–pave the way toward the gapless surveillance of contents, be it online, in e-mail traffic or for the scouring of private computers for content. Retrieval research and practice can, without a doubt, work out algorithms that make the content of e-mails searchable, but the question is whether it should. If governmental regulations threaten aspects of privacy (e.g. the U.S. "Patriot Act"), it must be considered whether the loss of privacy (to be deemed a negative aspect) is made up for by the protection of society from criminal or terrorist activity (positive) (Lilly, 2005). According to Rainer Kuhlen (2004, 195), the object is

> to maintain the balance between the justified demand for security and the right for privacy and informational self-determination. ... The ambivalence is clear: there will be no privacy if security is not safeguarded. However, security is worthless if there is no more privacy, or if it is too restricted.

Search engine providers evaluate search arguments and accessed websites gleaned from personalized access in order to adjust the retrieval service to each individual user, thus optimizing it. E-commerce companies save their customers' transaction information in order to be able to use it in the context of recommender systems–also for the user's benefit. In Customer Relationship Management, it becomes possible to pointedly address the individual customer (Gurau, 2008). Collaborative services in Web 2.0 evaluate user information in order to bring together users with similar interests into a community. All these services are only made possible by the consequent tracing of person-related information. In many cases, the resulting services–optimized research, specific product recommendations, communities–are useful for the persons concerned, if not expected (particularly in Web 2.0).

The collection of person-related data–by government authorities as well as the private sector–is reminiscent of George Orwell's *Nineteen Eighty-Four* (Severson, 1997, 73 et seq.):

> If "Big Brother" denied us all personal privacy, our self-identities would be destroyed just as Winston Smith's was in Orwell's *Nineteen Eighty-Four*. Privacy is one of the necessary ingredients of self-identity.

The least we can expect from services that deal with person-related data and traces is, according to Severson (1997, 74):

> (1) that they get permission before using private information for secondary purposes; and (2) that they provide people with free opportunities to correct inaccuracies in their records.

If a person knows or suspects that their privacy is being invaded, the result is an interesting specific moral problem: is it justified to lie under such conditions (Al-Fedaghi, 2005)? **Lying** can mean, in this case, making false person-related statements, but it can also consist of knowingly generating entirely senseless search terms (in case of suspected surveillance), entering invalid URLs etc., in order to obscure one's actual behavior via static. Is the person-related information of an individual their (intellectual) property, which only they can decide how to use (Moore, 2005)?

Securing privacy means, in the end, acting discreetly–even in digital space. **Discretion** is regarded as a "virtue of the information age" (Nagenborg, 2001, 123), both for public authorities and for the internet's private users. Everybody should stand behind the things they reveal of themselves; nobody, though, should make private information about others public (at least not without their consent), or acquire such information in an untoward manner (e.g. via tracing on the internet). According to Michael Nagenborg (2001, 124) the following holds for the individual:

> We must learn to adequately disengage from the internet if we want to create something like privacy.

Discretion does not mean turning a blind eye to illegal action–on the contrary. Nagenborg (2001, 124) states:

> Discretion must not be confused with arrogance. Illegitimate information (e.g. incitement to criminal acts) must be reacted to in the same manner as in the urban public.

To clarify, Helmut F. Spinner (2001, 28) introduces the concept of "information encroachment". This is an analogous construct to "normal" encroachment, such as murder or assault.

> Knowledge can cause harm in other ways, which are often of no less consequence and possibly even harder to heal. Private confrontation and political struggle strike wounds; confessions are often embarrassing; denunciations are nefarious … .

Information encroachment can be imperative (in the case of the digital observation of a crime), but in most cases, it is forbidden (Spinner, 2001, 30):

> A case of information encroachment that is to be forbidden in any case is one that concerns the publication of false, misleading or exaggerated information *that causes harm to others* or, conversely, the concealment of true facts, as is the case in everyday insults, libel, defamation, breach of secrecy … etc.

"Informational self-determination", then, is the defense from "heteronomy by information encroachment" (Spinner 2001, 86)–a conception that goes far beyond codified data protection. Informational self-determination also means that every person must be informed about every kind of information encroachment and have the possibility to either delete or correct information regarding themselves, and know, furthermore, "to what extent and under what conditions (others) may use this knowledge" (Kuhlen, 2004, 189).

Privacy means the privacy of *one* person. But what if one individual has built up several "identities" in different digital spaces? Different names (e.g. for chatting) and **avatars** are not unusual. Stephan Werner (2003, 103-104) compares avatars and aliases with puppets:

> (T)he chosen chat name can be regarded as an agent of the individual. It appears as an autonomous (virtual) object, which can be clearly identified and, in consequence, has its own identity with its own specific attributes that are not the individual's. The relationship between it and the individual can thus be likened to a puppet's relationship to its puppeteer. "Virtual Identity" is thus the identity of the software agent, who in this instance serves as the individual's proxy.

Similarly to a puppet, though, the avatar/alias is as legally incompetent in e-commerce as it has no just claim on "its" intellectual property, as these characteristics are only "its" individual's. according to Werner (2003, 110), people are thus granted a "chance for individuality", in the positive sense (which can be, on the other hand, a pathological "chance" at schizophrenically splitting up one's personality); in the negative sense, this "encompasses a lack of reliability in social relationships" (Werner, 2003, 110). Avatars (or computer systems) are not the subject of information ethics—information ethics is always aimed at people, or—as Bernd Frohmann (2002, 50) expresses it:

> I argue that cyberethics has to do with bodies, not bytes.

6.5   Intellectual Property

Intellectual property is owning an intangible, ideal object, such as an invention or a work of art. In information law, the protection of intellectual property comprises copyright as well as commercial legal protection (regarding patents, utility models, brands and designs). Professional information ethics come out in favor of protecting intellectual property. In the ACM (1992, 1.5; 1.6), we read:

> [As an ACM member, I will ...] (h)onour property rights including copyright and patents; (g)ive proper credit for intellectual property.

This is also obvious for the American Library Association (ALA, 2008, IV):

> We respect intellectual property rights and advocate balance between
> the interests of information users and right holders.

Western societies have been protecting intellectual property for centuries; the reasons behind this are largely economic in nature. Richard W. Severson (1997, 32) emphasizes:

> Since the Middle Ages, Western societies have attempted to protect intellectual property rights through legal means. The primary mechanisms for such protection are trade secrecy, copyright, and patent laws. The legal protection of intellectual property has always been commercially motivated.

If a small company produces a groundbreaking invention and wants to exploit it by itself, it requires a protective mechanism, since otherwise, large companies could take up this invention immediately after its release to the public and, due to their market power, be able to exploit it much more effectively than its inventor. Commercial protective rights grant our small company a monopoly on using its innovation, at least for a certain period of time. Without such protective rights, there would hardly be any reason for freelance inventors as well as small to mid-size companies to even go into research and development at all. This **utilitarian argument** for intellectual property protection (Palmer, 1997) emphasizes the value for all members of society, which would not be given without such protective mechanisms. The value argument is double-edged, though, since it is perfectly possible to claim (and possibly to prove) that it is always more beneficial to a society if intellectual works belong to nobody, being everyone's property "in the public interest".

Apart from utilitarianism, there are three further lines of argument that speak in favor of intellectual property protection. (1.) Works are the expression of indivuals' **efforts**. Without legal protection, they would be deprived of the fruits of their labor. If someone develops, designs or discovers something new, he deserves protective authorship rights. Tom Palmer (2005, 131) expresses this as follows:

> When one has improved what was before unimproved (or created what
> before did not exist), one is entitled to the results of one's labor. One deserves it.

(2.) The works of a creator are an expression and a part of his **personality**. Without protection, it would hardly be possible for the author to take responsibility for his works, because in that case, they would not belong to him (Palmer, 2005, 143):

> In fact, the relationship between creator and creation is so intimate that when the personality of the former changes, so too can the treatment of the latter.

This becomes particularly clear in the case of a work of visual art: the destruction of a painting does indeed affect the personality of the artist. At this point, we have to stop and ask ourselves what a "work" is, since it is the only concept that is so closely tied to the person of its creator. According to the IFLA (1998), we distinguish between two aspects of a document's content ("work" and "expression") as well as two aspects of its physical form ("manifestation" and "item"). The work is the author's creation, which is concretely realized as an "expression" (e.g. as an illustrated book or a translation into a foreign language). The manifestation is effectively the "embodiment" of an "expression", it is a certain edition with special characteristics (e.g. a softcover book). The item, finally, is the concrete book of a manifestation. If you, dear reader, think that the book you are in the process of reading is "your" book (i.e. your property), what you mean is that the item in question is yours. If we, as its authors, claim that it is "our" book (and thus our property), we are not contradicting you, since we refer to the level of the work. The discussion about intellectual property always revolves around works. Thus authors are the owners of their works, whereas translators are not the owners of the translated text (we are now on the level of "expressions"); the translation, too, remains the authors' intellectual property.

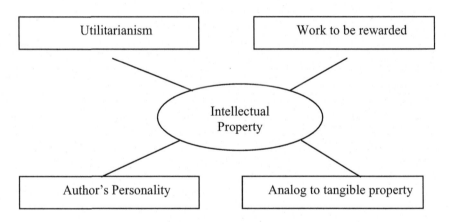

Figure 6.2: Lines of Argument for the Protection of Intellectual Property.

(3.) Ownership of intangible goods is nothing other than **"normal" ownership** of a tangible good. Just as a person owns a piece of land or a house, the Coca-Cola Company–to take a random example–owns the formula for its drink (which, by the way, was never patent-protected–such a patent would have long since run out–but has been and always will be a company secret) (Palmer, 2005, 150):

> If a chemist for the Coca-Cola company were to reproduce the formula for Coca-Cola (...) on leaflets and drop them over New York, the Coca-Cola company would have uncontestable grounds for (drastic) legal action against the violator of their secret and any of his conspirators.

The damage for Coca-Cola would be gigantic, since anyone who would find such a leaflet, read and understand the formula and then use it in his own soft-drink company cannot be legally tried (as there is no patent). In such cases, intellectual property must be treated in the same way as any other property. Palmer (2005, 149) calls this line of argument "piggybacking", as intellectual property is basically carried into legal protection on the back of normal ownership rights. Figure 6.2 charts the four theories defending ownership rights for intangible goods.

Intellectual property is a **privilege** of the owner (Palmer, 2005, 126) to dispose of his property at his guise. But is such private ownership of ideal objects really that unproblematic, ethically speaking? To whom does knowledge belong (Kuhlen, 2004, 311 et seq.)? Let us consider the case of an online research. The researcher has bought a certain amount of data sets from a provider of digital information and downloaded them onto his computer. He now wants to send the result of his research to a colleague via e-mail, i.e. make a digital copy of it. The provider DIALOG states, in its General Terms and Conditions:

> Under no circumstances may Customer, or any party acting by or through Customer, copy, transmit or retain data retrieved from DIALOG service in machine-readable form.

Our researcher is thus prohibited from digitally transmitting his (paid-for) research result. Is this ethically sound? Weckert and Adeney (1997, 68) initially defend payment for content with regard to the value provided by a company such as DIALOG:

> Having databases is useful. They are expensive to build and maintain. Unless the vendors get a reasonable return for their efforts, there will be no databases. Given the structure of our society, they must make their profit from the users, so users must pay for the service.

On the other hand, prohibiting the transmitting of the information thus gleaned is not ethically defendable, since no (notable) economic damage is to be expected by the company as a result of it (Weckert & Adeney, 1997, 69):

> People generally undertake online searching to find material on some particular interest of theirs. It is unlikely that many others will want just

those specific results, so it is hard to see that profits would be much affected. Thus we have no good reasons for the restrictions that are in place on online search results.

Now we will slightly tweak our example. Let us assume digital full texts of scientific articles, and the practice of inter-library loans. Now, one single library in all of Germany has subscribed to this particular journal. The others, who have not, will order single articles via inter-library loan, by individual requests from users. As in the above DIALOG example, digital copies of a journal (already paid-for) are transmitted. Here, though, the publisher must expect considerable economic damage. If only one single subscription (at "normal" prices, and not under consortium or national licenses, which let publishers break even) is made per country (or per library network), the publisher will not recoup its expenses (and as a consequence, have to cancel the magazine). This, in turn, is not only a disadvantage for the publisher, but also for the scientific community in question. In this second case (which is precluded by German copyright law), the transmission of information is not ethically defensible.

From an ethical perspective, the first example represents a **fair use** of intellectual property, whereas the second one does not. This "fair use", seems to be one of the keys for dealing with intellectual property (Severson, 1997, 50-51):

> Fair-use doctrine protects the often overlooked societal aspects of copyright law by ensuring the right of researchers, teachers, and ordinary citizens to use copyrighted materials freely for specific purposes. ... Suppose you want to read a magazine article at the public library. You could sit down and read it there, or you could make a photocopy and take it home to read later. Under fair-use guidelines, it is acceptable to photocopy articles–even books–if the photocopy is for temporary personal use. On the other hand, it would not be acceptable to make ten copies and distribute them at your PTA meeting.

"Fair" also means asking **fair prices** for information goods. If members of certain (poor) countries or (poor) social groups are unable to pay the asking price for information on the sole basis of their economic situation, they will be excluded from free access to knowledge. "Fair" may mean, in this context, to layer prices in a group-specific manner, i.e. to offer different prices for citizens of developing countries and those of the First World, or for the economic elite and the socially underprivileged (Ponelis, 2007, 5).

Crawling the Web consists of searching, copying, indexing and saving websites for use in search engines. There is no question of respecting ownership rights. Thelwall and Stuart (2006, 1775) observe:

> Crawlers ostensibly do something illegal: They make permanent copies of copyright material (Web pages) without the owner's permission.

This practice is particularly delicate in the case of the Internet Archive (arc-hive.org), as it saves "historic" websites, and thus occasionally those that have been consciously overwritten or deleted by the owner of this intellectual property. Search engines such as the Internet Archive refer to the Robots.txt protocol, in which website owners give crawlers instructions for dealing with their site (e.g. NOINDEX or NOFOLLOW). Also, site owners are allowed to request deletion by the Archive. The practice of search engines to copy everything not explicitly excluded in Robots.txt, and to remove only when asked to, seems to be widely tolerated (and can–as it is in the U.S.A.–be regarded as "fair use"). As far as the sites contain information that can be abused (e.g. e-mail addresses for sending spam), this practice definitely has its disadvantages for users and is, ethically or even legally speaking, at least problematic. Evidently, it is regarded as extremely desirable at the moment or a crawler to illegally copy websites that are technically protected by copyright, following the principle "Esse est indicato in Google" (Hinman, 2005).

What about the legal protection of intellectual property in the case of collaboratively created software and content (such as Wikipedia)? According to Lawrence M. Sanger (2005, 193), this is a case of **shopwork** ("*sh*ared *op*en *work*"). Shopwork has two main characteristics: such works are freely available (open source, open content), and they have been created in strict collaboration. If collaboratively created software and collaboratively created content are important for a society (as is often claimed), the society in question must take responsibility for the ability of the creators of software and content to be able to make a living from their work, which is obviously valuable. This does not lead to a new copyright for shopwork, but instead to the (pretty extreme) ethical maxim of sufficiently financing the authors (Sanger, 2005, 200):

> (T)he law should actually *support* such works, either through funding or
> other special legislative support.

For Milton Mueller (2008), there is no contradiction between knowledge regarded as property (**information capitalism**) and publicly accessible knowledge (**information communism**). Especially on the internet, both forms of dealing with knowledge can co-exist without a problem: commercially distributed software or commercially distributed content (protected by commercial property rights) is pitted against free software and free content (only protected via Creative Commons, for example). According to Mueller (2008), the challenge is in finding the "right" application for both approaches:

> One could even argue that the success of liberal-democratic governance
> hinges on finding the right place for each model and exploiting the crea-
> tive relationship between the two.

It is thus ethically justifiable to rate the author's right to his work more highly than the right of all others to access to this knowledge (Himma, 2008, 1160). This in no way excludes the possibility of the author deliberately waiving some of his rights and making his work publicly accessible. If a country wants to strengthen authors– even economically–they must create an artificial shortage (as for tangible goods) for knowledge goods (here via commercial property rights) (Palmer, 2005, 157):

> Tangible goods are clearly scarce in that there are conflicting uses. It is that scarcity that gives rise to property rights. Intellectual property rights, however, do not rest on a natural scarcity of goods, but on "artificial, self-created scarcity". That is to say, legislation or legal fiat limits the use of ideal objects in such a way as to create an artificial scarcity that, it is hoped, will generate greater revenues for innovators.

6.6   Conclusion

- Information ethics is a specified ethics that deals with all ethical aspects of information processing. It has become necessary due to the transition to the "multimedia culture" in the course of the advent of the information society with its novel power factors (e.g. software producers' or search engines').
- According to Rawls, the goal of ethics is to create justice. In this respect, information ethics works toward information justice. Kant's Categorical Imperative teaches us to consider the consequences of our (information) actions as far as they affect other people.
- Information ethics can be segmented into four subject areas, which are partly interlinked, and partly work in opposite directions: professional information ethics, free access to information, privacy and intellectual property.
- Professional information ethics regulates the professional behavior of information scientists and professionals. It is laid down in the professional organizations' respective "codes of ethics".

- Free access to information is closely related to freedom of communication. This latter consists of the subnorms of the right to read and the right to write. Censorship prevents free access to information. It seems ethically reasonable to prohibit censorship, with some exceptions (damage to specific individuals, representations of sex with children).
- The individual's privacy is threatened, in digital environments, by ongoing person-related information (name, age, gender) as well as digital traces. It becomes controversial when digital traces are pursued via spyware, since on the one hand, the summarization of (one's own, or someone else's) behavior is partly expected by the user, to optimize research or shopping systems (in personalized services or recommender systems), and feared–particularly in case of abuse (e.g. spamming)–on the other. Discretion becomes the virtue of the information society.
- Is intellectual property justified? Four theories (utilitarianism, reward for work, creator's personality and "piggybacking") provide arguments for the protection of intangible and ideal objects. Intellectual property is a privilege that should be dealt with fairly. Information capitalism (with strong ownership components, even of knowledge goods) does not contradict information communism (with strong components of publicly accessible knowledge); rather, both forms co-exist and find their respective "correct" usage.

6.7   Bibliography

ACM (1992). ACM Code of Ethics and Professional Conduct.

ALA (2008). Code of Ethics of the American Library Association.

Al-Fedaghi, S. (2005). Lying about private information: An ethical justification. Communications of the International Information Management Association, 5(3), 47-56.

ASIS&T (1992). ASIS&T Professional Guidelines.

Balkin, J.M. (2005). Digital speech and democratic culture: A theory of freedom of expression for the information society. In Moore, A.D. (ed.), Information Ethics. Privacy, Property, and Power (pp. 297-354). Seattle, London: University of Washington Press.

Capurro, R. (1988). Informationsethos und Informationsethik–Gedanken zum verantwortungsvollen Handeln im Bereich der Fachinformation. Nachrichten für Dokumentation, 39, 1-4.

Capurro, R. (2003). Ethik im Netz. Wiesbaden: Steiner.

Capurro, R. (2004). Informationsethik–eine Standortbestimmung. International Journal of Information Ethics, 1, 1-7.

Carbo, T., & Smith, M.M. (2008). Global information ethics: Intercultural perspectives on past and future research. Journal of the American Society for Information Science and Technology, 59(7), 1111-1123.

Floridi, L. (1999). Information ethics: On the philosophical foundations of computer ethics. Ethics and Information Technology, 1, 37-56.

Fröhlich, G. (2006). Plagiate und unethische Autorenschaften. Information–Wissenschaft und Praxis, 57, 81-89.

Froehlich, T.J. (1992). Ethical considerations of information professionals. Annual Review of Information Science and Technology, 27, 291-324.

Frohmann, B. (2002). Cyberethik: Bodies oder Bytes? In Hausmanninger, T., & Capurro, R. (eds.), Netzethik. Grundlegungsfragen der Internetethik (pp. 49-58). München: Fink.

Gurau, C. (2008). Privacy and online data collection. In Quigley, M. (ed.), Encyclopedia of Information Ethics and Security (pp. 542-548). Hershey, PA: Information Science Reference.

Hauptman, R. (2002). Ethics and Librarianship. Jefferson, NC, London: McFarland.

Henrichs, N. (1995). Menschsein im Informationszeitalter. In Capurro, R., Wiederling, K., & Brellochs, A. (eds.), Informationsethik (pp. 23-36). Konstanz: UVK .

Hill, J.B., & Johnson, E.W. (2004). Ethical issues in digital reference. In Mendina, T., & Britz, J.J. (eds.), Information Ethics in the Electronic Age (pp. 99-106). Jefferson, NC, London: McFarland.

Himma, K.E. (2008). The justification of intellectual property: Contemporary philosophical disputes. Journal of the American Society for Information Science and Technology, 59(7), 1143-1161.

Hinman, L.M. (2005). Esse est indicato in Google: Ethical and political issues in search engines. International Review of Information Ethics, 3, 19-25.

IFLA (1998). Funetional Requirements for Bibliographie Records. München: Saur.

Kant, I. (1985[1788]). Critique of Practical Reason. New York, NY, London: Macmillan. (Original: 1788).

Kerr, I., & Gilbert, D. (2004). The role of ISPs in the investigation of cybercrime. In Mendina, T., & Britz, J.J. (eds.), Information Ethics in the Electronic Age (pp. 163-172). Jefferson, NC, London: McFarland.

Kuhlen, R. (2004). Informationsethik. Umgang mit Wissen und Information in elektronischen Räumen. Konstanz: UVK.

Lilly, J.R. (2005). National security at what price? A look into civil liberty concerns in the information age under the USA Patriot Act. In Moore, A.D. (ed.), Information Ethics. Privacy, Property, and Power (pp. 417-441). Seattle, WA, London: University of Washington Press.

Moore, A.D. (2005). Intangible property: Privacy, power, and information control. In Moore, A.D. (ed.), Information Ethics. Privacy, Property, and Power (pp. 172-190). Seattle, WA, London: University of Washington Press.

Moore, A.D., & Unsworth, K. (2005). Introduction. In Moore, A.D. (ed.), Information Ethics. Privacy, Property, and Power (pp. 11-28). Seattle, WA, London: University of Washington Press.

Mueller, M. (2008). Info-communism? Ownership and freedom in the digital economy. First Monday, 13(4).

Nagenborg, M. (2001). Diskretion in offenen Netzen. IuK-Handlungen und die Grenze zwischen dem Privaten und Öffentlichen. In Spinner, H.F., Nagenborg, M., & Weber, K. (eds.): Bausteine zu einer Informationsethik (pp. 93-128). Berlin, Wien: Philo.

Palmer, T.G. (1997). Intellectual property rights: A non-Posnerian law and economics approach. In Moore, A.D. (ed.), Intellectual Property: Moral, Legal, and International Dilemmas (pp. 179-224). New York, NY: Rowman & Littlefield.

Palmer, T.G. (2005). Are patents and copyrights morally justified? The philosophy of property rights and ideal objects. In Moore, A.D. (ed.), Information Ethics. Privacy, Property, and Power (pp. 123-168). Seattle, WA, London: University of Washington Press.

Ponelis, S.R. (2007). Implications of social justice for the pricing of information goods. International Review of Information Ethics, 7, 1-5.

Rauch, W. (1998). Informationsethik. Die Fragestellung aus der Sicht der Informationswissenschaft. In Kolb, A., Esterbauer, R., & Ruckenbauer, H.W. (eds.), Cyberethik. Verantwortung in der digital vernetzten Welt (pp. 51-57). Stuttgart, Berlin, Köln: Kohlhammer.

Rawls, J. (1971). A Theory of Justice. Cambridge, MA: Harvard Univ. Press.

Reichmann, G. (1998). Informationsrecht in Österreich. In Kolb, A., Esterbauer, R., Ruckenbauer, H.W. (eds.), Cyberethik. Verantwortung in der digital vernetzten Welt (pp. 135-152). Stuttgart, Berlin, Köln: Kohlhammer.

Sanger, L.M. (2005). Why collaborative free works should be protected by the law. In Moore, A.D. (ed.), Information Ethics. Privacy, Property, and Power (pp. 191-206). Seattle, WA, London: University of Washington Press.

Severson, R.W. (1997). The Principles of Information Ethics. Armonk, NY, London: Sharpe.

Smith, M.M. (1997). Information ethics. Annual Review of Information Science and Technology, 32, 339-366.

Smith, M.M. (2001). Information ethics. Advances in Librarianship, 25, 29-66.

Spinner, H.F. (2001). Was ist ein Informationseingriff und was kann man dagegen tun? In Spinner, H.F., Nagenborg, M., & Weber, K.: Bausteine zu einer Informationsethik (pp. 11-91). Berlin, Wien: Philo.

Stafford, T.F. (2008). Spyware. In Quigley, M. (ed.), Encyclopedia of Information Ethics and Security (pp. 616-621). Hershey, PA: Information Science Reference.

Thelwall, M., & Stuart, D. (2006). Web crawling ethics revisited: Cost, privacy, and denial of service. Journal of the American Society for Information Science and Technology, 57(13), 1771-1779.

Weckert, J., & Adeney, D. (1997). Computer and Information Ethics. Westport, Conn., London: Greenwood.

Werner, S. (2003). Aspekte der Individualität im Internet. In Hausmanninger, T. (ed.). Handeln im Netz. Bereichsethiken und Jugendschutz im Internet (pp. 95-112). München: Fink.

Part C

Digital Information Goods

Chapter 7

Business, Market and Press Information

7.1 Digital Information Products for and about Business and the Press

We will begin our discussion of information goods with digital business, market and press information. Scientific information are factored out and will be discussed separately, in the context of STM information (Chapter 9). In this chapter, we will address three kinds of information: business information, structural and market information as well as press information ("news"). This information is available both in text form and in the form of numerical data (Ainsworth, 2009). Figure 7.1 sums up our breakdown of business and press information.

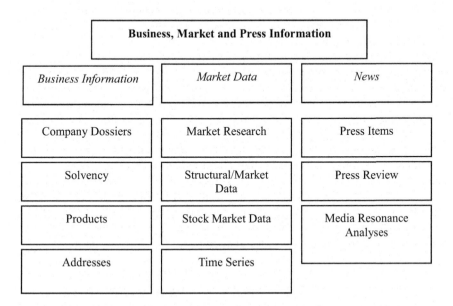

Figure 7.1: Classification of Digital Goods of Business and Press Information.

7.2 Clients on the Market for Business, Market and Press Information

On the demanders' side of this submarket of digital information we almost exclusively see companies. Knowledge-intensive service providers in particular, like banks, insurance companies, large offices or management consultancies, as well as knowledge-intensive industrial firms (such as major enterprises in the chemical and pharmaceutical industry), are the main group of customers.

Business and press information serve, on the one hand, to monitor known enterprises, and on the other, to scan new companies previously unknown to the researcher. Reasons for the **monitoring** of known companies include assessment on the part of new business partners (or–if this has not happened prior to the beginning of a contractual relationship–in case of outstanding charges to a business partner) as well as the ongoing observation of companies directly above and below one's own in the value chain (suppliers and clients). Added to this is research in case of planned investment or takeovers and for observing competitors, respectively. Monitoring is in the name of the company, or its number in company databases (such as the D-U-N-S number of D&B, previously Dun & Bradstreet, which definitely identifies every company). In **scanning**, we do not know the company name (yet), which is why any search must be performed via characteristics. Scanning can be used to spot new players on one's own market, locate new suppliers and clients as well as contact persons and their addresses for mailing purposes (Stock, 2001). Apart from the monitoring and scanning of companies, there is also research for markets and industries, one's own and neighboring. Aspects of science and technology, such as the surveillance of competitors' patenting activities, can also catch the eye of the researchers. Since these are STM information, we will discuss this aspect in Chapter 9.

We can observe three **organization strategies** for dealing with business and press information (and perhaps any further information, such as STM) in demanding companies. (1.) Companies rely on end consumer research. Information professionals or knowledge managers make the suitable information services available in the company in short-term projects, train employees and then withdraw from the daily running of the research. The "end consumers", i.e. the staff, look for information on their own. (2.) Companies bundle information know-how in an individual work unit (with a name like "Information Research Center", "Knowledge & Research Center" or "Research & Information"). Generally, its task is to both manage internal knowledge and to consult–just-in-time–external knowl-edge. The objective is not (or not only) to research documents and make them available to specialists, but to process found information. Noack, Reher and Schiefer (2009, 430) emphasize, for management consultancies:

> The fundamental objective is to first purify information and then pass it on. Simple information transmission is no longer the main concern, since by now, pretty much everyone is capable of finding information. The actual value added by an IRS [information retrieval service, A/N] is

the compression of information, which consultants seldom have time to do.

Noack, Reher and Schiefer (2009, 425) report, for German consultants, of a build-up (however reticent still) of staff numbers in such work units. For British companies, Foster (2009, 19) points to the outsourcing of several information tasks, preferably to Asian countries (particularly India). Organization variant (3.) is a compromise between (1.) and (2.) end consumers assume light research tasks, the result of which flow directly into their work; the difficult, or company-critical work of information compression is left to information professionals.

7.3   Business Information

What is business information? We will adhere to the definition by Corsten (1999, 5):

> Business information refers to all information that can be gathered (…) about a company without having to its their premises or talking to its staff.

Digital Business Information–which is the only kind that interests us in this book–is business information available via the WWW (or CD-ROM, in exceptional cases).

Although a lot of business information are scattered throughout the Web, general search engines are little suited to the required research. Statements by companies themselves (apart from annual reports) are entirely unverified, crucial aspects (like solvency) go unreported on the internet and search engines do not allow some necessary formulations, such as "all companies within an industry, from a certain level of manpower and income upward". This is rather the domain of professional providers of business information in the four market segments (Stock & Stock, 2001a, 2001b):

- Company Dossiers (with relevance for the German information market: Creditreform and Hoppenstedt, among others),
- Solvency Information (Bürgel, Creditreform and D&B),
- Product Information (e.g. Kompass and Wer liefert was?),
- Addresses (AZ Direct by Bertelsmann and Schober).

7.4   Company Dossiers

Company dossiers fall into various different categories, which provide, in total, a (more or less) satisfactory representation of the enterprise. **Financial information** is ideally gleaned from balance sheets, which are annual accounts with a comparison of the forms (assets) and sources (liabilities) of property, statements on receipts and expenditures as well as further economic characteristics. Balances of companies that are required to publish, but also those of several other companies, are entirely retrievable via balance databases. Depending on the country, there are different laws regulating the publication requirement. Green (2007) distinguishes between countries with a more protestant tradition (such as the United Kingdom), in which many company data are publicly accessible, and others, who tend to retain data. The purposes of publishing company information differ relative to the group a country belongs to (Green, 2007, 91):

> *Anglo-Saxon countries* [including Denmark and the Netherlands, A/N]: to provide existing or potential shareholders with a true and fair view of the company.

> *Continental countries*: to provide the authorities with information for taxation and statistics and to offer a protection to the credit grantors.

In Germany, companies are required to publish by the Transparency and Disclosure Act, if two of the three following traits are in evidence (PublG §1 (1)):

- the total of the annual statement exceeds €65m,
- sales revenue exceeds €130m,
- the company employs more than 5,000 people.

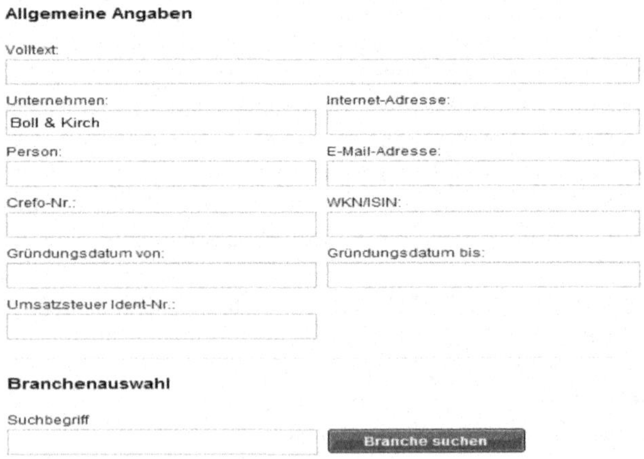

Allgemeine Angaben

Volltext:

Unternehmen:	Internet-Adresse:
Boll & Kirch	

Person:	E-Mail-Adresse:

Crefo-Nr.:	WKN/ISIN:

Gründungsdatum von:	Gründungsdatum bis:

Umsatzsteuer Ident-Nr.:

Branchenauswahl

Suchbegriff

Branche suchen

Figure 7.2: Search for Company Information with Creditreform (Extract). Source: Creditreform.

The reports are published in the Federal Gazette. In the U.K., all "limited companies" are required to disclose. These reports are then stored in "Company Houses".

For all companies that are not required to disclose, the producers of business information are called upon to at least research fundamental financial information themselves.

Although business information is fixated upon the financial situation of companies, further **basic data** is collected additionally. The key data are: official business name (perhaps the business number), legal form, object of the company, address, bank connection, memberships, production sites and branches etc. This is supplemented by information concerning the industries in which the company is active (indexed via industry classification systems), statements about investments and acquisitions (Mergers & Acquisitions: "M&A Data"), information about ownership and management as well as employee numbers over the last few years (Stock, 2001, 27).

For German companies, the **sources of company dossiers** are, apart from annual reports in the Federal Gazette, voluntarily published business reports, all information in the commercial and insolvency registers, reports in the economic press as well as–extremely importantly–self-disclosure of parties concerned. Dossier databases for German firms are, among others, "Firmenwissen" of Creditreform or the "Hoppenstedt Firmendatenbank" (Stock & Stock, 2001, 28-30; Stock, 2002).

For the data pool of economic information services, **quality criteria** apply (Stock, 2001; Stock & Stock, 2001a, 2001b):

* completeness,
* up-to-dateness,
* correctness,
* indexing depth and consistency,
* adequate retrieval interface.

Completeness consists of two dimensions: on the one hand, there is the coverage of registered companies as against all the companies in the country (degree of coverage), on the other hand, there is the ready availability of as many data as possible about a company (dept of analysis). Considering the country-specific variants of duty to disclose and readiness to inform, the degree of coverage of business information varies considerably. For example, the large financial databases of Bureau van Dijk contains more than 2.2m dossiers about British companies, but only around 800,000 about German companies. Up-to-dateness means a database producer's ability to react to changes in the observed companies. The ability to react depends on the number of sources as well as their speed of evaluation. For seldomly requested company dossiers, the data pool is only updated when a specific research is on hand. Correctness is if the statements in the unit of documentation match reality, as well as the clear definition of what is being registered in any given instance (as in the statements concerning manpower: are persons being counted, who are, after all, able to work part-time, or full-time equivalents?). Indexing depth and consistency concern the allocation of suitable classes to company activities. This relates to both the knowledge organization systems used (can these even represent all industries and markets?) as well as their application (is every economic activity represented adequately and consistently?) The retrieval interface represents the intersection with the customer. Are all fields searchable via adequate operators (such as Boolean or algebraic operators)? An example of a system's retrieval interface for searching business information is provided in Figure 7.2.

Does digital business information facilitate the development of a "transparent" company? For Corsten (1999, 51), the answer is no: "There still exist too many black spots". For large companies, the state of information is generally better than for mid-size or even small firms. "But the data that a company wants to keep secret at any price can seldom be ascertained" (Corsten, 1999, 51).

7.5   Credit Information

Databases with credit information enrich company dossiers by stating each respective firm's solvency. At this point, we would like to represent the solvency index of Creditreform (Creditreform, 2009). The demander receives a characteristic value, which, apart from "normal" financial information, also takes into consideration the company's payment record. Research into a business partner's solvency is inevitable, particularly in the case of new suppliers or clients, or for outstanding charges. The same goes for any kind of credit transaction.

The solvency index considers both qualitative and quantitative risk factors, which enter the final statement weighted according to their relevance. The following factors are considered (their weighting, as percentage, in brackets):

- subjective credit opinion (25%),
- payment method (20%),
- corporate development (8%),
- order situation (7%),
- legal form (4%),
- industry (4%),
- age of the company (4%),
- revenue per employee (4%),
- equity (4%),
- asset turnover (4%),
- payment performance of the company (4%),
- payment performance of the clients (4%),
- shareholder structure (4%),
- revenue (2%),
- number of employees (2%).

Creditreform obtains the important data concerning the payment method from the accounts receivable departments of certain member companies. The data available is by no means complete, but is a (more or less pertinent) sample at best. It must additionally be taken into consideration that the industry risk–which does not regard the specific situation of the company in question at all–also enters the score. A value of between 100 and 600 will result from the sum of all weighted risk factors. The solvency index correlates with a company's default risk. For an index value of between 100 and 149, the default risk (within one year; all figures for 2008) is at 0.09%, a medium solvency of between 251 and 300 points to 1.36% default risk and a very weak solvency (351-499) carries a default risk of more than 13%. For the year 2008, the average default risk in Germany was 2.22% (Creditreform, 2009).

Solvency information about German companies is offered, apart from Creditreform, by the information producers Bürgel as well as D&B (Stock & Stock, 2001a, 26-28).

7.6   Product Information

Some databases give a detailed representation of the products of the companies they index. Generally, this involves business-to-business products, and not wares for end customer markets. As product databases always inform about the companies that offer the products, they are also carriers of general company information.

Product information services' criterion of demarcation from other company information is the presence of a specific knowledge organization system of product classes and single products. The classification system of the information service Kompass works with three hierarchy levels. On the top level are (marked in double digits) the industries (e.g. 44 for *Machines and Facilities for the Pulp, Paper and Printing Industry; Office Machinery and Facilities for Electronic Data Processing*), the medium level allocates product groups (in triple digits) to their industries (44141 for *Printing Presses and Accessories / Part 2*), and level 3 records (in double digits once more) the single products (4414151 for *Cylinders for Printing Presses*). Additionally, a user of Kompass can research importers (I) and exporters (E) on the product group level, and for producers (P), distribution companies (D) and service providers (S) on the product level. Particularly in product searches, it is important to distinguish producers of an economic good from their dealers and service companies.

Figure 7.3 is an extract from a unit of documentation, which was found in a search for *Producers* of *Corking Machines for Bottles*. We are told that the indicated company is an exporter of, among other products, filling plants for bottles and that the line of products it manufactures goes from bottle cleaning machines to crown cap machines. Additionally, the company acts as dealer (and exporter) of metal caps for bottles. Apart from self-disclosures, which are of equal importance here, Kompass conducts after-investigations in various sources to safeguard the correctness of the statements as far as possible. Providers of product information are, other than Kompass, Sachon Industriedaten as well as Wer liefert was? (Stock & Stock, 2001a, 30-32).

>> Haupt-Produkte und Dienstleistungen

          Kompass-Produktbezeichnung
   ⊟   E   **Maschinen und Anlagen für das Abfüllen von Flaschen**
   └   P   Flaschenabfüllanlagen, komplett
   └   P   Reinigungsmaschinen und Waschmaschinen für Flaschen
   └   P   Trockenmaschinen für Flaschen
   └   P   Kontrollmaschinen für Flaschen
   └   P   Flaschenabfüllmaschinen
   └   P   Abfüllmaschinen und Abkapselmaschinen für Flaschen
   └   P   Kapselmaschinen für Flaschen
   └   P   Korkmaschinen für Flaschen
   └   P   Kronenkorkmaschinen / Kronenkorker für Flaschen
   └   P   Verdrahtungsmaschinen für Flaschenkorken
   └   P   Verschliessmaschinen für Flaschen
   └   P   Flaschenkapseln, Herstellungsmaschinen
   └   P   Aufsetzmaschinen für Flaschenkapseln
   └   P   Förderanlagen und Beschickungsanlagen für Kronenkorkenverschlüsse
   └   P   Ausrichtmaschinen für Flaschen
   └   P   Flaschenabfüllanlagen und -ausrüstungen für die Getränkeindustrie
   └   P   Sterilisiermaschinen für Flaschen, für die Getränkeindustrie
   └   P   Abfüllanlagen und -ausrüstungen für Weinflaschen
   └   P   Flaschenabfüllanlagen und Zusatzausrüstungen für Brauereien

>> Weitere Produkte und Dienstleistungen

          Kompass-Produktbezeichnung
   ⊟   E   **Verschlüsse, Kappen und Verpackungstuben aus Metall**
   └   D   Kapseln, Metall
   └   D   Kapseln, Metall, für Flaschen
   ⊟   E   **Maschinen und Anlagen für die Weinerzeugung, Kellereimaschinen**
   └   P   Schaumweine / Sekt, Herstellungsmaschinen und Herstellungsanlagen
   └   P   Förderanlagen und Transportanlagen für Sektflaschen
   ⊟   E   **Etikettiermaschinen und Markiermaschinen**
   └   P   Etikettiermaschinen für selbsthaftende Etiketten
   └   P   Etikettiermaschinen für Flaschen
   ⊟   E   **Maschinen und Anlagen für die Nahrungsmittel- und Getränkeindustrie, Handel**
   └   D   Maschinen und Anlagen für die Weinerzeugung / Kellereimaschinen, Handel

Figure 7.3: Product Display of a Company in Kompass. Source: Kompass.

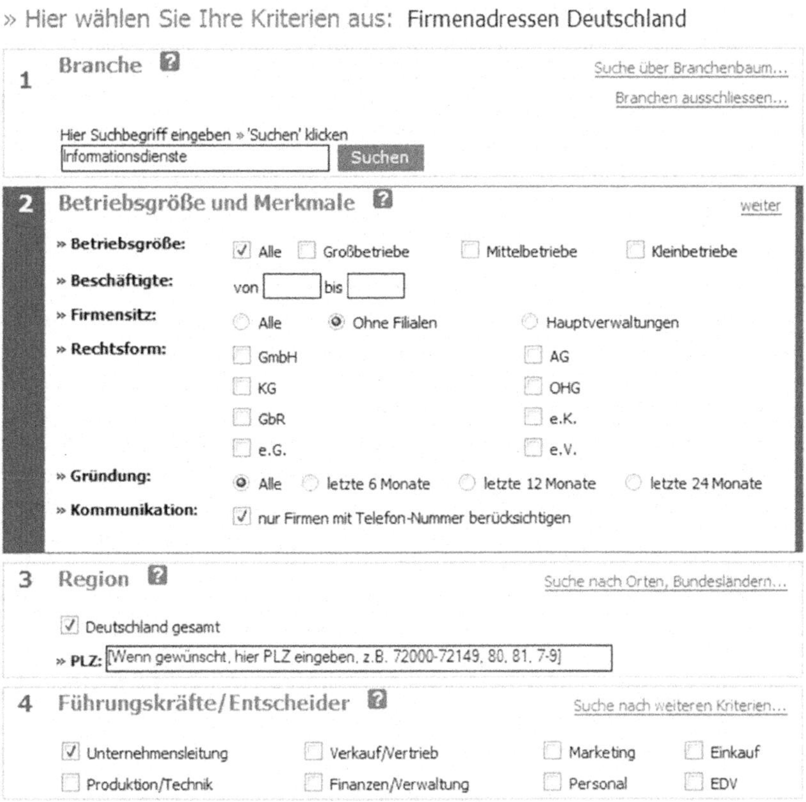

» Hier wählen Sie Ihre Kriterien aus: Firmenadressen Deutschland

Figure 7.4: Searching for Addresses on Schober. Source: Schober.

7.7   Addresses

When using address databases, the customer's goal is normally a marketing activity. For a mailing campaign, one requires private or company addresses, in the latter case as accurate as possible, including contact person. In addition, one can either use information services with company dossiers (such as the Hoppenstedt Company Database or Creditreform's Firmenwissen) or the respective marketing divisions from these databases (e.g. the product MARKUS by Bureau van Dijk on the basis of data from Creditreform). Marketing databases have, compared to "simple" address databases, the advantage of including analytic tools for data preparation (such as the geographic distribution of customer addresses as points on a map), thus providing raw materials for market research.

Address databases like AZ Direct by Bertelsmann Avato or Schober (Stock & Stock, 2001a, 32-33) allow searches by industry (but not by product), region, company size and management. Important for the applications are places where research results intersect–e.g. via Comma Separated Values (CSV)–with Office applications, in order to be directly embedded in form letters.

7.8   Market Data

Market and industry documents in text form can be found with providers of "Market Intelligence Reports". Profound offers reports by Frost and Sullivan or Datamonitor, for instance, which are offered as either complete documents or chapter-by-chapter/chart-by-chart. These reports contain processed data from secondary research as well as data producers' own data (primary research). Additionally, there are information products on marketing (e.g. the database FAKT; Stock, 2000, 208 et seq.), which separate specific rankings (e.g. the top 20 ads on TV, separated by industry) or time series (e.g. the development of German chemical companies' employment records 1994-2008) from specialist literature and offer them separately on the information market.

If a customer does not want to access processed data, he has the task of acquiring the pertinent numerical information from digital information services. Here we distinguish between (general) structural, market and industry data, numerical information on individual companies (stock market information) and time series for products, industries and parameters of national accounts, such as official statistics and research institutes have available.

7.9   Structural, Market and Industry Data

As an example for the fundamental structural, market and industry data required by marketing, we will sketch the information products provided by GfK GeoMarketing. The GfK (previously "Gesellschaft für Konsumforschung" = Society for Consumer Research) is one of the largest market research companies worldwide. Among its information products are, for instance, data on purchasing power and population structure in Germany.

Information on purchasing power and regions' as well as municipalities' retail turnover, respectively, are a tool for companies' location planning as well as the performance reviews of field service. The databases on purchasing power indices are arranged by region (in Germany) and postcode areas. They represent an indicator for the economic attractiveness of a location. The single databases each register different aspects of purchasing power:

- retail-relevant purchasing power (demand-oriented part of purchasing power),
- point-of-sales revenue for retail.

Our example in Figure 7.5 is the result of a search for the retail-relevant purchasing power of the community of Wandlitz in the state of Brandenburg, researched with the information provider GENIOS. We receive numerical information about population and household numbers, their purchasing power (absolute and relative values) and index values (where the average of all German citizens has been set to 100).

Ebene Gemeinde

Gemeinde/Gebiet Wandlitz

Gebietsschlüssel 12060269

Stand (Jahr): 2008

Einwohner:	20760
Einwohner in Promille:	0,252
Haushalte:	9441
Haushalte in Promille:	0,241
EH-Kaufkraftsumme in Mio. EUR:	109,6
EH-Kaufkraft in Promille:	0,238
EH-Kaufkraft je Einwohner:	5279
EH-Kaufkraftindex pro Einwohner:	94,2

GfK Einzelhandelsrelevante Kaufkraft nach Verwaltungseinheiten
8600, GKER, 06.02.2009, Words: 1, NO: 12060269

Figure 7.5: Data of Retail-Relevant Purchasing Power According to GfK. Source: GENIOS / GfK GeoMarketing.

Comprehensive basic information on the population of single areas, with special allowance made for household size, age of "heads" of household, their status / net income as well as buildings in the region is promised by GfK's population structure database. Figure 7.6 exemplifies the variety of this data with reference to the example of Wandlitz.

Area Code 12060269   Region of Wandlitz
Population: 20,760
Population per mille: 0.252
Households (01/01/2006). 9,441
Average household size: 2.20
Single households absolute: 3,128
Single households, proportionately: 33.13

Single households, index: 86.7

Multi-person households with no children, absolute: 3,096

Multi-person households with no children, proportionately: 32.79

Multi-person households with no children, index: 107.1

Multi-person households with children, absolute: 3,217

Multi-person households with children, proportionately: 34.07

Multi-person households with children, index: 109.3

Immigrant households, absolute: 116

Immigrant households, proportionately: 1.23

Immigrant households, index: 15.4

Age of head of household under 30, absolute: 1,086

Age of head of household under 30, proportionately: 11.50

Age of head of household under 30, index: 100.2

Age of head of household 30 under 40, absolute: 1,458

Age of head of household 30 under 40, proportionately: 15.44

Age of head of household 30 under 40, index: 88.4

Age of head of household 40 under 50, absolute: 2,750

Age of head of household 40 under 50, proportionately: 29.13

Age of head of household 40 under 50, index: 137.0

Age of head of household 50 under 60, absolute: 2,248

Age of head of household 50 under 60, proportionately: 23.81

Age of head of household 50 under 60, index: 142.9

Proportion age of head of household 60 years and more, absolute: 1,899

Proportion age of head of household 60 years and more, proportionately: 20.11

Proportion age of head of household 60 years and more, index: 60.7

Average age of head of household: 48.91

Status low: HH net income of no more than €1,100, absolute: 585

Status low: HH net income of no more than €1,100, proportionately: 6.20

Status low: HH net income of no more than €1,100, index: 44.1

Status medium: HH net income of between €1,100 and €1,500, absolute: 647

Status medium: HH net income of between €1,100 and €1,500, proportionately: 6.85

Status medium: HH net income of between €1,100 and €1,500, index: 56.2

Status medium: HH net income of between €1,500 and €2,000, absolute: 1,009

Status medium: HH net income of between €1,500 and €2,000, proportionately: 10.69

Status medium: HH net income of between €1,500 and €2,000, index: 79.5

Status medium: HH net income of between €2,000 and €2,500, absolute: 1,609

Status medium: HH net income of between €2,000 and €2,500, proportionately: 17.04

Status medium: HH net income of between €2,000 and €2,500, index: 115.3

Status high: HH net income of between €2,600 and €4,000, absolute: 4,158

Status high: HH net income of between €2,600 and €4,000, proportionately: 44.04

Status high: HH net income of between €2,600 and €4,000, index: 175.6

Residential buildings, total: 6,542

Mixed buildings commercial/private: 59

Commercial buildings: 235

Proportion of 1-to-2 family homes, absolute: 6,119

Proportion of 1-to-2 family homes, proportionately: 93.53

Proportion of 1-to-2 family homes, index: 113.0

Proportion of 3-to-6 family homes, absolute: 324

Proportion of 3-to-6 family homes, proportionately: 4.95

Proportion of 3-to-6 family homes, index: 44.5

Proportion of 7 and more family homes, absolute: 97

Proportion of 7 and more family homes, proportionately: 1.48

Proportion of 7 and more family homes, index: 26.5

20 and more family homes, absolute: 2

20 and more family homes, proportionately: 0.03

GfK Population Structure Data per Administration Unit

8600, GKBR, 02/26/2009, Words: 439, N°: 12060269

Figure 7.6: Population Structure Data of the GfK. Source: GENIOS / GfK GeoMarketing.

The individual numerical information (on single households, multi-person households with and without children, immigrant households etc.) contain both absolute values (for example, there are 3,128 single households in Wandlitz), relative values (33.13% of all households in Wandlitz are single households) and index values, measured against the German average (with an index value of 86.7, there are significantly fewer single households in Wandlitz than in the average German community).

Figure 7.7: Stock Market Information Alongside Links to Financial Blogs and Digital News. Source: Google Finance.

7.10   Stock Market Information

Price information on listed companies are available (as with the commercial provider Bloomberg) from a multitude of stock markets or–for free–from Web search engines (James, 2009a, 2009b, 2009c). The data are both historically oriented (course movements over the last years) and in real time, i.e. they are published directly from the stock market system. Generally, providers additionally furnish their customers with current news and analysts' reports on the company (Figure 7.7). A portfolio tracker, as offered by Bloomberg, serves as an alert service for all companies one wishes to survey.

7.11   Time Series

Time series are collections of numerical values, arranged according to time. Thus for instance, the number of unemployed people in Germany between the years 1960 and 2010 can be represented as a time series with the respective yearly averages. In the economic sector, the basic values for time series are collected both by official statistics and by economic research institutes. Official statistics refers to its legislative mandate: those asked *must* answer. The other surveys are voluntary in nature, and response rates are generally below 100%.

The values of the time series can be compressed into different levels of aggregation, where values from subunits are summarized into wholes. Such a subunit can be, for instance, the volume of labeling machines exported from Germany to Japan; a superordinate aggregate would be the export of these machines from all EU countries to Japan, or the export of all engineering products from Germany to Japan.

Time series have different periodicities. Variables can be collected daily, monthly, quarterly or yearly. Via calculation, one can obtain rough coverage from a fine-grained one, but not the other way around, obviously. Generally, economically oriented time series have three aspects regarding content:
- region,
- industry or product,
- indicator.

Our example above thus refers to the regions of Germany and Japan, to the product labeling machine and to the indicator export volume.

Time series designate either absolute numbers (example: monthly income of an average German household for the years 1990 to 2010, expressed in Euros of the year 2008) or index values (here a value is standardized to 100 and all others referred to it). Partly, time series can be used to show seasonal influences that recur every year. Such distortions can be calculated out via statistical procedures. The time series that result from these then show seasonally adjusted values.

When researching time series, the demand for information is to be adjusted to the possibilities of these information collections: what region(s), industry(ies), indicator(s) are we dealing with? What level of aggregation is needed? What periodicity? Absolute or index values? Is seasonal adjustment required? The spectrum of time series information is varied. It goes from detailed information (e.g. producer prices for milk) to highly aggregated macroeconomic data (Gross Domestic Product of Germany).

We would like to consider the construction of a time series more closely. We are dealing with an economic indicator for the German economy, collected by the ifo Institut für Wirtschaftsforschung (Institute for Economic Research) in Munich: the so-called "economic climate" (Goldrian, ed., 2004). This example is meant to demonstrate that a time series has various preconditions for definition, collection and calculation, i.e. that comprehensive prior knowledge is absolutely required for their interpretation or processing. This note should also be understood as a warning not to approach information from time series indiscriminately.

The ifo economic climate index is an early indicator for the economic development of Germany. In contrast to "solid" indicators, which are collected by the Federal Bureau of Statistics (e.g. the production volume of industries), for instance, these are "soft" indicators, based on personal opinions and hence representing a mood variable.

The questions on the economy are embedded in the monthly ifo economic test. This survey has pursued two goals since its inception (in 1949). The ifo institute wants, firstly, to obtain information from German companies about their assessment of the economic situation and development on their markets. The companies then receive, secondly, information concerning the development of their markets (around 500 product groups at this time). This simultaneous give and (partly exclusive) take of information explains the great readiness of companies to regularly participate in the surveys. Around 7,000 German companies are surveyed; if the questionnaire is not submitted in time, there will be a telephonic follow-up. Not all economic sectors are covered by the ifo economic test. Collected are assessments about the industry, construction, wholesaling and retail. Agriculture and large areas of the tertiary sector are thus not represented.

The assessment of the economy may be distorted by short-term disruptive influences. The participants thus take care not to let seasonal fluctuations or irregularly high or low results affect their estimate. The results thus provide "monthly information about the current state of the economy and its current development that is more reliable than other indicators" (Lindlbauer, 1989, 123). The questionnaire is conceived so as to take as little time to fill out as possible. To safeguard this,

- only those variables that the management is already being constantly briefed on are asked about;
- the possible answers–mostly three–are already specified, the correct one only has to be ticked off;
- the questionnaires are kept as short as possible, one A4 page being sufficient most of the time (Lindlbauer, 1989, 125).

The questions are about the business situation (good / satisfactory (seasonal) / bad) and plans and expectations (mostly favorable / more or less the same / mostly unfavorable). The companies' single reports are then processed. The statements are given a different weighting, relative to company size. The single statements of a company are multiplied with a company-specific value, where the multiplier is set in dependence of the industry and the manpower class of the company. The following example should illustrate the procedure (cf. Lidlbauer, 1989, 126):

Company	Report	Weighting	Distribution of weighted answers		
			good	satisfactory	bad
A	satisfactory	6		6	
B	good	9	9		
C	good	3	3		
D	bad	2			2
Sum:		20	12	6	2
Percentage:		100%	60%	30%	10%

Four companies of different sizes submitted reports. One company (A) reports "satisfactory", two companies (B and C) sum up their estimate as "good" and one (D) is doing "badly". The different company sizes mean that the value "good" has a much higher weighting for the (large) company B than the value "bad" does for the (small) company D.

Das ifo Geschäftsklima für die Gewerbliche Wirtschaft

(seit Jan. 1991)

Lange Zeitreihen für das ifo Geschäftsklima in der gewerblichen Wirtschaft Deutschlands und seine beiden Komponenten Geschäftslage und -erwartungen

Indexwerte (2000=100, Gewerbliche Wirtschaft, Deutschland, saisonbereinigt)
R 1 : Geschäftsklima
R 2 : Geschäftsbeurteilung
R 3 : Geschäftserwartungen
Salden (Gewerbliche Wirtschaft, Deutschland, saisonbereinigt)
R 4 :Geschäftsklima
R 5 :Geschäftsbeurteilung
R 6 :Geschäftserwartungen

Zeit	R 1	R 2	R 3	R 4	R 5	R 6
1,09	82,9	86,7	79,3	-34,7	-29,8	-39,3
2,09	82,7	84,3	81,1	-35,2	-34,6	-35,8
3,09	82,2	82,7	81,8	-36,1	-37,7	-34,4
4,09	83,8	83,5	84,1	-32,9	-36,1	-29,7
5,09	84,4	82,6	86,2	-31,7	-37,8	-25,4
6,09	86,1	82,5	89,8	-28,4	-38,1	-18,1
7,09	87,6	84,5	90,8	-25,4	-34,1	-16,1
8,09	90,7	86,3	95,3	-19,2	-30,6	-7,0
9,09	91,4	87,1	95,8	-17,8	-29,0	-5,9
10,09	92,0	87,4	96,8	-16,5	-28,4	-3,9
11,09	93,8	89,2	98,7	-12,9	-24,9	0,0
12,09	94,6	90,4	98,9	-11,5	-22,6	0,2

Figure 7.8: Time Series Display: ifo Economic Climate for the Year 2009 in Excel Format. Source: ifo Institut für Wirtschaftsforschung.

Balances are being calculated for the aggregation into product groups, industries etc., up to the two comprehensive economic climate indicators for the German economy. The median values, i.e. "satisfactory" for the current business estimate or "more or less the same" for expected future developments, do not enter the calculation. Such reports are deemed "neutral" and do not influence the result of the evaluation. The two other values are added, where the (already weighted) percentages for "good" and "mostly favorable" are regarded as a positive sign, respectively, and the percentage for "bad" or "mostly unfavorable" as a negative one. In our example, the result is +60–10 = +50.

The ifo economic climate consists of the two components "assessment of the current business situation" and "assessment of the business situation over the next half year". Both balances are used to calculate the geometric mean, i.e. both balance values are multiplied and the square root drawn from the product. The two components of the economic climate, as well as the geometric mean, can vary between the extremes of +100 and –100. +100 is reached when all answerers vote positively; –100 when everyone's vote is negative.

Figure 7.9: Time Series Display: ifo Economic Climate and Production Index as a Graphic. Source: ifo Institut für Wirtschaftsforschung.

The goal is to name a specific problem. Since it is impossible to draw the square root of a negative digit, the constant 200 is added to both balance values and then subtracted again from the result. This allows us to calculate freely, but seems counterintuitive. If, for example, the two balance values are +50 and –50, we expect the mean to be 0, just as we do for +100 and –100. However, the results are -6 for +50/ –50) and 27 (for +100/–100), respectively. Hence, the more different both balances are, the more the geometric mean deviates from the arithmetic mean.

The calculation path for +50/ –50 is:

(1) $+50 + 200 = 250$
(2) $-50 + 200 = 150$
(3) $250 * 150 = 37,500$
(4) $(37.500)^{1/2} \approx 194$
(5) $194 - 200 = -6.$

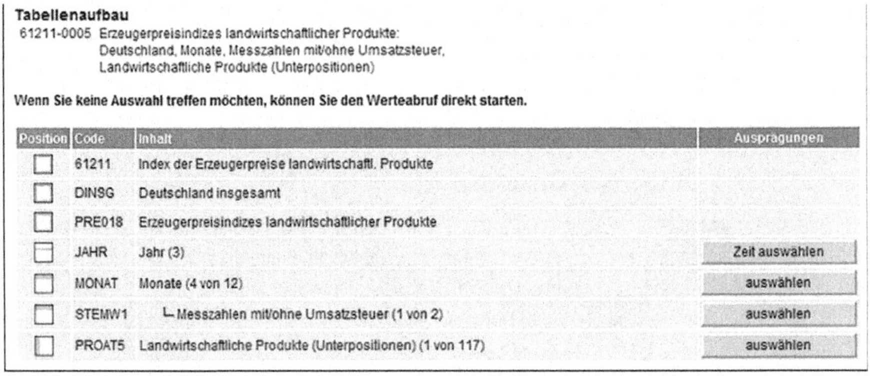

Tabellenaufbau
61211-0005 Erzeugerpreisindizes landwirtschaftlicher Produkte:
            Deutschland, Monate, Messzahlen mit/ohne Umsatzsteuer,
            Landwirtschaftliche Produkte (Unterpositionen)

Wenn Sie keine Auswahl treffen möchten, können Sie den Werteabruf direkt starten.

Position	Code	Inhalt	Ausprägungen
☐	61211	Index der Erzeugerpreise landwirtschaftl. Produkte	
☐	DINSG	Deutschland insgesamt	
☐	PRE018	Erzeugerpreisindizes landwirtschaftlicher Produkte	
☐	JAHR	Jahr (3)	Zeit auswählen
☐	MONAT	Monate (4 von 12)	auswählen
☐	STEMW1	└ Messzahlen mit/ohne Umsatzsteuer (1 von 2)	auswählen
☐	PROAT5	Landwirtschaftliche Produkte (Unterpositionen) (1 von 117)	auswählen

Figure 7.10: Time Series Research. Search for Producer Price Indices for Milk in Germany. Source: GENESIS Online.

Time series with the geometric mean of the balances and the index values are shown in Figure 7.8. According to them, the balances of the economic climate and within them, the business expectations, developed positively over the year 2009. Looking at the index values (Basis: 2000), we can see that the values for 2009 are below those for 2000.

▦ Tabelle

Erzeugerpreisindizes landwirtschaftlicher Produkte: Deutschland, Monate, Messzahlen mit/ohne Umsatzsteuer, Landwirtschaftliche Produkte (Unterpositionen)				
Index der Erzeugerpreise landwirtschaftl. Produkte Deutschland Erzeugerpreisindizes landwirtschaftlicher Produkte			(2000=100)	
Landwirtschaftliche Produkte (Unterpositionen)	Januar	April	Juli	Oktober
	Indizes einschließlich Umsatzsteuer	Indizes einschließlich Umsatzsteuer	Indizes einschließlich Umsatzsteuer	Indizes einschließlich Umsatzsteuer
2007				
Milch	93,7	94,0	111,2	139,7
2008				
Milch	133,2	113,9	114,6	108,7
2009				
Milch	87,6	78,3	74,5	83,9

Figure 7.11: Time Series Display: Producer Price Indices for Milk in Germany. Source GENESIS Online.

It turns out (Figure 7.9) that the ifo economic indicators may be ahead of official statistics by a few months, which makes them suitable–with reservations–for prognoses (Vogt, 2007).

In Germany, the "solid" data of official statistics are available for research online via the GENESIS database of the Federal Bureau of Statistics. The search is oriented by charts (or their headings). In a second step, the values are adjusted (e.g. for yearly or monthly values) (Figure 7.10). The requested values are displayed as a chart (Figure 7.11). A local storage of the research results is available for further processing in different formats (as Excel chart, in HTML format or as CSV).

7.12   News

Press information comprises all articles in daily and weekly newspapers, consumer publications, business newspapers, industry newsletters and–published in real time and stored in archival databases–news reports from press agencies. News items initiated by institutions themselves may also be of importance, independently of whether a press outlet has reported on them or not. Several broadcast stations offer transcripts of their radio and TV programs, making these researchable also.

In news, we distinguish between three information products:

- press reports,
- press reviews,
- media resonance analyses.

In digital products for **press reports**, we can distinguish between two approaches. One, used by Google News, works with the concept of topic detection and tracking. A pool of selected digital sources–if available–is trawled for new topics and the articles belonging to them are summarized into a unit of documentation. The source pool mainly comprises online versions of newspapers as well as a few blogs. The user always searches the articles' full text, the arrangement criteria are relevance (as also applied in Google) and date. Google News provides an alert service, which allows for the surveillance of a topic of one's choosing.

Figure 7.12: Search Interface of the Press Database Factiva. Source: Stock/Stock, 2003a.

The second approach, as pursued in Factiva or LexisNexis, is based on the (mostly automatic) indexing of all articles via a faceted thesaurus (Factiva) or a classification system (Nexis). The user thus finds a controlled vocabulary on companies, industries, geographical terms and topics in "his" language, with which he can research all documents–no matter what language they are written in (Figure 7.12). Apart from all of the world's top economic newspapers (among them the *Wall Street Journal*), important agencies (like Dow Jones and Reuters), Factiva processes around 28,000 sources in total. Alerts are as common as the embedding of Factiva data sets into corporate knowledge management systems (Stock & Stock, 2003a). Generally, the unit of documentation only comprises the continuous text of the articles from the original print versions. All images are removed (and sometimes saved in a separate database), layout and placement in a magazine are no longer evident. Some providers (among them GENIOS for some of its sources; Stock & Stock, 2003b) proceed to keep available a PDF of the original pages, or at least of the excerpt in question (as does the *New York Times*). Completeness cannot be expected by either Google News or the commercial information providers (Weaver & Bimber, 2008).

7.13   Media Observation: Press Reviews and Media Resonance Analyses

A **press review** is a periodical compilation of press articles on any one topic, often on one's own company, products and competitors. Press reviews are either compiled by the company in question itself, or commissioned from a service provider. The basis for research in German newspapers is the database of the PMG (Presse Monitor GmbH), which disposes of 568 of the 627 German newspapers online (beginning of 2010) and also holds the rights for licensing press reviews. In a simple variant, the articles that concern the topic in question are printed from the digital version. More elaborated variants have more user-friendly options:

The articles are researched via PMG, but digitally cut out from the digitized newspapers, leaving the article's layout intact.

If one wants to publish the press review very early (e.g. around 8am on work days), intellectual research (skimming newspapers) must likewise be made early–perhaps even as early as the previous evening.

The single press clippings also serve as the basis for **media resonance analyses** (Raupp & Vogelsang, 2009). The goal is an information compression of press reviews concerning the topic over time. The press presence is documented in presence reports. The topic's presence shares are calculated relative to all publications over a given period of time, as is the articles' distribution, e.g. by position on the page (relative to one's visual perspective), by category, region, form of journalistic representation and sentiment (positive, neutral, negative). The user is additionally provided with information about the circulation of the newspapers that discuss his topic and is thus able to estimate the scope of the information. Service providers in media observation generally do not restrict themselves to press reports, but also take into consideration contributions to Web 2.0 services (particularly blogs and evaluation services).

7.14   Providers' Pricing Strategies

Information providers pursue three pricing strategies: (1.) free offers, (2.) subscriptions and (3.) single sales of units of documentation ("pay as you go").

Market data such as stock market prices are, apart from free services like Google Finance, normally distributed as subscriptions (Ainsworth, 2009, 86). The basis for the calculations are the number of employees with access privileges (sometimes with simultaneous access privileges) and time, i.e. for five employees per month or year. As far as time series are offered by official institutions, like the Federal Bureau of Statistics, the customer can access them for free.

Media observation services principally work with the subscription model. There are hardly any free services for business information. In this area, professional special providers dominate, their pricing models being subscriptions and pay-as-you-go. Sometimes, you can find pared-down versions of databases (with far fewer search options, or less display fields), sort of like "appetizers", for free on the Web–such as the Hoppenstedt Firmendatenbank (Stock, 2002, 23).

In pay-as-you-go distribution, the price span is very large per document. Newspaper articles go (beginning of 2010 from GENIOS) from €2.38 (e.g. for an article from *Rheinische Post*) and €3.87 (*F.A.Z.* article). The GfK offers its purchasing power and structure information for around €10 per data pool. A complete market research report from MarketResearch.com's Profound service can go up to several thousand Euros, even though most clients do not buy complete reports but mainly single chapters. (In Profound, a certain sum is generally paid in advance per year, from which the single purchases are deducted; Nutting, 2009) A company dossier (from Creditreform, purchased via GENIOS) is set at €11.30, a balance sheet at €44.62 and solvency information at €59.50, each for a company with offices in Germany.

In the view of free products (such as Google Finance or Google News), information providers that charge money for similar content problems face. There is a predatory competition favoring providers of free information products currently at work on such submarkets for economic and press information. Certain providers, among them *Wer liefert was?*, have already ceased charging for content and gone over to exploiting users' attention.

7.15 Conclusion

- Digital information products for and about the economy and the press can be put into the three product groups Business Information (Company Information), Market Data and Press.
- Consumers of economic and press information are (almost exclusively) companies, which use the information to monitor known competitors, scan new players as well as observe markets and industries.
- The customers organize this information demand either via end user concepts, information retrieval services or a mixture of both services.
- Company information is distributed via different digital products: Company Dossiers (key data next to financial information), solvency (information on credit status), products and addresses.
- The different cultures of companies' publishing behavior mean that business information for Anglo-Saxon countries is much more comprehensive than for continental states.

- Quality criteria for company information are degree of coverage and depth of analysis, the provider's ability to react to current changes, the correctness of all data, indexing depth and consistency for industry and product classification as well as the suitable retrieval system.
- Market data can be found in information products such as market research reports, structure and industry information, stock market information and time series. Numerical statements generally require explanation and interpretation, which means that their research and analysis depends on relevant expert knowledge.
- Press information is obtained wither via providers working with Topic Detection and Tracking, or via services using elaborate search tool (including controlled vocabularies).
- Media observation is conducted via press reviews (periodical compilation of articles on any given topic) and media resonance analyses, which compress individual information.
- Providers of economic and press information pursue three different pricing strategies, with free offers, subscriptions and single sales of units of documentation.

7.16   Bibliography

Ainsworth, M. (2009). Market data and business information. Two peas in a pod? Business Information Review, 26(2), 81-89.

Corsten, R. (1999). Das gläserne Unternehmen? Firmeninformationen in kommerziellen Online-Archiven. Köln: FH Köln. Kölner Arbeitspapiere zur Bibliotheks- und Informationswissenschaft; 20.

Creditreform (2009). Bonitätsindex. Neuss: Verband der Vereine Creditreform e.V.

Foster, A. (2009). Battening down the hatches. The business information survey 2009. Business Information Review, 26(1), 10-27.

Goldrian, G., ed. (2004). Handbuch der umfragebasierten Konjunkturforschung.– München: ifo Institut für Wirtschaftsforschung. ifo Beiträge zur Wirtschaftsforschung; 15.

Green, L. (2007). Deficiencies in European company information. Business Information Review, 24(2), 89-111.

James, S. (2009a). Mining company information from stock exchange web sites. Part 1: Basic principles of disclosure. Business Information Alert, 21(6), 1-6.

James, S. (2009b). Mining company information from stock exchange web sites. Part 2: Stock exchange sites and how to use them. Business Information Alert, 21(7), 1-7.

James, S. (2009c). Mining company information from stock exchange web sites. Part 3: Listed company sources. Business Information Alert, 21(8), 1-7.

Lindlbauer, J.D. (1989). Konjunkturtest. In Oppenländer, K.H., Poser, G. (eds.), Handbuch der Ifo-Umfragen (pp. 122-187). Berlin: Duncker & Humblot.

Noack, D., Reher, S., & Schiefer, J. (2009). Die Bedeutung von Informationsvermittlungsstellen in deutschen Unternehmensberatungen. Information - Wissenschaft und Praxis, 60(8), 421-430.

Nutting, D. (2009). VIP Report: Product Review of MarketResearch.com's Profound. Ashford, Midlesex: Free Pint.

PublG. Gesetz über die Rechnungslegung von bestimmten Unternehmen und Konzernen (Publizitätsgesetz) vom 15. August 1969, last amended on May 25th 2009.

Raupp, J., & Vogelsang, J. (2009). Medienresonanzanalyse. Eine Einführung in Theorie und Praxis. Wiesbaden: VS Verlag für Sozialwissenschaften.

Stock, M. (2002). Hoppenstedt Firmendatenbank. Firmenauskünfte und Marketing via WWW oder CD-ROM. Die Qual der Wahl. Password, N° 2, 20-31.

Stock, M., & Stock, W.G. (2001a). Informationsqualität: Professionelle Informationen über deutsche Unternehmen im Internet. Password, N° 11, 26-33.

Stock, M., & Stock, W.G. (2001b). Firmeninformationen: Professionelle Informationen über deutsche Unternehmen im Internet: Eine komparative Analyse. Password, N° 12, 18-25.

Stock, M., & Stock, W.G. (2003a). Von Factiva.com zu Factiva Fusion: Globalität und Einheitlichkeit mit Integrationslösungen–auf dem Wege zum Wissensmanagement. Password, N° 3, 19-28.

Stock, M., & Stock, W.G. (2003b). Online-Hosts für Wirtschaft und News auf dem deutschen Informationsmarkt. Eine komparative Analyse. Password, N° 7+8, 29-34.

Stock, M., & Stock, W.G. (2005). Digitale Rechts- und Wirtschaftsinformationen bei LexisNexis. JurPC, Web-Dok. 82/2005.

Stock, W.G. (2000). Informationswirtschaft. Management externen Wissens. München; Wien: Oldenbourg.

Stock, W.G. (2001). Informations-TÜV: Qualitätskriterien für Firmeninformationen im Internet. Password, N° 10, 23-28.

Vogt, G. (2007). Analyse der Prognoseeigenschaften von ifo-Konjunkturindikatoren unter Echtzeitbedingungen. Jahrbücher für Nationalökonomie und Statistik, 227(1), 87-101.

Weaver, D.A., & Bimber, B. (2008). Finding news stories. A comparison of searches using LexisNexis and Google News. Journalism and Mass Communication Quarterly, 85(3), 515-530.

Chapter 8
Legal Information

8.1 Legal Documents and Their Demanders

Carriers of legal information can be separated into three groups (Arewa, 2006, 801et seq.). Primary legal information comprises all documents of written law (laws, regulations) as well as all important judgments (cases from all instances). Secondary legal information comes about via expert commentaries as well as jurisprudential research results in expert magazines. As a lot of documents concerning primary and secondary legal information lie scattered around, tertiary legal information is used to uncover the connections between the documents. This regards both formal citations and "related" documents. Figure 8.1 summarizes our classification of digital legal information in a schema:

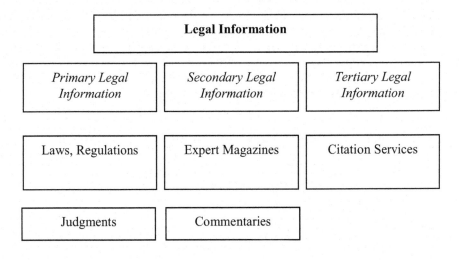

Figure 8.1: Classification of Digital Goods for Legal Information.

Customers of legal information are mainly to be found in three areas:
- Commercial enterprises:
    o offices and
    o legal departments of companies,
- public institutions:
    o courts of law and
    o public administration,
- institutes of higher education (jurisprudential faculties, in the U.S.A.: "law schools").

Sometimes, private individuals might also be allowed to research legal information.

Information producers (and providers on information markets) are "those responsible" for the information–legislative (publishers of legal texts) and courts (publishers of verdicts) as well as publishing houses (secondary and tertiary information). An important role is played by information providers that specialize in law (e.g. Juris in Germany or Westlaw and LexisNexis in the U.S.A.) as well as providers of Web search engines (Google Scholar), as they bundle the single pieces of information. Customers have access both to the producers' data (if separately for every information pool) as well as to the aggregated and interlinked information from legal hosts and search engines, respectively.

The law is always aligned nationally (Christiansen, 2002); even within the European Union, one cannot (yet) assume any "harmonized" law of all member states (Ritaine, 2006). In contrast to STM and economic information, a provider of legal information must always cater to exactly one national market–in its official language. Yet, as a consequence of globalization, users are often required to be familiar with several national legal systems (Germain, 2007). If a customer is interested in different legal systems (let us say: in German and American law), he is required to address different legal information products (in our example, he might consult the Wolters Kluwer product Jurion for German and Lexis.com for American legal information; Stock & Stock, 2005). National law is joined by "transnational" law, such as universal human rights or international trade law.

8.2   Primary Legal Information I: Legal Norms

Laws and regulations for German law exist on three levels:
- legal norms of the European Union,
- Federal Law,
- laws of the 16 states.

Figure 8.2 shows an excerpt from a legal norm of the state Northrhine-Westphalia, as it was published in the law and ordinance gazette. In this decree, a pre-existing legal norm is modified. Occasionally, there are "article laws", which contain changes to several norms at the same time. This makes it difficult for the user to compile the full text of a law. **Consolidated laws** provide relief; here, the changes to the legal texts are included. Kuntz (2006b, 1) points out:

These consolidated collections of laws have no official character; only the legal text published in the gazettes is official.

Gesetz und Verordnungsblatt (GV. NRW.)

Ausgabe 2010 Nr.1 Seite 1 bis 14

Dritte Verordnung zur Änderung der Studienbeitrags- und Hochschulabgabenverordnung

Normstruktur :

| Normkopf |
| Norm |
| Normfuß |

221

Dritte Verordnung zur Änderung
der Studienbeitrags- und Hochschulabgabenverordnung

Vom 14. Dezember 2009

Auf Grund der §§ 6 Satz 2 und 3, 19 Absatz 1, 2 und 4 des Studienbeitrags- und Hochschulabgabengesetzes vom 21. März 2006 (GV. NRW.S.119), zuletzt geändert durch Artikel 3 des Gesetzes vom 13. März 2008(GV. NRW. S.195), § 29 Absatz 4 Satz 3, 4 und 6 des Hochschulgesetzes vom 31. Oktober 2006(GV. NRW. S.474), zuletzt geändert durch Artikel 2 des Gesetzes vom 28. Oktober 2009(GV. NRW. S.516), sowie § 26 Absatz 4 Satz 3 und 4 des Kunsthochschulgesetzes vom 13. März 2008(GV. NRW. S. 195), zuletzt geändert durch Artikel 14 des Gesetzes vom 21. April 2009 (GV. NRW. S. 224), wird im Einvernehmen mit dem Finanzministerium und mit Zustimmung des Ausschusses für Innovation, Wissenschaft, Forschung und Technologie des Landtags verordnet:

Artikel 1

Die Studienbeitrags- und Hochschulabgabenverordnung vom 6. April 2006(GV. NRW. S. 157), zuletzt geändert durch Verordnung vom 17. November 2007(GV. NRW. S. 600), wird wie folgt geändert:

Figure 8.2: Full Texts of State Laws for Northrhine-Westphalia. Source: Ministry of the Interior of the State Northrhine-Westphalia; recht.nrw.de.

Consolidated laws are worked out by publishers as well as legislative institutions. The "laws on the internet" provided by Juris, or the legal texts edited by the publishing house of C.H. Beck, are such consolidated versions (Kuntz, 2006c). If a user requires the current status of a legal norm, the consolidated version will help him; if an earlier version is required, though (because the respective case goes back a while, for instance), the changes must be traced back.

In Germany, full texts of legal norms are offered on the information market by Juris, Beck-online, Jurion (Stock & Stock, 2005) as well as by the legislative institutions (the latter as Open Accessory publications) (Kremer, 2004; Münch & Prüller, 2004; Schulz & Klugmann, 2005, 2006). In the United States, LexisNexis (as a workspace of Reed Elsevier) and Westlaw (belonging to the Thomson Reuters corporation) dominate in the commercial arena (Arewa, 2006).

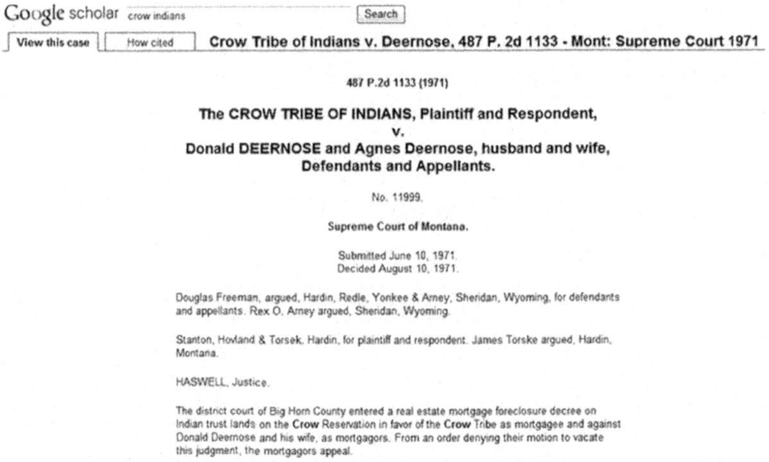

Google scholar crow indians [Search]

View this case | How cited | Crow Tribe of Indians v. Deernose, 487 P. 2d 1133 - Mont: Supreme Court 1971

487 P.2d 1133 (1971)

The CROW TRIBE OF INDIANS, Plaintiff and Respondent,
v.
Donald DEERNOSE and Agnes Deernose, husband and wife, Defendants and Appellants.

No. 11999.

Supreme Court of Montana.

Submitted June 10, 1971.
Decided August 10, 1971.

Douglas Freeman, argued, Hardin, Redle, Yonkee & Arney, Sheridan, Wyoming, for defendants and appellants. Rex O. Arney argued, Sheridan, Wyoming.

Stanton, Hovland & Torsek, Hardin, for plaintiff and respondent. James Torske argued, Hardin, Montana.

HASWELL, Justice.

The district court of Big Horn County entered a real estate mortgage foreclosure decree on Indian trust lands on the Crow Reservation in favor of the Crow Tribe as mortgagee and against Donald Deernose and his wife, as mortgagors. From an order denying their motion to vacate this judgment, the mortgagors appeal.

Figure 8.3: Full Text of a Verdict in Montana. Source: Google Scholar.

8.3 Primary Legal Information II: Cases / Decisions

Depending on the dominant legal system, what is currently considered to be "good law" is gleaned primarily from either the legal norms (as in Germany) or jurisdiction (as in the United States). Of course, leading decisions (in Germany) are also relevant, as are laws (in the U.S.A.).

Verdicts are published both in their **full text** (as seen in Figure 8.3) as well as, occasionally in an abridged version (e.g. reduced to the principle). Courts publish **press reports** (Figure 8.4), which may also be of importance to the researcher. While the text of the verdict–as is common in Germany–the document has been rendered anonymous (i.e. the name "Verena Becker" does not appear and, as a consequence, is not searchable), the press agency has distanced itself from the anonymization. In the U.S.A., anonymization is a foreign concept, and thus every name can be researched.

The **publication density**, the degree of coverage of all verdicts contained in a database relative to all decisions worthy of documentation, heavily depends upon the respective instance. The definition of "worthiness of documentation" (or "worthiness of publication", respectively) is the crucial factor for its decision (Walker, 1998, 2):

> Deemed worthy of publication is … any court decision that takes a position in a question of law (legislative decision) and any decision that makes a statement that goes beyond the immediate proceedings, thus being of interest to, and indeed understandable for, those involved.

The Federal Courts' publication density is much higher than that of the courts of instance, where a maximum of 5% of all settled proceedings are published (Kuntz, 2006a, 43). But even the verdicts of the upper Federal Courts, as well as those of the Federal Constitutional Court, are not always wholly documented.

Bundesgerichtshof

Mitteilung der Pressestelle

Nr. 261/2009

Verena Becker der Beihilfe zum Mord an Generalbundesanwalt Buback und seinen Begleitern dringend verdächtig

- Haftbefehl jedoch aufgehoben

Das ehemalige "RAF"-Mitglied Verena Becker befindet sich seit August 2009 wegen des Vorwurfs der Mittäterschaft an der Ermordung von Generalbundesanwalt Buback und seinen Begleitern in Untersuchungshaft. Auf ihre Beschwerde hat der 3. Strafsenat (Staatsschutzsenat) des Bundesgerichtshofs den Haftbefehl aufgehoben. Er hält Verena Becker zwar der Beihilfe zu diesem Anschlag für dringend verdächtig, sieht jedoch keinen für die Anordnung von Untersuchungshaft zwingend erforderlichen Haftgrund.

Am 7. April 1977 lauerten zwei Mitglieder der "RAF" dem Dienstwagen des Generalbundesanwalts Buback auf der Fahrt zum Dienstgebäude der Bundesanwaltschaft auf. Sie verwendeten ein Motorrad, das von dem damaligen "RAF"-Mitglied Sonnenberg angemietet worden war. Als das Dienstfahrzeug kurz nach 9.00 Uhr an einer Verkehrsampel anhalten musste, fuhren die Täter rechts neben dem PKW. Die Person auf dem Soziussitz gab mit einem Selbstladegewehr eine Serie von mindestens 15 Schüssen durch die Seitenfenster auf die drei Insassen des Dienstfahrzeugs ab. Generalbundesanwalt Buback und sein Fahrer Göbel verstarben noch am Tatort. Erster Justizhauptwachtmeister Wurster erlag am 13. April 1977 den schweren Schussverletzungen, die er bei dem Attentat erlitten hatte.

Figure 8.4: Report from the Press Office of the Federal Court of Justice.

Leading decisions from Germany are distributed commercially by Juris, Beck-online and Wolters Kluwer (Jurion). They are joined by the (free) publications of the individual courts. In the area of verdicts, too, the commercial market for legal information in the U.S.A. is dominated by the duopoly (Arewa, 2006, 821) Lex-isNexis and Westlaw. However, their commercial offers are under massive attack from Google (with its product Google Scholar), which offers a free search interface. All U.S. providers dispose of the verdicts from the District and Appellate Courts as well as the Supreme Court.

8.4   Secondary Legal Information: Expert Annotations and Specialist Literature

The offer of secondary legal information is the domain of specialist publishers. These offer both entire books, as e-books (Figure 8.5), and contributions to specialist magazines digitally. The German market is dominated by the product Beck-online. While LexisNexis and Westlaw differ only marginally in their offer of legal norms and verdicts, there are–particularly due to the different affiliations to publishers–notable differences in specialist literature. Thus the documents of the Legal Library of Martindale-Hubbell (an area of the LexisNexis Group of Reed Elsevier) are available digitally with LexisNexis, but not with its competitor West-law. It must be noted, in addition, that the full texts of jurisprudential specialist magazines are also available with other (non-legal) STM information providers (such as EBSCO) (Koulikov, 2010). The subject area of secondary legal informa-tion does not restrict itself to "pertinent" legal literature. In the end, attorneys and courts cite all types of literature–up to and including Wikipedia (Zosel, 2009).

IBR Reihe

Sicherheiten für die Bauvertragsparteien

von

Rechtsanwalt Dr. Claus Schmitz, München

letzte Aktualisierung: 09.06.2009

id Verlags GmbH

Mannheim

- Sicherheiten für die Bauvertragsparteien
  - Einführungstext
  - 1. Vorwort des Herausgebers
  - 2. Vorwort des Autors
  - I. Einleitung
  - II. Der richtige Umgang mit Bürgschaften
  - III. Chancen und Risiken des § 648a BGB
  - IV. Forderungsabtretungen
  - V. Bauhandwerkersicherungshypoth gemäß § 648 BGB
  - VI. Durchgriffshaftung zugunsten des Auftragnehmers gegen Organe des vermögenslosen Auftraggebers

Figure 8.5: E-Book in Beck-Online. Source: Beck-Online.

8.5   Tertiary Legal Information: Citations and Other Refer-ences

Legal Norms, court decisions, annotations and specialist articles are interlinked via formal citations. In products such as Shepard's (in LexisNexis) or KeyCite (in Westlaw), such citation connections are registered and evaluated intellectually. In Google Scholar, they are processed via automatic citation indexing, where there can obviously be no evaluation (Figure 8.6). Both are variants of citation indexing. The assessment of verdicts does not stay the same, after all, but is subject to changes over time. This change of perspectives and evaluations must be docu-mented (Spriggs & Hansford, 2000; Taylor, 2000).

| View this case | How cited | Crow Tribe of Indians v. Deernose, 487 P. 2d 1133 - Mont: Supreme Court 1971 |

How this document has been cited

" —the court found a state court lacked jurisdiction over a real estate foreclosure action concerning trust land located on the reservation. "
- in Montana Tribal Courts: Influencing the Development of Contemporary Indian Law and 4 similar citations

" —state courts would not be available for the foreclosure of mortgages involving **Indian** land (in this case, curiously, involving a foreclosure by the **tribe** against one of its members). "
- in Law and the American Indian and 2 similar citations

" This view is also held by a number of state courts which have denied state jurisdiction over reservation **Indians** on the ground that the state had not accepted Congress' invitation to take jurisdiction under Public Law 280. "
- in Wildcatt v. Smith, 1984 and one similar citation

" These enactments by Congress are certainly illustrative of the detailed regulatory standards which Congress has imposed on any extension of state jurisdiction, whether civil or criminal, to actions in which **Indians** are parties arising in **Indian** country. "
- in State Securities, Inc. v. Anderson, 1973

" As our discussion above indicates state authority within the exterior boundaries of an **Indian** reservation is limited. "
- in LaRoque v. State, 1978

" Justices White and Stewart, in dissent, argued that Congress could not have intended to prevent the tribes from authorizing state court concurrent jurisdiction. "
- in Sovereignty, Citizenship and the Indian

" "- .. Provided Further, That until the issuance of fee-simple patent allottees to whom trust patents all shall be issued shall be subject to the exclusive jurisdiction of the United States...." "
- in The Native American Credit Problem

" "It is abundantly clear that state court jurisdiction in **Indian** affairs on reservations does not exist in the absence of an express statutory grant of such jurisdiction by Congress together with strict compliance with the provisions of such statutory grant. Illustrative of this principle is the 1971 case Kennerly "
- in Blackwolf v. DISTRICT COURT OF SIXTEENTH JUD. DIST., 1972

Cited by

[CITATION] Handbook of federal Indian law: with reference tables and index
FS Cohen - 1942

Public Law 280: The Limits of State Jurisdiction Over Reservation Indians
CE Goldberg - UCLA L. Rev. 1974

[CITATION] Law and the American Indian
ME Price - 1973

Judicial Enforcement of the Federal Restraints on Alienation of Indian Land ...
RN Clinton ... - Me. L. Rev. 1979

State ex rel. Iron Bear v. District Court
512 P. 2d 1292 - Mont: Supreme Court 1973

all 43 citing documents »

Related documents

Blackwolf v. DISTRICT COURT OF SIXTEENTH JUD. DIST.
493 P. 2d 1293 - Mont: Supreme Court 1972

State ex rel. Kennerly v. District Court
466 P. 2d 85 - Mont: Supreme Court 1970

Martin v. Denver Juvenile Court
493 P. 2d 1893 - Colo. Supreme Court 1972

Ghahate v. Bureau of Revenue
451 P. 2d 1002 - NM: Court of Appeals 1969

State ex rel. Iron Bear v. District Court
512 P. 2d 1292 - Mont: Supreme Court 1973

Figure 8.6: Citations of Verdicts in Google Scholar. Source: Google Scholar.

KeyCites (Figure 8.7) distinguishes between the "direct" history (within the proper channel of one and the same case) and its "indirect" version (citation of the case outside proper channels). The number of stars (at most four) shows how intensively a verdict has been discussed. The user here sees at first glance–just as in the competing product Shepard's (Stock & Stock, 2008, 323-325)–whether a verdict still holds: a red flag signals that the decision has since been reversed, and a yellow flag shows that there is at least the danger of the decision no longer representing "good law".

Google's automatic indexing recognizes verdicts from their typical form of citation and lists both the citing sources (Figure 8.6, top right) and the text environment of the footnote (left). An automatic indexing of the document, and the use of important search arguments found therein, lead to a research for "related" documents. One such service is offered by Google Scholar (Figure 8.6, bottom right) and LexisNexis ("More like this!"; Stock, 2007, 485-487).

A quality criterion of legal information products is the linking to all documents interlinked via citations. If, for instance, a court decision cites a legal norm, there will be a link to the text of the norm (and what's more, precisely to the paragraph, passage etc.)–and vice versa. If a specialist article links to a verdict, there will be a link to the full text of that decision.

Negative Indirect History (U.S.A.)

·*Overruled by*

▷ 2 Hapka v. Paquin Farms, 458 N.W.2d 683, 59 USLW 2113, 12
    UCC Rep.Serv.2d 60, Prod.Liab.Rep. (CCH) P 12,545 (Minn.
    Aug 03, 1990) (NO. C4-88-410) ★ HN: 2 (N.W.2d)

·*Declined to Follow by*

▷ 3 Held v. Mitsubishi Aircraft Intern., Inc., 672 F.Supp. 369, 24
    Fed. R. Evid. Serv. 103, Prod.Liab.Rep. (CCH) P 11,736
    (D.Minn. Aug 14, 1987) (NO. CIV. 4-85-1148) ★ ★ ★ HN:
    1,2 (N.W.2d)

·*Overruling Recognized by*

▶ 4 Marvin Lumber and Cedar Co. v. PPG Industries, Inc., 1998
    WL 1056973 (D.Minn. Aug 06, 1998) (NO. CIV.4-95-739
    ADM/RLE) ★ ★ ★ **HN: 1,2 (N.W.2d)**

Figure 8.7: KeyCites in Westlaw. Source: Westlaw (Note: The Upper Two Flags Are Yellow in the Original, the Bottom One Red).

8.6   Providers' Pricing Models

We can find three pricing models in the area of digital legal information: Open Access, subscription and a special provision for law schools. Free access to information is granted by public institutions (legislative, judiciary), but certain legal specialist magazines come with open access, such as the *International Journal of Legal Information* via Cornell University's Law Library (Arewa, 2006, 837) or–in Germany–*JurPC*. Another aggregation of open access materials, also free of charge, is offered (but only for the U.S. market at this moment) by search tools like Google Scholar.

Commercial providers of legal information like Juris, LexisNexis and Westlaw prefer subscriptions. Single sales of documents via pay-as-you-go is rejected as a business model; demand on the side of the end users is apparently too low for this model. The prices are negotiated in various differentiated ways. Generally, there are differences between economic enterprises and institutions as customers. A subscription of Juris costs attorneys €1,200 per user and per year ("Juris Standard") and municipalities (in the version "Juris Kommune Premium") €850, also per user per year.

The information providers LexisNexis and Westlaw, operating in America, grant institutes of higher education large discounts. Arewa (2006, 829) describes this subsidization of law schools as beneficial for all parties involved:

> This differential pricing structure means that professors and students have relatively low cost access to the legal materials on Lexis and Westlaw. Commercial users, who pay high prices for Lexis and Westlaw access, subsidize this relatively open access within the law schools.

The benefits of this market and pricing structure flow to all parties in-volved: law students become trained in the use of Lexis and Westlaw and arrive at their post-law school employment at least conversant with using the Lexis and Westlaw databases. Although law firms pay a high cost, they benefit by getting new employees who are already trained in the use of Lexis and Westlaw. Lexis and Westlaw, which invest signifi-cant amounts of resources in the legal market, benefit by getting early access to future generations of potential Lexis and Westlaw users.

8.7   Conclusion

- Primary legal documents are legal norms (laws, regulations) and verdicts, secondary documents include annotations and specialist magazines, terti-ary documents uncover connections (primarily citations) between the le-gal documents.
- Customers of digital legal information include offices, economic enter-prises' legal departments, courts of law, institutions of public administra-tion as well as institutes of higher education.
- Legal systems are always aligned nationally, meaning that legal informa-tion products are also tailored to individual national requirements. Legal systems define what "good law" is valid in any given instance either via written law (in Germany) or leading decisions (case law, in the United States for example).
- Legal norms are published in binding form in publishing gazettes. An overview over the valid version of a law is granted by consolidated laws.
- The publication density in Germany depends upon the instance: whereas courts of instance publish at most 5% of their decisions, the density is much higher at the federal level, even though no complete coverage is ever achieved. German verdicts (but not the press reports of those ver-dicts) are rendered anonymous, so that names of individuals cannot be re-searched.
- Secondary legal information is put on the market by publishing houses, acting as information producers, and–downstream–by information pro-viders, as e-books or digital versions of specialist articles.
- Tertiary legal information means evaluating citation indices (such as Shepard's or KeyCite) or alternatively (in Google Scholar) automatically compiled citation connections. The quality criterion of all legal informa-tion products is the interlinking of all cited passages (in legal norms, ver-dicts, articles, annotations etc.).

- Providers of digital legal information work either in the area of open access (legislative institutions, courts of law, but also publishers of specialist magazines) or offer subscriptions. An interesting provision is made, in the U.S., for law schools (which are attractive for the providers), which are granted access to all legal information by LexisNexis and Westlaw practically for free. Such a procedure is considered profitable for the jurisprudential training institutions, for the companies and for the information providers.

8.8   Bibliography

Arewa, O.B. (2006). Open Access in a closed universe. Lexis, Westlaw, law schools, and the legal information market. Lewis & Clark Law Review, 10(4), 797-839.

Christiansen, C. (2002). Electronic law journals. International Journal of Legal Information, 30, 337-353.

Germain, C.M. (2007). Legal information management in a global and digital age: Revolution and Tradition. International Journal of Legal Information, 35(1), 134-163.

Koulikov, M. (2010). Indexing and full-text coverage of law review articles in nonlegal databases: An initial study. Law Library Journal, 102(1), 39-57.

Kremer, S. (2004). Die großen Fünf. Professionelle Online-Dienste für Juristen im Test. JurPC, Web-Dok., 205/2004.

Kuntz, W. (2006a). Quantität gerichtlicher Entscheidungen als Qualitätskriterium juristischer Datenbanken. JurPC, Web-Dok., 12/2006.

Kuntz, W. (2006b). Überlegungen zur Nutzung von Gesetzessammlungen. JurPC, Web-Dok., 93/2006.

Kuntz, W. (2006c). Die Praxis der Konsolidierung von Gesetzen im Bund und in den Ländern. JurPC, Web-Dok., 152/2006.

Kuntz, W. (2007). Publikation von Gerichtsentscheidungen des Bundesverfassungsgerichts und der obersten Bundesgerichte aus den Jahren 2000–2006 im Internet und in juristischen Datenbanken im Vergleich. JurPC, Web-Dok., 189/2007.

Münch, J.B., & Priller, K. (2004). Vergleich der führenden juristischen Onlinedienstleister in Deutschland. JurPC, Web-Dok., 175/2004.

Ritaine, E.C. (2006). Harmonising European private international law: A replay of Hannibal's crossing of the Alps? International Journal of Legal Information, 34(2), 419-439.

Schulz, M., & Klugmann, M. (2005). Der Markt elektronischer Rechtsinformationen. Aktueller Stand und Zukunftsperspektiven. Computer und Recht, 21(4), 316-320.

Schulz, M., & Klugmann, M. (2006). Mit dem „Google-Prinzip" durch die virtuelle Bibliothek? Neue Entwicklungen im Markt der elektronischen Rechtsinformationen. Computer und Recht, 22(8), 568-572.

Spriggs II, J.F., & Hansford, T.G. (2000). Measuring legal change: The reliability and validity of *Shepard's Citations*. Political Research Quarterly, 53(2), 327-341.

Stock, M., & Stock, W.G. (2005). Digitale Rechts- und Wirtschaftsinformationen bei LexisNexis. JurPC, Web-Dok., 82/2005.

Stock, W.G. (2007). Information Retrieval. Informationen suchen und finden. München, Wien: Oldenbourg.

Stock, W.G., & Stock, M. (2008). Wissensrepräsentation. Informationen auswerten und bereitstellen. München: Oldenbourg.

Taylor, W.L. (2000). Comparing KeyCite and Shepard's for completeness, currency, and accuracy. Law Library Journal, 92(2), 127-141.

Walker, R. (1998). Die Publikationsdichte–ein Maßstab für die Veröffentlichungslage gerichtlicher Entscheidungen. JurPC, Web-Dok., 36/1998.

Zosel, R. (2009). Im Namen des Volkes: Gerichte zitieren Wikipedia. JurPC, Web-Dok., 140/2009.

Chapter 9

STM Information

9.1   Information in Science, Technology and Medicine

The term "STM information" summarizes the totality of all knowledge from
- Science,
- Technology and
- Medicine.

This concerns the full texts of the documents in question as well as their bibliographic references, including metadata (Stock & Stock, 2008, Ch. 6) as well as STM facts (Stock & Stock, 2008, Ch. 7). Figure 9.1 provides an overview of the different products of digital STM information.

The **documents** can be separated into the following groups:
- articles in journals with Peer Review,
- articles in journals without Peer Review,
- contributions to proceedings of conferences (generally with Peer Review),
- books, patents and utility models.

A fundamental element of scientific-technical-medicinal publishing is Peer Review. This is a process of anticipated quality assurance and consists of assessing the scripts prior to their publication. Assessment as a legal act is practiced for patents, which are only granted after a thorough examination.

The world's most comprehensive database on periodicals, Ulrichsweb, currently holds more than 300,000 magazine titles. However, among them are journals without any STM characteristics. British Library holds around 40,000 titles of ongoing STM magazines (Stock, 2009). As this institution does not subscribe to all journals with STM content, this figure will serve as a lower estimate for the total amount of STM periodicals. Among them, around 25,000 are academic STM magazines in the narrow sense (i.e. those with continuous Peer Review) (Ng, 2009, 31). Apart from niche disciplines or smaller publication languages, most magazine articles are available in digital form–next to their print versions, which generally appear alongside them. Ng (2009, 31) reports of around 17,000 digital magazines (as of 2009), a number that is steadily rising.

The case is similar for contributions to conferences and eBooks. For the documents of technical protective rights (patents and utility models), we can assume–at least for the big industrial countries–the existence of complete databases, which hold the full text of all documents, unbroken from patent N° 1 to the current status. Apart from formal communication in magazines, conference contributions, books and protective rights documents, there also exist in STM informal channels such as cooperation between colleagues, mailing lists, message boards, weblogs, news groups etc. Apart from certain humanistic research areas, STM research today, in the age of "Big Science" (Solla Price, 1963), is mainly accomplished in teams.

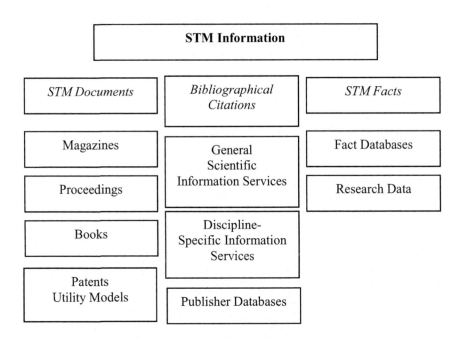

Figure 9.1: Classification of the Digital Goods of STM Information.

Bibliographic references–currently offered online throughout–are found in the following information products:
- general scientific information services (with no restrictions to scientific disciplines, like Web of Knowledge or Scorpus),
- discipline-specific literature databases (e.g. Chemical Abstracts for chemistry, INSPEC for physics or Compendex for engineering science),

- publisher databases (with references for their own articles and books, such as Elsevier's Science Direct or SpringerLink).

These are joined by information resources with **STM facts**, which are on the one hand, in the context of e-science ("enhanced science"), databases with research data that could not be included in the publications (due to a lack of space), and specific fact databases on the other (e.g. Beilstein for organic chemistry or Gmelin for inorganic chemistry).

There also exist, in the World Wide Web as well as the Deep Web (Stock, 2007, 108-111) search tools that specialize on STM information. These products will be discussed in Chapter 10.

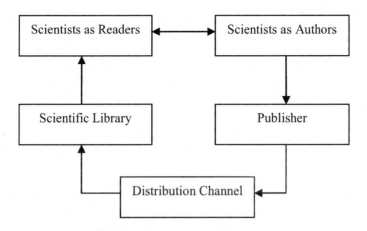

Figure 9.2: Value Chain of STM Information. Source: by analogy with Ball, 2004, 416.

The **value chain** of STM information (Figure 9.2) has a surprising–when compared to other economic value chains–characteristic: the producers are also the consumers. Scientists write for scientists, scientists read what colleagues have written. As profit-oriented publishers are involved in the value chain, this results in a "suspenseful" constellation: the science system must buy back its own results–sometimes at relatively high prices.

What distinguishes an **STM publication**? It is always written by domain experts (accounted for by their statement of affiliation, i.e. their address information), follows a formal structure (e.g. IMRaD: Introduction, Methods, Results and Discussion; Stock & Stock, 2008, 392), contains an Abstract as well as a(n ideally complete) list of all preparatory work relevant for the publication, usually as a bibliography in standard format (such as APA, the citation format of the American Psychological Association) (Figure 9.3).

Science and technology in the region:
The output of regional science and technology,
its strengths and its leading institutions

NICOLE ALTVATER-MACKENSEN, GREGOR BALICKI, LUCIE BESTAKOWA,
BIANCA BOCATIUS, JOHANNES BRAUN, LARS BREHMER, VERENA BRUNE,
KIRSTINA EIGEMEIER, FÜSÜN ERDEM, RALF FRITSCHER, ANNE JACOBS,
BERND KLINGSPORN, MARCIN KOSINSKI, JULIA KUNTZE, JU-RA LEE,
ANNA OSTERHAGE, MARTIN PROBOST, THORSTEN RISCH, TOBIAS SCHMITT,
WOLFGANG G. STOCK, ANJA STURM, KATRIN WELLER, KERSTIN WERNER

Heinrich-Heine-University Düsseldorf, Department for Information Science, Düsseldorf (Germany)

We operationalize scientific output in a region by means of the number of articles (as in the SciSearch database) per year and technology output by means of the number of patent applications (as in the database of the European Patent Office) per priority year. All informetric analyses were done using the DIALOG online-system. The main research questions are the following: Which scientific and technological fields or topics are most influent within a region and which institutions or companies are mainly publishing articles or holding patents? Do the distributions of regional science and technology fields and of publishing institutions follow the well-known informetric function? Are there – as it is expected – only few fields and few institutions which dominate the region? Is there a connection between the economic power of a region and the regional publication and patent output? Examples studied in detail are seven German regions: Aachen, Düsseldorf, Hamburg, Köln (Cologne), Leipzig – Halle – Dessau, München (Munich), and Stuttgart. Three different indicators were used, science and technology attraction of a region (number of scientific articles and patents), science and technology intensity (articles and patents per 1,000 inhabitants), and science and technology density (articles and patents per 1 billion EURO gross value added). Top region concerning both attraction and intensity is Munich, concerning density it is Aachen.

References

AKSNES, D. W., SIVERTSEN, G. (2004), The effect of highly cited papers on national citation indicators, *Scientometrics*, 59 : 213–224.
AUDRETSCH, D., FELDMAN, M. (1996), R&D spillovers and the geography of innovation and production, *American Economic Review*, 86 : 630–640.

Figure 9.3: Characteristics of STM Information on the Example of a Magazine Article: Account of Expertise, Abstract, References. Source: Scientometrics.

Within the large area of STM, there are heavily compartmentalized submarkets, which lead to **knowledge gaps**. It can be observed for several scientific disciplines that scientists who work in companies or other non-academic institutions are isolated from academics–and vice versa. Certain magazines thus preferentially address scientific practitioners, whereas others prefer academics as their target group. There is hardly any information exchange between the two groups (Schlögl & Stock, 2008, 661, for the area of Library and Information Science, LIS):

There is only a low level of information exchange between practitioners and academics. Each of the two groups uses mainly its particular communication channels, i.e. practitioners (as authors) write primarily for practitioners, academics (as authors) write mainly for academics. As a consequence, there is a gap between the communities of LIS academics and LIS practitioners.

Practitioners–not only in LIS but also in other disciplines, e.g. medicine–do not make adequate use (or none at all) of the respective current scientific results, while academics often abstract from problems set by "real life". The information stream between both parties is massively impaired, to the detriment of both (Figure 9.4). The criteria of scientific publications are pointed differently for practically oriented magazines than for academic ones: the number of references is higher for the latter, as is the number of members of the editorial board, whereas magazines for practitioners often carry advertisements (Schlögl & Stock, 2008, 654).

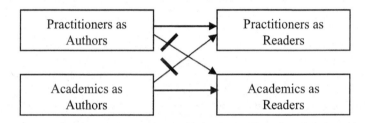

Figure 9.4: Scientists as Practitioners and as Academics.

Relief might be provided by the so-called **evidence-based** approach, in which one looks for the best possible evidence for the solution to any given problem. Evidence-based medicine is the most famous example, but there is also evidence-based library and information practice (Booth & Price, ed. 2004), evidence-based management and evidence-based knowledge management (Gust von Loh, 2009, Ch. 3). Gust von Loh (2009, 2) emphasizes:

> The principle of evidence-based information practice is the closing of gaps between theory and practice via the best possible evidence.

Apart from the gaps between academics and practitioners, there exist further obstacles in the flow of STM information. Disciplinary and language barriers impede the ideal information supply. Within LIS, for instance, German-language contributions are practically ignored entirely by the Anglo-American community, but even in the opposite direction, English-language articles are only seldomly cited by German library and information scientists (Schlögl & Stock, 2004). The cross-discipline transmission of STM information fails due to the individual disciplines' different foci, and due to the respective differences in terms' meanings. In this complex of problems, relief may be provided by so-called **Informing Science**, as Cohen (2009, 1) pictures it:

> The transdiscipline of Informing Science ... explores how best to inform clients using information technology. ... The essence of the Informing Science philosophy is the transfer of knowledge from one field to another: breaking down disciplinary boundaries that hinder the flow of information.

Both evidence-based approaches and Information Science name existing problems of STM information, but they have yet to prove their practical applicability.

9.2   The Production Process of STM Information

We will now describe the process of producing a magazine and conference contribution, respectively (Ware & Mabe, 2009). Both procedures run in similar ways and always involve–at least for academic magazines and conferences–a Peer Review (Figure 9.5). After completing the manuscript, the author (or, for teams, the Corresponding Author) sends it to the journal that is most relevant for the topic in question and promises the best publicity for the research results. Conferences (and, within, specific sessions) are selected according to the same criteria (here the touristic attractiveness of the conference location might also play a role). After the evaluation of formal and fundamental content criteria (e.g. whether the contribution fits the organ's thematic profile), three assessment variants are possible:

- assessment by committees of the magazine,
- blind Peer Review,
- double-blind Peer Review.

In the first case, the editor himself, or members of the editorial board, decide the article's acceptability; consequently, there will be no real Peer Review. Blind Peer Review means that the author is not told the names of his assessors. Double-blind Peer Review strives toward keeping secret the authors' identities from their assessors; this is hardly possible in practice, as any assessor who knows his way around a subject area (which, after all, he should do) would probably be able to guess the authors merely by looking at the references in the contribution. For LIS magazines, 26% of decisions are made by magazines' committees, 36% prefer blind Peer Review and 33% apply double-blind Peer Review (5% did not provide any information on the assessment method used) (Schlögl & Petschnig, 2005, 13).

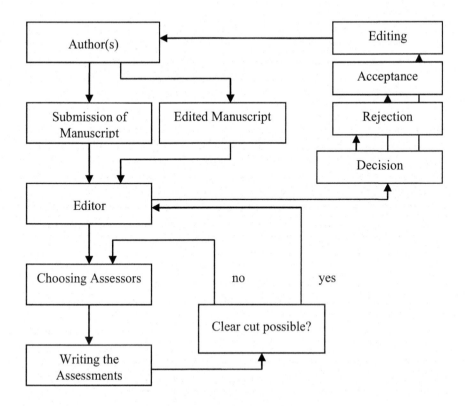

Figure 9.5: Schematic Representation of a Peer Review Procedure.

If external assessors are brought in, there will be generally two of them. If they do not agree, a third peer will be consulted. Some publishing organs also work with three assessors from the start. In cases where the assessors' evaluations differ radically, some magazines will consult a "top advisor". On the basis of the evaluations, the editor decides whether to reject, edit or directly accept a contribution. Depending on the prominence of a magazine or conference, there may be rejection quotas of more than 90%. If a redraft is required, the authors will be returned their annotated manuscript. The new drafts will then run through the assessment process once more. Bornmann and Daniel (2010) report, on the example of *Angewandte Chemie–Internation Edition*, that up to seven steps were necessary until a decision could be made, but that two steps were enough for 50% and three for another 30% of articles. The editors pursue a "clear-cut rule" (Bornmann & Daniel, 2010, 11):

> If the ... editors decide on a manuscript using only initial external review, they generally follow a so-called clear-cut rule: Only those manuscripts are accepted for publication that were positively assessed by the reviewers (in most cases, two) with regard to the importance of the results and the suitability of publication of the manuscript.

The assessors assume the role of "gatekeepers" in this (pro bono) task. The editors of magazines from the large scientific publishers here primarily rely on scientists from the United States (for Elsevier magazines, for instance, 49.5% of all Peers are from the U.S.A., 11.9% from the U.K. and 6.4% from Germany) (Braun & Dióspatonyi, 2005, 115). The Peer Review procedure is not uncontroversial. It can be protracted, and the consistency of different assessors' votes on the same script is not always very high; also, subjective influences on the side of the peers and of the editors cannot always be excluded (Bornmann, 2010)–but: there is no better alternative in the STM production process.

After a contribution has been accepted, time passes before the article is published. In the area of LIS, this will be six months for many magazines, while in extreme cases, idle periods of up to 21 months have been reported (Schlögl & Petschnig, 2005, 15). Before the print magazine is published, its digital version is generally released (from several weeks up to a few months) beforehand, initially without pagination, which is entered up for the print version's distribution. For conferences, accepted contributions are published in the proceedings, which are available at the beginning of the sessions (mostly only in digital form, though).

If a manuscript is rejected by a magazine, the team of authors will, in all probability, submit it to another journal for publication, and the procedure will begin anew. In this case, several years may pass between the moment the research results are first specified and the article's date of publication.

9.3   Digital and Print Products

The stream of STM information in the pre-internet era was informal (on a few conferences and personal meetings) as well as formal, via print media (full texts and bibliographies) (Vickery, 1999, 480). With the advent of the internet, the number of informal channels (such as blogs or message boards) broadened–central, however, is the location- and time-independent access to all formal STM publications (Vickery, 1999, 514). For this, two things must be ensured:

- all STM information are available in digital form,
- all scientists have access to this information from their workplace.

Ng (2009, 230) sketches the world of digital STM information:

Traditional print journals have passed their golden age despite failing to achieve the Utopian ideals that the scientific publishing world envisioned, viz:

Online availability of the entire full-text refereed research corpus.

Availability on every researcher's desktop, everywhere, 24 hours a day.

Interlinking of all papers and citations.

Fully searchable, navigable, retrievable, impact-rankable research papers.

Access to research data.

For free, for all, forever.

Disregarding the last point, all of these ideals are realizable today–and have been realized, for the most part.

Journal of the American Society for Information Science and Technology

See Also:
Journal of the American Society for Information Science

© 2010 ASIS&T

View all previous titles for this journal

* Get Sample Copy
* Recommend to Your Librarian
* Save journal to My Profile
* Set E-Mail Alert
* Email this page
* Print this page
* RSS web feed (What is RSS?)

Published on behalf of

asis&t

American Society for Information Science and Technology

Go to the ASIS&T homepage now

Journal Home
Product Information | Editorial Board | For Authors | Subscribe | Advertise | Contact | Online Submission | Virtual Issues

ISSUE NAVIGATION Early View | **Current Issue** | 2010 | 2009 | 2008 | 2007 | 2006 | ALL ISSUES (1950 - 2010)

Current Issue

Previous Issue | Next Issue

Volume 61 Issue 3 (March 2010)

Research Articles
Doctors' online information needs, cognitive search strategies, and judgments of information quality and cognitive authority: How predictive judgments introduce bias into cognitive search models (p 433-452)
Benjamin Hughes, Jonathan Wareham, Indra Joshi
Published Online: Nov 24 2009 9:40AM
DOI: 10.1002/asi.21245

Abstract | References | Full Text: HTML, PDF (Size: 239K) | Supporting information
Save Article

Effects of granularity of search results on the relevance judgment behavior of engineers: Building systems for retrieval and understanding of context (p 453-467)
Panos Balatsoukas, Peter Demian
Published Online: Dec 10 2009 2:53PM
DOI: 10.1002/asi.21268

Figure 9.6: Table of Contents of the Digital Version of a Magazine. Source: Wiley InterScience.

The large **scientific publishers**, such as Elsevier or Springer, continuously pursue the product policy of offering digital versions alongside the established print products of their STM magazines. Their stock has been largely retrodigitalized, i.e. all articles, starting from issue N° 1 of a periodical, are available in the PDF format (for a full-text example, see Figure 9.3; the table of contents of a magazine is reproduced in Figure 9.6). Older contributions that have been scanned and are only stored graphically here are not full-text-searchable, so that OCR (Optical Character Recognition) procedures are used additionally. For more recent years, whose digital versions have been produced directly within the production process ("digital born papers"), full-text search is of course available throughout. The same goes for the proceedings of conferences in the STM area.

Astrophysics

Measurement of the pressure dependence of air fluorescence emission induced by electrons

AIRFLY Collaboration

(Submitted on 6 Mar 2007)

The fluorescence detection of ultra high energy (> 10^18 eV) cosmic rays requires a detailed knowledge of the fluorescence light emission from nitrogen molecules, which are excited by the cosmic ray shower particles along their path in the atmosphere. We have made a precise measurement of the fluorescence light spectrum excited by MeV electrons in dry air. We measured the relative intensities of 34 fluorescence bands in the wavelength range from 284 to 429 nm with a high resolution spectrograph. The pressure dependence of the fluorescence spectrum was also measured from a few hPa up to atmospheric pressure. Relative intensities and collisional quenching reference pressures for bands due to transitions from a common upper level were found in agreement with theoretical expectations. The presence of argon in air was found to have a negligible effect on the fluorescence yield. We estimated that the systematic uncertainty on the cosmic ray shower energy due to the pressure dependence of the fluorescence spectrum is reduced to a level of 1% by the AIRFLY results presented in this paper.

Subjects:	Astrophysics (astro-ph)
Journal reference:	Astropart.Phys.28:41,2007; Astropart.Phys.28:41-57,2007
DOI:	10.1016/j.astropartphys.2007.04.006
Cite as:	arXiv:astro-ph/0703132v1

Submission history

From: Paolo Privitera [view email]
[v1] Tue, 6 Mar 2007 22:22:02 GMT (197kb)

Download:
• PDF
• PostScript
• Other formats

Current browse context:
astro-ph
< prev | next >
new | recent | 0703

References & Citations
• SLAC-SPIRES HEP
  (refers to | cited by)
• NASA ADS
• CiteBase

Bookmark(what is this?)

Figure 9.7: Evidence of an Article on arXiv. Source: arXiv.

The production process from finished manuscript to published article takes a (sometimes very) long time. An additional way besides formal publication in a magazine or conference proceedings has been found in **Preprint archives**. A significant example is arXiv (Ginsparg, 2007; Haque & Ginsparg, 2009), focusing on physics, mathematics and IT, which is operated by the department of information science at Cornell University. Authors upload their script directly after finishing it, in order to effectively provide advance information about their research results. The scientific communication process can begin now–and not just months or years later. Thus, the article in Figure 9.7 had already been uploaded to arXiv in March 2007, even though the paper only appeared formally, in a specialist magazine, in September 2007. arXiv offers free access to the preprint (via "Download", top right) as well as to the published article (via the Digital Object Identifier, DOI, and the publisher's portal; bottom left, next to DOI).

Preprint archives are very popular in certain scientific disciplines–such as physics–but hardly play any role at all in other areas (chemistry for example) (Velden & Lagoze, 2009). Articles in arXiv may receive more citations that contributions that do not appear in preprint archives (for methodological reasons–there is a lack of comparative figures–such statements are not very reliable), and download figures on the scientific publishers' portals decrease (Davis & Fromerth, 2007). The user of preprint archives faces the task of scrutinizing contributions that have not been published formally (i.e. in a magazine / in proceedings with Peer Review), as these have not (or not yet) successfully cleared the hurdle of "quality assurance". Zhao (2005, 1414) emphasizes:

> Web-publishing is not as well controlled as journal publishing...

However, a lack of control cannot fundamentally be taken as a signal for lack of quality.

The process of continuous digitalization of publications in the humanities and social sciences is not as advanced as it is in natural sciences and medicine. This is not merely due to scholars' (at least sporadic) preferences for paper, but to financial restrictions on the (often very small and technically under-equipped) publishers. The Knight Higher Education Collaborative (2002, 215) demands either the parallel marketing of magazines and conference contributions in print and online for these sciences, too–or, for budgetary reasons, the establishment of e-only versions to replace the original print products.

Publisher-independent digital archives provide relief for all those periodicals whose publishers cannot, or do not want to, create digital versions of their magazines under their own steam. A successful example for such an archive is JSTOR (Journal Storage) (Garlock, Landis & Piontek, 1997; Guthrie, 1997; Spinella, 2008). JSTOR stores periodicals from N° 1 up to the respective current edition. The limitation for inclusion is reached with the expiration of an embargo period (of several months or a few years). In this time, the magazine's publisher holds the exclusive rights over their articles, so as not to endanger subscriptions. Spinella (2008, 80) formulates the goals of JSTOR:

> The initial mandate was to develop a trusted archive of the complete
> runs of scholarly journals, and to expand online access to those works
> as broadly as possible.

JSTOR scans the articles. Images are required for the display, the text, gleaned via OCT, is available for full-text search (Guthrie, 1997). JSTOR is a non-commercial project that seeks an advantage for all involved: scientists are provided online access to materials (which are often hard to get otherwise), librarians save storage space for the print versions and publishers are offered the possibility of digitally marketing their products. Since JSTOR started cooperating with Google, searches for articles are conducted primarily via this search engines as Spinella (2008, 81) reports:

> Researchers do discover JSTOR through many different channels, but
> we cannot overstate the impact of being indexed by Google.

Password-protected access to the articles' full texts (PDFs) is granted via JSTOR's portal.

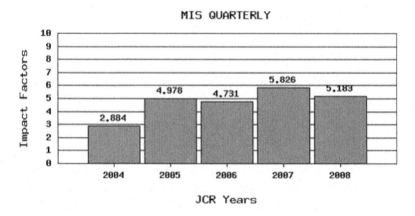

Figure 9.8: Time Series of the Impact Factor for the Magazine MIS Quarterly. Source: Journal Citation Reports.

9.4   Journal Impact Factor

One characteristic value has established itself for the evaluation of the importance of academic magazines: the Journal Impact Factor, formulated as early as 1963 by Garfield and Sher (Garfield & Sher, 1963, 200) and finalized in its current edition by Eugene Garfield in 1972. The Impact Factor is an indicator of central importance for journal scientometrics (Juchem, Schlögl & Stock, 2006). It takes into consideration both the number of publications in a magazine as well as the number of these publications' citations. The Impact Factor IF of a magazine M is calculated as a fractional number. The numerator is the number of citations for exactly one year t, which name articles from magazine M from the two preceding years (i.e. t–1 and t–2). The denominator is the number of source articles in M for the years t–1 and t–2. Let the number of source articles from M for t–1 be S(1), the number for t–2 be S(2), and the number of citations of all articles from M for the years t–1 and t–2 in the year t be C. The Impact Factor for M in t will be:

$$IF(M,t) = C / [S(1) + S(2)].$$

The values of the Impact Factor are published in Journal Citation Reports as part of "Web of Knowledge" by Thomson Reuters (Stock, 2001). There may be several variants of Journal Impact Factors by now, such as the Eigenfactor Score (reminiscent of Google's PageRank) (Stock, 2009), but Garfield's classical Impact Factor has lost nothing in significance. Figure 9.8 shows the progress of an academic magazine's Impact Factor; one can observe a steep increase of *MIS Quarterly*'s significance between the years 2004 and 2007. Figure 9.9 is a ranking of all magazines in the class "Information Science and Library Science" listed in Journal Citation Reports, structured according to their Impact Factor values for the year 2008.

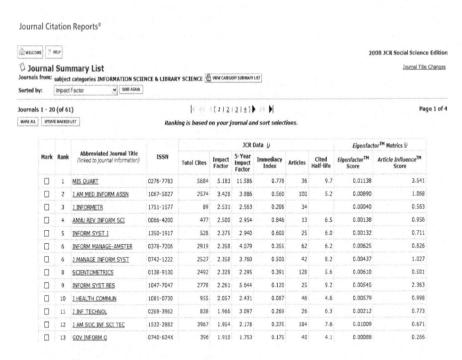

Figure 9.9: Magazines of the Class "Information Science & Library Science", Arranged According to Impact Factor. Source: Journal Citation Reports.

The Impact Factor helps libraries in developing their stock, gives scientific publishers pointers to the location of their magazines, provides authors (as far as they do not already know "their" magazines) with publishing options and even plays a role (although methodologically highly dubious) (Stock, 2001) in the evaluation of institutions' and authors' research performances. As the citation habits of scientists from different disciplines can differ greatly, it is methodologically inadmissible to compare the IF values of periodicals across disciplines without any further normalization. Thus for example, the top medical magazine, the *New England Journal of Medicine*, has an Impact Factor of 44.0 for the year 2005 (Brown, 2007), whereas top information science journals, such as the *Journal of Documentation* or the *Journal of the American Society for Information Science and Technology* can only boast values of 1.52 and 1.29 (average values for the years 1997 through 2000) (Schlögl & Stock, 2008).

It cannot be concealed that the Impact Factor, too, has methodological problems (Stock, 2001). For certain disciplines (such as history), the time window (year of publication and the two preceding years) is far too short, the denominator of the IF formula restricts itself to "citable sources" (thus ignoring "letters to the editor", for instance), whereas the numerator includes citations of all contributions (including the letters). Also, neither the country-specific nor the discipline-specific representativeness is always very balanced. Some countries (including the U.S.A. and several EU states) are represented disproportionately highly, some others (e.g. China) are underrepresented. Certain disciplines (e.g. chemistry) are sufficiently represented, others (many areas of humanities and the social sciences) are not. A statistical problem must be taken into consideration. The IF is an arithmetic mean, which may only be calculated if the values approximately follow a Gaussian bell curve. The distribution of journal articles, though, is extremely lopsided to the left: a few articles are cited highly, whereas many are cited little or not at all. We can thus regard the IF exclusively as an estimated value for a magazine as a whole; any conclusion drawn for single articles is principally inadmissible. The separation into classes in Web of Knowledge can be slightly arbitrary. The two topmost magazines in Figure 9.9 hardly belong to the area of information and library science; *MIS Quarterly* is better described as a business informatics magazine, and the *Journal of the American Medical Information Association* represents medical informatics. To interpret the IF, the user is thus always required to possess expert knowledge in order to avoid misinterpretations.

9.5   STM eBooks

Digital books–eBooks–are electronic versions of books, to be consumed either on a normal computer (PC, laptop) or a specific device, such as Amazon's Kindle, which is very popular in the United States (Bedord, 2009). A further international prevalence of eBooks in the entertainment area is currently impeded by the different types of reading device as well as different and not always compatible formats (such as Amazon's AZW format for Kindle).

In contrast to the market for eBooks of fiction, some broadly accepted formats have already established themselves in the STM area. All important scientific publishers offer their books–mostly chapter-by-chapter–either in the PDF format, ePub (based on XML) or directly in the XML format (Göbel, 2010). The production and distribution of chapters from eBooks proceed analogously to the publication process of magazine articles. Publishers generally offer their digital products, i.e. magazine articles as well as eBooks, via a single interface (as, for example, the publisher de Gruyter does with its digital Portal Reference Global; see Figure 9.10).

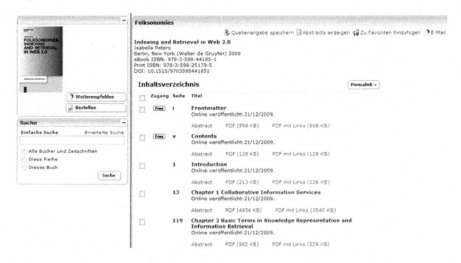

Figure 9.10: Chapter-by-Chapter Sales of an eBook. Source: De Gruyter Reference Global.

In the case of eChapters, it is important for authors and publishers that these represent a(n at least somewhat) coherent product, which can stand on its own. One mistake that can be observed from time to time is the omission to add a bibliography to the chapters. Hence, the book you are reading right now is suitable for eBook publication, as the bibliographies are printed chapter by chapter, leaving the individual chapters able to stand on their own.

Textbooks, too, are available as eBooks in the area of STM. Here it is shown that the students mainly use the digital versions to search for small sections of a book or specific facts. They are not read as a whole in this way; for this purpose, the students still buy (in some cases even more than before) the printed version (Nicholas, Rowlands & Jamali, 2010).

9.6   Patents and Utility Models

As concerns protective rights documents, we are lucky to have the patent and trademark offices of all major countries offer the totality of their documents for free usage, generally in the PDF format. Apart from the non-technical protective rights documents (brands and designs), all technical documents, patents as well as utility models, are thus available digitally (see above, Ch. 5). Figure 9.11 shows, on the example of the database of the German Patent and Trademark Office (DPMA; "Deutsches Patent- und Markenamt"), the process of research for a patent (sought here: the first German patent). The research (formulated in a search mask as represented in the graphics below, or in the search syntax) leads to a hit list, from which the suitable documents and the bibliographical data are selected.

Step 1: Search for Patents

Recherche formulieren		
Veröffentlichungsnummer DE 1		DE 4446098 C2 / DE 4446098
Titel		Mikroprozessor
Anmelder		Heinrich Schmidt
Erfinder		Lisa Müller
Veröffentlichungsdatum		12.10.1999
Bibliographische IPC		F17D5/00
Reklassifizierte IPC		F17D5/00
Anmeldedatum		15.05.1998
Prüfstoff-IPC		A01B1/02
Suche im Volltext		Fahrrad

Step 2: Display of Hit List

Trefferliste Einsteigerrecherche

Suchanfrage:

DE000000000001?/PN

Zurück zur Recherche

TREFFERLISTE: TREFFER: 1 (GESAMTTREFFER: 1) ANGEZEIGTE TREFFERLISTE HERUNTERLADEN				
Nr.	Veröffentlichungs-Nummer ▲	Titel	Anzeige PDF	Familien-Recherche
1	DE000000000001A	[DE] Verfahren zur herstellung einer rothen ultramarinfarbe	📄	Suchen

Step 3: Release of Patent Document (PDF)

KAISERLICHES PATENTAMT

PATENTSCHRIFT

№ 1.

JOH. ZELTNER

In Firma: NÜRNBERGER ULTRAMARIN-FABRIK.

VERFAHREN ZUR HERSTELLUNG EINER ROTHEN ULTRAMARINFARBE.

Figure 9.11: Research for Patents and Utility Models. Source: Deutsches Patent- und Markenamt / DEPATISnet.

Finally, one arrives at a facsimile of the requested documents. The DPMA database provides comprehensive search options–e.g. via the notations of the International Patent Classification (IPC) (Stock & Stock, 2008, 215)–as well as the joining of members of a patent family.

9.7   Digital Object Identifiers (DOI)

Scientists cite different literature, which has been used in the preparation and execution of their research activities. It is of fundamental importance for the user to be able to navigate directly to the full text of the cited work from an article's references. This requires a unique label for each and every STM object. One such function is filled by the **Digital Object Identifiers** (DOI) (Mader, 2001), which are managed by the International DOI Foundation. Thus for instance, the above article in Figure 9.6 is uniquely labeled via the number *10.1002/asi21245*. The DOI always stays the same, even if a magazine changes publishers or moves to a different URL. The arguments before the slanted mark are the prefix and contain information about the registration agency (currently always *10*) and a combination of digits that describes an applicant (it is irrelevant whether this is a publisher, an imprint or a single magazine). The suffix behind the slanted mark is a freely definable combination of digits, which uniquely describes the object. Objects are not only text documents, but can be everything that is uniquely identifiable. Saved and publicly accessible research data thus also have DOIs. For the scientific arena, the company CrossRef processes the citation links between STM documents via DOIs and offers these to publishers as services rendered; there is a similar service, TIB DataCite (to which the Technical Information Library in Hanover has contributed decisively) for research data. The user merely clicks on the DOI (e.g. within a bibliography) and is thus led to his destination (Figure 9.12).

Sets & Subsets:

- Irino, T; Tada, R (2009): Chemical and mineral compositions of sediments from ODP Site 127-797. *Geological Institute, University of Tokyo.* [doi:10.1594/PANGAEA.726855]

Earthquake Event, Authored by Automated System:

- Geofon operator (2009): GEOFON event gfz2009kciu (NW Balkan Region) *GeoForschungsZentrum Potsdam(GFZ).* [doi:10.1594/GFZ.GEOFON.gfz2009kciu]

Mapped Visualisation of a Dataset:

- Kraus, Stefan; del Valle, Rodolfo (2008): Geological map of Potter Peninsula (King George Island, South Shetland Islands, Antarctic Peninsula). *Instituto Antártico Chileno, Punta Arenas, Chile & Instituto Antártico Argentino, Buenos Aires, Argentina.* [doi:10.1594/PANGAEA.667386]

Video of eye operation that supplements a medical journal:

- B. Kirchhof (2009) Silicone oil bubbles entrapped in the vitreous base during silicone oil removal, *Video Journal of Vitreoretinal Surgery.* [doi: 10.3207/2959859860]

Figure 9.12: Navigation Between STM Objects. Above: Literature (via CrossRef), below: Research Data (via TIB DataCite). Source: International DOI Foundation.

9.8　Information Services with Bibliographic References to STM Publications

The totality of all STM publications comprises several hundred million documents–and counting. In practical work, it is impossible for scientists, engineers and physicians to get an overview or even to remember a temporarily valid status without consulting information services with bibliographic references. In, respectively before the acceptance of an STM project, it is thus absolutely required to consult relevant information services. We distinguish, roughly, between three different types of STM information services:

- general scientific information services,
- discipline-specific information services,
- publisher-specific information services.

Among the **general scientific databases**, there are three products that divide the market among themselves: Web of Science (WoS) by Thomson Reuters, Scopus by Elsevier and Scholar by Google (Bakkalbasi, Bauer & Wang, 2006; Falagas, Pitsouni, Malietzis & Pappas, 2008; Jacso, 2005), with the former two available for a fee in the Deep Web and the search engine Google Scholar available for free in the Surface Web. All three information services are citation databases, i.e. they work with citation indexing as a method of knowledge representation (Stock & Stock, 2008, Ch. 18). Web of Science and Scopus only consider contributions in academic journals and conference proceedings for their source documents, while Google Scholar locates documents that are available digitally and transport STM content (with a few blurry edges). Web of Science covers around 10,000 periodicals and contributions to roughly 110,000 conferences, Scopus processes around 16,500 evaluated journals, 350 book series as well as conference literature (as of spring 2010). There are broad overlaps in the sources, but all three information services must be used in practical application, as only in this way can a satisfactory literature base be realized. The great difference between Google Scholar and the two other products lies in their coverage of sources (disregarding any accidents and mistakes during production, WoS and Scopus process the sources from cover to cover, whereas Google Scholar is dependent upon the digital availability of single articles on the Web) as well as in the extent of their functionality (which is very restricted in Google Scholar's case).

We will now explicate some of the professional, general scientific information services' functions. Researchable are source articles (via the terms in title and Abstract as well as keywords specified by the author) as well as articles that cite an author or a specific work. The hit list provides context-specific options for refining the search according to scientific domain, author, language, document type etc. Desired aspects are automatically linked via AND as additional search arguments, undesirable ones are excluded from further searches via NOT. Additionally, there is the function of structuring the results according to date of publication or amount of citations received. For the individual bibliographical data pools, the user has the options of navigating "forward" (to the articles doing the citing), "backward" (to the passages that are cited) and (in WoS) to "related" documents (via bibliographical coupling; Stock & Stock, 2008, 335-337). Various tools facilitate simple informetric analyses (Stock, 2007, Ch. 11), such as stating the h-index (Stock, 2007, 443-444) or (again in WoS) creating rankings and time series.

Discipline-specific information services are available–in varying quality–for all scientific disciplines. For the "big" sciences, it can be assumed that the respective databases will use the respective terminology (via a nomenclature, a classification system, a thesaurus or the combination of several methods) for search and retrieval and that the databases are (more or less) exhaustive. Examples for "big" discipline-specific information services are (with statements on provider and extent as of mid-2010 in brackets):

- Biology: BIOSIS (Thomson Reuters / 21m citations),
- Chemistry: CA (Chemical Abstracts Services / 29m),
- Engineering Science: Compendex (Elsevier / 10m),

- Agriculture: CABA (CAB International / 6m),
- Medicine: Medline (U.S. National Library of Medicine / 19m) and EMBASE (Elsevier / 14m),
- Economics: ECONIS (Deutsche Zentralbibliothek für Wirtschaftswissenschaften / 3m),
- Patents and Utility Models: Derwent World Patents Index (Thomson Reuters / 19m patent families),
- Physics: INSPEC (Institution of Engineering and Technology / 12m).

In Figure 9.13, we see a typical discipline-specific bibliographic citation, which we researched in the medical database Medline, hosted by Ovid. The central quality traits are indexing via technical terms (in this field MeSH, "Medical Subject Headings", via descriptors; Stock & Stock, 2008, 241-243) and the informative content of the Abstract.

Unique Identifier	19213266
Record Owner	From MEDLINE, a database of the U.S. National Library of Medicine.
Status	MEDLINE
Authors	Millstein CB.
Authors Full Name	Millstein, Charles B.
Institution	Tufts University School of Dental Medicine, MA, USA. jeanmill74@aol.com
Title	Technology transfer: Kuwait--a quarter-century of progress.
Source	Journal of the History of Dentistry. 56(3):140-4, 2008.
Abbreviated Source	J Hist Dent. 56(3):140-4, 2008.
NLM Journal Name	Journal of the history of dentistry
Publishing Model	Journal available in: Print Citation processed from: Print
NLM Journal Code	9609747, cj7, 9609747
Journal Subset	D, Q
Country of Publication	United States
MeSH Subject Headings	Developed Countries *Developing Countries History, 20th Century History, 21st Century Kuwait *Pediatric Dentistry / hi [History] *Preventive Dentistry / hi [History] *Technology Transfer United States
Personal Name as Subject	Hein J. DePaola P. Soparkar P. Al-Mutawa S. Al-Duwairi YS.
Abstract	The transfer of knowledge, skill, and technology from resource-rich countries to resource-constrained countries is a valuable tool in improving global health. During an important period in dental history, one individual made this type of transfer a reality. John W. Hein was director of the Forsyth Dental Center in Boston when he wrote a short article in 1986 defining technology transfer. For it to be successful, either within a first-world, developed country or in a third-world, developing country, he determined that certain proven procedures should be followed, maintained, and updated. This paper will outline the development of his strategy for technology transfer, as well as its successful application in Kuwait.
ISSN Print	1089-6287
ISSN Linking	1089-6287
Publication Type	Biography. Historical Article. Journal Article. Portraits.
Language	English

Figure 9.13: Discipline-Specific Bibliographic Citation. Source: Medline / Ovid.

Publisher databases of the big scientific publishers, such as SpringerLink or ScienceDirect (by Elsevier) offer their own bibliographical information services. Elaborate services (such as ScienceDirect in Figure 9.14) are hardly distinguishable from general scientific databases in terms of appearance (ScienceDirect, for instance, allows for reference searches and facilitates the context-specific restriction of retrieval results). Their advantage is the free offer (there is only a charge for full texts), their disadvantage the restriction to products from the publisher in question. Since most publishers offer STM documents across several disciplines, they are not able to offer their users access via the respective scientific domains' terminologies (as the discipline-specific services do).

Figure 9.14: Bibliographical Record of a Publishing House Database. Source: ScienceDirect.

Bibliographic citations contain metadata on documents, but not the full texts themselves. What is required–if the user is not to be left sitting with the "hors d'œuvre"–is a link to a PDF of the full text. For publisher databases, this link is self-evident; for all other information services, it must be created. Generally, libraries run **link servers** (such as SFX; Van de Sompel & Beit-Arie, 2001) for their customers (scientists and students both) using DOIs, CrossRef or further proprietary services. If the customer finds a bibliographic citation in a general scientific or discipline-specific database, he is led–as far as the library has licensed the magazine or the book–directly to the full text; failing that, to the publisher database with its option of purchasing the document. A further service enters the fray: it must be checked whether the user (or the computer he is using) is authorized to access the desired source. Such tasks are performed by **authentification services** such as Shibboleth (Mikesell, 2004; Needleman, 2004).

9.9   STM Facts

For STM facts, we distinguish between two groups of information services. Fact databases record facts that are intellectually extracted from specialist literature, whereas information services with research data collect unpublished raw data that have been compiled in the context of research projects. In many areas of STM, users require both, literature and facts (Losoff, 2009).

```
Beilstein Records (BRN):      2498107
Beilstein Pref. RN (BPR):     127-91-3
CAS Reg. No. (RN):            127-91-3, 18172-67-3, 19902-08-0, 23089-32-9
Chemical Name (CN):           (1R)-pin-2(10)-ene, (+)-nopinene,
                              (+)-.beta.-pinene
Autonom Name (AUN):           6,6-dimethyl-2-methylene-
                              bicyclo<3.1.1>heptane
Molec. Formula (MF):          C10 H16
Molecular Weight (MW):        136.24
Lawson Number (LN):           4055
File Segment (FS):            Stereo compound
Compound Type (CTYPE):        isocyclic
Constitution ID (CONSID):     1226038
Tautomer ID (TAUTID):         2323395
Beilstein Citation (BSO):     3-05-00-00378, 4-05-00-00456, 5-05, 6-05
Entry Date (DED):             1989/07/05
Update Date (DUPD):           2001/07/25
```

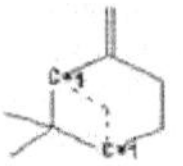

Figure 9.15: Document from a Fact Database (Extract). Source: Beilstein / STN International.

STM fact databases are diverse. We meet them in all the places where a purposeful search for single factual information can be conducted, e.g. for materials, gene sequences, inorganic and organic chemical structures and reactions (Stock, 2007, 503-505; Stock & Stock, 2008, 131-133). Our example in Figure 9.15 shows a small extract from a fact document on beta-pinene ($C_{10}H_{16}$), which lists the different designations of this material. Chemical characteristics and toxicity are also listed.

The global, Web-supported scientific cooperation–particularly for data-intensive endeavors (e.g. in high-energy physics, climate research or bioinformatics)–is called **e-science** (enhanced science) or (particularly in the United States) **cyberinfrastructure** (Hey & Trefethen, 2005; Newman, Ellisman & Orcutt, 2003). Large-scale scientific projects can thus be executed in different locations. Collections of **research data** came about, more as a side product of e-science, which are made available for further use by the scientists that originally collected the data. This involves the claim for the citability of such collections in publications derived from them (and that the data have been processed in such a way that even project outsiders can understand them). In Figure 9.16, we printed a research data pool (with the chart heavily abridged).

Citation: **White, J (2009): Stable Isotope Stacked Record of ice core GRIP913. doi:10.1594/PANGAEA.712617,**
In Supplement to: **White, James WC; Barlow, L K; Fisher, D; Grootes, Pieter Meiert; Jouzel, Jean; Johnsen, Sigfus J; Stuiver, Minze; Clausen, Henrik B (1997):** The climate signal in the stable isotopes of snow from Summit, Greenland: Results of comparisons with modern climate observations. *Journal of Geophysical Research,* **102(C12),** 26425-26440, doi:10.1029/97JC00162

Reference(s): **Steig, Eric J; Grootes, Pieter Meiert; Stuiver, Minze (1994):** Seasonal precipitation timing and ice core records. *Science,* **266 (5192),** 1885-1886, doi:10.1126/science.266.5192.1885 ⌕

Stuiver, Minze; Grootes, Pieter Meiert; Braziunas, TF (1995): The GISP2 d18O Climate Record of the Past 16,500 Years and the Role of the Sun, Ocean, and Volcanoes. *Quaternary Research,* **44(3),** 341-354, doi:10.1006/qres.1995.1079 ⌕

GRIP/GISP (1997): The Greenland Summit Ice Cores CD-ROM and new data archived since 1998. *National Snow and Ice Data Center, University of Colorado at Boulder, and World Data Center for Paleoclimatology, National Geophysical Data Center, Boulder Colorado,* http://www.ngdc.noaa.gov/paleo/icecore/greenland/greenland.html ⌕

Project(s): **Greenland Ice Core Project/Greenland Ice Sheet Project** (GRIP/GISP) ⌕

Coverage *West: -37.6422 * East: -37.6422 * South: 72.5872 * North: 72.5872*

*Minimum Age: -0.029 ka BP * Maximum Age: 0.178 ka BP*

Event(s): **GRIP913** ⌕ * *Latitude:* 72.5872 * *Longitude:* -37.6422 * *Date/Time:* 1991-06-01T00:00:00 * *Location:* Greenland ⌕ * *Campaign:* GRIP ⌕ * *Basis:* Sampling/drilling ice ⌕ * *Device:* Drilling ⌕ * *Comment:* core from the GRIP camp drilled in 1991

Comment Dating control as in White et al. (1997). GISP2 timescale is NOTidentical to official GISP2 timescale in the file gisp2age. Cal year1986=summer1985-summer1986

Parameter(s):

# Name	Short Name	Unit	Principal Investigator	Method	Comment
1☐ AGE ⌕	Age	ka BP			Geocode
2☐ Age ⌕	Age	year AD	White, James ⌕		
3☐ delta 18O, water ⌕	d18O H2O	per mil SMOW	White, James ⌕		

Size 416 data points

1☐	2☐	3☐
Age [ka BP]	Age [year AD]	d18O H2O [per mil SMOW]
-0.029	1979	-36.43
-0.028	1978	-35.83
-0.027	1977	-33.35
-0.026	1976	-34.02
-0.025	1975	-36.74
-0.024	1974	-35.26
-0.023	1973	-36.21
-0.022	1972	-33.56
-0.021	1971	-32.43
-0.020	1970	-34.45
-0.019	1969	-33.96
-0.018	1968	-35.12
-0.017	1967	-35.37
-0.016	1966	-33.79
-0.015	1965	-34.10
-0.014	1964	-34.81
-0.013	1963	-35.88
-0.012	1962	-36.43
-0.011	1961	-35.82
-0.010	1960	-34.74
-0.009	1959	-34.12

Figure 9.16: Access to Research Data (Extract). Source: PANGAEA. Publishing Network for Geoscientific and Environmental Data.

9.10   The STM Market: Publishers, Libraries and Scientists

Users of STM information are, in most cases, scientists–in a university, a private or public research institution or a company. These users, though, generally do not appear on the information market as (buying) customers. This function is predominantly fulfilled by libraries, i.e. college libraries, specialist research libraries and company libraries. The libraries face the task of satisfying the information needs of "their" scientists as exhaustively as possible on a limited budget. This is not always possible. Academic journals and databases get more expensive by the year, and scientists keep requesting new periodicals to subscribe to. Moore-Jansen, Williams and Dadashzadeh (2001, 54) report of price increases for products of scientific publishers of 15% per year on average over the period from 1995 to 2000. The reasons for the price increases are the high production costs (e.g. for high-resolution images), increasing page numbers per year, the low circulation of some magazines and probably also certain publishers' high profit expectations.

If the libraries' acquisition budgets cannot keep up with the costs, this will invariably lead to a thinning of each respective institution's offer. This relation is called the **serials cancellation crisis** (Chrzastowski & Schmidt, 1997). The search for ways out of this unpleasant situation occasionally leads to innovative business models.

Publishers offer their digital versions of magazines and their eBooks in different variants:
- Subscription per journal title:
  - o   Subscription to print and digital version (price of the print subscription plus a small extra charge),
  - o   e-only (subscription to the digital version only),
- Subscription to a thematic bundle (or to the entire offer) of a publisher (digital),
- Pay-per-view.

General scientific and discipline-specific information services both offer libraries subscriptions, almost to the exclusion of any other offers. The costs for print versions are, for academic periodicals for use in libraries, between several hundred and several thousand Euros per year. The price for digital access varies depending on the number of employees or the number of scientific employees of an institution. For pay-per-view, the prices for an article vary between a few Euros to more than 30 Euros.

STM magazines and books are brought on the market either by profit-oriented **publishers** or by non-profit organizations, mostly **scientific societies** (Galyani-Moghaddam, 2006). Among the commercial publishers, a few big companies (e.g. Elsevier, Springer or Wiley-Blackwell) dominate the market. For the pricing of a periodical, its provenance–commercial publisher or scientific society–plays a remarkable role: on average, commercial publishers charge 2.8 times more than non-profit publishers (Galyani-Moghaddam, 2006, 115). But there are also exceptions. Thus the magazines of the American Physical Society (e.g. *Physical Review B*) are in the high-price segment, for instance.

For the electronic versions of periodicals and books, production and distribution costs are lowered (Varian, 1998), leading to an entirely new business model: the so-called **long tail business**. This is derived from the known curve distribution of an inverse power law, in which very few items (let us say magazines) are manifested very strongly (in the example: by number of readers) (Stock, 2007, 76-78). After a steep decline of the Y-values, the curve moves into the "long tail". Here, there are very many items, which are manifested weakly, respectively. But even the low manifestations add up to considerable amounts–the long tail is, indeed, very long. "The future of business is selling less of more", Chris Anderson claims (2004, 2006). Thomas H.P. Gould (2009) applies this idea to academic publishing. The market–according to Gould–can handle a lot more (cheap, i.e. digitally produced) magazines. Such magazines are profitable for a publisher, providing it publishes a sufficient amount of titles, even with very low subscription figures.

In purely digital solutions, the libraries are no longer "in possession" of "their" stock, as they merely license access to it. **Digital licenses** have the disadvantage of coming with the insecurity about the guarantee of long-term access to the titles. However, it is deemed an advantage that hundreds of meters of shelf space are saved, which would normally be filled with magazines and books.

In order to strengthen their negotiating power, libraries join up and form **consortiums**, negotiating with publishers as a unit. Any hoped-for savings are hardly realizable, but the results are a significantly larger offer for a relatively low surcharge (Filipek, 2009, 145). Another option of licensing STM literature for large user circles is represented by **national licenses** (Filipek, 2009, 76 et seq.). Two models can be distinguished: in the Icelandic model, the entire population, independently of their location (thus including home PCs) is provided with access to the licensed literature. The competing model only provides for access from select institutions (e.g. universities), but nation-wide. A mixed form of both approaches is pursued in Singapore; free access to the digital resources is provided to the citizens of this city-state either on their own computer at home, the computers in all libraries or those in selected libraries (Chellapandi, Han, & Boon, 2010; Sharma, Lim, & Boon, 2009). Marketing is used to try to safeguard that all citizens are aware of these information services (Dresel & Kaur, 2010).

We distinguish three distribution channels between publishers and libraries:

- Libraries (or their consortium leaders, respectively) negotiate directly with publishers.
- Libraries outsource the management of their periodicals, leaving the tasks of subscribing, controlling access to magazines etc. to **agencies** (such as Swets; Prior, 1997). The agencies, for their part, work together with the publishers in order to be able to offer an ideal range of STM literature. Libraries manage all their subscriptions via a single interface.
- Libraries contract the services of **hosts**, which bundle the single databases under one interface and also (at least partially) offer full texts (see Chapter 10). The borders between agencies and hosts can be blurry, as agencies also offer hosting services.

A broad discussion is conducted, in the process of scientific publishing, around the subject of **open access** to STM documents (Ball, 2004; Mann, von Walter, Hess, & Wigand, 2009). We can observe different approaches to granting customers free access:

- the publisher, or the publishing institution, carries the costs itself and offers the documents online for free ("golden road"),
- instead of the user, the author (or, respectively, his library or a library consortium, thus saving subscription costs) pays for the publication, which can now be offered for free (used, for example, by the publishing group BioMedCentral) (let us call this the "silver road"),
- authors or their institutions archive their documents themselves, on their homepages, so that open access is created–with high distribution on the internet ("green road").

All three models presuppose a "normal" production process of STM literature, i.e. including Peer Review. The "green" road is controversial in terms of copyright, at least if the author puts the PDF of the published article online, unless his publisher agrees to the "green" by-document. But this procedure is often tolerated, as it creates publicity for the source. Articles with open access have more readers on average, and more citations, than "closed-off" documents (Harnad & Brody, 2004).

How can a publisher guarantee the financing of its open access publications? Crow (2009, 9) specifies the following ways:

- the authors pay a fee for every contribution,
- the authors pay for a specific contribution to an otherwise commercial magazine, allowing this article to appear with open access,

For financing the "golden" road:

- the publication is financed via advertising, which is, unusual, however, particularly for academic journals (Schlögl & Petschnig, 2005), and is thus not exhaustively implemented (Frantsvåg, 2010),
- there is a sponsor,
- the publisher utilizes cross-subsidization (e.g. using profits from successful commercial publications),
- non-cash benefits and personnel services by scientific institutions (the most frequent case): a scientist (or a team of scientists) commits a part of his working hours (sometimes also his free time) to the publication of an open access magazine.

The value chain of STM publications from publisher to user is roughly schematized in Figure 9.17. Not all steps must necessarily be taken. The library can consult a subscription agency, but does not have to; in open access (the "green" road), the user can forego the services of a library.

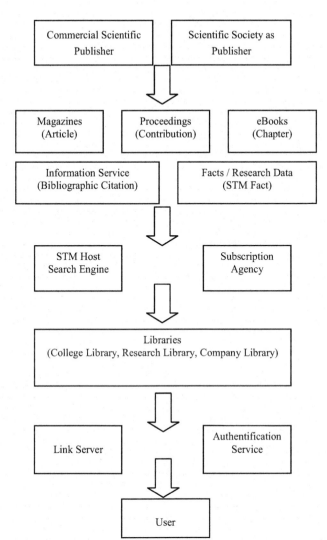

Figure 9.17: Value Chain Between Publisher and User for Digital STM Documents.

9.11   Conclusion

- Information from science, technology and medicine (STM) comprises STM documents (journals, proceedings, books, patents and utility models), bibliographic records of these documents as well as STM facts.
- A particularity of the market for STM information is that scientists are both the producers as well as end consumers of the information. The scientific system buys back its own results.
- STM publications are written by domain experts, adhere to a formal structure, contain an Abstract as well as a list of used sources in a fixed format.
- Gaps can be detected in the STM information stream. The gap between theory and practice is meant to be closed via evidence-based action, the gap between different disciplines via Informing Science.
- Scientific magazines are distinguished by an evaluation of their articles via Peer Review. As this process is very time-consuming, preprint archives have established themselves for some scientific disciplines (e.g. in the service arXiv for physics).
- The big scientific publishers uniformly distribute their magazines and book series in parallel print and digital versions. Publisher-independent archives (such as JSTOR) are available for further titles.
- A crucially important characteristic value for the influence of an academic journal is its Impact Factor, which is a quotient of the number of citations of an article from a magazine from the two years preceding the year under review and the number of source articles from those two years. In interpreting the Impact Factor, its methodological subtleties and problems must be taken into consideration.
- Compared to eBooks in fiction, eBooks in the STM area are already fully established.
- Patents and utility designs are fully available in digital form for all of the world's most important countries.
- Each STM document, no matter whether it is a text, a fact etc., is uniquely labeled via a Digital Object Identifier (DOI). This facilitates interlinking between documents.
- Since there are several hundred million STM documents, bibliographical information services provide an overview (with their metadata). We distinguish between general scientific information services (which are always also citation databases: Web of Science, Scopus and Google Scholar), discipline-specific information services (always with indexing via the respective domain's terminology) and publisher databases (restricted to the respective in-house products).

- STM facts are intellectually extracted from publications and offered in domain-specific fact databases. Some scientists offer their research data, used in their publications, for further use (via their scientific societies and libraries).
- The STM market comprises three main groups of players: publishers (profit-oriented scientific publishers and non-profit scientific societies), libraries and the scientists themselves. As a reaction to the serials crisis, interesting new business models appeared, such as the Long Tail Business, library consortiums, national licenses and open access.

9.12   Bibliography

Anderson, C. (2004). The long tail. Wired, 12(10).

Anderson, C. (2006). The Long Tail: Why the Future of Business is Selling Less of More. New York, NY: Hyperion.

Bakkalbasi, N., Bauer, K., Glover, J., & Wang, L. (2006). Three options for citation tracking: Google Scholar, Scopus and Web of Science. Biomedical Digital Libraries, 3(7).

Ball, R. (2004). Open Access–Die Revolution im wissenschaftlichen Publizieren? In Bekavac, B., Herget, J., & Rittberger, M. (eds.), Informationen zwischen Kultur und Marktwirtschaft. Proceedings des 9. Internationalen Symposiums für Informationswissenschaft (pp. 413-432). Konstanz: UVK,.

Bedord, J. (2009). Ebooks hit critical mass. Online, 33(3), 14-18.

Booth, A., & Brice, A., eds. (2004). Evidence Based Practice for Information Professionals. London: Facet.

Bornmann, L. (2010). Does the journal peer review select the „best" from the work submitted? The state of empirical research. IETE Technical Review 27(2), 93-95.

Bornmann, L., & Daniel, H.D. (2010). The manuscript reviewing process. Empirical research on review requests, review sequences, and decision rules in peer review. Library & Information Science Research, 32, 5-12.

Braun, T., & Dióspatonyi, I. (2005). The journal gatekeepers of major publishing houses of core science journals. Scientometrics, 64(2), 113-120.

Brown, H. (2007). How impact factors changed medical publishing–and science. British Medical Journal, 334(7593), 561-564.

Chellapandi, S., Han, C.W., & Boon, T.C. (2010). The National Library of Singapore experience: Harnessing technology to deliver content and broaden access. Interlending & Document Supply, 38(1), 40-48.

Chrzastowski, T.E., & Schmidt, K.A. (1997). The serials cancellation crisis: National trends in academic library serials collections. Library Acquisitions: Practice & Theory, 21(4), 431-443.

Cohen, E.B. (2009). A philosophy of Informing Science. Informing Science. The International Journal of an Emerging Transdiscipline, 12, 1-15.

Crow, R. (2009). Income Models for Open Access: An Overview of Current Practice. Washington, D.C.: Scholarly Publishing & Academic Resources Coalition (SPARC).

Davis, P.M., & Fromerth, M.J. (2007). Does the arXiv lead to higher citations and reduced publisher downloads for mathematics articles? Scientometrics, 71(2), 203-215.

Dresel, R., & Kaur, N. (2010). Marketing eResources. International Conference on Digital Libraries (ICDL). Shaping the Information Paradigm (pp. 460-467). New Delhi: TERI; IGNOU.

Falagas, M.E., Pitsouni, E.I., Malietzis, G.A., & Pappas, G. (2008). Comparison of PubMed, Scopus, Web of Science, and Google Scholar: Strengths and weaknesses. FASEB Journal, 22(2), 338-342.

Filipek, D. (2009). Konsortialverträge zwischen Bibliotheken zwischen und Verlagen. Ein erfolgsversprechendes Modell? Hamburg: Kovač.

Frantsvåg, J.E. (2010). The role of advertising in financing open access journals. First Monday, 15(3).

Galyani-Moghaddam, G. (2006). Price and value of electronic journals. A survey at the Indian Institute of Science. Libri, 56, 108-116.

Garfield, E. (1972). Citation analysis as a tool in journal evaluation. Science, 178, 471-479.

Garfield, E., & Sher, I.H. (1963). New factors in the evaluation of scientific literature through citation indexing. American Documentation, 14(3), 195-201.

Garlock, K.L., Landis, W.E., & Piontek, S. (1997). Redefining access to scholarly journals. A progress report on JSTOR. Serials Review, 23(1), 1-8.

Ginsparg, P. (2007). Next-generation implications of open access. CTWatch Quarterly, 3(3).

Göbel, R. (2010). eBooks. Eine Übersicht für die professionelle Nutzung. Password, N° 3, 4-5.

Gould, T.H.P. (2009). The future of academic publishing. Application of the long-tail theory. Publishing Research Quarterly, 25, 232-245.

Gust von Loh, S. (2009). Evidenzbasiertes Wissensmanagement. Wiesbaden: Gabler.

Guthrie, K.M. (1997). JSTOR. From project to independent organization. D-Lib Magazine, 3 (7/8).

Haque, A., & Ginsparg, P. (2009). Positional effects on citation and readership in arXiv. Journal of the American Society for Information Science and Technology, 60(11), 2203-2218.

Harnad, S., & Brody, T. (2004). Comparing the impact of open access (OA) vs. non-OA articles in the same journals. D-Lib Magazin, 10(6).

Hey, T., & Trefethen, A. (2005). Cyberinfrastructure for e-science. Science, 308(5723), 817-821.

Jacso, P. (2005). As we may search–Comparison of major features of the *Web of Science*, *Scopus*, and *Google Scholar* citation-based and citation-enhance databases. Current Science, 89(9), 1537-1547.

Juchem, K., Schlögl, C., & Stock, W.G. (2006). Dimensionen der Zeitschriften-szientometrie. Information–Wissenschaft und Praxis, 57(1), 31-37.

Losoff, B. (2009). Electronic scientific data & literature aggregation. A review for librarians. Issues in Science and Technology Librarianship, Fall 2009.

Mader, C.L. (2001). Current implementation of the DOI in STM publishing. In Schlembach, M.C. (ed.), Information Practice in Science and Technology (pp. 97-118). Binghamton, NY: Haworth Information Press.

Mann, F., von Walter, B., Hess, T., & Wigand, R.T. (2009). Open access publishing in science. Communications of the ACM, 52(3), 135-139.

Mikesell, B.L. (2004). Anything, anytime, anywhere: Proxy servers, Shibboleth, and the dream of the digital library. Journal of Library Administration, 41(1/2), 315-326.

Moore-Jansen, C., Williams, J.H., & Dadashzadeh, M. (2001). Is a decision support system enough? Tactical versus strategic solutions to the serials pricing crisis. Serials Review, 27(3/4), 48-61.

Needleman, M. (2004). The Shibboleth authentification/authorization system. Serials Review, 30(3), 252-253.

Newman, H.B., Ellisman, M.H., & Orcutt, J.A. (2003). Data-intensive e-science frontier research. Communications of the ACM, 46(11), 69-77.

Ng, K.H. (2009). Exploring new frontiers of electronic publishing in biomedical science. Singapore Medical Journal 50(3), 230-234.

Nicholas, D., Rowlands, I., & Jamali, H.R. (2010). E-textbook use, information seeking behaviour and its impact: Case study business and management. Journal of Information Science, 36(2), 263-280.

Philip, D., & Michael, F. (2007). Does the arXiv lead to higher citations and reduced publisher downloads for mathematics articles? Scientometrics, 71(2), 203-215.

Prior, A. (1997). Managing electronic serials: The development of a subscription agent's service. The Serials Librarian, 32(3/4), 57-65.

Schlögl, C., & Petschnig, W. (2005). Library and information science journals. An editor survey. Library Collections, Acquisitions, & Technical Services, 29, 4-32.

Schlögl, C., & Stock, W.G. (2004). Impact and relevance of LIS journals. A scientometric analysis of international and German-language LIS journals–Citation analysis versus reader survey. Journal of the American Society for Information Science and Technology, 55(13), 1155-1168.

Schlögl, C., & Stock, W.G. (2008). Practitioners and academics as authors and readers. The case of LIS journals. Journal of Documentation, 64(5), 643-666.

Sharma, R.S., Lim, S., & Boon, C.Y. (2009). A vision for a knowledge society and learning nation: The role of a national library system. The ICFAI University Journal of Knowledge Management, 7(5/6), 91-113.

Solla Price, D.J. de (1963). Little Science, Big Science. New York, NY: Columbia University Press.

Spinella, M. (2008). JSTOR and the changing digital landscape. Interlending & Document Supply, 36(2), 79-85.

Stock, W.G. (2001). JCR on the Web. Journal Citation Reports: Ein Impact Factor für Bibliotheken, Verlage und Autoren? Password, N° 5, 24-39.

Stock, W.G. (2009). The inflation of impact factors of scientific journals. ChemPhysChem, 10(13), 2193-2196.

Stock, W.G. (2007). Information Retrieval. Informationen suchen und finden. München, Wien: Oldenbourg.

Stock, W.G., & Stock, M. (2008). Wissensrepräsentation. Informationen auswerten und bereitstellen. München: Oldenbourg.

The Knight Higher Education Collaboration (2002). Op. cit. Publishing in the humanities and social sciences. Learned Publishing, 15(3), 205-216.

Van de Sompel, H., & Beit-Arie, O. (2001). Open linking in the scholarly information environment using the OpenURL framework. D-Lib Magazine, 7(3).

Varian, H.R. (1998). The future of electronic journals. Journal of Electronic Publication, 4(1).

Velden, T., & Lagoze, C. (2009). Communicating chemistry. Nature Chemistry, 1(9), 673-678.

Vickery, B. (1999). A century of scientific and technical information. Journal of Documentation, 55(5), 476-527.

Ware, M., & Mabe, M. (2009). The STM Report. An Overview of Scientific and Scholarly Journal Publishing. Oxford: International Association of Scientific, Technical and Medical Publishers.

Zhao, D. (2005). Challenges of scholarly publications on the Web to the evaluation of science. A comparison of author visibility on the Web and in print journals. Information Processing & Management, 41, 1403-1418.

Chapter 10
Search Tools and Content Aggregators

10.1 Typology of Search Tools and Content Aggregators

In Chapters 7 through 9, we got to know various specialized information products, each of them catering to specialized markets. In the **Deep Web** (Bergman, 2001)– also called "Invisible Web" (Sherman & Price, 2001)–there are thousand of databases, which offer highly specialized information. Added to this are the billions of pages in the **Surface Web** (Stock, 2007, 108-111). The Surface Web comprises all digital documents that are *within* the Web (and are generally interlinked), while the Deep Web summarizes all digital documents that are integrated in to their own respective information collections (databases), the start pages of which are accessible *via* the WWW (Stock & Stock, 2004c, 3-13).

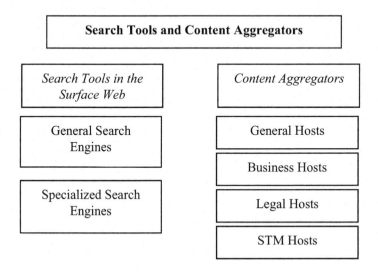

Figure 10.1: Classification of Search Tools and Content Aggregators.

Search and retrieval in the Surface Web is performed via **search engines**, which are either aligned to Web contents in general (like Google), or which retrieve specific documents (such as Google News or Google Scholar). The variety of databases in the Deep Web is bundled via Content Aggregators. Such so-called **hosts** summarize (anywhere between hundreds and thousands of) individual databases under one single retrieval system and one single user interface. Depending on the content on offer, we distinguish between general hosts (with no thematic emphasis) and–analogously to information services (Chapters 7-9)–hosts for economic, legal and STM information.

Web search engines cater to mass markets and offer their services free of charge, securing their funding by marketing customers' attention via adverts. Hosts act on (sometimes very small) niche markets. As a critical mass of attention that could bind advertising customers is seldomly reached here, the hosts sell both digital content, i.e. the full texts, bibliographic citations or fact documents they provide, and their services of searching and retrieving content. It can occasionally be observed that operators of Deep Web databases (e.g. JSTOR) deposit their documents for search (but not for display) with search tools in the Surface Web (here: in Google).

10.2   Online Search Engines

In pretty much every country of the world, the market for general Web search engines follows an inverse power law: one single company dominates the market in question, the competitors following some distance behind. In the U.S.A., around two thirds of all Web searches (around 15bn in total) are conducted via Google, with the closest competitor (Yahoo!) accounting for 17% (source: comScore, data for February 2010). In Germany, the distance between the market leader (again Google, this time with 89%) and the second-placed player (T-Online, 3%) is even more extreme (source: Webtrekk, data for June 2009). In China, we can observe the same form of distribution, but with different players: here, 61% of all searches are performed via Baidu, with Google.cn coming in second place with 27% (source: Internet World Business, data for September 2009). The market for search engines thus very impressively demonstrates the "winner takes all" principle. For companies (and all other parties whose websites are meant to be retrieved on the internet), this means that they have to safeguard their sites' visibility with the respective search engine market leader. This is done in two ways via **search engine marketing** (von Bischopinck & Ceyp, 2007):

- Search engine optimization (SEO),
- Sponsored Search.

SEO serves to construct a website in such a way that it will land as high up in the hit list as possible (ideally in first place) if certain search arguments are being used. Sponsored Search (as part of online advertising) pursues the goal of leading potential customers to one's own Web presence via short advertising texts that are displayed, context-specifically, for the search arguments that are used (see Chapter

15). SEO requires technical and content-related measures to be applied to one's own website, Sponsored Search requires financial means (next to the best possible advertising copy and the acquisition of the right search arguments). Whether via SEO or advertising, the central goal of companies is to get their websites (with their products, services, self-projection etc.) retrieved and displayed for the suitable search arguments.

SEO can be performed in the company itself; however, there are also external service providers that specialize in search engine optimization. We distinguish between **on-site optimization** (measures applied to one's own site, e.g. using the correct terminology in the continuous text as well as in the title, number and distribution of crucial terms in the text or in subheadings, the folder structure for the entire site or the placement of internal links) and **off-site optimization** (links to one's own site from external sources and their anchor texts, as well as the number of clicks to one's own site). All optimization measures require detailed knowledge of computer and information science, both for the measures applied in information linguistics as well as the search engines' sorting algorithms used. Only the method of on-site optimization is fully subject to the optimizers' control, off-site methods requiring the help of others. Here, one can very quickly encounter dubious practices (such as the managing of link farms) that are considered spam (Stock, 2007, 125-128) and–if recognized–result in a deletion of the websites by search engines.

Operators of search engines (in most countries at the moment Google) pursue the task of constructing and expanding the broadest possible mass of users for their **advertising customers** (which are, after all, their sole source of profit). All products, be it general search engines (Google.com or, specifically for Germany, Google.de), specialized search engines (Google Scholar, Google News, Google Books etc.) or additional offers (such as Gmail or Google Earth) serve the sole purpose of binding the search engine's users to this research tool in the long term. This is achieved by satisfying the users' information needs via sophisticated search technology and the right content–without charging the users a Cent. In Google's annual report (2009, 1), we read:

> We will do our best to provide the most relevant and useful search results possible, independent of financial incentives. Our search results will be objective, and we do not accept payment for search result ranking or inclusion.
>
> We will do our best to provide the most relevant and useful advertising. Advertisements should not be an annoying interruption. If any element on a search result page is influenced by payments to us, we will make it clear to our users.
>
> We will never stop working to improve our user experience, our search technology, and other important areas of information organization.
>
> We believe that our user focus is the foundation of our success to date.

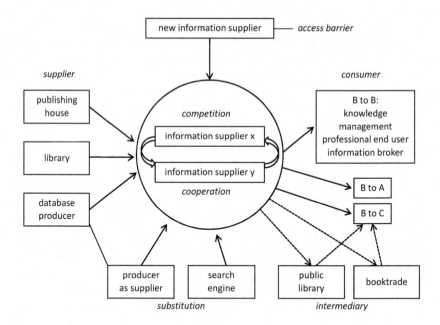

Figure 10.2: Industry Structure of Content Aggregators. Source: Stock & Stock, 2004b, 20.

10.3   Content Aggregators (Hosts)

Online hosts bundle the content of various different databases under one surface and using one retrieval system. For the user, this bears the advantage of having all the important information collections in front of one at a single glance, and only having to speak one retrieval language. However, such search languages are not always easy to use, which is why hosts offer both relevant courses and a help desk for any urgent questions.

The Content Aggregators' suppliers are
- publishers (with their digital content),
- libraries with their document delivery services (for content that is not available digitally and must thus be acquired in the form of a print copy),
- providers of bibliographical information services.

Hosts can be separated into **general information providers** without any thematic restrictions (such as DIALOG or–with an emphasis on magazines' full texts–EBSCO*host*) and **specialist providers**. The latter act in the area of either economic, market and press (e.g. Factiva, Nexis, Profound or–with a particular emphasis on the German economy–GENIOS) (Stock & Stock, 2003), legal (Lexis,

Westlaw and–for German law–Juris) (Kremer, 2004) or STM information (Stock & Stock, 2005). Among STM hosts, there are once more, apart from general STM providers (such as STN International or Thomson Reuters with its product Web of Knowledge), specialists, e.g. DIMDI and Ovid for medical information or Questel for information of commercial legal protection (Stock & Stock, 2006). Hosts act on niche markets, which makes it very difficult for new providers to successfully establish themselves on the information market. The market has been in the hands of the established players for years–the online hosts' roots go back to the year 1972 (Stock, 2007, 43-46).

A problem of many hosts is that the **suppliers** also market their information services themselves, thus binding many possible customers. Search engines are regarded as a threat with some justification: Google News is a competitor on the market for press information, Google Scholar, for court decisions (i.e. "Legal Opinions and Journals"), is at least a competitor of the American legal hosts, and Google Scholar (in the segment "Articles and Patents") competes with STM hosts.

On the **customers' side**, B-to-B business models dominate, i.e. companies act as customers. Here, three strategies are pursued in the context of operational knowledge management (see Chapter 7 above): end user research, installation of an information retrieval service or a mixed form of both strategies. Particularly in the area of legal information, but also for resort-specific information (e.g. medical information from DIMDI for the German Federal Ministry of Health), we can find B-to-A business models, in which public administrations act as customers. Due to the lack of end users' willingness to pay, B-to-C business models are hardly realizable. Attempts to incorporate public libraries or stationary book trade into the value chain as a further sales intermediary (Bieletzki & Roth, 1998) must be deemed failures.–An overview of the industry structure of content aggregators is provided by Figure 10.2.

For the **pricing models**, many online hosts prefer subscriptions–either to their entire offer or to individual databases. However, it is also an option for registered customers to selectively access hosts' offers after paying a basic fee, and then paying for them on an individual basis. Thus, the host STN International charges €120 for one hour's access to the database *Compendex*, or €475 for *World Patents Index* (as of 2010). For each bibliographic citation, *Compendex* charges €2.85; viewing the display of a patent document in the *World Patent Index* costs €7.91. Searches to survey a thematic profile (SDI; Selective Dissemination of Information; Stock, 2007, 154-156) are an important product of hosts. Weekly SDI searches in *Compendex* cost €3.50, and €57.60 in the *World Patents Index* (displayed documents are charged additionally). Special commands lead to charges shown separately. The command ANALYZE (for up to 50,000 data pools to be processed), important for informetric analyses (Stock, 2007, Ch. 11), costs €43.90 in STN. Some online hosts (such as GENIOS) do not charge users' access time, which means that only the documents users view generate costs. To safeguard the transparency of these (not inconsiderable) costs, GENIOS shows the fee that is incurred before any document is displayed.

Due to the competition between (free) Web search engines and (commercial) Content Aggregators, it was suggested (Bock, 2000) to use **certification marks** in order to effectively designate the latter as quality information, signaling users that online hosts provide a different kind of information–of higher quality. Highly specialized technical information in particular always represent credence goods for laymen, as they will not be able to exhaustively determine the quality of these economic goods before or after the purchase. Certification marks (e.g. registered as a collective mark) have not (yet) been able to assert themselves for online hosts. How to operationalize the quality of digital information services in such a way that they can be registered via quantitative characteristic values, leaving us able to actually drawing a clear line between quality information and all the rest, is an unresolved problem.

The Content Aggregators' companies can only survive by establishing **unique selling propositions** vis-à-vis competitors on their own market as well as substitute products from other industries (Stock & Stock, 2004b). Such propositions, in the sense of critical success factors, are, for online hosts:

- exclusive content (at least a few of the host's databases are only available here),
- the "right" selection of required databases, from the customer's perspective (for reasons of time and economy, customers prefer one-stop shopping, which means that all relevant sources that are required need to be available via the host),
- the power of the retrieval system used (search and retrieval are conducted on a professional level, which means that the research options must stand out strongly against regular search engines),
- unified knowledge organization systems (thesauri, classification systems etc.) in restricted thematic areas (across the borders of singular bibliographic databases),
- synergies between bibliographical databases, full texts and facts.

Hosts bank on strategic alliances with their suppliers and, partly, with customers (which are asked for their expertise during product development), but also on **cooperation with competitors** (Stock & Stock, 2004a). Only in cooperation is it possible, in some areas of this niche market, to create marketable products in the first place. Joint venture partners, such as the FIZ Karlsruhe and the Chemical Abstracts Service (CAS), make up the STM host STN International in cooperation with the Japan Association for International Chemical Information (JAICI). FIZ Karlsruhe and CAS distribute their own respective databases via STN (apart from various third-party products), CAS with its *Chemical Abstracts* and FIZ Karlsruhe with its own smaller databases. The STN interfaces are very elaborate and address both information professionals (with STN on the Web or the client software STN Express) and professional end users (with STN Easy) at the same time. With the end user product *SciFinder*, CAS markets its *Chemical Abstracts* all over again, past STN, and thus becomes a competitor (especially of STN Easy). For the weaker partner–in this case FIZ Karlsruhe–such a combination of partner and competitor can become a serious burden.

10.4 Conclusion

- Access to documents on the Surface Web is granted by search engines. These are either directed to broad Web user groups (general search engines, like Google) or to users with specific information needs (specialist search engines, like Google Scholar).
- For providers of websites, it is essential to be found by search engines. When relevant search arguments are used, one's own site should be displayed as high up as possible on the hit list (ideally in first place). Search engine marketing means either Search Engine Optimization or Sponsored Search.
- Search Engine Optimization means the design of a website (text, entries in meta-tags, layout) in such a way that the algorithms of information linguistics and Relevance Ranking used in the search tool are able to correctly index the content of the site. We distinguish between on-site optimization (measures applied to one's own site) and off-site optimization (linking of one's own site in the context of the entire WWW). Specialized service providers can be consulted for search engine optimization.
- For those companies that run search engines, it is essential to bind large user groups to themselves by providing a free offer of popular general and specialized research tools. Their attention is marketed to advertising customers in the context of Sponsored Links.
- In the Deep Web, there are thousands of domain-specific databases, which are bundled by Content Aggregators (also called online hosts). Hosts summarize the most diverse databases under one search interface and one retrieval system. Hosts market both their content as well as their research services (generally in the high-price segment).
- Suppliers of online hosts are publishers, providers of bibliographic databases as well as libraries (as document delivery services); their customers are mainly companies and public administrations. B-to-C business models are not successful.

10.5 Bibliography

Bergman, M.K. (2001). The Deep Web: Surfacing hidden value. JED–The Journal of Electronic Publishing 7(1).

Bieletzki, C., & Roth, K. (1998). Online-Hosts in Öffentlichen Bibliotheken. Neue Nutzer–neue Märkte. Köln: FH Köln. (Kölner Arbeitspapiere zur Bibliotheks- und Informationswissenschaft; 12).

Bock, A. (2000). Gütezeichen als Qualitätsaussage im digitalen Informationsmarkt, dargestellt am Beispiel elektronischer Rechtsdatenbanken. Darmstadt: STMV S. Toeche-Mittler.

Google (2009). Annual Report for the Fiscal Year Ended December 31, 2009. Google Inc. Washington, DC: United States Securities and Exchange Commission. Form 10-K.

Kremer, S. (2004). Die großen Fünf. Professionelle Online-Dienste für Juristen im Test. JurPC, Web-Dok., 205/2004.

Sherman, C., & Price, G. (2001). The Invisible Web. Medford, NJ: Information Today.

Stock, M., & Stock, W.G. (2003). Online-Hosts für Wirtschaft und News auf dem deutschen Informationsmarkt. Eine komparative Analyse. Password, N° 7/8, 29-34.

Stock, M., & Stock, W.G. (2004a). Kooperation und Konkurrenz auf Märkten elektronischer Informationsdienste: Mit dem Wettbewerber zusammenarbeiten? Password, N° 1, 20-25.

Stock, M., & Stock, W.G. (2004b). Kritische Erfolgsfaktoren von Anbietern elektronischer Informationsdienste. Password, N° 4, 16-22.

Stock, M., & Stock, W.G. (2004c). Recherchieren im Internet. Renningen: Expert.

Stock, M., & Stock, W.G. (2005). Online-Hosts für Wissenschaft, Technik und Medizin auf dem deutschen Informationsmarkt. Eine komparative Analyse. Password, N° 2, 18-23.

Stock, M., & Stock, W.G. (2006). Intellectual property information. A comparative analysis of main information providers. Journal of the American Society for Information Science and Technology, 57(13), 1794-1803.

Stock, W.G. (2007). Information Retrieval. Informationen suchen und finden. München, Wien: Oldenbourg.

Von Bischopinck, Y., & Ceyp, M. (2007). Suchmaschinen-Marketing. Konzepte, Umsetzung und Controlling. Berlin: Springer.

Chapter 11

Web 2.0 Services

11.1 Social Software

In the early 21st century, services in the World Wide Web develop which are predicated upon the active participation of broad masses of users. The keyword for such services has come to be accepted as "**Web 2.0**" (O'Reilly, 2005). This should not be regarded as akin to an update number, as of software, but rather as signifying the growing importance of the WWW after the collapse of the "first" internet economy (O'Reilly & Batelle, 2009). The focus of Web 2.0 is the hoped-for or actual intelligence of the masses. Tim O'Reilly and John Batelle (2009, 1) define:

> Web 2.0 is all about harnessing collective intelligence. Collective intelligence applications depend on managing, understanding, and responding to massive amounts of user-generated data in real-time.

The term "Web 2.0" is a hyperonym of "social software", the corresponding technical basis (such as Ajax or RSS) and the information-legally significant aspect of open access (such as Copyleft or Creative Commons) (Peters, 2009, 15).

In Web 2.0 services, the user acts both as producer of information and as its consumer–a role that Toffler (1980) described as that of the "**prosumer**". The kinds of information thus produced are various; they range from short biographical statements (e.g. on Facebook), films (YouTube) and images (Flickr) up to one's personal genome (e.g. in 23andMe, a genetics company tied to Google, which executes genome analyses for customers and wants to make the data–which is first rendered anonymous–available to scientific research (Prainsack & Wolinsky, 2010).

How can Web 2.0 be evaluated from a sociological perspective? Collectives are, following Tönnies (1887), either societies or communities. If the individual orients himself by the collective and shares its goals or purposes, we have a "community". In a "society", the individual tries to achieve his own personal goals or purposes. Prosumers in Web 2.0 are characterized by shared goals (e.g. to create a comprehensive encyclopedia in Wikipedia, or to make images available for use by the collective on Flickr), which means that what we have is a **commu-nity**. Since these activities principally take place online, they are "virtual com-munities" or "online communities". Long before the advent of Web 2.0, Rhein-gold (1993, 5) defined:

> Virtual communities are social aggregations that emerge from the Net
> when enough people carry on those public discussions long enough,
> with sufficient human feeling, to form webs of personal relationships in
> cyberspace.

In online communities, it is not to be expected that its members share the work-load equally. Rather, the opposite is the case: very few (let us say: 1% of the community) are responsible for a large part of activities (e.g. writing articles for Wikipedia), a few (roughly 9%) collaborate by contributing small services (e.g. correcting Wikipedia entries), and the majority of members (i.e. the remaining 90%) are mostly users, or "lurkers", following Jakob Nielsen (2006).

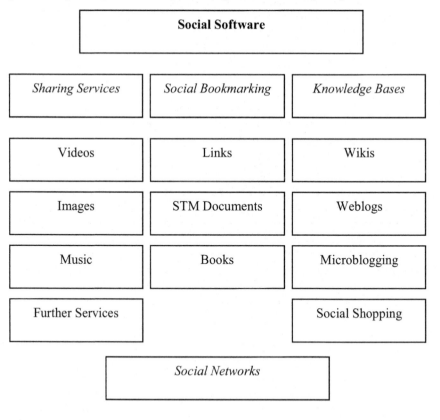

Figure 11.1: Classification of Web 2.0 Services.

We speak of "**social software**" if there are information services in which the prosumers (and not the "lurkers") form a virtual community. In many cases, of course, others can also profit from these services. We distinguish, roughly, between four classes of social software (Figure 11.1):

- Sharing Services allow for the depositing, online, of certain types of resources (such as videos or images), thus sharing them with others,
- Social Bookmarking Services serve the management (one's own as well as others') of any (Web) resources of one's choosing,
- Knowledge Bases create collections of documents, which are made available to others–some of them in real time,
- Social Networks are, in their narrow definition, platforms for communicating with other members of the community.

Since the resources always carry statements about their producers (such as their real name or a pseudonym), all sorts of social software allow for the construction of networks between the parties involved, i.e. social networks in their broad definition.

Social networks, broadly defined, have two manifestations. On the one hand, prosumers collaborate directly (digitally, which means that they do not have to know each other in person) and create a shared product. The paradigm of this form is a Wiki: an author writes a first draft of an article, a second author adds something, a third corrects a detail, which is deleted again by the first, etc., until the article temporarily "stands". We call this "collaborative intelligence", following Vander Wal (2008). In the second manifestation, prosumers act independently of each other. A clear example of this is provided by the bookmarking service del.icio.us. Here, users tag Web documents with keywords of their own choosing, everybody for himself. In their totality, these tags form "typical" distributions, which allows the system to distinguish important keywords from unimportant ones. This is what is called "collective intelligence" (Peters, 2009, 166-170), which is the exclusive result of (e.g. statistical) algorithms. Only in this way–thus Peters (2009, 169)–is the "wisdom of crowds", and nothing else, at play. This is in contrast to collaborative intelligence, which can also (under bad circumstances) mutate into the "madness of crowds". Surowiecki (2005, 10) names four criteria that tendentially preclude the madness of crowds: diversity of opinion (each individual should have his or her own subjective background information), independence (each person acts independently of all others), decentralization (the individuals are spatially separated from each others and can thus bring in local knowledge) and aggregation (the algorithmic processing of single pieces of information mentioned above). However, there is no guarantee that this will result in a wisdom of crowds. "One cannot simply state that a definition is incorrect only because it is hardly used", Spyns et al. (2006, 745) point out. All information gleaned from social software services thus require a critical examination.

All **business models** in Web 2.0 presuppose free usage of the platforms. Only sporadically are costs incurred by the users for premium offers, which provide services that exceed the standard applications' by far. A source of income for providers of lucrative databases lies in the licensing of their content for search engines. For the microblogging service Twitter, the provision of its database for use in Bing and Google represents its main source of income (Talbot, 2010). Occasionally, donations improve the financial basis of a platform (e.g. for Wikipedia). A method that is used almost continuously is the marketing of users' attention via advertising, in the form of both context-specific (the superimposed ads match the search request or the displayed content) and context-independent ads (e.g. banners that are displayed in certain areas of the screen with no relation to the specific content on show).

11.2   File-Sharing Services

We distinguish sharing services by their type of document: we will provide an example of a service for each type. Selecting such a paradigmatic service was not hard, as the markets tend to be dominated by one single platform:

- videos (YouTube),
- images (Flickr),
- music (Last.fm),
- further services.

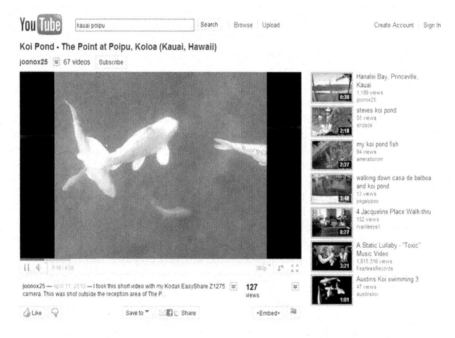

Figure 11.2: Display of a Video on YouTube.

11.2.1 Video on Demand

YouTube (a subsidiary of Google) is a platform for videos, in which the prosumers can upload (original as well as third-party) content (Peters, 2009, 80-87). YouTube accepts various media formats for uploads, but the clips are always played back in Adobe's Flash Video Format (FLV) (Figure 11.2). Every Web user can view the videos; uploading, rating or commenting, though, is only possible after registration, by creating one's own "channel". Apart from a few older or certain specifically designated accounts, users are not allowed to upload videos that are longer than ten minutes or larger than 2 GB. The average clip length is four minutes (calculated from a sample), the average rating (from a maximum of five stars) is relatively good for most productions, with an average of 4 (Gill et al., 2007). The videos are either created by the prosumers themselves or taken from other sources (legally or–in terms of copyright–illegally). Sometimes, films are uploaded to YouTube multiple times, which leads to duplicates. Even audio content that is already available elsewhere can be found on YouTube, occasionally enhanced with original animation. The work is done by laymen as well as professional media enterprises (Kruitbosch & Nack, 2008). The films are described, content-wise, by the uploader–and no-one else–with a title, a short description and tags, in the sense of a Narrow Folksonomy.

On the user side, there is a massive selection of videos. The first 10% of clips (arranged by views) make up for a total of 80% of all clicks, so that usage of the resources is distributed with an extreme slant to the left. This typical power-law distribution is explained by the well-known Matthew Principle ("the rich get richer, the poor get poorer"). 90% of the videos are viewed at least once on their upload date; 40% even get more than ten views. If a clip does not manage to be viewed enough times in its first few days, it is improbable that it will grow popular in the future (Cha et al., 2007).

Prosumers' interaction on YouTube–be it via video posts, reciprocal comments or lists of subscribers and friends–creates communities (Rotman, Golbeck, & Preece, 2009). In such social networks, defined broadly, two tendencies can be detected (Lange, 2007): in the first variant ("publicly private"), the author reveals his identity (by stating his real name), whereas in the second variant ("privately public"), the emphasis is on anonymity.

11.2.2 Images

Flickr is a sharing service for digital images and is operated by Yahoo! (Peters, 2009, 69-80). Registered prosumers upload their photos to Flickr, choose their status (only private, only for friends or family and publicly, as the standard, respectively), put them into photostreams (if they wish to do so) and index them via tags of their own choosing (as well as–for photos regarding specific locations–with geotags, i.e. latitude and longitude data). Friends can add further tags, which makes Flickr's method of knowledge representation an Extended Narrow Folksonomy. Camera information (such as type of camera or time and date of photography) is adopted and saved automatically. It is also possible to place images into thematically oriented "groups". The service is used by both laymen and professional photographers. Flickr can also be used for one's own, exclusively private purposes, e.g. for organizing one's photos and sending them only to certain other persons (if at all). Flickr's API (Application Programming Interface) is used frequently in order to embed resources saved there in other services, as mash-ups (combinations of content from various different sources). Thus, one can enter suitable photos, as sights, for display on a service for maps (such as Google Maps).

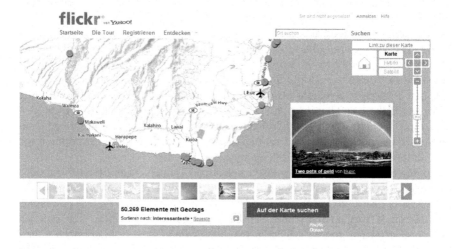

Figure 11.3: Research for Geographically Relevant Images on Flickr via Map and Geotags.

Quantitatively, Flickr must be regarded as a success, in the face of its gigantic amount of resources (several billion photos). However, the majority of images is viewed, or commented, very seldomly (Cox, 2008). Similarly to YouTube, it is very few resources that are viewed very often, which means that here, too, the predominance of a power law is demonstrated impressively. All images will reach their maximum number of views per day after around two days. The (eventually) successful images are discovered as early as three hours after being uploaded, which is mainly due to the uploader's networking. Van Zwol (2007, 190) reports: "People that are highly interconnected will have their photos viewed many times". If an image manages to be viewed very often, this will be due to users around the globe. Less successful images (less than 50 views over 50 days) only appeal to viewers from one geographic area (Van Zwol, 2007).

A special search option is the use of maps. Here, images with geotags, or whose (language) tags specify a location, can be researched by clicking on the map (Figure 11.3). A further usage option provided by photos' sense of place is represented by the informetric compression of spatial information. Thus, for instance, the most-photographed metropoles (at the moment: New York City), or the most photographed sights in a metropolitan area (e.g. the "Cloud Gate" sculpture in Chicago) can be named (Crandal et al., 2009). In this way, representative images for a region can be created, or the photographers' movements be charted (via the time of creation of photographs with geographic information). The latter is used for the discovery of typical tourists' routes: "One can even see the route of the ferries that take tourists from Lower Manhattan to the Statue of Liberty" (Crandall et al., 2009).

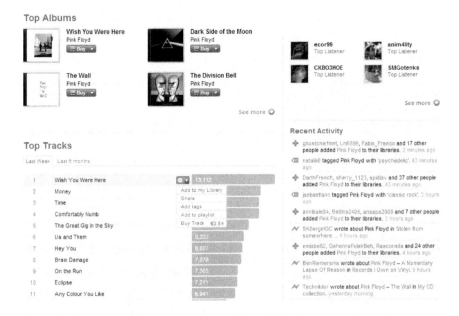

Figure 11.4: Display of Albums, Tracks, Listeners and Current Information as the Result of a Search for Pink Floyd on Last.fm.

11.2.3   Music

Even though not every user can upload music on this platform, **Last.fm** (belonging to CBS) is still a typical Web 2.0 service (Peters, 2009, 49-55). Artists and record labels are invited to make their music available for broad usage, all others participate via content descriptions or comments ("shots") (Haupt, 2009). Last.fm is thus a file-sharing service for **music** as well as an internet radio (as signified by the domain ".fm", which designates the website of the London-based company as originating in the Federated States of Micronesia). Prosumers' tags are often genre descriptions. As each user may re-allocate already used tags, this is a Broad Folksonomy, which allows for a ranking of the resources via number of tags. This fact, and the number of music titles listened to, provide the criteria for arranging hit lists. Thus, in Figure 11.4, we see displays for albums and single tracks arranged by popularity. If available, a suitable YouTube clip will be played as a mash-up feature. An aspect of social networks (in the broad definition) lies in the recommendation, based on a user's preferences (music played, tags allocated etc.) of other, similar users, which facilitates personal contact. The most important aspect, though, is discovering new good music.

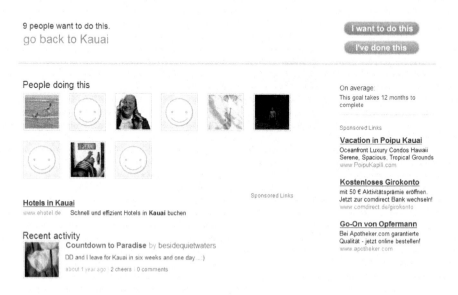

Figure 11.5: Display of Users on 43Things with the Goal of Returning to Kauai at Some Point. Displayed on the Right: Context-Specific Ads.

11.2.4   Further File-Sharing Services

A very specific sort of "resource" is managed collaboratively on **43Things**: personal **goals** and the ways of reaching them (Peters, 2009, 90-95). The users upload to-do lists (with a maximum of 43 goals) to the platform; if they are accomplished, this can also be stated (Smith & Lieberman, 2010). In Figure 11.5, we learn that nine people pursue the goal of returning to Kauai, and that they have taken this step after twelve months on average. On 43Things, it is less the saving and sharing of resources which is at the center of attention, but the creation of virtual communities based on certain goals.

From the multitude of further sharing services, we will point to the collaborative compilation of an **event calendar** (Upcoming) and the selection of **news** (Digg or Reddit).

11.3   Social Bookmarking

Social Bookmarking services collect prosumers' **bookmarks** in one single plat-form (Peters, 2009, 23-36). For the individual, this has the advantage of being able to manage his bookmarks outside of his own computer; for the community, this collection of resources represents a search tool with intellectually indexed content for Web documents and–depending on the service–for printed resources. We dis-tinguish between general Social Bookmarking platforms with no domain-specific restrictions (Hammond et al., 2005) and services for scientific resources. Among general platforms, a standard service has already established itself in del.icio.us, whereas several scientific bookmarking services are in co-existence.

11.3.1   Bookmarking in General

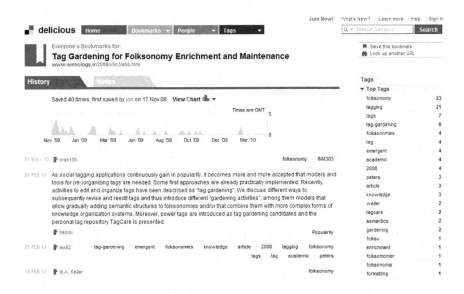

Figure 11.6: Hit List with Trend Information on Indexing Date and a List of Tags Used on Del.icio.us.

Del.icio.us, a Yahoo! company, allows registered prosumers to collect and man-age their bookmarks (Peters, 2010, 26-30). Since every prosumer may tag any re-source multiple times, this is a Broad Folksonomy, the statistical analysis of which impressively demonstrates Collective Intelligence. In the example in Figure 11.6, we see a classic example of an inverse-logistical distribution for the list of tags ar-ranged by frequency: two terms (*folksonomy* and *tagging*) dominate the entire list pretty evenly, serving as "power tags" (Peters & Stock, 2010). A few tags lie in the vicinity of the curve's turning point (*tags, tag-gardening*), after which begins the "long tail" of entries that are used very seldomly to describe the content of this resource. The list also shows some problems of folksonomies. Entries such as *peters* or *weller* refer to the authors, *2008* to the year of publication and *article* to the document type–none of which are characteristics that represent the content. In the broad column on the left, all tagging prosumers are displayed with all of the tags they have used (in descending chronological order), so that the user is able to click on other users as well as on other tags.

Social Bookmarking is a complement to algorithmically operating **search engines** (Lewandowski & Maaß, eds., 2008). While the latter process far larger amounts of documents due to their automatic processes, Social Bookmarking services have advantages for particularly active sites (those where the content is often changed) as well as new resources that have so far remained hidden to the search engines (Heymann, Koutrika, & Garcia-Molina, 2008).

11.3.2   STM Bookmarking

Bookmarks for **STM literature** (Reher & Haustein, 2010) are managed, among others, by

- BibSonomy (independent) (Hotho et al., 2006),
- CiteULike (with support by Springer) (Emamy & Cameron, 2007),
- Connotea (run by the Nature Publishing Group) (Lund et al., 2005),
- 2collab (run by Elsevier) (Liu & Wu, 2009).

With the exception of BibSonomy, the STM bookmarking services are produced, or at least supported, by the big scientific publishers. These services work analogously to del.icio.us, i.e. allow the saving and tagging of URLs (here: of scientific-technical-medical literature). Many scientific journals provide users with the option of storing an article, whose bibliographic citations are currently being viewed, on Social Bookmarking services "with one click of the mouse", provided the prosumer has an account with the service in question. Here, the article's entire metadata (magazine title, DOI, statements on volume and page numbers etc.) are adopted automatically. Entering the metadata–even of non-digital documents–manually is also an option (e.g. on BibSonomy).

Among the scientific bookmarking services, none has asserted itself as the standard as of yet (mid-2010), allowing us to observe a "combat zone" (Figure 11.7). At the beginning of or time series, all four platforms we observed were on pretty much the same, very low, level. Then, CiteULike was able to pull clear temporarily, but remained at its new level until mid-2010, while Connotea and BibSonomy steadily increased their usage and moved past CiteULike. 2collab was not able to significantly increase its usage figures over the entire time span. Critical mass, apparently, has not been reached by any of the platforms (for contrast: in Alexa's statistic, del.icio.us is positioned above Conotea and BibSonomy by one decimal place, with a value of more than 0.01% of all page views).

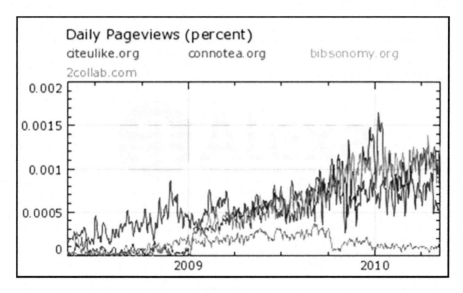

Figure 11.7: Relative Frequencies of Site Views of CiteULike, Connotea, BibSonomy and 2collab between Mid-2009 and Mid-2010. Source: Alexa.

11.3.3 Collective Compilation of a Library Catalog

Beside the digital world, there exists the realm of printed resources. The management and content description of books is granted by the platform **LibraryThing** (Peters, 2009, 61-68). LibraryThing is an electronic catalog, known from actual libraries, only that the "library" here only exists virtually and that prosumers (not librarians) do all the work. Here, too, Collective Intelligence is used via a Broad Folksonomy. The cataloguing of up to 200 books is free for private individuals as well as companies, with (small) charges being incurred for any more resources than that. The (commercial) version for libraries (LibraryThing for Libraries) permits a mash-up of the local catalog with information from LibraryThing. From the librarians' perspective, such a procedure has been described as "helpful", as the tags provide new access paths to resources and additionally recommend the user similar books to the ones he searches for (Westcott, Chappell, & Lebel, 2009).

The use of Social Bookmarking services is very cheap in comparison with commercial cataloguing or documentation software. As a consequence of the **"digital divide"**, there are countries in the world whose information facilities and library systems do not work very effectively. The use of proprietary software is hardly an option, purely for economic reasons. Trkulja (2010) expressly recommends such countries to use Social Bookmarking, e.g. BibSonomy (for representing the content of scientific articles produced in those countries) and LibraryThing (for cataloguing the books available in their libraries).

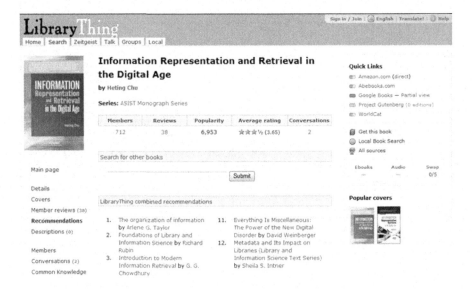

Figure 11.8: Recommendations of Similar Resources on the Basis of a Search Result on LibraryThing.

11.4   Collaborative Construction of a Knowledge Base

We now come to the collaborative services. These do not deal–as collective platforms do–with the statistical processing of single pieces of information, but with the actual collaboration between members of a community with the goal of collaboratively working out a common knowledge base. We distinguish the following four approaches to reaching such a goal:

- Wikis (Wikipedia),
- Weblogs (Blogger, WordPress) as well as search engines for blogs (such as Technorati),
- Microblogging (Twitter),
- Others; among them recommender services and further collaborative services in e-commerce, such as "Social Shopping" (Grange & Benbasat, 2010), which we will not address here, however, and which do not figure among i-commerce.

11.4.1 Wiki

A **Wiki** (Hawaiian for *fast*) collects–similarly to an encyclopedia–articles on concepts and entities, while providing users with the option of continuously editing these articles. There is a mass of domain-specific wikis, the most famous of which being the domain-spanning internet encyclopedia **Wikipedia**. Wikipedia is structured according to language; within the linguistic areas, articles range from thousands to hundreds of thousands in number. The German version of Wikipedia contains 1.1m articles as of mid-2010, while the English-language variant already boasts 3.3m entries. The authors remain anonymous; everybody can work on the articles and discuss their evolution up to date. According to Wikipedia's editing policy, no new (research) results are published; instead, existing knowledge about a subject is compiled and backed up via sources. Adherence to these criteria is guaranteed by (equally anonymous) "editors". Collaboration is (relatively) simple; from a technical point of view, it merely requires rudimentary knowledge of HTML. Many templates facilitate the formatting work. A typical Wikipedia entry is shown in Figure 11.9.

Figure 11.9: Entry on "Cloud Gate" on Wikipedia.

Can the user rely on the veracity of the statements in the articles? A small sample of articles on scientific subjects displayed an error rate that was only insubstantially above that of the established "Encyclopaedia Britannica" (Giles, 2005). Neither do further comparative studies–e.g. with the German "Brockhaus" encyclopedia–result in evidence of any serious flaws in Wikipedia's content (Hammwöhner, 2007). However, gaps–and blatant ones at that–can be detected in the way the statements are supported. This concerns both the number of references as well as the selection of sources backing up the specified data. Luyt and Tan (2010, 721) report:

> Not only are many claims not verified through citations, those that are suffer from the choice of references used. Many of these are from US government Websites or news media and few are to academic journal material.

However, it is an open question as to what constitutes information quality in the first place. Stvilia et al. (2008) thus do not refer to individual specific quality dimensions (such as the citations mentioned above), but evaluate the way Wikipedia's quality assurance is organized. They arrive at a positive result (Stvilia et al., 2008, 1000):

> Results of the study showed that the Wikipedia community takes issues of quality very seriously. Although anyone can participate in editing articles, the results are carefully reviewed and discussed in ways very similar to open source programming projects.

What must be emphasized is the open discussion on revisions to articles, which can be viewed, with no restrictions, by every reader–this is a significant difference to traditional encyclopedias, where nothing is reported on the selection and editing of their entries. Haider and Sundin (2010) describe this open discourse as a "remediation" of the genre of encyclopedias:

> This remediation brings with it a change of site and the encyclopaedic notion is transferred from its personification in the printed book to being a space in which people meet, quarrel, negotiate and collaborately build knowledge.

In traditional encyclopedias, there is selection (if only for reasons of space), which is why only particular, or "top-priority" (Anger, 2002, 41) knowledge, and no specialist knowledge, is included. Thus it was "something special" to be included in the Brockhaus. This has been left out of Wikipedia. In the English version of Wikipedia, we find–as we do in the Brockhaus, or the Encyclopaedia Britannica–an entry on *Chicago*, but there is also an extensive entry on *Midway (CTA)*, a subway station of the Orange Line in Chicago (e.g. with the information that there are 299 parking spaces available). Where readers of printed encyclopedias had to wait for the next edition in order to learn new knowledge, this happens almost in real time on Wikipedia; knowledge is processed and made retrievable quickly (hence *wiki*).

In view of these assessments, it is hardly surprising that in a survey of students, 100% of those asked admitted to using Wikipedia. These students are, for the most part, aware of the risk of possible misinformation (Denning, et al., 2005) and do not "blindly" trust the entries, instead using them as their entry point into a new subject matter in order to then research further (possibly more reliable) material (Lim, 2009). Scientists also use Wikipedia, as well as other wikis. In a survey by Weller et al. (2010), a total of 6.3% of respondents stated that they did not consult wikis. Concerning their motives, the researchers state (Weller, et al., 2010):

> (O)f those participants who use wikis or Wikipedia 78.3% stated to use 'Wikipedia as a work of reference', 17.0% use wikis for 'knowledge organization within working groups' and 22.6% for 'personal knowledge management', 4.7% claimed to use wikis for collaborative editing of publications and finally 30.2% use Wikipedia for 'checking students' texts for plagiarism' (another 1.9% 'other purposes').

11.4.2   Blogs

Weblogs are sites on the World Wide Web with single entries (posts) that are arranged in descending chronological order. These posts have a fixed URL (permalink), which is sometimes created for each individual post or for the entire blog (with a jump label to the individual post). If a post is discussed on another blog, this will be recorded on the cited post as a trackback. It is possible to allow comments on one's posts. Users are offered the option of subscribing to blogs (e.g. via RSS or Atom Feeds), so that they will be informed of the latest posts as they are published. There are platforms on the Web (such as Blogger or WordPress) that facilitate the publishing of weblogs. The totality of all weblogs is called the "blogosphere". Blogs represent a genre on the internet, which has established itself between the medial form of a fixed website and computer-mediated communication (e.g. via e-mail or instant messaging) (Herring et al., 2004). Blogs and posts are researchable via specialist search engines such as Technorati (Peters, 2009, 96-100) or Google Blogs.

We separate weblogs analytically into four classes:

- personal blogs (documentation of daily life in the sense of a diary, posting of private comments, "outlet" for thoughts or feelings or even artistic contributions, like poetry or prose; Nardi et al., 2004),
- blogs by companies and other institutions (PR campaigns on behalf of the company or individual products, e.g. "Frosta-Blog"; blogs by political parties or individual politicians, e.g. the "Obama Blog"),
- political blogs (blogs with political content, occasionally–especially in countries with authoritarian governments–with highly critical views),

- professional blogs (thematically oriented contributions aimed at a professional audience, e.g. "resource shelf" as a blog for information professionals).

Figure 11.10: Post on the Professional Weblog "resource shelf".

Professional blogs (for an example, see Figure 11.10) play a role that is not to be underestimated in the communication of the respective communities, as Bar-Ilan (2005, 305) observed:

> 'Professional' blogs are excellent sources of secondary and tertiary information. Most information (...) can be easily found elsewhere, but these blogs concentrate and filter it, and they can be viewed as one-stop information kiosks or information hubs. The postings are mainly on information appearing in other weblogs, news items and press releases. Often, in addition to pointing to information sources, the bloggers provide commentary and express their opinion on the issues at hand.

Within the blogosphere, the information contained in the posts is deemed pretty much uniformly credible–even more so than other sources, such as newspapers, television and radio (Johnson & Kaye, 2004). The blogosphere's evaluation with regard to the individual's participation in society (as required by Critical Theory, for instance) is divided. Jürgen Habermas, as the main advocate of Critical Theory, gives the blogosphere a negative assessment, as he regards weblogs to play "a parasitical role of online communication" (Habermas, 2006, 423), which contributes to the fragmentation of the public sphere. Fuchs (2008, 134) makes out dangers in blogs run by companies and political institutions:

> This shows that Web 2.0 can be incorporated into big politics (as well as big business) that can result in a destruction of its participatory potentials. In such cases, Web 2.0 is colonized in the Habermasian sense of the word by power and money.

Kline and Burstein (2005, XIV), on the other hand, bank on the "participatory potential" of weblogs, as blogging can move others to participate: "to restoring the lost voice of the ordinary citizen in our culture".

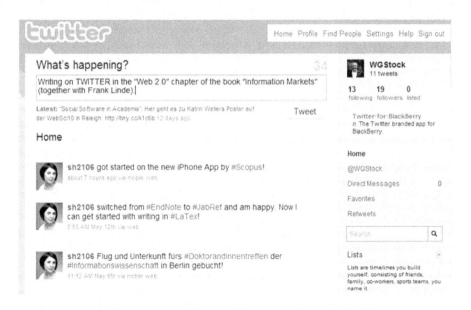

Figure 11.11: Homepage on Twitter with Current Tweets.

11.4.3 Microblogging

A variant form of blogging is **microblogging**, represented most prominently by **Twitter**. Every registered prosumer is able to send messages ("tweets") (restricted to 140 characters) from his computer or cell phone. One can "follow" other users (thus becoming their "follower") and is shown their tweets. If a user wants to send a message to a certain recipient in person, ha can also do so (via @user) (the public can see these tweets too, though). (Purely private tweets are sent as "direct messages") The ratio of personal @-tweets is around 25% of all posts (Huberman, Romero, & Wu, 2009). Occasionally, there are efforts toward establishing a controlled vocabulary. In order to always give a concept (let us say a conference or a product) the same name, "hashtags" are used (as in Figure 11.11 #Scopus). The counterpart to the forwarding of e-mails is called "retweeting" on Twitter (Boyd, Golder, & Lotan, 2010).

Twitter's advantage is the shortness of posts, which means a very low effort is required on the part of both the author and his followers (Zhao & Rosson, 2009). However, one can always incorporate a link into one's tweet. "The ability to include links in a post means that richer content is only a click away" (Martens, 2010, 149). The flexible content is regarded as another advantage, as all that is required (apart from laptop and cell phone) is an internet connection. The use of mobile end devices makes Twitter a very fast medium of information distribution.

As searches on Twitter itself are suboptimal, and less than the entire database is made available for research, one has to take recourse to search engines (such as Bing or Google), which process both the current tweets as well as Twitter's entire public archive. The contents of Twitter are also saved by the Library of Congress.

The four classes of blogs can also be detected in microblogging. Mainka (2010) demonstrates this for microblogs run by companies and political parties, which means that here, too, there is a partial kind of "colonization" of Web 2.0 with the aid of money and power. Professional microblogs, for example, can be observed in scientific conferences (Letierce et al., 2010). From time to time, there are two discussions during and after lectures, one taking place in the room, the other on Twitter. Statements regarded as important are distributed in real time, lecturers refer to their set of slides on Slideshare, to their blog posts or to the lecture's full text in the proceedings, and there is the occasional lunch or dinner date.

Twitter, too, is a medium of social networking in the broader sense. The precise statements on followers and followees make it relatively easy to create graphs of communities via network analysis, which emphasize the role of the individual prosumers very clearly. Java et al. (2007) work with the algorithms on hubs and authorities known in information retrieval to determine the status of a single agent (Kleinberg, 1999; see Stock, 2007, 375-382); an alternative is Google's PageRank (Stock, 2007, 382-386). The basis of Java et al.'s calculations are the number of followers (to determine the degree of authority) as well as the number of followees (manifestation of the hub). As in the Kleinberg algorithm, analog calculations are performed for followers and followees. For an authority, it is thus not only of importance how many users follow them, but also *who* follows (a follower with, say, 1,000 followers of his own is thus more important than one with only 10).

11.5   Social Networks

Social networks in the narrow definition serve the user's self-representation on personal sites, the nurturing of social relationships as well as other (partly collaborative) activities (such as games). Boyd and Ellison (2007) define the term as follows:

> We define social network sites as web-based services that allow individuals to (1) construct a public or semi-public profile within a bounded system, (2) articulate a list of other users with whom they share a connection, and (3) view and traverse their lists of connections and those made by others within the system.

We will distinguish general social networks from interest-led networks. In general networks, there are country-specific platforms (e.g. VKontakte in Russia or studiVZ in Germany), but international domination—even at the cost of the national versions—has been achieved by Facebook. For interest-led communities, MySpace music is a very prevalent service.

11.5.1   General Social Networks

On **Facebook**, prosumers create a site about themselves, which can be accessed either by all or only by "friends". A friend relationship in this sense is always mutual, which means that requests must be explicitly accepted. In addition to the personal sites, one can also create sites of which users become "fans" (see Figure 11.12). The fan relationship is one-sided; it does not have to be confirmed. Facebook allows the posting of messages to a user's "wall", the uploading of photos or video clips and the commenting of friends' activities. On the sites of one's friends, one can find a complete list of their respective friends and a highlighted subset of mutual friends. There are various applications, particularly games (Rao, 2008), such as Farmville. The majority of users visits "their" social network once or several times a day (Khveshchanka & Suter, 2010, 74).

Motives for participating in general social networks include the nurturing of social contacts and simply the fact that they are fun to use. There are users "who are looking for fun and pleasure while 'hanging around' on the WWW" (Hart et al., 2008, 474). Social contacts are established in independence of geographical constraints. This also has repercussions in the non-digital world, as Ellison, Steinfield and Lampe (2007) report:

> The strong linkage between Facebook use and high school connections suggests how SNSs (Social Network Services, A/N) help maintain relations as people move from one offline community to another. It may facilitate the same when students graduate from college, with alumni keeping their school email address and using Facebook to stay in touch

with the college community. Such connections could have strong pay-offs in terms of jobs, internships, and other opportunities.

Informationswissenschaft Heinrich Heine Uni Düsseldorf Düsseldorfer
Studenten der Informationswissenschaft halten auf Hawaii Fachvorträge

Zum 43. Mal fand im Januar 2010 die renommierte Hawaii International Conference
on System Sciences statt. Sie gilt als ein Mega-Event bei Informationsspezialisten.
Diesmal trafen sich rund 800 Wissenschaftler aus über 30 Ländern zum Erfah...
Mehr anzeigen

27. Januar um 15:26 · Kommentieren · Gefällt mir · Teilen

Nils Werner, Katrin Weller und Kochanek Rafael gefällt das.

Schreibe einen Kommentar ...

Informationswissenschaft Heinrich Heine Uni Düsseldorf Düsseldorfer
Studenten der Informationswissenschaft halten auf Hawaii Fachvorträge.

HICSS Hawaii 2010
9 neue Fotos

27. Januar um 15:14 · Kommentieren · Gefällt mir nicht mehr · Teilen

Dir und Katrin Weller gefällt das.

Figure 11.12: Extract from the Fansite of the University of Düsseldorf's Department of Information Science on Facebook.

What circumstances would move users to switch social networks? On the pull side, the influence of peer groups dominates; a significant push factor is represented by dissatisfaction with usage conditions (Zengyan, Yinping, & Lim, 2009). Users stay faithful to Facebook if they are happy, with this happiness depending on their expectations being exceeded by the platform (i.e. if there is positive disconfirmation). Shi et al. (2010) were able to determine stay factors:

The findings suggest that the positive disconfirmations of maintaining offline contacts, information seeking and entertainment all significantly affect users' continuance intention to use Facebook which are mediated by their satisfaction with Facebook.

Regarded as a problem is the lack of **privacy**–the publishing of private and rather confidential personal statements. Young users in particular, and those who seek a relationship, tend to put highly sensitive and potentially stigmatizing information (such as their sexual orientation or religious beliefs) on Facebook (Nosko, Wood, & Molema, 2010). In contrast with German studiVZ users, American Facebook users are more aware that any published personal information can be misinterpreted or otherwise used to the publisher's disadvantage (Krasnova & Veltri, 2010, 5). However, this does not prevent them from revealing more information than their German counterparts (Krasnova & Veltri, 2010, 9). In a detailed analysis of the publication of private data on social networks, Khveshchanka and Suter (2010, 74) found out that American users show their photos on their site in 92% of cases, whereas the figures for Russian and German users are 72% and 53%, respectively.

Facebook has functions that are also offered by other Web 2.0 services: the user can upload photos or videos and communicate with others. We thus have a case of competition between the platforms of social software.

11.5.2 Interest-Led Networks

There are further social networks, which mainly cater to their users' common interests. Thus there is Xing for business contacts or **MySpace** for music. Prosumers occasionally use different networks for different purposes, e.g. Xing for professional interests, Facebook to communicate with friends and MySpace to promote their band.

In the case of MySpace Music, Rossi and Teli (2009) speak of a "virtual scene" instead of an online community. MySpace Music is used by both established artists and unknown (so far) bands. Smaller bands (Figure 11.13) benefit from the fact that songs can be uploaded without an accompanying video. On the profile pages, there are statements about the artists, music titles can be played back (with or without a video), there are blogs and notes on upcoming gigs. Friendships are– as on Facebook–bilateral. "Top Friends" are a handpicked amount of (up to) 40 people, whose names are displayed ("normal" friends are not listed). For musicians, there are advantages to participating in MySpace (Antin & Earp, 2010, 954):

Participating in MySpace Music has the potential to convey a variety of benefits on musicians. Musicians are likely to use MySpace Music to explore musical styles, to find new music and collaborators, to organize gigs, and form communities around musical genres or geographic locations.

For top artists, a correlation can be detected between their number of friends on MySpace Music and their CD sales and profits (Dhar & Chang, 2009).

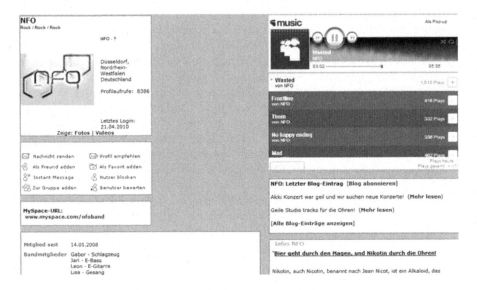

Figure 11.13: Profile Page of the Independent Düsseldorf Rock Band NFO on MySpace.

11.6   Conclusion

- Web 2.0 services are platforms on the internet on which the members of a virtual community collaborate in the creation and expansion of each respective service, thus becoming prosumers (producers as well as consumers). The prosumers of Web 2.0 services form social networks in the broad sense. If prosumers collaborate directly, there is "collaborative intelligence", and if individual contributions are algorithmically processed, we speak of "collective intelligence". In no case is there any guarantee of correct information.
- The Web 2.0 business models have free usage of the platforms at their core. Profits are generated from premium offers, licensing the database, donations or advertising.

- In sharing services, prosumers share certain documents with the virtual community. Depending on the type of resource, we distinguish sharing services for videos (YouTube), images (Flickr), music (Last.fm) and goals (43Things). On each respective market, one single service is dominant. Users with identical or similar preferences can be identified via uploaded resources or allocated tags and recommended by the system.
- Social Bookmarking platforms unite prosumers' collections of bookmarks. In this way, they become search tools for intellectually indexed content, which have advantages vis-à-vis search engines that work algorithmically, particularly for websites that are very active or new. In Social Bookmarking for websites of all genres and for books, standards have established themselves in the form of del.icio.us and LibraryThing, whereas the market for STM Bookmarking is currently a combat zone (as of mid-2010).
- Knowledge bases in Web 2.0 are built collaboratively. A wiki collects entries on concepts and entities, which can be modified at any point. The advantages of such a service (such as the online encyclopedia Wikipedia) are the quickness with which new knowledge is put online; a disadvantage is represented by gaps in backing up the veracity of the information via sources. Blogs are websites for publishing opinions, which are occasionally very idiosyncratic. A variant of blogging is microblogging (with the standard Twitter), with very short messages and the advantage of access via all kinds of mobile end devices, which makes microblogs a very speedy medium for disseminating information.
- Social networks, narrowly defined, serve to record a user-specific personal profile and, particularly, communication with friends and the nurturing of social contacts. General social networks (such as Facebook) address all prosumers on the Web, whereas interest-led platforms (such as MySpace Music) only reach certain groups of people. Under heated discussion is the privacy (or–depending on one's perspective–the lack thereof), i.e. the extent of available person-related information.

11.7 Bibliography

Anger, E. (2002). Brockhaus multimedia 2000 Premium auf CD-ROM und DVD. Rösch, H. (ed.), Enzyklopädie im Wandel. Schmuckstück der Bücherwand, rotierende Scheibe oder Netzangebot (pp. 36-65). Köln: FH Köln. (Kölner Arbeitspapiere zur Bibliotheks- und Informationswissenschaft; 32).

Antin, J., & Earp, M. (2010). With a little help of from my friends. Self-interested and prosocial behavior on MySpace Music. Journal of the American Society for Information Science and Technology, 61(5), 952-963.

Bar-Ilan, J. (2005). Information hub blogs. Journal of Information Science 31(4), 297-307.

Boyd, D., & Ellison, N.B. (2007). Social network sites. Definition, history, and scholarship. Journal of Computer-Mediated Communication, 13(1), art. 11.

Boyd, D., Golder, S., & Lotan, G. (2010). Tweet, tweet, retweet. Conversational aspects on retweeting on Twitter. Proceedings of the 43rd Hawaii International Conference on System Sciences. Washington, DC: IEEE Computer Society Press.

Cha, M., Kwak, H., Rodriguez, P., Ahn, Y.Y., & Moon, S. (2007). I tube, you tube, everybody tubes. Analyzing the world's largest user generated content video system. Proceedings of the 7th ACM SIGCOMM Conference on Internet Measurement (pp. 1-14). New York, NY: ACM.

Cox, A.M. (2008). Flickr. A case study of Web2.0. Aslib Proceedings 60(5), 493-516.

Crandall, D., Backstrom, L., Huttenlocher, D., & Kleinberg, J. (2009). Mapping the world's photos. Proceedings of the 18th International Conference on World Wide Web (pp. 761-770). New York, NY: ACM.

Denning, P., Horning, J., Parnas, D., & Weinstein, L. (2005). Wikipedia risks. Communications of the ACM, 48(12), 152.

Dhar, V., & Chang, E.A. (2009). Does chatter matter? The impact of user-generated content on music sales. Journal of Interactive Marketing, 23(4), 300-307.

Ellison, N.B., Steinfield, C., & Lampe, C. (2007). The benefits of Facebook "Friends". Social capital and college students' use of online social network sites. Journal of Computer-Mediated Communication, 12(4), art. 1.

Emamy, K., & Cameron, R. (2007). Citeulike. A researcher's social bookmarking service. Ariadne 51.

Fuchs, C. (2008). Internet and Society. Social Theory in the Information Age. New York, NY: Routledge.

Giles, J. (2005). Internet encyclopaedias go head to head. Nature, 438, 900-901.

Gill, P., Arlitt, M., Li, Z., & Mahanti, A. (2007). YouTube traffic characterization. A view from the edge. Proceedings of the 7th ACM SIGCOMM Conference on Internet Measurement (pp. 15-28). New York, NY: ACM.

Grange, C., & Benbasat, I. (2010). Online social shopping: The functions and symbols of design artefacts. Proceedings of the 43rd Hawaii International Conference on System Sciences. Washington, DC: IEEE Computer Society Press.

Habermas, J. (2006). Political communication in media society. Does democracy still enjoy an epistemic dimension? The impact of normative theory on empirical research. Communication Theory, 16, 411-426.

Haider, J., & Sundin, O. (2010). Beyond the legacy of the Enlightenment? Online encyclopaedias as digital heterotopias. First Monday, 15(1).

Hammond, T., Hannay, T., Lund, B., & Scott, J. (2005). Social bookmarking tools (I). A general review. D-Lib Magazine, 11(4).

Hammwöhner, R. (2007). Qualitätsaspekte der Wikipedia. kommunikation@gesellschaft, 8, Beitrag 3.

Hart, J., Ridley, C., Taher, F., Sas, C., & Dix, A. (2008). Exploring the Facebook experience. A new approach to usability. Proceedings of the 5th Nordic Conference on Human-Computer-Interaction: Building Bridges (pp. 471-474). New York, NY: ACM.

Haupt, J. (2009). Last.fm. People-powered online radio. Music Reference Services Quarterly, 12, 23-24.

Herring, S.C., Scheidt, L.A., Bonus, S., & Wright, E. (2004). Bridging the gap. A genre analysis of weblogs. Proceedings of the 37th Hawaii International Conference on System Sciences. Washington, DC: IEEE Computer Society.

Heymann, P., Koutrika, G., & Garcia-Molina, H. (2008). Can social bookmarking improve Web search? Proceedings of the International Conference on Web Search and Web Data Mining (pp. 195-206). New York, NY: ACM.

Hotho, A., Jäschke, R., Schmitz, C., & Stumme, G. (2006). Bibsonomy. A social bookmark and publication sharing system. Proceedings of the Conceptual Structure Tool Interoperability Workshop at the 14th International Conference on Conceptual Structures (pp. 87-102).

Huberman, B.A., Romero, D.M., & Wu, F. (2009). Social networks that matter. Twitter under the microscope. First Monday, 14(1).

Java, A., Finin, T., Song, X., & Tseng, B. (2007). Why we twitter. Understanding microblogging usage and communities. Proceedings of the 9th WebKDD and 1st SNA-KDD Workshop on Web Mining and Social Network Analysis (pp. 56-65). New York, NY: ACM.

Johnson, T.J., & Kaye, B.K. (2004). Wag the blog. How reliance on traditional media and the Internet influence credibility perceptions of weblogs among blog users. Journalism & Mass Communication Quarterly, 81(3), 622-642.

Khveshchanka, S., & Suter, L. (2010). Vergleichende Analyse von profilbasierten sozialen Netzwerken aus Russland (Vkontakte), Deutschland (StudiVZ) und den USA (Facebook). Information–Wissenschaft und Praxis, 61(2), 71-76.

Kleinberg, J. (1999). Authoritative sources in a hyperlinked environment. Journal of the ACM 46(5), 604-632.

Kline, D., & Burstein, D. (2005). Blog! How the Newest Media Revolution is Changing Politics, Business and Culture. New York, NY: CDS Books.

Krasnova, H., & Veltri, N.F. (2010). Privacy calculus on social networking sites: Explorative evidence from Germany and USA. Proceedings of the 43rd Hawaii International Conference on System Sciences. Washington, DC: IEEE Computer Society Press.

Kruitbosch, G., & Nack, F. (2008). Broadcast yourself on YouTube–really? Proceedings of the 3rd ACM International Workshop on Human-Centered Computing (pp. 7-10). New York, NY: ACM.

Lange, P.G. (2007). Publicly private and privately public. Social networking on YouTube. Journal of Computer-Mediated Communication, 13(1), art. 18.

Letierce, J., Passant, A., Decker, S., & Breslin, J.G. (2010). Understanding how Twitter is used to spread scientific messages. Proceedings of the Web Science Conference 2010, April 26-27, 2010, Raleigh, NC, USA.

Lewandowski, D., & Maaß, M., eds. (2008). Web-2.0-Dienste als Ergänzung zu algorithmischen Suchmaschinen. Berlin: Logos.

Lim, S. (2009). How and why do college students use Wikipedia? Journal of the American Society for Information Science and Technology, 60(11), 2189-2202.

Liu, W., & Wu, L. (2009). 2collab. Journal of the Medical Library Association, 97(3), 233-234.

Lund, B., Hammond, T., Flack, M., & Hannay, T. (2005). Social bookmarking tools (II). A case study–*Connotea*. D-Lib Magazine, 11(4).

Luyt, B., & Tan, D. (2010). Improving Wikipedia's credibility. References and citations in a sample of history articles. Journal of the American Society for Information Science and Technology, 61(4), 715-722.

Mainka, A. (2010). Twitter: "Gezwitscher" oder gezielte Informationsvermittlung? Information–Wissenschaft und Praxis, 61(2), 77-82.

Martens, E. (2010). Twitter for Scientists. ACS Chemical Biology, 5(2), 149.

Nardi, B.M., Schiano, D.J., Gumbrecht, M., & Swartz, L. (2004). Why we blog. Communications of the ACM, 47(12), 41-46.

Nielsen, J. (2006). Participation Inequality. Encouraging More Users to Contribute. (Online).

Nosko, A., Wood, E., & Molema, S. (2010). All about me. Disclosure in online social networking profiles. The Case of FACEBOOK. Computers in Human Behavior, 26, 406-418.

O'Reilly, T. (2005). What is Web 2.0? (Online).

O'Reilly, T., & Battelle, J. (2009). Web Squared: Web 2.0 Five Years on. (Online).

Peters, I. (2009). Folksonomies. Indexing and Retrieval in Web 2.0. Berlin: De Gruyter Saur. (Knowledge & Information. Studies in Information Science).

Peters, I., & Stock, W.G. (2010). "Power Tags" in Information Retrieval. Library Hi Tech, 28(1), 81-93.

Prainsack, B., & Wolinsky, H. (2010). Direct-to-consumer genome testing: Opportunities for pharmacogenomics research? Pharmacogenomics, 11(5), 651-655.

Rao, V. (2008). Facebook applications and playful mood. The construction of Facebook as a "Third Place". Proceedings of the 12th International Conference on Entertainment and Media in the Ubiquitous Era (pp. 8-12). New York, NY: ACM.

Reher, S., & Haustein, S. (2010). Social bookmarking in STM. Putting services to the acid test. Online, 34(6), 34-42.

Rheingold, H. (1993). The Virtual Community. Homesteading on the Electronic Frontier. Reading, MA: Addison-Wesley.

Rossi, C., & Teli, M. (2009). Music collectivities and MySpace: Towards digital collectives. Proceedings of the 42nd Hawaii International Conference on System Sciences. Washington, DC: IEEE Computer Society Press.

Rotman, D., Golbeck, J., & Preece, J. (2009). The community is where the rapport is. On sense and structure in the YouTube community. Proceedings of the 4th International Conference on Communities and Technologies (pp. 41-50). New York, NY: ACM.

Shi, N., Lee, M.K.O., Cheung, C.M.K., & Chen, H. (2010). The continuance of online social networks. How to keep people using Facebook? Proceedings of the 43rd Hawaii International Conference on System Sciences. Washington, DC: IEEE Computer Society Press.

Smith, D.A., & Lieberman, H. (2010). The why UI. Using goal networks to improve user interfaces (pp. 377-380). Proceedings of the 14th International Conference on Intelligent User Interfaces. New York, NY: ACM.

Spyns, P., de Moor, A., Vandenbussche, J., & Meersman, R. (2006). From folksonomies to ontologies. How the twain meet. Lecture Notes in Computer Science, 4275, 738-755.

Stock, W.G. (2007). Information Retrieval. Informationen suchen und finden. München; Wien: Oldenbourg.

Stvilia, B., Twidale, M.B., Smith, L.C., & Gasser, L. (2008). Information quality work organization in Wikipedia. Journal of the American Society for Information Science and Technology, 59(6), 983-1001.

Surowiecki, J. (2005). The Wisdom of Crowds. Why the Many are Smarter than the Few and How Collective Wisdom Shapes Business, Economics, Societies, and Nations. New York, NY: Anchor Books.

Talbot, D. (2010). Can Twitter make money? Technology Review 113(2), 52-57.

Tönnies, F. (1887). Gemeinschaft und Gesellschaft. Leipzig: Fues.

Toffler, A. (1980). The Third Wave. New York, NY: Morrow.

Trkulja, V. (2010). Die Digitale Kluft. Bosnien-Herzegowina auf dem Weg in die Informationsgesellschaft. Wiesbaden: VS Verlag für Sozialwissenschaften / Springer Fachmedien.

Van Zwol, R. (2007). Flickr. Who is looking? Proceedings of the IEEE/WIC/ACM International Conference on Web Intelligence (pp. 184-190). Washington, DC: IEEE Computer Society.

Vander Wal, T. (2008). Welcome to the matrix! Gaiser, B., Hampel, T., & Panke, S. (eds.), Good Tags–Bad Tags. Social Tagging in der Wissensorganisation (pp. 7-9). Münster: Waxmann.

Weller, K., Dornstädter, R., Freimanis, R., Klein, R.N., & Perez, M. (2010). Social software in academia: Three studies on users' acceptance of Web 2.0 services. Proceedings of the Web Science Conference, April 26-27, 2010, Raleigh, NC, USA.

Westcott, J., Chappell, A., & Lebel, C. (2009). LibraryThing for libraries at Claremont. Library Hi Tech, 27(1), 78-81.

Zengyan, C., Yinping, Y., & Lim, J. (2009). Cyber migration. An empirical investigation on factors that affect users' switch intentions in social networking sites. Proceedings of the 42nd Hawaii International Conference on System Sciences. Washington, DC: IEEE Computer Society Press.

Zhao, D., & Rosson, M.B. (2009). How and why people twitter. The role that micro-blogging plays in informal communication at work. Proceedings of the ACM 2009 International Conference on Supporting Group Work (pp. 243-252). New York, NY: ACM.

Chapter 12

Online Music and Internet TV

12.1 Commercial Music Distribution on the World Wide Web

For a long time, the traditional line of music distribution, via physical sound carriers (be it LPs or CDs) dominated the music business. The consumers were quick to recognize that music stored on CDs was very easy to copy, and began "sharing" this music. Over the years, a functioning illegal information market for music developed in this way (see Chapters 24-26). The music industry tried to make their products uncopiable via Digital Rights Protection (DRM) (which also incurred the wrath of "honest" customers, who were left unable to make backup copies) and to criminalize the "pirates". Some artists (such as *The Grateful Dead*) actively supported the free sharing of their music, hoping to generate profits from live concerts and merchandising products. In view of the illegal market's proper functioning, it seems difficult to establish successful models for the commercial distribution of music via the World Wide Web–consumers had to wait a long time for (legal) online offers. In this chapter, we will discuss (commercial) information products on the market for digital music (Peitz & Waelbroeck, 2005; Hougaard & Tvede, 2010), which take their place beside the illegal markets and Web 2.0 services (such as Last.fm and MySpace Music) and even cooperate (particularly with the latter).

Regarded as sensible strategies for the successful placement of commercial products are the lowest possible prices on the one hand (Buxmann, Strube, & Pohl, 2007) and the abolishment of DRM measures on the other. Since online sales also stimulate sales of physical media (and vice versa), and since these sales are correlative with concerts and merchandising, "multi-channel management" is what is called for (Buxmann, Strube, & Pohl, 2007, 38). The online market can also be viewed as a testing ground for determining whether the publication of physical media–for new artists or for new songs–will be profitable (Fox, 2005).

The value chain of digital music comprises four links: artists, music labels (where the market is dominated by the four companies Universal Music Group, Warner Music Group, Sony-BMG and EMI), online aggregators and, in the end, the customers. Figure 12.1 shows four versions of this value chain. In the bottom variant, music labels and aggregators exit the chain, allowing the artists to distribute directly to the customer. This should only be the case if the artist knows his (rather small number of) fans. In the next option, there is no intermediate music label, but there is an aggregator. This is the case, for instance, with MySpace Music for independent artists. In the third variant, there is no aggregator, i.e. the music label itself offers its customers online music. This model is hardly in use at all at the moment. The last option is also used the most in the commercial arena. Music labels market music titles online with the help of an aggregator. The dominant aggregator on the market is Apple iTunes (Voida et al., 2005).

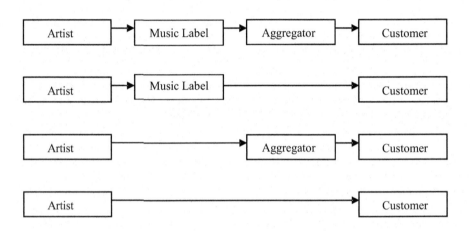

Figure 12.1: Value Chains for Online Music. Source: Following Premkumar, 2003.

iTunes offers digital music and digital videos for purchase (Figure 12.2); as of mid-2010, around 11m titles can be chosen from. Music is offered per album (e.g. *Machine Head* by *Deep Purple* in Figure 12.2) or per song (such as *Smoke on the Water*). The prices for the individual tracks vary–depending on the music labels' preferences–between €0.69 and €1.29; no DRM is used. Additionally, iTunes offers videos, both as complete films and as episodes from TV shows (for €1.99) and audiobooks. The intersection between the shopping system and the user is a special software, which must be downloaded (for free) by every customer. This software also allows the user to manage his resources and synchronize them with his MP3 player.

Figure 12.2: Shopping Interface on iTunes.

12.2 Internet Television

In contrast to Web 2.0 productions (e.g. distributed exclusively via YouTube), we speak of internet TV when either established broadcasting institutions use the WWW as a distribution channel for their content or when (commercial or independent) producers regularly distribute their own content on the Web. As with music (and videos, too), the border between internet TV and Web 2.0 services is blurred, as one and the same content can be available both on internet TV (e.g. in a channel's Web offer) and Web 2.0 (probably–cut into ten-minute segments–on YouTube).

Internet TV (also called Web TV or IPTV) means the integration of television and the World Wide Web (Hart, 2004; Katz, 2004; Noll, 2004; Tanaka, 2007). In order to realistically gauge the possibilities of internet TV, we should first find out the habits connected to regular TV consumption. Television is a structured medium (Simons, 2009); it dictates when to watch (time), what to watch (content) and where to watch (location). Web TV can break up these structures by saving programs (or circumscribable parts thereof), making them available for consumption independently of time and place. TV is a social medium, it is either watched or discussed with others. The disadvantage of internet TV lies in "fracturing the audience", as Nele Simons (2009, 220) calls it, its advantage the creation of new (virtual) communities via online media (such as blogs)–right up to the "quasi-intimacy" of chatting with TV stars (Bowen, 2008). Television is regarded as a "lean-back medium" (Simons, 2009), which is often consumed in living rooms, whereas PCs stand in offices or bureaus–a problem that hinders the amalgamation process of both worlds. The following options are being discussed for internet TV (Waterman, 2004):

- (conventional) TV is distributed in real time via the internet protocol (and can be viewed in a window on one's PC screen, e.g. in parallel to one's work applications),
- TV programs are stored by the respective station and can be accessed online (for an example, see Figure 12.3),
- original programs are created for the internet (e.g. by small local channels).

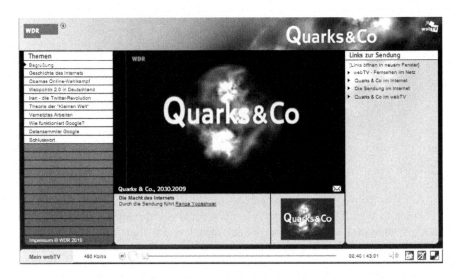

Figure 12.3: Access to a Program of the WDR.

Producers (Einav, 2004) are TV channels, film studios, independent creative people (among them producers of pornography) as well as laymen, where the latter tend to release their videos on YouTube rather than via their own Web presence. The customers profit from additional offers to programs, e.g.–as in the case of *Quarks & Co.* by the WDR (West German Broadcasting)–the segmenting of longer programs into circumscribable parts, or written descriptions of the program's content.

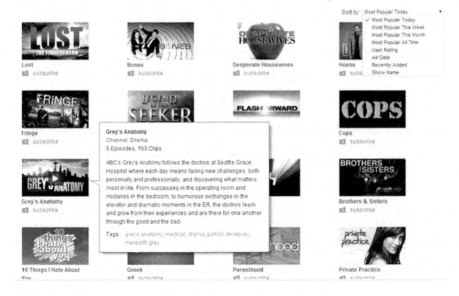

Figure 12.4: Selection of TV Shows on the American TV Aggregator Hulu.

Since there is a multitude of channels that digitally provide programs, here too, content aggregators are called upon to bundle the content. In the United States, Hulu (Figure 12.4) has already established itself. Hulu allows for searches, retrieval and (free) playback of programs from various (American) TV channels (Perenson, 2008, 106).

A new form of "broadcasting" TV programs is broadcasting to mobile end devices. The (really very restricted) size of the screen and the (pretty short) usage period (e.g. in commuter trains on one's way to work or home) in particular mean that only certain types of programs are suitable. Kaasinen et al. (2009) discuss news; Miyauchi, Sugahara and Oda (2009) also observe the consumption of news reports, but also of entertainment contents.

12.3 Conclusion

- In iTunes, a content aggregator for music (to be paid for) has established itself as the standard, which means that in this segment, a legal, "normal" market has joined the long-dominant illegal market.
- Internet TV means either the transmission of programs on the WWW in real time, the storage of programs for the purposes of time- and location-independent access or the production of shows solely for distribution via the Web.

> - As with the music offer, internet TV also profits from or actually requires an aggregator that bundles TV programs and offers them on a single platform if market success is to be achieved.

12.4   Bibliography

Bowen, T. (2008). Romancing the screen. An examination of moving from television to the World Wide Web in a quest for quasi-intimacy. The Journal of Popular Culture, 41(4), 569-590.

Buxmann, P., Strube, J., & Pohl, G. (2007). Cooperative pricing in the digital value chains. The case of online music. Journal of Electronic Commerce Research 8(1), 32-40.

Einav, G. (2004). The content landscape. In Noam, E., Groebel, J., & Gerbarg, D. (eds.), Internet Television (pp. 215-234). Mahwah, NJ: Lawrence Erlbaum.

Fox, M. (2005). Technological and social drivers of change in the online music industry. First Monday Special Issue #1: Music and the Internet.

Hart, J. (2004). Content models. Will IPTV be more of the same, or different? In Noam, E., Groebel, J., & Gerbarg, D. (eds.), Internet Television (pp. 205-214). Mahwah, NJ: Lawrence Erlbaum.

Hougaard, J.L., & Tvede, M. (2010). Selling digital music. Business models for public goods. Netnomics, 11.

Kaasinen, E., Mulju, M., Kivinen, T., & Oksman, V. (2009). User acceptance of mobile TV services. Proceedings of the 11th International Conference on Human-Computer Interaction with Mobile Devices and Services (art. 34). New York, NY: ACM.

Katz, M.L. (2004). Industry structure and competition absent distribution bottlenecks. In Noam, E., Groebel, J., & Gerbarg, D. (eds.), Internet Television (pp. 31-59). Mahwah, NJ: Lawrence Erlbaum.

Miyauchi, K., Sugahara, T., & Oda, H. (2009). Relax or study? A qualitative user study on the usage of live mobile TV and mobile video. ACM Computers in Entertainment, 7(3), art. 43.

Noll, A.M. (2004). Internet television. Definition and prospects. In Noam, E., Groebel, J., & Gerbarg, D. (eds.), Internet Television (pp. 1-8). Mahwah, NJ: Lawrence Erlbaum.

Peitz, M., & Waelbroeck, P. (2005). An economist's guide to digital music. CESifo Economic Studies, 51(2/3), 359-428.

Perenson, M.J. (2008). The best TV on the Web. PC World 26(Sept.), 105-112.

Premkumar, G.P. (2003). Alternative distribution strategies for digital music. Communications of the ACM, 46(9), 89-95.

Simons, N. (2009). „Me TV". Towards changing TV viewing practices? Proceedings of the 7th European Conference on European Interactive Television (pp. 219-222). New York, NY: ACM.

Tanaka, K. (2007). Research on fusion of the Web and TV broadcasting. 2nd International Conference on Informatics Research for Development of Knowledge Society Infrastructure (pp. 129-136). Washington, DC: IEEE Computer Society,

Voida, A., Grinter, R.E., Ducheneault, N., Edwards, W.K., & Newman, M.W. (2005). Listening in. Practices surrounding iTunes music sharing. Proceedings of the SIGHCI Conference on Human Factors in Computing Systems (pp. 191-200). New York, NY: ACM.

Waterman, D. (2004). Business models and program content. In Noam, E., Groebel, J., & Gerbarg, D. (eds.), Internet Television (pp. 61-80). Mahwah, NJ: Lawrence Erlbaum.

Chapter 13
Digital Games

13.1 Console and PC Games

Let us, first and foremost, make a terminological distinction. When we talk about games in this book, we refer to results from **game research** (Simons, 2007), which is only marginally related to **game theory**, a mathematical theory concerning rational decisions in the presence of several agents.

Digital games require hardware in order to be played at all. Here we distinguish between console games (when using a console or a cell phone) and PC games, which are (alone or–using internet services–with others) played on one's computer (Kerr, 2006, 54 et seq.).

Console games can be distinguished into three main groups. Console games, narrowly defined (e.g. for PlayStation or Wii) require an external screen (e.g. a television). Handheld consoles have an integrated screen (e.g. Gameboy, Nintendo DS or PlayStation Portable). Cell phone games are generally simple games of skill (e.g. *Nature Park* or *Snake*), which only require the smallest displays.

PC games are either "simple" board or card games or games of skill, which are also played in the real world, games of chance equally transferred from the real to the digital world (if legally dubious), video games (with several genres), "Massively Multiplayer Online Role Playing Games" (MMORPGs), Social Games (generally as extensions to social networking platforms) as well as "games with a purpose", which are games that serve the indexing of Web resources, for instance. A classification of digital games is provided in Figure 13.1.

In accordance with our definition of the information market (Table 1.2), in this book we will exclusively consider PC games. Our delineation is blurred, though, since several console games have internet compatibility by now. Until the advent of MMORPGs, the market for digital games was dominated by console games (Nielsen, Smith, & Tosca, 2008, 13 et seq.), even though these were more expensive, compared to their PC counterparts. This is because for PC games, the game manufacturers' licensing fees to the console manufacturers disappear. Nielsen, Smith and Tosca (2008, 17) assume that the easy (illegal) copiability of PC games resulted in a certain pricing pressure, which had a favorable result on consumer prices.

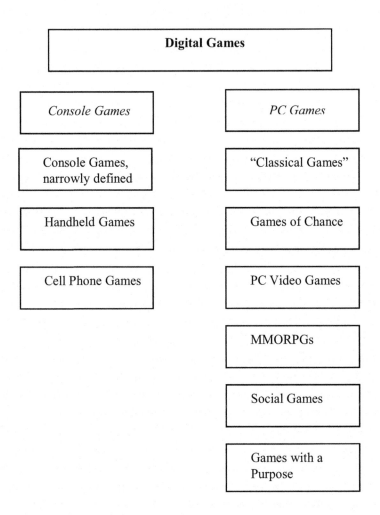

Figure 13.1: Classification of Digital Games.

All digital games run through three phases in their **development** (Nielsen, Smith, & Tosca, 2008, 18 et seq.). In the conceptional phase, the idea for the game is formulated, its (hopefully) attractive functions explained. Added to this are a market analysis and budget planning. The design phase is dominated by software development, in which the functional and technical specifications are discussed and realized. At the end of the design phase, there is a preliminary prototype, which represents a fragment of the envisioned game containing all its essential features. Only in the production and testing phase is the prototype equipped with graphics and sound. The users expect games to employ 3d technology and color ("3D true color graphics") (Choi & Kim 2004, 21). The alpha version thus created now runs through a series of tests regarding simplicity of usage and playability, leading to a "Gold Master" and thus to the first commercially distributed version of the game.

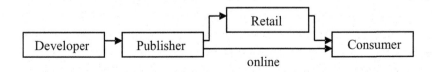

Figure 13.2: Value Chain of the Digital Gaming Industry

The Gold Master is either marketed by the developer itself or–particularly in the case of smaller developing companies–by a publisher. The game *Rez* (a shooter), for example, has been developed by UGA and distributed by Sega, whereas in the case of *The Sims*, Maxis assumed both roles (Nielsen, Smith, & Tosca, 2008, 16). Finally, the games are sold either via stationary retail (as DVDs) or online, or on a subscription basis (e.g. with monthly usage fees). Several online games can be played for free. The value chain of the digital gaming industry can be seen in Figure 13.2.

The evaluation of information systems has been working with two variables that cause the systems' user acceptance ever since Davis' (1989) classical results: *Perceived Ease of use* and *Perceived Usefulness*. Not so for the evaluation of digital games: ease of use is still there, but the usefulness factor is replaced by *Perceived Enjoyment* (Hsu & Lu, 2007). **Fun** becomes the critical success factor. Castronova (2007, 82) even laments the lack of an "economy of fun", which he believes is required here.

13.2   Digital Versions of "Traditional" Games

We will now speak of PC games. A first group among these consists of games that are also played outside the digital sphere and have only been turned into digital copies. These are board games (such as chess or Go), card games (e.g. Solitaire; Figure 13.3), games of skill (pinball) or other simple games (e.g. Battleship). Some of these games are preinstalled on new (Windows) computers. Such games have been developed by Microsoft, partly in cooperation with Oberon Games.

There are single-player games (such as Solitaire), multi-player games, where players take turns (pinball), multi-player games played on the WWW (e.g. chess against a player somewhere in the world) and man-against-machine games (also in chess).

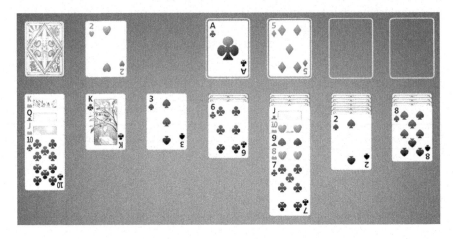

Figure 13.3: PC Version of Solitaire (Oberon Games / Microsoft)–a Typical Single-Player PC Game.

13.3   Gambling

Online gambling involves virtual adaptations of games of chance known from the real world. The main difference to casino and sports gambling lies in players' ability to keep playing around the clock (Griffith, 2003). We distinguish between two main groups of online games of chance:

- Casino Games (LaBrie et al., 2008), among them Blackjack, Roulette, slot machines and Poker (LaPlante et al., 2009) (see Figure 13.4) and
- Betting, particularly on sports events (LaPlante et al., 2008).

In games of chance, the danger of addiction is particularly high compared with other games. McBride and Derevensky (2009) report that in a random sample of customers of online gambling sites, around a quarter are to be regarded as "problem players". These play–compared to "hobby players"–longer sessions and bet higher sums–and losing more money in consequence. Problem players have a tendency toward "Problematic Internet Use" (PIU) (see Chapter 4 above).

Online gambling (including bets on future events, among them sports) are illegal in many countries. In Germany, the prohibition is regulated by the Interstate Gambling Treaty (GlüStV) (since 2008). In the U.S.A., there has been an "Unlawful Internet Gambling Enforcement Act" (UIGEA, 2006) since 2006, which prohibits financial transactions (e.g. credit card payments) in favor of (domestic or foreign) organizers of such games (Morse, 2009). In certain countries, though, online gambling is legal; among them Gibraltar (home of PartyCasino), Malta and several Central American countries. In Canada, the Kahnawake Mohawk First Nation (in Quebec) has declared itself independent in gambling matters and legalized these activities. Kahnawake is, at the moment, the host of the most internet gambling sites in the world (Williams & Wood, 2007, 11).

Figure 13.4: Selection of Online Games of Chance on PartyCasino.

13.4   Video Games

Video games tell a story and allow the player to actively participate in the events they depict. Occasionally, the objective is even to anticipate the "real" plot and to control the characters one plays accordingly. We distinguish five genres of video games:

- Sports Games (e.g. *Snooker* or *Formula 1*),
- Action Games (e.g. *Tomb Raider*, *Call of Duty*),
- Adventure Games (e.g. *Myst*, *Monkey Island*),
- Strategy Games (e.g. *Dune II: The Building of a Dynasty*, *Command & Conquer*),
- Process-oriented games (e.g. *Ultima Online*); this also includes all MMORPGs, whom we will grant an entire section.

It must be noted that "storytelling" has another meaning in video games than it does in novels or films. In the traditional case of **narrativity**, the recipient is outside of the plot–however badly one wants, one cannot help Luke Skywalker fight Darth Vader. In video games, this is possible (even if–compared to film–only in short, select sequences). Video games' interactivity influences their narrativity, however, which is why Jesper Juul (2001) emphasizes:

> You can't have narration and interactivity at the same time; there is no such thing as a continuously interactive story. (...) The relations between reader/story and player/game are completely different–the player inhabits a twilight zone where he/she is both an empirical object outside the game and undertakes a role inside the game.

For Tavinor (2005, 202), online video games form a hybrid genre consisting of narrativity and interactivity: "Video games are *interactive fictions*".

If a video game is based on a film (like the game *Enter the Matrix*, based on *The Matrix*), licensing fees must be paid to the rights holder (Kerr, 2006, 69 et seq.). This, of course, also works in the opposite direction (e.g. for the film *Lara Croft: Tomb Raider*, based on the *Tomb Raider* games).

Especially for first-person video games (e.g. shooters), it is important to provide the player with as realistic an impression as possible of the game's world– from the "subjective" point of view of the avatar (Steinicke et al., 2009). Research into the direct translation of the player's movements (in the real world) into the actions of the (virtual) avatar is ongoing (Mazalek et al., 2009).

13.5   Massively Multiplayer Online Role Playing Games (MMORPGs)

A dominant position in the online gaming world is currently held by Massively Multiplayer Online Role Playing Games (Achterbosch et al., 2008). What exactly are such games? Let us decipher the abbreviation MMORPG (Chan & Vorderer, 2006, 79):

- M   (Massively): lots of players play a game simultaneously,
- M   (Multiplayer): the game is principally played with other people; there are thus no offline versions of the game,
- O   (Online): the game is played on the internet,
- RP   (Role Playing): every player assumes a certain role in the game, which he can–within a certain set of rules–freely define and which is represented in the game by an avatar,
- G   (Games): here the definition becomes a little blurred, as there are definitely games in the narrow definition of the word (such as "World of Warcraft"), but also digital worlds with no predominant gaming character (such as "Second Life") or pedagogically oriented "Serious Games" (Zyda, 2005; Bellotti et al., 2009), such as the edutainment world "Wissenheim" (Baeuerle, Sonnenfroh, & Schulthess, 2009).

Figure 13.5: Scene from World of Warcraft. Source: Blizzard Entertainment.

We will briefly describe the rules of probably the most successful of the MMORPGs, **"World of Warcraft"** (WoW) (Figure 13.5), developed by Blizzard Entertainment. In an environment reminiscent of medieval legend or J.R.R. Tolkien's "Lord of the Rings", the player chooses one of the two factions "Alliance" or "Horde", then selects one of the races available (e.g. blood elves or night elves) and a class (e.g. mages, warlocks or hunters). The game is played on decided servers that are not interconnected. There are servers on which persons play against persons (and can kill each other), and servers on which persons play against the software. Furthermore, it is possible to engage in role-playing games on the servers. The goal here is to perform tasks ("quests"), in order to be rewarded with pieces of equipment, playing money ("gold") and experience. Experience points gained by fighting avatars or exploring uncharted territory affect a player's "level". Currently, one can work one's (avatar's) way up to level 80. Players mostly form groups ("guilds") and perform their tasks together. Communication with members of one's own faction is possible via chats; communication with members of the enemy faction, though, is not an option. Another aspect worthy of mention is the "raids", where the players must (mandatorily) meet at certain times, since the tasks cannot be performed otherwise.

Experience points make the avatar increasingly valuable, and are translated into a player's renown within the game (Smahel et al., 2008). Playing in a guild and–particularly in the case of raids–collaborative actions may increase the feeling of solidarity, but they require a not inconsiderable amount of playing time. Thus, the possibility of MMORPGs such as WoW leading to **problematic internet usage**–depending on each player's disposition and motivation (Yee, 2006)–cannot be dismissed.

Let us expand our view a little and consider digital world in general. Edward Castronova (2005, 22) defines "**virtual**" or "**synthetic worlds**" as

> any computer-generated physical space, represented graphically in three dimensions, that can be experienced by many people at once.

For Castronova (2005, 18), the connection of game and massive computer usage forms the basis for the creation of something like a "new Earth":

> Add computing power to a game world and you get a place that's much bigger, much richer, and much more immersive. The robots running around in it, humanoid and unhumanoid, are smarter and act more and more like real people and real monsters (if there is such a thing). Add immense computing power to a game and you might get an incredibly realistic extension of Earth's reality itself. The place that I call "game world" today may develop into much more than a game in the near future. It may become just another place for the mind to be, a new and different Earth.

In virtual worlds, there exists a "**virtual economy**" (Castronova, 2003). In contrast to the "normal" economy, in an "avatar economy", an authority can determine and regulate the prices for the (digital) goods. The work (of the avatar) is fun (otherwise there would be no players). A thing like economic growth is not even mentioned. In the final analysis, the normal economy confines people to certain roles, whereas in the avatar economy, a change of profession or race, and even the decision as to whether one wants to live or, rather, be dead for a while (of course with the option of changing this status at any time) is always possible.

Societal and legal **norms** in virtual worlds–i.e. in the underlying software–are seen as particularly strongly regulated. Thus, Lessig (2006, 24) argues:

> In MMOG space is "regulated", though the regulation is special. In MMOG space regulation comes through code. Important roles are imposed, not through social sanction, and not by the state, but by the very architecture of the particular space.

Whether this is science fiction or merely fiction is anyone's guess. The question of whether such a parallel digital world is even worth striving for should also be an open one. However, the quotes by Castronova and Lessig hint at the direction in which game research is currently being conducted.

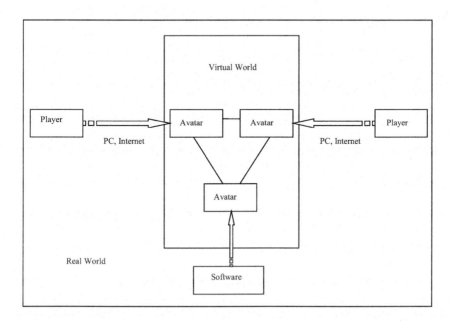

Figure 13.6: Elements of an MMORPG. Source: Following Kolo & Baur, 2004.

In a virtual world (schematically simplified in Figure 13.6), there are both human **players** who play with or against each other via their **avatars**, but there are also avatars who join the action as "non-player characters" (NPCs), exclusively controlled by the **software**. The real world in which the players reside is explored by empirical game research via surveys of players. Thus, we know that subscribers of WoW play for ten hours a week on average (Ducheneault et al., 2006, 286) and that the gaming time rises in tandem with one's experience level (Ducheneault et al., 2006, 287). However, it is also possible for game research to observe the "behavior" of the avatars in the virtual world (knowing, of course, that real people are behind their actions). Ducheneault et al., observed, for example, WoW's "in-game demographics". The ratio of Allicance avatars and their Horde counterparts is two to one. As for the races, humans (25%) and night elves (23%) dominate, while orcs only account for 7% of WoW's virtual world's inhabitants (Ducheneault et al., 2006, 293). The largest proportion of female avatars is represented by night elves (with around 40%), whereas 90% of dwarves are male. Ducheneault et al. (2006, 296-297) cite aesthetic reasons to explain this situation:

> The aesthetic preferences ... seem to be reinforced when taking in-game gender into account, with players clearly favoring the "sexy" female Night Elves (...) to their perhaps less visually pleasing Dwarven counterparts.

When regarding both worlds, the "identity tourism" (Ducheneault et al., 2006, 297) between player and avatar catches the eye; this tendency is expressed by male players choosing female avatars and vice versa.

Such virtual worlds are–economically speaking–a product (the software as such) as well as a service (insofar as the software offers "services" within the game) (Ruch, 2009). Both product and service are entirely useless, however, if the players do not interact. MMORPGs function exclusively in the triangle constellation of product–service–player. This is also emphasized by Ström and Ernkvist (2007, 641):

> The major difference between MMOG games and stand alone games are the social interaction on a massive scale and the persistent nature of the world.

How large is the number of participants in MMORPGs? A game like WoW is subscribed to by several million people, but in actuality, only a small number of people (between five and sixty) play with each other. The "right" players must find each other in order to really take part in the game.

Another form of MMORPGs is represented by virtual worlds with no predominant gaming ingredient. The great difference to the games (like WoW) lies in the absence of goals (e.g. defined by the rules of the game). The best-known example of such a virtual world is probably the platform **Second Life** (Kumar et al., 2008), created by LindenLab (Malaby, 2009). Here, a "mingling" between the real and the virtual world is definitely in evidence, insofar as real-world institutions (libraries, universities, companies etc.) create dependencies in Second Life.

Two fundamental **pricing strategies** have established themselves on the market for MMORPGs (Nojima, 2007). on the one hand, there are fixed monthly subscription fees (as for WoW; currently around €13 per month), and on the other hand sales of digital goods within the game (as in Second Life). Occasionally, both pricing strategies are used jointly. In the case of WoW, there is also the price for the DVD of the game.

It is also possible for players to earn money via MMORPGs. In Second Life, this is a stated objective (Papagiannidis et al., 2008), whereas in WoW this is against the rules. Nevertheless, gold farmers "earn" the WoW currency of gold (which is needed to buy certain pieces of equipment) within the game, and then sell it (e.g. via eBay) to "lazy" players–for real money, of course.

13.6   Social Games

Social Games are digital games that are typically played via **social networks** (such as Facebook)–generally among friends. Examples include games developed by Zynga, such as **FarmVille** (Figure 13.7). Such games are normally free, but also provide the option of buying in-game currency for real money. The in-game currency can also be earned by collecting points (with no monetary but a lot of time effort). Players can make their friends virtual presents or perform certain tasks on their "land". The player performs services (in FarmVille, for example, harvesting fruit) and is rewarded with points. The points are then used to build houses and cultivate farmland. Thus, a strawberry field can be planted, but after a time the strawberries must be picked. Conformity (here the punctual picking of the fruit) is rewarded (with points), lack thereof (e.g. forgetting to pick the fruit) results in the forfeiture of the currency invested.

Figure 13.7: Private Farm, Surrounded by Friendly Neighbors, in Zynga's FarmVille.

Social Games can certainly be regarded as **complementors** of social networks: Facebook users–who, after all, have a list of defined friends–can play FarmVille with them (and of course with others) in their free time and should also regard this as added value. Social Games lead to a feedback of players' actions, which are meant to accomplish certain goals in the game, and certain members (particularly friends) in the original social network (Järvinen, 2009). Thus the number of neighboring plots (owned by friends) is of advantage for a player, and he will thus strive to increase the number of his neighbors. Playing social games also leads to increased logins to the respective social network. There are also "gifts" for one's FarmVille property (such as a stray llama) that appear in the Facebook user's profile and which must be snapped up quickly before they expire.

Most of the time, though, the user will play alone; this, too, can be viewed as a worthwhile leisure activity. A problem is certainly the time pressure for some actions, which can lead the player–if he cedes to the pressure–into a certain loose dependence of the game.

13.7   Games with a Purpose

Games can occasionally serve a purpose, which is effectively a by-product of the game. In the area of the World Wide Web, there are many tasks that can be better accomplished by men than by machines. This is the point of origin of Luis von Ahn's and Laura Dabbish's (2008, 58) "Games with a Purpose":

> Many tasks are trivial for humans but continue to challenge even the most sophisticated computer programs. Traditional computational approaches to solving such problems focus on improving artificial intelligence algorithms. Here, we advocate a different approach: the constructive channeling of human brainpower through computer games.

Figure 13.8: The ESP Game as an Example of a Game with a Purpose.

The players do not play in order to solve an open problem of computer science, they play because it is fun. An open problem, for example, consists of making images and other non-textual documents retrievable on the Web via suitable keywords. This is the approach of the ESP Game (also on Google, licensed as "Google Image Labeler") (von Ahn & Dabbish, 2004). Two randomly selected players are shown the same image (Figure 13.8). They are asked to find matching words to describe the image's content. The goal of the players is to collect as many points as possible via high agreement rates in a set period of time; the game's purpose is to gain content-descriptive metadata for the images. When a threshold value for players' agreement is reached, the tag thus generated is saved and the document thus made retrievable on the internet. If the same image is displayed again in the ESP Game, tags already generated are displayed as "taboo words" and can no longer be used.

13.8   Conclusion

- We consider digital games from the perspective of game research. These games are distinguished into console games (classed, according to their hardware, into console games in the narrow sense, handheld and cell phone games) and PC games. The latter are "classical" games, games of chance, video games, MMORPGs, Social Games and Games with a Purpose.
- The development of a game comprises three phases: conception, design and production. The value chain of the digital gaming industry includes the developers, publishers, retail (which is excluded in the case of online distribution) and, at the end of the chain, the consumers.
- "Traditional" PC games are digital versions of games that are also played in non-digital environments (e.g. board games, card games, games of skill).
- Also from the non-digital world are the templates for online games of chance, in the two main categories of casino games (e.g. Blackjack, Roulette or Poker) and betting (particularly on sports events).
- Internet gambling is forbidden in many countries (including Germany and the U.S.A.). Other countries (such as the Kahnawake Mohawk territory in Canada) have no such prohibition and host various digital gambling services.
- Video games provide stories. The narrativity of the games is of a different kind than the narrativity of films or novels, as the player can affect the action. The incorporation of motifs from films into games (and vice versa) is subject to payment of licensing fees.

- A dominant position in online video gaming is currently held by Massively Multiplayer Online Role Playing Games (MMORPGs). Here, virtual worlds are created for players to interact in via their avatars. There are, additionally, avatars in some MMORPGs that are "played" by the game's software. We distinguish between games with prescribed rules and goals (such as "World of Warcraft"), those without any such objectives (e.g. "Second Life") and Serious Games, which serve pedagogical purposes, for instance.
- Social Games are typically offered by a social network (such as Facebook) and played by its members, alone or in a weak form of interaction with friends.
- Games with a Purposes are fun to play, but serve another underlying purpose. Thus, for example, the ESP Game facilitates the indexing of the content of images on the Web.
- In some variants of games, the possibility of certain players displaying symptoms of "Problematic Internet Use" (PIU) cannot be excluded. The most dangerous games in this regard are deemed to be games of chance and MMORPGs.

13.9   Bibliography

Achterbosch, L., Pierce, R., & Simmons, G. (2008). Massively Multiplayer Online Role-Playing Games. The past, present, and future. ACM Computers in Entertainment 5(4), art. 9.

Baeuerle, T., Sonnenfroh, M., & Schulthess, P. (2009). Wissenheim. An interactive 3D-world for leisure and learning. Proceedings of the International Conference on Education, Research and Innovation (ICERI2009).

Bellotti, F., Berta, R., De Gloria, A., & Primavera, L. (2009). Enhancing the educational value of video games. ACM Computers in Entertainment 7(3), art. 23.

Castronova, E. (2003). On virtual economics. Games Studies. The International Journal of Computer Game Research, 3(2).

Castronova, E. (2005). Synthetic Worlds. The Business and Culture of Online Games. Chicago: University of Chicago Press.

Castronova, E. (2007). Exodus to the Virtual World. How Online Fun is Changing Reality. New York, NY: Palgrave MacMillan.

Chan, E., & Vorderer, P. (2006). Massively multiplayer online games. Vorderer, P., Bryant, J. (ed.), Playing Video Games. Motives, Responses, and Consequences (pp. 77-88). Mahwah: Lawrence Erlbaum.

Choi, D., & Kim, J. (2004). Why people continue to play online games. In search of critical design factors to increase customer loyalty to online contents. CyberPsychology & Behavior, 7(1), 11-24.

Davis, F.D. (1989). Perceived usefulness, perceived ease of use, and user acceptance of information technology. MIS Quarterly, 13, 319-339.

Ducheneault, N., Yee, N., Nickell, E., & Moore, R.J. (2006). Building an MMO with mass appeal. A look at gameplay in World of Warcraft. Games and Culture, 1(4), 281-317.

GlüStV (2008). Staatsvertrag zum Glücksspielwesen in Deutschland (Glücksspiel-staatsvertrag–GlüStV) dated 01/01/2008.

Griffith, M. (2003). Internet gambling. Issues, concerns, and recommendations. CyberPsychology & Behavior, 6(6), 557-568.

Hsu, C.L., & Lu, H.P. (2007). Consumer behavior in online game communities. A motivational factor perspective. Computers of Human Behavior, 23, 1642-1659.

Järvinen, A. (2009). Game design for social networks. Interaction design for playful dispositions. Proceedings of the 2009 ACM SIGGRAPH Symposium on Video Games (pp. 95-102). New York, NY: ACM.

Juul, J. (2001). Games telling stories? A brief note on games and narratives. Games Studies. The International Journal of Computer Game Research, 1(1).

Kerr, A. (2006). The Business and Culture of Digital Games. London: Sage.

Kolo, C., & Baur, T. (2004). Living a virtual life. Social dynamics of online gaming. Games Studies. The International Journal of Computer Game Research, 4(1).

Kumar, S., Chhugani, J., Kim, C., Kim, D., Nguyen, A., Dubey, P., Bienia, C., & Kim, Y. (2008). *Second Life* and the new generation of virtual worlds. Computer / IEEE Computer Society, 41(9), 48-55.

LaBrie, R.A., Kaplan, S.A., LaPlante, D.A., Nelson, S.E., & Shaffer, H.J. (2008). Inside the virtual casino. A prospective longitudinal study of actual Internet casino gambling. European Journal of Public Health, 18(4), 410-416.

LaPlante, D.A., Kleschinsky, J.H., LaBrie, R.A., Nelson, S.E., & Shaffer, H.J. (2009). Sitting at the virtual poker table. A prospective epidemiological study of actual Internet poker gambling behavior. Computers in Human Behavior, 25, 711-717.

LaPlante, D.A., Schumann, A., LaBrie, R.A., & Shaffer, H.J. (2008). Population trends in Internet sports gambling. Computers in Human Behavior, 24, 2399-2414.

Lessig, L. (2006). Code. Version 2.0. New York, NY: Basic Books.

Malaby, T.M. (2009). Making Virtual Worlds. Linden Lab and Second Life. Ithaca, NY: Cornell University Press.

Mazalek, A., Chandrasekharan, S., Nitsche, M., Welsh, T., Thomas, G., Sanka, T., & Clifton, P. (2009). Giving your self to the game. Transferring a player's own movements to avatars using tangible interfaces. Proceedings of the 2009 ACM SIGGRAPH Symposium on Video Games (pp.161-168). New York, NY: ACM.

McBride, J., & Derevensky, J. (2009). Internet gambling behavior in a sample of online gambler. International Journal of Mental Health and Addiction, 7, 149-167.

Morse, E.A. (2009). Survey of significant developments in Internet gambling. The Business Lawyer, 65, 309-316.

Nielsen, S.E., Smith, J.H., & Tosca, S.T. (2008). Understanding Video Games. The Essential Introduction. New York, NY: Routledge.

Nojima, M. (2007). Pricing models and motivations for MMO play. Situated Play. Proceedings of DiGRA 2007 Conference (pp. 672-681). Digital Games Research Association.

Papagiannidis, S., Bourlakis, M., & Li, F. (2008). Making money in virtual worlds. MMORPGs and emerging business opportunities, challenges and ethical implications in metaverses. Technological Forecasting and Social Change, 75, 610-622.

Ruch, A. (2009). World of Warcraft. Service or space? Games Studies. The International Journal of Computer Game Research, 9(2).

Simons, J. (2007). Narrative, games, and theory. Games Studies. The International Journal of Computer Game Research, 7(1).

Smahel, D., Blinka, L., & Ledabyl, O. (2008). Playing MMORPGs. Connections between addiction and identifying with a character. CyberPsychology & Behavior, 11(6), 715-718.

Steinicke, F., Bruder, G., Hinrichs, K., & Steed, A. (2009). Presence-enhancing real walking user interface for first-person video games. Proceedings of the 2009 ACM SIGGRAPH Symposium on Video Games (pp. 111-118). New York, NY: ACM.

Ström, P., & Ernkvist, M. (2007). The unbound network of product and service interaction of the MMOG industry. With a case study of China. Situated Play. Proceedings of DiGRA 2007 Conference (pp. 639-649). Digital Games Research Association.

Tavinor, G. (2005). Video games, fiction, and emotion. Proceedings of the 2nd Australasian Conference on Interactive Entertainment (pp. 201-207). Sidney: Creativity & Cognition Studios Press.

UIGEA (2006). 31 U.S.C. §§5361-5367 („Prohibition on Funding of Unlawful Internet Gambling").

von Ahn, L., & Dabbish, L. (2004). Labeling images with a computer game. Proceedings of the SIGHCI Conference on Human Factors in Computing Systems (pp. 319-326). New York; NY: ACM.

von Ahn, L., & Dabbish, L. (2008). Designing games with a purpose. Communications of the ACM, 51(8), 58-67.

Williams, R.J., & Wood, R.T. (2007). Internet Gambling. A Comprehensive Review and Synthesis of the Literature. Report prepared for the Ontario Problem Gambling Research Centre, Guelph, Ontario, Canada. Lethbridge, Alberta: Alberta Gaming Research Institute.

Yee, N. (2006). Motivations for play in online games. CyberPsychology & Behavior, 9(6), 772-775.

Zyda, M. (2005). From visual simulation to virtual reality to games. Computer / IEEE Computer Society, 9, 25-32.

Chapter 14
Software

14.1   The Software Market

"Software" refers to programs that can be run on hardware (generally a computer). These programs are in code. The market for software (Mowery, 1995) is distinguished by virtue of its particular complexity: there is not only a wealth of applications, but also a multitude of respective new versions following each other chronologically or variants, offered at the same time, which differ in terms of their functionalities. For many programs, it is important that they be attuned to each other. To comprehensively describe the products of such a market in the context of a single chapter does not appear possible, which is why we will content ourselves with a general overview and concentrate on describing the creation of software.

As complex as the market is in terms of products, it is extremely simple from the companies' perspective. For commercial software, there are a select few companies who dominate–we need only consider Microsoft's monopoly status. However, in the single market segments, too, there is often a single company that "calls the tune". Thus, there is a clear market leader, in SAP, for programs of Enterprise Resource Planning (ERP); the market for database system is dominated by Oracle. Apart from commercial products, we can find Open Source software–which is just as highly developed–such as Linux' or Apache's, which is the product of voluntary (and unpaid) cooperation between software developers. From a user perspective, the choices represented here are not summed up as "either/or", but increasingly as "not only but also", since products from both worlds are often interoperable (Baird, 2008).

Dominant companies, and dominant products within market segments, provide for a high functionality in the programs, but also to a great vulnerability, since standard programs in particular are susceptible to attack (this is where the criminal's work investment "pays off"). Among the quality criteria for software are thus both optimal functionality and an equally optimal software security.

In a first rough classification (Buxmann et al., 2008, 4), we can distinguish **system software** (e.g. operating systems, network software or programming languages), **machine-oriented software** such as Middleware ("connecting" software, which allows programs to interact) and database and **application software** (e.g.

retrieval systems). Within application software, we also differentiate **individual software** (which is "tailor-made" for a specific task in a company) and **standard software**, which is produced for the mass market. For the latter, we classify via the kind of usage, and are left with software for commercial usage, such as ERP or knowledge management systems (with a multitude of programs, such as systems for document, project, customer relationship or customer knowledge management) (Gust von Loh, 2009), software for commercial and private usage (browsers, office software) and software for purely private implementation (such as games or software for looking at and editing pictures). Figure 14.1 collects all these aspects in one classification.

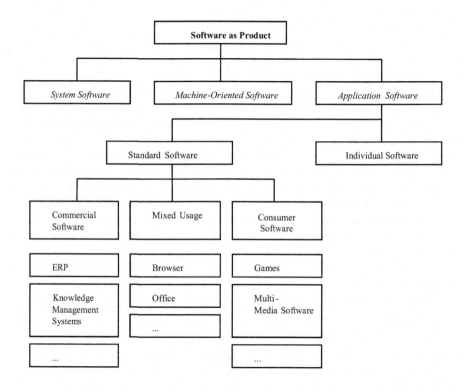

Figure 14.1: Rough Classification of Software.

The software products are joined by software services. Here, we distinguish between consulting and implementation services and the operation of application software as a service. **Consulting and implementation services** are often necessary when there is insecurity concerning the kind of software to be used or when the required software is difficult to implement in the company (Buxmann et al., 2008, 7). Such service providers appear in the form of IT service companies, system integrators or systems houses. Some consulting services also specialize in software selection and implementation.

Certain companies decline to acquire application software and use it in-house, instead outsourcing this operational procedure to third parties. Such companies host application software and offer their services on a subscription basis. Here, we speak of **Software as a Service** (SaaS) (Buxmann et al., 2008, 8et seq.). Figure 14.2 shows our classification of software services.

Software companies generate their revenue either by selling licenses for their products or by offering services (or from both areas).

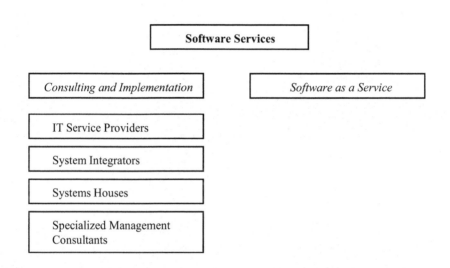

Figure 14.2: Rough Classification of Software Services.

14.2   Software Development

Depending on our starting point, we distinguish between five kinds of software development (the first three following Ruparelia, 2010, 12):
- on the basis of specifications (Cascade model, b-model, V-model),
- on the basis of risk (to be avoided) (spiral model),
- on the basis of concrete scenarios (simplified model),
- on the basis of the development process (agile software development),
- component-based development (can be combined with one of the above methods).

Every software development must be both effective and efficient (Zave, 1984, 112-113). Effectiveness ("are we doing the right things?")–called "Validation (Building the Right System)" by Zave–is demonstrated by customers successfully implementing the software in solving their problems, where the users are familiar with the intended applications, but not with computer systems. Efficiency ("are we doing things the right way?"), or "Verification (Building the System Right)", means that the system thus created fulfils the formulated expectations and specifications, but it also means that the (financial or personal) means applied during production have been used ideally.

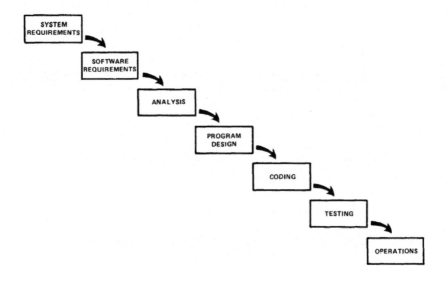

Figure 14.3: The Cascade Model of Software Development. Source: Royce, 1970, 329.

At the beginning of the traditional models of software development are the specifications, in other words, what the system to be created is expected to offer in terms of functionality. As early as 1956, Benington introduced a corresponding model (Benington, 1987), which was fleshed out by Royce into the **Cascade model** in 1970 (Figure 14.3). The way from the requirements to the working system proceeds via several stages, which much each be planned and staffed. On the basis of the specifications for the entire system (which also comprises hardware), the software specifications are separated and analyzed in such a way that they become programm*able*. Only after the program's design has been conceived does the actual programming ("coding") of the desired solution begin. This is then tested extensively and, in case of positive results, released. One should not imagine this to be a linear and one-track process, however. Rather, there is a feedback to previous stages every step of the way. Of particular importance is the interplay of software specifications and program design, since it is decided only during the conception of the software whether the requirements even make sense and, particularly, if they are realizable. A further central feedback loop is located between testing and product design, since here it is shown how the design "runs" during operation. Royce (1970, 332) emphasizes the importance of project documentation, since detailed notes on the acquired status of the project are necessary at every step of the software development. To avoid errors in the product, Royce (1970, 334) recommends repeating the entire process ("do it twice"), the goal being, firstly, the prototype, and the operative product second. In conclusion, Royce (1970, 338) sets out five "golden rules" of software development:

> Complete program design before analysis and coding begins.
>
> Documentation must be current and complete.
>
> Do the job twice if possible.
>
> Testing must be planned, controlled and monitored.
>
> Involve the customer.

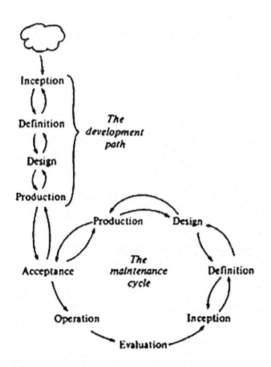

Figure 14.4: The b-Model of Software Development. Source: Birrell & Ould, 1985, 4.

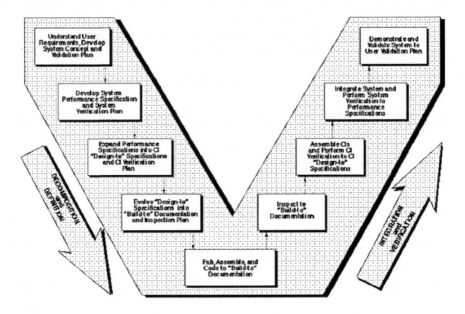

Figure 14.5: The V-Model of Software Development. Source: Forsberg & Mooz, 1995, 5. CI = Configuration Item.

Birrel and Ould (1985) split the production process in two fundamental stages in their **b-model** (Figure 14.4). The first stage–the development path–is laid out analogously to the Waterfall model. Birrel and Ould emphasize that a software is never "final", but requires constant maintenance and further development. In this respect, the second stage–the maintenance cycle–must be heeded, leading as it does to a sequence of versions of the original software.

The **V-model** by Forsberg and Mooz (1995), as used by NASA, also follows the Cascade model at first, but splits the overall process into two subphases (Figure 14.5). The process starts at the top left, with the users' information requirements, and ends up at the top right, with the information system as accepted by the user. On the left-hand side of the V, user specifications are disassembled into "configuration items" and defined as precisely as possible, in order to be assembled in an integrated way–as software items–on the right-hand side. Here, the single (horizontal) levels correspond to each other: user requirements are opposed by the system, as positively evaluated by the users (topmost level), the system architecture by the integrated system and the design work corresponds with the system integration work (levels 3 and 4), so that comparisons between the different stages of the requirements (left-hand side) and the stages of system development (right-hand side) can be made at any given time.

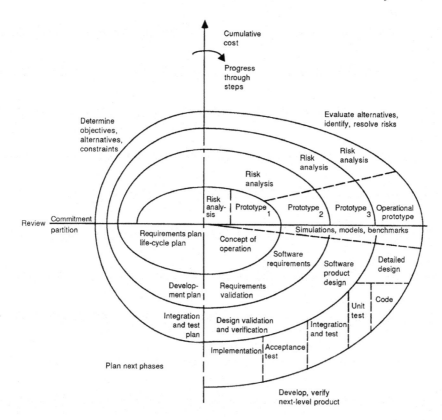

Figure 14.6: The Spiral Model of Software Development. Source: Boehm, 1988, 64.

Software development is an expensive and risky business. Boehm's **spiral model** (1988) (Figure 14.6) always keeps this risk in mind, being characterizable via "start small, think big" (Ruparelia, 2010, 10). The elements of the Waterfall are still granted great importance, but they are no longer run through in their entirety at the beginning. The Cascade model's top-down approach is replaced by a look-ahead perspective. The first prototype is the result of a feasibility study and is thus very primitive, but it is meant to make it possible to estimate whether the risk of starting the project is worth it in the first place. In the second run, the requirements are specified and analyzed. At the end of this run, there is again a prototype, which is subjected to a risk analysis. Bit by bit–secured via a risk analysis after each round–an operative prototype is developed, which can be fleshed out into a product. The great advantage of the spiral model is its continuous risk estimate, and thus its cost control of software development

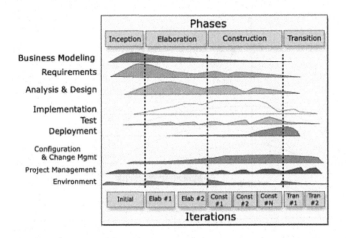

Figure 14.7: The Unified Model of Software Development. Source: Jacobson et al., 1999 and Intelligent Systems.

The **unified model** by Jacobson, Booch and Rumbaugh (1999) starts with the concrete case of software development and unifies aspects of both the Cascade and the spiral model (Figure 14.7). Within the four phases (beginning, conceptional elaboration, software construction and transition to the market phase), several rounds of iteration are run through, as in the spiral model. Differently weighted according to the phase, the objective is to run through six core disciplines of software development: moulding the business model, specifications, analysis and design, implementation, testing and practical application. Here we recognize the building blocks of the Cascade model without any difficulty. Complementing the core process, attention is also granted to accompanying activities such as change management or project management.

The approaches to software development sketched thus far can be summarized as being "plan-driven"–they pursue an elaborate plan and document every step. Not so the "light-weight" methods, such as the Dynamic Systems Development Method, Feature-Driven Development or Extreme Programming, which, put together, we call **agile software development**. This method is distinguished via a non-linear process, in which frequent, short feedback loops occur between developers, among each other, and between developers and customers, in the sense of "inspect-and-adapt" (Williams & Cockburn, 2003, 40). The "manifest of agile software development" formulates four fundamental behavioral guidelines:

> individuals and interactions over processes and tools,
>
> working software over comprehensive documentation,
>
> customer collaboration over contract negotiation,
>
> responding to change over following a plan.

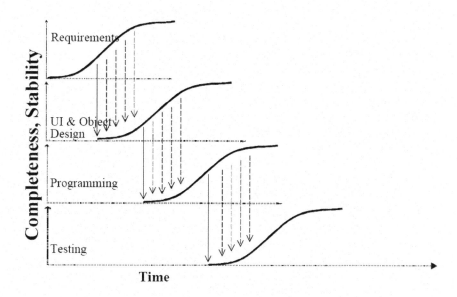

Figure 14.8: Agile Software Development with Overlapping Project Phases. Source: Cockburn, 2000.

One orients oneself more on people and communication than on set plans in project management (Cockburn, 2000, 8). Communication itself–since it is always less than perfect–must be guided. This is how software development becomes a game, which is played in a team and pursues goals. Alistair Cockburn (2000, 33 and 40) describes agile software development as a "goal-directed cooperative game" and as a "game of invention and communication". The group of developers starts their work as early as possible, so that project phases, which are normally worked through one after the other, overlap. Here it is essential for the information of each previous stage to be constantly updated (indicated in Figure 14.8 via the dashed arrows). Updates are made via direct communication and not via written documentation. This is expressed particularly clearly in Extreme Programming (XP): we deliver software, not documentation (Cockburn, 2000, 141).

Since it is dependent on direct communication, agile software development is suited for small teams (less than 50 developers) and companies that are not certified according to the quality management norm ISO 9000, because ISO 9000 prescribes strict documentation. However, it is possible to combine agile software development with one of the plan-based methods (Boehm & Turner, 2003).

Software consists of components–for instance, a text processing software will have the integrated components of spellchecking or hyphenation (Brereton & Budgen, 2000). It is advisable to use such components multiple times and incorporate them into systems. This is the basic idea of **component-based software development**, which dates back to McIlroy (1969). Component-based development can be combined with any of the previously introduced models of software production.

What does software development look like in practice? We will briefly sketch this on the example of **Microsoft**. There are loosely linked small teams of developers, who frequently synchronize their work results and stabilize the product in development. Added to this are continuous tests of the software. This "Synch-and-Stabilize" approach (Cusumano & Selby, 1997, 54) knows different project phases (planning, development, stabilization), but it does not run through the stages of the Cascade model one after the other, instead pursuing an interative approach. Cusumano and Selby (1997, 55) report:

> The waterfall model has gradually lost favor, ..., because companies usually build better products if they can change specifications and designs, get feedback from customers, and continually test components as the products are evolving. As a result, a growing number of companies in software and other industries–including Microsoft–now follow a process that iterates among design, building components, and testing, and also overlaps these phases and contains more interactions with customers during development.

Thus it can definitely happen that more than 30% of specifications in the planning phase are amended during later development stages (Cusumano & Selby, 1997, 56). The products are offered on the market as long as they are "good enough". In other words, one does not wait until something becomes "perfect" (Cusumano & Selby, 1997, 60).

14.3   Globalization and "Offshoring"

The software industry is aligned internationally. Programs can–at least in principle–be developed anywhere, with transport costs, in contrast to the value chain of physical goods, being negligible. The **globalization** of this industry is not only of importance for the labor markets, but also for distribution. There are hardly any national "home markets" for software; rather, software can be sold the world over (Buxmann et al., 2008, 156 et seq.).

If we want to make the international buying and labor markets usable for software production, we must decide whether to found subsidiaries abroad (or enter joint ventures with domestic enterprises) or whether to contract a third party. The latter method is called–no matter what country is concerned–"outsourcing". Outsourcing activities abroad is either "nearshoring", when the countries are close by (from the U.S.A.'s perspective Canada or Mexico, from the German perspective the Czech Republic, Poland, Hungary and Slovakia), or "offshoring", when far-

away countries are concerned (such as India, for companies with their seat in
Germany or the U.S.). Table 14.1 summarizes these definitions.

Outsourcing *Nearshoring* *Offshoring*			*Contractee has its seat...*	
		domestically	*in neighboring countries*	*overseas*
Shifting of internal activities to...	associated enterprises	---	Nearshoring without Outsourcing	Offshoring without Outsourcing
	foreign enterprises	Outsourcing	Nearshoring with Outsourcing	Offshoring with Outsourcing

Table 14.1: Systematization of Outsourcing, Nearshoring and Offshoring. Source: Following Mertens et al., 2005, 2.

The shifting of internal activities abroad without outsourcing means the founding
of subsidiaries or entering joint ventures with domestic companies. The goals are
cost savings via lower salaries in the target country as well as the option of tapping the respective foreign markets. Since the creation of one's own subsidiary
"from the bottom up" in an unknown country requires a lot of effort, joint ventures
with established enterprises from the target country allow a company to profit
from their knowledge of the country and preliminary work. Here the difference
between nearshoring and offshoring becomes clear. In nearshoring, the cultural
(but also the temporal) distance is far shorter than in offshoring, which means that
subsidiaries make more sense in closer proximity. The shifting of one's activities
to foreign companies, i.e. outsourcing, can be done domestically or aim for close-
by countries (with similar cultures) or far-off countries (with the disadvantage of
cultural differences). The software industry makes use of nearshoring, offshoring
and outsourcing like few other branches of the industry. India in particular has become an important exporter of software and partner of foreign software companies.

What are the motives that lead software companies to practice outsourcing as
well as nearshoring/offshoring? Buxmann, Diefenbach and Hess (2009, 165 et
seq.) detect five bundles of motives:

- Cost savings (lower salaries in the nearshore and offshore locations, but
  connected to a higher coordination effort–particulary offshore),
- Higher flexibility (in outsourcing, services can be bought precisely when
  needed, thus reducing one's own fixed costs),
- Concentration on core competencies (shifting more peripheral activities
  abroad while dealing with the important aspects oneself),

- Acquiring know-how (India in particular has many and well-trained information specialists, which are not available in the national labor markets of, for instance, Germany and the U.S.–in such numbers at least),
- "Follow the Sun" (Development and Service Centers intelligently placed around the world allow for service around the clock, due to the different time zones).

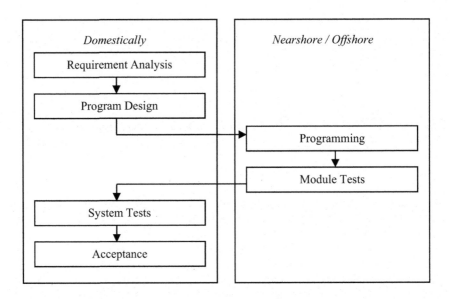

Figure 14.9: Phases of Software Development Domestically and Nearshore/Offshore. Source: Following Buxmann et al., 2009, 178.

If we regard the steps of software development, we can see that not all stages of the creation process are suitable for nearshoring or offshoring. Buxmann et al. (2009, 178) discuss the option of preferentially shifting abroad routine tasks such as programming (following detailed specifications) and tests of the programmed modules, while keeping the other steps in-company (Figure 14.9).

What are the effects of globalization on **SAP**? This company, based in Walldorf, Germany, produces business software and is the worldwide market leader within this segment (Schuster et al., 2009). The stage of requirement analysis is distributed internationally by SAP (to subsidiaries as well as independent companies), since proximity to the respective customers allows the company to meet an optimum of specific requirements. The rough planning for the project is done in Walldorf, while the concrete program design, programming and testing are done in SAP's development centers, scattered around the world (Schuster et al., 2009,

191). Apart from various smaller development centers, SAP keeps four large centers: (in order of their strategic importance) in Walldorf, Bangalore, Montreal and Palo Alto. As far as it does not touch upon highly sensitive areas, programming can be shifted to India. For software tests, SAP keeps a test team in Pune (India) (Buxmann et al., 2008, 180-181.). This distributed processing results in the project teams' high creativity level, due to employees' different cultural backgrounds and–via the "Follow the Sun" principle–project working times of 24 hours every day. The headquarters in Walldorf supervises the process of the decentralized activities and integrates the individual work packages. The software is implemented on location, by the customer. Customer service and system support are guaranteed around the clock by three call centers in Walldorf, Philadelphia and Singapore. Here, "Follow the Sun" is essential, as Schuster, Holtbrügge and Heidenreich (2009, 192) report:

> Since SAP often supports all of a company's business processes, such a company will be unable to operate in case of system failure, which makes around-the-clock service availability a decisive competition factor for the customer.

14.4   Conclusion

- The software market is very complicated from the product side; however, if we focus on companies, it becomes more simple, since many market segments are dominated by a single company, respectively.
- We differentiate the market for software products into system software, machine-oriented software and application software. Software is either individual software (tailor-made for one specific use scenario) or standard software (conceived for the mass market). Standard application software is conceived for either commercial, private or combined use in both the above areas. Software services regard both consulting and implementation as well as Software as a Service.
- Software development follows classical models. The Waterfall model (as well as its variants, the b-model and the V-model) operates on the basis of the specifications; the spiral model focuses on risk assessment and thus bases an iterative development path. In the unified model, aspects of the other two models are combined, on the basis of the specific case. Component-based development strives toward using existing software modules (components) multiple times.
- Microsoft works iteratively while pursuing a synch-and-stabilize approach.

- The software industry always works internationally, both on buying and labor markets and on sales markets. Outsourcing is frequently practiced. Subsidiaries, joint ventures with domestic enterprises and outsourcing can also be found on foreign markets.
- We distinguish between nearshoring (foreign countries that are close to home and have a similar culture) and offshoring (overseas countries– India being particularly popular).
- SAP uses the advantages of nearshoring and offshoring. By using "Follow the Sun", both software creation teams and service personnel can work 24 hours every day.

14.5   Bibliography

Baird, S.A. (2008). The heterogeneous world of proprietary and open-source software. Proceedings of the 2nd International Conference on Theory and Practice of Electronic Governance (pp. 232-238). New York, NY: ACM.

Benington, H.D. (1987). Production of large computer programs. Proceedings of the 9th International Conference on Software Engineering (pp. 299-310). Los Alamitos, CA: IEEE Computer Society Press.

Birrell, N.D., & Ould, M.A. (1985). A Practical Handbook to Software Development. New York, NY: Cambridge University Press.

Boehm, B.W. (1988). A spiral model of software development and enhancement. Computer / IEEE, Sept., 61-72.

Boehm, B., & Turner, R. (2003). Using risk to balance agile and plan-driven methods. Computer / IEEE, 36(6), 57-66.

Brereton, P., & Budgen D. (2000). Component-based systems. A classification of issues. Computer / IEEE, Nov., 54-62.

Buxmann, P., Diefenbach, H., & Hess, T. (2008). Die Softwareindustrie. Ökonomische Prinzipien, Strategien, Perspektiven. Berlin, Heidelberg: Springer.

Cockburn, A. (2000). Agile Software Development. (Online).

Cusumano, M.A., & Selby, R.W. (1997). How Microsoft builds software. Communications of the ACM, 40(6), 53-61.

Forsberg, K., & Mooz, H. (1995). The Relationship of System Engineering to the Project Cycle. Cupertino, CA: Center for Systems Management.

Gust von Loh, S. (2009). Evidenzbasiertes Wissensmanagement. Wiesbaden: Gabler.

Jacobson, I., Booch, G., & Rumbaugh, J. (1999). The Unified Software Development Process. Reading, MA: Addison-Wesley.

McIlroy, M.D. (1969). Mass produced software components. Naur, P., & Randell, B. (ed.), Software Engineering. Report on a Conference Sponsored by the NATO Science Committee (pp. 138-155). Garmisch, Germany, 7th to 11th October 1968. Brussels: NATO.

Mertens, P., Große-Wilde, J., & Wilkens, I. (2005). Die (Aus-)Wanderung der Softwareproduktion. Eine Zwischenbilanz. Erlangen, Nürnberg: Friedrich-Alexander-Universität. (Arbeitsberichte des Instituts für Informatik. Friedrich-Alexander-Universität Erlangen Nürnberg; 38,3).

Mowery, D.C. (1995). International Computer Software Industry. New York, NY: Oxford University Press.

Royce, W.W. (1970). Managing the development of large software systems. Proceedings of the 9th International Conference on Software Engineering (pp. 328-338). Los Alamitos, CA: IEEE Computer Society Press.

Ruparelia, N.B. (2010). Software development lifecycle models. ACM SIGSOFT Software Engineering Notes, 35(3), 8-13.

Schuster, T., Holtbrügge, D., & Heidenreich, S. (2009). Konfiguration und Koordination von Unternehmungen in der Softwarebranche. Das Beispiel SAP. In Holtbrügge, D., Holzmüller, H.H., & von Wangenheim, F. (eds.), Management internationaler Dienstleistungen mit 3K. Konfiguration–Koordination–Kundenintegration (pp. 174-202). Wiesbaden: Gabler.

Williams, L., & Cockburn, A. (2003). Agile software development: It`s about feedback and change. Computer / IEEE, 36(6), 39-43.

Zave, P. (1984). The operational versus the conventional approach to software development. Communications of the ACM, 27(2), 104-118.

Chapter 15
Online Advertising

15.1 Forms of Advertising on the Internet

Online advertising means advertisements scattered throughout the internet. Many website operators, among them all large search engine providers, offer their services for free, which allows them to generate large numbers of visits and visitors to their sites. Their customers' attention is sold (or auctioned) to advertising customers. This principle is known from commercial television, having merely been transferred to the World Wide Web, as Evans (2008, 359) describes:

> Many web sites settled on the traditional „free-tv" modell: generate traf-
> fic by giving away the content and sell traffic to advertisers.

Internet advertisement has two goals (Hollis, 2005):
- building up and maintaining a brand,
- selling products via the internet (e-commerce).

The basic forms of online advertisements (Faber et al., 2004) are banners (and other graphically oriented elements), which are displayed on websites independently of the person of the user and of any search arguments, e-mails (generally in the form of newsletters), which are sent to limited target groups with the explicit consent of the recipients, and context-specific ads, which appear on the basis of subscribed search arguments, when users enter appropriate queries. Context-specific advertising is called "**search advertising**", banner advertising is called "**display advertising**" (Evans, 2008, 363). Special forms of advertising are viral marketing ("contagious advertising") as well as advertising in digital games. Figure 15.1 summarizes this rough classification of online advertising in an overview.

From a technical point of view, advertising resources on the Web (thus excluding newsletters, which are sent out in the form of e-mails) are
- graphics (typically banners),
- websites in themselves (typically pop-up windows or interstitials),
- text displays (typically Sponsored Links in search engines).

According to Faber, Lee and Nan (2004, 456), some forms of Web advertising re-produce known patterns from non-digital media. Banners resemble posters, pop-ups and particularly ads that interrupt processes (interstitials) are reminiscent of advertising breaks in commercial television (Barnes & Hair, 2009). Depending on how strongly the forms of advertising impede the user's intended activities on the Web, they are rejected as more or less of an "intrusion". This negative attitude is directed toward the ads themselves, but also to the website that displays them (McCoy et al., 2007).

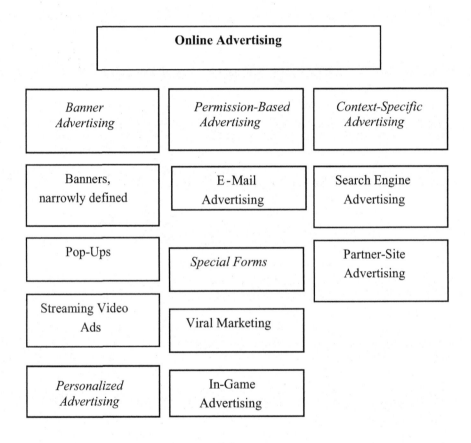

Figure 15.1: Classification of Online Advertising.

It is important for the advertiser to create an ideal **target site**, to which the ad directs the user (von Bischopinck & Ceyp, 2007, 145 et seq.). This site serves, depending on the goal that is being pursued, either brand management or ventures or a first step toward a transaction in e-commerce and, eventually, the creation of a longer-term customer relationship.

The business models for online advertising provide for three different **settlement bases** (Mangàni, 2004):

- Cost per View (CPV) or Cost per Impression (CPI), generally billed per thousand ads as "thousand-contact price" (TCP),
- Cost per Click (CPC), billed per number of clicks on the ad,
- Cost per Action (CPA), billed as a sort of realtor fee for sales in e-commerce (Hu et al., 2010), but with the downside that the strategy of brand building, which does not lead to direct profits, is not taken into consideration.

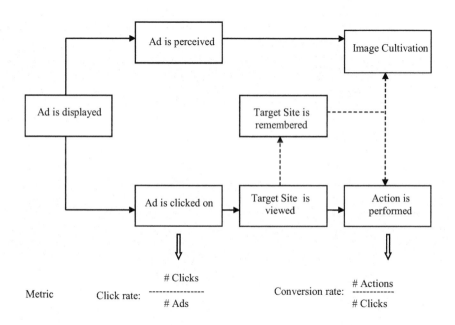

Figure 15.2: Stages of an Online Ad and its Metrics. Note: # : Number.

How does the **customer dialog** for an online ad work (Figure 15.2)? The ad, i.e. the banner or context-specific text, is displayed to the user. If the ad is not clicked on, but still perceived, this serves the advertised product's, or the advertising company's, image cultivation. In the ideal case, though, the ad is clicked on and the target site accessed. Here, we must distinguish between two subsequent paths:

in the first case, an action is directly performed, something is bought or the customer signs up for a newsletter (which, in turn, mutates into permission-based e-mail advertising), whereas in the second case, not direct action takes place, but the customer remembers the website (or product or company), which both image cultivation and can also lead–at a later date–to actions (Manchanda et al., 2006).

We take into account three **metrics**, which serve as the success factors of an online campaign (von Bischopinck & Ceyp, 2007, 237 et seq.):

- Click Rate, as the relative frequency of clicks on an ad with regard to all of its displays: #Clicks / #Ads,
- Conversion Rate, as the relative frequency of user actions (online sales, qualified customer contacts via subscription to a newsletter and similar "leads") with regard to all visits to the website initiated via the ad: #Actions / #Clicks,
- ROI (Return on Investment) as the quotient of the profit (generated via the actions) and the total cost of the marketing campaign: Profit / Costs of Online Advertising.

The crucial value, from an economic perspective, is the last one. Here, we need to be in the black, as the advertising campaign would create a loss otherwise. Let us suppose that a click on "our" ad costs €1, and that 1,000 clicks would generate €1,200 in e-commerce revenue. Not taking into account the costs in our own company, we would then have spendings of €1,000 and a profit of €1,200 - €1,000 = €200. The ROI of this campaign is at €200 / €1,000 = 0.2.

Companies occasionally choose the path of outsourcing their online advertising. Especially for the area of context-specific advertising, **search engine advertising agencies** (which offer both search engine advertising and search engine optimization among their services) have established themselves as their own small industry (von Bischopinck & Ceyp, 2007, 150 et seq.) (see Chapter 10 above).

15.2   Banner Advertising

Every medium has its own advertising standards, e.g. the 30-second commercial on TV or the quarter-page ad in the newspaper. In the early days of online advertising, banners were such a standard (and still are, partly). Depending on size and placement, we can distinguish between four basic forms (Plummer et al., 2007, 83):

- Full Banner (normally 468 * 60 pixels; Half Banner: 234 * 60 pixels),
- Leaderboard (728 * 90 pixels),
- Rectangle (normally 180 * 150 pixels; Large Rectangle: 336 * 280 pixels; Medium Rectangle: 300 * 250 pixels; Square: 125 * 125 pixels; Micro Bar: 88 * 31 pixels),
- Skyscraper (normally 120 * 600 pixels; Wide Skyscraper: 160 * 600 pixels).

In Figure 15.3, we indicate the size and typical placement of the basic banner forms. Instead of graphically oriented banners, there can also be video playbacks–in the Rectangle form.

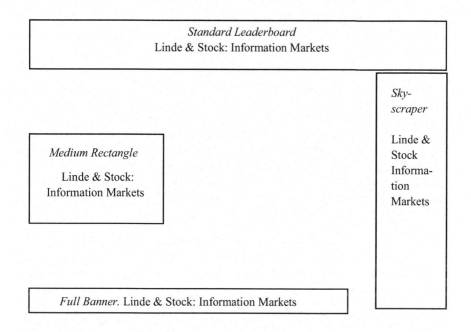

Figure 15.3: Typical Sizes and Placements of Banners.

For banners, we distinguish between **content** and **design** (Lohtia et al., 2003), which both have cognitive and affective dimensions. Cognitive content factors are stimuli, such as competitions, cognitive design options are represented by offers of interactive forms (such as a search function). Affective content factors are emotional tones (suggestions of joy, fear etc.), affective design elements are color and animation. Lohtia et al. distinguish banners addressed to companies (B-to-B advertising) from those directed at the end customer (B-to-C). In an extensive empirical study of the influence of the content and design elements described above on the manifestation of the Click-Through Rate (CTR), the following results arose (Lohtia et al., 2003, 416):

> 1. ... the presence of incentives and interactivity lowered the CTR of banner advertisements. This was especially true for B2B banner advertisements than B2C banner advertisements.

2. ... the presence of emotion and animation increased the CTR for B2C banner advertisements and decreased the CTR for B2B banner advertisements.

3. Medium level of color was better than low or high levels of color for B2B and B2C banner advertisements.

4. B2B banner advertisements had higher CTR than B2C banner advertisements.

Banners do not have to appear, rigidly in place, throughout the duration of a campaign, but can also adjust to the daily rhythm of the customers. Plummer et al. (2007, 21 et seq.) report of successful customer responses depending on the time of day. The brewery Budweiser, for instance, displays certain beer banners every Friday afternoon due to the notion that this will lead customers to preferentially shop for beverages at the end of their working week. Kentucky Fried Chicken successfully displayed ads for a new product, adjusted for the different American time zones, just before the respective lunch hour.

15.3   Target-Group Specific Online Advertising

Certain banners (or other forms of online advertising) are only offered to selected users. In such cases, we speak of **target-group specific online advertising**. This is only possible when the operator of the website has enough information on his users. Basic information is gleaned via statements made by the customer during registration. Additionally, one can collect the user's digital traces, by, for instance, storing and accessing the URLs of all of the websites he has visited with the help of a "toolbox". In social networks such as Facebook, in particular, a lot of very detailed person-related data are collected–depending on the individual users' communicativeness. The customer's profile, collated from basic information and digital traces, is exploited for advertising by having only the ads be displayed that best match the customer profile. If the user is provided the option (as on Facebook) of clicking away ad banners, and if he gives his reasons for doing so ("... is uninteresting", "... is misleading" etc.), the operator can further optimize the user profile and is able to perform **personalized online advertising**. Personalized advertising, the main source of revenue for the operators of social networks, is quick to clash with the protection of privacy (Fuchs, 2010; Tucker, 2010).

15.4   Advertising in Digital Games

A specific area of digital advertising can be observed in "in-game advertising" (Gaca, 2007; Thomas & Stammermann, 2007). In contrast to click-oriented online advertising, it is not possible in this example to click away the ad (as with pop-ups) or to skip it (as with search engine and partner site advertising). There are static ads which are firmly integrated into the game and are not changeable, and there are dynamic ads, which is varied depending on the situation. Herman and Kaiser (2005, 25) explain this difference on a few examples:

> Where the industry used to work with "static" in-game displays, which were meant to make the game environment more "life-like"–billboards in the city, perimeter advertising in sports stadiums, product placement, theater marquees, a trip by the game's protagonist to McDonald's–now there is the possibility of "dynamic" ads. A game's protagonist might drink a Coke at 2pm, but later in the day, the otherwise identical cut-scene will see him ordering a beer or whiskey, all depending on what company bought the corresponding advertising slot.

We distinguish between three forms of in-game advertising:
- Poster advertising, perimeter advertising, illuminated advertising etc.,
- Product placement,
- Advergames.

Poster, illuminated and **perimeter advertising** (the latter particularly in sports games) simulate real-world advertising forms in the digital realm (Figure 15.4). Providing the dynamic concept is being used, this form can be adjusted to target groups with particular ease. Thus, one can offer a German player (registered, in online games, via the point of presence in the internet) can be offered German products, an American player will, however, be shown "his own". In a virtual world, such as Second Life, this sort of advertising is made extensive use of (Barnes, 2007).

Product placement (Ip, 2009) in games works analogously to product placement in film. We distinguish the passive placement of a branded item in the game's world (e.g. a can of a certain soft drink, placed on a desk somewhere but serving no purpose) from active placement. Actively dealing with a product lets the protagonist "experience" a certain company or product (Gaca, 2007, 12). This includes the aforementioned scene set in a fast food restaurant. Another example is the way Red Bull is advertised in the game Worms 3D: if the player's avatar drinks Red Bull, he enjoys various benefits–he is given wings, can run faster, fly higher etc. The player cannot possibly ignore this, since he needs Red Bull within the game–and is, at the same time, "provided with everything that makes up the image of Red Bull" (Herman & Kaiser, 2005, 29). Product placement is generally static.

Figure 15.4: Poster Advertising in a Digital Game. Source: Herman & Kaiser, 2005, 25.

Advergames are digital games created around a certain product. Here it is not the game, but the product which is in the foreground (Gaca, 2007, 12-13). Thus, for example, Chrysler developed driving games with which customers can "test drive" the company's latest products virtually (Herman & Kaiser, 2005, 28).

Initial results of empirical research into in-game advertising (Cauberghe & De Pelsmacker, 2010) show that players tend to remember brands thus advertised, but that there is no effect on their attitude toward them. If a game is played multiple times, however, this can lead to a negative influence on one's attitude toward the brand, which indicates a short wearout period. The repetition of static advertising in particular is subject to quick rejection by the player for being too obtrusive.

15.5   E-Mail Advertising

Advertising via e-mail is strictly regulated in most countries, and can only be implemented in special cases. Such advertising is allowed if the recipient has given his permission, which can be rescinded at any point (see Chapter 10). Correspondingly, such forms of advertising are termed "**permission-based**" (Godin, 1999). Compared with other forms of advertising, e-mail marketing is cheap and effective at the same time (Drèze, 2005). However, in order to be granted the permission to furnish customers with ads, it is imperative that the customers trust the advertiser to provide them with useful information. E-mail advertising is usually done in the form of **newsletters**, which reports on products or activities (e.g. training) and contains links to several target sites, and which, for legal reasons, has a specific link allowing the recipient to cancel his subscription to the newsletter ("opting out"). Occasionally, newsletters are used as websites. Three advantages speak in favor of permission-based e-mail advertising (Marinova et al., 2002, 62):

- The recipients enter themselves into mailing lists and thus signal at least a potential interest in accepting certain advertising information.
- The advertiser knows his recipients by name is thus able to personalize the ads ("One-to-One Marketing").
- The ad messages represent (in the ideal case, i.e. if there is a latent information need for the content provided) an information benefit or (in case the information is not currently relevant) at least no particularly sever burden.

The advertiser can never be sure that the customers have ordered the newsletter with their "real" mailing account. Some users deliberately create "spam accounts", from which they conduct certain transactions, but which they never use for communication. It can also never be assumed that the current recipients will tell the advertiser that they have changed their e-mail address. In this respect, the building and maintenance of **qualified mailing lists** are very important tasks (Tezinde et al., 2002, 30).

The goal of e-mail advertising campaigns is to achieve as high a click rate on the links as possible (and, in consequence, the performing of actions). The e-mail's content and design should lead the user to click on at least one of the links it contains. In any case, the most basic goal is to prevent the user from unsubscribing. Newsletters which are sent too often, in too short a time ("overtouching") increase the probability of customers opting out (Ansari & Mela, 2003, 144).

15.6 Context-Specific Advertising

If users work with search engines, they expect to be presented appropriate search results that satisfy their information needs. This fact leads to **context-specific search engine advertising** in marketing. Since we know, in this case, what a user is researching, we will show—in exact accordance with the search arguments entered by the user—advertising texts that might also satisfy the stated information need. Scattering losses are pretty minimal in this case, since the ad matches the query. The market leader in the area of context-specific search engine advertising is Google, with its **AdWords** service (Davis, 2010; Geddes, 2010) (Figure 15.5; the top three results and all results on the right-hand side are ads, marked as "sponsored links").

Travel Insurance	Search

About 95,600,000 results (0.31 seconds)   Advanced search

Cheap Travel Insurance   Sponsored links
WorldNomads.com/Travel-Insurance   Save 50% off travel agents prices ! Buy, extend and claim online, 24/7.

Travel Insurance online
www.worldwideinsure.com   Travel Insurance for E.U residents and Expats **Travel Insurance**.

Travel Insurance
www.WorldEscapade.com   Travel on a Budget & Save Up to 50% Coverage From 1,20€/ Day. Buy Now!

News for **Travel Insurance**

Standard travel insurance does not cover oil spill - 10 hours ago
She was told her travel insurance would not cover her air fare. "I figured that we would be qualified to receive reimbursement or credit for a future flight ...
New York Times   eTaiwan News - 12 related articles »

Travel Insurance | Compare Cheap Holiday Insurance Quotes ...
Compare travel insurance quotes from just £3 with moneysupermarket.com, Britain's no1 comparison site. Search over 450 policies and buy your cover online.
www.moneysupermarket.com/travel-insurance/ - Cached

Travel Insurance: Travel Guard - Trip, Medical/Health & Accident ...
Travel Guard is travel insurance and assistance that travels with you. Coverages include: Trip cancellation and delay, lost baggage, medical emergency, ...
www.travelguard.com/ - Cached - Similar

Sponsored links

Travel Health Insurance
U.S Expats & Citizens on the move
Renewable **Travel** Health **Insurance**
www.TravelHealthInsurance.com

Low Cost **Travel Insurance**
Save with Lonely Planet !
Be covered by our trusted provider.
www.lonelyplanet.com

Schengen **travel insurance**
Visiting Europe With A Visa?
Travel Insurance from 0.9 euro/day
www.AXA-Schengen.com/travel

Travel Health Insurance
ihi Bupa **Travel Insurance** Trusted
Across The World For Over 30 Years.
www.IHI.com

Low Cost **Travel Insurance**
Travel Insurance For Expats & E.U.
Residents. Simple, Clear Policies.
www.SunSelection.co.uk

Travel Insurance
Instant Quotes or buy online
Travel Medical or Trip Cancellation
www.internationalbenefits.com

Figure 15.5: Context-Specific Search Engine Advertising on the Example of Google AdWords. Source: Google.

Which keywords should be selected to lead to the ad display? This is a problem of knowledge representation: one indexes one's target site via expressive terms, which represent the content adequately. Additionally, one chooses words of which one assumes that users could use them to search for the target site. Google offers four formal options for defining a **keyword**:

- Exact match: [Apple Pie]. The Ad is only displayed if exactly the same search argument has been entered.
- Phrase match: "Apple Pie". The ad is displayed if that phrase occurs in the search argument.
- Broad match: Apple Pie. The ad is displayed if the terms occur somewhere in the search argument.
- Negative match (in conjunction with one of the above variants: — cinnamon. The ad is not displayed if the term occurs somewhere in the search argument.

The focus in selecting the terms is on **terminological control** over the keywords. Homonyms must be selected so as to prevent their polysemy from taking effect. If, for instance, a company that organizes trade fairs uses the keyword *fair*, its ad will also be displayed if a user searches for *carnival fair*. There are tools for finding synonyms and quasi-synonyms, which suggest (more or less appropriate) terms.

Here, one works either with analyses of log data from search requests, knowledge organization systems (such as thesauri) or with an analysis of co-occurring terms in the ad database at hand (Saramento et al., 2009; Kaiser, 2010, 139 et seq.).

Apart from the keywords, the advertising customer chooses further parameters (Kaiser, 2010, 102):

- Targeting (regional selection, target languages, time zones, exclusion of certain URLs),
- Budget (generally the setting of a daily budget),
- Bid (maximum offer),
- Distribution (AdWords, AdSense, ads in Gmail etc.).

If several advertisers have "booked" a keyword, Google will create a **ranking of ads**. Since it is known from empirical studies (Ghose & Yang, 2009) that both the click and the conversion rate correlate with the ranking (the higher the ranking, the higher the click and conversion rates), it is important for advertisers to place their ad text as high up as possible. The allocation of keywords is an auction procedure, specifically a variant of Second-Price Auctions, also called **Vickrey Auction** (following Vickrey, 1961), in which the winner does not pay the sum of his own offer but that of the bidder closest to himself.

The auction for keywords is fundamentally different from auctions for physical goods (Kaiser, 2010, 150). In the latter, there is only one winner, whereas the former auctions off rankings, which means that there is a winner, but also a second, third etc. A traditional auction ends with the winner getting the prize. The keyword auction, on the other hand, is continual, and the procedure changes with each new bid on the keyword. The search engine has the role of the auctioneer; the advertising customers are the bidders.

Google's Ad Rank is no pure price ranking, but also takes into consideration the "quality" of the text display. To calculate the retrieval status value e of the ad, the maximum price per click (max CPC) that is bid on is multiplied with the ad text's Quality Score (QS):

$$e_{Ad} = \max CPC_{Ad} * QS_{Ad}.$$

The Quality Score has several components, of which the most important is the ad's previous click rate. When an ad text is displayed for the first time, there can be no click rate. Such a cold-start problem (Richardson et al., 2007) can be resolved if the click rates of the same keywords in other advertisers as well as the click rates of similar (quasi-synonymous) terms are used as estimated values.

To calculate the price to be paid per click, Google takes the retrieval status value e of the nearest co-competitor and divides this value by the Quality Score of the current ad (plus 1 Cent). In Table 15.1, we execute the procedure on an example (let the minimum price for an ad be $0.04).

Rank ing	Cus- tomer	Max CPC	QS	e	Price Calculation	Price
1	A	$0.40	1.8	0.40 * 1.8 = **0.72**	0.65 / 1.8 + 0.01 = 0.3711	**$0.37**
2	B	$0.65	1.0	0.65 * 1.0 = **0.65**	0.375 / 1.0 + 0.01 = 0.385	**$0.39**
3	C	$0.25	1.5	0.25 * 1.5 = **0.375**	Minimum Offer: 0.04	**$0.04**

Table 15.1: Calculation of Ranking and Price in Google AdWords. Source: Following Kaiser, 2010, 160.

If an ad has a high Quality Score, one may have to pay less than one's competitors and still achieve a higher ranking (like customer A in Table 15.1). By taking into account the Quality Score, what we have now is no longer a classical Vickrey Auction; however, one still orients oneself on the principles of a Second-Price Auction (via the next-placed ad's retrieval status value). This calculation rewards ads that promise the highest profit for Google in comparison with their competitors with a high ranking.

Google offers **context-specific partner site advertising** via **AdSense**, which draws upon the ad database of AdWords. The billing of the site owner is either done via Cost per Click or Cost per View. The website that registers the ad is automatically indexed by Google and algorithmically reduced to (quantitatively) important words. The ad texts are then displayed in accordance with these extracted terms. Target sites for AdSense can also be blogs (Fox et al., 2009). In the example from Figure 15.6, the terms *Kaua'i* (as well as *Kauai*) and *Hawaii* (and *Hawaiian* and *HawaiiWeb*) occur multiple times on the website of HawaiiWeb. The four ads (visible in the Figure) displayed by Google either thematize *Hawaii* or *Kauai*. The selection and arrangement of the ad displays are given their foundation by their retrieval status value. Since ads by competitors might fit the content of one's own site, but one does not want to advertise the competition on one's own Web presence, Google provides a filter with which to pointedly reject ads by certain customers.

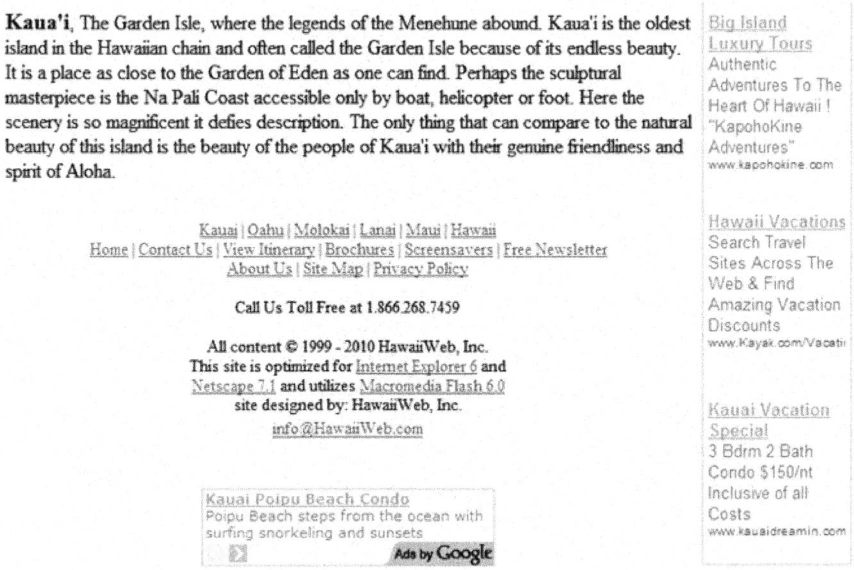

Kaua'i, The Garden Isle, where the legends of the Menehune abound. Kaua'i is the oldest island in the Hawaiian chain and often called the Garden Isle because of its endless beauty. It is a place as close to the Garden of Eden as one can find. Perhaps the sculptural masterpiece is the Na Pali Coast accessible only by boat, helicopter or foot. Here the scenery is so magnificent it defies description. The only thing that can compare to the natural beauty of this island is the beauty of the people of Kaua'i with their genuine friendliness and spirit of Aloha.

Big Island Luxury Tours
Authentic Adventures To The Heart Of Hawaii !
"KapohoKine Adventures"
www.kapohokine.com

Kauai | Oahu | Molokai | Lanai | Maui | Hawaii
Home | Contact Us | View Itinerary | Brochures | Screensavers | Free Newsletter
About Us | Site Map | Privacy Policy

Call Us Toll Free at 1.866.268.7459

All content © 1999 - 2010 HawaiiWeb, Inc.
This site is optimized for Internet Explorer 6 and Netscape 7.1 and utilizes Macromedia Flash 6.0
site designed by: HawaiiWeb, Inc.
info@HawaiiWeb.com

Kauai Poipu Beach Condo
Poipu Beach steps from the ocean with surfing snorkeling and sunsets
Ads by Google

Hawaii Vacations
Search Travel Sites Across The Web & Find Amazing Vacation Discounts
www.Kayak.com/Vacati

Kauai Vacation Special
3 Bdrm 2 Bath Condo $150/nt Inclusive of all Costs
www.kauaidreamin.com

Figure 15.6: Context-Specific Partner Site Advertising on the Example of Google AdSense. Source: HawaiiWeb.

Neither AdWords nor AdSense are fraud-proof. Competitor Click Fraud (in Ad-Words) and Publisher Click Fraud (in AdSense) are regarded as deviant information behavior (see Chapter 4.5.3 above) and are not reconcilable with prevailing law (see Chapter 5.10 above). Google works with a filter system for "invalid" clicks (which, however, is only able to recognize clear patterns) and does not charge the customer for these clicks (Kaiser, 2010, 126 et seq.).

15.7   Viral Marketing

Certain news spread fast and far, others remain virtually unnoticed. The driving force in the case of wide distribution is mouth-to-mouth propaganda. The exploitation of this force in advertising is called "viral marketing". Stuckmann (2010, 97) lists its advantages:

> The advertising message or the product are discovered by the customer and deemed so interesting that he wants to tell others of it, and thus passes his discovery on (…). The consumers reached in this way receive the message with good-will, since it does not reach them via trivial channels, such as TV or radio, but from their circle of friends and acquaintances.

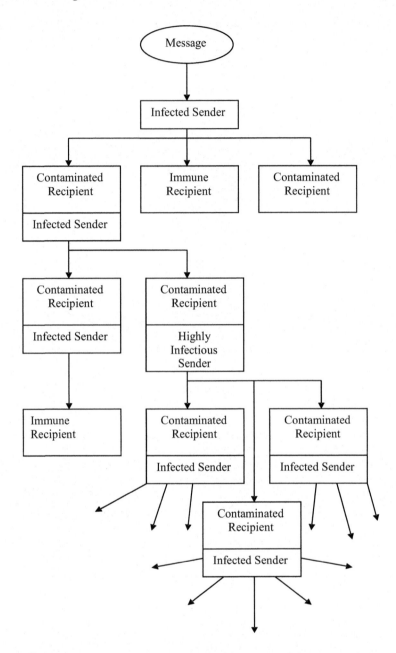

Figure 15.7: Spreading of a Message in Viral Marketing.

Viral information distribution can be observed not only in advertising, but concerns all manner of knowledge. We distinguish two forms:

- self-initiated viral information distribution: the author (e.g. a company for an advertising message) provides the initiative himself,
- foreign-initiated viral information distribution: some third party provides the initiative, where the message may be either positive or negative.

Also and especially on the internet, many forms of viral information distribution are possible. They can be particularly pronounced in recommender services (such as Amazon) (Leskovec et al., 2007; Richardson & Domingos, 2002), weblogs or videosharing services (YouTube) (Stuckmann, 2010), message boards and micro-blogging (Twitter) (Jansen et al., 2009). Foreign-initiated negative information distribution must be noticed by the enterprise concerned as early as possible in order to be counteracted, ideally via self-initiated actions.

A central role in digital viral marketing is played by the **users**, both as recipients and as senders (Subramani & Rajagopalan, 2003). In Figure 15.7, we want to exemplify this schematically. The "virus" is, in our case, the message. A recipient can be susceptible to this virus and "catch it", i.e. absorb the message; another recipient, on the other hand, might be "immune" against it and pay it no further attention. For the "viral carriers", there are three cases to be differentiated: (1.) the recipient does not pass on the message (as the person on the top right-hand side in Figure 15.7), (2.) the recipient passes on the message but the persons he sends it to do not, (3.) a "highly infectious" sender–possibly a respected individual due to his position in the community–sends the message on, with the consequence that his own recipients in turn massively distribute the message. In self-initiated viral marketing, it is important to use such highly infectious senders, in the sense of a Seed List.

15.8   Conclusion

- Advertising via the internet pursues the goals of creating and cultivating a brand as well as to make sales in e-commerce. The basic forms of online advertising are banners (display advertising), permission-based e-mail advertising and context-specific (search) advertising. Depending on how obtrusive the ads are to the user' workflow, it will be rejected or accepted, where, in the former case, the negative opinion concerning the ad are transferred to the website carrying the ad.
- The invoice bases for online advertising are Cost per View (displays), Cost per Click and Cost per Action (realtor fee on sales in e-commerce).
- Three metrics are suited for measuring the success of online campaigns: click rate, conversion rate and Return on Investment.

- Banner advertising is graphically oriented and is offered in four basic forms (full banner, leaderboard, rectangle, skyscraper). Both content and design of the banner should appeal to the customer.
- E-mail advertising requires, for legal reasons, the permission of the customers, which makes it a form of permission-based marketing.
- Context-specific advertising starts on the basis of a search request or a website and operates appropriate ads on exactly this basis. Search engine advertising (as in Google AdWords) contains a short ad text and keywords under which the text is displayed. If several advertisers use the same keyword, Google will create a ranking that depends upon the maximum price offered and on a Quality Score (mainly of the click rate). In the sense of a Vickrey auction, the retrieval status value of the next highest bidder is used as the basis for calculating the click price. Partner site advertising (such as Google AdSense) uses the ads from the AdWords database and displays them on thematically appropriate partner sites.
- Viral marketing banks on mouth-to-mouth propaganda, and thus on users' active role in information diffusion. On the Web–particularly in Web 2.0 services–viral information distribution can often be observed.

15.9   Bibliography

Ansari, A., & Mela, C.F. (2003). E-Customization. Journal of Marketing Research, 40, 131-145.

Barnes, S.B. (2007). Virtual world as a medium for advertising. The DATA BASE for Advances in Information Systems, 38(4), 45-55.

Barnes, S.B., & Hair, N.F. (2009). From banners to YouTube. Using the rear-view mirror to look at the future of internet advertising. International Journal of Internet Marketing and Advertising, 5(3), 223-239.

Cauberghe, V., & De Pelsmacker, P. (2010). Advergames. The impact of brand prominence and game repetition on brand responses. Journal of Advertising, 39(1), 5-18.

Davis, H. (2010). Google Advertising Tools. Cashing in with Adsense, Adwords, and the Google APIs. 2nd ed. Beijing: O'Reilly Media.

Drèze, X. (2005). Lessons from the front line. Two key ways in which the internet has changed marketing forever. Applied Stochastic Models in Business and Industry, 21, 443-448.

Evans, D.E. (2008). The economics of the online advertising industry. Review of Network Economics, 7(3), 359-391.

Faber, R.J., Lee, M., & Nan, X. (2004). Advertising and the consumer information environment online. American Behavioral Scientist, 48(4), 447-466.

Fox, D., Smith, A., Chaparro, B.S., & Shaikh, A.D. (2009). Optimizing presentation of AdSense ads within blogs. Proceedings of the 53rd Human Factors and Ergonomics Society Annual Meeting (pp. 1267-1271).

Fuchs, C. (2010). Facebook, Web 2.0 und ökonomische Überwachung. Datenschutz und Datensicherheit, 34(7), 453-458.

Gaca, C. (2007). Markenmanagement in Video- und Computerspielen. Saarbrücken: VDM Verlag Dr. Müller.

Geddes, B. (2010). Advanced Google AdWords. Hoboken, NJ: Wiley.

Ghose, A., & Yang, S. (2009). An empirical analysis of search engine advertising. Sponsored search in electronic markets. Management Science, 55(10), 1605-1622.

Godin, S. (1999). Permission Marketing. Turning Strangers into Friends, and Friends into Customers. New York, NY: Simon & Schuster.

Herman, D., & Kaiser, S. (2005). Die Eroberung eines neuen Werbekanals. GDI_Impuls, 2(05), 24-31.

Hollis, N. (2005). Ten years of learning on how online advertising builds brands. Journal of Advertising Research, 45(2), 255-268.

Hu, Y., Shin, J., Tang, Z. (2010). Pricing of online advertising. Cost-per-click-through vs. cost-per-action. Proceedings of the 43rd Hawaii International Conference on System Sciences. IEEE Computer Science Press.

Ip, B. (2009). Product placement in interactive games. Proceedings of the International Conference on Advances in Computer Entertainment (pp. 89-97). New York, NY: ACM.

Jansen, B.J., Zhang, M., Sobel, K., & Chowdury, A. (2009). Twitter power. Tweets as electronic word of mouth. Journal of the American Society for Information Science and Technology, 60(11), 2169-2188.

Kaiser, C. (2010). Suchmaschinenwerbung. Sponsored Links als Geschäftsmodell der Suchwerkzeuge. Mit einer Fallstudie über chinesische Suchdienste. Hamburg: Kovač.

Leskovec, J., Adamic, L.A., & Huberman, B.A. (2007). The dynamics of viral marketing. ACM Transactions on the Web, 1(1), art. 5.

Lohtia, R., Donthu, N., & Hershberger, E.K. (2003). The impact of content and design elements on banner advertising click-through rates. Journal of Advertising Research, 43(4), 410-418.

Manchanda, P., Dubé, J.P., Goh, K.Y., & Chintagunta, P.K. (2006). The effect of banner advertising on internet purchasing. Journal of Marketing Research, 43, 98-108.

Mangàni, A. (2004). Online advertising. Pay-per-view versus pay-per-click. Journal of Revenue and Pricing Management, 2(4), 295-302.

Marinova, A., Murphy, J., & Massey, B.L. (2002). Permission e-mail marketing as a means of targeted promotion. Cornell Hotel and Restaurant Administration Quarterly, 43, 61-69.

McCoy, S., Everard, A., Polak, P., & Galletta, D.F. (2007). The effects of online advertising. Communications of the ACM, 50(3), 84-88.

Plummer, J., Rappaport, S., Hall, T., & Barocci, R. (2007). The Online Advertising Playbook. Proven Strategies and Tested Tactics from The Advertising Research Foundation. Hoboken, NJ: Wiley.

Richardson, M., & Domingos, P. (2002). Mining knowledge-sharing sites for viral marketing. Proceedings of the 8th ACM SIGKDD International Conference on Knowledge Discovery and Data Mining (pp. 61-70). New York, NY: ACM.

Richardson, M., Dominowska, E., & Ragno, R. (2007). Predicting clicks. Estimating the click-through rate for new ads. Proceedings of the 16th Conference on the World Wide Web (pp. 521-529). New York, NY: ACM.

Sarmeno, L., Trezentos, P., Gonçalves, J.P., & Oliveira, E. (2009). Inferring local synonyms for improving keyword suggestion in an on-line advertisement system. Proceedings of the 3rd International Workshop on Data Mining and Audience Intelligence for Advertising (pp. 37-45). New York, NY: ACM.

Stuckmann, M. (2010). Einsatzmöglichkeiten von Web 2.0 Tools im Marketing: Virales Marketing. Information–Wissenschaft und Praxis, 61(2), 97-101.

Subramani, M.R., & Rajagopalan, B. (2003). Knowledge-sharing and influence in online social networks via viral marketing. Communications of the ACM, 46(12ve), 300-307.

Tezinde, T., Smith, B., & Murphy, J. (2002). Getting permission. Exploring factors affecting permission marketing. Journal of Interactive Marketing, 16(4), 28-36.

Thomas, W., & Stammermann, L. (2007). In-Game Advertising. Werbung in Computerspielen. Strategien und Konzepte. Wiesbaden: Gabler.

Tucker, C. (2010). Social Networks, Personalized Advertising, and Privacy Controls. Working Papers / NET Institute No. 10-07.

Vickrey, W. (1961). Counterspeculation, auctions, and competitive sealed tenders. Journal of Finance, 16(1), 8-27.

Von Bischopinck, Y., & Ceyp, M. (2007). Suchmaschinen-Marketing. Konzepte, Umsetzung und Controlling. Berlin: Springer.

Part D

Competitive Strategies
of Information Providers

Chapter 16
Strategic Framework

16.1 Porter's Model of Industry Structure Analysis

What distinguishes an industry, and what must be taken into consideration when analyzing an industry? The work of Michael E. Porter (2004), who developed the model of the "Five Forces" at play in an industry, was groundbreaking in this regard. Before getting into this subject in more detail, we still need to explain what an industry is in the first place. Porter (2004, 5) explains an industry as

> the group of firms producing products that are close substitutes for each other.

To differentiate industries, he thus takes as his basis substitute competition. If we are to look at different industries, however, such as the pharmaceutical industry, the travel industry or even the information industry, we will soon recognize that a multitude of different products are on offer within an industry–and hence, within sub-industries or markets (Grant & Nippa, 2006, 125 et seq.). In the information industry, this might be online games or business news, which represent totally different markets and cannot be deemed to form a substitute relation. Now, the concept of the relevant market also normally uses the substitute relation as a criterion for differentiation (Backhaus, 2007, 127 et seq., Hungenberg, 2006, 98 et seq.); hence, it appears pertinent for our analytical purposes to relate the Five Forces model developed by Porter, as well as the Value Net model by Nalebuff and Brandenburger (1996)–to be introduced in the following–not only to an industry as a whole, but also to the (sub-)markets that might exist in an industry.

The basis of Porter's model is the industrial organisation approach (Tirole, 1999), which assumes that the attractiveness of a market from a company's perspective is mainly dependent on the market structure. In order to cover the industry systematically, Porter recommends considering five essential forces which, when added together, make up the industry's attractiveness. Individually, they are the competition between the companies within the industry, the suppliers' as well as the consumers' market power and the threat posed by substitute products and potential competitors (Porter, 2004, 4).

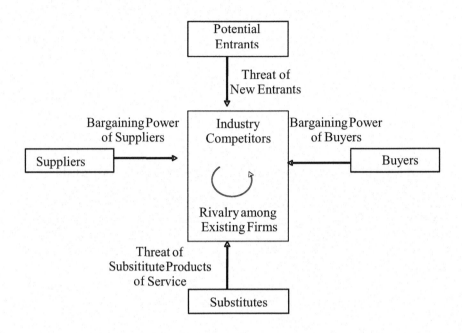

Figure 16.1: The Five Forces Driving Industry Competition According to Porter. Source: Porter, 1999, 34.

Even though an empirical proof of Porter's approach was only partially conclusive (Welge & Al-Laham, 2003, 204 et seq.), it wielded enormous influence on the scientific debate on enterprise strategy. One clear disadvantage of the model, however, is the implication that companies within an industry are automatically in competition with the other companies in the market, and that they can only gain an advantage in this way. Porter's basis is a classical understanding of the value-added chain, in which a company buys component parts from suppliers, assembles them and sells them on to its customers. The other players in the market, which produce the same or a similar amount of added value, are viewed as a threat to one's own profitability. The way markets actually work, however, shows that companies can also seek to gain an advantage via select cooperation with customers, suppliers or competitors (Hungenberg, 2006, 109 et seq.). This is where Nalebuff's and Brandenburger's Co-Opetition model starts off.

16.2   Nalebuff's and Brandenburger's Value Net

Nalebuff and Brandenburger (1996) want to emphasize that there are not only competitive but also cooperative relationships in the market, which are of equally great importance to achieving success in business. This combination of competition and cooperation–i.e., co-opetition–creates, in contrast to Porter's model, a slightly different model of market analysis. Nalebuff and Brandenburger speak not only of forces that threaten profitability, but also of a "Value Net", in which different agents can also create values together.

If we go back to Chapter 3's considerations of indirect network effects, we can use them in the Value Net–as opposed to Porter's model. An example for this are complementary goods such as hardware and software. More powerful hardware encourages customers to use more computer-intensive programs. More complex programs, in turn, require more powerful hardware. Windows XP simply runs better with an Intel Centrino processor than it does on a Pentium-run computer. The constellations do not have to be bilateral, though–they can have many sides. Let us consider the example of ProShare by Intel (Nalebuff & Brandenburger, 1996, 15). Intel's management was dissatisfied with the speed of the development of products using the processors to capacity. In order to encourage its customers to keep updating their equipment, Intel pushed forward one of the most CPU-intensive applications, namely video transmissions, and invested, in the mid-nineties, in a system for video conferences by the name ProShare (Intel, 2007a). Similarly to the situation for fax machines, which we considered above (Chapter 3), Intel was confronted with a significant problem in the starting phase: what is the use of a video conference system if there aren't enough people to hold a conference? It had to be Intel's mission to build up a market presence and to lower the cost of units. To do so, Intel tried to find other companies with similar interests. This turned out to be, on the one hand, telephone companies, who wanted to sell higher cable capacities. ProShare was a good way of promoting ISDN or, as today, DSL connections. Faster connections sold better if customers wanted to use certain applications. Thus some telephone companies subsidized ProShare in order to sell their packages (Nalebuff & Brandenburger, 1996, 16). As a further cooperation partner, Intel identified the computer manufacturer Compaq, who preinstalled ProShare in all of its computers destined for business purposes. Offering video conferences allowed Compaq a distinguishing feature vis-à-vis their competition. At the same time, ProShare's market presence was increased and the acquisition cost of the software for the end customers lowered significantly. All of the players mentioned had recognized their complementary relationships. Intel wanted to increase demand for higher CPU capacity, the telephone companies wanted to sell higher data transmission capacities and Compaq was looking for an advantage over its competitors. All three interests could be bundled in ProShare's package.

Intel's ProShare went on to become the market leader for PC-supported video conference systems. Further cooperations, as with Deutsche Telekom AG, BMW AG and Erasmus University in Rotterdam, as well as a development partnership with the video conference provider PictureTel, were to follow (Intel, 2007b; WP, 1999).

The recent acquisition of the game developer Havok by Intel had the same motivation (Iwersen, 2007). Havok is a software developer world-famous for its programming of so-called physics engines, which produce physically accurate, photographic images of reality and are considered the best the gaming industry has to offer. Their great advantage from Intel's perspective: they require huge amounts of CPU capacity.

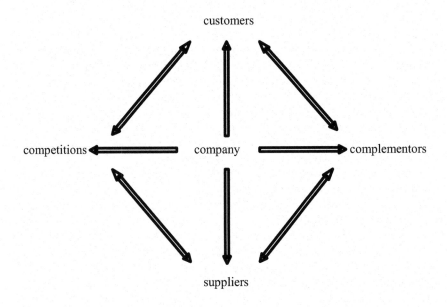

Figure 16.2: The Value Net's Basic Pattern According to Nalebuff and Brandenburger. Source: Nalebuff & Brandenburger, 1996, 30.

16.3   The Value Net's Elements

How can such complementary relationships be displayed in the Value Net? Like Porter, Nalebuff and Brandenburger (1996, 16) initially orient themselves, in the vertical direction, on the flow of goods from the suppliers through the observed company and on to the end consumer. Resources, such as materials or manpower, flow to the company from the suppliers' side, and products and services flow on to the customers from there. Money flows in the opposite direction. The suppliers are paid for their services by the companies; for the customers, one must define by case. Traditionally, they pay for the license to use a company's choice of products. Particularly in the information market, though, there are often constellations where it is not the customers but third parties who pay and thus finance or at least subsidize the product. This is the case for ad-financed free TV: the channels finance their product from advertising revenue, and the customer pays not with money, but with attention.

In the horizontal direction, not only competitors are regarded, as in Porter, but also complementors. These are companies who through their offer add value to the offer of the company observed. Complementors–as opposed to suppliers–mostly perform their services at their own expense.

For the question of who a company's competitors are, Nalebuff and Brandenburger additionally try to overcome Porter's rigid industry differentiation. They allow all active players in the market to qualify as possible competitors. They say:

> The more [...] one strives to solve customers' problems, the more the industry perspective loses meaning. As people think more in terms of solving their customers' problems, the industry perspective ist becoming increasingly irrelevant.

> The customers are interested in the end result, not in what industry the company that gives them what they want belongs to.

An example: if one considers two airlines, such as Lufthansa and British Airways, the enhanced perspective makes it clear that they compete not only within the industry, but also with industry outsiders, for instance, like Intel, which offers a substitute for air travel in the form of video conferences.

In order to account for both of these aspects, Nalebuff and Brandenburger explicitly draw on Game Theory. Game Theory (Neumann, 2007 [1944]) assumes that there is a structural similarity between parlor games and markets. The players try to maximize their own profit, but are dependent on the other players. They know this, and accommodate these interdependencies in their decision-making. Game Theory is used in strategic management to analyze the effects of one's own actions and/or those of one's competitors.

In this context, both competitors and complementors are regarded from two perspectives, the customers' and the suppliers'.

For the "player" competitor, it holds, from the customers' point of view on the one hand, and the suppliers' on the other (Nalebuff & Brandenburger, 1996, 18, 20):

> A player is your competitor if customers value your product *less* when they have the other payer's product than when they have your product alone.

> A player is your competitor if it is *less* attractive for a supplier to provide resources to you when it's also supplying the other player than it's supplying you alone.

With complementors, the case is analogous. Nalebuff and Brandenburger (1996, 18 et seq.) define, again from two points of view:

> A player is your complementor if customers value your product *more* when they have the other payer's product than when they have your product alone.

> A player is your complementor if it is *more* attractive for a supplier to provide resources to you when it's also supplying the other player than it's supplying you alone.

Competition for customers and suppliers, this must be stressed again and again, often takes place beyond industry borders. Companies compete for financial resources, materials or manpower, by now often on a global scale.

The relationships between companies on the market can have many different faces. They can be competitive, as the one between Coca-Cola and Pepsi, or complementary with highly aligned interests, such as the one between Microsoft and Intel, who both profit reciprocally from the other's product innovations. Often, however, companies assume several roles at once, thus being competitor and complementor at the same time (Nalebuff & Brandenburger, 1996, 20). Airlines, for instance, compete for limited landing rights and airport space. At the same time, they are jointly interested in key aircraft suppliers making them attractive offers for next-generation airplanes. For Boeing or Airbus, it would be much cheaper to develop a plane for both airlines than to produce different versions. The principals could cooperatively contribute to the development costs, thus lowering the cost of units far more quickly, which would of course be of benefit to them.

Let us regard another value net, that of an institution of higher education (Nalebuff & Brandenburger, 1996, 23 et seq.). The **customers** of a university are its students. As they often do not pay for their own education, though, financiers enter the scene as further customers: parents, providers of scholarships, creditors. They all expect their investments to be profitable, i.e. that the graduates later get a job with adequate pay providing financial independence and enabling them to repay their debts. Donators are another customer group: they expect their donation to be rewarded in the form of influence or prestige. The awarding of a research assignment can also create a customer relationship.

The **suppliers** of a university are its employees, the academic staff, the administration etc. Furthermore, information suppliers such as publishers and database providers belong on this list.

The **competitors** of a university are, on the side of demand, other private or public purveyors of education competing for students, funds or research assignments. On the supply side, there is competition between the different schools, and also private enterprises, for personnel.

The **complementors** of a university are manifold. All institutes of education providing preparatory training belong on this list. The better this training, the more students will profit from higher education. Other complements are technical facilities (computers, internet etc.), boarding and infrastructure. All environmental aspects influencing the university are to be deemed complementary, in short.

16.4 Value Nets for Information Goods

The Value Net is a good basic framework for capturing the players in a market and their competitive and complementary relationships. Now, the focus of our investigations is on information goods. As we learned in Chapter 3, information goods display four particular characteristics. Specifically, these are the character of public goods, the domination of fixed costs, information asymmetries as well as (direct and indirect) network effects.

These characteristics can be viewed as mechanisms effective on information markets. As we saw in Chapter 3, they contain the potential for market failure. In a value net for information markets, these mechanisms are to be given explicit consideration.

The network effects in particular play a prominent role for information goods. Here it is not only important whether the information good has a broad installed base today, but also whether the customers expect it to be widely used in the future. The **expectations** of market participants are the central factor (Katz & Shapiro, 1985, 425). In order to influence these, companies can send signals. These can be product previews, for example, meant to signal to the customer that it is worth their while to postpone their purchase, as a better offer will be available in the near future. For the value net, this means that not only customers must be given explicit consideration, but also their expectations.

In order for information markets to function–and the fact that they do is easily verifiable–special institutional regulations have developed over time, such as copyright, for example. Additionally, trading with digital information goods is based on a multitude of technological developments that make their exchange possible in the first place (Fritz, 2004, 86 et seq.). Information needs a data carrier to be stored (CD, DVD, hard drive), must be formatted in a certain way before they can be transmitted (MP3, MP4, HTML) and require a transmission path, which these days is mainly the internet with the appropriate protocol TCP/IP. For information to be protected, other technologies are required, such as CSS (Content Scrambling System) or digital watermarks. Institutions and technologies both influence players' courses of action in the value net, but they cannot be directly influenced by them. Laws and regulations take shape in political processes, which are often very drawn out. The situation for technologies is similar, if they exist as (public or de facto) standards. New technologies can of course be invented at any time, but on the one hand, a single invention does not change the entire technological environment, and on the other hand, an open process decides whether it will in fact assert itself on the market. In each value net, but for information markets in particular, institutions and technologies must thus be considered as environmental factors.

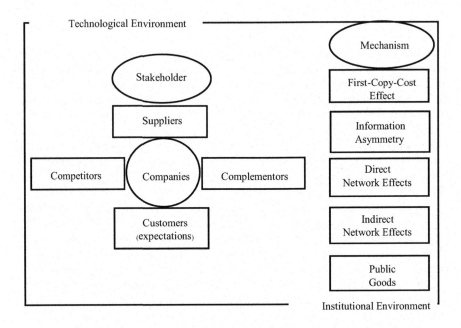

Figure 16.3: Enhanced Value Net for the Analysis of Information Markets.

16.5   Business and Business Field Strategies

Having established a value net, we must ask ourselves what the agents' scope of influence over the information markets is. How and where can they begin building up their business field, respectively their value net?

In each case, we are dealing with typical strategy questions. What is meant by strategy? From among the many possible definitions, we have taken the one by Bruce Henderson (1989, 3), the founder of Boston Consulting Group:

> Strategy is a deliberate search for a plan of action that will develop a
> business's competitive advantage and compound it.

A discussion of strategy is normally held on several levels (e.g. Grant & Nippa, 2006; Hungenberg, 2006). On the top level, strategies for the entire company are being developed. Such (overall) business strategies deal with the company's field of operation: what should be offered on which markets in which industries? Subordinate are the so-called business field strategies, which involve the company's course of action on single markets within the competition. Our further deliberations will focus exclusively on business field, or also competitive, strategies.

	Companies	**Business Field**
Environment Analysis	Analysis of the **macro-environments**, e.g. •Legal-political •Technological •Economical	**Industry and Market Analyses**, e.g. •Five Forces (Porter) •"The New Forces" (Downes/Mui) •Value Net (Nalebuff/Brandenburger)
Business Analysis	Financial Analyses, e.g. •Business value •Value drivers Portfolio Analyses, e.g. •Market growth / market share •Market appeal / Business field strength **Competences across business fields**	Financial analyses, e.g. •Revenue and cost structure •Result situation •ROI **Business-field-specific competences**

Figure 16.4: Objects and Methods of Strategic Analysis.

Each kind of strategy does not merely exist pre-made, but must be developed in-house. To do so, one generally delineates different phases in the process of strategic management (Remer, 2004, 25 et seq.) There is, both on the company and the business field level, an initial analysis phase, before strategy alternatives are developed, evaluated and selected.

Always featured in a strategic analysis are (e.g. Hungenberg, 2006; Welge & Al-Laham, 2003) the view to the company's and the business field's respective environment on the one hand and their interior on the other. Both levels and both perspectives are displayed in Figure 16.4.

This overview makes it pretty clear where the focus will be placed. Our unit of analysis is initially the individual business field, and particularly its environment analysis.

16.6   Competitive Advantages

In every strategy text book (e.g. Grant & Nippa, 2006; Hungenberg, 2006), strategic considerations on the business field level lead to the question: what is the basis on which companies achieve their competitive advantages? Here, too, the doyen of strategy, Michael Porter (1980), has exerted decisive influence. He shaped strategic management by stating that companies fundamentally possess two strategic alternatives for achieving competitive advantages: differentiation strategy and cost/price leadership strategy. Companies that work with the differentiation strategy offer their customers a performance advantage, allowing them to achieve a bonus vis-à-vis their competition. A cost/price leader, on the other hand, offers his customers a price rebate while furnishing merely adequate quality. Porter's approach, it must be noted, was also criticized. Practice has shown that companies must keep a close eye on both price and performance. The comprehensive instalment of quality management in particular has led to the possibility of realizing high quality as well as relatively low costs at the same time, eliminating the restriction of having to choose one or the other (Grant & Nippa, 2006, 313). Providers of digital goods in particular have the option of overcoming the contrast between differentiation and cost orientation. They can quickly profit from unit cost reduction when unit quantities rise. At the same time, the customer relationship can be managed interactively online. Information providers can–other then in the traditional mass markets–practice customer-individual (one-to-one) marketing. Even in case of large quantities, such an individualization of the range of services is relatively easily achieved (Fritz, 2004, 171 et seq.). A customer-specific differentiation and reduction of costs can both be achieved at the same time in this way. The competitive advantage thus shifts to the competence of being able to make individual, personalized offers to one's customers (Albers, 2001, 16). We will take up this point later, in the course of our more in-depth elucidation of product and price differentiation.

The goal of our deliberations here is to work out–on the business level–strategic options for providers of information goods. In the following, we will introduce a set of (strategic) variables available to information providers in order to act in their business field. Porter's fundamental considerations on positioning persist for the traditional markets, but information goods require other competitive strategies than conventional products (Klodt, 2003, 108). Porter's strategy alternatives are not made obsolete, but can be implemented as new variants in information markets (Shapiro & Varian, 1999, 25).

16.7   Strategic Variables for Designing Value Nets

What specific strategic variables can information providers use to design their value net, or their business field, respectively? If we are precise, there is of course a huge difference here, since the value net is only a model of the business field. Hence, the design objectives relate to the value net only superficially, always concerning, in the end, the actual business field behind. For our purposes, both terms can be used synonymously.

The starting point of our deliberations is the seminal book "Information Rules" by Carl Shapiro and Hal R. Varian (1999 [1998]). In their "Strategic Guide to the Network Economy", the authors offer multiple starting points that are of huge significance for information providers' strategy development. Their work has strongly influenced strategy discussion, particularly from the software industry's point of view. There is, however, a lack of systematics, e.g. there is no model that serves as the basis of Shapiro's and Varian's considerations. As a consequence, it does not become clear which strategic variables have been selected for what reason and what their significance is.

Here the work of van de Kaa et al. (2007) helps us: they investigated 103 publications on standardization under the viewpoint of which factors have been named and how important they were deemed in order to win a fight for standardization. They came up with the result of 31 factors in all, to be placed in five categories: superior design, mechanisms, stakeholders, dominant agent and strategy.

After Suarez, standardization in the industry for information and communication technologies is to be viewed as a process consisting of five phases. At the beginning, there is product development (Phase One) and technological feasibility (Phase Two), which is followed by the development of the market by one or several competitors fighting to create an installed base in Phase Three. In the fourth decision phase, network effects begin to operate and to influence the customers' decision-making. In the last phase, a standard has been established and is stabilized via the pre-existing network effects as well as switching costs.

These threads can now be very easily combined with one another. According to Suarez (2004, 283), the strategic behavior of a company is decisive for market success. It is the key to influencing stakeholders (e.g. the installed (customer) base) and the mechanisms (e.g. network effects) at play on information markets. If the strategic variables mentioned by Shapiro and Varian (1999) are then squared with those by van de Kaa et al. (2007), we can work out a total of seven strategic variables apart from product quality, which always plays an important role. They are:

- Timing of market entry,
- Pricing,
- Compatibility management (standardization),
- Complement management,
- Copy protection management,
- Signaling,
- Lock-in management.

These seven aspects are strategic variables because they are "manageable", i.e. under the entrepreneurial influence. Such decision variables, or action parameters, can be used by companies in such a way that targets such as market share, brand awareness or profit can be reached.

In this way, a frame of reference (Grochla, 1978, 62 et seq.) containing factors and relations relevant for our investigation of information providers' competitive strategies can be constructed.

The strategic variables directly and strongly affect the stakeholders, who in turn affect the mechanisms. There are weaker relations between the strategic variables and the mechanisms, as well as for reachback.

In the following chapters, we will describe the strategic variables one by one and in detail, and demonstrate their correlations with stakeholders, mechanisms and other variables.

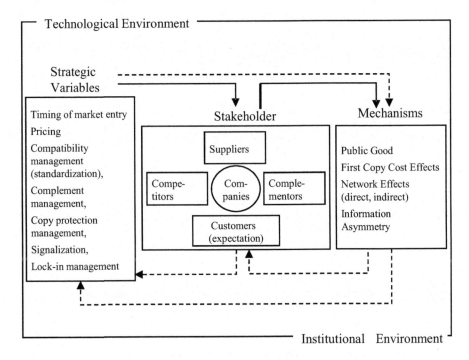

Figure 16.5: Frame of Reference for the Analysis of Information Markets.

16.8   Conclusion

- Industry structure analysis according to Porter concentrated on the Five Forces. Other companies on the market are regarded as threats to one's own profit.

- In the Value Net according to Nalebuff and Brandenburger, not only competitive relationships are regarded as possible performance indicators, but cooperative relationships as well.
- Value nets for information goods should supplementarily take into consideration the mechanisms at play in an information market (public goods, domination of fixed costs, information asymmetries, network effects) as well as the technological and institutional environment.
- Market and industry analysis are that part of a business field strategy which deals with the environment analysis.
- Competitive advantage, according to Porter, can be achieved via cost/price leadership or differentiation strategies.
- Information providers are successful on the market when they use the strategic variables in order to influence stakeholders as well as mechanisms in their favor.

16.9   Bibliography

Albers, S. (2001). Besonderheiten des Marketings mit interaktiven Medien. Albers, S., Clement, M., Peters, K., & Skiera, B. (eds.), Marketing mit interaktiven Medien. Strategien zum Markterfolg (pp. 11-23). 3. Aufl. Frankfurt am Main: IMK (Kommunikation heute und morgen, 31).

Backhaus, K. (2007). Industriegütermarketing. 8th, fully revised ed. München: Vahlen (Vahlens Handbücher der Wirtschafts- und Sozialwissenschaften).

Downes, L., & Mui, C. (1998). Unleashing the Killer App. Digital Strategies for Market Dominance. Boston, Mass: Harvard Business School Press.

Fritz, W. (2004). Internet-Marketing und Electronic Commerce. Grundlagen - Rahmenbedingungen - Instrumente. 3rd ed. Wiesbaden: Gabler (Gabler-Lehrbuch).

Grant, R. M., & Nippa, M. (2006). Strategisches Management. Analyse, Entwicklung und Implementierung von Unternehmensstrategien. 5th ed. München: Pearson Studium (wi - wirtschaft).

Grochla, E. (1978). Einführung in die Organisationstheorie. Stuttgart: Poeschel (Sammlung Poeschel, 93).

Henderson, B. D. (1989). The Origin of Strategy. Harvard Business Review, November - December, 139-143.

Hungenberg, H. (2006). Strategisches Management in Unternehmen. Ziele - Prozesse - Verfahren. 4th ed. Wiesbaden: Gabler (Lehrbuch).

Intel (2007a). Intel(R) ProShare(R) Products - Index. (Online).

Intel (2007b). Die Intel Geschichte. (Online).

Iwersen, S. (2007). Spieler sind bessere Kunden. Handelsblatt, 180, 09/18/2007, 12.

Katz, M. L., & Shapiro, C. (1985). Network externalities, competition, and compatibility. American Economic Review, 75(3), 424-440.

Klodt, H. (2003). Wettbewerbsstrategien für Informationsgüter. Schäfer, W., & Berg, H. (eds.), Konjunktur, Wachstum und Wirtschaftspolitik im Zeichen der New Economy (pp. 107-123). Berlin: Duncker & Humblot.

Nalebuff, B.J., & Brandenburger, A.M. (1996). Co-opetition. New York, NY: Doubleday.

Neumann, J. v. (2007 [1944]). Theory of Games and Economic Behavior. Princeton, NJ.: Princeton Univ. Press (Princeton Classic Edition).

Porter, M. E. (2004 [1980]): Competitive strategy. Techniques for analyzing industries and competitors. New York, NY: Free Press.

Remer, A. (2004). Management. System und Konzepte. 2nd ed. Bayreuth: REA-Verl. Managementforschung (Schriften zu Organisation und Personal, 16).

Shapiro, C., & Varian, H. R. (1999 [1998]). Information Rules. A Strategic Guide to the Network Economy. [repr.]. Boston, MA: Harvard Business School Press.

Suarez, F.F. (2004). Battles for technological dominance: an integrative framework. Research Policy, 34(2), 271-286.

Tirole, J. (1999). Industrieökonomik. 2nd ed. München: Oldenbourg.

van Kaa, G. de; Vries, H. J. de; van Heck, E., & van den Ende, J. (2007). The Emergence of Standards: a Meta-analysis. 40th Annual Hawaii International Conference on System Sciences.

Welge, M. K., & Al-Laham, A. (2003). Strategisches Management. 4th ed. Wiesbaden: Gabler (Lehrbuch).

WP (1999). Zusammenarbeit bei Videoconferencing. funkschau, 5, 15. (Online).

Chapter 17

Timing of Market Entry

17.1　Innovators and Imitators

Companies that want to enter a market with their product are either innovators or imitators. An innovatation, according to Grant & Nippa (2006, 418), is

> the initial commercialization of inventions via the manufacturing and marketing of new products or services or use of a new production method.

A company is thus innovator, pioneer or first mover if it is the first to come up with a new market offer (Lieberman & Montgomery, 1988, 51). Imitators, followers or second movers are those companies that enter the market with a similar product or a similar service after the innovator. Whether a company is pioneer or follower thus depends heavily on the definition of the relevant market.

Let us take the example of the online auction platform eBay. In September of 1995, Pierre Omidyar founded eBay in the USA, under the name of Auction Web. It was renamed eBay in May of 1996 (Cohen, 2004; eBay, 2004). 1997, 1998 and 1999 gave rise to three German counterparts called Feininger, Ricardo and Alando. Feininger is the pioneer on the German market (Möllenberg, 2003, 162) and is still active on the market today. The follower Alando is taken over by eBay a mere six months after its foundation, in July of 1999, and becomes eBay's German marketplace. Ricardo, on the other hand, focused mainly on auctioning new goods in Business-to-Consumer (B2C) auctions. The Consumer-to-Consumer (C2C) auctions also offered by eBay serve mainly to increase customer loyalty (Möllenberg, 2003, 163). In November of 2003, Ricardo ceased holding auctions in Germany. As part of the European e-commerce group QXL Ricardo plc, based in London, Ricardo today successfully operates an auction platform in Switzerland, amongst other ventures. According to Ricardo (2007), they are market leaders there.

Who was the first mover in the market for internet auctions, then? The question must be answered differently, according to market differentiation. If we assume that there is a world market for internet auctions, then eBay must surely be regarded as pioneer (Möllenberg, 2003, 154). Principally, anyone in the world could have participated in the auctions. However, it must be noted that eBay's service was only available in English at the beginning, making such an offer relatively uninteresting for people who do not speak the language. Added to this is the fact that the shipping of goods beyond US borders is, in most cases, very expensive in relation to product costs. It would thus make sense to differentiate the American market from the German market, i.e. to perform a spatial market differentiation (Backhaus, 2007, 128 et seq.). Hence Feininger would have to be regarded as another first mover. Here, then, we encounter a problem that affects digital information goods in general. Every information good is, principally, available worldwide, due to its digital availability. There may, as displayed above, be restrictions and inconveniences, but the relevant market–as long as the provider itself allows it– must always be objectively defined, that is to say the world market must be observed. For our example, this means that there is only one real pioneer, which is eBay. Feininger is an imitator, who can only be seen as a first mover on the German market. The first commercialization of the idea of online auctions has already been performed by eBay. Even if it does not make much of a difference for the second mover, when it is founded, that another company is already active, in a (spatially) different market, it will be well advised to take into consideration the fact that, objectively speaking, it is the same market. Feininger should thus list eBay as a competitor in its value net.

If we differentiate between B2C and C2C auctions, however, Ricardo is the first mover in the market for B2C auctions. Here we can see very clearly how important market differentiation is for determining the pioneer position. It also becomes clear that to be successful, it is not enough to be the pioneer. eBay began, as a second mover on the German market, to offer B2C auctions in the year 2000 and was able, in time, to establish itself as market leader in this area as well (Möllenberg, 2003, 158 et seq.). In the end, Ricardo had to strike their colors in Germany.

The analysis of Alando, on the other hand, is wholly unambiguous: the company is a second mover for internet auctions in every regard–spatially and objectively.

17.2 Advantages and Disadvantages for First Movers

As we can see, the decision of when to enter a new market has great strategic meaning. Risk and opportunity lie side by side. Will the attempt to win the market as first mover succeed, perhaps even resulting in a lasting position of dominance, or will the new product fail? In that case, it might be prudent to enter the market as second mover. In the following, we will investigate the advantages and disadvantages of a first mover –first generally speaking and then relating to information markets–and whether this position is the decisive magnitude of influence for market success. Simplified, the question is: is it enough to be the first on the market in order to keep one's competitors at a distance in the long term?

Every pioneer creates market entry barriers for the follower. These can have many causes. Lieberman & Montgomery (1988) name the following possible advantages for the pioneer: name recognition and image, a head start in experience, the implementation of standards on the market, monopoly-based pioneer profits (e.g. via patents and copyrights), the building up of a loyal customer basis and the resulting switching costs or the securing of resources (e.g. employees) which can be deducted only with great difficulty later. However, this position does not only hold advantages. Disadvantages faced by first movers are free rider effects, where the follower profits from the pioneer's investments (e.g. in R&D, infrastructure), the difficulty of estimating the exact market potential, or changes of customer needs and technological change. As shown in Figure 17.1, there are advantages and disadvantages to both the first and second mover positions.

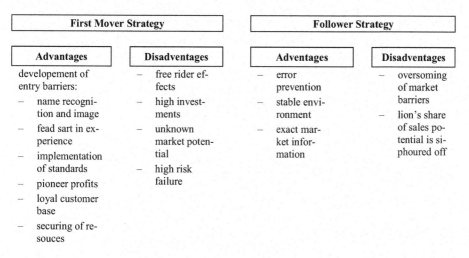

First Mover Strategy		Follower Strategy	
Advantages	**Disadventages**	**Adventages**	**Disadvantages**
developement of entry barriers: – name recognition and image – fead sart in experience – implementation of standards – pioneer profits – loyal customer base – securing of resouces	– free rider effects – high investments – unknown market potential – high risk failure	– error prevention – stable enviromment – exact market information	– oversoming of market barriers – lion's share of sales potential is siphoured off

Figure 17.1: General Advantages and Disadvantages of the First Mover and Follower Strategy. Source: Following Wirtz, 2006, 654.

One can be successful as innovator or as follower (Oelsnitz & Heinecke, 1997), but there are no universally valid statements concerning as to what makes the difference between the two positions (Srinivasan et al., 2004, 41 et seq.). As shown in Figure 17.2, there are examples where the first mover was successful and able to appropriate a large part of the innovation benefit. At the same time, counterexamples prove that the costs and risks of tapping a new market were too high in many cases, and the pioneers could not establish themselves.

Product	Innovator	Follower	The Winner
Commercial jet aircrafts	De Havilland (Comet)	Boeing (707)	Follower
Floating glas process	Pilkington	Corning	Innovator
X-ray apparatus	EMI	General Electric	Follower
Office PC	Xerox	IBM	Follower
Video recorder	Ampex/Sony	Matsushita	Follower
Diet Cola	R. C. Cola	Coca-Cola	Follower
Immediately picture camera	Polaroid	Kodak	Innovator
Pocket calculator	Bowmar	Texas Instruments	Follower
Microwave stove	Raytheon	Samsung	Follower
Normal paper photocopier	Xerox	Canon	open
Fiber optic cable	Corning	many companies	Innovator
Video game consoles	Atari	Nintendo/Sega	Follower
Throwing away daipers	Procter & Gamble	Kimberly-Clark	Innovator
Ink-jet printer	IBM and Siemens	Hewlett Packard	Follower
Internet browser	Netscape	Microsoft	Successor
MP3 player	Diamond Multimedia	Apple (IPod)	Follower
Operating systemes for digital handhelds	Palm and Symbian	Microsoft (CE/Pocket PC)	Follower

Figure 17.2: Examples for Successful Pioneer and Follower Strategies. Source: Grant & Nippa, 2006, 431 based on Teece, 1987, 186-188.

If we then turn our investigation to information goods, we can find proof of both variants in the aforementioned examples as well. Thus the follower Microsoft took over market predominance for internet browsers from the pioneer Netscape and has held on to it until today. In the market for operating systems for digital handhelds, however, Palm and Symbian were able to hold their own for a long time. Microsoft probably still carried the day in 2004, when, in the declining market for handhelds, more units with Windows Mobile were sold than units with the Palm Operating System (Lehmann, 2004). The market for Smartphones is different; here Symbian OS is keeping its competitors Microsoft, Apple and Palm at a clear distance (Postinett, 2008).

A large part of Microsoft's success is surely owed to its superior resource basis, particularly in the areas of product development, marketing and sales (Grant & Nippa, 2006, 433). Perhaps the most decisive point, however, is the installed base that Microsoft profits from. The huge number of Windows operating systems in the private as well as business environment leads to distinct indirect network effects in Microsoft's favor. In using Internet Explorer as well as Windows-based handhelds, the customer has clear advantages through their compatibility with his PC's operating system. Thus it is much easier for owners of handhelds to exchange data with the preconfigured Office programs than to have to install separate programs such as "Palm Desktop".

17.3　First-Mover Advantages on Information Markets

Which of the first-mover advantages are specifically relevant for information markets, then? To be the first to enter a market provides a head start in customer acquisition. The company that is the first to start building up its customer base has two decisive advantages it can profit from both upcoming network effects and customer loyalty effects, which are created via switching costs.

A growing number of customers makes the product more valuable for everyone via (direct) **network effects** (Lieberman, 2005, 9), and not only for the pre-existing–and this is where customers' expectations play a large role–but also for potential customers who have not made up their minds to buy yet. Indirect network effects serve as additional entry barriers for possible followers. A large customer basis creates an impetus for complementors to bring out complementary products to the basic good. If, on the other hand, the second mover has only negative prospects for gaining a large customer basis, it will be an unattractive option for complementors to support such a competing offer. Indirect network effects create even stronger barriers for followers when the established provider makes bundled offers, i.e. offering basic product and complement in one package (Peitz, 2006). If the follower is unable to be a one-stop shop, it will prevent him from entering the market. This becomes truer the more insecure the prospects for business success become. A second mover specializing only on one product from the bundle will regularly decide against market entry when financial straits must quickly be navigated or the prospects for future gains are not positive enough to justify market entry costs (Choi & Stefanadis, 2003, 2). If the new competitors' products are, in addition, incompatible with those of the established provider, and if the product's reproduction costs are near zero, the emergence of a natural monopoly–i.e. the monopolist is able, due to constantly sinking average costs, to always offer lower prices than two or more companies–is heavily encouraged (Sundararajan, 2003, 27).

The second advantage is in the existing customers being confronted with **switching costs** after their buying decision (Dietl & Royer, 2000, 327; Lieberman, 2005, 8-9), which tendentially rise further as time goes by, and may become prohibitive in the end. This results in a lock-in, i.e. it becomes economically unattractive for the customer to switch providers because the costs of such a switch would not warrant the expected gain. For the follower–this is shown by Farrell & Klemperer (2006) via model studies–it might still be relatively easy under these conditions to gain previously uncommitted customers by offering low prices, yet the building up of a comprehensive customer basis becomes markedly more difficult. If the second mover is dependent on the pioneer's customers in order to succeed, the market entry barrier can prove insurmountable.

It must further be noted that due to the dominant fixed costs for information goods the **economies of scale** that occur are disproportional (Dietl & Royer, 2000, 327; Shapiro & Varian, 1999, 168). Since they occur not only for the basic good but also for the complements, however (Ehrhardt, 2001, 28), it becomes even harder for a second mover to implement the cost reduction necessary for an attractive offer.

Another advantage enjoyed by first movers is in the establishment of **standards**. A (communication) standard means the totality of rules that form the foundation of human or machine interaction (Buxmann et al., 1999, 134). Such standard could be the grammar of a language or the rules of Hypertext Markup Language (HTML). Standardization is the process that leads to compatibility. Compatibility in turn means that products can work together. Companies that have already heavily invested in development, market entry and the establishment of a standard have a vested interest in their chosen standard's eventual success (Dietl & Royer, 2000, 327). This readiness to fight for a standard is a very credible signal to the stakeholders (customers, competitors, suppliers, complementors). Potential customers form positive expectations toward the prospects of the offered product and thus contribute to the creation of (direct) network effects.

> If consumers expect the product to become popular, the network will grow relatively large (Lee & O'Connor, 2003, 251).

Competitors might decide not to enter the market with a competing product but to follow the standard. Suppliers will choose the purportedly more successful producer, and the complementors will also decide to align their offer to the basic product that promises the greatest distribution. This will speed up the creation of indirect network effects.

The entry into network effect markets is further benefited by the size and thus comprehensive **resource endowment** of a company. Smaller first movers are thus well advised to seek partners rich in resources (Srinivasan et al., 2004, 55), as it takes time and effort to finance, produce and market innovations, and not only in network effect markets. To be successful, a variety of complementary resources are needed, such as finances, marketing, personnel etc. (Grant & Nippa, 2006, 424 et seq.).

> Thus Chester Carlson may have invented Xerography, but he was unable over the course of many years to make his product ready for the market, since he lacked the resources to further develop his invention, to produce, distribute and furnish it with the necessary service (Grant & Nippa, 2006, 424).

The first mover then has the advantage of being able to collect the resources necessary for market success at an early stage. What is meant here is not the geographical localities and physical resources relevant for traditional goods, as these are mostly irrelevant for information providers (Lieberman, 2005, 5). Localities can only be spoken of figuratively, e.g. when considering domain names or access to a customer basis.

> As an example, Monster.com paid AOL $100 million in 1999 for the right to serve as AOL's sole provider of recruitment services for four years. This preemptive move blocked rivals' access to a leading consumer portal and helped build brand recognition and referrals for Monster.com (Lieberman, 2005, 6).

Very recently, for instance, AOL made a deal with Hewlett Packard. Both companies agreed that in the future, the PC manufacturer would preinstall the AOL header with search interface on all new computers (as of 2007).

Certain advantages with respect to the resource endowment can arise in human resources. Key personnel who are under contract with the pioneer are–at least in the short term–unavailable to competitors (Heindl, 2004, 247).

It is of large importance for information providers, however, to be noticed by the customers. We remember that information goods carry with them distinct experience qualities. In order to relieve the quality insecurities that these entail, a good **reputation** of the provider is of enormous help. Brands, as Shapiro and Varian (1999, 5) observed, play an important role:

> The brand name of the *Wall Street Journal* is one of its chief assets, and the Journal invests heavily in building a reputation for accuracy, timeliness, and relevance.

In order to make a brand widely known, it must be built up and maintained with care over a long period of time, which already brings us to the decisive point: a first mover cannot create the positive attributes of a brand ad hoc, he must first build them up, which takes time and money (Heindl, 2004, 232; Besanko et al.,

2004, 439). And the fact that the latter cannot replace the former can be seen in the example of many dotcom companies spending many millions of Dollars on marketing endeavors during the time of the bubble, only to end up, in many cases, practically throwing it away.

> Despite huge outlays on advertising, product discounts, and purchasing incentives, most dot-com brands have not approached the power of established brands, achieving only a modest impact on loyalty and barriers to entry (Porter, 2001, 69).

There can be no real mention of a true advantage in brand-building enjoyed by a first mover over his follower in this regard. There could, however, be an advantage for a pioneer in generating publicity and a positive reputation, which are both prerequisites for brand-building (Fritz, 2004, 195).

> From the perspective of learning theory, the first comer will profit from a series of attention, image and recognition advantages. The [new, A/N] brand of a first party is received more attentively by the consumer, it is remembered better and, overall, rated more highly (Oelsnitz, 1998, 26 with reference to Alpert & Kamins, 1995).

If the pioneer manages to leverage these attention advantages into a good reputation and thus customer loyalty, this will represent an advantage. For second movers, this can represent a market entry barrier, as they know that they will have to make heavy marketing investments in order to overcome the innovator's more favorable position. In case of failure, these would be irrevocably lost as sunk costs. Three of today's best-known internet brands were successful first movers in this regard: Yahoo, eBay and Amazon. On the opposite scale we can find eToys, for example, who made enormous advertising endeavors in order to make their brand known but failed nevertheless (Lieberman, 2005, 6).

17.4   Empirical Proofs for First-Mover Advantages

The first-mover advantages mentioned above are comprehensively substantiated and, in individual cases, even supported by model analysis. Now, though, it is interesting to see what empirical proofs we can find for the existence of first-mover advantages. There are relatively many studies that stem from general pioneer research (for an overview, cf. Heindl, 2004, 65 et seq.), but there are only a few more specific analyses that apply for information providers. Thus Lieberman (2005) investigates internet companies in terms of how first-mover advantages have a positive on the company's success measured against the development of market capitalization and profit. Since the analysis deals to a large degree with information providers, we can admit the results to be valid for our considerations. Lieberman makes out two very interesting points. To be the first to enter a market bears advantages both when network effects are at play and when the offer is secured by legal protection, particularly patents (Lieberman, 2005, 28).

In segments with very distinct network effects, such as the ones observed by market makers or brokers (e.g. eBay, E*Trade, Expedia, Monster, DoubleClick), a first mover has measurable advantages (Lieberman, 2005, 29). Providers as well as demanders here have a vested interest in meeting the largest possible number of market participants from the opposite spectrum of the market. This will favor the creation of a single, dominant platform, which in most of the observed cases is the first mover's. The pioneer thus has a good chance of being the first to reach critical mass and dominate the market.

The success of internet pioneers is also measurably greater if they protect their offer legally and build up a large portfolio of patents, such as Amazon or Yahoo have done, for example (Lieberman, 2005, 30).

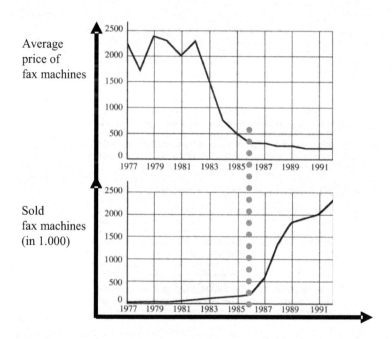

Figure 17.3: Market Development for Fax Machines. Source: Following Varian, 2004, 654.

On the exact opposite seems to be, at first glance, the central assertion of the empirical analysis by Srinivasan et al., (2004, 54).

> First, network externalities have a strong negative effect on the survival
> duration of pioneers.

Firstly, this supports the point, well known to us, that it is hard to assert oneself on network effect markets. There is a great risk of not reaching critical mass and thus failing to profit from the lock-in effects of the installed base. It is known from several markets that there is a long lead time of minimal growth for network products before the market really takes off. Varian demonstrates this via the example of the fax machine (Figure 17.3).

Must the general recommendation thus be: do not be the first in markets with strong network effects? It appears to be of advantage to let others go in front of oneself and, personally, merely to prepare for one's market entry at the time it becomes clear that the market really gets going. Now there are definitely first movers who are very successful in network effect markets. What marks them out? According to Srinivasan et al., there are three critical success factors that play a central role for survival in such markets dominated by network effects.

First movers increase their chances of survival every time they offer **technology-intensive products with a high degree of innovation**. This can be very clearly demonstrated via the example of CD technology introduced by Sony (Srinivasan et al., 2004, 54):

> Because of its laser-based, computerized technology, the CD-player offered virtually noiseless sound quality that was impossible to achieve with the prevalent audiocassette player, thereby providing a breakthrough in sound reproduction. Not affected by the scratches, smudges, and the heat warping that afflict audiocassettes. CDs maintained their original sound quality for a long time. The CD player was revolutionary and, as an industry analyst *(San Diego Tribune* 1987, p. BI) notes, was "the most dramatic development in sound reproduction since Edison."

This radically new technology created high market entry barriers that have secured a dominant position for Sony to this very day.

However, pioneers that already offer innovative products must take care not to invest half-heartedly in new products and technologies. This is called "technological inertia" (Christensen, 2007), frequently observed in established companies. This attitude is characterized by a resistance to make large investments in new technologies which would threaten their precursors. A good example for this is the Encyclopædia Britannica, which for several centuries was practically the byword for reference books. However, the book version was clung to for too long, and the step toward an online version made so late that Microsoft, with its digital Encarta encyclopedia, was able to gain a large market share in a short amount of time.

A second aspect is **company size**, which bears a positive relation to success in network effect markets. A pioneer with a comprehensive resource endowment will find it a lot easier to be the first to survive in the market (Srinivasan et al., 2004, 55). It is thus recommended for smaller innovators to strengthen their resource basis through collaborations.

Perhaps the critical success factor for pioneers that have survived is that they offer their customers **extrinsic value** (Srinivasan et al., 2004, 54; Lee & O'Connor, 2003, 251). They concentrate not only on a product's intrinsic value but simultaneously make sure that direct and indirect network effects occur. Again, Sony provides a nice example with its introduction of the CD player in 1982 (Srinivasan et al., 2004, 54):

> Sony worked extensively to develop the CD format accepted by the music industry and entered into extensive licensing agreements for other firms to manufacture the CD player. Sony also recognized that the availability of music titles on CDs was crucial for delivering utility to customers of the CD player, so it leveraged its Columbia Records label and its collaboration with Philip's PolyGram Records, two of the world's largest music producers at the time, to ensure the availability of music titles on CDs. When Sony introduced its first CD player, Columbia Records simultaneously released the world's first 50 music CD titles.

In order to generate extrinsic value, companies must think not only of marketing their own product but develop the network in parallel. To do so, they can license their product, support the development and marketing of complements and perhaps even secure downward compatibility with pre-existing networks in order to keep switching costs low.

Network effects are quite clearly a critical aspect. The more pronounced they are, the more they can negatively influence the pioneer's chances of survival (Srinivasan et al., 2004, 54-55).

This is shown in Figure 17.4 via the negatively inclined main effect. This effect is heightened if the pioneer is already the provider of the preceding product generation. In that case, there is a danger of investing too little into the new product in order to limit the cannibalization effect vis-à-vis the old product. Network effects are beneficial if the degree of innovation of the new product and its technology intensity are high, the company has a good resource endowment and knows how to make the customer understand the extrinsic value.

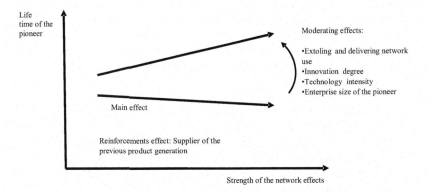

Figure 17.4: Influence of Network Effects on the Length of a Pioneer's Survival. Source: Following Srinivasan et al., 2004, 45.

17.5   Second-Mover Advantages

We can summarize that there is no general advantage for internet pioneers (Lieberman, 2005, 8, 28). There are special challenges to innovators, particularly in network effect markets, if they not only offer their product but at the same time make sure that there is a sufficient number of attractive complements. Due to the initial reticence of customers (to buy) and suppliers (to make offers), it becomes even less important, when offering products with pronounced network effects, to be the first in the market at any cost than it is to be the first to build up a large installed base in a short period of time (Lee & O'Connor, 2003, 246-247). If the second mover succeeds in establishing swift distribution via extensive use of resources, this may even overcompensate for pre-existing first-mover advantages (Tellis & Golder, 1996, 2002). Related to a product's intrinsic value, first-mover advantages are less important in network effect markets than they are in markets without network effects (Lee & O'Connor, 2003, 247). In such markets–to emphasize once more–it is far more important to quickly establish an installed base and to offer attractive complements in parallel to the basic product.

A propitious moment for second movers to enter the market should be every time technological changes occur. In the software market, such a window opened e.g. when graphical user interfaces appeared. The hitherto dominant spreadsheet application Lotus 1-2-3 lacked the corresponding features, so Microsoft was able to enter and take over the market with Excel (Brynjolfsson & Kemerer, 1996). The first-mover advantage on its own is thus definitely not enough to be successful in the long term. The pioneer must also continually work at securing his position by creating further competitive advantages (Fritz, 2004, 167). In a study, Liebowitz (2002, 44 et seq.) uses the example of Yahoo and AOL, among others, to show that they offered a markedly higher product and service quality, respectively, than the market average, which was probably the critical factor for their success. Some other factors that favor the second mover's success are, according to Gerpott (2005, 20), good access to a large customer basis, sufficient financial power for comprehensive advertising measures and an offer that is part of the established array of products' core business. The example of Google's entry into the market for electronic classifieds shows the established providers, such as newspaper publishers and eBay, do not have a permanently secure market position:

> With more than 400 million permanent users worldwide, enormous profit margins in the regular business and a good image due to the quality of its search results, Google meets all three requirements with ease (Gerpott, 2005, 20).

Generally, followers are in the so-called free-rider position (Lieberman & Montgomery, 1988), i.e. they can profit from the pioneer's work at no cost. Followers can generally manage to attaint the pioneer's knowledge without having to make the same research endeavors, be it through the publication of copyright-protected knowledge that is nevertheless used by the follower via engineering around or by poaching key personnel (Specht, 2001, 143). Followers are also favored by the advancing infrastructure expansion. For i-commerce offers, this means cheap offers for hardware and software, available (micro) payment systems, prevalent internet access and PC availability as well as a general acceptance of the product. Another advantage enjoyed by followers is market insecurity decreasing over time. Innovators must accept the risk that it will only become clear what product properties are particularly preferred by the consumers after the product's introduction on the market. It can be of great advantage to only enter a market once it is clear which standard will assert itself.

Hence even if the first-mover position can be of benefit, it cannot do all the work (Oelsnitz & Heinecke, 1997, 39), and will not be enough, in the long run, to beat competitors who have better products or manage to create an installed base more quickly. Even when established companies dominate markets with free offers, there is a chance at a successful market entry with a priced product if the added value in terms of quality or endowment is made sufficiently clear to the customer (Gallaugher & Wang, 1999, 82et seq.). Quality, up-to-dateness and exclusivity are identified by Stahl et al. (2004, 59) as critical success factors for information goods in particular. According to Weiber and Kollmann (2000, 58 et seq.), traditional positioning as cost or quality leader is less important for information goods than a differentiation as speed leader or topical leader. The speed leader can offer information to potential demanders more quickly than the competition. His competitive advantage is a head start in information availability. An early market entry is of advantage for this strategy. The "quality leader in the sense of high-quality information acquisition" (Weiber & Kollmann, 2000, 60) positions himself less through the speed of information provision than through the kind and content of the information provided. This strategy particularly comes to bear on special information that needs high-grade processing (studies, test reports). The provider must draw his competitive advantage from having better content that the competition. This way is still eminently realizable after a later market entry.

For a successful market entry, it is thus important to carefully weigh the risks and opportunities of the first- and second-mover positions. The more pronounced network effects are, the more important it becomes to concentrate on the network effect value for the consumer.

First-Mover Advantages	**Second-Mover Advantages**

• Above-average economies of scale, scope and experience
• Creation of network effects, switching costs and Lock-Ins
• Establishment of a Standard
• Perception/Reputation
• Securing of scarce strategic resources
	• Free-rider effects
	  - Appropriation of (legally unprotected) technological knowledge
	  - Infrastructure development
	• Lesser market insecurity (development of a standard)

Figure 17.5: First- and Second-Mover Advantages of information providers.

17.6   Conclusion

- To determine the first mover, it is essential to identify the relevant market according to objective criteria.
- First movers generally have temporal advantages in creating a customer basis. This makes the early development of network effects and switching costs, the establishment of a standard, the appropriation of critical resources and the building of a good reputation possible.

- It can be empirically proven that network effects negatively influence the survival chances of first movers, particularly when they already offer the new product in the preceding product generation. Network effects can be of benefit for the survival of the innovator when the degree of innovation and technology intensity of the new product are high and when he has a good resource endowment and knows how to make the network effect value clear to demanders.
- Second movers profit from the pioneer's groundwork. (Technological) Knowledge is more easily available, there is an infrastructure and the customers are attuned to the new product. Second movers can delay their market entry until it is clear which standard will establish itself.
- Competitive advantages can be built up via the speed of information acquisition as well as the quality of the content. It is critical for market success that product and service quality (intrinsic value) and network effect value (extrinsic value) that are offered to customers be well aligned.

17.7 Bibliography

Alpert, F.H., & Kamins, M.A. (1995). An empirical investigation of consumer memory, attitude, and perceptions toward pioneer and follower brands. Journal of Marketing, 59(10), 34-45.

Backhaus, Klaus (2007). Industriegütermarketing. 8th ed. München: Vahlen (Vahlens Handbücher der Wirtschafts- und Sozialwissenschaften).

Besanko, D., Dranove, D., Shanley, M., & Schaefer, S. (2004). Economics of Strategy. 3rd ed. Hoboken, NJ: Wiley.

Bliemel, F., Fassott, G., & Theobald, A. (eds.) (2000). Electronic Commerce. Herausforderungen - Anwendungen - Perspektiven. 3rd ed. Wiesbaden: Gabler.

Brynjolfsson, E., & Kemerer, C.F. (1996). Network externalities in microcomputer software. An econometric analysis of the spreadsheet market. Management Science, 42(12), 1627-1647.

Buxmann, P., Weitzel, T., & König, W. (1999). Auswirkung alternativer Koordinationsmechanismen auf die Auswahl von Kommunikationsstandards. Zeitschrift für Betriebswirtschaft, Ergänzungsheft 2, 133-151.

Choi, J. P., & Stefanadis, C. (2003). Bundling, Entry Deterrence and Specialist Innovators. Department of Economics, Michigan State University, East Lansing, MI. (Online).

Christensen, C. M. (2007). The Innovator's Dilemma. New York, NY: Collins Business Essentials.

Cohen, A. (2004). Mein eBay. Geschichte und Geschichten vom Marktplatz der Welt. Berlin: Schwarzerfreitag.

Dietl, H., & Royer, S. (2000). Management virtueller Netzwerkeffekte in der Informationsökonomie. Zeitschrift für Organisation, 69(6), 324-331.

eBay Deutschland - Presse Service Center (2004). (Online).

Farrell, J., & Klemperer, P. (2006). Coordination and Lock-in. Competition with Switching Costs and Network Effects. Nuffield College, Oxford University, Oxford, England. (Online).

Fritz, W. (2004). Internet-Marketing und Electronic Commerce. Grundlagen - Rahmenbedingungen - Instrumente. 3rd ed. Wiesbaden: Gabler (Gabler-Lehrbuch).

Gallaugher, J. M., & Wang, Y. M. (1999). Network effects and the impact of free goods: an analysis of the web-server market. International Journal of Electronic Commerce, 3(4), 67-88.

Gerpott, T. J. (2005). Unterschätzter Nachahmer. Handelsblatt, 219, 20.

Grant, R.M., & Nippa, M. (2006). Strategisches Management. Analyse, Entwicklung und Implementierung von Unternehmensstrategien. 5th ed. München: Pearson Studium (wi - wirtschaft).

Heindl, H. (2004). Der First Mover Advantage in der Internetökonomie. Hamburg: Kovač (Strategisches Management, 18).

je (2007). AOL besiegelt Reorganisation. Handelsblatt, 180, 17.

Lee, Y., & O'Connor, G. C. (2003). New Product Launch Strategy for Network Effects. Journal of the Academy of Marketing Science, 31(3), 241-255.

Lehmann, J. (2004). HP überholt Palm bei Handhelds - Absatz aller Mobilgeräte legt in EMEA um 62 Prozent zu. Winhelpline Forum (ed). (Online).

Lieberman, M. B. (2005). Did First-Mover Advantage Survive the Dot-Com Crash. Anderson Graduate School of Management, UCLA, Los Angeles, CA. (Online).

Lieberman, M. B., & Montgomery D. B. (1988). First-mover advantages. Strategic Management Journal, Special Issue, 9, 41-58.

Liebowitz, S. J. (2002). Re-thinking the Network Economy. The True Forces that Drive the Digital Marketplace. New York, NY: AMACOM.

Möllenberg, A. (2003). Internet-Auktionen im Marketing aus der Konsumentenperspektive. Braunschweig: Eigenverlag.

Oelsnitz, D. von der (1998). Als Marktpionier zu dauerhaftem Erfolg. Harvard Business Manager, 4, 24-31.

Oelsnitz, D. von der, & Heinecke, A. (1997). Auch der Zweite kann gewinnen. io management, 66(3), 35-39.

Peitz, M. (2006). Bundling May Blockade Entry. University of Mannheim. (Online).

Porter, Michael E. (2001). Strategy and the Internet. Harvard Business Review, March, 62-78.

Postinett, A. (2008). Apple überholt Microsoft. Handelsblatt.com. (Online).

ricardo.ch - über uns (2007). (Online)

Shapiro, C., & Varian, H.R. (1999). Information Rules. A Strategic Guide to the Network Economy. [repr.]. Boston, MA: Harvard Business School Press.

Specht, M. (2001). Pioniervorteile für Anbieter von Informationsgütern im Electronic Commerce. München: FGM-Verl. (Schriftenreihe Schwerpunkt Marketing, Bd. 56).

Srinivasan, R., Lilien, G.L., & Rangaswamy, A. (2004). First in, first out. The effects of network externalities on pioneer survival. Journal of Marketing, 68(1), 41-59.

Stahl, F., Siegel, F., & Maass, W. (2004). Paid Content - Paid Services. Analyse des deutschen Marktes und der Erfolgsfaktoren von 280 Geschäftsmodellen. Universität St. Gallen.

Sundararjan, A. (2003). Network Effects, Nonlinear Pricing and Entry Deterrence. Leonard N. Stern School of Business, New York University. (Online).

Teece, D. J. (1987). The Competitive Challenge. Strategies for Industrial Innovation and Renewal. Cambridge MA: Ballinger.

Tellis, G. J., & Golder, P. N. (1996). First to market, first to fail. Real causes of enduring market leadership. Sloan Management Review, 37, 65-75.

Tellis, G. J., & Golder, P. N. (2002). Will & Vision. How Latecomers Grow to Dominate Markets. New York, NY: McGraw-Hill.

Varian (2004). Grundzüge der Mikroökonomik. 6th ed. München: Oldenbourg.

Weiber, R., & Kollmann, T. (2000). Wertschöpfungsprozesse und Wettbewerbsvorteile im Marketspace. Bliemel, F., Fassott, G., & Theobald, A. (eds.), Electronic Commerce. Herausforderungen - Anwendungen–Perspektiven (pp. 47-62). 3rd ed. Wiesbaden: Gabler.

Wirtz, B.W. (2006). Medien- und Internetmanagement. 5th ed. Wiesbaden: Gabler.

Chapter 18
Pricing

18.1 Product and Pricing Policy

As is the case for traditional goods, information providers must consider which product they want to offer to their customers at what price. Product policy, i.e. the presentation of the service offer (Meffert, 2005, 327), and pricing policy (Diller, 2008, 21 et seq.) are two of the central setscrews in a company's marketing mix. The close connection of these two entrepreneurial action parameters becomes clear in the economical price definition (Diller, 2008, 31), in which the price is represented as a quotient of remuneration and scope of services. This exemplifies on the one hand that the customer always considers the relation between the remuneration for and service of an offer. In this sense, prices can only be too high when the corresponding service is inadequate. On the other hand, the quotient makes the diametrically opposed interests of suppliers and customer very clear. Suppliers are interested in a particularly high price quotient, customers in a particularly low one.

Here, too, the context of our considerations will allow us only the mention of product and pricing policy's particularities as relevant for information providers. Comprehensive analyses of marketing in general can be found in Meffert (2005) or, for pricing policy specifically, Diller (2008), among others. We on the other hand wish to exemplify how information providers can design their products and prices with regard to high fixed and low variable costs, information asymmetries, uncontrollable propagation tendencies and network effects. These economical characteristics pose particular challenges to product design and pricing, but at the same time, digital goods lead to much more variable forms of product and price differentiation than traditional goods.

The focus of this section is the pricing of information offers. Information providers generally have different income streams available to them (Wirtz, 2006, 70 et seq.). Next to the recipient or user markets, they often service advertising and licensing markets as well. Thus search engines or online portals integrate ads into their online presence, for example. Book publishers in possession of the exploitation rights to a bestseller give out licenses for softcover editions. Film or music producers sell regional or outlet-specific exploitation rights. Here, too, prices must be set. The mere sale of rights does not represent an information good and thus will not play a role in the following. Advertisements, on the other hand, are generally not requested for their own sake but are offered to the user as a forced bundle, i.e. as a comination of desired and more or less undesired information goods. Advertisements are thus regarded as a particular form of complement. If we orient ourselves on the definition of information goods anything that is or can be digitized and for which there is willingness to pay, we will be able to clearly mark when advertisements are an information good and not an unsolicited nuisance (information bad), which is when it has value for the user and he or she would principally be ready to pay. For example, there are entry charges for the cinematic presentation of advertising films that have received critical recognition or awards.

Product policy is only considered when it is in close relation to pricing policy, i.e. in price differentiation. For further aspects of product design, read the sections on Complement Management, Compatibility, Copyright Management and Signaling.

> Pricing policy is one of the *most potent (kind of) marketing weapons* in the marketing mix. This potency comes as a result from the strong *effects* (*"Price Response"*) it can be used to achieve on the market. Customers as well as competitors often react drastically to changes in price. Market share shifts in the double digits are not uncommon, particularly as prices are easily communicable and arouse the interest of many customers who view budget buys as the central purpose of their economic behavior (Diller, 2008, 21).

Prices for information goods can be formed in several ways. For digital offers, there are new pricing vistas vis-à-vis traditional goods. Here Figure 18.1 provides an overview. **Fixed-price offers** are generally accepted. In this static procedure, the price is dictated by one side of the market, usually the provider. An innovation in static procedures is Reverse Pricing, where the customer dictates the price. Here it must be distinguished between such procedures where the provider sets a minimum price that must not be lowered (Name your own price–NYOP) and procedures that bank on completely unregulated pricing by the customer (Pay what you want–PWYW).

Such a demand-oriented pricing with a (covert) set minimum price (NYOP) is practiced by priceline.com, for example. The demander tells Priceline the maximum price he is willing to pay for a particular service (plane ticket, hotel, rental car etc.), whereupon Priceline searches for the corresponding offer (Kwasniewski, 2003; Bernhardt et al., 2005). An analogous offer can lately be found on eBay, with its "Best Offer" function. Here the buyer may make up to three price offers below the publicly set minimum price. If one of his offers is above the minimum determined by the seller, which is invisible to buyers, he will win the item.

A totally new variant of determining prices from the demanders' side is the (open) Pay What You Want. Here the provider foregoes a minimum price and accepts the customer's price offer without reservation (Kim et al., 2009). Such offers are more and more frequent as of late, e.g. from music groups such as Radiohead and Nine Inch Nails, who make their music available for download for a certain period of time, merely providing the option of a voluntary payment.

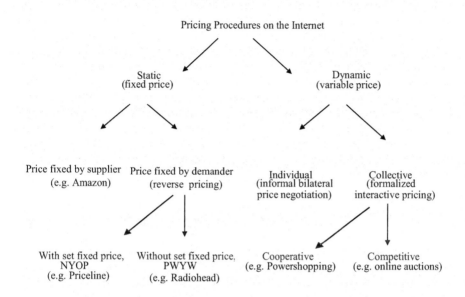

Figure 18.1: Alternative Pricing Procedures. Source: Following Fritz, 2004, 203 with reference to Möllenberg, 2003, 36.

Then there are the dynamic procedures of pricing (Fritz, 2004, 202 et seq.). Here the price is only determined over the course of the transaction between supplier and demander. Individual price negotiations have been in use for a long time as so-called invitations to tender, particularly in public administration (Wirtz, 2001, 459). With the advent of the internet and electronic payment services, e-market-places have established themselves for business-to-business transactions over the past few years. However, the hopes that had originally been nurtured concerning the great economic importance of these trade platforms were disappointed. Covisint, for instance, an electronic marketplace of the automotive industry launched at great expense, was sold by its founding company a few years after its inception due to a lack of success (Zillich, 2004). Individual business-to-consumer price negotiations are only gradually coming up.

Collective procedures, and specifically competitive ones, such as online auctions, are used far more often. We will address this issue below, under Price Differentiation. Cooperative pricing by buying communities bundles the demanders' buying power in order to create bulk discounts. A product becomes cheaper as more interested parties make an offer online. This pricing variant has not established itself, though, as a lack of customer acceptance and legal problems (Zeix, 2006) have led to even the leading representatives of power shopping, such as powershopping.de or letsbuyit.com, leaving the market.

Due to their fixed-cost-intensive cost structure, it makes sense for information providers to aim for prices that create large quantities of sales and thus the desired unit cost reduction. If the provider then wants to let the network effects related to information goods come into play, it is recommended to concentrate, in pricing, on a quick distribution. Both these aspects point in the same direction: prices must not be set in a cost-oriented, but in a market-oriented way (Fritz, 2004, 204). This can be achieved with a view to competition, which is heavily favored by the internet's price transparency, or with a view to the customer. Here either the customer's willingness to pay must be determined via (online) market research or the customers must be given the option–at least in part–to reveal what their ideal price would be. Here the instrument of price differentiation offers an entire arsenal of possibilities.

18.2   Forms of Price Differentiation

From a current perspective, we can already say that it will be an entirely new and central challenge, even for information providers, to not so much set one's preferred price than ideally determine the pricing mechanisms to be used (Skiera et al., 2005, 292). Here we are on the topic of price differentiation. Its basic idea is to sell fundamentally the same product to different customers at different prices (cf. e.g. Diller, 2008, 227 et seq.). From a company's perspective, this would ideally mean that consumer surplus could be skimmed off in its entirety. Of course, price differentiation only makes sense if there are actual different use values and thus different willingnesses to pay for the offered goods on the customers' side. This is well established in everyday life, but does it hold for information offers? For internet users, it is apparent that priced information offers are still being largely rejected. Heil (1999, 246) recognizes, focusing on a survey of internet users by the GVU Center, that more than 40% reject priced offers because there is, in their opinion, still a sufficient amount of free alternatives available. The results are similar for music-sharing platforms. Walsh et al. (2002, 216) show that a good two thirds of the surveyed filesharing site users are not willing to pay for services hitherto free of charge. It must thus be assumed that for information offers, there is a larger fraction of users unwilling to pay. The reverse conclusion, however, might be that there is definitely willingness to pay on information markets. Also it can be observed that willingness to pay for digital goods is tendentially increasing, with growth rates particularly high in Germany (Stahl et al., 2004, 13, 31). Broadband users in particular have a high acceptance of the purchase of digital products

(Theysohn et al., 2005, 174). Thus it makes entrepreneurial sense to siphon off the existing willingnesses to pay via differentiated pricing (Fritz, 2004, 207).

There are three basic forms of price differentiation, which go back to Arthur Cecil Pigou (1929). They are distinguished by the party that sets the price and how the buyer groups are separated.

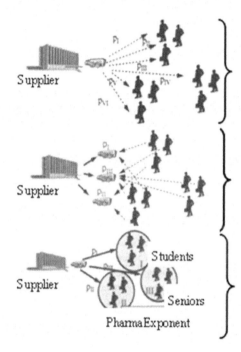

1st Degree Price Differentiation
(also called complete price differentiation).
The ideal form of price differentiation: customers are made an offer that matches their individual willingness to pay

2nd Degree Price Differentiation
Principle of self-selection:
customers select from several alternatives according to their individual willingness to pay

3rd Degree Price Differentiation
Principle of Segmentation:
customers are made an offer according to their target group affiliation

Figure 18.2: Basic Forms of Price Differentiation. Source: Following Schumann & Hess, 2006, 70-71.

1st Degree Price Differentiation represents the ideal form, where the provider tries to get every customer to pay the maximum price he is willing to pay. Before the advent of electronic trade, this form of price differentiation had been regarded as not very practicable. It could be implemented in individual price negotiations (Diller, 2008, 236), by haggling or in auctions, but only the internet created the means for using individual price differentiation not only in single transactions but in mass business (Diller, 2008, 222-223). The different forms of online auctions, to be addressed later, in particular are a suitable instrument for finalizing transactions on the basis of individual willingnesses to pay.

In 3rd Degree Price Differentiation, the aim is to overcome the problem of individually determining willingnesses to pay via target group segmentation. Customer groups are formed, e.g. students or senior citizens, whose members are assumed to have similar willingnesses to pay, and which can be clearly differentiated from the other groups.

> As an example, let us consider a medical journal. As it is well regarded by doctors, the publisher can charge them a relatively high price. For students of medicine, the journal's value is less high, and they typically have lesser financial means. For this reason, the publisher offers its future core target group a reduced student subscription. A special price for members of the pharmacological industry can be set in a similar way (Schumann & Hess, 2006, 70).

This variant leaves the customers no choice between offers and prices. The problem of this form of differentiation is in the clean separation of the customer groups and in the occurrence of arbitrage. To wit, if customers from the group charged a low price sell the product on to those who would normally pay more, the company is deprived of consumer surplus it would receive by selling the product to the more solvent customers itself.

The last of the three forms of price differentiation mentioned–and displayed in Figure 18.2–is 2nd Degree Price Differentiation.

Price Differentiation (PD)							
PD 1st Degree		PD 2nd Degree			PD 3rd Degree		
Price individualization		Perfor-mance obtain PD	Quantita-tive PD	Price Bundle (PB)	Personnel PD	Spatial PD	Tempo-ral PD
Price negotia tions	e.g. Auc-tions	Delivery vs. collections price, Seat categories	e.g. Quantity discounts Boni, Multi-stage rates Esti-mated prices	e.g. Set-price, Package tours, Acces-sory packages	e.g. Student rates, Official rates or Senior rates	e.g. Internat. PD, Station prices	e.g. Week-end fares, Noctur-nal tariffs

Figure 18.3: Examples of Price Differentiation. Source: Diller, 2008, 229.

Contrary to the 1st and 3rd Degree Forms of Price Differentiation, the provider here does not make a fixed offer to a single customer or target group (segmentation). Instead, the company offers the services in such a differentiated way that the customers will buy at different prices of their own volition. This principle of self-selection allows them to decide which combination of price and performance they want their product to have. This price differentiation can be based on differences in performance (e.g. classes of reservation for airplane travel), on a difference in quantity (e.g. bulk discounts, flatrates) or it can take the form of a price/product bundle (e.g. all-expense tours). Figure 18.3 provides an overview of these options.

The different forms of price differentiation will now be discussed with regard to information offers. For the 1st Degree Price Differentiation, we will deal with the different variants of **online auctions**. For 2nd Degree Price Differentiation, we will present **windowing, versioning** and **bundling**. 3rd Degree Price Differentiation will involve "**follow-the-free**" pricing. These five forms of pricing are generally very relevant for internet marketing (Fritz, 2004, 200 et seq.), and specifically for electronic trade with digital content (Stahl, 2005, 285 et seq.).

18.2.1   Online Auctions

An individual pricing that takes into consideration customers' willingness to pay is very desirable for companies. As opposed to standard-price offers, this form of **1st Degree Price Differentiation** allows for the complete transformation of consumer surplus into profit. Next to the above-mentioned individual price negotiations, auctions are a suitable instrument for revealing willingness to pay (McAfee & McMillan, 1987). The bidding procedure frequently makes bidders go to the very limit of their willingness to pay or–in the case of "overbidding" (Sattler & Nitschke, 2003)–even beyond. Until a few years ago, auctions didn't play a particular role in economic life. They were predominantly used in selling rarities, used items or on the stock market (Diller, 2000, 300). The internet has changed this, though, hence online auctions are one of the most popular sales methods today (Fritz, 2004, 210). Apart from the usefulness for companies to reveal customers' willingness to pay (Fritz, 2004, 204 with further sources), auctions offer the customers a certain price experience. The success of eBay and other auction platforms confirms this.

The auction theory differentiates between four central types of auctions (McAfee & McMillan, 1987, 702; Wirtz, 2001, 453 et seq.), which can all be found in electronic business transactions. A fundamental difference between them is whether they are conducted publicly or whether they are hidden.

The different auction types' prevalence rate varies strongly. Well suited for mass business and by far the dominant variant on the internet is the English Auction. Dutch Auctions are also used quite often. Hidden auctions are seldomly found, with the Vickrey auction only playing a role in online advertising (e.g. in Google AdWords).

Public Auctions	Hidden Auctions
English Auction	Highest Price Auction
Increasing the offers until there is only one bidder left. The last bidder wins the item and pays the price of his last bid. E.g. eBay.com; hood.de	Each bidder submits exactly one hidden bid. The highest bidder wins the item and pays the price of his bid. E.g. murphyauctions.net
Dutch Auction	Vickrey Auction
A preset starting price is lowered until the first bidder accepts it. This bidder will then win the item. E.g. intermodalex.com; azubo.de	Special form of highest price auction, where all bidders submit exactly one hidden bid. The highest bidder wins the item and pays the price of the second highest bid.

Figure 18.4: Auction Types.

18.2.2   *Windowing*

So-called windowing deals with the problem of bringing a finished information good, like a book or a film, on the market in different packages and at different points in time (Owen & Wildman, 1992, 26-37). Starting from one and the same first copy, the master, customers–and this is the decisive point–are offered different modes of transmission, i.e. carrier media, over time. Films are not only shown in cinemas but also enter the market–with delays–as DVDs, on Pay-TV and free TV.

We remember that **2nd Degree Pricing** means that companies make different offers, where customers then choose the one that is most attractive to them. The offers satisfy different needs, which is why customers are prepared to pay different prices. Customers, for instance, who want to see a new film in the cinema, are willing to pay more than those who want to see it as a rental DVD or on TV.

At the foreground of this form of price differentiation is the temporal aspect. Information providers try to exploit the different "profit windows"–hence: windowing (Zerdick et al., 2001, 70et seq.)–to the full. If they didn't grade their offers, cannibalization effects would kick in: many customers go to the cinema or rent a DVD because they have to wait a long time to see a film on TV, which is why there are clear waiting periods between the single windows. In Europe, there are generally six months between a film's entering the video market and the Pay-per-View program. In the USA, this period is much shorter, usually between 40 and 90 days (Zerdick et al., 2001, 71). Free-TV offers are right at the end of the exploitation chain, as the customers found here are the ones with the least willingness to pay. Accordingly, they are the ones who have to wait the longest for the free, because ad-financed, transmission. If films on free TV were shown before they aired on Pay-TV, a large part of the customers willing to pay would be lost. After a film has been shown free of charge, consumers are ready to pay only very little, or nothing.

The single exploitation windows' positioning depends on their potential for profit. Even though profit from ticket sales in cinemas has gone down significantly in recent years, it is still the most important source of revenue.

Furthermore, films have a high strategic meaning for the overall exploitation's success.

> The more successful and prominent a film was in cinemas, the easier (and more profitable) its exploitation in the following profit windows is going to be (Zerdick et al., 2001, 71).

The largest profits are made in home entertainment these days, where DVDs have largely replaced video tapes, and sales are more profitable than rentals (Wirtz, 2006, 267). When the exploitation chain has been completely run through, the films are additionally offered via syndication and program archives (Zerdick et al., 2001, 71).

The greater the danger of cannibalization, the more clearly the exploitation windows must be separated from each other and planned without any temporal overlaps. If the gaps between the windows are too small, the customers may wait for the lower-priced offer (DVD instead of cinema). But within the TV windows, too, repeats must not air too frequently, as interested audiences will not be excited for repeat viewings (Schumann & Hess, 2006, 74 et seq.).

It is still an open question how new offers will fit into this chain. Just as the home entertainment market pushed back ad-financed TV to last place with its introduction at the beginning of the nineteen-eighties (Zerdick et al., 2001, 71), new digital offers on the internet will make space for themselves. Video-on-Demand is slowly beginning to unfold, encountering a clientele that has a tendentially higher willingness to pay because this sort of offer reduces transport and search costs for them (Wirtz, 2006, 308). Streaming films before, during or shortly after their cinematic launch could also address customers who are ready to pay a little more for this offer. When Video-on-Demand has fully established itself, it is to be expected that it will be positioned at the forefront, possibly even in first place, of the value chain (Litman, 2000, 100).

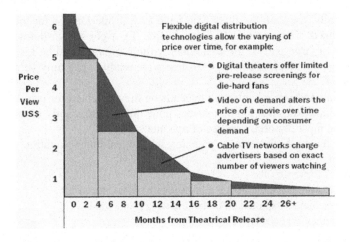

Figure 18.5: Revenue Potentials for Digital Film Distribution. Source: Cap Gemini Ernst & Young, 2001, 14.

Here some interesting perspectives with regard to the creation of network effects open up. If it is so important that a new film generates a lot of initial publicity so that the subsequent exploitation can profit in terms of quantity and price, digital offers can make an important contribution if they are measurable and thus as communicable as box office data. In such a case, it might be the legal–and possibly even illegal–download figures that are used for advertisements. Digital paid content in each case bears "digital potential" (Wirtz, 2006, 308), i.e. the chance of making–in combination with windowing–a clear step toward perfect price differentiation. Prices can, as shown in Figure 18.5, be variably set over time in order to siphon off film, DVD or TV audiences' different willingnesses to pay.

Upon closer inspection, it is noticeable that windowing is no entirely pure form of temporal price differentiation. It may be with regard to identical content, which is exploited repeatedly in the different windows, but not with regard to the form of the offer. The customer, it is easy to recognize, receives a clearly different product, depending on whether he watches a film in the cinema or at home on his TV or PC. Here the relation to another form of price differentiation that is increasingly being used for information goods, namely performance-oriented price differentiation (versioning), becomes clear. It used to be too complicated to change information products in order to sell them to different target groups after they had been created, which is why temporally graded distribution via different channels–as it is also practiced in publishing, for example, with its hardcover and softcover editions–played such an important role. With the digitalization of information products, an entirely new arena is opening up. Products can be reassembled with little effort and tailor-made for ever smaller target groups. The fact that this can be done to a much greater degree of differentiation is shown by the following example from publishing.

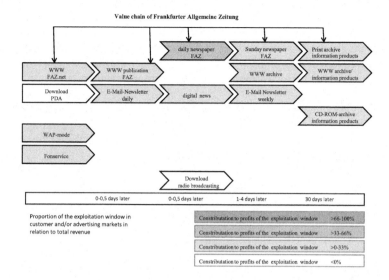

Figure 18.6: Exploitation Chain of the Frankfurter Allgemeine Zeitung. Source: Following Schumann & Hess, 2006, 75.

As can be very clearly recognized in Figure 18.6, there is a total of fifteen exploitation windows, which are divided into five stages. Of all the offers, only three are print-based, and eleven–twelve if we also count the telephone offer–are electronic. The main earner is still the print version of the daily newspaper. All other offers either bring in no (PDA, radio offer) or little revenue, up until a maximum of 33%.

18.2.3   Versioning

With this, we will leave windowing and turn to performance-oriented price differentiation, i.e. versioning, as another form of **2ⁿᵈ Degree Price Differentiation**. We can find two points that may serve as separation criteria between windowing and versioning, the identity of the product and the timing of the offer. Windowing is traditionally based on a once-created first copy being offered via different distribution channels, in principally identical form–i.e., apart from some minor edits. Additionally, the different offers are temporally graded, meaning that there exist temporal exploitation windows that can be clearly separated so that the information offers can only be used after a certain time has elapsed in each case.

If the customer can choose from different variants generated from a first copy, and if these are available to him at the same time, we are dealing with versioning.

Windowing approaches versioning when the offers are adjusted for single channels. Thus it is often the case that DVDs are outfitted with additional features, e.g. languages, extended versions, or background material.

Windowing and versioning as forms of 2nd Degree Price Differentiation are again distinguished from temporal 3rd Degree Price Differentiation, which we will address further on, by the provider varying the prices in relation to the time of the offer if there are identical offers. To wit, if telephone conversations are more expensive during the daytime than evenings or nights, there is a temporal price differentiation.

In versioning, the company thus offers its product in different versions and leaves it to the customer to select the variant best suited to him. Versioning is based on performance differences in information offers noticeable to the customer, be it films, music, books or software.

> Your goal in versioning your information product is to sell to different market segments at different prices. By creating low-end and high-end versions of your product, you can sell the same thing to customers with significantly different levels of willingness to pay (Shapiro & Varian, 1999, 61-62).

The provider must thus aim to design the product services in such a way that they meet customers' expectations as exactly as possible on the one hand, and that the asking price matches the customers' willingness to pay. This form of performance-oriented price differentiation comes close to product differentiation, yet remains *price* differentiation because

> The goal of performance-oriented price differentiation is to achieve a higher perception of gain, and thus a greater willingness to pay, in a section of one's clientele via relatively minor changes in the range, or quality, of services that result in no significant cost consequences. In this respect, performance-oriented price differentiation is always use-oriented. The more elastically demanders react to corresponding differentiations in their sense of values and the willingness to pay that is predicated on it, the better it will succeed (Diller, 2008, 237).

The versioning of information goods is thus a form of price and not product differentiation, because it aims to match to customers' different senses of usefulness while incurring minimal differentiation costs. Let us take the example of an E-Mail program, of which there are three versions that address different customer needs. The underlying price differences, e.g. for more free text messages, better virus protection or more disk space, are very low for the provider. The case is slightly different, though, when information offers are coupled to different service levels, for example. This can lead to noticeable additional costs if the pre-existing service capacities are insufficient and must be augmented specifically for the premium offers.

For the development of the different product versions, Deneckere and McAfee (1996) as well as Shapiro and Varian (1999, 69) recommend that the high-end version be created first, from which versions with reduced quality can then be derived. This creates two advantages:

On the one hand, the low-end version can be used to advertise the qualitatively superior product. The users of stripped-down versions of mailing programs, encyclopedias or database offers are very quick to recognize the added value of the higher-priced offers. Every user of Adobe's free Reader will quickly come to appreciate the usefulness of being able to create PDF-documents oneself, which requires the priced version of Adobe Acrobat. Providers can use the low-priced versions to reduce information asymmetries quite easily and to build up trust on the customers' side (Wirtz & Olderog, 2001, 199).

On the other hand, the range of reactions to competition is larger when the highest-quality version is developed first. Should the competition offer high quality at relatively cheaper prices, the already available premium offer can quickly be repositioned. The new, or re-development of a high-end version from a version of low or medium quality is much more time-consuming.

How many versions should the customers be offered? In theory, one could fashion an individual version for each customer if versioning costs are negligible, which would allow one to achieve the ideal of perfect price differentiation. Too many product versions bring with them two disadvantages, however. On the one hand, the provider incurs more costs if he must manage many offers at the same time ("menu cost"; Wu & Chen, 2008, 165). On the other hand, there is the danger of a too large variety of offers confusing the customers (Iyengar & Lepper, 2000). The consumers must be able to clearly recognize the service differences in order to base their shopping decision on them. If the perceptible difference is not sufficient, there is a danger of the higher-quality offers not being recognized as such and thus not bought (Zerdick et al., 2001, 188). The provider must thus tread carefully between answering customers' demands on the one hand and necessitating rising service costs as well as possibly making excessive demands on the customer on the other hand.

There are several empirical analyses according to which at least three versions should generally be offered (e.g. Simonson & Tversky, 1992; Smith & Nagle, 1995). At least three versions because consumers tend to the middle, usually avoiding the extremes.

> When buying products, consumers normally try to avoid extreme choices–they fear they'll have to pay too much if they go for the most expensive version, and the worry they'll get too little if they opt for the cheapest. They are drawn instead to a compromise choice–a version in the middle of the product line (Shapiro & Varian, 1998, 114).

According to Simonson and Tversky (1992), buyers follow to the Extremeness Aversion Hypothesis:

> The extremeness aversion hypothesis derives from the notion that disadvantages loom larger than the respective advantages, which extends the notion of loss aversion (Simonson & Tversky, 1992, 292).

If the buyer only has two offers to choose from, he will frequently choose the cheaper one. If, on the other hand, there is a high-end, gold, maxi or premium version, this will promote the medium–formerly most expensive–version. The goal of the introduction of a third, high-quality variant is not primarily to sell it in huge quantities, but to change customers' perceptions regarding the cheaper versions and to make low-end buyers settle for the higher-value (medium) product.

> Adding a premium product to the product line may not necessarily result in overwhelming sales of the premium product itself. It does, however, enhance buyers' perceptions of lower-priced products in the product line and influences low-end buyers to trade up to higher-priced models (Smith & Nagle, 1995, 107).

The middle products thus gain acceptance. It can even be empirically demonstrated that sales of the second, respectively next-to-last, product can be boosted by increasing the number of versions from two to three or more (Stahl, 2005, 202).

When developing the product offer, however, Bhargava and Choudhary (2004) recommend that information providers pay close attention to the way customers' willingnesses to pay are distributed. The introduction of a low-end version only makes sense if more customers are won for this offer than are "lost", i.e. than no longer buy the higher-grade version.

> Introduction of a low quality product into the market has two effects: it causes some low-value consumers (who would not otherwise have purchased the product) to enter the market, but it also causes some high-value consumers to shift to the low quality product ... When marginal costs are negligible, the reduction in revenue is equivalent to a reduction in profit ... The overall reduction in profit makes price discrimination suboptimal (Bhargava & Choudhary, 2004, 5).

There are many information offers that exist in exactly three versions, e.g. tax programs such as Lexware (2011) with Basic, deluxe and Home&Business, or Adobe products with their differentiation of Standard, professional and 3D. A key factor in designing the top version is that it be clearly different to the lower ones. In order to safeguard this, one might even offer software features that go far beyond most buyers' needs (Shapiro & Varian, 1999, 73; Simonson & Tversky, 1992, 293-294). Even if versioning results in noticeable costs, it is always recommended to offer a clearly distinguishable high-end version and–if costs are not too high–lower-quality versions (Sundararajan, 2004, 1671). A further argument for the offer of premium versions is in their quality perception. High-priced offers are frequently regarded as high-quality by customers (Völckner, 2006; Stahl, 2005, 297). The premium offer's positioning can thus positively influence the perception of the entire offer.

In pricing, it should be noted that demand for the high-grade premium versions can be increased in different ways. When working with linear price increases, quality and extent must increase disproportionately (Heitmann et al., 2006, 11). Even better, though, is not working with linear price increases. As Heitmann et al. (2006, 12) show with the example of telephone providers, it is recommended to increase only the services offered in a linear way and to increase the prices less than proportionately. This is because customers glean the value of an offer from the relation of price and performance, where the performance serves as a reference value. The bigger performance package is then seen as relatively cheaper. If, on the other hand, there is definitely not enough performance in the larger package, customers will still tend to buy the cheaper version.

Now, what does the other side of the versioning spectrum look like? How many versions should be offered at most? Shapiro and Varian (1999, 70) regard the absolute upper limit as the number of clearly distinguishable customer segments that should all be served with different versions as long as they are perceived as clearly separate from each other. With regard to cognitive costs for the customers and the provider's costs of maintaining the range of services, Hui et al. (2008) recommend offering a manageable number of versions. They also regard three as sufficient.

Some more concrete statements are found in Stahl (2005). He observes, on the basis of an empirical analysis of digital content, that a very large number of versions can result in sales increases if they are reduced to a number smaller than ten. From a dynamical perspective, a reduction of versions will first lead to a reduction in sales, but this will be overcompensated for in the following periods. Stahl (2005, 203) suspects that a reason for this is that customers have to recover their bearings after the known version falls away before they buy again, from the reduced catalog this time. He (317) calculated six to be the number of versions for which sales and profit are maximized.

Depending on what kind of information good we are dealing with, and what value it is deemed to have by the customer, the provider's decision as to how many versions to offer–in the context of the envisaged bandwidth–will vary. Due to the low versioning costs for digital information costs (Zerdick et al., 2001, 191), however, this is not a problem. For companies, versioning is thus a suitable field of experimentation for achieving increased sales (Shapiro & Varian, 1998, 113-114.).

Versioning is a form of 2nd Degree Price Differentiation, because buyers reveal their individual willingnesses to pay via their choice of version. Economically, this is the **Principle of Self-Selection** (Shapiro & Varian, 1999, 54). The provider no longer has to find out, in detail, what value his customers ascribe to his products. Versioning can be an effective strategy, particularly when customers cannot be clearly distinguished on the basis of external characteristics (Klein & Loebbecke, 1999).

Versioning can be performed in different ways, as displayed in Table 18.1. As can be clearly recognized, versioning costs only play a subordinate role.

Form of Versioning	Degree of Versioning	Examples
Up-to-dateness	Immediate or delayed access	Onvista: Stock exchange information in real time or with time delay (onvista.de) Ökotest: Price according to the test's age (oekotest.de)
Availability of information	Unimedial or multimedial Access possibilities	Falk: Road and city maps as printouts or E-Mail LexisNexis-Databases: On-Screen or as downloads; Database access on-campus or off-campus (lexisnexis.de)
Range of services	Few or many functionalities Low or high depth of information Extent of support	Adobe Photoshop CS3 or CS3 extended with many additional functionalities (adobe.com) OpenBC/Xing: Comprehensive Research options with premium membership (xing.com) Dialog Web vs. Dialog Professional with differing extents of background information (dialog.com) Abstract vs. full text of a market study Shop software xt:Commerce with and without support
Friendliness of design	Low or high image resolution	Fotolia: Price grading in dependence of pixel size (de.fotolia.com)
Processing speed	Low or high speed	Mathematica: Performing the symbolical, graphical and numerical operations at different calculating speeds (wolfram.com)

Table 18.1: Forms of Versioning.

18.2.4 Bundling

Another form of **2nd Degree Price Differentiation** is bundling: two or more (information) goods are summarized in one single offer and sold as a package or set at a (generally lower) total price. There is price and product bundling; both forms are two inseparable sides of the same coin, as we are dealing with the creation of different offer services and the simultaneous price determination in the same breath (Diller, 2008, 240). We will regard bundling as price bundling in this context.

Adams and Yellen (1976) were the first to comprehensively analyze this pricing strategy. The core aim of bundling is to reduce the variance of consumers' appreciation of, and thus their willingness to pay for, a good in comparison with retail. How well this works depends on how the willingnesses to pay for the single goods within the bundle correlate to each other. A precondition here is that the products not be (moderate or strong) substitutes; they must be either independent or complementary (Tellis, 1986, 155; Venkatesh & Kamakura, 2003, 229).

A positive correlation is when customers who are ready to pay a lot for a good in the bundle also have a high willingness to pay for the other good (Figure 18.7). This is also valid on a lesser price level, i.e. if there is a low willingness to pay for both goods. One speaks of negative correlation, on the other hand, when willingness to pay is high for one good and low for the other. Simple statistical calculations can demonstrate that bundling results in a homogenization of willingness to pay. This is more pronounced the more negatively willingnesses to pay correlate.

> Consumer's valuation for a collection of goods typically has a probability distribution with a lower variance per good compared to the valuations for the individual goods. The larger the number of goods bundled, the greater the typical reduction in the variance (Bakos & Brynjolfsson, 1999, 1614).

The stronger the homogenization resulting from bundling, the greater the provider's revenue potentials will be. In Figure 18.8, this can be recognized in the extension of the profit area when comparing Bundle I (not very pronounced homogenization, or heterogeneous demand structure, respectively; Figure 18.) and Bundle II (very pronounced homogenization, or homogeneous demand structure, respectively).

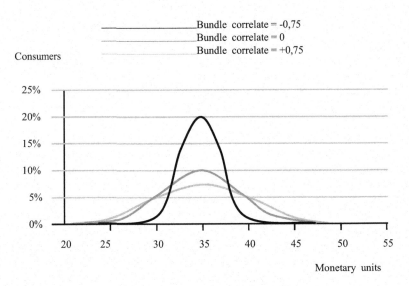

Figure 18.11: Correlations of Willingnesses to Pay and the Homogenization Effect. Source: Olderog & Skiera, 2000, 143.

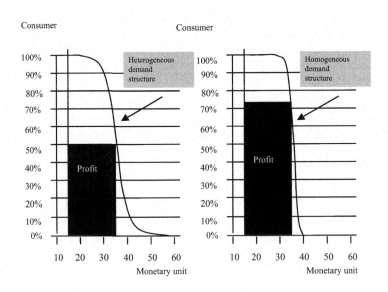

Figure 18.8: Forms of Bundling. Source: Olderog & Skiera, 2000, 143.

Bundling is a profitable variant of price differentiation for digital information goods in particular, as marginal cost for adding a further good to a bundle are negligible (Varian, 2003, 19). Conversely, it has been empirically proven that bundling becomes increasingly unattractive as marginal cost rises, e.g. for information offers on data carriers such as video cassettes or DVDs, but also for physical goods (Bakos & Brynjolfsson, 1999, 1626).

If we consider the example of two Microsoft products, like Word and Excel, and two customers with different valuations of these products, it can be clearly recognized how the dispersion of willingnesses to pay are reduced by bundling (Shapiro & Varian 1999, 75 et seq.).

	Word	Excel
Customer A	€ 120	€ 100
Customer B	€ 100	€ 120

Table 18.2: Willingnesses to Pay for Software Products. Source: Following Shapiro & Varian, 1999, 75.

Depending on how prices are configured, the provider will achieve different profits. If he chooses uniform fixed prices for the products, e.g. €100 or €120, he will earn either €240 or €400. In the first case, the customers only bought either Word or Excel, in the second case each bought both. Now the company is considering offering a package consisting of both programs. As willingness to pay is the same, in sum, a price of €220 for the "Office Suite" would result in a 10% increase to profit, to €440. The company is exploiting the fact that dispersion of willingnesses to pay is less pronounced for the bundle than it is for the single components. The interesting thing is that customers allocate the single prices individually. A receives, from his point of view, the less valuable Excel for €100, B the less valuable Word, yet both value the bundle exactly the same.

The result, according to Bakos and Brynjolfsson (1999), is a "predictive value of bundling", i.e. bundling reduces the insecurity of the provider with respect to customers' subjective valuation. Even without an exact knowledge of customers' individual ratings, bundling can provide for a demand-oriented price determination. It is easier to estimate the customers' valuation for a whole set of goods than for each good individually. This is generally valid, as long as the goods offered in the bundle are not too closely related and their reciprocal valuation by the customer does not influence itself too significantly (Bakos & Brynjolfsson, 2000, 63):

> As a result, a seller typically can extract more value from each information good when it is part of a bundle than when it is sold separately. Moreover, at the optimal price, more consumers will find the bundle worth buying than would have bought the same good sold separately.

We can now differentiate between different forms of bundling (Wirtz & Olderog, 2001, 200-201). In **pure bundling**, also called tying, there are only product packages with multiple components. This is the preferred method for newspapers and magazines, as articles are not sold individually but only as part of the entire issue. The counterexample, which strictly speaking is not an example of bundling at all, is **pure unbundling**. Here the services are only sold individually. This procedure is interesting in so far as here services are often offered now that previously were only available in a package. The download options for music (formerly only complete cassettes, LPs, CDs) or press products must be mentioned in this respect. **Mixed bundling** offers the customers both variants, i.e. they can buy the package or the individual offer. Mixed bundling is often found for software, when, as in the case of Microsoft Office, the single programs are offered separately and in sets for private individuals, professional users or companies.

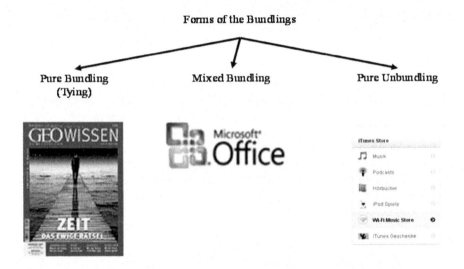

Figure 18.9: Forms of Bundling.

Via bundling consumers' willingnesses to pay can be skimmed off. This is more successful the closer one comes to perfect (1st degree) price differentiation. Adams and Yellen (1976, 481) observe three optimality conditions:

- Customers whose willingness to pay is below marginal cost should be prohibited from buying (Exclusion),
- Customers whose willingness to pay is above marginal cost should be encouraged to buy (Inclusion) and
- Transactions should not result in consumer surplus (Complete Extraction).

We can see that next to the dispersion of willingnesses to pay, variable costs have a decisive influence on whether and how a bundling strategy can be used.

For information providers, bundling is generally very suitable (Bakos & Brynjolfsson, 1999, 1626). Let us consider once more the software offers Excel and Word, this time focusing on a customer C, whose willingness to pay is €40 for Excel and €140 for Word. It is clearly observable how the package offer leads to the so-called "transfer of consumer surplus" (Wirtz & Olderog, 2001, 203 et seq.). Let us assume that the asking price for each of the products Word and Excel is €110. In the case of individual prices, customer C would only buy Word, perhaps because he is a journalist, but not Excel, because at that price, he would prefer to settle his finances with a text processing program. Without variable costs, the provider aims at a contribution margin of €110. This violates two of the above conditions, as the customer does not buy Excel even though his willingness to pay exceeds marginal cost (Inclusion) and he achieves €30 of consumer surplus when buying Word (Extraction). So what happens if the company changes its pricing strategy and offers a package at €180? Here it must be noted that the bundle price is not merely a result of the addition of individual prices but is calculated via an autonomous optimization procedure on the basis of willingness to pay (Olderog & Skiera, 2000, 140 et seq.). The total price of a bundle is frequently below the sum of the individual prices. If, however, the single components are worth less in isolation than they are in the bundle, that is if an added benefit is created, e.g. via seamless interplay, the bundle price can also be more than the sum of the individual prices (Huber & Kopsch, 2002, 619).

In our context, the sum of the customer's willingnesses to pay corresponds exactly to the price for the bundle and the optimality conditions are completely fulfilled. In his mind, the customer transfers the consumer surplus applicable for Word in comparison with its individual price to the lesser-valued Excel. The provider arrives at a contribution margin of €180 and there is, all in all, no more consumer surplus. If the provider's price does not meet the sum of willingnesses to pay as exactly as in this example, the customer will either not pay (sum of willingnesses to pay < package price) or create consumer surplus (sum of willingnesses to pay > package price). Even if the latter is not ideal from the provider's perspective, as the condition of Extraction is not met, he can still use bundling to appropriate the consumer surplus transferred from one product to the other by the customer and must merely do without the part that goes beyond.

What pricing strategy is the most advantageous, then: the determination of single prices (pure unbundling), pure bundling or the combination of both in mixed bundling? For the case of two products offered, it can be said (without considering the costs), with regard to the distribution of customer preferences on a demand curve (Simon & Fassnacht, 2009, 303 et seq.):

- Pure unbundling is recommended if the customers' willingnesses to pay for the offered products are at the outer ends of the demand curve, i.e. if the preference for one of the two products is dominant and the preference for the other product is very low or even zero.

- If the willingnesses to pay for both products are rather balanced, i.e. if the customers are interested in both products and thus have a relatively high preference for the bundle, too, pure bundling is recommended.
- If there are multiple customer groups with both extreme and balanced willingnesses to pay for both products, mixed bundling is of advantage.

Mixed bundling is frequently the strategy of choice, because it is able to combine the advantages of both pure pricing strategies:

> The advantage of pure bundling is its ability to reduce effective buyer heterogeneity, while the advantage of unbundled sales is its ability to collect a high price for each good from some buyers who care very little for the other. Mixed bundling can make use of both of these advantages by selling the bundle to a group of buyers with accordingly reduced effective heterogeneity, while charging high mark ups to those on the fringes of the taste distribution who are mainly interested in only one of the two goods (Schmalensee, 1984, 227).

What happens if there are still variable costs, if, for example, both products are offered in elaborate packaging with a booklet included, but the market situation precludes the raising of prices? In such a situation, variable costs result in a short-term reduction of the provider's contribution margins. This is problematic in bundling when the marginal cost is above the customer's willingness to pay for one of the products in the bundle (Excel in Figure 18.10). In such a case, the condition of Exclusion is violated (Wirtz & Olderog, 2001, 205), i.e. there are customers who buy products even though their willingness to pay is below the marginal cost. The provider thus consciously incurs losses with regard to the individual product. He can only appropriate the consumer surplus of the higher-rated product as long as the marginal cost for the lower-rated product is beneath the corresponding willingness to pay. Otherwise, he must use it to "cross-subsidize" the Exclusion violation, i.e. to make up for the difference between willingness to pay and marginal cost. This he can keep up for as long as there is sufficient consumer surplus available. If, however, this difference is greater for the lesser-valued product but greater than the available compensatory consumer surplus, the contribution margins will come under attack. As can be clearly seen in Figure 18.10, this is the case: the consumer surplus for Word is insufficient to compensate for the lack of willingness to pay for Excel.

Nevertheless, it can be sensible to offer while incurring a loss, e.g. when the goal is to build up an installed base. When Sony offers its Playstation 3 below marginal cost, the positive contribution margins of games that are offered as part of the package are used for cross-subsidization. The same goes for mobile telephone providers, who only offer their end product cheaply in a package with a contract, generally running two years. The providers' goal is to compensate for the losses of today with future winnings. It becomes very clear, though, that the larger marginal cost, the more it restricts the provider's scope of action. This goes for cross-subsidization within the bundle, but also for possible bundle discounts.

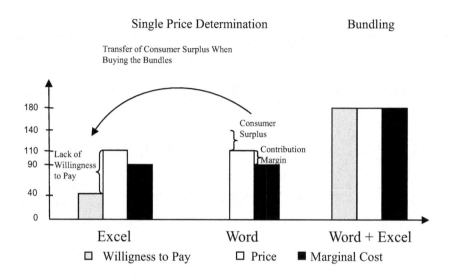

Figure 18.10: Transfer of Consumer Surplus. Source: Following Wirtz & Olderog, 2001, 204.

If we take another look at Figure 18.10, this statement can be made very clear. If the provider sets prices per unit, he will only sell Word to customer C for €110, and only registers a contribution margin of €20, because marginal cost is €90. In the case of pure bundling, for the package price of €180, the customer will receive both products, but the provider is left with no contribution margin. He must use both the consumer surplus transferred in comparison with unit prices (€30) and his contribution margins (€40) in order to compensate for the lack of willingness to pay for Excel (€70). From the buyer's point of view, this looks a little different: he subtracts from the package price (€180) what the maximum price he would pay for the more valuable product (Word, €140), and thus gets–to his thinking–the price he is required to pay for Excel (€40), and which he is prepared to pay. The missing difference to marginal cost (€90) must be "financed" by the provider by transferring consumer surplus (€30) and by foregoing a contribution margin for Word (€20). The provider is thus in a worse position than he would be when selling only one product. If he were then to opt for mixed bundling and offer a package price of, say, €200, customer C would be someone who will decide against the bundle and only buy Word.

Marginal contribution

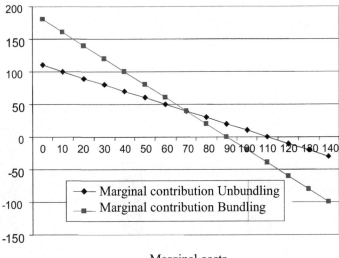

Marginal costs

Figure 18.11: Profit Comparison of Word and Excel in Case of Bundling at €180 and Unbundling at €110.

The influence that marginal cost has on the profits to be expected is displayed in Figure 18.15. What is compared is the profit from selling to customer C that is made in case of bundling and in case of unbundling when marginal cost for both products rises concurrently. The break-even point is reached when marginal cost is €70; after that, the bundled offer at €180 is no longer profitable compared to the single offer at €110. This point even shifts further forward as the unit price is set higher. If it is not at €110 but, for instance, at €140, marginal cost of €40 will already make the single product offer more profitable.

Hence, if not only the potential customers' willingness to pay is considered, as above, but also the variable costs of goods and services, the following additional insight can be gained for the assessment of bundling:

Rising marginal cost shifts the advantage of a bundling strategy in favor of the setting of unit prices. The reason for this is that a violation of the Exclusion condition (release of the product below marginal cost) in the bundle becomes ever more probable. When setting unit prices, this cannot happen unless aimed for.

> The chief defect of pure bundling is its difficulty in complying with Ex-
> clusion. The greater the cost of supplying either good, the greater the
> possibility of supplying some individuals with commodities for which
> reservation price falls short of cost (Adams & Yellen, 1976, 482).

From the provider's perspective, only thing left to do is decide whether pure un-bundling or mixed bundling is the better alternative.

> Like pure bundlers, therefore, mixed bundlers face a trade-off between more complete extraction and more complete exclusion. The dilemma is simply less pronounced in the case of mixed bundling (Adams & Yellen, 1976, 483).

According to Chuang and Sirbu (2000) it is generally to be assumed that mixed bundling is the ideal pricing strategy for information goods. Whether pure bun-dling or pure unbundling is to be preferred as the next best thing depends on mar-ginal cost and the economies of scale that can be implemented via bundling (Chuang & Sirbu 2000, 155). As soon as marginal cost enters the scene and cannot be significantly lowered via economies of scale (via bundling), there is the danger, described above, of violating the Exclusion condition. The provider must thus weigh the implications of saving expenditures via bundling and incurring losses to contribution margins due to insufficient willingness to pay on the part of a group of customers. The higher the cost of violating the Exclusion condition, the more pure unbundling is recommended (Chuang & Sirbu 2000, 155; Adams & Yellen 1976, 488).

Applied to the market for scientific journals, Chuang and Sirbu (2000, 161 et seq.) recommend that a publisher always offer single articles next to the custom-ary bundles. A further increase in profits can be realized when additional "super-bundles" are offered, which comprise several magazines or online accesses. The option of general access (site license) as the largest possible bundle goes in the same direction (Bakos & Brynjolfsson 2000, 129 et seq.). Recently, there have also been all-in-one offers, such as Napster's music flatrate (www.napster.com), for which there is not a one-off but a monthly fee. In creating music bundles, one should take care not to merely combine one or a few attractive titles with several weak ones. This leads to customers–if they have the choice–picking out the good songs and ignoring the album. Profits will be lower than they would be for pure bundling (Elberse, 2009).

The advantages of bundling thus depend on the relation of willingness to pay and variable cost (Buxmann et al., 2008, 117; Olderog & Skiera, 2000, 144). The smaller this difference, the more unbundling seems like the better option.

Hitt and Chen (2005) recommend so-called customized bundling as another, relatively new variant next to mixed bundling. If marginal cost is low but not zero, and buyers' preferences are directed at a relatively small (and perhaps diverse) number of single products, they suggest to leave it to the customer to decide which package, limited only by number, from the complete offer he wishes to choose. This could be, for a newspaper, 25 online articles, or for a music platform, 10 al-bums or 50 songs at a fixed price. Customized bundling is generally preferable to pure bundling, because it is better suited for dealing with heterogeneous groups of buyers. There is only one price for the entire bundle. This offer is unsuitable for doing justice to customers with different budgets, nor can it adequately cater to buyers who want a different number of goods (in the package) (Wu et al., 2008). The example of music buyers can serve to explicate the first case: one only buys music sporadically and would be prepared to spend €100, while another consumes €1,500 worth of music per year. The second case fits customers of commercial television, for example, where one only wants a small package of movies while another wishes to use the entire range of offers.

> As long as customers differ in the number of goods they positively value, customized bundling dominates pure bundling and individual sale and enhances welfare (Wu et al., 2008, 610).

A specialized form of customized bundling can be found in the recommendation by Altinkemer and Bandyopadhyay (2000). They take the example of music and suggest analyzing customers' buying habits and fixing corresponding bundles on the basis of these insights. Other than the completely free compilation via the customers, which comes closer to a bulk discount, this option allows the provider to accommodate less popular songs or new, as yet unknown offers in the bundle. This is only possible, however, as long as customer preferences for the admixtures aren't too low or even negative.

Bundling is a pricing strategy that can entail advantages for both the provider and the customer. Apart from the previously named aspects, bundling leads to further advantages from the provider's point of view (Tillman & Simon, 2008, 523 with additional literature). On the one hand, it bears the potential for cost reduction (Point 1 in Figure 18.12). If packages are made up of several goods, this can lead to a reduction of manufacturing, transaction, information or even complexity costs. On the other hand, bundling contains potentials for increasing profits (Point 3). In empirical studies, these are set at between 5 and 40 per cent compared to unit pricing.

How large should bundles be made? In a model-based approach, Bakos and Brynjolfsson (2000, 120 et seq.), state that the demand curve for information goods with a heterogeneous valuation becomes more elastic as the size of the package increases. This is due to the fact that the more goods a package comprises, the greater customers' average valuation is concentratedund the median.

> For example, some people subscribe to America Online for the news, some for stock quotes, and some for horoscopes. It is unlikely that a single person has a very high value for every single good offered; instead most consumers will have high values for some goods and low values for others, leading to moderate values overall (Bakos & Brynjolfsson, 2000, 121).

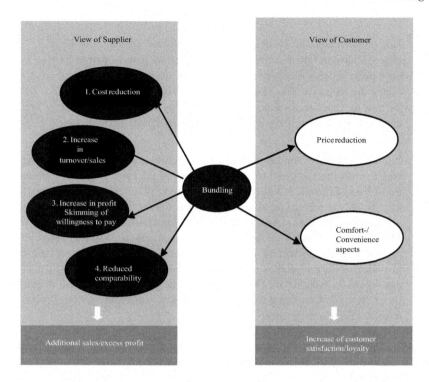

Figure 18.12: Bundling Advantages for Provider and Customer. Source: Tillmann & Simon, 2008, 523.

Geng et al. (2005) qualify this by noting that the making of large packages is only ideal in the case that the valuations of the individual goods on offer decreases slowly. Nevertheless, we can draw some far-reaching conclusions for the competitive position of information providers from the analyses of Bakos and Brynjolfsson (2000). For content and software providers we can generally say that providers of large bundles enjoy competitive advantages, vis-à-vis both smaller "bundlers" as well as, more pronouncedly, providers of individual products on services. In detail, this means that:

- Providers of large bundles have advantages in shopping, e.g. for content. They can offer higher prices because their profit expectations through sales are higher (Bakos & Brynjolfsson, 2000, 70).
- Providers of large bundles have particular advantages vis-à-vis providers of single information goods. They can demand higher prices and realize a greater market share as well as higher profits (Bakos & Brynjolfsson, 2000, 72). For new competitors, this worsens the prospects of a successful market entry, even if they have a cheaper cost structure and higher-quality products (Bakos & Brynjolfsson, 2000, 76).

This phenomenon can be observed in the software markets. For instance, Microsoft Office includes numerous printing fonts as part of its basic package. This is easy to do given the low marginal cost of reproducing digital goods. This strategy has drastically reduced the demand for font packages sold separately while allowing Microsoft to extract some additional value from its Office bundle (Bakos & Brynjolfsson, 2000, 72).

- Providers of large bundles can enter new markets at relative ease, if they add an information good to their pre-existing package (e.g. via cooperation or acquisition) that is offered on its own by an established competitors. In an extreme case, that competitor can even be forced off the market via the selling of bundles (Bakos & Brynjolfsson, 2000, 77).
- The impetus to innovate and enter new markets is systematically less pronounced for providers of individual services. The danger alone of providers of large bundles incorporating the new product into their package serves as a deterrent. Conversely, bundle providers can achieve profits on new markets more easily, which makes innovation more attractive to them (Bakos & Brynjolfsson, 2000, 78).

These insights have been formulated without taking into consideration network effects. What vistas will open up if network effects are explicitly incorporated? Lee and O'Connor (2003) dealt with the repercussions of network effects on the introduction of new products in detail, as well as, specifically, with the role played by bundling (Lee & O'Connor, 2003, 249). On network effect markets, the compatibility of basic goods and complements plays an important role. Bundled offers are a good instrument for decreasing customer insecurity as to whether all components work well together. A further appeal of the package is a product warranty that holds for the entire bundle. Thus it is much more attractive for the normal user, for reasons of usability, to buy Microsoft's Office Suite containing Excel, Word, PowerPoint and Access than it is to compile their own package–which might even be more powerful due to the special functions of its applications–from, say, Lotus 1-2-3, Word Perfect, Coreldraw and Dbase Plus. Bundling is also well suited for forcing sales of the basic product by bundling it with complements. As we have seen above, bundling decreases the dispersion of willingnesses to pay and facilitates higher turnover. Bundling can be used not only as a structuring instrument, but also for the further building up of an installed base, if, for example, new software versions are offered at a moderate price together with attractive complements. Microsoft practiced this–albeit contentiously, from a legal standpoint–in developing its operating systems, from DOS to Windows, Windows 95 etc., by bundling them with different applications (Arthur, 1996, 106), such as Internet Explorer or Windows Media Player.

The situation is slightly different for established networks: if standardization is well on its way and the customer can choose from different manufacturers' compatible complements, it can be hazardous to make pure bundling offers (Simon 1998, 143). In such a case, customers can compile their single (compatible!) products or services, with complete disregard as to who provides them, individually. Were a provider to only ever offer his PCs as a bundle of CPU, monitor, keyboard and mouse, he would have to expect that many customers will either choose another provider's package, perhaps because they prefer a certain monitor, or prefer an individual solution–almost invariably with other providers' components (Brandtweiner, 2001, 108).

Brooks et al. (2001) demonstrate, on the example of an experimentally tested model, that bundling strategies must be regarded as dynamic, not static, if profits are to be maximized. They thus recommend keeping a permanent eye on the market and always making sure that the bundle offers are suited to the market conditions.

Bundling is to be used particularly cautiously if you are the dominant provider on the market, as it can lead to complications with competition law (Köhler, 2003). The recent sentencing of Microsoft for bundling its operating system with its server software or Windows Media Player is a prominent example.

We can record, as a general statement, that bundling is only profitable if the demanders' willingness to pay for the single components of the package are above their marginal cost (Olderog & Skiera, 2000, 157).

Bundling verges–as windowing does–on versioning. A specific form of versioning is the offer of an unchanged first copy of an information good in different packages. This is common practice in music, where finished songs are often featured on different albums. The concurrent offer of different bundles can be termed versioning bundling (Schumann & Hess, 2006, 72). Here it must be noted that this is only versioning on the level of the entire package, not of the single product. However, further versioning options come up here, particularly for information goods, i.e. if the single information good must be modified before entering a bundle.

18.2.5   Follow-the-free

In **3rd Degree Price Differentiation**, as displayed in an overview in Figure 18.2 above, the provider does not leave the choice of products to the customer but separates the customer groups himself and makes them group-specific offers. An overview of this was provided in Figure 18.3. Of the three traditional forms of 3rd Degree Price Differentiation (personal, spatial, temporal), we are particularly interested in the last, the temporal form in connection with information goods. In general, we speak of temporal price differentiation when the same product or service is offered at different prices over the course of a certain period in time (Simon & Fassnacht, 2009, 276). This form of pricing is recommended if demand fluctutates heavily in dependence of time. In order to take advantage of the temporary differences in demanders' preferences, they are charged different prices at different times of the day (telephone, electricity), days of the week (cinema, car rental), seasons (airplane, hotel room) or in dependence of the product's life cycle (special prices at new products' market entry) (Meffert, 2005, 556). As temporal arbitrage is eliminated in most cases, the market segmentation is fully effective.

Skimming strategy	Penetration strategy
- Realisation of high short term benefits, less affected by discounting - If there are real innovations, benefits in the course of time with a monopolistic market position, reduction of long term competitive risk, rapid amortisation of R&D-expenditure - Profit realisation in early stage of life cycle, reduction of obsolescence risk - Establishment of a downward price potential, exploitation of positive price change effect possible - Gradual skimming of consumers willingness to pay is possible (temporal price differentiation) - risk of price increase prevented (secure calculation) - High price as a positive indicator of prestige and quality - Prevention of high capacities, lower demands on financial resources	- High aggregate profit margin with faster sales growth despite low unit contribution margin - Constitution of a long term strong und predominant market position due to positive intra-personal (consumer item) or inter-personal (consumer good) carryover effects (higher prices and/or higher sales volume in the future) - Exploitation of static Economies of Scale, short term cost reduction - Fast rise of the cumulative amount due to a fast "shut down" on the experience curve, achievement of a cost advantage difficult to overcome for the competitors - Risk of failure reduced due to a low offering price and minor flop percentage - Deterrence of potential competitors to enter the market

Figure 18.13: Skimming vs. Penetration Strategy. Source: Simon & Fassnacht, 2009, 329.

The latter variant, setting market entry prices, is particularly significant for information goods. The two variants for setting prices previous to market entry, long known, are the skimming strategy and the penetration strategy (Dean, 1951; Diller, 2008, 289). In skimming, the provider initially sets high prices and then gradually lowers them in order to slowly address new layers of customers. In the penetration strategy, low entry prices are set, with the goal of raising them later, after the market has been covered accordingly and a strong market position is achieved. A comparison of both strategies can be found in Simon and Fassnacht (Figure 18.13).

A central difference of both strategies is in the profit expectations, which are initially high and then low in skimming, and are vice versa by the penetration strategy.

Skimming represents the traditional pricing strategy for introducing innovative products, in which companies try to operate as cost-effectively as possible from the outset by using high prices to address the customers with a high willingness to pay (Lee, 2003, 248).

For digital information goods, however, the penetration strategy is more common (Reibnitz, 2003, 13). It is often found as a special form called "Follow-the-free" (Zerdick et al., 2001, 191), or Dynamic Pricing (Wendt et al., 2000, 2), in which products are sold for an extremely low price or even for free. Prominent examples are Avira's antivirus programs, Netscape's and Microsoft's browsers or Acrobat Reader.

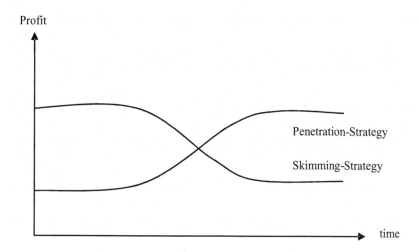

Figure 18.14: Profit Expectations of Skimming and Penetration Strategy. Source: Simon & Fassnacht, 2009, 330.

This strategy, seemingly irrational at first glance, has a solid economical background: Follow-the-free is the consequent implementation of the strategy, suggested as early as the mid-nineteen-seventies by Henderson (1974), of the very low starting price. He propagates the acceptance of early losses in the introductory phase and the building up of a head start in terms of cost vis-à-vis the competition by lowering unit costs as quickly as possible via experience curve effects. He identifies the preconditions as high price elasticity, in order for low prices to rapidly effect increased consumption, as well as pronounced degression effects. As soon as unit prices sink below the selling price, sales become profitable and a certain pricing leverage is realized vis-à-vis the competitors.

Cost degression is famously very pronounced for information goods, and if the products are not sold but given away, the provider will have to ask himself the question whether the saturation quantity–and thus the market potential–will be enough for him overall.

There are further reasons for using the Follow-the-free strategy for information goods, though. Due to the relatively unpronounced search qualities, offering products free of charge is a suitable measure for giving buyers the opportunity to check their quality.

> Free products are provided to overcome the problem of quality uncertainty and, ultimately, to generate profits (Choi et al., 1997, 243).

However, the central role in this form of price differentiation is played by the creation of network effects. The provider wants to use the free offer to build up an installed base as quickly as possible. The plan is two-pronged: as long as the initial (extrinsic) network effect value is low, willingness to pay is low. Only when the number of customers increases will network effects make the offer more and more attractive to new customers. In marketing, one speaks of carryover effects when sales in one period influence sales over the following periods (Diller, 2008, 293). For network effects, we can say: the higher sales are in the previous period, the higher they will be in the period to follow. Besides, network effects create switching costs for the existing customers, which in an extreme case scenario lead to a Lock-In effect. For customers that have already gotten used to a product (e.g. Windows) that is used by many others, and who perhaps have already incurred additional expenses in the form of hardware or applications, it costs money to move to another provider. Apart from any costs of buying the new product, the customer must get used to a new layout, for example, different formats or even new functionalities, as well as lost the advantage of having acquaintances who use the known, compatible products. If these costs are prohibitive, the customer is in a Lock-In, switching products is no longer economically rational (Shapiro & Varian, 1999, 103 et seq.; Varian, 2003, 20 et seq.). We will address the different forms of switching costs in more detail in the section dedicated to Lock-In.

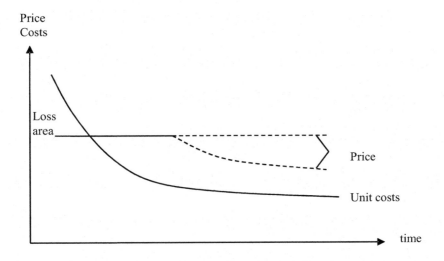

Figure 18.15: Strategy of the Extremely Low Starting Price. Soure: Simon & Fassnacht, 2009, 332.

But how does the product that is given away earn money? The decisive point is always the same: will the company succeed in creating network effects? If so, there are different courses of action.

First, one might proceed as provided in the penetration strategy and raise prices. If the network is attractive enough, new as well as existing customers will be ready to pay. Based on a simulation, Xie and Sirbu (1995, 914) observe that

> the optimal pricing path [...] is *increasing* if the positive effect of the installed base in the potential demand is strong.

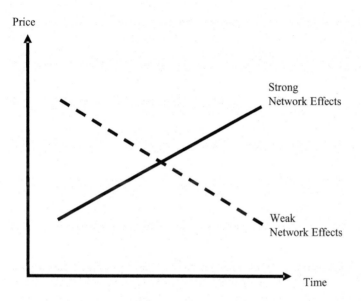

Figure 18.16: Development of the Ideal Price Path for Strong and Weak Network Effects. Source: Following Xie & Sirbu, 1995, 921.

Network effects are responsible for increasing new customers' willingness to pay so that prices can be raised. If in addition to this, existing customers are in a Lock-In, the danger of losing customers must be viewed as negligible in spite of the raised prices. This procedure has been successfully put into practice by eBay. In the beginning, its services were free of charge, until at the end of January, 2000, listing fees were introduced (Möllenberg, 2003, 171). eBay was able to make up for the initial sharp decline because many sellers returned to eBay as other platforms did not offer them the same chances of making a profit. Other auction platforms such as Andsold, eHammer or iTrade did not manage to take this step successfully and had to give up (Möllenberg, 2003, 172). Here a possible problem of the Follow-the-free strategy reveals itself: the customers get used to, or are already used to free offers from the internet. If the network effects are not strong enough, raising the prices is either impossible or at least extremely difficult to achieve. If there is a fundamental willingness to pay, one should avoid surprising customers with a price increase. It is recommended to communicate the phase of low prices or free offers as Promotional Pricing (Fritz, 2004, 207), i.e. to make it abundantly clear that these are (introductory) offers for a limited time only. Such limits can be temporal (30-day trial version, as for Salesforce) or quantitative: the accounting software QuickBooks by Intuit can be used for 20 clients, above which number a priced version must be bought (Anderson, 2008).

If direct price increases for existing customers cannot be implemented, there are various other possibilities for combining Follow-the-free with other price differentiation strategies such as versioning or bundling with complements.

Versioning, for one, provides some very interesting starting points: as a provider, one can offer the existing customers more up-to-date (upgrade) and/or higher-performance (premium) product versions (Zerdick et al., 2001, 193):

> Network Associates (formerly McAfee) initially distributed their anti-virus programs free of charge. This allowed them to win a third of the market for virus protection software. From this strong market position, they achieved significant profits from selling upgrades. A further positive side effect of free product offers is the voluntary incorporation of users in the further product development. Due to the sizeable installed base and the high customer loyalty, a multitude of viruses is recognized, which can then be disabled via upgrades. These indirect network effects improve product performance and thus stabilize the market position.

On the other hand, profits can also be generated via sales of complementary services (separately or in a package). If this is profitable enough, it will even be advisable to offer the basic good (such as Acrobat Reader or RealPlayer) free of charge (Parker & Van Alstyne, 2000, 34). This path has been chosen by Sun, for instance, with their free offer of Java to support server sales.

> The free product may persuade adopters to employ standards-supported or complementary goods offered by the firm, thereby fueling network externalities in related markets (Gallaugher & Wang, 1999, 70).

A variant of this tactic is used in the reverse direction by both Microsoft and Google, who make free additional offers (antivirus programs and word processing programs, respectively)–even in markets with priced offers–in order to bolster sales or the use of their core products (operating systems and search).

In many cases, Follow-the-free apparently works permanently well for **software**. The resulting network effects can also be used to plausibly explain other success stories, such as ICQ's (Fritz, 2004, 192) or the Apache Web Server's (Zerdick et al., 2001, 194; Web Server Survey, 2007).

Generally, open-source products have the best preconditions for bringing about network effects in terms of price. As development costs are spread over many heads and there are no aspirations to recoup them via sales, the products can generally be distributed free of charge, even from an economical perspective. Ollhäuser (2007, 196) thus speaks of the open-source principle as a "Free for all". Whether these products will assert themselves against the established, priced competing products (e.g. Linux vs. Windows; Fritz, 2004, 192-193) is thus at least no longer a question of cost price. Here the customer may assume that the open-source software of his desire will be available free of charge permanently. Providers of proprietary software cannot readily and convincingly claim that they will not raise the price of their software after an introductory period in order to redeem the development costs.

From this perspective, one might assume that providers of proprietary software wouldn't have a prayer in asserting themselves on the market against open-source products and generating income from selling licenses. This statement becomes relative, though, if we consider how open-source products actually make money. Financing is mostly via sales of complementary services, such as implementation services, support or schooling. As bundling with advertisements is rejected within the open-source community, donations are used as an alternative source of funding (Sabel, 2007, 205-206).

There are thus two cost components for the customer; pure acquisition costs and oncosts following from usage. The so-called Total Cost of Ownership is thus relevant for the customer. Maaß (2006, 131-132) was able to demonstrate, on the example of the market for server/system software, that this total cost plays the most important role in the decision to make an investment. As training and support costs can significantly exceed acquisition costs, the isolated amount of the introductory price only plays a subordinate role within this industry segment. This is reinforced by the segment-specific short innovation and product life cycles, which make it harder to enforce a price increase for ageing products over several periods. A penetration pricing strategy is thus not generally advisable. Its application depends on the concrete product and market circumstances.

Now how does this apply to **content**, which is not meant for repeat usage, like software, but is tendentially consumed only once to a few times? Stahl (2005, 237 et seq.) demonstrates empirically that the Follow-the-free strategy is of advantage for the offering of digital content, as well. The more comprehensive–seen from a static point of view–the offer of free content is, the greater sales of priced contents will be. Furthermore, it is also the case dynamically that extending the free offer in period one will increase sales of priced content in the following period. This form of pricing thus generates network effects, switching costs and Lock-In effects for content, too.

The named effects are particularly advantageous if a specific form of bundle is being "sold", namely the connection between the information good, normally of benefit, and corresponding (frequently undesired) advertisements. Many cost-free offers are not based on making profits from the product itself, but from advertising revenue. Profits in the newspaper and magazine market only consist partly of sales of the information good, but consist to more than 50% of advertising revenue (Wirtz, 2006, 179). Free newspapers offered via the Follow-the-free strategy, for example, even eliminate sales revenue altogether and generate nothing but advertising revenue. The case is similar for (private) television and radio channels, here, too, 90% of profits are from advertising (Wirtz, 2006, 360, 427). Owen et al. (1974) stated as early as the nineteen-seventies that TV channels were not there to produce programs.

> TV Stations are in the business of producing *audiences*. These audiences, or means of access to them, are sold to advertisers. The product of a TV station is measured in dimensions of people and time. The price of the product is quoted in dollars per thousand viewers per minute of commercial time (Owen et al., 1974, 4).

Advertising as a form of revenue has long been used on the mass markets for content. Lately, though, it has started to be used in an individualized way and been transferred to software. Google's business model is mainly based on context-specific ad displays, largely for the search results. Since the acquisition of You-Tube, Google has been working more intensively on individualized ads for video clips. The same principle is employed by flickr, where the viewing of images is accompanied by ads. Adobe, on the other hand, is considering ad-financed software offers (Koenen, 2007).

Obtaining customers' profiles in return for the free usage of information goods is of benefit for financing via advertising, facilitating addressee-specific ads. As far as the profiles have been created truthfully, individualized advertising offers have the opportunity to go from an undesirable information "bad" to a useful information "good" and the combination of requested information and customer specific, substantial advertising will effect an increase in usefulness for the consumer. New forms of advertising are moving in this direction. Under the term "user-initiated online advertising", for example, the customer can actively click on objects in videos in order to be shown ads for them. This can go as far as money being paid for specific advertisements (Anderson, 2008). The reciprocity between the amount of users and informative advertising offers can lead to a mutual benefit, which is termed "promotional circulation spiral" (Hass, 2007) in media economics.

What a complement strategy of cost-free (including ads) and priced offers might look like for content is shown in the cross-media concept of "Deutschland sucht den Superstar" (DSDS, the German version of "American Idol") (Schumann & Hess, 2006, 62 et seq.):

> Apart from the TV show "Deutschland sucht den Superstar", which formed the core of the product line, the media that were mainly served

are magazines, CDs, DVDs and the internet; mobile applications were also developed. The DSDS product line thus encompasses several TVs shows (including the DSDS show as well as interviews, short segments etc.), a DSDS print magazine, the CD albums "We Have a Dream", "United" and "Take Me Tonight", the internet presence "deutschland-suchtdensuperstar.rtl.de" as well as a series of merchandise articles (T-Shirts, mgs etc.).

All in all, it becomes clear that the network effects that occur for information goods facilitate, but at the same time require, new and manifold pricing variants. Versioning in particular plays a prominent role. The general recommendation here was to offer several versions as a matter of principle. If this statement is linked to the realization that free offers are of great advantage for network goods, it is an obvious choice for companies to always check whether a basic version might not be offerable at a low price or evevn free of charge (Wirtz & Olderog, 2001, 199-200). As Jing (2000) shows formally even for the monopoly scenario, profits from high-quality information goods can, in case of existing network effects, be increased precisely by distributing lower-quality versions free of charge.

> The free low-quality product is essential for expanding market coverage
> and enhancing consumer valuation of the high quality (Jing, 2000, 2).

The cannibalization effects that occur (buying the lower-quality product instead of the higher-quality one) are overcompensated for by the network effects and the resulting increased willingness to pay for the higher-quality product. The low-quality good is thus the gateway drug, so to speak, because

> the low quality helps inflate the network and the high quality extracts
> the network benefits and is the primary source of revenue (Jing, 2000,
> 8; originally in italics).

The more pronounced the network effects are, the higher the price can be set for the premium offer. Brynjolfsson and Kemerer (1996) found out, for the market for spreadsheet programs (without versioning), that an increase of the installed base by 1% was concurrent with a price increase of 0.75%.

For software offers, Gallaugher and Wang (1999, 81) empirically observed that it is very well possible to ask premium prices if one makes simultaneous trial offers. In the web server market they investigated, companies with trial offers were able to surcharge up to 60% compared to companies without trial versions.

Network effects represent a certain protection for the established provider. In order to gain market share as a second mover, the Follow-the-free strategy can be easily implemented. Buxmann (2002) shows, with the help of simulations, that this is the case first and foremost if the established provider's installed base is large and the network effects pronounced. If they are very strong, it may even make sense not only to give away the product, but even to pay for it in order to attack a securely established provider. This way, we can easily explain why Microsoft was able to win the browser wars with Netscape relatively easily. It was because of the help of strong network effects and a large installed base of operating systems and Office applications. In the same way, though, the market for business software, which is characterized by weak network effects, shows that low-price strategies are of little help in this latter case (Buxmann, 2002, 14 et seq.).

A particular variant of price differentiation is used by companies who tolerate pirated copies. Many private individuals, for example, use software in infringement of copyright law, whereas companies and administrations generally opt for legal usage. Even if companies go on the record to criticize this situation, it can be assumed that they would practice price differentiation of their own volition under perfect legal circumstances. On the one hand, this is because private individuals' willingness to pay is generally far below companies', and on the other hand because of habituation effects. If pupils and/or students illegally use software, it is not wholly improbable that they will, once they become decisionmakers in a company, buy these products. A relatively low price for the one target group (pupils and students) thus leads to increased sales in the other target groups (companies) (Wiese, 1991, 49). A further reason is the network effects that are generated if the installed base is large. We will address this line of argument in more detail in the chapter devoted to copyright management.

In conclusion, the different forms of 2nd and 3rd Degree price differentiation are summarized in Table 18.3. However, we must particularly emphasize the role played by versioning, which is especially easily implemented for information goods. It represents an autonomous form of 2nd degree price differentiation, but can also be combined with other variants of price differentiation, be it as versioning windowing or versioning bundling. The former is practiced if, for example, the DVD contains additional material compared to the film that ran in cinemas, which is meant to increase willingness to pay. The latter exists as rebundling (Stahl et al., 2004, 60) or as compilation (Heitmann et al., 2006, 11). In rebundling, single newspaper articles on a certain subject are compiled and offered as a package online, for example. A compilation contains songs by different artists. In both cases, an increase in demand is to be expected, because bundling levels the different preferences. The consumers accept the fact that they will buy, in a larger package, articles or songs for which they have a very low willingness to pay, or even none at all, individually. Versioning can also be easily combined with the Follow-the-free strategy, which is then applied to the low-end version only.

Object / Form of Price Differentiation (PD)	Information Content (First Copy) identical	varying	Medium identical	varying	Timing of the Offers sequential singular	recurring	simultaneous
2nd Degree							
Windowing	Traditionally unchanged original product	Different versions along the exploitation chain	May change between the individual exploitation windows		Set sequence of offers in the different exploitation windows	Partly: TV reruns	Partly: Video/ DVD remains available in parallel to subsequent offers
Versioning		Different versions of the same original product	Choice of media as a form of versioning (availability of information)				Simultaneous choice of alternatives for customers
Bundling	Package offer with unchanged original products	Versioning: - identical product in different packages (Rebundling, Compilation) - Product variants in the package offer	Traditionally identical medium				For several bundles: simultaneous choice of alternatives for customers
3rd Degree							
Follow-the-free	Traditionally unchanged original product	As a bundle in connection with advertising or other complements. Versioning: Follow-the-free only for the basic version	Traditionally identical medium		Standard price at one time only		

Table 18.3: Special Forms of Price Differentiation for Information Goods.

A variant, recently proposed by Chang and Yuan (2008), is Collaborative Pricing. They suggest a model in which the customer compiles his own personal bundle from the company's range of products, and is even able to make versioning suggestions. We would label this versioning Customized Bundling: the provider makes a price offer on the basis of the customer data (customer profile, buying history etc.) and the specific versioning effort, which the customer may accept or reject. In case of a rejection, the process will begin anew. This is a very far-reaching and innovative form of individual dynamic pricing:

> An interactive pricing process can be considered as a combination of
> collaborative prototyping, needs prediction, price estimation, and profits
> maintenance (Chang & Yuan, 2008, 638).

The allocations in the chart below relate to finished information goods, but can also be applied to information goods yet to be created. The entries in italics are the more recent variants of versioning that are based on digitalization and can be implemented in relation with other forms of price differentiation. The represented forms of price differentiation not only contain the known textbook variants, such as quantitative, personal or spatial differentiation. These are also applicable, but do not represent an exception.

18.3   Conclusion

- Pricing policy is a crucial setscrew in the marketing mix.
- Information providers have very variable options of price determination. Particularly new are the different forms of reverse pricing, in which the customer makes pricing suggestions, and collective forms of interactive price determination, above all online auctions.
- The ideal form of price differentiation is 1st Degree Price Differentiation. In this individual form of price differentiation, the consumer surplus can be skimmed off in its entirety (e.g. in online auctions).
- 2nd Degree Price Differentiation is based on the principle of self-selection. From several alternatives, the customers choose the one that is best suited to them in terms of their willingness to pay.
- Windowing, versioning and bundling are special forms of 2nd Degree Price Differentiation for information goods.
- In windowing, a finished information good (film, book etc.) is launched on the market at different times as part of different offers (e.g. hardcover, softcover).

- Information providers try to exploit the different profit windows as fully as possible. High-priced offers (e.g. tickets for the cinema) are found at the beginning, low-priced or free offers (e.g. broadcasts on free TV) at the end of the exploitation chain. The decisive factor is customers' willingness to pay, which is high at the beginning and low at the end.
- In performance-oriented price differentiation, that is versioning, the customer is simultaneously offered different variants of an information good at different qualities, which have been generated from an original version.
- According to empirical analyses, at least three versions should be offered, as customers tend to the middle. The maximum amount of versions on offer should not exceed six.
- When two or more (information) goods are put together in a package and sold at a total price, we speak of bundling.
- Simple statistical calculations show that bundling leads to a homogenization of willingnesses to pay, which will be more pronounced in proportion to how negatively willingnesses to pay are correlated. The stronger the homogenization that results from the bundling, the larger the provider's potential profits.
- Even without an exact knowledge of customers' individual willingnesses to pay, bundling can be used to assert demand-oriented pricing.
- In bundling, we decide between pure and mixed bundling, as well as pure unbundling. In pure bundling, only product packages are on offer, in pure unbundling only single products. Mixed bundling combines both approaches and lets the customer choose between single products and package offers.
- Pure unbundling is advisable if customers' willingness to pay is extremely pronounced, i.e. either very high and very low, or even, for one of the products, null.
- If willingnesses to pay are rather balanced, pure bundling is recommended.
- Mixed bundling should be used if there are customer groups with partly extreme and partly balanced willingnesses to pay.
- The advantages of bundling depend on the relation of willingness to pay and variable costs. The lower this difference is, the more unbundling is preferable. Bundling is generally only profitable if the demanders' willingnesses to pay for the single components of the package are above the marginal cost.
- Providers of large bundles have competitive advantages vis-à-vis both providers of smaller bundles and providers of individual services.
- In 3rd Degree Price Differentiation, the target group is segmented. Single customer groups are made specific offers.

- Follow-the-free is a variant of 3rd Degree Price Differentiation, which is popular for information goods. It is a special form of the penetration strategy, in which products are distributed at an extremely low price or even for free.
- The company can use the free offer to build up an installed base as quickly as possible. This is maximized if the product is not sold but given away. A large installed base creates network effects, which in turn lead to increased willingness to pay and switching costs.
- Providers who apply the Follow-the-free strategy forego profits from product sales. Alternative sources of revenue are, for example, price increases after the successful creation of an installed base, sales of higher-end versions or offers of complementary services. Specifically the "complement" advertising represents an attractive source of revenue in many cases.

18.4   Bibliography

Adams, W.J., & Yellen, J.L. (1976). Commodity bundling and the burden of monopoly. Quarterly Journal of Economics, 90(3), 475-498.

Albers, S., & Herrmann, A. (eds.) (2002). Handbuch Produktmanagement. Strategieentwicklung - Produktplanung - Organisation - Kontrolle. 2nd ed. Wiesbaden: Gabler.

Altinkemer, K., & Bandyopadhyay, S. (2000). Bundling and distribution of digitized music over the internet. Journal of Organizational Computing and Electronic Commerce, 10(3), 209-224.

Anderson, C. (2008). The Long Tail - Wired Blogs. (Online).

Arthur, B.W. (1996). Increasing returns and the new world of business. Harvard Business Review, 74, 100-109.

Bakos, Y., & Brynjolfsson, E. (1999). Bundling information goods: Pricing, profits, and efficiency. Management Science, 45(12), 1613-1630.

Bakos, Y., & Brynjolfsson, E. (2000). Aggregation and disaggregation of information goods. Implications for bundling, site licensing, and micropayment systems. In Kahin, B., & Varian, H.R. (eds.), Internet Publishing and Beyond. The Economics of Digital Information and Intellectual Property (pp. 114-137). Cambridge, MA: MIT Press.

Bernhardt, M., Spann, M., & Skiera, B. (2005). Reverse pricing. Die Betriebswirtschaft, 65, 104-107.

Bhargava, H.K., & Choudhary, V. (eds.) (2001). Second-Degree Price Discrimination for Information Goods under Nonlinear Utility Functions.

Brandtweiner, R. (2001). Report Internet-pricing. Methoden der Preisfindung in elektronischen Märkten. Düsseldorf: Symposion Publ.

Brooks, C.H., Das, R., Kephart, J.O., MacKie-Mason, J.K., Gazzale; & Durfee, E.H. (2001). Information bundling in a dynamic environment. Proceedings of the 3rd ACM Conference on Electronic Commerce (pp. 180-190). New York, NY: ACM.

Brynjolfsson, E., & Kemerer, C.F. (1996). Network externalities in microcomputer software. An econometric analysis of the spreadsheet market. Management Science, 42(12), 1627-1647.

Buxmann, P. (2002). Strategien von Standardsoftware-Anbietern. Eine Analyse auf Basis von Netzeffekten. Zeitschrift für betriebswirtschaftliche Forschung, 54, 442-457.

Buxmann, P., Diefenbach, H., & Hess, T. (2008). Die Softwareindustrie. Ökonomische Prinzipien, Strategien, Perspektiven. Berlin, Heidelberg: Springer.

Cap Gemini Ernst & Young (2001). Business Redefined. Connecting Content, Applications, and Customers. Cap.

Chang, W.L, & Yuan, S.T (2008). Collaborative pricing model for bundling information goods. Journal of Information Science, 34(5), 635-650.

Choi, S.Y., Stahl, D.O., & Whinston, A.B. (1997). The Economics of Electronic Commerce. Indianapolis, IN: Macmillan Technical Pub.

Chuang, C.I. J., & Sirbu, M. (2000). Network delivery of information goods. Optimal pricing of articles and subscriptions. In Kahn, B., & Varian, H.R. (eds.), Internat Publishing and Beyond. The Economics of Digital Information and Intellectuell Property (pp. 138-166). Cambridge, MA: MIT Press.

Dean, J. (1951). Managerial Economics. Englewood Cliffs: Prentice-Hall.

Deneckere, R., & McAfee, R.P. (1996). Damaged goods. Journal of Economics and Management Strategy, 5(2), 149-174.

Diller, H. (2000). Preispolitik. 3rd ed. Stuttgart: Kohlhammer (Kohlhammer-Edition Marketing).

Diller, H. (2008). Preispolitik. 4th ed. Stuttgart: Kohlhammer (Kohlhammer Edition Marketing).

Elberse, A. (2009). Bye Bye Bundles: The Unbundling of Music in Digital Channels. Harvard Business School. (Online).

Fritz, W. (2004). Internet-Marketing und Electronic Commerce. Grundlagen - Rahmenbedingungen. 3rd ed. Wiesbaden: Gabler (Gabler-Lehrbuch).

Gallaugher, J.M., & Wang, Y.M (1999). Network effects and the impact of free goods: An analysis of the web-server market. International Journal of Electronic Commerce, 3(4), 67-88.

Geng, X., Stinchcombe, M.B., & Whinston, A.B. (2005). Bundling information goods of decreasing value. Management Science, 51(4), 662-667.

GMX - Mail-Produkte (E-Mail, SMS, Fax). GMX GmbH. (Online).

Greco, A.N. (ed.) (2000). The Media and Entertainment Industries. Readings in Mass Communications. Boston, MA: Allyn and Bacon (Media economics series).

Hass, B.H. (2007). Größenvorteile von Medienunternehmen: Eine kritische Würdigung der Anzeigen-Auflagen-Spirale. MedienWirtschaft, 4, Sonderheft, 70-78.

Heil, B. (1999). Online-Dienste, portal sites und elektronische Einkaufszentren. Wettbewerbsstrategien auf elektronischen Massenmärkten. Wiesbaden: Dt. Univ.-Verl. (Gabler Edition Wissenschaft).

Heitmann, M., Herrmann, A., & Stahl, F. (2006). Digitale Produkte richtig verkaufen. Harvard Business Manager, August, 8–12.

Henderson, Bruce D. (1974). Die Erfahrungskurve in der Unternehmensstrategie. Frankfurt a.M.: Herder & Herder.

Huber, F., & Kopsch, A. (2002). Produktbündelung. In Albers, S., & Herrmann, A. (eds.), Handbuch Produktmanagement. Strategieentwicklung - Produktplanung - Organisation–Kontrolle (pp. 615-646). 2nd ed. Wiesbaden: Gabler.

Hui, W., Byungjoon, Y., & Tam, K.Y. (2008). The optimal number of versions: Why does goldilocks pricing work for information goods. Journal of Management Information Systems, 24(3), 167-191.

Hutter, M. (ed.) (2001). e-conomy 2.0. Management und Ökonomie in digitalen Kontexten. Marburg: Metropolis (Wittener Jahrbuch für ökonomische Literatur, N° 6).

Iyengar, S.S., & Lepper, M.R. (2000). When choice is demotivating: Can one desire too much of a good thing. Journal of Personality and Social Psychology, 79(6), 995-1006.

Jing, B. (2000). Versioning Information Goods with Network Externalities. Proceedings of the twenty first international conference on Information systems. Brisbane, Queensland, Australia. (Online).

Kahin, B., & Varian, H.R. (eds.) (2000). Internet Publishing and Beyond. The Economics of Digital Information and Intellectual Property. Cambridge, MA: MIT Press.

Kim, J.Y, Natter, M., & Spann, M. (2009). Pay what you want: A new participative pricing mechanism. Journal of Marketing, 73(1), 44-58.

Klein, S., & Loebbecke C. (1999). Signaling and segmentation on electronic markets. Innovative pricing strategies for improved resource allocation. Paper presented at the Research Symposion on Emerging Electronic Marketes. Münster, Germany.

Koenen, J. (2007). Adobe peilt einen Internet-Thron an. Handelsblatt, 216, 20.

Köhler, H. (2003). Koppelungsangebote (einschließlich Zugaben) im geltenden und künftigem Wettbewerbsrecht. Gewerblicher Rechtsschutz und Urheberrecht, 729-738.

Kwasniewski, N. (2003). Billig ins Luxusbett. Die Zeit, 49(2003), 79. (Online).

Lee, Y., & O′Connor, G.C. (2003). New product launch strategy for network effects. Journal of the Academy of Marketing Science, 31(3), 241-255.

Lexware.de (2011). Lexware. (Online).

Linde, F. (ed.) (2007). Markttheoretische und wettbewerbsstrategische Aspekte des Managements von Informationsgütern. Institut für Informationswissenschaft der Fachhochschule Köln. (Kölner Arbeitspapiere zur Bibliotheks- und Informationswissenschaft, 53). (Online).

Litman, B.R. (2000). The structure of the film industry: Windows of exhibition. In Greco, A. N. (ed.), The Media and Entertainment Industries. Readings in Mass

Communications (pp. 99-121). Boston, MA: Allyn and Bacon (Media Economics Series).

Maaß, C. (2006). Strategische Optionen im Wettbewerb mit Open-Source-Software. Berlin: Logos-Verlag.

McAfee, R.P., & McMillan J. (1987). Auctions and bidding. Journal of Economic Literature, 25, 699-728.

Meffert, H. (2005). Marketing. Grundlagen marktorientierter Unternehmensführung; Konzepte, Instrumente, Praxisbeispiele; mit neuer Fallstudie VW Golf. 9th ed., Wiesbaden: Gabler (Meffert-Marketing-Edition).

Möllenberg, A. (2003). Internet-Auktionen im Marketing aus der Konsumentenperspektive. Braunschweig: Eigenverlag.

Olderog, T., & Skiera, B. (2000). The benefits of bundling strategies. Schmalenbach Business Review, 52(2), 137-159.

Ollhäuser, B. (2007). Follow the free als Preisstrategie. In Linde, F. (ed.), Markttheoretische und wettbewerbsstrategische Aspekte des Managements von Informationsgütern (pp. 181-199). Institut für Informationswissenschaft der Fachhochschule Köln. (Kölner Arbeitspapiere zur Bibliotheks- und Informationswissenschaft, 53).

Owen, B.M., Beebe, H.J., & Manning, W.G. (1974). Television Economics. Toronto, London: Lexington.

Owen, B. M., & Wildman, S. S. (1992). Video Economics. Cambridge, MA: Harvard Univ. Press.

Parker, G.G., & Van Alstyne, M.W. (2000). Information Complements, Substitutes, and Strategic Product Design. Tulane University. New Orleans. (Online).

Pigou, A. C. (1929). The Economics of Welfare. London: MacMillan.

Reibnitz, A. v. (2003). Pricing von Paid Content und Paid Services. Berlin: VDZ (Dokumentation Publikumszeitschriften).

Sabel, T. (2007). Follow the free. Erfolgsmodelle kostenfreier Informationsangebote. In Linde, F. (ed.), Markttheoretische und wettbewerbsstrategische Aspekte des Managements von Informationsgütern (pp. 200-215). Institut für Informationswissenschaft der Fachhochschule Köln. (Kölner Arbeitspapiere zur Bibliotheks- und Informationswissenschaft, 53).

Sattler, H., & Nitschke, T. (2003). Ein empirischer Vergleich von Instrumenten zur Erhebung von Zahlungsbereitschaften. zfbf, 55(6), 364-381.

Scheerer, M. (2007). Kotau vor den Kartellwächtern. Handelsblatt, 180 (09/18/2007), 2.

Schmalensee, R. (1984): Pricing of Product Bundles. Gaussian Demand and Commodity Bundling. The Journal of Business, 57(1), 211-230.

Schumann, M., & Hess, T. (2006). Grundfragen der Medienwirtschaft. Eine betriebswirtschaftliche Einführung. 3rd ed. Berlin: Springer. (Springer-Lehrbuch).

Shapiro, C., & Varian, H.R. (1999 [1998]). Information Rules. A Strategic Guide to the Network Economy. Boston, MA: Harvard Business School Press.

Simon, H. (1998). Preismanagement kompakt. Probleme und Methoden des modernen Pricing. Repr. Wiesbaden: Gabler.

Simon, H., & Fassnacht, M. (2009). Preismanagement. Strategie, Analyse, Entscheidung, Umsetzung. 3rd ed. Wiesbaden: Gabler.

Simonson, I., & Tversky, A. (1992). Choice in context: Tradeoff contrast and extremeness aversion. Journal of Marketing Research, 29(3), 281-295.

Skiera, B., Spann, M., & Walz, U. (2005). Erlösquellen und Preismodelle für den Business-to-Consumer-Bereich im Internet. Wirtschaftsinformatik, 47(4), 285-293.

Smith, G.E., & Nagle, T.T. (1995). Frames of reference and buyers' perception of price and value. California Management Review, 38(1), 98-116.

Stahl, F. (2005). Paid Content. Strategien zur Preisgestaltung beim elektronischen Handel mit digitalen Inhalten. Wiesbaden: Dt. Univ.-Verl.

Stahl, F., Siegel, F., & Mass, W. (2004). Paid Content - Paid Services. Analyse des deutschen Marktes und der Erfolgsfaktoren von 280 Geschäftsmodellen. Herausgegeben von Universität Gallen.

Sundararjan, A. (2004). Nonlinear pricing of information goods. Management Science, 50(12), 1660-1673.

Tellis, G. J. (1986). Beyond the many faces of price: An integration of pricing strategies. Journal of Marketing, 50(4), 146-160.

Theysohn, S., Prokopowicz, A., & Skiera B. (2005). Der Paid Content-Markt - Eine Bestandsaufnahme und Analyse von Preisstrategien. MedienWirtschaft: Zeitschrift für Medienmanagement und Kommunikationsökonomie, 2(4), 170-180.

Tillmann, D., & Simon, H. (2008). Preisbündelung bei Investitionsgütern. zfbf, 60, 517-538.

Varian, H.R. (2003). Economics of Information Technology. University of California, Berkeley. (Online).

Venkatesh, R., & Kamakura, W. (2003). Optimal bundling and pricing under a monopoly: Contrasting optimal bundling and pricing under a monopoly: Contrasting complements and substitutes from independently valued products. Journal of Business, 76(2), 211-231.

Völckner, F. (2006). Determinanten der Informationsfunktion des Preises. Eine empirische Analyse. Zeitschrift für Betriebswirtschaft, 76(5), 473-497.

Walsh, G., Frenzel, T., & Wiedmann, K.-P. (2002). E-Commerce-relevante Verhaltensmuster als Herausforderung für das Marketing, dargestellt am Beispiel der Musikwirtschaft. Marketing ZFP, 24(3), 207-223.

Web Server Survey - SecuritySpace. E-Soft Inc. (Online).

Wendt, O., Westarp, F. v., & König, W. (2000). Pricing in Network Effect Markets. Institute of Information Systems. Frankfurt/Main. (Online).

Wiese, H. (1991). Marktschaffung. Das Startproblem bei Netzeffekt-Gütern. Marketing ZFP, 13(1), 43-51.

Wirtz, B.W. (2001). Electronic Business. 2nd, ed. Wiesbaden: Gabler (Lehrbuch).

Wirtz, B.W. (2006). Medien- und Internetmanagement. 5th ed. Wiesbaden: Gabler.

Wirtz, B.W., & Olderog, T. (2001). E-Pricing: Die neue Herausforderung für das Preismanagement. In Hutter, M. (ed.), e-conomy 2.0. Management und Ökonomie in digitalen Kontexten (pp. 187-219). Marburg: Metropolis (Wittener Jahrbuch für ökonomische Literatur, N° 6).

Wu, S.Y., & Chen, P.Y. (2008). Versioning and piracy control for digital information goods. Operations Research, 56(1), 157-172.

Wu, S.Y., Hitt, L.M., & Chen, P.Y., Anandalingam, G. (2008). Customized bundle pricing for information goods: A nonlinear mixed-integer programming approach. Management Science, 54(3), 608-622.

Xie, J., & Sirbu, M. (1995). Price competition and compatibility in the presence of positive demand externalities. Management Science, 41(5), 909-926.

Zeix - Internet-Lexikon (2006). Powershopping. Herausgegeben von Zeix AG. (Online).

Zerdick, A. et al. (eds.) (2001). Die Internet-Ökonomie. Strategien für die digitale Wirtschaft. 3rd ed. Berlin: Springer.

Zillich, C. (2004). Covisint - ein 500-Millionen-Dollar-Flop. computerwoche, 04/05/2004. (Online).

Chapter 19

Managing Compatibility and Standardization

19.1   Compatibility Standards and Standardization

Compatibility standards have long played a significant role in many areas of the economy. Some examples are railway track widths, voltages, weight or length measurements or even transmission and communication protocols in telecommunication (Knieps, 2007, 117). The burden of defining, introducing and changing standards has so far been shouldered by engineers and lawyers; only recently has it come to the attention of economists.

Compatibility (Farrell & Saloner, 1987, 1 et seq.), often referred to alternatively as interoperability (Choi et al., 1997, 513), generally means that different systems (products, individuals or organizations) are capable of cooperating via a common point of intersection. Among such compatible systems are trains and tracks, hydrants and hoses, or cameras and lenses. Compatibility generally refers to two aspects (Knieps, 2007, 118). On the one hand, there is the compatibility of entire networks, e.g. of rail, telecommunication or language networks. If two networks are compatible on the basis of a common standard, such as the German and French rail networks, the extent of the direct network effects is determined by the sum of users of **both** networks. Conversely, this means that all agents that use a common standard form a network (Picot et al., 2003, 63-64). On the other hand, the availability of products that are compatible with a network is relevant. The more comprehensive and diverse the offer of such complements (e.g. rail vehicles), the stronger indirect network effects will be.

Considering examples such as PCs and their peripheral units, the different components of a stereo system including data carriers (CD, DVD etc.), the terminal devices in a telephone network or the internet, or even a common national language, they all fundamentally concern the exchange of information. One needs concrete specifications of a data carrier, such as a CD, or a telephone/internet protocol, in order to make communication possible. Even information exchange between two people requires a common standard. In Chapter 17 we have defined a (communication) standard as the totality of rules that form the basis of communication for people or machines (Buxmann et al., 1999, 134). In short, it is the rules that create compatibility.

Here we do not refer to standards of quality or security, that is requirements which a product or production must meet (Hess, 1993, 18 et seq.), or standards for reducing diversity (e.g. DIN A4) or information/product description standards (e.g. for describing fuels) (Blind, 2004, 20 et seq.). We are exclusively concerned with standards of compatibility.

A standard often stands for a technology, a method or a code that dominates the market, thus representing "the" standard (Burgelman et al., 1996, 311). This very narrow conception is not the basis of our considerations either, as it would blind out the development toward a standard and the competition of standards.

In connection with compatibility standards, there is often talk of technology, i.e. technical/technological standards. A very broad view of technology, such as the English language's, generally refers to procedural agreements, which are found in many areas of human activity, e.g. in service creation processes, but also, more generally, in human co-existence.

Compatibility between participating systems comes about via a process of standardization (Farrell & Saloner, 1987, 3). In such a collective process, the unification of intersections or protocols, a certain variant is selected from a pool of options and accepted by a certain amount of people for a certain period of time (Borowicz, 2001, 14). Compatibility as a result of standardization thus means, in short, that products are able to work together.

19.2   Relevance of Standards

Why are standards so significant?

> Companies that have set industry standards, or are in a position to influence these, are able to achieve innovation profits that no other competitive advantage can come close to obtaining (Grant & Nippa, 2006, 437).

Standards play an outstanding role on information markets not only for this economic reason, but also due to technological aspects. Digital information goods always have a certain storage format, their transmission is subject to a format and even their output is technologically specified. This means that a functioning market offer of information goods always requires (communication/compatibility) standards.

In the days before the internet's prevalence, most standards were created by public institutions or legislative and administrative acts (of the post or telecommunication) as so-called de jure standards.

In the internet economy, almost all standards are the results of processes of self-organization (the internet's self-administration) and of de facto assertion on the market (e.g. operating systems, browsers, communication services). Thus the process of standardization is given an entrepreneurial character (Picot, 2000).

Standards have become increasingly open to influence, meaning companies who have succeeded in setting standards–such a Microsoft and Intel (Wintel PC Standard), Qualcomm (CDMA Standard) or Cisco (IP Standards)–generate above-average shareholder value. For the IT world, it is generally to be assumed that it is changing from a product-based world to one based on standards. In such a world, it is not important who provides a program, only that it be able to process open formats (Postinett, 2009, 11).

19.3 Forms of Standards

In observing standards, one must take into consideration the supply as well as the demand side. Standards must first be developed by their providers; this is how they acquire ownership rights over it. Depending on the mode of access, one differentiates between provider-specific (proprietary) or cross-provider (open) standards (Ehrhardt, 2001, 12 et seq.). A standard is deemed **proprietary** if the network of products and complements applies to the technology of only one company. This is the case for video game consoles by Nintendo, Sony or Microsoft. Other manufacturers are prohibited from selling compatible hardware, precluding the possibility of substitution. If you want to play Halo 3, you must buy Microsoft's Xbox. As soon as companies form coalitions, one speaks of an **open proprietary standard** (Borowicz, 2001, 99). This can be a simple alliance of two companies, such as Philips' and Sony's for the CD-ROM format, or entire groups, such as the ones facing off over the succession of DVD. The decisive factor is that access to the technology is controlled by a company. If access to a standard is possible without any significant restrictions, this is an **open** standard. Examples for this are CD-ROM, ISDN, HTML or Linux. An open standard always means that intellectual access is free; usage, though, can very well incur licensing fees. These must merely be set in such a way that they represent no serious hurdle for access (Hess, 1993, 27; Maaß, 2006, 158).

It is definitely possible for several (proprietary or open) standards to compete for dominance on a market. If, however, an entire industry serves a unified standard, we speak of an **industry standard** (Ehrhardt, 2001, 13). Such a standard is found, for instance, on the market for stereo systems: equipment from the most diverse of manufacturers can be assembled into a functioning aggregate.

However, the demand side also plays an important role in the establishment of a standard. In the final analysis, the consumers decide on the actual acceptance and prevalence of a standard (Hess, 1993, 36 et seq.). Is there an industry-wide standard dominating the market or are there fragmented standards that compete on a market? According to Suarez (2004, 281) a standard can be called dominant if

(a) there is a clear sign that the most closely competing alternative design has abandoned the active battle, thus acknowledging defeat directly or indirectly;

(b) a design has achieved a clear market share advantage over alternative designs and recent market trends unanimously suggest that this advantage is increasing.

Some dominant standards are VHS for video recorders, Windows for PC operating systems and the Adobe Portable Document Format (pdf). Further examples are shown in the table below.

Enterprise	Product category	Standard
Microsoft	Operating systems of PCs	Windows
Intel	Microprocessors for PCs	*86 series
Matsushita	Video cassette recorder	VHS system
Sony/Philips	CDs	CD-ROM format
Iomega	PC diskette drives with higher storage capacity	Zip disk drives
Intuit	Software for online finance transactions	Quicken
Sun Microsystems	Programming language for web pages	Java
Rockwell and 3 Com	56 K modems	V 90
Qualcomm	Digital mobile telephone communication	CDMA
Adobe Systems	General file format for the construction and account of electronic documents	pdf

Table 19.1: Examples of Companies who Control Standards. Source: Grant & Nippa, 2006, 437.

19.4   Determining Factors of Standardization

Whether there are several standards that compete for a market or whether a single standard will achieve dominance depends on both the supply and demand conditions. Shapiro and Varian (1999, 186 et seq.) detected two central factors that decide whether a market tends to a single standard or not. They describe such markets as "tippy markets" (176).

Supply / Demand	Low Cost Degression Effects	Pronounced Cost Degression Effects
Homogeneous Customer Preferences	Low	High
Heterogeneous Customer Preferences	Improbable	Possible

Table 19.2: Standardization Potential. Source: Following Shapiro & Varian, 1999, 188.

Homogeneous customer preferences are the best precondition for the forming of a unified standard. If, in addition, there is interest on the provider's side, because increasing output quantity would allow him to significantly reduce his overhead, the probability of dominant standard emerging is to be deemed high. Both effects are often in effect at the same time, particularly for information goods (Shapiro & Varian, 1999, 189). The situation looks different when customers have very different desires and do not want to settle for a small amount of product offers. In this case, different products, and thus incompatible standards can stay on the market (Borowicz, 2001, 70). Apple's MAC computers have asserted themselves against IBM-compatible PCs up to this day because Apple users have certain demands on the product functionalities that have not been satisfactorily met by IBM PCs. Only recently has Apple begun trying to tap into its competitor's large installed base via the installation of Boot Camp, an additional, Windows-compatible operating system, on its computers.

The trend toward standardization is stronger in proportion to how pronounced the occurring network effects are (Stango, 2004, 3; Borowicz, 2001, 67 et seq.). These are, of course, ubiquitous in information goods, but can turn out weaker or stronger. While, for instance, the basic value is the most important aspect of standard business software, companies regard data exchange software (EDI) more from the viewpoint of whether their business partners also use it (Buxmann, 2002). In the second case, the specific product requirements are eclipsed by the network effect value. Standardized products are important for the customer in this case. A similar relation applies to the value of the basic good and the complements for the customer. Church and Gandal (1992) used a game-theoretical model to ob-

serve, on the example of software, that when customers highly value a diverse as-
sortment of complements in comparison with the variety of the basic good of
hardware technology, this will lead to a de facto standardization in the hardware
market. Heterogeneous customer desires with regard to the complement of software, on the other hand, lead to the co-existence of different incompatible hardware offers.

The potential for standardization is more pronounced depending on the overall
strength of the network effects, i.e. the higher the demand for intensive exchange
(direct network effects) and/or complementary services (indirect network effects)
is in comparison with the specific requirements to the basic good. Gupta et al.
(1999, 414) thus recommend, for the analysis of markets with indirect network effects, to first analyze the competing basic goods, then the complementary offers as
well as the complementors that offer them, and finally customer expectations with
regard to their notions concerning both aspects (hardware and complement offer).
Barring the suppliers, neglected here, this corresponds exactly to the constellation
of the value net we proposed for analyzing information markets.

For planning standardization, providers must thus take into consideration three
factors (Hess, 1993, 36 et seq.):

- The degree of standardization: how comprehensively should compatibility be created? What product functions should be standardized and to
  what other products or systems should compatibility be formed?
- The competitors' access to the standard: how open is access to the standard? How strongly is the product protected?
- The standard's prevalence with the buyers: how are the potential customers' standardization expectations being influenced positively?

Standards can be spread in different ways. If it is done via the market and without
being legally binding, we speak of an informal or de facto standard. If standards
are made binding by regulatory instances, like the government or standardization
committees (Deutsches Institut für Normung: DIN, Comité Européen de Normali-
sation: CEN, International Organization for Standardization: ISO), this is called a
formal or de jure standard (Blind, 2004, 17; Ehrhardt, 2001, 14).

The importance of attaining a high prevalence with the help of a standard for
the success of a technology is shown by examples where new technologies failed
due to incompatibilities. Ehrhardt (2001, 162 et seq.) here names the introduction
of AM Stereo technology (Medium Wave) as well as Quadrophony, a four-
channel-sound technology that was meant to replace stereophonic sound. Currently, we have the example of Digital Rights Management (DRM) in the music industry. Here the various providers of different technologies did not succeed in set-
tling on a common standard.

> There have also been significant brakes on the digital music sector: the
> lack of interoperability between services and devices due to different
> providers' digital rights management (DRM) standards (Bundesverband
> Musikindustrie, 2008, 5).

As a consequence, the music industry has decided to forego DRM entirely and to offer music without any copy protection in the future.

19.5   Standards on Information Markets

The above deliberations already made clear why standards play a decisive competitive role, particularly for providers of information goods. This is down to two reasons: on the one hand, the use and exchange of information (goods) always presupposes compatibility. Secondly, standards are always important when goods with network effects are concerned (Grant & Nippa, 2006, 439). In goods that become more valuable for the users with increasing prevalence, standards have great advantages for customers and suppliers, but also for the provider. Let us consider the above example of DRM. For buyers of music, it is of advantage if there is a large user community using the same DRM technology. This increases the options for sharing music. Thus for example, all titles that users bought on iTunes were protected by the DRM system fairplay until recently. The protected titles are only compatible with the corresponding music players (iPods) and their software. A user of this software might discuss the music with users of another network, such as customers of the former online service Connect by Sony, but cannot share it. Here both direct and indirect network effects become visible: direct ones where data exchange is concerned and indirect ones with regard to the complements necessary for playing the music. This corresponds to two different forms of compatibility that can generally prevail for information goods, with regard to substitutability on the one hand and to complementarity on the other (Borowicz, 2001, 10 et seq.).

The size of a network depends on the quantity of available **substitutes**, for one. Gabel (1987, 94) here talks of "multivendor compatibility", as for example when hardware is characterized as IBM-compatible. Hence, if the single DRM systems and storage formats had been compatible, and thus substitutable, there could have been one single, large network of listeners. The struggle for a unified DRM standard for music is now over, yet the standard for the storage format is still being fought over. As long as various incompatible formats are used for storing music, there will be different networks that will prevent the direct network effects from blossoming.

On the other hand, the size of a network is influenced by the indirect network effects. They, too, can only come into effect if compatibility is a given, this time with regard to the available **complements**. An online music service thus has advantages if there is a large number of compatible products on which the buyers can listen to their music. The number of complements grows in proportion with the size of the respective network. In our example, two-sided (indirect) network effects even come into play when the number of iPod buyers buys the music offered on iTunes and, conversely, a large community of music listeners on iTunes leads to a greater wealth of variants in MP3 players.

Chou and Shy (1996) here developed a dynamic model, in which they observe the effects of exclusively incorporating third-party providers into the production of complements. In their model, the consumers can choose between two basic technologies (hardware), and their value depends–with a given budget–on the number of available complements (software). If the basic technologies are incompatible, the value for the consumers depends on how many complements are available for the platform in question. Due to their constrained budget, they will choose the cheaper basic product in order to have more money available for additional applications. An intense price competition between the providers of the basic technologies is to be expected. The case is similar when basic good and complements are available from a single source. Here, too, there is no impetus for the provider to raise prices in order to force those consumers who only request the basic good off the market (Economides & Viard, 2004, 3). This may also explain why Microsoft charges a lot less for Windows than for the Office package: users who want to use Windows together with other applications should not be scared off the basic good. With strong network effects, it can even be profitable to lower the price of the basic product to zero and to draw one's profits from the increasing requests for complements (Clements, 2002).

The logical consequence, then, is that incompatible offers and exclusive applications are more interesting for large companies than for smaller ones (likewise Haucap, 2003, 34, with a model-based analysis of the telecommunication market). They can try to force newcomers off the market, which they will probably accomplish if they have a strong head start on the market and the new provider's cost advantage is low (Maaß, 2006, 80 with further sources). Also of advantage for the established provider in this situation are a higher reputation and customer preferences in favor of his product (Katz & Shapiro, 1994, 111).

For smaller providers, it is thus recommended to open up and seek compatibility with the established competitor in order to draw on his installed base. Orienting oneself on the dominant standard further makes a price premium possible, which Gallaugher and Wang (1999) observe in an empirical analysis of the web server market:

> In a market where more than one standard can be employed, products
> that support dominant standards were shown to exert a price premium
> (Gallaugher & Wang, 1999, 83).

There is one danger to be faced, though: third-party providers of complements may develop few or no products that are entirely tailor-made for the newcomer's offer. Dranove and Gandal (2003) investigated the case of DD vs. DivX. DivX players had a one-way compatibility, i.e. they could read DVDs, whereas DVD players did not recognize the DivX format. It was thus more profitable for providers of the respective complements (films) to only offer the format both were able to use (Dranove & Gandal, 2003, 385). This again might lead to the basic product being unpopular due to its lack of a multitude of specific complements (Chou & Shy, 1990).

The decision in favor of compatibility is thus at the same time a decision against an intra-standard competition. Katz and Shapiro (1986) investigated this in a model and arrived at the following conclusion:

> The most striking result is that firms may use product compatibility as a means of reducing competition among themselves. By choosing compatible technologies, the firms prevent themselves from going through an early phase of extremely intense competition where each firm tries to build up its network to get ahead of its rival (Katz & Shapiro, 1986, 164).

However, competitive intensity only decreases at the beginning of the product life cycle. In the case of compatible products, none of the providers will be able to dominate the market on his own, and so the competition's intensity will rise in later phases (Katz & Shapiro, 1994, 110 et seq.).

For the provider, the question of compatibility with others is a fundamental decision, which in turn leads to the question of whether he himself believes he is capable of creating a sufficient amount of network effects. The competition on network effect markets

> ... is prone to tipping, there are likely to be strong winners and strong losers under incompatibility. Therefore, if a firm is confident it will be the winner, that firm will tend to oppose compatibility (Katz & Shapiro, 1994, 111).

19.6   Effects of Compatibility Standards

Apart from network effects, there is a series of further advantages that compatibility brings and which makes the establishment of a standard something to strive for. If a dominant standard exists, this will decrease both transaction and switching costs for the customers (Graumann, 1993; Picot et al., 2003, 64). Different product offers can be more easily found and compared. This means that the **decision time** is decreased and the **decision quality** rises. The costs for switching from one compatible product to another sink likewise. A printer does not become worthless if you buy a different PC, and you can also continue using your saved weblinks when switching browsers. In such cases, however, it must be noted that dominant standards may lower the switching costs for using the standardized products, yet at the same time significantly raise them with regard to alternative offers. Existing, but also future offers that are not compatible, will have a much harder time asserting themselves on the market. Dominant standards, no matter whether they are open or proprietary, decrease switching costs within a standard but raise them outside of it. In this way, not only individuals but also industries, even entire societies can find themselves in a Lock-In, as has been the case with Microsoft Windows for some time (Shapiro & Varian, 2003, 57).

Established standards increase **decision certainty** for all involved: consumers, suppliers and manufacturers all have a higher certainty of their investments possessing long-term value and not leading to high switching costs in a short time. The higher the switching costs are, bringing the customer closer to a Lock-In, the longer a standard will prevail. Even solutions that are technologically superior or that are more user-friendly, cannot assert themselves if too many customers face prohibitive switching costs (in a Lock-In).

A much-cited example for this is the Anglo-American QWERTY (or German QWERTZ) keyboard (David, 1985). This allocation of keys on a typewriter, developed in 1873, aimed at a slow typing speed in order to avoid blocking the typebars in case of simultaneous keystrokes. Even though this problem could be solved technically, and a significantly more efficient and faster keyboard, the "Dvorak Simplified Keyboard Technology (DSK)" was patented in 1932, the originally introduced de facto standard has survived to this very day. As many millions of people have become used to a certain arrangement of letters, the switching costs are far too high for them to consider a new standard. This phenomenon, termed path dependency in the literature on strategic management, also makes providers shrink back from bringing a changed product onto the market.

High, or even prohibitive switching costs, lead to customers continuing to use the product once bought and not changing providers. The creation of such a standard is not necessarily, according to Arthur (1989), the result of a product's technological superiority, but is often due to chance ("historical events"). Products such as DOS, Java or VHS have become successful mainly because they had, at a certain point in time, a larger installed base than the competing products MAC OS, ActiveX or Betamax (Arthur, 1998). Thus it is not necessarily the better offer which will assert itself on the market—it can also be a worse product (seen in isolation, without considering network effects) or technology that reaches Lock-In.

Manufacturers as well as suppliers of a standardized good profit from a greater **market volume**. This means higher sales potentials as well as cost minimizing potentials in R&D, production or even marketing. A standard will solidify the market position of all providers involved and leads to market entry barriers for providers of diverging product standards.

19.7   Upwards and Downwards Compatibility

Specifically on network effect markets, a second dimension, apart from access to a technology, plays an important role for the provider: upward and downward compatibility ("multivintage compatibility"; Gabel, 1987, 94), or even vertical compatibility with other products or systems of the same provider. The company must determine whether a new product offer is compatible with existing offers in networks or whether it will break with the old standards, thus attempting to generate a new market, or to establish a new network. Next to the decision on compatibility with complements, this is the second aspect of the degree of standardization. This is a specific form of substitutability.

If a new product, e.g. a computer or a gaming console, is downwards compatible, software or games of the older model can still be used. Sony's Playstation 3 (PS3) originally offered **downward compatibility**. PS2 games could also be played on the PS3. In order to force sales of new games for the PS3, Sony ended the compatibility–much to the customers' sorrow–in late 2007 (Postinett, 2007). If users of the old product are, in reverse, not able to process protocols, files etc. of the new model, it lacks the corresponding **upward compatibility**. When Microsoft, for example, brought the new Word 97 on the market (Shapiro & Varian, 1999, 193-194), the Word 95 files could still be read but users of the old product were not able to process the new file type. Microsoft wanted to exploit its dominant market position and force all users to upgrade to the 97 version as quickly as possible. When this strategy became known, though, there were significant delays in the adaption and Microsoft had to release two free applications, a Word Viewer for reading the 97 files and a Word Converter for turning them into 95 files. The situation was similar in the case of Office 2007, which introduced entirely new formats (e.g. docx instead of doc for Word). The users of older Office versions were initially unable to process the new formats, and a corresponding converting tool had to be developed.

A great danger of the continued guarantee of compatibility is that new products lose performance ability. dBase is a good example for this (Shapiro & Varian, 1999, 192 et seq.). In order to stay compatible with older product versions, the newer versions contained ever more complicated hierarchies of programming code, which affected the performance. Microsoft was then able to use its relational database application Access to relatively easily assert a new, revolutionary and dBase-incompatible standard. The new product's performance ability was so much higher that Microsoft was able to develop its own large installed base even in the face of existing switching costs.

19.8 Strategies of Standardization

Both dimensions of standardization, that of access and that of compatibility, can be combined in a strategy matrix. Shapiro and Varian (1999, 191 et seq.) here see two possible alternatives: an evolutionary and a revolutionary strategy. The former offers a migration path, the latter breaks with existing offers while promising a much higher performance or value level. The evolutionary strategy has the great advantage of the installed base, i.e. all members of the network who use the same standard with all the corresponding network effects, still being usable. To proceed revolutionarily means to enter a new product on the market that is in competition with the previous standard. This was the case with Access vs. dBase. Subsequent compatible product versions of the same program are then, of course, part of an evolutionary strategy. Innovations that create an entirely new market must be ascribed to the revolutionary strategy, though.

Evolutionary strategies always build on existing standards or previous versions of a product and bank on its further development. This can be driven by a single company (en bloc migration), as Microsoft or Adobe do with their respective new product versions. They are in control of everything. In order to share the risk more strongly, and to increase their chances of asserting themselves there are often alliances between several partners (controlled migration). This was the case with Toshiba and NEC, who created HD DVD, and Sony and Matsushita, who created Blu-Ray, both in order to supply the standard replacing DVD. There may be several parties involved, who have to reach an understanding as concerns the standard that is aimed at, but they can control the development jointly. If direct control is foregone, one is in the environment of open standards (open migration). These are freely accessible and can be used by everybody, be it in order to offer one's own standards (e.g. fax machines) according to this standard or to develop it further together with others, as is the case with Linux or Open Office.

Access ╲ Compatibility	Proprietary – closed	Proprietary - open	Open
Compatible (evolutionary)	En Bloc Migration	Controlled Migration	Open Migration
Incompatible (revolutionary)	Power Play Discontinuity	Cooperative Discontinuity	Open Discontinuity

Table 19.3: Standardization Strategies. Source: Following Shapiro and Varian, 1999, 204.

If a new standard is created that is incompatible with existing products, technologies or conventions, one enters the field of discontinuous, **revolutionary strategies**. If they are pursued by a single company, we are dealing with the very risky Power Play strategy. There are many examples of an innovator trying to assert his standard on the market. Very successful examples, such as Apple's iTunes or the Nintendo Entertainment System in the eighties, stand opposite an equal number of cases in which a company completely failed to establish its standard. A prominent example is Sony with its Betamax video recorders, no longer existent today. In many cases, however, companies have succeeded in creating a durable standard, which did not become the dominant industry standard but only play a supporting role. Among these companies are Palm with its Palm Operating System for Personal Digital Assistants (PDAs) and Apple with its Macintosh operating system, or also Sony's MiniDisc, which today is of significance only in Japan. Often, companies introduce their new, incompatible standards while banking on cooperation with others (cooperative discontinuity). This can be during the development phase, as for the CD (Sony and Philips), or also by licensing the format, as JVC/Matsushita did, when they were able to win Philips and Sharp, among others, in order to build up VHS as the dominant standard on the market for video recorders. Freely accessible, open standards to be newly introduced (open discontinuity) were the internet protocol TCP/IP, the text-based markup language for content on the Web (HTML), the MP3 format for compressing audio files, or GSM as a standard for digital cellular networks.

If several standards are in competition with each other and try to achieve dominance in order to become the industry standard, we also speak of a format war, or "Standards War" (Shapiro & Varian, 1999, 261 et seq.) In such struggles, there are different approaches to asserting one's own, preferred standard. They correspond with access rights and are differentiated according to whether a company strives to actively assert its standard as developer or technology leader, or whether it acts passively and conforms to a standard in the role of follower or adopter. The access to a standard is not, as above, a question of whether a new standard should be compatible with other products or not (evolutionary vs. revolutionary), but of whether one chooses to pursue the quest for market dominance either on one's own or in cooperation with others. The degree of openness itself is thus a strategic option (Grindley, 1995). Companies must thus consciously decide whether they want to keep their technology exclusively for themselves (proprietary–closed), open up part-way (proprietary–open) or make it accessible for everyone. In the proprietary-open strategy, the developer of a technology at least has the option of controlling access, granting or restricting it at his discretion. The proprietary-closed strategy always springs from marketary or market-similar (closed forums, consortiums etc.) competitive processes, whereas open standards are always the result of the work of recognized councils (including open forums). If access to a standard is public, it cannot be denied anyone (Borowicz, 2001, 99).

As a basic rule for a successful standardization, Hess (1993, 28) recommends making the licensing sufficiently generous for critical mass to be reached in any event.

> As anyone who has purchased property knows, the three guidelines for success in real estate are: location, location, and location. Three guidelines for success in industries where standards are important and increasing returns exist are: maximize installed base, maximize installed base, and maximize installed base (Hill, 1997, 10).

Access / Role	Proprietary-closed	Proprietary-open	Open
Active	Monopoly Strategy	Awarding Strategy	Sponsorship Strategy
Passive	Circumvention Strategy	Licensee Strategy	Copycat Strategy

Table 19.4: Behavior Options in the Standardization Competition. Source: Following Borowicz and Scherm, 2001.

19.9   Options of Proactive Behavior

The active behavior options of primary interest to us all aim at establishing a dominant standard. Network effects play the decisive role here (van de Kaa et al., 2007). There are two different approaches for a company: to initiate network effects via market processes, thus supporting the emergence of a de facto standard, or conversely, to strive for the negotiation of de jure standards. This will provide for a unified basis for the subsequent market offer and benefits the occurrence of network effects.

There are now a series of factors that influence the choice of one of the three active behavior options displayed in Table 19.4, in which the underlying legal conditions play an important role. If there is a regulator who sets the standard, all possibility of choice is precluded from the outset. If there is a preset standard, it must be noted whether protective rights (patents) may be established. The more comprehensively and effectively these can be used, the more a proprietary strategy will be favored. These two legal factors are widely prespecified, however, and cannot be extensively influenced by a single company.

More relevant are the factors that can be actively influenced by a company, also called success factors. These are subject to the (strategic) decision sphere of the individual company. They are viewed as the cause of a provider achieving dominance in the standardization competition with his chosen behavior option. Borowicz (2001, 113)–and, in precisely the same way, Suarez (2004), focusing specifically on information and telecommunication technologies–identify four of these: pricing policy, timing of market entry, signaling and organization of external relations. The first three factors are well known to us as action parameters in the context of information providers' competitive strategies, and will as such each be discussed in their own chapter. Only the **organization of external relations** shall be elaborated on a little more here. It can go in three directions: cooperation for the complement offer, for the offer of the basic good and in standardization councils. The discussion of complement management will follow in the next chapter. The latter two points have already been addressed at various points in the previous chapter. The various different associated aspects can be very clearly summarized via the example of the introduction of the Digital Compact Cassette (DCC) by Philips (Hill, 1997, 13). In 1992, Philips introduced its DCC technology on the market. To support this digital audio technology, Philips cooperated with Matsushita. Matsushita guaranteed the marketing under its own brand names Panasonic and Technics and provided a collection of recorded DCC cassettes via its in-house music label MCA. This measure meant that the central complement for the market introduction was available in sufficient amounts. The signal that Philips' music label PolyGram and MCA both banked on DCC was sufficiently convincing for a series of other labels to jump on the bandwagon, among them EMI, Warner and CBS.

This case exemplifies how varied the positive effects of an alliance can be. The basic technology can be distributed faster, potential competitors–who might (have been) develop(ing) their own products–can be won as cooperation partners, and at the same time, strong signals are being sent to the other providers to the effect that a new standard will probably assert itself. Market insecurity decreases and the readiness of other companies to invest in the development of complements rises. For a discussion of the risks and aspects of the formalization of alliances, e.g. in the form of joint ventures, we refer to the extensive literature on this subject (for an introduction Borowicz, 2001, 153 et seq., Ehrhardt, 2001, 137 et seq.).

Even though Philips did many things right in introducing DCC, and access to the technology was made open enough, DCC was not able to assert itself on the market because the buyers were not addressed enough. Although Philips invested a lot of energy to provide downwards compatibility (DCC players were able to play analog cassettes as well), there was a lack of purposeful marketing.

> Philips' failure to establish the DCC as a new standard can be attributed in part to consumer confusion over the benefits of digital recording technology. Philips' poor product launch advertising–which failed to mention the issue of backward compatibility and did not highlight the benefits of a digital recording technology–did nothing to dispel this confusion (Hill, 1997, 16).

Success Factors \ Active Role	Monopoly Strategy	Allotment Strategy	Sponsorship Strategy
Penetration Pricing a) Starting Prices b) Price Development	a) Very low, close to variable costs b) Raise prices with increasing network effects and switching costs	a) Low, but higher than would be possible in a monopoly due to greater market power and fewer competing technologies b) Raise prices, but perhaps stay below monopoly price due to intra-standard competition	Penetration prices of secondary importance if the standardization council's reputations is high and there is no council competition
Price Differentiation (PD)	All forms of PD that facilitate network effects, particularly versioning and bundling	Product and price differentiation via company-specific offers	Regional PD, corresponding to the standardization council's sphere of influence
Timing of Market entry	Early (Pioneer) and building of barriers (e.g. installed base, distribution channels)	As early follower: Use of market power, financial power and capacities in order to offset the possibly already installed base As late follower only with significantly improved or advanced technology	Influence council's work in one's own favor (Beginning, Participants, Procedure)
Signalization a) Main addressees b) Signal contents	a) Customers, trade b) above all assurances, guarantees	Customers, trade	Councils
Cooperation Relationships (Alliances)	With providers of complements, if there is no solitary system provider	Competing providers of basic good and providers of complements	Competing providers of basic good, providers of complements and possibly standardization councils

Table 19.5: Success Factors of Active Standardization Strategies.

Additionally, Philips entered the market with relatively high end product prices ($900-1,200 per device) instead of pursuing a penetration strategy. On top of that, there was at the beginning only one kind of terminal device available, for home use; portable devices or devices for use in cars were missing. A further problem was probably the Minidisc, which Sony brought on the market as a competing technology at the same time (Hill, 1997, 16 et seq.).

This case makes it very clear how important it is to take into consideration all three factors for planning the standardization. In addition to the decision as to how extensively compatibility should be provided, it must be carefully planned in what capacity to involve the competition and how to address the demanders' side.

In closing, we will once more, briefly, take up the four success factors and summarize the central statements–allocated to the three active behavior options (Borowicz, 2001, 113 et seq.)–in Table 19.5, on order to show how they can be used in the standardization competition.

19.10 Options of Passive Behavior

If companies pursue a passive standardization strategy (see Table 19.4), their aim is to adopt another provider's standard. Their goal is market entry. Depending on the form of access, the following three passive options are available.

The **circumvention strategy** (Borowicz, 2001, 103 et seq.) is used by companies who want to gain access to a proprietary technology, which the holder does not want to provide. He is keen on keeping this information good exclusively to himself and not letting it become public property. As we have already found out in Chapter 3, the exclusion principle can be asserted for information goods only via secrecy or legal protection (e.g. patents). In order to get the desired information anyway, the copycat may get a hold of the parts of an information good that are for sale and try to imitate it. Such reverse engineering would mean, for example, buying software and trying to recreate it. Here it is difficult to decrypt the secret parts of the software, as the source code or specific interface information are not typically provided by the manufacturer. Information that are not offered on the market would then have to be appropriated in other–more or less legal–ways, by spying on the monopolist or directly poaching knowledge carriers. If information goods are freely accessible but patent-protected, there is the possibility of challenging or leveraging the patent. If the patent is still undergoing the examination procedure, a competitor may try to prevent its acceptance by contesting it. One may file a suit against existing patents or try to circumvent them by engineering around. An extensive empirical analysis by Debons et al. (1981, 913) showed that–even if patenting generally increases the cost of imitation–60% of patented innovations were circumvented within four years.

If the holder of a technology pursues a proprietary-closed approach and lets other companies share in while being controlled by him, an interested company may choose a **licensee strategy** (Borowicz, 2001, 105 et seq.). The following aspects are of note for licensing:

The decision on the degree of exclusivity that is striven for and the time of licensing have a particularly large effect on risk and market position. The more exclusively and the earlier licensing is completed, the greater the licensee's entrepreneurial risk will be, as the market is not yet fully developed. His risk situation then resembles a first mover's. The broader and the later one invests in a technology via licensing, the smaller the risks, but also the chances of economic success will be.

Degree of Exclusivity	Exlusive license (usage only by licensee)	Semi-exclusive license (usage only by licenser and licensee)	Simple licenses (right to use the technology alongside others)
Time of Licensing	Before market entry	After market entry, before standardization	After standardization
Extent of Licensing	Individual license	---	Package license
Licensing Compensation	Flate rate	Running costs	License exchange

Table 19.6: Aspects of Licensing.

The passive **copycat strategy** (Borowicz, 2001, 108 et seq.), corresponding with public access, is not, as the former two do, subject to marketary processes but is powered by the adoption of standards that have already been approved and made publicly accessible by councils.

19.11   Opening a Standard as Trade-Off Issue

As we can see, active and passive behavior options have different goals in the standardization competition. A passive behavior is directed toward market entry. As a consequence, there is an intra-standard competition, a **competition within the market** between providers of the same standard. If the offers are reciprocally compatible, network effects only occur with regard to the entire market, and not for the individual provider.

Active behavior options aim toward the inter-standard competition, i.e. the **competition for the market** (Borowicz, 2001, 112). Here network effects are of great significance for the individual provider and must be taken into consideration when choosing one's strategy. Shapiro and Varian (1999, 186-187) demonstrate this via the example of internet service providers (ISP). In the early days of the internet, AOL, Compuserve and other ISPs offered proprietary services such as e-mail or newsgroups. It was very complicated, or even impossible, to send an e-mail from one provider to another. The customers were thus very interested in belonging to a large network. The commercialization of the internet has led to the availability, today, of standardized protocols for browsers, e-mail or chat applications, and the network one affiliates oneself with does not affect transmission anymore. The competition for the ISP market has made way for a competition within the market. The establishment of common standards has led to an integration of the different networks.

However, network effects can also be revived on standardized markets, if new technologies are developed. These can either satisfy given needs better, or also satisfy completely new needs, thus creating a new market. AOL is an excellent example with its instant messaging system ICQ. In order to use this proprietary technology, one must become a customer of AOL after all. As long as the different instant messaging services (e.g. by Yahoo! or Microsoft) stay incompatible with each other, network effects are again of great importance. Whether a new, incompatible offer will win the struggle is fundamentally dependent on whether the (old) users are in a Lock-In. Even if the new offer is better, a Lock-In can prevent its market acceptance. More on this in Chapter 23.

As we have seen, a provider must think very carefully about what sort of competitive situation to commit himself to. Any opening of a standard has several consequences. The competitive relationships will, in all probability, be positively affected: if several companies cooperate on the basis of a(n) (proprietary-)open technology, they will be more likely to succeed, as a faster assertion on the market and a greater market volume are to be expected. However, the higher competitive intensity brings along several disadvantages for the single provider. He must take into account lower market share and, over the course of the product life cycle, a stronger price competition, i.e. lower contribution margins (Grindley, 1995, 45 et seq.). This relation is schematically represented in Figure 19.1.

If we express this in a simple formula, we get (Grindley, 1995, 45 et seq.):

Potential Gains = Market Size x Market Share x Contribution Margin

The decision in favor of more openness thus means a trade-off between a greater market volume on the one hand and a stronger competition within the market on the other hand. The latter has a positive effect for an individual provider on balance, if he has been able to assume a dominant position in the competition or the market has developed so positively due to the standardization that it overcompensates for the provider's loss of market share.

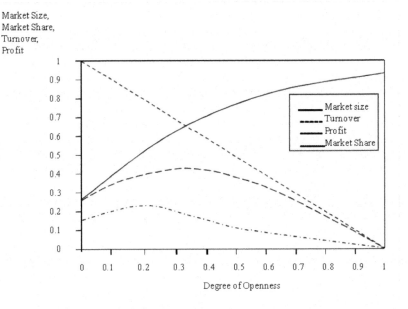

Figure 19.1: Effects of the Opening of a Standard on Sales and Profit. Source: Following Grindley, 1995, 46.

Specifically for the allotment strategy (Table 19.4), there is also the recommendation by Economides (1996) to make the licensing fee dependent on the strength of the network effects. The stronger the expected network effects are, the lower the licensing fees should be set in order to quickly reach critical mass and to initiate positive reinforcing effects. In case of very strong network effects, he even recommends not only the granting of licenses free of charge but their subsidization.

Similarly to the discussion of market entry strategies, we can say for standardization, too, that standards, once established, do not guarantee any lasting competitive advantages or monopoly positions (Borowicz, 2001, 55 et seq.). The material and immaterial investments of all parties involved may work toward a Lock-In, but the market and technology development can make a standard obsolete in a short time. The software-as-a-service offers or the Open-Source movement, with Linux and Open Office, are examples of how quickly established networks can run into difficulties. Here, too, it must thus be noted that the providers' power of innovation and potential for renewal remain of critical importance.

19.12 Conclusion

- A standard is the totality of rules which create compatibility.
- Standardization is a collective process of unifying intersections and protocols, respectively, in which a certain variant is picked from a pool of options and accepted by a certain amount of people for a certain period of time.
- Standards can arise from marketary processes, in which case one speaks of de facto standards. If they are set by regulatory instances, they are de jure standards.
- Compatibility is the result of a process of standardization and generally means that different systems are capable of working with each other via a common point of intersection.
- Standards play a crucial role on digital information markets for technological as well as economic reasons. A (communication/compatibility) standard is always required for a technologically functioning market offer of information goods. As de facto standards, they have also become increasingly influenceable and thus bear, from an economic perspective, potential gains that are well above the average. Standards are always highly important for network effect goods.
- If two networks are compatible on the basis of a common standard, the extent of direct network effects is determined via the sum of both networks' users. The more comprehensive and varied the offer of complements for a network, the stronger indirect network effects will be.
- The provider of a standard has ownership rights and can decide who has access to this standard (degree of openness). The demanders decide, via their consumer behavior, how far a standard will in fact be accepted and become prevalent.
- A standard is dominant if there is no close competitor (anymore) and if it manages to keep alternative offers on the market at a clear distance for now and likely in future.
- Homogenous customer preferences and pronounced cost degression effects are the best preconditions for the establishment of a unified standard.
- Access to a standard and compatibility to other systems are the two decisive strategy elements of standardization.
- If several standards are in competition with each other and try to beat the respective others in order to become the dominant (industry) standard, we speak of a format war. Companies may behave actively or passively in such conflicts, depending on whether they want to force acceptance of a standard they have developed or adjust to someone else's standard.

> - The decision in favor of more openness means a trade-off between a greater market volume on the one hand and stronger market competition on the other hand. The latter makes itself felt positively for a single provider, on balance, if he can assume a dominant position within the competition or if standardization makes the market develop positively enough to overcompensate for the provider's own loss of market share.

19.13 Bibliography

Arthur, W. B. (1989). Competing technologies, increasing returns, and lock-in by historical events. The Economic Journal, 99(394), 116-131.

Arthur, W. B. (1998). The pretext interview. Pretext. (Online).

Blind, K. (2004). The Economics of Standards. Theory, Evidence, Policy. Cheltenham: Elgar.

Borowicz, F. (2001). Strategien im Wettbewerb um Kompatibilitätsstandards. Frankfurt am Main: Lang (Europäische Hochschulschriften, Reihe 5, Volks- und Betriebswirtschaft, N° 2802).

Borowicz, F., & Scherm, E. (2001). Standardisierungsstrategien. Eine erweiterte Betrachtung des Wettbewerbs auf Netzeffektmärkten. Zeitschrift für Betriebswirtschaft, 53, 391-416.

Bundesverband Musikindustrie (ed.) (2008). Digital Music Report 2008. (Online).

Burgelman, R.A., Maidique, M.A., & Wheelwright, S.C. (1996). Strategic Management of Technology and Innovation. 2nd ed. Chicago: Irwin.

Buxmann, P. (2002). Strategien von Standardsoftware-Anbietern. Eine Analyse auf Basis von Netzeffekten. Zeitschrift für betriebswirtschaftliche Forschung, 54, 442-457.

Buxmann, P., Weitzel, T., & König, W. (1999). Auswirkung alternativer Koordinationsmechanismen auf die Auswahl von Kommunikationsstandards. Zeitschrift für Betriebswirtschaft, Ergänzungsheft 2, 133-151.

Choi, S.Y., Stahl, D.O., & Whinston, A.B. (1997). The Economics of Electronic Commerce. Indianapolis, IN: Macmillan Technical Pub.

Chou, C.F., & Shy, O. (1990). Network effects without network externalities. International Journal of Industrial Organization, 8, 259-270.

Chou, C.F., & Shy, O. (1996). Do consumers gain or lose when more people buy the same brand. European Journal of Political Economy, 12, 309-330.

Church, J., & Gandal, N. (1992). Network effects, software provision, and standardization. The Journal of Industrial Economics, 40(1), 85-103.

Clements, M. T. (2002). System components, network effects, and bundling. Topics in Economic Analysis & Policy, 2(1). (Online).

David, P.A. (1985). Clio and the economics of QWERTY. American Economic Review, 75(2), 332-337.

Debons, A., King, D.W., Mansfield, U., & Shirley, D.L. (1981). The Information Profession: Survey of an Emerging Field. New York, NY: Marcel Dekker.

Dranove, D., & Gandal, N. (2003). The DVD vs. DIVX standard war: Empirical evidence of network effects and preannouncement effects. Journal of Economics and Management Strategy, 12(3), 363-386.

Economides, N. (1996). Network externalities, complementarities, and invitations to enter. European Journal of Political Economy, 12, 211-233.

Economides, N., & Viard, V.B. (2007). Pricing of Complements and Network Effects. New York, NY and Beijing: New York University and Cheung Kong Graduate School of Business.

Ehrhardt, M. (2001). Netzwerkeffekte, Standardisierung und Wettbewerbsstrategie. Wiesbaden: Dt. Univ.-Verl. (Gabler Edition Wissenschaft : Strategische Unternehmungsführung).

Farrell, J., & Saloner, G. (1987). Competition, compatibility and standards. The economics of horses, penguins and lemmings. In Gabel, H.L. (ed.), Product Standardization and Competitive Strategy. (Advanced Series in Management, 11) (pp. 1-22). Amsterdam: North-Holland.

Gabel, H.L. (1987). Open standards in the european computer industry: the case of X/Open. In Gabel, H.L. (ed.), Product Standardization and Competitive Strategy. (Advanced Series in Management, 11) (pp. 91-123). Amsterdam: North-Holland

Gallaugher, J. M., & Wang, Y. M. (1999). Network effects and the impact of free goods: an analysis of the web-server market. International Journal of Electronic Commerce, 3(4), 67-88.

Grant, R.M., & Nippa, M. (2006). Strategisches Management. Analyse, Entwicklung und Implementierung von Unternehmensstrategien. 5th ed. München: Pearson Studium (wi - wirtschaft).

Graumann, M. (1993). Die Ökonomie von Netzprodukten. Zeitschrift für Betriebswirtschaft, 63(12), 1331-1355.

Grindley, P. C. (1995). Standards Strategy and Policy. Cases and Stories. Oxford: Oxford Univ. Press.

Gupta, S., Jain, D.C., & Sawhney, M. S. (1999). Modeling the evolution of markets with indirect network externalities: An application to digital television. Marketing Science, 18(3), 396-416.

Haucap, J. (2003). Endogenous switching costs and exclusive systems applications. Review of Network Economics, 2(1), 29-35.

Hess, G. (1993). Kampf um den Standard. Erfolgreiche und gescheiterte Standardisierungsprozesse - Fallstudien aus der Praxis. Stuttgart: Schäffer-Poeschel.

Hill, C.W.L. (1997). Establishing a standard: Competitive strategy and technological standards in winner-take-all industries. Academy of Management Executive, 11(2), 7-25.

Katz, M.L., & Shapiro, C. (1986). Product compatibility choice in a market with technological progress. Oxford Economic Papers, 38(11), 146-165.

Katz, M.L., & Shapiro, C. (1994). Systems competition and network effects. Journal of Economic Perspectives, 8(2), 93-115.

Knieps, G. (2007). Netzökonomie. Grundlagen - Strategien - Wettbewerbspolitik. Wiesbaden: Betriebswirtschaftlicher Verlag Dr. Th. Gabler, GWV Fachverlage GmbH Wiesbaden (Springer-11775 /Dig. Serial]).

Maaß, C. (2006). Strategische Optionen im Wettbewerb mit Open-Source-Software. Berlin: Logos-Verlag.

Picot, A. (2000). Die Bedeutung von Standards in der Internet-Ökonomie. Selbst-organisation ersetzt den hoheitlichen Akt. Frankfurter Allgemeine Zeitung, 11/16/2000, 30.

Picot, A., Reichwald, R., & Wigand, R. T. (2003). Die grenzenlose Unternehmung. Information, Organisation und Management. 5th ed. Wiesbaden: Gabler (Gabler-Lehrbuch).

Postinett, A. (2007). Showdown unterm Weihnachtsbaum. Handelsblatt, 204, 10/23/2007, 14.

Shapiro, C., & Varian, H.R. (1999 [1998]). Information Rules. A Strategic Guide to the Network Economy. Boston MA: Harvard Business School Press.

Shapiro, C., & Varian, H.R. (2003). The information economy. In Hand, J.R.M., & Lev, B. (eds.), Intangible assets. Values, Measures, and Risks (pp. 48-62). Oxford: Oxford Univ. Press.

Stango, V. (2004). The economics of standards wars. Review of Network Economics, 3(1), 1-19.

Suarez, F.F. (2004). Battles for technological dominance: an integrative framework. Research Policy, 33(2), 271-286.

van Kaa, G. de, Vries, H.J. de; van Heck, E., & van den Ende, J. (2007). The emergence of standards: a meta-analysis. Proceedings of the 40th Hawaii International Conference on System Science. (Online).

Chapter 20

Complement Management

20.1 Kinds of Complementary Relationships

As we have already seen in many places, information goods require, today, increasingly technological devices for their creation. Pross (1972, 128) speaks of secondary media

> ...that transport a message to the recipient without that latter needing a device for decoding its meaning... .

Newspapers, magazines, books etc. are such secondary media which require machines for their production, but not their reception. In the days of the internet, such information goods are available not only physically, but also online, thus automatically becoming tertiary media (Pross, 1972, 128),

> ...which in order to use, both transmitter and recipient require devices...

or even quaternary media, which, employing information and communication technologies, are determined

> ...by the global system of telepresences... (Faßler, 2002, 147).

The resulting consequence is that information goods must always be offered in conjunction with other goods: entertainment media require a playback device, software cannot go without an operating system and hardware, and music or videos can only be downloaded from the Web if means of transmission and output devices are provided. As a consumer using information goods, one is practically always dependent on complements. Thus, it is no longer individual products which are in competition with each other, but systems of goods.

> A system is a bundle of complementary and intercompatible goods that
> stand in a context of utilization and which the customer considers joint-
> ly in his purchase decision (Stelzer, 2000, 838).

Among such systems are the Windows or Macintosh worlds already known to us
from the chapter on standardization, the different gaming consoles or the competing DVD successors HD DVD and BluRay. Customers must be aware during their
purchase that they will settle not on a single product, but on a whole package of
complementary products, and perhaps even services. As we already know, indirect
network effects are at play in such cases. The prevalence of a system component
(e.g. of an operating system) benefits sales of complementary components (e.g.
antivirus programs, organizers, installation services), and often vice versa. In this
context, we must differentiate between components with limited and components
with strong complementarity (Huber & Kopsch, 2002, 624). If components are of
limited complementarity, they will increase another component's usefulness, but
are not a requirement for its usage. The owner of a television set, like the owner of
a Windows operating system, is able to choose from a multitude of programs, neither of which is individually necessary for the operability of the hard-
ware/software. Not so if the relation is **strictly** complementary. Any given application will not be able to run without an operating system, a computer without an
input unit or a set-top box without coded transmissions are worthless. A specific
kind of complement is absolutely required in this case. Should there be no selection of options in the choice of this required complement (e.g. an application that
will only run on the Macintosh operating system or the TV programs that can only
be decrypted with a specific decoder), and the components only be compatibly in
exactly one constellation, we can speak of **strictest** complementarity. This used to
be the case, for example, in the music platform Sony Connect, closed since March
2008. The music, which was offered in Sony's own ATRAC format, could only be
played on devices offered by Sony and a few licensees.

It is of stellar importance for the buyer of a system component–we will refer to
the first-bought component as the primary or basic good–whether any complements are available to him, and if so how many. The decision in favor of a DVD
player or a gaming console is that much easier if a comprehensive collection of
films or games is available.

> Despite higher prices, consumers can be better off because compatibil-
> ity allows them to assemble systems that are closer to their ideal con-
> figurations (Gilbert, 1992, 1).

The providers' endeavor must thus be to recognize complementary relations between single components and to achieve indirect network effects (Fritz, 2004,
193). In case of limited complementarity, additional components are very useful,
and in case of strict complementarity they are even required, since without them
the basic good would not be bought. The provider's paramount concern is thus to

put (indirect) network effects in motion in the first place. He must make sure that all the strictly complementary components are available to the customers.

20.2   Starting Points for Creating Indirect Network Effects

A possibility for exploiting complementary relationships between different components for creating network effects which we already know is the bundling strategy, in which two or more components are offered in a package and offered at a total price.

> A bundling strategy can be used by the firm to link the primary product
> with other compatible ancillary products, reinforcing positive feedback
> and thereby increasing the demand for both (Lee & O'Connor, 2003,
> 249).

Should a provider be unable to offer the required (strict) complements from his own product line, he must strike up appropriate cooperative partnerships. Nokia chose this path for its gaming cellphone N-Gage and cooperated with game providers in order to be able to make an attractive system offer for the launch of their product. In parallel, Nokia developed the online platform Ovi as a limited complement.

In general, it is to be assumed that without an attractive (minimum) offer of complements, system products will not be economically successful (Dietl & Royer, 2000, 328). Schilling (2002) was able to confirm this empirically on the example of diverse hardware and software offers.

However, indirect network effects now lead to a "chicken-and-egg" problem if hardware and software are offered by different companies and the provider of the basic good must rely on independent complementors (Gupta et al., 1999, 397 with further sources).

> The chicken-and-egg problem arises because hardware firms want
> complementors to spur sales of new hardware products by offering a
> wide selection of software for the new products, but complementors in
> turn want to wait until the new hardware products have achieved sig-
> nificant market penetration, before committing to the new hardware
> platforms. Neither the hardware firms nor the software complementors
> want to move first to invest in market creation (Gupta et al., 1999, 397).

This problem can be found on many markets (see Table 20.1). As of now, we can observe it in Amazon's endeavors in the establishment of eBooks. Amazon offers access to several hundred thousand electronically available titles for its hardware, the Kindle 2.0, as well as subscriptions to magazines and blogs (Postinett, 2009). In order for indirect network effects to arise, the basic good and the complements are needed simultaneously, as the customer would want to buy them at the same time and not with a time delay between the two. Compared with the first eBook reader, the Rocket eBook, which entered the market in 1999 and left it shortly afterward, Amazon has a good starting position regarding their technology and their content base. The bargaining power as the world's biggest bookseller secures the basic offer of content, which is so important for success. Whether the small variety of reading devices–apart from Amazon, Sony has a large market share–and the prominently book-based content will be enough to lead to success, remains to be seen. Google is competing strongly, currently making around 1.5m titles available for cellphones via Google Book Search (Postinett, 2009). A new standardization struggle is in the works.

Market	Basic Good Provider	Complement Provider	Form of "Chicken-and-Egg" Problem
DVD Players	Hardware providers, e.g. Sony, RCA, Philips	• Film studios • Video rental services	Sales of DVD players vs. content and availability of rental movies
Personal Digital Assistants (PDAs)	Hardware providers, e.g. Apple, 3Com, Casio	• Independent software providers	PDA sales vs. software applications
eBooks	Hardware providers, e.g. Softbook, RocketBook, Everybook	• Book publishers	Prevalence of eBooks vs. availability of content
Network Computers	Hardware providers, e.g. Oracle, IBM, Sun	• Independent Java software programmers	Sales of network computers vs. Java-based applications
Operating Systems	Providers of operating systems, e.g. Microsoft, Apple, Sun	• Hardware providers • Independent software providers	Installed base of operating systems vs. availability of hardware and software

Table 20.1: Examples for Chicken-and-Egg Problems on Markets with Indirect Network Effects. Source: Following Gupta et al., 1999, 398.

Gupta et al. (1999) demonstrate how existentially important an attractive offer of complements is on the example of television. Sales of color television sets, which for a long time had proceeded rather slowly, increased abruptly after a broad offer of TV programs in color became available (Gupta et al., 1999, 412 et seq.). The authors arrive at the conclusion that the same principle holds for digital television (HDTV):

> HDTV will be a niche product, and will diffuse slower than originally
> expected due in part to the lack of programming (Gupta et al., 1999,
> 396).

As long as there is an insufficient range of complements, lowering the price for the basic good that is the HDTV television set will not be the key to success either. Other than during the introduction of the fax machine, where direct network effects were meant to take hold and lowered prices managed to act as drivers, the focus here is on indirect network effects. The customers want television and programming. Premature price reductions will only lead to unnecessary losses, and not to a fast upgrading of the complement offer (Gupta et al., 1999, 411 et seq.).

A very central role in dealing with complements is taken by signaling. Product announcements in particular are an extremely effective instrument for making complementors provide an appropriate range of complements for a basic good. This will be discussed further in Chapter 22 on Signaling.

20.3 Strategic Variants of the Complement Range

Here, too, a provider must decide–similarly to the behavior options in the standardization competition described in Chapter 19–how the offer of complements should come about. The fundamental variants to choose from are the sole provider strategy and the cooperation strategy (Ehrhardt, 2001, 170 et seq.).

The **sole provider** creates a minimum offer of complementary goods by himself. This is the case, for example, if the manufacturer of a basic good, such as a gaming console or a CD/DVD player, provides a sufficient amount of video games, music or films in time for the product launch. This is what Nintendo does in developing its own games, and Sony in providing Blu-Ray discs with in-house content (Sony-BMG). If the provider does not have sufficient competences for creating complements by himself, but sufficient financial means, forward integration will be an option, in which other companies are taken over as strategic acquisitions. This is the path Sony chose in order to provide content for the CD and the Minidisc: in 1987, it bought CBS Records. The purchasing price of $2bn, which was extremely high at the time, showed what great significance Sony ascribed to the offer of complementary products (Grindley, 1995, 121). If the offers of the basic good and the complements come from a single source, the possible innovation transfer will bring about clear advantages. One reason for the strong market position of Microsoft Office as a complement for the operating system Windows is the fact that Microsoft knows earlier than other providers which new features will appear in a Windows update, meaning that the development of the application software can be adjusted much earlier and more precisely (Kurian & Burgelman, 1996, 283). The risk of engaging in two markets is double, though, as apart from the basic good, one has to assume the burden of any malinvestments in developing the range of complements.

The **cooperation strategy** is different: the more partners one can get on board for providing complements, the more broadly the risk can be spread. A very successful example of cooperation is that of Microsoft and AOL (Ehrhardt, 2001, 173 et seq.). Microsoft's Internet Explorer became the standard browser for AOL in 1996 via a cooperation agreement. In return, AOL was allowed to place its logo on the Windows interface instead of Microsoft Network (MSN) and was thus made the default online service. The annoying competitor Netscape was thus relegated to runner-up, even though Microsoft entered the browser market at a relatively late stage. Such strategic partnerships or alliances can also involve many different parties. Toshiba and Sony both chose this path in supporting their DVD successor technologies, rallying companies from consumer electronics as well as the computer, gaming and media industry round them in order to support their format. Sony managed to build the more potent alliance and emerged victorious.

Additionally, Shapiro and Varian (1999, 23) recommend that the provider of a basic good create as lively a competition for complementary offers as possible. An intense competition should lead to a differentiated product range and low prices, which will ultimately benefit sales of the basic good. The strategies used here can, but don't have to, involve providing complements oneself. Microsoft, for instance, has for years been pursuing the strategy of buying up successful product developments (Shapiro & Varian, 1999, 23). Many startups in the software industry even actively pursue the goal of being taken over by Microsoft after a successful start.

Another variant of invigorating the market can consist of subsidizing complementors. 3DO, the first provider of 32-bit CD-ROM hardware and software technology for video games, pursued this path (Nalebuff & Brandenburger, 1996, 113 et seq.). In order to heat up the competition between the hardware providers, licenses for manufacturing hardware were given out for free, whereupon a crowd of providers entered the market. In order to force sales, sluggish at first, and to build up an installed base more quickly, 3DO began to additionally subsidize the hardware prices. The necessary impetuses for price reduction consisted of investment offers in 3DO and the software licensing fees. In order to support the range of games on offer, 3DO began developing their own. In spite of this sophisticated strategy, 3DO was unable to dominate the market, as Sega and Sony established themselves as competitors too early, before Nintendo took the next technological step shortly after in developing its 64-bit hardware.

Here we can link to our previous deliberations in standardization. The creation of standards is a very effective option for driving the creation of complementary offers by third parties forward. Here it is not the compatibility between different basic goods, but that between basic good and complement which is important.

Compatible components benefit the occurrence and effectiveness of indirect network effects:

> Standardization feeds the reinforcing cycle between primary and ancillary products, since compatibility is normally maintained by adhering to a common technological standard (Lee & O'Connor, 2003, 243).

20.4   Conclusion

- In order to create, transmit and play information goods, they pretty much always require technical devices. As a consumer, one is thus dependent on appropriate complements. The competition is thus between systems of goods.
- Without an attractive minimum offer of complements, economic success for system products is not to be expected.
- Depending on the necessity of co-usage, there is limited, strong and strongest complementarity.
- The range of complements necessary for system goods can be provided in different ways. As a sole provider, the one can do so oneself. In the cooperation strategy, one seeks out partners for providing the range of complements jointly.

20.5   Bibliography

Dietl, H., & Royer, S. (2000). Management virtueller Netzwerkeffekte in der Informationsökonomie. Zeitschrift für Organisation, 69(6), 324-331.

Ehrhardt, M. (2001). Netzwerkeffekte, Standardisierung und Wettbewerbsstrategie. Wiesbaden: Dt. Univ.-Verl. (Gabler Edition Wissenschaft: Strategische Unternehmungsführung).

Faßler, M. (2002). Was ist Kommunikation. 2nd ed. München: Fink.

Fritz, W. (2004). Internet-Marketing und Electronic Commerce. Grundlagen - Rahmenbedingungen - Instrumente. 3rd ed. Wiesbaden: Gabler (Gabler-Lehrbuch).

Gilbert, R. J. (1992). Symposium on compatibility: Incentives and market structure. The Journal of Industrial Economics, 40(1), 1-8.

Grindley, P. C. (1995). Standards Strategy and Policy. Cases and Stories. Oxford: Oxford Univ. Press.

Gupta, S., Jain, D.C., & Sawhney, M. (1999). Modeling the evolution of markets with indirect network externalities: An application to digital television. Marketing Science, 18(3), 396-416.

Huber, F., & Kopsch, A. (2002). Produktbündelung. In Albers, S., & Herrmann, A. (eds.), Handbuch Produktmanagement. Strategieentwicklung - Produktplanung - Organisation–Kontrolle (pp. 615-646). 2nd ed. Wiesbaden: Gabler,.

Kurian, T., & Burgelman, R. A. (1996). The operating-system software industry in 1994. In Burgelman, R. A., Maidique, M. A., & Wheelwright, S. C. (eds.), Strategic Management of Technology and Innovation (pp. 275-295). 2nd ed. Chicago, Il: Irwin.

Lee, Y., & O´Connor, G.C. (2003). New product launch strategy for network effects. Journal of the Academy of Marketing Science, 31(3), 241-255.

Nalebuff, B. J., & Brandenburger, A. M. (1996). Coopetition - kooperativ konkurrieren. Mit der Spieltheorie zum Unternehmenserfolg. Frankfurt am Main: Campus-Verlag.

Postinett, A. (2009). Amazon bringt verbesserten E-Bookreader. Handelsblatt, 28, 02/10/2009.

Pross, H. (1972). Medienforschung. Film, Funk, Presse, Fernsehen. Darmstadt: Habel.

Schilling, M. A. (2002). Technology success and failure in winner-take-all markets: the impact of learning orientation, timing, and network externalities. Academy of Management Journal, 45(2).

Shapiro, C., & Varian, H.R. (1999). The art of standards wars. California Management Review, 41(2), 8-32.

Stelzer, D. (2000). Digitale Güter und ihre Bedeutung in der Internet-Ökonomie. WISU, 6, 835-842.

Chapter 21

Copy Protection Management

21.1 Development of Copyright for Information Goods

Information goods satisfy information needs. Whoever wants to make money by selling information goods has a great interest in the consumer acquiring his desired information in the designated fashion, and not just taking it without supervision: music providers want to sell their CDs or downloads, publishers their books and magazines and the film industry their films, on DVD or in the cinema. Unpaid copying is the bête noire of all these kinds of providers. The most common term is piracy, which is incorrect from a legal point of view as no violence is used by the copier's appropriation of an information good. It seems more appropriate to speak of bootlegging.

If we look back in history, we can see that from the ancient world up until the middle ages, it was common practice to take information that one had acquired and alter or develop it further at one's guise. A document or book wasn`t allowed to be stolen in those days, but its content was not subject to protection. The invention of the printing press in the mid-15th century then made it relatively easy to create larger numbers of copies. This facilitated the distribution of information goods, but created financial problems for the printers, who were the providers. They had to invest in their machinery, and in their authors' work, but could not be sure that their product would not be copied by others once it became available. In consequence, printers demanded protective rights, which they were also increasingly granted (Neubert, 2005, 9). Later, the authors were also granted ever-increasing rights to their intellectual work, which they could cede to a publisher for money (Gehring, 2008). At the beginning of the 18th century, the first modern copyright law was passed in England in the form of the Statute of Anne (Tallmo, 2003).

The development of copyright was and is a permanent balancing act between private and public interests. The creator of a work has an interest in its valorization on the market, as he wants to be (financially) compensated for its usage. The possible danger of a continued, gratuitous usage lies in the creator of a work losing interest in further production, which can lead to a shortage of information goods. The public, on the other hand, has an interest in the most comprehensive and cheap–ideally free–distribution of a poem, painting or piece of music etc.

The legal protection of intellectual property was introduced for the benefit of the creator. It was adjusted and readjusted over time, with the tendency toward more strictness. A fundamental reason for this is due to the increasingly easier possibilities for reproducing information goods. Where it used to be a long and arduous process, for example, to copy books, the invention of the photocopier has made it extremely easy to reproduce documents. The copy problem has been exacerbated by the unending march of digitalization; copies of digital information goods can be made with no loss in quality, which leads to no differences between original and copy being distinguishable.

21.2   Digital Rights Management Systems (DRMS)

The providers of information goods are meeting the simplified means of reproduction in two ways. On the one hand, they have an interest in strengthening legal protection. This can be clearly recognized in the changes to German copyright and the industry associations' commentaries. The 1965 version still allowed the fashioning of a copy for private consumption. In the current version, however, a private copy is only allowed if no copy protection measures must be circumvented to create it. Nevertheless, industry lobbyists still regard copyright as not restrictive enough. Another approach to safeguarding one's rights is through patents. They play an important role as software patents, or patents of computer-implemented inventions, for example, in order to secure a product–or at least the parts of it that represent a technological innovation.

Apart from legal protection, information providers also have means of protecting their products technologically. These aim at preventing the unlawful use of information goods, making copying impossible or at least being able to track which original spawned which copies. The copy protection system Lenslok was used for game software as early as the 1980s, for example. Here the user had to enter a code, displayed on the screen in encrypted form, which could only be read through a special pair of glasses–which were part of the software package–before he could start playing. Another example is the analog copy protection method for VHS video systems developed by Macrovision in 1983. Here an interfering signal is added during recording, making further copies of the same tape impossible with devices that used the method.

If technological and legal components are used together in order to allow the copyright holder to manage the rights to his information goods, we speak of Digital Rights Management (DRM) (Picot, 2005, 3). This refers to

> procedures that help protect rights to digital products in the same way that we are accustomed to from intellectual property tied to physical media. Copy and circulation must be tied to the copyright holder's, i.e. the content provider's, rules (Grimm, 2003, 97).

If we look back on the public-good problem of information goods, we can see quite clearly what the use of digital rights management is meant to achieve: it is supposed to make it possible to exclude unlawful usage and thus prevent the mutation of originally private goods to public goods. Information goods to be distributed commercially do not suffer from the problem of usage rivalry–in fact, they show positive network effects in most cases–but from the lack of excludability, which makes it very hard, or impossible even, for the copyright holder to make usage of his information good contingent upon the payment of a fee.

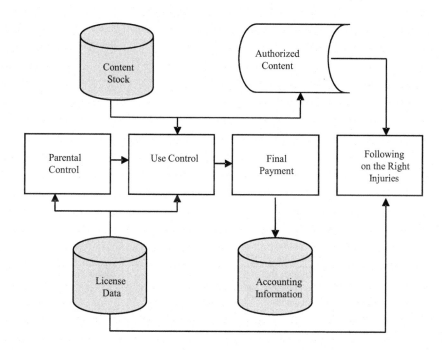

Figure 21.1: Architecture of DRM Systems. Source: Hess, 2005, 19.

In order to secure these rights, digital information goods require the simultaneous management of several functions (Hess et al., 2004a, 55). Information providers must pre-emptively control access (who is using?) and usage kind (how is it being used?), while at the same time–downstream of usage–being able to trace copyright infractions.

Complementary billing functions pave the way toward generating usage-dependent revenue (Hess, 2005, 19). If all these functions are technologically integrated in a system, we speak of Digital Rights Management Systems (DRMS).

Function	Short Description	Protection Technology	Application Examples
Access and usage control	Controls who has access to the content and how the content is being used.	• Encryption • Passwords • Product activation	• Video DVDs (Content Scrambling System–CSS) • Online games • Software
Protecting authenticity and integrity	Securing the content via security tags that are inseparably connected to the information good.	Digital watermarks, digital fingerprints, digital signature	Photos, audio/video files Audio/video/text files
Identification via metadata	Allows the exact identification of an object such as digital content, copyright holder and user.	--	--
Rights Expression Language	Describes the kind and extent of access and usage rights as well as the necessary billing information in a machine-readable fashion.	Xtensibl Rights Markup Language (XrML), Open Digital Rights Language (ODRL)	--
Copy recognition systems	Search engines that scour the networks for illegal copies.	Search engines, watermarks	Audio, video
Payment systems	Legitimization procedure for payment settlement.	User registration, credit card authentification	Online shops
Special hardware and software	Hardware and software in terminal devices used to protect digital information goods from unlawful usage.	Set-top boxes/ Smart cards Dongles Music management software	Pay-TV Software iTunes

Table 21.1: Functions and Protection Technologies of DRMS.

In order to be able to really control access and usage, the provider must consult the corresponding licensing data that define usage rights. To recognize copyright infractions, it is necessary for information goods to contain identifications that should be unremovable, if possible, and for the billing procedure, the required user data must be available for identification and completing the payment process. There are different protection technologies available for each of these functions in a DRMS (Fetscherin & Schmid, 2003, 317; Fränkl & Karpf, 2004, 29 et seq.), an overview of which is provided in Table 21.1.

How a DRM system is built up in specific detail is shown in Figure 21.2 on the example of the Windows Media Player. This application is available for free, and is preinstalled on many Windows PCs. It serves to play video and audio files on one's computer. The Media Player's DRMS functionalities are contained within the Microsoft Media Rights Manager.

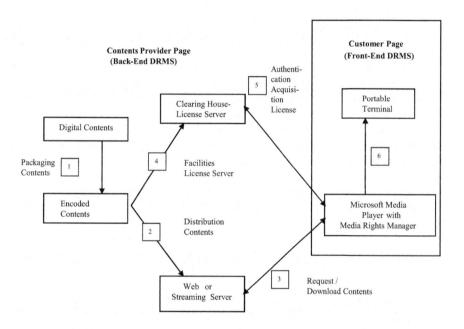

Figure 21.2: Architecture of Microsoft's Windows Media Player. Source: Schumann & Hess, 2006, 104, following Pruneda, 2003.

The functionality is as follows (Pruneda, 2003): In Step 1, the digital content is encrypted by the provider as a Windows Media File. Next (Step 2), the content is offered, securely, via web or streaming servers. In Step 3, the users can download the content. The user's software recognizes that the content is protected and establishes a connection with the licensing server (Step 4), through which the user (Step 5) can acquire a license for a fee. After the payment is received, the license is released and the user can play the content (Step 6). If the user sends the Media File to another user via e-mail, the latter must buy his own license before being able to access the file.

21.3   Advantages and Disadvantages of DRMS

Now what advantages and disadvantages can be observed in the use of DRM systems? Generally, there is a fundamental difference between the interests of customers and those of the providers. Let us first consider the **customers**:

> Consumers generally reject any control over their media consumption and request interoperable and user-friendly solutions, if anything (Hess et al., 2004a, 55).

It can be shown empirically that customers highly value the up-to-dateness and exclusivity of content. Willingness to pay is reduced strongly, though, if the transmission or usage entails technological difficulties (Fetscherin, 2003, 309). Such difficulties might be that the acquired information good is not playable on all devices. If the music CD can be played on a CD player, but will not run on a PC or in the car, consumers will regard this as a major nuisance. Additionally, the installation of DRM clients, which may even have to be separately acquired in the first place, whose functionality must be learned and for which licensing conditions may have to be checked, all significantly curtail the product's usefulness in the consumer's mind (Hess et al., 2004a, 56). Figure 21.3 clearly shows that the rejection rates for different kinds of usage constraint are very high.

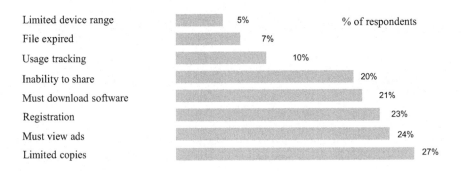

Which constraints would you accept?

	% of respondents
Limited device range	5%
File expired	7%
Usage tracking	10%
Inability to share	20%
Must download software	21%
Registration	23%
Must view ads	24%
Limited copies	27%

Figure 21.3: Acceptance of Usage Constraints. Source: Fetscherin, 2003, 316.

The DRMS currently in use are generally to be considered as user-**un**friendly (Bizer et al., 2005, 196 et seq.). They are mutually incompatible and generate severe data protection problems. An extreme example of the implementation of providers' interest in protection is the Super Audio CD:

> Heard of DVD-Audio or Super Audio CD? Probably not, yet both formats were touted earlier this decade as successors to the Compact Disc, each offering superbly detailed audio and music in surround sound. There are many factors to blame for the general lack of interest in the DVD-A and SACD, but it was probably the need to connect six(!) individual analog cables between the player and the rest of the system that convinced most everyday consumers to stick it out with their old-fashioned CDs. The record companies were so paranoid that a digital connection would make it too easy to clone a disc that they insisted on a hookup that required a spaghetti bowl of wires and a degree in electrical engineering to configure properly. Most people couldn't be bothered, so they stayed away (Pachal, 2006).

The use of protection mechanisms is accepted by the consumer if it serves to increase usefulness. This is the case, for instance, if protected songs or films that cannot be copied are pre-released. In June of 2002, the music industry, using DRM, tried out such a form of Follow-the-free with the band Oasis:

> On June 23, nearly two million Britons opened their Sunday edition of the London Times and found a free CD containing three not-yet-released song clips from the band's new album. But this was no ordinary promotional CD: Using new digital content controls, Sony had encoded it with instructions that, in effect, banned people from playing the three clips for more than just a few times on their home PCs. Fans also were unable to copy the music file and post it to file-sharing networks—thereby making it harder to steal. Oasis fans who wanted to hear more had to link to the band's Web site and preorder the new album from U.K.-based retailer HMV—or wait until it was released. The idea: Use software code not to ban, but to create buzz for new products without getting burned in the process. Did it work for Oasis? Preorders of the album exceeded company expectations by 30,000 during the week following the Sunday Times' promotion, and Oasis' record company gained data from 50,000 fans who registered online—new information that could be used to sell more CDs in the future. HMV was able to raise the number of visitors to its retail Web site, and even the Sunday Times was able to score a win in the deal: Circulation that day was 300,000—its second-highest Sunday circulation ever (Marks, 2002).

This free audio sample generated network effects that benefited not only the band, but also the participating complementors. As this example does not represent a usage constraint on a bought good but on a free offer, i.e. a sort of gift, the use of DRM did not meet the kind of rejection mentioned above in this case.

As opposed to the customers, **information providers** have a vested interest in preventing the usage of their goods counter to specifications. DRMS can help, as–depending on how restrictively the system is designed–only legitimized users have access. In such a case, bootleg copies can only be created with great effort, contingent upon the circumvention of the protection mechanisms at work.

Information providers face a certain dilemma in using DRM, as DRM aims for the bootlegger but always hits–as collateral damage–the paying customers via the control and usage constraints that ensue. In the most favorable case–assuming a perfectly functioning DRMS–the customers could merely say that they are not worse off with DRM than without it. To use DRMS is also only worth the effort if the excluded bootleggers actually have a willingness to pay of greater than zero, thus representing a potential source of revenue. Should this not be the case, the resulting effects will be negative on balance: the company downgrades the offer to interested customers while failing to compensate for the loss of profit by excluding bootleggers.

Information providers must thus consider carefully which access and usage conditions they want their products to enter the market with. Let us consider, following Shapiro and Varian (1999, 98 et seq.), the initial case of a provider who offers his information goods with DRM and makes a certain profit (A: initial case).

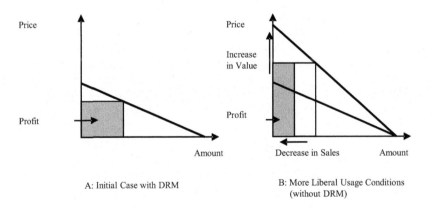

A: Initial Case with DRM

B: More Liberal Usage Conditions (without DRM)

Figure 21.4: Trade-Off Between the Increase of the Use Value and the Sales Figures. Source: Following Shapiro & Varian, 1999, 99.

If this provider were now to go without DRM, this would increase the use value for the customers. As we have already seen above, this is a very realistic perspective, as the demanders can then use the information good (film, music title etc.) on any device, without any technological restrictions, and even copy (on a small scale), lend or resell it, all within the framework of the applicable copyright, of course. The higher use value thus leads to a greater willingness to pay, and the demand curve goes up (Case B). If sales stay the same, the profits will increase. In the displayed model, the demand rises twofold, i.e. profits would double.

Strube et al. (2008) show, via an empirical analysis of online music, that these model statements are correct. Foregoing DRM raises the use value for the customer, as would sound quality or lower prices–further, less important parameters. An unchanged price of 99 cents per song will, without DRM, more than quintuple profits. Thus without DRM, there are possibilities for raising prices, which favors further increases in profit.

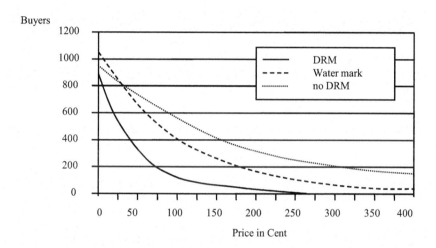

Figure 21.5: Price-Sales Function for Different Degrees of DRM Protection without Bootleg Copies. Source: Strube et al., 2008, 1053.

However, foregoing DRM also has other effects on sales figures. If we assume that the absence of DRM will lead to more (legal and bootleg) copies and fewer sales, turnover will decrease. The above model estimates that sales will be halved. How this affects profits depends on the relation between the decrease in sales and the price increase. In our example, profits stay the same. Without DRM, half the amount is sold at twice the price. This, according to Shapiro and Varian, represents a trade-off: more liberal offer conditions facilitate a higher-priced offer while leading to fewer sales. However, Shapiro and Varian assume, in their model, that the overall demand will remain unchanged, i.e. that the saturation quantity stays the same. Against this, we can say that the absence of DRM will not only increase the use value for the existing interested potential buyers, but that there is also as a yet unused market potential. We are talking about people who–even at a price of zero–had shown no previous interest in a DRM-protected product, e.g. because the terminal device compatibility was unsatisfactory, or because the creation of copies is prohibited. If this customer circle then unveils further demand, the saturation quantity will shift to the right and the market will even grow. If we look once more at the results of Stube et al. (2008, 1053-1054)'s analysis, we can say that the higher profits resulting from the absence of DRM more than makes up for the losses incurred by illegal copies. On the one hand, customers' willingness to pay is much higher; on the other hand, the saturation quantity is increased significantly, i.e. there are more buyers.

However, there is yet another approach to increasing the use value and thus the market volume: easing the rights. So far, we have concentrated on the renunciation of technological copy protection methods, which will then no longer have to be circumvented. Yet as information provider, one also has the option of easing the existing legal regulations oneself, by defining oneself the degree of (legal) protection regarding content. In addition to the known legal regulations, Creative Commons, already mentioned in Chapter 5, here provide an alternative framework for the release and distribution of digital media content in the form of tiered licensing agreements.

21.4   Copy Protection and Network Effects

Now there are some interesting cases in which a provider may even draw a profit from a free distribution of his product via either legal or illegal copies by the end consumers. To wit, it is always of great advantage for the provider to have a large installed base when selling goods that demonstrate pronounced network effects.

Conner and Rumelt (1991) show, on the example of **software**, that piracy can make a positive contribution, particularly for programs that are complex and difficult to operate, which require a customizer, or which lend themselves to simultaneous use by many users (Conner & Rumelt, 1991, 137). This includes spreadsheet applications, more complex text processors, as well as database or desktop publishing programs. In these cases, the product's protection leads to a diminished installed base that is of disadvantage for both customer and provider, when customers either abstain from buying or (bootleg) copying. It can thus be of advantage for the provider to accept piracy as an additional cheap distribution path next to traditional sales. Distribution via copies even gives the provider a cost advantage, as he can save marketing expenses (Peitz & Waelbroeck, 2004), and it is not him but the user who invests time and money in the creation and distribution of the copies (Conner & Rumelt, 1991, 137). If we then assume that these are mainly people with no, or a very small, willingness to pay, who could not have been enticed to buy in any case, this is a viable alternative for quickly building up a large installed base. Model-supported analyses for software by Shy (2000), Blackburn (2002), as well as Gayer and Shy (2003), confirm this assumption. It can be shown that goods displaying strong direct or indirect network effects can profit from bootlegging, as the installed base will grow faster with than without illegal copies. This increases consumers' willingness to pay and thus enables the provider to compensate for lost profits. Tolerating bootlegging thus facilitates a kind of price differentiation in which the provider gives customers with a low willingness to pay the (tolerated) option of acquiring the desired product via copying. In this way, the provider can profit from a growing network without having to offer a uniformly low price to all customers. As the network increases in size, he can then enforce measures of product protection and perhaps even increase prices (Sundararajan, 2004, 302 et seq.).

For providers who carry both the basic good and its necessary complements, it may be advisable to turn a blind eye to bootlegging. Gürtler (2005) analyzes this via a model of the video game market. Here it transpires that the

> ...enabling of product piracy is a device to shift reservation prices from the software market to the more important market for video games hardware (Gürtler, 2005, 22).

Caution should be exercised when using this strategy, however, if the overall offer of games suffers from piracy, i.e. if other software companies are less inclined to produce games for hardware providers that tolerate bootlegging.

If the provider holds a strong position on the complementary market, wholesale copying may even represent an alternative to sales (Blackburn, 2002, 86). This approach, which is tantamount to giving the product away (Follow-the-free), is profitable if it leads to increased demand on the complementary market, which overcompensates for lost profits from the basic good. Here we can link to our remarks on versioning in Chapter 18, where the basic good (e.g. Acrobat Reader) is given away and the higher-end product version (Acrobat Writer) is sold.

There are also some interesting examples for **content**, where the free distribution–via legal copies in this case–has led to a market success that would likely not have been achieved otherwise.

The label Reprise–a subsidiary of Warner–offered a few songs from the second album of their band My Chemical Romance (Anderson, 2007, 123-124) for free on websites such as AbsolutePunk.net or MySpace five months before the release date. The persons in charge were able to observe how the band's fans began downloading and sharing the songs. This information served as a pointer to which single should be released next. That song was soon played on the radio due to further fan support and later became the hit of that summer. The following tour was complemented by further audio and video material, which led to the album becoming one of the year's biggest sellers.

A similar case is Radiohead, who, after their contractual obligations to EMI ceased, put their seventh album on the market by themselves. It could be downloaded for free on a special website (www.inrainbows.com); an innovative feature was that the users could set their own price. Information provided by the online service Comscore (Gavin, 2007) revealed that around 40% of users worldwide were willing to pay for the download. The average price was £2.93. For the band, this amounted to an average profit well above the usual $1 that is earned via record-label distribution of an album (Schmalz, 2009, 72).

In both of these cases, the bands commanded a fan base they were able to activate via the free offers and which then helped them succeed in the long run.

The British band Arctic Monkeys even managed to succeed without this basis (Heilmann, 2006). Their debut album immediately soared to the top of the English charts, buoyed by extensive concert tours and free downloads via MySpace.

The band Nine Inch Nails recorded a similar success with their album Ghosts I-IV, which is offered under a Creative Commons license. Despite free online access, the album led the list of bestselling CDs on Amazon in 2008 (Gehlen, 2009). Currently, all songs from Ghosts are streamed on the band's homepage, the first nine titles can be downloaded for free and the different album versions bought for between $5 and $300 (Nine Inch Nails, 2011). The limited ultra-deluxe version alone netted the band around $750,000.

Common to all the above examples is that they went without product protection. Instead, their motto is "please copy". This form of offer generates reach, an installed base, and thence positive network effects that lead to a quickened proliferation of the songs. Once the threshold to the mass media radio and TV has been crossed, further success is very probable.

As an information provider, one now has the heavy task of estimating what concrete effect a loosening of copyright will have on one's sales figures. Should one go without DRM and rely on pure legal protection ("all rights reserved"), but energetically enforce it? Or should one officially invoke one's rights yet be secretly grateful for the bootleggers' support? Or does one aggressively build an installed base, exploit one's product for free–wholly or in part–and perhaps even waives a part of one's protective rights by using Creative Commons licenses ("some rights reserved")?

Let us again draw upon Shapiro's and Varian's thoughts on trading-off: if willingness to pay and sales change proportionally, profits will stay the same. In that case, the provider could happily save the costs of DRM and thus increase his overall profit. If, on the other hand, only (bootleg) copies increase, there will be no profits in sales and the use of DRM would be advisable for the provider. Yet if sales without DRM, or using Creative Commons licenses, only decrease less than proportionately, or market volume actually increases and network effects are created, it will be extremely recommendable to offer information goods without any particular protection.

Conversely, the introduction of DRM to a previously unprotected product does not merely represent the opposite case. On the one hand, the use value is decreased by the technological and legal restrictions, which in turn decreases willingness to pay. The provider should thus always take care to design DRM systems in such a way that they do not encroach on the product's use value for legal users (Sundararajan, 2004, 303). On the other hand, it cannot be simply assumed that sales of legal copies will just increase as intended. This is only the case if there is a corresponding number of bootleggers who have a positive willingness to pay for the information good and are prepared to turn to legal consumption.

So far, though, there are no concrete recommendations that could give an information provider specific advice. More generally, King and Lampe (2002) observe, on the subject of profitable piracy in the face of network effects, that it is always better to actively practice price differentiation than to tolerate bootlegging. They regard the danger of customers with a high willingness to pay resorting to illegal copies as too high. If a company has the option of differentiating between potential bootleggers and potential customers, it should, according to them, also protect the product and make an attractive offer of payment to the former as well, even on a low level. If the contingent of bootleggers is not too large and their willingness to pay for the product is low, it is even advisable to give the product away for free (King & Lampe, 2002, 16 et seq.).

> Price discrimination allows the firm to exploit any network benefits from spreading use of their product while also raising revenue (King & Lampe, 2002, 24).

It is highly recommended to combine price differentiation with versioning, which is very easy to implement for information goods. For instance, if customers value complementary services to a product, they will only be able to buy the desired product, as these services are not available for an illegal copy. Gayer and Shy (2003, 200 et seq.) demonstrate on a simple model that the free distribution of lower-quality versions of information goods has a positive effect on sales and profits of the priced version.

If customer group differentiation, and hence price differentiation, is not an option, tolerating piracy can represent a profit-increasing alternative, but only if the ability to bootleg is in inverse proportion to willingness to pay; i.e., if it is to be assumed that those who are able to create illegal copies with ease are the ones who would not be willing to pay for the product anyway. Castro et al. (2008, 80) here speak of an "overlap" between the legal and illegal markets, which must not become too large if profitability is to be protected.

> The greater the overlap between the markets of customers for legal versions of the product and customers for pirated versions, the more piracy reduces sales of legal versions.

On the other hand, potential bootleggers must not gain too large a share of the overall market (King & Lampe, 2002, 5). It can be added here that the price level has an influence on the readiness to not buy information goods but to copy them (illegally), which increases in proportion to the product prices (Gehrke et al., 2002).

It must also be noted that the usual, usage-restricting use of DRMS leads not only to rising transaction costs, but also increases manufacturing costs. If these are passed down to the customers in the form of higher prices, the effect will be reduced sales. In the extreme case, the use of DRMS may even render the exchange of certain information goods no longer economically viable (Gehrke et al., 2002).

In summary, we can say so far that looser product protection increases the use value for and thus the willingness to pay of the customers. Furthermore, it is to be assumed that market volume will increase correspondingly. Increased sales volumes (including (bootleg) copies) will then also lead to increased network effects. This means that the average consumer's valuation of the information good will increase due to its increasing prevalence. Blackburn speaks, on the example of music, of an awareness effect:

> This awareness effect is essentially a network effect–however, rather than increasing the valuation of individual customers, the increased number of listeners increases the share of the consumers who are aware of the artist, thus raising the valuation of the average customer (Blackburn, 2004, 10).

This, in turn, contributes to further (legal and/or illegal) distribution. How pronounced this distribution caused by network effects will be should, among other factors, depend on their strength. Apart from this, the sampling effect surely plays a role, as once an information good (song, film, game etc.) has been tried out and experienced with no strings attached, any positive valuation of it will only make a purchase more probable (Blackburn, 2004, 9; Strube et al., 2008, 1045).

Wu and Chen (2008, 170) explicitly recommend using versioning in combination with legal and technological measures of protection to defend against bootlegging. On the one hand, this will allow companies, via market expansion, to gain customers who would not have committed to buying the product without versioning, and on the other hand bootleggers will be at least partially scared off as the costs of producing illegal copies rise.

> The benefits of versioning ... can come from two sources: from accommodating more customers to the market and from converting pirates into buyers (or discouraging piracy) (Wu & Chen, 2008, 170).

The more noticeable the costs of bootlegging, the better versioning will work. In this respect, the introduction or tightening of legal and/or technological protection methods play into the hands of the versioning provider. Network effects, initially blanked out by Wu and Chen, benefit the profitability of versioning even further.

Thus the circle to the pricing instruments, including versioning, that were already discussed in Chapter 18, and with the help of which customers can be made a very cheap or even free offer in order to build a large installed base, is complete. The higher-grade and more expensive versions that profit from this are then only available for a price. Here again it is shown that the old marketing adage, that the customer is never influenced purely by price or service but by their relation to each other, still holds. Hence this is a broad field for information providers to experiment in.

Common to all the examples of the effects of copying on the provider's profits mentioned above is that they refer to the end consumer who engages in (bootleg) copying. The recommendations concerning the use of copy protection are different if **commercial providers** are active on the market. Poddar (2006) demonstrates on a simple model that it is always advisable for software providers to protect their products as comprehensively as possible, even independently of the quality and reliability of the (commercial) bootlegs. If commercial bootlegs appear alongside the original offer, the result will still be network effects and increased demand for the original product, but the difference to bootlegging by end consumers is that this scenario results in a real competitive situation (Poddar, 2006, 3 et seq.). The consumer can now decide between different, very similar or even identical offers at different prices. The original provider will experience price abatement, meaning that sales will rise but profits drop. According to Poddar (2006, 9), this effect even arises independently of the strength of the network effects. An information provider must then incorporate the additional determinant of whether commercial bootleggers are active on the market in question. This is a regular occurrence, particularly in countries with less-developed economies (Poddar, 2006, 2).

21.5   Media Asset Value Maps

A pragmatic approach to determining the degree of technological protection via DRM is represented by Hess et al. (2004b, 56 et seq.)'s "Media Asset Value Maps". They suggest determining an information good's economic worthiness of protection from both the customer's and the company's perspective. From the **customer's perspective**, it is necessary to weigh the potential for illegal copying, which is influenced by the general interest in the product and the options for technological access. The **interest** represents the desire for, and the **access** the capability of producing copies. Some factors contributing to the desire are the consumers' willingness to pay, the illegal copy's potential loss of added value due to the lack of complements (e.g booklets or call-centre support), transaction costs (search, download, danger of being detected) as well as the presence of substitute goods. The capability, on the other hand, is influenced by the potential copier's technological know-how and specs (dataline bandwidth, hardware equipment). For music, this might mean that it appears more sensible to provide better protection for music aimed at a young, tech-savvy audience than for older listeners with little technological affinity. Thus it can be observed of the–mostly older–fans of German schlager music:

> As opposed to young listeners of pop music, they almost never illegally
> download songs online or copy CDs (Rüdel, 2007).

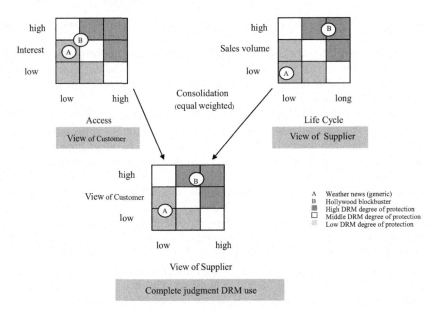

Figure 21.6: "Media Asset Value Maps" from the Customer's and the Company's Perspective. Source: Hess et al., 2004b, 57.

From the **company's perspective**, it is advisable on the one hand to assess **sales potentials** and the **duration of the product life cycle**, up to the end of which profits may be generated, on the other. In terms of profit, one should–departing from Hess et al. (2004b)–not only prognosticate expected sales without bootlegs but also the difference to sales including bootlegs. To determine this difference, the considerations on the effects of bootlegging with regard to network effects mentioned above may be drawn upon. This is to say that only when potential sales including bootlegging are significantly lower should the next step be taken and both perspectives be consolidated in order to arrive at a recommendation for the use of DRM for the information good in question.

For weather reports, which command mid-sized customer interest, have minimal technological access options, small sales potentials and a short life cycle, it is thus not recommended to implement protection methods. For large Hollywood movies, on the other hand, which from a similar customer perspective have high sales potentials as well as a long life cycle, and for which a provider assumes that increased revenue via network effects will not outweigh lost revenue due to piracy, a high degree of DRM protection should be aimed for. Another verdict would apply to music by unknown artists, for which uncontrolled distribution creates network effects, which then lead to profits, in the first place. Here the estimated profits with copy protection should, from the company's perspective, lie below those in which no protection mechanism is used.

The questions of copy protection, so prevalent at the time, might lose weight in the future. On the software market, for instance, there is a trend toward Software on Demand, where the customer no longer has to buy and install the applications; instead, they run on the provider's servers and access is gained online. In such a constellation, bootlegging is no longer possible, and what's more, the provider can even see in detail, via tracking programs, who is using his services to what extent and base his pricing models and bills on the insights thus gleaned. The case is similar for streaming media offers, where the audio or video files are accessed via on-demand or live streams and can be saved on one's PC only with great technological effort.

21.6   Conclusion

- The development of copyright was and is a permanent balancing act between private and public interests.
- Where technological and legal components are used together in order to allow the rights to information goods to be managed by the holder of the rights, we speak of Digital Rights Management (DRM).
- The use of Digital Rights Management Systems (DRMS) is problematic from the customer's perspective. It leads to a lower willingness to pay, as these systems represent a control over media usage and create technologically barriers in the transmission and consumption of content.
- Information providers have a vested interest in quelling any unlawful usage of their goods.
- The use of DRM contains a potential conflict of goals: not using DRM allows higher-priced offers, but can lead to lower sales due to the resulting bootleg copies.
- The use of DRM weakens the occurrence of network effects that could otherwise serve to increase the success of software and content.
- DRM should generally be used if illegal copies are offered commercially.
- Versioning in connection with technological and/or legal protection measures is well suited to increase profitability.
- "Media Asset Value Maps" represent a pragmatic approach to using DRM to determine the degree of technological protection vis-à-vis the end customer.

21.7   Bibliography

Anderson, C. (2007). The long tail. Nischenprodukte statt Massenmarkt. Das Geschäft der Zukunft. München: Hanser.

Becker, E., Buhse, W., & Günnewig, D., et al. (eds.) (2003). Digital Rights Management. Technological, Economic, Legal and Political Aspects. Berlin: Springer (Lecture Notes in Computer Science, 2770).

Bizer, J., Grimm, R., & Jadzejewski, S. (2005). privacy4DRM. Datenschutzverträgliches und nutzungsfreundliches Digital Rights Management. Studie im Auftrag des Bundesministeriums für Bildung und Forschung. Fraunhofer-Institut für Digitale Medientechnologie (IDMT). Unabhängiges Landeszentrum für Datenschutz, Institut für Medien- und Kommunikationswissenschaft. Ilmenau und Kiel. (Online).

Blackburn, D. (2002). Complementarities and network externalities in casually copied goods. Estudios de Economía, 29, 71-88.

Castro, J.O. de; Balkin, D., & Sheperd, D. A. (2008). Can entrepreneurial firms benefit from product piracy. Journal of Business Venturing, 23(1), 75-90.

Conner, K. R., & Rumelt, R.P. (1991). Software piracy. An analysis of protection strategies. Management Science, 37(2), 125-139.

Fetscherin, M. (2003). Evaluating consumer acceptance for protected digital content. In Becker, E., Buhse, W., Günnewig, D., & Rump, N. (eds.), Digital Rights Management. Technological, Economic, Legal and Political Aspects (pp. 301-320). Berlin: Springer (Lecture Notes in Computer Science, 2770).

Fetscherin, M., & Schmid, M. (2003). Comparing the usage of digital rights management systems in the music, film, and print industry. In Sadeh, N. (ed.), ICEC 2003. Fifth International Conference on Electronic Commerce, 50, (pp. 316-325). New York, NY: ACM.

Fränkl, G., & Karpf, P. (2004). Digital Rights Management Systeme. Einführung, Technologien, Recht, Ökonomie und Marktanalyse. 2nd. München: PG Verlag.

Gavin, J. (2007). Nearly Half of all U.K. Downloaders Pay for New Radiohead Album. Comscore (ed.). (Online).

Gayer, A., & Shy, O. (2003). Internet and peer-to-peer distributions in markets for digital products. Economics Letters, 81(2), 197-203.

Gehlen, D. von: Kontrolle ist schlechter. Published by Süddeutsche Zeitung. (Online).

Gehring, R.A. (2008). Einführung ins Urheberrecht. Eine kurze Geschichte. In Djordjevic, V., Gehring, R. A., Grassmuck, V., Kreuter, T., & Spielkamp, M. (eds.), Urheberrecht im Alltag. Kopieren, bearbeiten, selber machen (pp. 239-251). Bonn: Bundeszentrale für Politische Bildung (iRights.INFO, 655).

Gehrke, N., Burghardt, M., & Schumann, M. (2002). Eine mikroökonomische Analyse des Raubkopierens von Informationsgütern. In Weinhardt, C., & Holtmann, C. (eds.), E-Commerce. Netze, Märkte, Technologien (pp. 21-42). Heidelberg: Physica-Verlag.

Grimm, R. (2003). Digital Rights Management. Technisch-organisatorische Lösungsansätze. In Picot, Arnold (ed.), Digital Rights Management (pp. 93-106). Berlin: Springer.

Gürtler, O. (2005). On Strategic Enabling of Product Piracy in the Market for Video Games. Bonn: University of Bonn. (Bonn Econ Discussion Papers, 36). (Online).

Heilmann, D. (2006). Per Internet an die Spitze der Charts. Handelsblatt, 67, 04/04/2006, 20.

Hess, T. (2005). Digital Rights Management Systeme: eine Technologie und ihre Wirkungen. In Picot, A., & Thielmann, H. (eds.), Distribution und Schutz digitaler Medien durch Digital Rights Management (pp. 15-22). Berlin: Springer.

Hess, T., Ünlü, V., Faecks, W.I., & Rauchfuß, F. (2004a). Digitale Rechtemanagement-Systeme. Technische Grundlagen und ökonomische Wirkungen. Information Management & Consulting, 19(3), 53-58.

Hess, T., Ünlü, V., Faecks, W.I., & Rauchfuß, F. (2004b). Rechtemanagement als Lösungsansatz aus dem Digitalen Dilemma. München: Cap Gemini, Ludwigs-Maximilinan Universität. (Online).

King, S. P., & Lampe, R. (September 2002). Network Externalities and the Myth of Profitable Piracy. Intellectual Property Research Institute of Australia. (03/02). (Online).

Marks, S. (2002). Digital Rights Management and the Bottom Line. (Online).

Neubert, C.U (2005). Grundlagen des Urheberrechts. Duderstadt: EPV Elektronik-Praktiker-Verl.-Ges. (IT-Praxis-Reihe für Aus- und Weiterbildung).

Nine Inch Nails (2009). Ghosts. (Online).

Pachal, P. (2006). HD DVD & Blu-Ray: Lessons from Format Wars Past. Dvice. (Online).

Peitz, M., & Waelbroeck, P. (2004). The effect of internet piracy on CD sales: cross-section evidence. CESifo Working Paper (1122). (Online).

Picot, A. (2005). Digital Rights Management - ein einführender Überblick. In Picot, A., & Thielmann, H. (eds.), Distribution und Schutz digitaler Medien durch Digital Rights Management (pp. 1-14). Berlin: Springer.

Poddar, S. (2006). Economics of Digital Piracy - Some Thoughts and Analysis. The Case of Software and Movie Piracy. Department of Economics. Singapore: National University of Singapore. (Onlilne).

Pruneda, A. (2003). Using Windows Media Encoder to Protect Content. Microsoft Corporation. (Online).

Rüdel, N. (2007). Musikindustrie: Die Angst vor weniger Volksmusik im Fernsehen. Welt Online, 08/11/2007. (Online).

Schmalz, G. (2009). No Economy. Wie der Gratiswahn das Internet zerstört. Frankfurt am Main: Eichborn.

Schumann, M., & Hess, T. (2006). Grundfragen der Medienwirtschaft. Eine betriebswirtschaftliche Einführung. 3rd ed. Berlin: Springer (Springer-Lehrbuch).

Shapiro, C., & Varian, H.R. (1999 [1998]). Information Rules. A Strategic Guide to the Network Economy. Boston, MA: Harvard Business School Press.

Shy, O. (2000). The economics of copy protection in software and other media. In Kahin, B., & Varian, H.R. (eds.), Internet Publishing and Beyond. The Economics of Digital Information and Intellectual Property (pp. 97-113). Cambridge, MA: MIT Press.

Strube, J., Pohl, G., & Buxmann, P. (2008). Der Einfluss von Digital Rights Management auf die Zahlungsbereitschaften für Online-Musik - Untersuchung auf

Basis einer Conjointanalyse. In Bichler, M. (ed.), Multikonferenz Wirtschafts-informatik 2008 (pp. 1043-1053). Berlin: Gito-Verlag.

Sundararjan, A. (2004). Managing digital piracy: Pricing and protection. Information Systems Research, 15(3), 287-308.

Tallmo, K.E. (2003). The History of Copyright: The Statute of Anne, 1710. (Online).

Wu, S.Y., & Chen, P.Y (2008). Versioning and piracy control for digital information goods. Operations Research, 56(1), 157-172.

Chapter 22
Signaling

22.1 Market Failure Due to Information Asymmetries

Information asymmetries are present when one side of the market is better informed than the other. Akerlof (1970) demonstrated on the example of used cars that market coordination no longer works as well as it could in such a case. Despite the willingness to buy or sell at a specific price, supply and demand find no way to meet. Such a market failure is the result of the consumer' inability to (adequately) recognize the product quality of an offer, and their willingness to pay thus being lower than would be required to pay the price demanded by the providers. No sale is accomplished, even though the consumers would be willing to pay the asking price if only they estimated the product's quality more highly. It is thus of crucial importance for companies who, compared to other providers, offer higher quality and set correspondingly higher prices, that the customer be able to recognize the former aspect. The customer requires clues to separate high-quality providers from others who sell lesser services, even if the latter pretend to sell high-grade wares, e.g. via advertisements promising quality. The existence of such black sheep leads to welfare losses if either the quality available on the market decreases due to the providers of said quality withdrawing, or if the services on offer deteriorate slowly over time, unnoticed by the customers (Linde, 2008, 39 et seq.). In the former case we speak of "adverse selection", in the latter of "moral hazard". Adverse selection means that the quality of an offer is unchanged from one transaction to the next; moral hazard can occur if providers are in a position to change the quality (Monroe, 2003, 77 et seq.). This is, of course, undesirable if it means deterioration.

22.2 Market Communication via Signals

How, then, can a provider show his customers that he is trustworthy, that his products are in fact as good as he claims they are? This is where signaling comes into play. Companies can use signals to communicate with market participants. Each company active on the market sends signals to the different market players via its behavior. A new product announcement, for instance, is a signal to the customers that they will soon be able to make an attractive purchase, which will be worth the wait. This might result in them abstaining from the competition's current offer. The competitors are signaled, via this announcement, that their product's market position will change due to the new offer. This may lead them to preemptively lower their prices or to speed up their own product development. Complementors and suppliers may be led by this signal to develop hopes for lucrative commissions and thus decline other requests. A mere communicative act can thus directly influence the behavior of the other market players. Signals can also be sent indirectly, for example if companies build production capacities at a particular location, change their prices or enter into an alliance with others.

The concept of signaling dates back to Spence (1973), who represents it as an opportunity to transmit information from the better-informed to the worse-informed market side in case of an asymmetrical distribution. For him, signals are observable characteristics that can yet be influenced by the sender. The duration and quality of a job applicant are examples for a signal in the context of this initial discussion started by Spence. Today, signals are seen as a multiform phenomenon, which is why Grant and Nippa (2006, 150-151) define, with a slightly broader perspective:

> The term signaling is used in order to describe the selective communication of information to competitors or customers [or other market participants, A/N], the aim being to deliberately change their perception, decision-making and behaviors, respectively, in order to provoke or avoid certain reactions.

The necessity of signaling results from existing information asymmetries. There is a downward gradient of information between two market players, in which one side–the company, in this case–is better informed than the others, i.e. customers, competitors etc. Information asymmetries can consist of the company being able to better gauge the quality of its products, or knowing more, earlier, about its strategic aims. Signals can be used to reduce, keep up or even increase such existing asymmetries (McLachlan, 2004). Signals always play a role for unobservable characteristics or intentions about which a creditable statement must be made. If, for instance, the buyer of a software application is not provided with a trial version to convince him of the product quality, one must work with signals instead, e.g. offer him a money-back guarantee or be able to produce good test reports. The customer is thus made more secure in hoping that the product will be as good as advertised. Signals are a tried and tested means for quality providers to show their product quality and thus justify a higher price.

The interests of lower-quality providers, though, swing another way entirely. They would rather conceal the fact that their offers are flawed or even harmful to the consumer. In this context, Parker (1995, 304) mentions the tobacco industry, associations promising life after death and manufacturers of anti-wrinkle creams as typical providers of "lemons", i.e. products that cannot keep their promise of quality or even harm the customer. Such providers have a vested interest in existing information asymmetries be maintained.

Here it becomes clear on the one hand that the quality signals already mentioned have a strategic dimension, and on the other hand that there are other kinds of signals, which are not directed merely to the customers but also to other market players (competitors, suppliers, complementors). Such strategic signals meant to influence the market are of particular significance if a new product is being introduced, a standard created or market entry barriers built up, for example. Signals used in these contexts can be meant to reduce or increase information asymmetries (Irmscher, 1997, 153-154). New product announcements, for instance, initially create market insecurity. The different players may ask themselves what exactly the product will look like, what it can do and how much it will cost on which market. Such a creation of a market asymmetry can be of advantage vis-à-vis the competition, if it helps prevent them from entering the market themselves. The customer, on the other hand, should be signaled early on that it is worth waiting for the new product instead of buying a competing one. If the company has a reputation for providing quality, this will show the customer that he can expect a good product, while the competition's insecurity is increased, as they have to assume that the announced product will, in all probability, be good and hence be accepted by the consumers.

It is obvious that the variety of signals must be handled strategically in order for them to work together to create the intended effects.

Of central importance for every kind of signal is its credibility, and this in turn is dependent on the costs of sending the signal. Signals become more credible in proportion to the costs that would result if they were untrue. Offering warranties is relatively straightforward for a company that produces high-quality wares, as they will be made very little use of. However, if a bad product is enhanced with a warranty in order to signal high quality, this can lead to ruin.

In the following, we will present signaling as a strategic instrument of communication. As such, it can be attributed to a company's communication policy. On the one hand, we will concentrate on **product-related quality signals**, and specifically only those that serve to decrease information asymmetries. An extensive economical discussion on this subject can be found in the literature concerning New Institutional Economics (e.g. Göbel, 2002). On the other hand, we will introduce **signals of strategic market communication**, which are mostly multivalent in their direction of effect, i.e. they affect the single market players in different ways. The origins of such strategic signaling activities are military in kind.

> The use of diversionary tactics and misinformation was well developed in military warfare. In the year 1944, such maneuvers worked so well that the German high command believed, even as the allies were landing in Normandy, that the main invasion would take place near Calais (Grant & Nippa, 2006, 151).

In the context of economics, signaling has become a subject of Game Theory, which has significantly developed it over the last few years. Here signals are regarded as an integral part of companies' strategic behavior (e.g. Nalebuff & Brandenburger, 1996).

22.3   Approaches to Reducing Product-Related Quality Insecurities

In the third chapter, we got to know the existence of information asymmetries as an economic particularity of information goods. They result from the problem of quality assessment, which can be very different when buying (information) goods, depending on their characteristics. According to Darby and Karni (1973, 69), we can distinguish between three information-economical characteristics:

> We distinguish then three types of qualities associated with a particular purchase: search qualities which are known before purchase, experience qualities which are known costlessly only after purchase, and credence qualities which are expensive to judge even after purchase.

Depending on what kind of information good is being bought, these three features are differently pronounced. Clearly pronounced search qualities can be found in strongly standardized information goods, such as price information (e.g. stock market and exchange rate information or offers by price agencies). Here the quality insecurities are very low (Linde 2008, 35-36). In a market research report, though, credence qualities prevail, as the buyer–even if he is an expert–cannot comprehensively determine how much effort and diligence were used in conducting the investigation. Strongly pronounced experience qualities, in turn, are displayed by most software offers. If the software has been bought and the user is able to collect his experiences with the product, it will be shown very soon whether it is as easily installable and usable as advertised.

Overall, most information goods display little search, but highly pronounced experience and credence qualities. It is thus generally difficult for the buyer to comprehensively gauge the product's quality before buying. For information providers who want to signal that they offer a certain quality, it is advisable to adjust their measures according to the three mentioned information-economical qualities. According to Adler (1996, 101 et seq., 134 et seq.), three approaches to reducing information asymmetries can be distinguished. Adler talks of performance-related information search, as well as performance-related information substitutes that relate to all services. Performance-related information search aims to make quality properties verifiable before buying. Such inspection offers directly reduce existing information asymmetries. They are not a form of signaling–we only speak of signals when a (cost-related) statement is made concerning a non-observable characteristic. These are information substitutes meant to signal product quality without making it tangible, as a substitute for direct product information, so to say.

22.3.1   Inspection Offers

If information asymmetries exist, the provider can first support the customer in terms of performance-related information search. This will reduce his insecurity, and he can better gauge the quality of certain of the desired information good's features (e.g. the style of an author, band or artist, the layout of a text or the entertainment factor of a game) before committing to buy. This can be done by offering parts of the information good or information about the good. The provider intends to make quality properties of the offer accessible to the customer for checking. The provider thus gives the customer options for inspecting the good, hence the term inspection offers. In the following, a few variants of inspection offers will be introduced:

In order to reduce information asymmetries, providers can make parts of the information good **directly** available for inspection via a preview (Varian, 1998, 4). Previewing an information good may consist of the customer being able to listen a part of a music title, read extracts from a book or test sections of an e-learning application. For software, the same effect can be created if test licenses or downgraded versions are made available. In this way, the provider can transform experience qualities of the good into search qualities. The customer will not find out that he doesn't like a CD or game after having bought it, since he can answer this question for himself before.

For providers, however, such offers are not so straightforward. They must take care not to make so much of the information good available that the demand is already satisfied during the trial period, before buying, thus drastically reducing or even eliminating the customer's willingness to pay. Arrow (1962, 615) points out this so-called information paradox, as

> ... there is a fundamental paradox in the determination of demand for information; its value for the purchaser is not known until he has the information, but then he has in effect acquired it without cost.

This problem particularly applies to content offers. If customers have read the computer magazine in the shop, or have obtained the address of the cheap provider they searched for, it is very probable that their willingness to pay is next to zero. However, the fact that this does not always have to be the case is shown by counterexamples of shareware providers asking the users to only pay for the product after downloading and using it or artists (e.g. Nine Inch Nails or Radiohead) who offer their music on the Web for free and leaving it to the customer whether and how much to pay for the download. Here it seems we can distinguish between information offers as commodities and as consumables (Linde, 2008, 9 et seq.). It is generally to be assumed that the decrease of willingness to pay for information goods that are "consumed" (e.g. a newspaper article) is more pronounced than it is for commodities (e.g. a video game).

Inspection offers for **commodities** are already widely available these days. Most software offers can be tested for a certain time, there are trial subscriptions for newspapers and magazines, and even music can frequently be listened to before buying. Such offers are often very extensive, and the customer can check the quality almost entirely. He only has to pay for lasting usage privileges or continued delivery.

Comprehensive inspection offers are possible for **consumables** as well, however. Varian (1998, 4) reports that online offers of books can have a positive effect on sales:

> The National Academy of Sciences Press found that when they posted the full text of book [sic!] on the Web, the sales of those books went up by a factor of three. Posting the material on the Web allowed potential customers to preview the material, but anyone who really wanted to read the book would download it. MIT Press had a similar experience with monographs and online journals.

Here it is shown how well versioning can be used: the information contents are made available to the customer in their entirety, but in a form that allows for quality verification while making actual consumption unattractive. The customer can get to grips with content, style and layout on his computer, but cannot read the book on his sofa, must make do–depending on the design–with a black-and-white version on the screen and may not have any access to supplementary features, such as an index. All of this he will only receive after buying. If, however, the customer is only in need of one information, an image or a text passage, this rudimentary version will suffice and he will steer clear of a purchase.

Free offers (Follow-the-free) or offers, in which customer only pay what they feel like (Pay-what-you-want) work in the same direction. They serve to surmount the problem of quality insecurity as a first step, in order to generate profits later (Choi et al., 1997, 243; Kim et al., 2009, 55). The non-assertion of existing copyrights can here be seen as an equivalent of very low introductory prices. Both variants have

> ...similar potential to signal high product quality (Takeyama, 2009, 292).

With regard to asymmetrical information concerning product quality, it is indeed rational for quality providers to make the introductory price very low, even zero, or abstain from asserting their copyrights and tolerating illegal copies. In both cases, a quality provider can signal that he is sure of compensating for lost profits later, because he knows about the quality of his product and has no reason to fear the users' experiences. For lower-quality providers, this would be irrational behavior.

Specifically the degree of product protection here becomes a quality signal (Takeyama, 2009).

If the customer is granted partial or full access to information goods, the provider should always take care to make a transfer of quality judgments from the free offer to the priced one easily realizable, as existing information asymmetries will not be sufficiently reduced otherwise. Finally, in order to generate profits, the free versions should be designed in such a way that quality judgments are made possible but the demand for consumption is not satisfied in full (Stahl, 2005, 290).

Now, quality information can be transmitted not only directly, by (partially) disclosing the information, but also **indirectly** as meta-information, such as the artist's name, title, year of release or publisher. This also comprises abstracts, which provide a compressed overview of text contents without making the original accessible.

Inspection offers are extremely effective in order to reduce buyers' insecurities regarding the quality on offer. However, they are also obviously limited in that they lead to the surrender of goods, either completely or in their vital parts. The danger, particularly for consumables, is of interest in the product, and hence willingness to pay, dissipating. If, then, it is not the company's intention to make its information offers available for free, it must retain at least parts of the good. Certain quality properties of the information good will, in that case, obviously be tried and judged only after a purchase has been made. These are the so-called experience qualities. It is very important for information providers to be aware of the fact that the search and experience qualities are not inherent to the product, but that they themselves can, as providers, determine which quality properties the customers can inspect before buying and which can only be accessed after buying. Central to this decision is the estimation of how the customer's willingness to pay will develop on the back of the inspection. The more it suffers, the more it is recommended to either work with different versions or to keep the inspection offers limited.

22.3.2 Service or Product-Related Information Substitutes

Now, what can a provider do in order to convince the customer of his product's quality without making inspection offers? He must try to reduce the customer's quality insecurity concerning the post-purchase situation. The customer must receive signals that convince him—despite buying the proverbial pig in a poke—that he will not experience any (quality) disappointment afterwards. This can be accomplished by offering information substitutes: signals that relate to the provider's marketing policy as perceived by the customer (Adler, 1996, 103). This sort of signal serves as a substitute for inspection offers, i.e. access to the information good itself.

Such performance-oriented information substitutes initially comprise all manner of **rating** (testimonials, reviews). Book reviews, editorships, forewords or comments by famous persons or institutions, customers' judgments, criticisms or product reviews, for example on opinion sites such as www.ciao.de are all opinions by third parties that point to the quality of a good. Trusting the evaluators and their ratings saves the customer the effort of directly testing the offer himself. The submission of ratings by professional critics–but increasingly also by the consumers themselves–is extremely prevalent for films, books and music. For video games, specifically, the great significance of external ratings as a signal of the product's quality is widely accepted. Video games are reviewed in a wide variety of magazines, with an increasing number of online portals, particularly in the USA, now taking over this task previously the domain of the specialized press (Jöckel, 2008, 60).

A similar function is performed by **honors** and awards that can be won by books, music or films. A literary prize, a gold record or a Grammy Award generate short-term attention, thus benefiting sales, and serve as a long-term quality signal, which can be empirically proven (Clement et al., 2008, 771).

The classical quality signal to reduce information asymmetries for experience qualities, as already proposed by Spence (1976), is the **warranty**. This signal, however, is only really effective if there is a negative correlation between warranty costs and assured quality (Spence, 1976, 592).

> For a signal to be effective, it must be unprofitable for sellers of low quality products to imitate it. That is, high quality sellers must have lower costs for signalling activities.

The offer of a warranty signals the consumer that the provider is sure of the quality of his product, as otherwise he would have to expect financial losses. This quality promise is secured by the commitment to correct any problems that arise over the duration of the warranty, up until to a full refund. Backhaus and Voeth (2007, 460 et seq.) point out that warranties only become a marketing instrument if they go beyond the legally regulated warranty obligations (§§ 433 et seq. German Civil Code). Such extensions can be made chronologically, by providing warranties that go beyond the legally regulated minimum periods. This can go right up to a lifetime warranty, which can exceed the maximum statute of limitations, as specified in the Civil Code, if it is exactly stated which (product) lifespan it is meant to refer to. Warranties can also be extended with regard to content, if they guarantee the functioning of certain or even all features of a product or a certain period. An unusual example of an extension of content was provided some time ago by an American automobile manufacturer. General Motors offered its customers that whoever

> ...buys an Oldsmobile has 30 days or 1500 miles to think about his decision. If he decides that he doesn't like the car, he can drive onto the seller's lot and have the deal annulled. [...] Initial fears that GM's generous warranty might be abused have not been validated. Of the 65,000 buyers, only 306 returned their Oldsmobile in the three months since the start of the campaign (Deysson, 1990, 47).

Another example is the company Northern Light, who in 1997 brought a search engine on the market that could not only search websites but also the full text of entire articles (Notess, 1998). The freely usable search engine was without ads; the necessary profits were meant to be generated from article sales. What was special about it was the money-back guarantee, where purchased articles could be returned for a full refund if they were not liked.

Journal of Business Strategy

Title:	Where style meets substance. *(corporate leadership)(includes related articles) (Special Focus: Leadership)*
Summary:	Management experts believe that leadership could be the number one strategic concern of businesses in the 21st century.

Source:	**Journal of Business Strategy**
Date:	01-02/1995
Price:	$2.95
Document Size:	Long (8 to 25 pages)
Document ID:	SL19970922040043754
Subject(s):	Leadership--Technique; Management--Technique
Citation Information:	(v16 n1) Start Page: p48(12) ISSN: 0275-6668
Author(s):	Davids, Meryl
Document Type:	Article

Return to Results

New Search

Accounts

Format for Print

Money Back Guarantee If you buy an article and you are not satisfied with it, let us know and we will refund your money - no questions asked. Please press the "Money Back Guarantee" link for additional information about this policy.

Figure 22.1: Money-Back Guarantee for Northern Light. Source: Northern Light.

In 2002, Northern Light withdrew from the free Web search business in order to concentrate on the more successful development of search engines for business customers. The reason given was that business with ad-financed search had developed better. Two weeks after this decision, the company was bought by Divine, who in turn announced an agreement to deliver premium content to Yahoo! (Hane, 2002). Whether excessive use made of the offered warranty played a decisive role in this development cannot be proven. For digital goods, in any case, the danger of fees being reclaimed is relatively high:

Unlike physical products, returning a digital product seldom prevents the consumer from using the product in the future (Choi et al., 1997, 244).

Warranties can relate to current purchases, but also to ones yet to make (Backhaus & Voeth, 2007, 461 et seq.). They are offered at the time of purchase, yet relate to future services. Such "performance bonds" (Backhaus & Voeth, 2007, 462) are made, for example, by porcelain manufacturers, who assure the customer that he can buy replacements for certain product lines over a specified period of time. The analog case for information providers is the granting, to subscribers of a magazine or information service, of the right to cancel their obligations at any time. The provider wants to signal, in this way, that the quality of his product will be just as high in the future.

Guarantees transform experience qualities into 'quasi-search qualities'. No more quality verification costs then need to be incurred for these qualities (Irmscher, 1997, 267).

The more product qualities are encompassed by the warranty, and the longer it runs, the better it vouches for high quality. The demander's insecurity relating to experience qualities can thus be reduced, even entirely in the case of a full warranty. The fact that providers hesitate to go in for the latter is due to another sort of information asymmetry; a moral-hazard problem is created on the side of demand (Cooper & Ross, 1985). If a provider offers a full warranty, the demanders no longer have any incentive to treat the products with proper care, or even deliberately induce the warranty case. This is the reason why full warranties do not exist.

A summary of empirical analyses of warranties by Adler (1996, 111 et seq.) confirms the relation between extent of warranty and quality: brands with an above-average warranty also scored above-average results in product tests. Besides, from the provider's perspective–top managers were being polled–warranty offers play a particular role for products that cost a lot, are viewed as technologically complex, are seldomly bought and produced by relatively unknown manufacturers. This also holds for the customers' perspective. Furthermore, warranties– at least for higher-grade products–are an important factor in customers' perception of quality. If warranties are offered, they represent a high product quality to the customers. Warranties enable quality providers to work with higher prices and thus increase their profit margin instead of having to enter price fights with lower-quality providers (Monroe, 2003, 85).

For the provider, it is advisable to align the extent of his warranty with the market standard. Shimp and Bearden (1982)'s "too good to be true" hypothesis empirically confirms the fact that very extensive warranties can even create the opposite effect and cause skepticism and mistrust in consumers, if the warranty promise goes too far above the market standard and is made by a provider with a bad reputation or none at all. It is thus not recommended to providers with a low market reputation who have solved their quality problems to offer extensive warranties in order to be accepted by demanders as providers of higher quality. A better way is to generally improve credibility in the customers' perception by making it clear what the cost would be for the provider if the signals transmitted were false (Boulding & Kirmani, 1993, 120).

Warranties directly affect the reduction of information asymmetries relating to a good's experience qualities. Apart from the signaling function, they serve at the same time a backup function (Adler, 1996, 131). In case of a failure to keep the performance promise, the customer is able–supported by the law–to take the provider up on his promise. Whether or not the provider has a reputation for being particularly reliable or service-oriented does not play any role here at first.

The case is slightly different if signals are only credible when they are accompanied by a corresponding reputation. A high **price**, for instance, is not a quality signal in itself, but only if the buyer can assume that it is set by a quality provider and is not merely a "rip-off". Klein and Leffler speak of a reputation mechanism that must be in play for certain signals to be credible. Next to the price, they mention incurred advertising costs as signals for reducing insecurity (Klein & Leffler, 1981, 618). A high price at first appears plausible from the customer's perspective, since high quality is generally accompanied by higher manufacturing costs. At the same time, it is a signal of service quality, as companies stand to lose more from high prices, if customers are unhappy and stay away from the company in the future (Göbel, 2002, 326). The fact that the price, besides representing a monetary restriction in purchases, also has an information function, being interpretable as a quality signal, was addressed by Scitovsky as early as 1945. However, the correlation between price and perception of quality cannot be directly verified. While there are many theoretical and empirical studies on the subject, they do not present a unified picture, a weak positive correlation can be assumed at best (Adler, 1996, 121). If, on the other hand, the conditions under which consumers tend to infer a correspondingly higher product quality from a higher price are taken into consideration,

> ...it can be regarded as proven fact, today, that the price serves *less* as an indicator of quality
>
> the more price, and the less quality, are weighted by the consumer as shopping criteria, and the less pronounced product involvement is,
>
> the greater the demander's shopping experience and level of knowledge are, which conversely means that the price serves particularly often as a quality signal for (real) innovators,
>
> the more and the more reliable other options for quality assessment are available,
>
> the less pronounced the range of variation of quality and prices are in the respective product category,

the fewer other quality indicators (e.g. brand, name of provider company etc.) are available and

the less important the prestige value of a product is in comparison with other quality properties (Diller, 2008, 151 with other sources).

Diller further points out that price-oriented quality assessment does not mean, in most cases, that a quality product is being purchased. It can even happen that the customer obtains a lower-quality by choosing a relatively expensive offer. As such, the price cannot be regarded as a reliable yardstick for quality.

> If consumers still frequently resort to it, then only because they overestimate the risk of low prices, or absolutely want to see their minimum quality requirements fulfilled, respectively (disjunctive assessment behavior), and/or the sacrifice of cash utility is still a relatively minor factor in the relevant quality range in case of increasing prices (Diller, 2008, 153).

Besides the price, the amount of **advertising expenses** is seen as a signal to reduce product-related quality insecurities. Nelson (1974) was the first to analyze the relevance of advertising as a signal for unknown product quality. Since the consumers cannot check the validity of the advertising promise prior to purchase, thus Nelson's line of thought (1974, 730 et seq.), the contents of the ads will be greeted with skepticism due to their presumed intent to manipulate. There is thus no direct information value inherent to advertisements–apart from their simple existence. However, information may be indirectly inferred. The extent of advertising can, in terms of experience qualities, be seen as a quality signal as well as an indicator for a good relation between price and quality. Kirmani and Wright (1989) base this on psychological factors, according to which most people believe that the level of performance brought to bear on any given task mainly hinges on one's belief in one's own success. Advertising expenses are viewed as an indicator for a provider's marketing efforts. Analogously, consumers infer that the provider has a lot of trust in his product's quality and subsequent success. This correlation is restricted, however, if the customers are aware that the provider has no interest in repeat purchases, or that advertising expenses only represent a small part of the overall budget, for example. Excessively high advertising costs are also counterproductive and create mistrust. Experimentally, an inverted-U function emerged for the expectation of quality vis-à-vis increasing perceived advertising expenses (Kirmani & Wright, 1989, 349). This means that quality expectation is only positive at a medium level of advertising expenses, and not at very low or very high levels. Kirmani and Wright also analyzed from which elements of an advertising campaign consumers infer the extent of advertising efforts: product ratings (testimonials) or the choice of advertising medium are crucial influence quantities.

Thus we have some first empirical results that attest to the extent of advertising expenses actually being used as a quality signal by the consumers under certain conditions (Tolle, 1994, 934).

Slightly differently conceived empirical analyses of the relation between advertising expenses and the quality/price ratio produce contradictory results, however. Here the question of whether there actually is a positive correlation, and consumers really interpret the amount of advertising costs as a signal for the relation between quality and price, stays open (Tolle, 1994, 930-931.).

Another quality signal is represented by a product's **market share** (Katz & Shapiro, 1985, 424). This idea was already substantiated in several model analyses (Haller, 2005, 226). Specifically for the audio-carrier market, Haller (2005, 226 et seq.) shows via a signaling model that consumers have the impetus, under certain conditions, to buy from the manufacturer who announces the highest expected sales figures, since this can be interpreted as a signal for the quality of the product. One of the conditions Haller analyzed is that the price differences for the different qualities available on the market must be relatively low. Also, the signaling costs for lower-quality providers, e.g. in the form of bad reviews and/or lower sales figures, must be significantly higher than for an audio-carrier producer who offers high quality (Haller, 2005, 236).

Market share can be seen not only as a quality signal, but also as a quality-induced cause of the occurrence of network effects (Katz & Shapiro, 1985, 424). A large market share creates positive network effects, as the information asymmetries for the goods concerned are reduced more effectively. There is a larger number of consumers who can exchange information about the product quality (Hutter, 2003, 267). Here it is insignificant whether this information stems from experiences with legally or illegally acquired products. Bootleg copies contribute to the reduction of information asymmetries just as much as legal ones (Takeyama, 2003).

22.3.3 *Information Substitutes Relating to All Services*

The use of performance-related information substitutes serves to reduce insecurities regarding a product's experience qualities. They are generally ineffective for credence qualities. Warranties, for example, presuppose that the customer can assess the respective feature after the purchase. How else could he determine that the warranty case has occurred? Warranties are thus largely useless in relation to credence qualities, as the consumer cannot check for the fulfillment/non-fulfillment of a promise. As an example for such a credence quality, let us consider the care with which a scientific study has been conducted. As a reader of the corresponding publication in a magazine, one is not able to determine whether it holds up to scientific quality criteria. This, then, is a credence quality of this information good. The customer must simply trust in the fulfillment of his expectations by the provider. This is why it is very important for him to find indicators that enable him to predict, with high probability, the trustworthiness of the provider, in this case the author's. From the provider's perspective, it is advisable to send signals that could not be sent by lower-quality providers (Göbel, 2002, 326). The building of a reputation as a quality provider, or test seals by independent institutions are such signals that can be used to reduce quality insecurities that cannot be elicited by the customer. Such signal may be termed information substitutes relating to all services (Adler, 1996, 133-134). They are not meant to directly attest to the quality of a specific product, but point beyond the individual service and signal that the provider is a provider of quality.

Test seals, or seals of approval, which have already been used on the information market, are certificates of successful quality management (according to ISO 9000), e.g. for FIZ Chemie (Rüller, 2000), or collective marks, as SEC for suppliers in E-Commerce. Bock (2000) suggests the use of seals of approval to signal quality information by professional providers in order for them to distinguish themselves from the tons of unchecked, free content offers available online.

The use of such signals not only affects insecurities regarding credence qualities, but always also reduces insecurities about experience and search qualities. Adler here speaks of downward compatibility (1996, 135), where the higher-ranking strategies for reducing information asymmetries always additionally assume functions of the lower-ranking qualities.

Let us go back to the example of the article: if the author publishes it in a journal which is renowned for its tough review process, he thus sends a signal about the quality of his work and the potential reader–trusting in this–will not undertake any further examination of this aspect. At the same time, this information substitute relating to all services serves as a signal that certain experience qualities will also be of the same quality. The reader will assume, e.g. due to the magazine's reputation, that only a certain kind of contribution, a specific style of citation or a particular layout of the individual article is to be expected. He can save himself the effort of pre-inspecting these traits, and he does not have to fear that his expectations will be disappointed, i.e. that he will have a bad experience. Hence if the information substitutes relating to all services are mighty, the provider can, partly or in whole, forego lower-ranking signals.

The central information substitute relating to all services is the provider's **reputation**.

> Information-economically speaking, reputation can be understood as a stock of past information containing the entirety of experiences connected to the brand name, such as advertising campaigns and themes, product successes and failures, quality experiences etc. (Irmscher, 1997, 193).

Brand names in particular play a very important role in order to gain a reputation online. Barwise et al. (2002, 543) detect a growing importance of brand names on the internet, because trusted brands may be even more important in a world of information overload, and money-rich, time-poor consumers, where product quality still cannot usually be reliably judged online.

Degeratu et al. (2000) here show that the less product information is available, the greater the brand name's value is in e-commerce. In markets with pronounced information asymmetries, the brand represents a great value, which is strongly linked to the company's economic success. Companies that already have a good reputation, acquired on other ("offline") markets, are in the advantage here, as they can transfer these to the new market. But here too, the transferred reputation can only be sustained if the quality of the services is accepted by the customers. Generally, the companies that are successful on the internet are the ones who invest in their reputation, as is the case with Yahoo!, for example (Choi et al., 1997, 240 et seq.).

We had already seen above that the reputation is a prerequisite for the effectiveness of certain signals, such as the price. Great trust in the provider then translates to great trust in his price information. However, reputation can also be regarded as a direct signal for high product quality.

> When product attributes are difficult to observe prior to purchase, consumers may plausibly use the quality of products produced by the firm in the past as an indicator of present or future quality (Shapiro, 1983, 659).

From this point of view, brand-loyal consumers base their quality assessment less on the price than on the brand. The reputation can thus work in both directions (Völckner, 2006, 479). In the following, we will take a closer look at the effects of reputation as an independent signal for the perception of quality.

A good reputation signals trustworthiness. The provider wants to make it clear that he will not behave in an opportunistic manner and instead prove himself worthy of the trust put in him. If he is able to implement a price premium for his quality offer, it will in fact be of advantage for him to keep the quality high in the long term instead of maximizing his profits in the short run by reducing quality (Shapiro, 1983, 660). For the customers, the reputation reduces the quality risk.

> By foregoing this strategy of quality reduction, and thus higher profits in the short term, the provider gains a reputation, which is expressed in the demanders' additional *willingness to pay* for future transactions (Adler, 1996, 126).

Brynjolfsson and Smith (2000) prove, on the example of electronic book sales, the significance of the brand name. They show that customers are willing to pay a premium if the provider is well known. Conversely, this means that customers will buy a product with the same price from the provider who is best-known and has the best reputation. Providers with a lesser reputation must thus lower their prices in order to gain customers. For electronic marketplaces, it can generally be shown via several studies that the reputation has a positive correlation to both price and profits and leads to a greater price diversification (Stahl, 2005, 254, 293-294). For e-trade with digital contents specifically, Stahl (2005, 267-268) demonstrates empirically that investments in the reputation have a disproportionate effect on the amount of selling transactions, on the profits and on the number of customers per day. The reputation (measured by the number of referencing weblinks), it was additionally shown, also has a positive, if weaker, correlation with customer loyalty (measured by the provider's share of "loyal" customers). In the end, the reputation is also a driver for the creation of network effects, as it is a suitable strategy for positively influencing the customer's product perception.

> In order to reach critical mass, the *subjective perception* of the product's advantages is the decisive factors for potential users (Rogers, 2003, following Picot et al., 2003, 365).

Trust in the provider is the central requirement for buying goods with credence qualities (Göbel, 2002, 329). Without trust, the customer will not be moved to buy, as he will never be able to assess the product quality for himself. However, trust also plays an important role for a good's experience qualities. Here, too, the customer must find the (initial) trust to let himself make the purchase. He must trust in his expectations not to be disappointed by post-purchase experiences. Yoon et al. (1993) demonstrate, on the example of business insurances, that the customer's assessment of different insurance offers absolutely depends upon the provider's reputation. The providers' information offers are thus judged to be less important. They summarize (Yoon et al., 1993, 225)

> ...that insurance is an experience or credence good– buyers' evaluation of an insurance program greatly depends on company reputation because program information is either not persuasive or credible in influencing behavior.

22.3.4   Strategies for Building Reputation

The reputation represents a strategic competitive factor of towering importance on information markets (Klodt, 2001, 43). There are several approaches to building reputation (Stahl, 2005, 291 et seq.). Establishing a brand name is the most prevalent and effective of these methods of building a good reputation for oneself as a provider or one's products.

> Investing in brand and reputation is standard practice in the information biz, from the MGM Lion to the Time magazine logo. This investment is warranted because of the experience good problem of information (Varian, 1998, 5).

Different studies prove the significance of reputation and brand names in e-trade. The significance of reputation was analyzed multiple times in the context of online auctions. On the example of eBay, it has been shown several times (Luo & Chung, 2002; Melnik & Alm, 2002) that sellers with a good rating, i.e. a high reputation, get higher bids and price premiums for their offers. The sellers' reputation correlates positively with the buyers' willingness to pay.

Malaga and Werts (2000, following Stahl, 2005, 253) compare different reputation mechanisms in online trading, such as sellers' warranties, product sales via third parties or brand effectiveness. Brand names, they find, are the most effective variant of gaining a reputation with buyers on the internet.

One's own reputation can also be strengthened by reputation transfers. Apart from the options they have themselves, e.g. between different business fields or between the online and offline worlds, providers can profit from third parties' reputations. A traditional path is via the quality assessments, addressed above, of their own products. If such reviews stem from recognized experts or famous personalities, a reputation transfer takes place. This form of transfer is cultivated intensively in the media and entertainment industry. There are often reviews of films, books or music that are disseminated by the provider as product assessments. The same goes for the review of scientific articles. The publisher vouches for the quality of the offer with his good name.

A special role in the building of reputation is played by institutions, who secure the quality of services and, particularly, information (Zerdick et al., 2001, 42). Warranties, as we have seen, contribute little to signaling the excellence of credence qualities, since the buyer cannot check the fulfilment of the services promised. Here signals must be used that cannot be transmitted by opportunistic providers. **Certification marks and quality standards** are such information substitutes relating to all services that are used for credence qualities. According to Bock (2000, 145), certification marks are

> ...means of tagging products according to their make.

For instance, if food carries a Bio seal of the EU, or is certified as a product from an ecological growers' association such as Bioland, the consumer knows that an independent third party has checked the preparation and thus confirmed the credence qualities. This trust-confirming function can be assumed by seals of quality, testing centers or other trust centers (Zerdick et al., 2001, 42). In Germany, the Deutsche Institut für Gütesicherung und Kennzeichnung e. V. (formerly Reichs-Ausschuss für Lieferbedingungen–RAL) as well as the Technische Überwachungs-Verein (TÜV) play an important role for the allocation of certification marks. The decisive factor is that the certification marks themselves are viewed as trustworthy. Here the independence and reputation of the certifying body is the decisive factor.

Certification marks can counteract the risk of diminishing average product quality. This increases providers' interest in their usage, as quality-relevant information becomes more redeemable this way. This is particularly the case if these marks are themselves trademarks and thus represent concrete content statements (Bock, 258 et seq., 303 et seq.). They are of particular significance on the digital online information market, as there are no information carriers and, often, no price (free offers, Follow-the-free) that provides consumers with a basis of their quality assessment.

The same statements hold for the use of quality standards, generally defined as guidelines for the design of products and services (Kleinaltenkamp, 1994, 198). For uninformed consumers, quality standards represent indicators for the quality of the products and services on offer. For informed customers, on the other hand, they provide options for quality assessment, as activities that would otherwise have stayed hidden can now be made visible and verifiable (Fließ, 2004, 40). The most important and best-known standards are the quality management systems of the ISO 9000 series of standards and of the European Foundation for Quality Management (EFQM).

As opposed to warranties, in which the provider only incurs costs in case of their utilization, the use of certification marks or quality standards costs money in every case. Kirmani and Rao (2000, 69) here distinguish between "Default-Independent" and "Default-Contingent Signals". The former, e.g. ads, brand building or low introductory prices, lead to expenses that are independent of any possible misperformance (Default-Independent). Signals such as the setting of price premiums and the granting of warranties only lead to costs if the provider cannot keep his service promise (Default-Contingent). The provider should select his signaling strategy depending on how easily the market can be segmented and how quickly after the purchase the product quality reveals itself (Kirmani & Rao, 2000, 73-74). In the case of certification marks and quality standards, this means the provider must check whether he can use established signals or may seek to build special standards.

Less expensive than the use of certification marks or quality standards and more broadly laid out is the product's **review by online communities**. Here the provider will not profit from individual famous persons; instead, the reputation is strengthened if a multitude of voices comment positively on the provider and his services. In this form of reputation transfer, however, the company largely cedes control of how the results will pan out. If reviews are individually commissioned, the results can indeed be influenced. Positive comments can be pointedly elicited and communicated outward. The more independent the writing of reviews or the collection and publication of customers' opinions, though, the less the provider can prevent critical comments or even a complete hatchet job.

The reputation can also be enhanced by **links**, i.e. having other high-quality providers reference one's own offer. The positive assessment of a website's quality is transferred to the website it links to (Stahl, 2005, 255).

As we have seen, companies can choose from a multitude of options for signaling the quality they offer. They can start with any kind of information asymmetry that may occur in relation to the quality of a product or a service: search, experience and credence qualities. Signals that are used to reduce information asymmetries in credence qualities (performance-related information substitutes) also mitigate search-related quality insecurities. The same goes for signals to reduce quality insecurities that result from experience qualities (information substitutes relating to all services); they complementarily cover experience- and search-related insecurities. In Figure 22.2, the mentioned signaling instruments are displayed according to their rank.

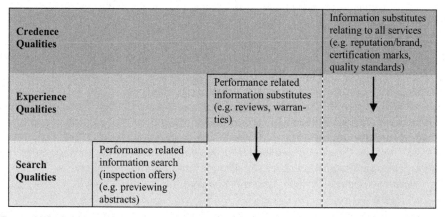

Figure 22.2: Spectrum of Action of Individual Instruments to Reduce Quality-Related Information Asymmtries. Source: Following Adler, 1996, 135.

22.4   Signals in Strategic Market Communication

The reduction of quality-related information asymmetries has so far been represented as a communication process between company and customer. Signals should convince potential buyers that the services offers correspond with the expected quality. However, signaling also plays an important role in the strategic context, as we noted at the beginning of this chapter. Monroe (2003, 89) speaks of competitive signals meant to influence the market in general:

> In essence, a competitive signal is a marketing activity that reveals insights into the unobservable motives for the seller's behavior or intended behavior. Such a signal alerts others about the product quality,

> reputation, business intentions, previews of potential actions, or even forecasts concerning the expected business conditions in the market.

In the context of strategic market communication, then, not only the quality signals discussed above are to be considered in their strategic dimension, but also those signals that are directed at other market players besides the customers.

For information goods as network effect goods in particular signals play a crucial role in surmounting critical mass up until the occurrence of network effects, creating a standard or, later, securing the provider's market position. The expectations of all market players are a central factor here. Katz and Shapiro (1985) formulate, from the customer's perspective:

> If consumers expect a seller to be dominant, then consumers will be willing to pay more for the firm's product, and it will, in fact, be dominant.

The company's goal is thus to influence the market participants' expectations in its favor. In the competition for reaching critical mass, and–going further–establishing compatibility standards, there is a whole line of signals that can be used to further one's success: product announcements (Farrell & Saloner, 1986; Shapiro & Varian, 1999a, 14), entering commitments as well as partnership or alliance announcements (Lilly & Walters, 1997), insurance offers (Dybvig & Spatt, 1983), but the direct communication of network growth in the form of sales figures, customers or market share can also play an important role here.

Whatever signals are sent, they must be credible in order to work.

> The receiver's assessment of the signal's credibility is influenced by the sender's reputation and the signal's potential reversibility (Monroe, 2003, 90).

The signaler's reputation again plays a crucial role. How reliable have past signals, e.g. concerning product or service quality, been? Have the promises been kept? After all, if the company has fulfilled the self-defined expectations of its services in the past, current signals are also to be deemed credible. The degree of signals' reversibility works in the same direction. Are they easily changeable, as for example the purely communicative announcement of an intended cooperation, or do they involve high (material or immaterial) costs? The latter scenario would be the case if the cooperation is contractually agreed upon, involves great communicative efforts and initial investments in joint manufacturing plants have already been made. A last-minute change would incur significant expenses. Such signals, based on observable behavior, are a lot more convincing and credible than those that are merely mentioned verbally (Monroe, 2003, 90). In the following, we will introduce the most important forms of signaling in the context of strategic market communication.

22.4.1   *Product Announcements*

Product announcements are of great significance in innovation management (Lilly & Walters, 1997), and also play a big role in connection with standardization processes (Maaß, 2006, 134 et seq., Shapiro & Varian, 1999b). Some examples: Bill Gates officially announced the new X-Box in March of 2000, even though it was slated to enter the market in the fall of 2001. Sony announced its PlayStation 2 twelve months before its market debut in Japan (Le Nagard-Assayag & Manceau, 2001, 204). Interestingly, this announcement took place exactly one week after Sega brought its new 128-bit Dreamcast console on the market. Other companies, such as Symbian, pursue a different strategy and avoid the creation of marketing hypes well in advance of the product launch (Suarez, 2004, 277).

A product announcement is

> a formal, deliberate communication before a firm actually undertakes a particular marketing action such as a price change, a new advertising campaign, or a product line change (Eliashberg & Robertson, 1988, 282).

Announcements comprise a description of the offer's features, possibly some price information as well as the probable launch date. For network goods in particular, their expected prevalence and compatibility with competing products are further typical information communicated as part of a product announcements (Köster, 1999, 21).

Announcing a product has several effects, which are differentiated according to who the announcement is aimed at.

Announcements that are primarily addressed to the **consumer** are designed to stir up curiosity and may further lead to the customers postponing their purchasing decision until the new product is available (Farrell & Saloner, 1986; Lilly & Walters, 1997). The announcement alerts them to the product earlier than an advertising campaign immediately prior to its launch would have done. Information concerning product qualities can be disseminated in the run-up and the press as well as other opinion leaders, e.g. on the internet, can comment or–if trial versions are available already–assess the product performance. The consumers can use the early information to plan their expenses in the long term, as well as minimize or distribute over a longer period any switching costs that may apply. It can be shown empirically that products involving high switching costs are regularly announced well before their launch. Announcements are also made more frequently (albeit with no statistical significance) if the new product involves high learning costs for the customer (Eliashberg & Robertson, 1988, 290-291).

The effectiveness of announcements heavily depends upon their timing. Well-timed product announcements can move up the product launch date. It would be of disadvantage, however, if as a consequence of the announcement sales of one's own predecessor product diminish, i.e. if cannibalization occurs. This danger is also referred to as the "Osborne Effect" (Besen & Farrel, 1994, 124). In the 1980s, the Osborne Computer Corporation had to file for bankruptcy due to the market launch of an already announced follow-up model to one of their computers being delayed by a year (Osborne & Dvorak, 1984).

Important influencing factors for a good timing of product announcements are the customers' buying frequency as well as learning and switching costs. Kohli (1999) demonstrates this empirically on the example of hardware and software. Badly timed–too early or too late–announcements cannot produce the desired effects. Late announcements are too close to the market launch, so they cannot create any strong effects anymore. They are then less announcements than early introductory advertising. Early announcements are also ineffective, as the announced product is then merely hot air, or "vaporware", i.e. products that are not available at the promised time (Bayus et al., 2001, 3). If insufficient information about the product is available, they fizzle out without effect (Kohli, 1999, 46).

Software companies often announce their products very early, in order to slow down the competition's sales and make customers aware of their own product.

> For example, Microsoft first announced that Windows NT 5.0® would
> be released in 1998 and then delayed its release of the product so long
> that it renamed its product Windows 2000®. Competitors accused Mi-
> crosoft of using vapourware tactics (Gans, 2008).

Bayus et al., (2001, 6) show that only around 50% of 123 software products announced between 1986 and 1995 actually entered the market within three months of the announcement being made. More than 20% of the products were even only available more than nine months after. The popular portal Wired releases a yearly list of the top ten vaporware products, in which hardware, software and video game offers occupy the top spots (Calore, 2008). 3D Realm's Duke Nukem Forever enjoys the epithet "King of Vaporware" due to its endless delays since 1998. Despite the flowing borders between an unintended delay in delivery and an intentionally early announcement, the customers' ire can cause lasting damage to a company's reputation as a reliable provider. Microsoft, for example, had to shoulder a decline in prices of 5.3% in late 1997 after it became clear that Windows 98 would not be available in the first quarter of 1998, as announced, but only in the second (Shapiro & Varian, 1999a, 275). With regard to its announcements, a company's reputation is also very important in this context. Companies that have a reputation to loose will refrain from making false announcements (Choi et al., 2006, 222).

Early announcements of new products can cause significant damage to not only the individual company, but also to an entire industry, if overall credibility is lost. Intentionally false announcements have thus been subject to prosecution in the USA recently (Bayus et al., 2001, 4 et seq.). In reaction to this, the Software and Information Industry Association has assessed the intentional misannouncement of products as detrimental in their eight principles of competition (Software & Information Industry Association, 2008).

Announcements can further aim in the direction of the **complementors**. They are thus made aware of new products and their planned market introduction and can develop appropriate complementary products at an early stage. If announcements are meant to be directed at complementors, they will typically not be released as press statements; the information tends to be confidentially passed on prior to the announcement, or be announced at a special event. Thus the X-Box was announced and demonstrated by Bill Gates at an annual meeting of game manufacturers. In the gaming industry, such announcements typically entail providing the manufacturers with development tools in order for a sufficient amount of compatible games to be available for the product launch (Le Nagard-Assayag & Manceau, 2001, 207). The announcements are meant to make complementors develop more complementary products for a basic goods than they would without this communication method.

Announcements are of particular importance if they involve network effect products. This explains why announcements are a widely used strategy in the information good industry (Choi et al., 2006, 208).

Managing (customer) expectations plays a crucial role for network effect products in particular (Shapiro & Varian, 1999a, 275). Companies have a vested interest in customers not merely expecting that the product will have a strong basic value for them, but that many others will also buy it, thus raising its network effect value.

> When network effects exist, the strategic reason for preannouncing is to gain a faster takeoff by managing consumers' expectations (Lee & O'Connor, 2003, 251).

Announcements represent a kind of psychological positioning strategy, which serves to convince customers that the new product will become the standard (Arthur, 1996).

According to a survey of experts from the music industry (Le Nagard-Assayag & Manceau, 2001, 209), a good's installed base is the most important factor for complementors' decision to manufacture compatible products. Complementors thus observe very precisely how the consumers assess these product announcements. They read journalists' comments and heed the recommendations made by retailers, market experts or even the potential buyers themselves. The internet's role in these processes is becoming increasingly important. The end consumer can make himself be heard very clearly and influences buying processes. Many Early Adopters are also internet users who glean their information from the Web. This played a huge role in the decision between the formats DVD and DivX. Dranove and Gandal (2003, 385 et seq.) found out that the information available on the internet was surprisingly accurate and that the unfavorable perspectives of DivX as a competing technology for DVD had been very well anticipated.

Le Nagard-Assayag and Manceau (2001) observed, on the basis of a model, what interdependencies there were between the expectations of consumers and those of complementors, and how product announcements affected the short- and long-term success of a network effect good. They make it clear that apart from direct network effects, indirect ones also play an important role. They demonstrate, on the example of hardware and software, that quick prevalence can best be achieved if both consumers (direct network effects) and complementors (indirect network effects) nurture great expectations concerning the product's success well ahead of its market launch.

> Microsoft, for instance, announces its new operating systems to program providers several years in advance in order to stimulate the design of software programs. A few months later, the firm makes a public pre-announcement at opinion leaders and potential customers to build favourable expectations about the forthcoming product (Le Nagard-Assayag & Manceau, 2001, 216).

They recommend placing a high priority on customer expectations, as these are the decisive factor for overall success. The complementors' expectations can effect different things. In the most favorable scenario, they are highly positive, in which case it is to be expected that the product will be a success in the short and in the long term. If the complementors' expectations are highly negative, this will impair short-term success, as fewer complementary offers will be available, which will be compensated for, however, once the complementors realize their misestimation and hurry to bring many offers onto the market. The worst-case scenario is a medium expectation of the product's success. In that case, the market will be steadily supplied with an average amount of complements and indirect network effects will be rather weak. Le Nagard-Assayag and Manceau (2003, 216-217) recommend orienting one's announcement strategy on how well complementors can be influenced. If it has to be assumed that no really high expectations can be created, one should instead focus only on the consumers and ignore the complementors' demurrals. Nevertheless, the complementors should not be completely forsaken. Of course they have to be provided with the necessary technological product information and the estimated market potential should also be announced. Additionally, the necessary lead time for product development should be made allowance for, so that complements will actually be available in time for the market launch.

Product announcements of network effect products work not only in the direction of the customers and complementors, but also have a large significance for the expectations of the **competitors**. They should, where possible, be prevented from entering the market in question. Such communication-induced market entry barriers can only be created, though, if the announcement does not stimulate but discourages competition. Eliashberg and Chaterjee (1985) derive, from different models, that the market leader will act more aggressively (e.g. via more ads) if he expects that the competitors' reaction will be weak or come with heavy delays and no clear direction.

There are thus correlations between the different groupings of addressees of product announcements, specifically consumers and competitors, which companies must take into account in their communication:

> A firm's decision of whether or not to preannounce a new product often results from a trade-off between the anticipation of increased future sales of the new product and the negative consequences related to freezing purchases, cannibalizing former products and stimulating competitive reactions (Le Nagard-Assayag & Manceau, 2001, 206).

Product announcements influence competitors' assessments regarding the chances for the swift building of an installed base:

> Under increasing returns, rivals will back off in a market not only if it is locked in but if they *believe* it will be locked in by someone else (Arthur, 1996, 107).

If network effects are at play, however, product announcements can be used strategically not only by the first mover, but also by a second, to achieve success in spite of the temporal disadvantage. Farrell and Saloner (1986) demonstrate this on a mathematical model. They refer to the switch from an existing technology to a new, incompatible one. Announcements by a market follower can obstruct the innovator's building of an installed base, or even prevent it.

> The timing of the announcement of a new incompatible product can critically determine whether the new product supersedes the existing technology (Farrell & Saloner, 1986, 942).

In this case, there are users who will, due to the announcement, not buy the already available product but wait for the new one and thus contribute–after its market entry–to that latter's increased building up of an installed base. This could be clearly observed in the introduction of DivX as a competing format for the DVD. The DivX announcement led to a decline in the adoption rate of DVD technology. This effect, however, only caused temporary market insecurity. DivX was found out very soon as an early product announcement, and neither was there any commitment on the part of the film industry to provide the necessary complementary content (Dranove & Gandal, 2003). In the end, DivX was not able to assert itself as the standard.

Following the same principle, then, a company can also protect its own, already established technology from a new competitor's market entry, of course, by announcing a follow-up technology, product enhancements or, as is common practice in the software industry, updates or upgrades.

Lemley and McGowan (1998, 505) detect even farther-reaching effects of product announcements, namely with regard to the creation of a standard:

> By preannouncing a product, a large company may therefore influence
> the outcome of a standards competition in an industry characterized by
> network effects.

Announcements thus play an important role in the question of whether a (competing) product reaches critical mass and whether network effects come into play. They are an important strategic instrument of communication, bearing opportunities as well as risks.

22.4.2   Commitment

Another way of sending strategic signals is via commitment, also called bonding (Göbel, 2002, 328). If companies assume certain externally visible obligations, e.g. by investing heavily in production facilities, this strategic commitment is meant to show which path they have chosen. Opportunistic behavior–i.e. doing something other than what was signaled–will profit them nothing after this. In the establishment of standards in particular, investing in large production facilities sends a signal for the lasting production of the new goods and the willingness for establishing a new standard. Investment announcements are particularly popular in cases where companies do not yet have the kind of reputation that could be damaged by opportunistic behavior. This was the case for Grundig, who announced the construction of large production facilities during the standardization competition for video recorder systems at the end of the 1970s in order to demonstrate their determination to establish Video 2000 as the standard. In view of the market potential at the time, it was clear that the volume which had been planned could only be sold if a dominant market position was attained (Heß, 1993, 65-66). Philips acted similarly during the establishment of the CD as the standard succeeding LPs (McGahan, 1991).

Another strategic signal in the form of commitment is when companies have committed customers and want to show the competition that, after a period of price competition, they now want to proceed to the phase where they milk their existing customers for all they're worth (Metge, 2008, 195). The (prohibitive) switching costs are used to exhaust one's own customers' willingnesses to pay, thus signaling the competition that the struggle for market share is coming to an end.

22.4.3 Cooperations

Potential customers' expectations can also be influenced by announcing different forms of cooperations. Innovators are always monopolists shortly after launching their new product. For potential customers, this bears the danger of monopolistic pricing, which in turn can lead to shopping reticence. In order to make it clear that that is not the sole provider's intention, access to a technology can be opened up. In this so-called "Second Sourcing", the modes of procurement are stretched out for the buyer by enhancing the production from one to two or more competing manufacturers. Second Sourcing is defined by Farrell and Gallini (1988, 673-674) as:

> Voluntary inviting competitors into the market, usually by licensing a product at low royalties or by using an "open architecture". This involves giving away part of the market, so it is not obvious that it will be profitable.

This opening up creates infra-technological competition, which makes it impossible for the individual company to artificially reduce its offer and set monopolistic prices. Furthermore, opening up access is a signal to providers of complementary products, for whom the security that sufficient basic offers will be made–even in case of the innovator's insolvency–is increased. This lowers the investment risk for the production of complements (Ehrhardt, 2001, 121-122). IBM is the classical example for the offer of an open system. IBM encouraged independent software providers to write IBM-compatible software in order to have sufficient complements available in time for market launch (Katz & Shapiro, 1994, 103).

The extent of opening up can reach from exclusive deals between only two companies up to large networks. Cooperation with big-name partners positively influences the expectations of the other market players.

> The most direct way to manage expectations is by assembling allies and making grand claims about your product's current or future popularity (Shapiro & Varian, 1999a, 275).

Prestigious companies often assume the role of opinion leaders. They are assumed to have large expertise and the ability of making a well-founded judgment on new products and technologies. Winning them as cooperation partners is thus extremely valuable. Sun Microsystems chose such a path, for example, by placing full-page ads in 1999, naming all the famous partners in their JAVA coalition (Shapiro & Varian, 1999a, 275-276). Likewise, the struggle for the follow-up standard to DVD was fought by building alliances and winning the big names of the participating industries.

In this sort of invitation to market entry (Second Sourcing), the monopolistic innovator (as was elaborated in detail above, in the chapter on Compatibility Management and Standardization) must weigh two effects against each other: the competitive effect and the network effect (Economides, 1996b, Ch. 4.1). The competitive effect means a decline of market share and a tendency toward decreasing prices and profits due to the increasing number of competitors. The (direct) network effects, on the other hand, cause an increasing willingness to pay and rising prices due to the high number of expected sales. If the network effects are strong enough, they will overcompensate for the disadvantages stemming from the increased intensity of competition (Economides, 1996a, 231). The network will grow much more strongly with competition than it would if the innovator were to go it alone. The same goes for the complements: their sales will also increase in line with the basic good's. If the original monopolist additionally offers complements, he will be able to profit from the network effects twofold.

22.4.4   Communicating the Network Growth

It is important, and thus has to be stressed once more, that the network effects are due not merely to the actual number of participants and availability of complements, but also to the expected size of the network and of the corresponding complementary offer in the planned period of participation (Katz & Shapiro, 1994). Thus it can come to a self-fulfilling prophecy, as the system which is expected to succeed will, in all probability, go on to do so (Picot & Scheuble, 2000, 251). Particularly if the market is in an unstable equilibrium (Linde, 2008, 125 et seq.), it can be the customers' expectations on their own that lead to a mushrooming of demand, up to a stable equilibrium, and thus decide whether a product succeeds or fails (Wiese, 1991, 46). This also makes it clear how important it is to continually keep communicating the status of network growth until success is confirmed. Apple practiced this to excess when launching iTunes in May 2003. In the following months, up to December, Apple released ten press statements meant to signal the success of the music service (Apple, 2003). How this can lead to an interplay of self-strengthening effects is clearly observable on the example of VHS video recorders (Dietl & Royer, 2000, 326). The growing offer of VHS recorders led to a growing offers of films in the corresponding format. The growing offer of films in turn led to increased demand for recorders. This lowered unit costs for both the hardware and complement providers, which facilitated price reductions and thus increased demand further. Additionally, the offer of the most diverse complements (recording devices for home videos, devices for programming the recorders etc.) increased, further strengthening the positive feedback.

22.4.5   Insurance Offers

A somewhat more specific signaling problem arises for the market launch of a network effect good. As long as critical mass is not reached, the provider faces the danger of setbacks if demand is not increased via direct and indirect network effects but customers instead decide to wait. In this penguin phase, early adopters will already be among the buyers, but the broad masses, who have a vested interest in the product's prevalence due to the network effects, are not yet ready to buy. They are insecure as to whether the product or the technology will in fact assert itself. A highly innovative solution, capable of solving the starting problem securely and free of charge is the insurance solution by Dybvig and Spatt (1983). They suggest giving every potential buyer of a network effect good insurance. Everyone who now decides to buy no longer has to run the risk of the desired network effects failing to establish themselves to an insufficient amount of other users. If that were the case, the insurance would come into effect and provide compensation. As the insurance largely reduces the insecurity, though, encouraging many consumers to buy the product, it will only be used minimally. Dybvig and Spatt regard the national government as the provider of such an insurance (1983, 238 et seq.), but the producer of a network effect good himself can also make such an offer (Wiese, 1991, 47). The problem of customer insecurity is transferred to the provider via this solution. As long as he is entirely certain of market success, the offering of insurance is in fact free–outside of the transaction costs for effecting and disseminating it. On the other hand, if demand does not grow as expected, the provider can incur significant expenses.

22.4.6   Limit-Pricing

Signaling also plays a large role during market entry, if the provider's goal is to keep the competition at arm's length. Low (penetration) prices set by the first mover send a clear signal that the market is unattractive for the follower(s). "Limit-Price" specifically designates the highest possible price that will still prevent the competition from entering the market (Wied-Nebbeling, 1994, 202 et seq.). Due to the existing information asymmetries between the first mover and his competitors, the followers are unable to accurately assess what the reasons for the pricing are (Wied-Nebbeling, 2004, 253 et seq.). Does the first mover have such a large pricing latitude due to low unit costs, or does he estimate demand to be so low that it can only be exploited via very low prices? Neither reason is an incentive for entering the market as follower and risk failing to reach one's minimum optimal company size.

Signaling, as was demonstrated, is a mighty but multivalent instrument. There is a multitude of available signaling options for influencing the various different stakeholders (customers, suppliers, complementors, competitors). As single signals can achieve different effects at the same time, though, good planning and careful coordination are imperative.

22.5   Conclusion

- Information asymmetries are in effect when one side of the market is better informed than the other. In that case, market coordination no longer works as well as it could, as supply and demand find no common ground despite being prepared to sell and buy at a set price, respectively. In the extreme case, this can lead to market failure.
- A provider can use signals to show the customers that he is trustworthy, and that his products actually possess the quality that is advertised.
- Signals always play a role for unobservable characteristics or intentions about which a credible statement must be made.
- Signaling is part of a company's communication policy. Besides product-related quality signals, signaling can also be used for strategic market communication.
- Overall, most information goods display very little search qualities, but highly pronounced experience and credence qualities. For the buyer, it is thus generally difficult to comprehensively gauge the product's quality prior to purchasing.
- Providers can reduce information asymmetries by offering parts of the information good. This can be done via direct access, e.g. via previews or test licenses, or indirectly, via meta-information.
- If direct inspection offers are made, the information paradox must be taken into consideration: by opening up (parts of) the information good prior to purchasing, demand can already be satisfied so extensively that the customer's willingness to pay regresses to zero.
- Performance-related information substitutes are signals that refer to the provider's sales policy design as perceived by the customer. They are substitutes for inspection offers, i.e. for access to the information good itself. They serve to reduce insecurities relating to a product's experience qualities.
- Information substitutes relating to all products and services do not directly signal the quality of a specific product but point beyond the single services and signal that the company is a quality provider.
- Signals that are used to reduce information asymmetries for experience qualities (performance-related information substitutes) also reduce search-related quality insecurities. The same goes for signals to reduce quality insecurities resulting from credence qualities (information substitutes relating to all services), which complementarily cover experience- and search-related insecurities (downward compatibility).
- The central information substitute relating to all producs and services is the provider's reputation.

- Crucial signals of strategic market communication are product announcements, commitments and cooperations.
- Product announcements are deliberate acts of communication effected by a company before performing a specific action on the market.
- A company is said to be committed if it takes on certain obligations, visible to the outside, in order to show which path it has chosen to follow.
- The expectations of potential customers can be influenced by announcing cooperations. Opening up access to a technology (second sourcing) creates competition, which reduces the customers' dependence.
- As complementary signaling methods of strategic market communication, providers can communicate network growth, make insurance offers or use limit-pricing.

22.6   Bibliography

Adler, J. (1996). Informationsökonomische Fundierung von Austauschprozessen. Eine nachfrageorientierte Analyse. Wiesbaden: Gabler (Neue betriebswirtschaftliche Forschung, 204).

Akerlof, G.A. (1970). The market for "lemons". Quality, uncertainty, and the market mechanism. Quarterly Journal of Economics, 84, 488-500.

Apple Inc. (ed.) (2003). Press Releases 2003. (Online).

Arrow, K.J. (1962). Economic welfare and the allocation of resources for invention. In The Rate and Direction of Inventive Activity. Economic and Social Factors. A Report by the National Bureau of Economic Research, New York (pp. 609-626). Princeton, NJ: Princeton University Press.

Arthur, B.W. (1996). Increasing returns and the new world of business. Harvard Business Review, 74, 100-109.

Backhaus, K., & Voeth, M. (2007). Industriegütermarketing. 8th ed. München: Vahlen (Vahlens Handbücher der Wirtschafts- und Sozialwissenschaften).

Barwise, P., Elberse, A., & Hammond, K. (2002). Marketing and the internet: A research review. In Weitz, B. A., & Wensley, R. (eds.), Handbook of Marketing (pp. 527-557). London: SAGE.

Bayus, B. L., Jain, S., & Rao, A. G. (2001). Truth or consequences: An analysis of vaporware and new product announcements. Journal of Marketing Research, 38, 3-11.

Besen, S.M., & Farrell, J. (1994). Choosing how to compete. Strategies and tactics in standardization. Journal of Economic Perspectives, 8(2), 117-131.

Bock, A. (2000). Gütezeichen als Qualitätsaussage im digitalen Informationsmarkt. Dargestellt am Beispiel elektronischer Rechtsdatenbanken. Darmstadt: STMV. (Beiträge zur juristischen Informatik, 24).

Boulding, W., & Kirmani, A. (1993). A consumer-side experimental examination of signaling theory: Do consumers perceive warranties as signals of quality. Journal of Consumer Research, 20, 111-123.

Brynjolfsson, E., & Smith, M. D. (2000). Frictionless commerce? A comparison of internet and conventional retailers. Management Science, 46(4), 563-585.

Calore, M. (2008). Cast your vote: Wired's 2007 vaporware awards. Compilerd from Wired.com. Wired News. (Online).

Choi, J.P., Kristiansen, E. G., & Nahm, J. (2006). Preannouncing information goods. In Illing, G., & Peitz, M. (eds.), Industrial Organization and the Digital Economy (pp. 208-228). Cambridge, MA: MIT Press.

Choi, S.Y., Stahl, D.O., & Whinston, A.B. (1997). The Economics of Electronic Commerce. Indianapolis, IN: Macmillan Technical Pub.

Clement, M., Hille, A., Lucke, B., Schmidt-Stölting, C., & Sambeth, F. (2008). Der Einfluss von Rankings auf den Absatz - Eine empirische Analyse der Wirkung von Bestsellerlisten und Rangpositionen auf den Erfolg von Büchern. Zeitschrift für betriebswirtschaftliche Forschung, 60, 746-777.

Cooper, R., & Ross, T. W. (1985). Product warranties and double moral hazard. Rand Journal of Economics, 16, 103-113.

Darby, M.R., & Karni, E. (1973). Free competition and the optimal amount of fraud. Journal of Law and Economics, 16, 67-88.

Degeratu, A.M., Rangaswamy, A., & Wu J. (2000). Consumer choice behavior in online and traditional supermarkets: The effects of brand name, price, and other search attributes. International Journal of Research in Marketing, 17(1), 55-78.

Deysson, C. (1990). Subtile Gehirnwäsche. Wirtschaftswoche, 44(5), 110-112.

Dietl, H., & Royer, S. (2000). Management virtueller Netzwerkeffekte in der Informationsökonomie. Zeitschrift für Organisation, 69(6), 324-331.

Diller, H. (2008). Preispolitik. 4th ed. Stuttgart: Kohlhammer (Kohlhammer Edition Marketing).

Dranove, D., & Gandal, N. (2003). The DVD vs. DIVX standard war: Empirical evidence of network effects and preannouncement effects. Journal of Economics and Management Strategy, 12(3), 363-386.

Dybvig, P.H., & Spatt, C.S. (1983). Adoption externalities as public goods. Journal of Public Economics, 20, 231-247.

Economides, N. (1996a). Network externalities, complementarities, and invitations to enter. European Journal of Political Economy, 12, 211-233.

Economides, N. (1996b). The Economics of Networks. (Online).

Ehrhardt, M. (2001). Netzwerkeffekte, Standardisierung und Wettbewerbsstrategie. Wiesbaden: Dt. Univ.-Verlag (Gabler Edition Wissenschaft : Strategische Unternehmungsführung).

Eliashberg, J., & Chatterjee, R. (1985). Analytical models of competition with implications for marketing: Issues, findings, and outlook. Journal of Marketing Research, 22(3), 237-261.

Eliashberg, J., & Robertson, T.S. (1988). New product preannouncing beavior: A market signaling study. Journal of Marketing Research, 25(3), 282-292.

Farrell, J., & Gallini, N.. (1988). Second sourcing as a commitment - monopoly incentives to attract competition. Quarterly Journal of Economics, 103, 673-694.

Farrell, J., & Saloner, G. (1986). Installed base and compatibility: Innovation, product preannouncements, and predation. American Economic Review, 76(5), 940-955.

Fließ, S. (2004). Qualitätsmanagement bei Vertrauensgütern. Marketing (ZFP) - Zeitschrift für Forschung und Praxis, 25, Spezialausgabe Dienstleistungsmarketing, 33-44.

Gans, J. (2008). Managerial Economics Online. Melbourne Business School. (Online).

Göbel, E. (2002). Neue Institutionenökonomik. Konzeption und betriebswirtschaftliche Anwendungen. Stuttgart: Lucius & Lucius.

Grant, R.M., & Nippa, M. (2006). Strategisches Management. Analyse, Entwicklung und Implementierung von Unternehmensstrategien. 5th ed. München: Pearson Studium (wi - wirtschaft).

Haller, J. (2005). Urheberrechtsschutz in der Musikindustrie. Eine ökonomische Analyse. Lohmar: Eul-Verl.

Hane, P. J. (2002). Divine acquires Northern Light, announces premium content agreement with Yahoo! Information Today, 19(3), 1.

Heß, G. (1993). Kampf um den Standard. Erfolgreiche und gescheiterte Standardisierungsprozesse - Fallstudien aus der Praxis. Stuttgart: Schäffer-Poeschel.

Hutter, M. (2003). Information goods. In Towse, R. (ed.), A Handbook of Cultural Economics (pp. 263-268). Cheltenham: Elgar.

Irmscher, M. (1997). Markenwertmanagement. Aufbau und Erhalt von Markenwissen und -vertrauen im Wettbewerb. Eine informationsökonomische Analyse. Frankfurt am Main: Lang (Europäische Hochschulschriften Reihe 5, Volks- und Betriebswirtschaft, 2081).

Jöckel, S. (2008). Videospiele als Erfahrungsgut. Der Einfluss von Online-Bewertungen auf den Erfolg von Videospielen. MedienWirtschaft, Sonderheft, 59-66.

Katz, M.L., & Shapiro, C. (1985). Network externalities, competition, and compatibility. American Economic Review, 75(3), 424-440.

Katz, M.L., & Shapiro, C. (1994). Systems competition and network effects. Journal of Economic Perspectives, 8(2), 93-115.

Kim, J.Y., Natter, M., & Spann, M. (2009). Pay what you want: A new participative pricing mechanism. Journal of Marketing, 73(1), 44-58.

Kirmani, A., & Rao, A.R. (2000). No pain, no gain. A critical review of the literature on signaling: Unobservable product quality. Journal of Marketing, 64, 66-79.

Kirmani, A., & Wright, P. (1989). Money talks: Perceived advertising expense and expected product quality. Journal of Consumer Research, 16, 344-353.

Klein, B., & Leffler, K.B. (1981). The role of market forces in assuring contractual performance. Journal of Political Economy, 89(4), 615-641.

Kleinaltenkamp, M. (1994). Technische Standards als Signale im Marktprozeß. In Zahn, E. (ed.), Technologiemanagement und Technologien für das Management. 55. Wissenschaftliche Jahrestagung des Verbandes der Hochschullehrer für Betriebswirtschaft e. V. an der Universität Stuttgart 1993 (pp. 197-226). Stuttgart: Schäffer-Poeschel.

Klodt, H. (2001). Und sie fliegen doch. Wettbewerbsstrategien für die Neue Ökonomie. In Donges, J.B., & Mai, S. (eds.), E-Commerce und Wirtschaftspolitik (pp. 31-48). Stuttgart.

Kohli, C. (1999). Signaling new product introductions: A framework explaining the timing of preannouncements. Journal of Business Research, 46(1), 45-56.

Köster, D. (1999). Wettbewerb in Netzproduktmärkten. Wiesbaden: Dt. Univ.-Verlag. (Beiträge zur betriebswirtschaftlichen Forschung, 89).

Le Nagard-Assayag, E., & Manceau, D. (2001). Modeling the impact of product preannouncements in the context of indirect network externalities. International Journal of Research in Marketing, 18, 203-219.

Lee, Y., & O'Connor, G.C. (2003). New product launch strategy for network effects. Journal of the Academy of Marketing Science, 31(3), 241-255.

Lemley, M., & McGowan D. (1998). Legal implications of network economic effects. California Law Review, 86, 481-611.

Lilly, B., & Walters, R. (1997). Toward a model of new product preannouncements timing. Journal of Product and Innovation Management, 14, 4-20.

Linde, F. (2008). Ökonomie der Information. 2nd ed. Göttingen: Univ.-Verl. Göttingen.

Luo, W., & Chung, Q. (2002). An empirical investigation of reputation and price dispersion in electronic commerce. Association for Information Systems, AMCIS 2002 Proceedings. (Online).

Maaß, C. (2006). Strategische Optionen im Wettbewerb mit Open-Source-Software. Berlin: Logos.

Malaga, R.A., & Werts, N. (2000). The use of reputation mechanisms in electronic commerce. An empirical investigation. Paper Presented at the Fifth American Conference on Information Systems. Milwaukee, WI.

McGahan, A.M. (1991). Philips' Compact Disc Introduction. Case Study. Boston, MA: Harvard Business School Publishing (Online).

McLachlan, C. (2004). Wettbewerbsorientierte Gestaltung von Informationsasymmetrien. Eine informationsökonomisch fundierte Analyse des anbieterseitigen Informationsverhaltens. Norderstedt: Books on Demand.

Melnik, M., & Alm, J. (2002). Does a seller's ecommerce reputation matter? Evidence from eBay auctions. Journal of Industrial Economics, 50(3), 337-349.

Metge, J. (2008). Wechselkosten, Marktzutritt und strategisches Unternehmensverhalten. Frankfurt am Main: Lang (Europäische Hochschulschriften Reihe 5, Volks- und Betriebswirtschaft, 3310).

Monroe, K. B. (2003). Pricing. Making Profitable Decisions. 3rd ed. Boston,MA: McGraw-Hill/Irwin.

Nalebuff, B.J., & Brandenburger, A.M. (1996). Coopetition - kooperativ konkurrieren. Mit der Spieltheorie zum Unternehmenserfolg. Frankfurt am Main: Campus.

Nelson, P. (1974). Advertising as information. Journal of Political Economy, 82, 729-753.

Notess, G. (1998). Northern Light: New search engine for the web and full-text articles. Database, 21(1), 32-37.

Osborne, A., & Dvorak, J. (1984). Hypergrowth. The Rise and Fall of Osborne Computer Corporation. Berkeley: Idthekketan.

Parker, P. M. (1995). Sweet lemons: Illusory quality, self-deceivers, advertising, and price. Journal of Marketing Research, 32(3), 291-307.

Picot, A., Reichwald, R., & Wigand, R.T. (2003). Die grenzenlose Unternehmung. Information, Organisation und Management. Lehrbuch zur Unternehmensführung im Informationszeitalter. 5th ed. Wiesbaden: Gabler (Gabler-Lehrbuch).

Picot, A., & Scheuble, S. (2000). Hybride Wettbewerbsstrategien in der Informations- und Netzökonomie. In Welge, M. K., Al-Laham, A., & Kajüter, P. (eds.), Praxis des strategischen Managements. Konzepte, Erfahrungen, Perspektiven (pp. 239-257). Wiesbaden: Gabler.

Rogers, E. M. (2003). Diffusion of Innovations. 5th ed. New York, NY: Free Press.

Rüller, C. (2000). Die Zertifizierung nach ISO 9000ff. in der Informationswirtschaft. Institut für Informationswissenschaft der Fachhochschule Köln. (Kölner Arbeitspapiere zur Bibliotheks- und Informationswissenschaft, 28).

Scitovsky, T. (1945). Some consequences of the habit of judging quality by price. Review of Ecomomic Studies, 12, 100-105.

Shapiro, C. (1983). Premiums for high quality products as returns to reputations. Quarterly Journal of Economics, 97, 659-679.

Shapiro, C., & Varian, H.R. (1999a). Information Rules. A Strategic Guide to the Network Economy. [repr.]. Boston, MA: Harvard Business School Press.

Shapiro, C., & Varian, H.R. (1999b). The art of standards wars. California Management Review, 41(2), 8-32.

Shimp, T.A., & Bearden, W.O. (1982). Warranty and other extrinsic cue effects on consumers´ risk perceptions. Journal of Consumer Research, 9, 38-46.

Software & Information Industry Association (2008). Sustaining Competition in the Software Industry: Enforcement of Current Laws is Key.

Spence, M. (1973). Job market signaling. Quarterly Journal of Economics, 87, 355-374.

Spence, M. (1976). Informational aspects of market structure: An introduction. Quarterly Journal of Economics, 90, 591-597.

Stahl, F. (2005). Paid Content. Strategien zur Preisgestaltung beim elektronischen Handel mit digitalen Inhalten. Wiesbaden: Dt. Univ.-Verlag. (Gabler Edition Wissenschaft).

Suarez, F.F. (2004). Battles for technological dominance: an integrative framework. Research Policy, 33(2), 271-286.

Takeyama, L.N. (2003). Piracy, asymmetric information and product quality. In Gordon, W. J., & Watt, R. (eds.), The Economics of Copyright. Developments in Research and Analysis (pp. 55-65). Cheltenham: Elgar.

Takeyama, L.N. (2009). Copyright enforcement and product quality signaling in markets for computer software. Information Economics and Policy, 21(4), 291-296.

Tolle, E. (1994). Informationsökonomische Erkenntnisse für das Marketing bei Qualitätsunsicherheit der Konsumenten. Zeitschrift für betriebswirtschaftliche Forschung, 46, 926-938.

Varian, H.R. (1998). Markets for Information Goods. Berkeley: University of California. (Online).

Völckner, F. (2006). Determinanten der Informationsfunktion des Preises: Eine empirische Analyse. Zeitschrift für Betriebswirtschaft, 76(5), 473-497.

Wied-Nebbeling, S. (1994). Markt- und Preistheorie. 2nd ed. Berlin: Springer (Springer-Lehrbuch).

Wied-Nebbeling, S. (2004). Preistheorie und Industrieökonomik. 4th ed. Berlin: Springer (Springer-Lehrbuch).

Wiese, H. (1991). Marktschaffung. Das Startproblem bei Netzeffekt-Gütern. Marketing (ZFP) - Zeitschrift für Forschung und Praxis, 1, 43-51.

Yoon, E., Guffey, H.J., & Kijewski, V. (1993). The effects of information and company reputation on intentions to buy a business service. Journal of Business Research, 27(3), 215-228.

Zerdick, A. et al. (eds.) (2001). Die Internet-Ökonomie. Strategien für die digitale Wirtschaft. 3rd ed. Berlin: Springer.

Chapter 23

Lock-In Management

23.1   Switching Costs and Lock-In

Besides acquisition costs, each mode of utilizing a(n information) good leads to familiarization costs, be they a website's navigation structure, the different uses of a software application or the page and subject layout of a(n online) newspaper. Getting to grips with a new product requires an effort on the part of someone who is used to a certain product. This can be minimal, if one only switches between different types of cell phone by the same provider, but it can become more complicated when dealing with a competing product's entirely new menu structure. The economist here speaks of switching costs, i.e. material (e.g. buying durable hardware) and immaterial costs (e.g. getting acquainted with a new program) incurred by the user when switching from one product to another. In the extreme case, switching costs can get so high for a user that the actual switch is no longer rationally justifiable: he is in a Lock-In (Shapiro & Varian, 1999, 103 et seq., Varian, 2003, 20 et seq.).

Porter (1980, 10) defined switching costs, or switching barriers, very early on as

> one time costs facing the buyer [when] switching from one supplier's product to another.

The first detailed discussion of the phenomenon of switching costs is found in Klemperer (1987). Generally, in any consideration of switching costs, costs are understood to include not merely a monetary but also a temporal, psychological and/or social commitment of resources. Switching costs thus include any genre of deterrents that make it harder, or even impossible, for consumers to switch providers (Staack, 2004, 151).

The user's switching costs can be separated into two components (Rams, 2001, 38). On the one hand, switching providers generates **direct**, palpable costs. These include the costs of any necessary contract cancellation, the transaction costs for selection and acquisition as well as set-up costs for installing, integrating etc. the new product. Also included are costs for organizational adjustments and the building up of human resources (e.g. via special training programs) in order to get used to the new product. On the other hand, **indirect** costs are incurred by foregoing any further use of the previous product. The indirect costs include all sunk costs, which are irreversible investments in hardware stocks or product-specific user training courses. Such investments cannot be reversed via decisions made in the present or future. The sole exception is investing in assets with resale value, such as used game or software licenses, or reusable hardware. Another component of indirect costs are the so-called opportunity costs. They represent–generally speaking–the value of foregoing a possible alternative. In case of a provider switch, for instance, the positive value of the previous business relationship is lost. Opportunity costs are particularly significant if the old and the new offer are only tangentially comparable. This is always the case when the previous offer has exclusive features, such as loyalty or patron discounts, which become forfeit when switching providers.

Besides the switching costs carried by the user, the new provider also faces expenses. Klemperer (1995, 518-519) distinguishes between transaction costs for administrating new customers, learning costs for working with the new customers and costs stemming from insecurity regarding their quality. Echoing Klemperer (1995, 519), Shapiro and Varian (1999, 112) thus speak of the "total cost of switching" being the costs to be carried by the customer and the new provider put together. It is thus of no import to their overall volume which of the two parties concerned must shoulder them. It is imperative to always incorporate the switching costs in their entirety, because only in this way can it be correctly analyzed whether the acquisition of new customers is worthwhile.

Apart from these **economic switching costs**, one can also identify psychological and social switching barriers (Peter, 2001, 120 et seq., Staack, 2004, 154 et seq.). **Psychological switching barriers** bind the customer through a positive emotional attitude vis-à-vis his current provider. From social psychology, it is known that people align their preferences in favor of the decisions they have made in order to reduce cognitive dissonance.

> Thus if consumers are initially indifferent between competing products, the fact of using one brand will change consumers´ relative utilities for the products so that they perceive a cost of switching brands (Klemperer, 1995, 518).

Benefit increases due to a new product are weighed by the potential buyer against benefit losses, which leads to an asymmetry: products, or product features already owned are usually rated higher than the possible benefits from switching products (Gourville, 2004, 4). The relationship of trust established between the parties concerned is the decisive factor here. Customer retention can also be the result of **social switching barriers**, which have been established via intensive social relationships (acquaintanceship, friendship etc.) between the market partners.

Switching costs, in the customer-supplier relationship, can be incurred not only by the customer but also by the supplier, in this case the provider (Messerschmitt, 2000, 239). Suppliers who have settled on a specific product design, software components and compatibilities cannot readily reverse these decisions. The switching costs are increased further if exclusive supplier relationships have been agreed upon in a single sourcing context.

Switching barriers for the customer are thus the result of investments made and needs satisfied. The focus of our further considerations will only be switching barriers with an economic aspect. In order to make this clear, we will speak of switching *costs* in the following.

23.2 Switching Costs in Information Good Economy

What kinds of switching costs typically occur in the information good economy? We have already addressed a series of (economic) switching costs above, and these also have a bearing on information goods. In the following, we will concentrate in some more detail on particular, information-good-specific switching costs. Shapiro and Varian (1999, 116 et seq.) name a few that are particularly significant for information goods.

Digital information goods are always stored in certain formats: Microsoft Word text files, for example, have the formats .rtf, .doc or .docx, music files have .wav or .mp3. When switching providers, one's **data stock** can be partly or wholly devalued if the new word processor or audio player is unable to read the files. A conversion of the data into a new format may be possible, but this always comes with a lot of work and the risk of data loss. Customers who have large data stocks in specific formats thus quickly find themselves in a Lock-In.

Each mode of utilizing digital information goods requires **compatible end devices**. The music collection from Sony's former online service Connect, in the ATRAC format, can only be played by Sony's portable players (or licensed products). Customers with a large music library are in a double Lock-In: if they switch providers, they will no longer be able to use their old stock, which requires specific devices in order to be accessed; devices which, again, cannot be used in connection with alternative products. A switch to iTunes or musicload thus becomes improbable. This great Lock-In risk was probably the decisive factor for Sony's music store Connect closing down in March 2008. Shortly prior, Sony had even opened up its playback devices for other formats so as not to endanger further sales.

In order to be used, every information good requires an end device that the user has to get accustomed to. This holds, on the one hand, for traditional information goods like a daily newspaper, with which one knows after a very short time where the weather forecast and the sports results can be found. It also holds, and far more strongly, for all sorts of software-supported output (e.g. via browsers) or software usage itself. The user is accustomed to certain navigation structures, functions or workflows, which makes it less attractive for him, over time, to switch to different displays and systems. Going beyond personal de- as well as habituation, there are often additional expenses for manuals, schooling or technical support incurred for **product-specific introductory training**.

Loyalty programs should be mentioned again, as these can be implemented particularly cheaply for information goods. The low variable costs make it easy for providers to make customers attractive offers (reduced purchasing costs, expanded offers etc.) in case of repeat purchases. Particularly in the online business, this practice is supported by the easily attainable and analyzable customer information, which is commonly registered (Shapiro & Varian, 1999, 127 et seq.).

According to Shapiro and Varian (1999, 110), switching costs are of paramount importance in information good economy:

> Switching costs are the norm, not the exception, in the information economy.

23.3   From Accidental Lock-In to Planned Lock-In

High or even prohibitive switching costs lead to customers continuing to use the product once they have bought it and not switch providers. In Chapter 19, Standardization, we chose as an example for a strong Lock-In the QWERTY keyboard. This case, together with the dominance of VHS in the video cassette market, are often named as examples where better offers (DSK keyboard, BetaMax) were available but could not beat the collective Lock-In (Grant & Nippa, 2006, 442; Beck 2002, 56 et seq., very critically, on the other hand, Liebowitz & Margolis, 1995). In this context, the question arises for companies whether they can influence the occurrence of a Lock-In.

Lock-In effects had been regarded for a long time as extraordinarily significant yet historically random events in the development of networks. Only in the 1990s did this view change fundamentally in network economics (Erber & Hagemann, 2002, 287), as it became clear that Lock-In effects could be controlled or even artificially created.

> Companies that knew of the significance of positive network externalities in markets for network effect goods were able to use this knowledge in the competition with others in order to leverage this *managed lock-in* strategy into a dominant market position (Erber & Hagemann, 2002, 288).

The costs incurred when switching network providers thus became an important strategic instrument for controlling the market. Particularly new was the realization that switching costs were no longer the result of specific technological distinctions or standards alone, but could be created artificially and deliberately, with the sole aim of making the switch harder for users (Erber & Hagemann, 2002, 288).

Next to the externally dictated exogenous switching costs, known and investigated for some time, we thus additionally have so-called **endogenous** switching costs, which can be controlled by the company itself. The latter have not been extensively researched so far (Haucap, 2003, 29). Nilssen (1992) regards artificial switching costs as typically endogenous. Among such artificial switching costs are, for example, discounts as well as loyalty or bonus systems (Metge, 2008, 8-9). Since goods that are ex ante relatively homogenous are made heterogeneous ex post by the existence of switching costs applying to the purchase, providers have the impetus to artificially create switching costs in order to differentiate the product (or service) on offer from its competing products (Klemperer, 1987, 375).

23.4   The Lock-In Cycle

How specifically does a Lock-In come about? Shapiro and Varian (1999, 131-132) regard the development of a Lock-In as a dynamic process over time, consisting of four phases. The starting point is product or **brand selection**–this can be an eBook, a Gameboy or visiting a job placement portal. The first time, this will be a decision by the consumer that is free from switching costs, as switching costs only occur as the consequence of certain decisions. In the second phase (**sampling**), the consumer decides to test the offer. He reads excerpts from the eBook, plays on the Gameboy for five minutes or browses the job portal. Pricing is an important instrument for this phase. Nothing is easier for information providers to make easy, free trial offers. The great danger inherent to this, however, is that the customer will content himself with the trial offer, ignoring the priced alternatives. Customers who assay the product beyond the trial phase enter the third phase of the Lock-In Cycle, the **entrenchment** phase. If the consumer learns to appreciate the author's writing style, likes the games as well as handling of the Gameboy or finds all the relevant information he needs on the job portal, he will get used to the new product and develop a preference, as against other alternatives. He might even make complementary investments. These could be additional games, or the personal configuration of the offers on the portal. This is where switching costs occur. The provider will try to draw this phase out for as long as possible, to prevent the customer turning to other offers; his goal is to let switching costs increase, ideally (from his perspective) until they become prohibitive and lead to a **Lock-In** in phase four. If this point is actually reached, the customer will stay loyal to his provider and, come the next purchase, merely consider other products without actually testing them. Any renewed **brand selection** in the second and all subsequent passages of the cycle will be significantly shaped by the switching costs that apply.

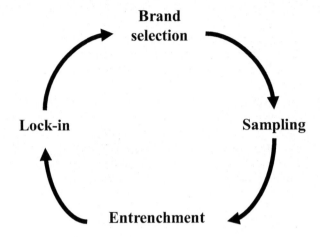

Figure 23.1: Lock-In Cycle. Source: Shapiro & Varian, 1999, 132.

For the provider, it is recommended to not merely look at the first passage of the Lock-In Cycle in order to evaluate a customer relationship, but to take into particular consideration the payment flows to come (Shapiro & Varian, 1999, 133). In this way, he can gauge how much he can invest in customer acquisition. This is particularly relevant if switching costs increase as time passes, as they do in the building of data stocks or in product-specific training. If, on the other hand, they decrease over time, as in the acquisition of hardware that will eventually be discarded, a Lock-In is increasingly less likely. The switching costs must be positive in sum for the provider in order to decrease the likelihood of customer defection.

Hence, Lock-In is a phenomenon that does not occur randomly, but can be actively triggered. In essence, companies can actively manage switching costs. As Lock-In effects are the result of a multitude of factors, however, it is important to exhaust all existing options to generate a Lock-In. Among these are the analysis of the switching costs that inevitably arise for the customer, the artificial creation of switching costs or the wholesale invention of new ones (Erber & Hagemann, 2002, 288).

Shapiro and Varian (1999, 142 et seq.) suggest three steps for strategically exploiting switching costs and Lock-Ins. Step one is the building of an installed base. Corresponding with the phases of brand selection and sampling in the Lock-In Cycle, the goal for information providers must be to build a large customer base as quickly as possible. They can then attempt to bind them by increasing switching costs (entrenchment). These switching costs will then ideally land the customers in a Lock-In. The Lock-In situation, thus the recommendation by Shapiro and Varian (1999, 142) for step three, should then be used economically.

> Maximize the value of your installed base by selling complementary products to loyal customers and by selling access to these customers to other suppliers.

In the following, we will discuss this three-step approach in more detail.

23.4.1   Building an Installed Base

A discussion of all approaches to building an installed base would be tantamount to a representation of all previous chapters on the competitive strategies of information providers. In light of this, previously discussed aspects will only be briefly sketched vis-à-vis new ones.

Let us begin with a demonstrative example. In 1995, Iomega developed the ZIP drive (Shapiro & Varian, 1999, 143). This is a removable disk storage system that works the same way as diskette drives and hard drives. These ZIP drives were very popular because they had large storage capacities, by the standards of the time, holding 100 MB, and were very easy to handle. Floppy Disks, still prevalent at the time, had a storage volume of 1.44 MB. ZIP drives were constructed to accept only ZIP-compatible diskettes, which in turn were exclusively manufactured by Iomega. Iomega's plan was to create an installed base of ZIP drives, in order to sell the diskettes–at a high price–to the locked-in customers. In order to implement this strategy, Iomega used extensive promotional pricing, offering large discounts on the drives, even selling below manufacturing costs. Iomega wanted to distance the competition (e.g. Syquest, Imation) quickly and hoped for positive network effects (e.g. via word of mouth) to occur and that the good diskette margins would lead to profits. Up until 2004, around 50m drives and more than 300m diskettes were sold.

From today's point of view, Iomega used its strategic options well. An innovative product with obvious added value was brought on the market. Penetration Pricing was used in order to push the basic good onto the market in order to create direct network effects. The selected pricing strategy signaled that Iomega was convinced of the quality of its offer and did not fear customers' valuation of its products. At the same time, information asymmetries were reduced via the relatively low introductory prices, which set the hurdle of buying a ZIP drive low. Profits were generated via the captive offer of complements. Cross-subsidization was implemented. The final goal for Iomega was probably to set a proprietary standard, which would have allowed it to realize above-average returns over a longer period.

The fact that this form of power play with a new, revolutionary, incompatible technology did not succeed was probably due to alternative, cheaper storage technologies such as (re)writable CDs and particularly USB flash drives being available too soon. Additionally, technical problems occurred after some time of using the ZIP products: a dirty or out-of-adjustment writing/reading head could damage or even destroy both diskette and drive. The news of the "click of death" (Festa,

1998) went around and created negative publicity. Besides, the price for the diskettes was and still is very high.

What can we learn from this case? An important factor in building an installed base is the market position. Can a provider enter the market as first mover, or is there already a competition that has tied a part of the customers to itself? The pioneer has a clear advantage with regard to acquiring new customers undisturbed by the competition. Nevertheless, there can be switching costs, namely via any existing predecessor products that are used by the customers. Many consumers, for instance, were in a Lock-In regarding LPs and acted very reticently during the transition to CD (Shapiro & Varian, 2003, 56 et seq.). Likewise, there were many employees who were very familiar with the spreadsheet application Lotus 1-2-3 and had little desire to switch (Shapiro & Varian, 2003, 57). When switching costs apply and the customers are tied–by predecessor products or the competition–the quick creation of an installed base becomes markedly more difficult. Here there are several approaches to persuading customers to switch anyway. A whole range of options is provided by signaling: product announcements, cooperations or the communication of a successful market entry are signals that can contribute to the acquisition of customers. Providing compatibility is another option. Here it may be necessary–as for example in mobile telephony, during the transition from GSM to GPRS or UMTS, respectively, or when Microsoft Office 2007 introduced new formats–to build bridges in the form of converters, or to design upward and downward compatibility in such a way that the customers will not shy away from the switch. The crucial question for customer acquisition is how compatible the desired product is, i.e. which standard one buys into when purchasing the product. Buyers with identical preferences generally have a high interest in compatibility. If there are several product alternatives, and the networks are equal in size, they will settle for the opener standard as it provides the greatest security for being able to use compatible products by different providers, even in the future.

For the provider, choosing the standard to which his products are tied (proprietary or open) is thus a very central criterion. Proprietary standards lead to high switching costs. As long as there are no alternatives, they allow the provider to pillage the market. Customers who want to own the product must shoulder the resultant switching costs. Open standards, on the other hand, are tied to low switching costs. If there is already one standard or more on the market, it is thus generally advisable for a new provider to either accept the standard and produce compatible products, or to offer a new standard as an open standard. This can be seen quite clearly on the market for server software: Microsoft profits from existing network effects for Windows and Office in selling its software. The competitors (e.g. Sun with Java or OMG with CORBA), on the other hand, all use open standards (Messerschmitt, 2000, 241).

The openness of standards cannot completely protect the consumer from a Lock-In, however. There may be competition and diversity within a(n open) standard, but when it becomes dominant, entire industries or even societies can end up in a Lock-In. This goes for open (e.g. Internet Protocol) as well as proprietary standards (e.g. IBM PC, Microsoft Windows) (Messerschmitt, 2000, 240-241).

Compatibility lowers the switching costs for the consumer, but simultaneously gives the provider the option of setting a higher starting price for the basic good (Haucap, 2003, 29). This pricing latitude results from the customers' ability to draw from a more varied offer of complements.

Differentiated pricing is advisable over the course of the Lock-In Cycle (Shapiro & Varian, 1999, 163 et seq.). It is to be assumed that one's own (existing) customers have a higher valuation of the existing offer than new customers do. Existing customers, thus the conclusion, are more prepared to accept higher prices than customers who have not previously shown any interest in the offer in question. The standard prices for one's existing customers are generally too high for acquiring new customers. New customers with a lower willingness to pay must thus be won over by lower introductory prices. Attractive–but temporary– introductory offers can make valuable contributions toward acquiring new customers. Many newspapers and magazines take this path and make low-priced introductory offers, which even frequently include a complementary gift, for instance when choosing a trial subscription.

For the sake of acquiring new customers, it is worth differentiating customers with no previous interest in a certain information good from those who already use an equivalent product, i.e. the competition's. While the latter have a higher valuation of willingness to pay for the information good, they are tied to their current provider by the switching costs. A possible approach here is to (partly) shoulder these switching costs. Borland, the provider of Quattro Pro, a spreadsheet application, worked with such offers and gave switchers a 70% discount if they chose Quattro Pro instead of the newer version of their previous product. This discount corresponded with the switchers' relatively high switching costs (Meisner, 2004, 40). This form of subsidizing a switch is also called the Pay-to-Switch Strategy, and it is opposed by the strategy of Pay-to-Stay (Shaffer & Zhang, 2000). Shaffer and Zhang (2000) recommend, on the basis of a model, targeting those customers (one's own or others') whose price elasticity is relatively high with low prices. These can be customers of the competition, whom one can hope to win over via attractively-priced offers, but they can also be one's own customers, who must be dissuaded from turning their back on the company.

How can price discounts, in the form of introductory offers or the subsidy of switching costs, be calculated? How much can be invested in the acquisition of a new customer without losing too much money? Shapiro and Varian recommend using the cash value from a customer relationship as the yardstick (1999, 113; further approaches to calculating switching costs can be found in Metge, 2008, 41 et seq.). Starting off with the switching costs in their entirety, i.e. those of the customer and those of the new provider, the discounts, benefits or bonuses etc. plus one's own costs must under no circumstances amount to more than the cash value from the new customer relationship. This makes an approximate calculation quite simple. Let us suppose that a customer who wants to switch database providers faces 50 Euros of switching costs. Setting the customer up costs the provider a further 25 Euros. Hence, the total switching costs in this case are 75 Euros. The cash value to be expected from the customer relationship should surpass this value, as losses would be incurred otherwise. If the cash value was 100 Euros, one might entice the customer to switch, e.g. by offering to let him use the product for free for two months, which would cost the company 25 Euros per month, for instance. This sum changes nothing in the absolute amount of the switching costs, but merely shifts it from the customer who is willing to switch to the provider. In other words, the customer's switching costs are 0 Euros, those of the provider 50 Euros (from the promised two months free of charge) plus 25 Euros for the set-up, i.e. 75 Euros in total. If we calculate the difference between the total switching costs (75 Euros) and the calculated cash value (100 Euros), we are left with 25 Euros of profit. Alternatively, the money could also be invested in advertisements enticing the customer to switch. If the expected cash value was a mere 70 Euros, however, one should hold back on measures of customer acquisition. If we further take into consideration that the cash value of a One-Euro profit made from a customer over 24 months–provided a monthly interest rate of 2% - is roughly 20 Euros per month, we can estimate fairly easily what the relation between revenue and expenditure will look like. If the company knows that it must make at least 75 Euros from a customer, the profit margin must not fall below 3.75 Euros, seen over 24 months. Assuming (discounted) costs of 1.25 Euros, the customer's monthly fee must be at least 5 Euros.

Total switching costs	€75
Cash value for €1 profit from a customer relationship over 24 months	€20
Necessary profit over 24 months to cover total switching costs	€75/€20 = €3.75
Running costs of customer relationship	€1.25
Minimum monthly fee required	€5

Table 23.1: Cash-Value-Related Approximate Calculation of a Customer Relationship.

An interesting variant to lowering the switching costs is when the provider can offer the customer services that are very cheap for him to make available but have a markedly higher market price. If the above two months free of charge, amounting to two time 25 Euros, only set the provider back 1 Euro, the switching costs are dramatically reduced from the provider's perspective. In that case, they are no longer 75 Euros but a mere 27; 25 Euros for set-up and 2 Euros for providing a service worth 50 Euros to the customer.

It generally holds, for markets with a very high level of switching costs, that for the customer, the added value of the new offer must be significantly higher, or the price, compared to the established offers, a lot lower, in order for a provider to be successful (Heil, 1999, 176; Shapiro & Varian, 1999, 146). The different pricing alternatives were already discussed in detail in Chapter 18 above. Generally, it is still to be noted that customers who have been poached from the competition via subsidies have a relatively high price elasticity and will not stay with the new provider for a very long time. Here it is hugely important to build switching barriers, so that the investment can be recuperated–at least during the stipulated duration.

23.4.2   *Customer Loyalty via the Creation of Switching Costs (Entrenchment)*

When a company has built up an installed base, it can go about attaching its customers. Switching costs–as we could see–are closely related to customer loyalty, which consists of two components. One the one hand, there is the aspect of voluntary loyalty. The customer feels **attached** to the company if the cooperation is pleasant, if he identifies with the provider or if he feels morally obligated, e.g. because the provider puts a lot of effort in. On the other hand, customer loyalty has an aspect of involuntary attachment. Customers feel **bound** if their freedom to act is impeded, e.g. via a lack of alternative offers or contractual obligations (Staack, 2004, 71). Both aspects lead to customers staying loyal to the provider, i.e. continuing the business relationship or broadening it, perhaps even recommending the provider to others (Staack 2004, 170).

Staack (2004, 318 et seq., 353 et seq.) demonstrates empirically that the economic switching barriers (switching costs) represent the crucial influencing factors for customer loyalty in eCommerce (similarly Peter, 2001, 232 for pharmaceutical wholesalers).

They contribute directly and indirectly to the customer's attachment: on the one hand, they directly and strongly influence the customer's boundness. The indirect effect occurs via the influence on the psychological switching barriers. Additionally, the economic switching barriers have a positive influence on customer satisfaction. The competing offer's attractiveness only plays a subordinate role for customer loyalty.

Remarkably, (customer) satisfaction is, overall, negligible in its effect on customer loyalty. It merely serves as a slight intensifier for psychological switching barriers. These, in turn, are only in a positive correlation with the attachment of online customers, but not with their boundness. The boundness of a customer then has a strong positive effect on his loyalty vis-à-vis the provider.

> Besides pure, "voluntary" provider loyalty, caused by a positive attitude (e.g. trust, satisfaction) toward the online shop, it is thus also the construction of switching barriers (and hence the state of "boundness") which leads to a feeling of attachment regarding the company in question (Staack, 2004, 319).

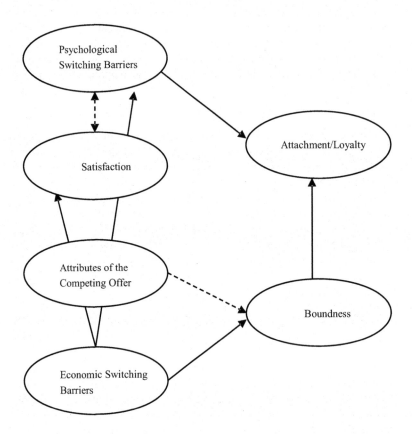

Figure 23.2: Elements of Customer Loyalty in eCommerce. Source: Following Staack, 2004, 318.

From the provider's perspective, it is thus highly advisable to concentrate on economic switching barriers, i.e. switching costs. Of the highest import in this context are those switching costs that can be influenced by the provider himself, namely artificial (endogenous) switching costs.

How can switching costs be influenced, specifically? First of all, the user's familiarity with a product plays an important role, as it generates switching costs. It is then possible for the provider to intensify these familiarization effects. Liebermann (2005, 7) gives the example of adjusting the product according to the customer's specifications (**customization**):

> One example is the loyalty of many buyers to Amazon.com: users grow
> accustomed to features of Amazon's site, which evolve to suit the indi-

vidual user's preferences. These factors allow experienced buyers to search more efficiently on Amazon than on the websites of competitors.

The same furrow is being ploughed by the various "My..." offers for the **personalization** of online portals (My Yahoo!), search engines (iGoogle) or software providers (MySAP). Customers who have individually configured their sites with a provider (e.g. by entering addresses, mailing contacts, dates) face relatively high switching costs–if the data is non-exportable.

Switching costs are not merely the result of individual configuration of or familiarization with an offer, but also of **interactivity**. If chatrooms, message boards or other community services are available on an online portal, one must relinquish any existing contacts when switching providers.

Above, we already addressed the high effectiveness of **customer loyalty programs**. By offering discounts or other benefits, customers are rewarded for their loyalty. The design of such loyalty offers is entirely under the provider's control. The increasing availability of customer data in particular allows for the tailoring of very individual offers. Payback is a well-known German customer loyalty programs spanning across providers. Provider-specific examples are, for instance, airlines' frequent-flier programs or the bonus program of Deutsche Bahn.

Such programs create two kinds of switching costs (Shapiro & Varian, 1999, 128). If a customer has already collected bonuses, these will be forfeit in case he decides to switch. The switching costs can only be minimized if he switches immediately after redeeming them. If, on the other hand, there are benefits for cumulative usage (e.g. discounts or special services), the entire switching costs will rise. It then becomes increasingly unattractive for the customer to switch providers, and more and more complex for the competition to entice the customer to switch, due to the switching costs increasing over the duration of usage.

> The variations on these discount programs are virtually endless. You can offer your customers a discount for buying exclusively from you or for committing to a certain minimum order size. You can offer discounts for customers who buy more than they did last year. You can utilize volume discounts to encourage customers to keep buying from you rather than sampling other suppliers (Shapiro & Varian, 1999, 129).

Contractual agreements represent another option of influencing customer loyalty. The longer the duration of the contracts, the more time the provider has to attach his customers for a long time. Especially in case of a foreseeably long-term Lock-In, it can be in the interest of the customer to sign correspondingly long-term contracts. This serves to protect them from unwanted changes to the company's terms and conditions. For the provider, shorter contracts are preferable, as they give him leverage–in case of high switching costs–and thus a good position for negotiating contract extensions. A popular tactic used by companies is to cut the first passage of the Lock-In Cycle short of their initiative in order to make the customers a new, longer-term contract (Shapiro & Varian, 1999, 170). This can frequently be observed in cell phone providers extending contract durations. Before the customer's switching costs are dramatically reduced as the contract nears expiry, the customers are presented with a new contract that includes a staying bonus.

(Free) offers of newer versions and **upgrades** are also effective means of extending the Lock-In Cycle by increasing the offer's usefulness right before its end.

Providers are further able to influence the **search costs**. The internet with its multitude of options has contributed to lowering search costs in general. For the individual provider, the main concern is to actually be found by potential customers. This involves not hiding from price comparisons and customer ratings online but facing them instead, by offering services with an attractive cost-benefit ratio. On the other hand, the cost of searching quality information can be lowered for the potential customer if the provider puts them into the package, i.e. juxtaposing the product itself with customer ratings, test results etc.

> ... reducing the cost of searching for quality information lowers price sensivity ...[and] ... increases the likelihood that consumers will purchase from that seller ... (Peng et al., 2009, 66).

Switching costs are automatically generated if the provider succeeds in selling his customers products that follow his own **compatibility standard**. Apple is a typical example of such a case. Whoever buys an iPod must buy and manage his music on iTunes. In order to run iTunes, it is necessary to install QuickTime, another Apple product. QuickTime changes browser settings so that music files in the .mp3 format will automatically be opened as QuickTime files. Music bought in the iTunes store is doubly protected: one the one hand via AAC, Apple's file format which is only compatible with iPod and iPhone, and by using the Fairplay DRMS, so far unlicensed to other providers (Gehring, 2007). A similar situation applies to the use of digital audiobooks (Stross, 2005). A large number of audiobooks can be bought in the iTunes store, courtesy of Audible Incorporated. These, too, are only playable on iPod and iPhone.

This interplay generates relatively high switching costs for the user in both cases: buying music or audiobooks in the iTunes store requires an iPod or iPhone in order to be played, while owners of such a device are in turn restricted to those products that are available in the iTunes store.

Driving the user's switching costs up and generating a Lock-In means walking a fine line. In case of a weak market position, high switching costs can lead to customers shying away from one's products. Providers with a strong market position, on the other hand, can use the creation of switching costs as an instrument for opening up additional pricing latitudes and attaching customers even further.

23.4.3 Exploiting Switching Costs and Lock-In

If a provider has managed to build a sufficiently large installed base and generated switching costs, he can then try to translate these into economic advantages. His goal is to make the investments he has made redeem themselves. The customers so far acquired and attached are at the center of all deliberations:

Locked-in customers are valuable assets (Shapiro & Varian, 1999, 144).

Switching costs, and Lock-In in particular, give a company the option of **raising prices**. Haucap and Uhde (undated, 8) show, on the example of American libraries who (must) exhibit scientific journals, that prices have increased massively over the years without a corresponding increase in subscriptions.

Besides simple price increases, there is a whole range of other options for generating revenue streams (Zerdick et al., 2001, 193-194), which have already been discussed in detail in Chapter 18 on Pricing. Among these are sales of complementary services or of product versions that are newer ("upgrades") or more powerful ("Premium"). Here are some examples:

In the area of mobile telephony, the cell phones are often highly subsidized. Profits are made from selling the complementary service "telephony" to bound customers.

Network Associates (formerly McAfee Associates) initially offered its McAfee antivirus programs for free. After winning a market share of one third, they were able to leverage this strong position to generate sizeable profits from selling upgrades. Another advantage was drawn by Network Associates by incorporating their users in the further development of its products for free. The large installed base and strong customer loyalty helped discover a multitude of viruses, which could then be neutralized in the newer product versions.

Many customers who use the Adobe Reader will later want to edit documents themselves, and go on to buy the required full version.

Apart from direct sales to existing customers, one can also sell **access to the installed base** to third parties. This is common practice in television, cinema, broadcasting or print media, in the form of advertisements. The channels, studios or publishers sell access to the viewer, listener or reader to the advertisers. This can lead to self-reinforcing effects when high dissemination leads to increased advertising revenue, which in turn is used for further dissemination. This reciprocal reinforcement is called a "circulation spiral" in media economics (Hass, 2007, 70). Goldfarb (2003) was able to demonstrate, based on a model, that Lock-In effects lead to increased revenue in ad-financed content offers because the provider can use the existing attachment to save money by providing worse quality.

Analogously, internet companies deal with the reciprocity between users and ads. AOL, for instance, sold access to its customers to Amazon a few years ago. The online merchant Amazon paid around $19m in order to gain the attention of 8.5m AOL customers (Shapiro & Varian, 2003, 52).

The Lock-In effects described are all cheap for the provider. In recording and exploiting the customer data, however, one must always pay attention to the applicable legal barriers, such as are formulated, for instance, in the German Bundesdatenschutzgesetz (Federal Data Protection Act, BDSG) (Peter, 2001, 262 et seq.).

On the basis of an empirical analysis in eCommerce, Staack (2004, 344 et seq.) recommends paying attention first and foremost to the factors, known from stationary trade, of cost-benefit ratio and quality/diversity of the products on offer in order to increase customer attachment.

> Online shops that make their customers a diverse offer of high-quality and attractively priced products and services reduce, in so doing, the relative attractiveness of other providers and thus raise the defection barriers of the economic kind, which in turn have a positive effect on the boundness of the users (Staack, 2004, 347).

Further aspects are the website's operability, quality of delivery in the form of quick and accurate shipping, clear statements on data protection as well as information on the offer, which may be implemented, next to text and image descriptions, via customer ratings, for example. Complementary added-value offers can further intensify the attachment effect. Among such offers are events (contests, vouchers etc.), exclusive benefits (premium systems, power shopping offers, advantage clubs etc.), personalized information or advice offers, comprehensive self-service tools, free complementary offers (information services via mail or SMS, calendar, entertainment etc.) or community services (virtual customer communities).

Lock-In effects are not only observable in priced information offers, but also in those that are free of charge, e.g. in free news portals such as SPIEGEL-Online or FAZ.net, which might explain why such providers are able to generate a part of their revenue via priced offers (Heitmann et al., 2006, 10).

Switching costs and the Lock-In resulting from them in the extreme case, it has become clear, are in a strong interdependency with the other strategic variables that information providers can use in order to assert themselves on the market. Switching costs are not a given, but result from interaction with the customer. The different strategic variables can be used along the Lock-In Cycle in order to attach the customer. Besides pricing, the timing of market entry, the complement offer and compatibility, network effects also have an influence on switching costs, be it directly, when goods have a network effect value that would be lost by switching, or indirectly, when there is a large complementary offer that would be inaccessible in case of a switch. The existence of switching costs in itself, however, influences the different strategic variables as well as, massively, the stakeholders. The decision premises by customers and competitors in particular are noticeably swayed by the occurrence of switching costs. For the provider, it can be stated as a general recommendation that the first order of the day is to build an installed base and create network effects. Switching costs rise as network effects increase in intensity. A large market share alone, however, is not a sufficient indicator for the existence of switching costs:

> High market shares don't imply high switching costs (Shapiro & Varian, 1999, 149).

Only the combination of a large market share and high switching costs can provide a certain degree of security that future profits, too, will be in line.

23.5   Conclusion

- Switching costs are material or immaterial costs incurred by a user when switching from one product to another. In the extreme case, switching costs can be so high for a user that switching is no longer rationally justifiable. In that case, he is in a Lock-In.
- Switching costs can be separated into direct, palpable costs as well as indirect costs resulting from the inability to continue using the previous product.
- Apart from economic switching barriers, there are also psychological and social switching barriers that may prevent customers from switching providers.
- Switching costs can be technological in nature and occur as dictated by external circumstances (exogenous). They can also be partly controlled by the company itself, in which case we speak of endogenous switching costs.
- The occurrence of a Lock-In is a dynamic process over time, with the four phases of Brand Selection, Sampling, Entrenchment and Lock-In.
- Switching costs and Lock-In may be put to use by a company if it builds an installed base, tries to attach its customers by raising switching barriers and finally exploits the resulting Lock-In economically.
- The building of an installed base is the first, and most important, step in offering network effect goods.
- The financial latitudes for calculating investments in (new) customer acquisition and attachment, respectively, can be derived from the cash value of a customer relationship.
- Customers feel attached to a company if cooperation is pleasant, if they identify with the provider or if they feel morally obliged to him. Customers feel bound if their scope of action is restricted.
- Economic switching barriers (switching costs) play a crucial role in creating customer loyalty.

23.6   Bibliography

Beck, H. (2002). Medienökonomie. Print, Fernsehen und Multimedia. Berlin: Springer.

Erber, G., & Hagemann, H. (2002). Netzwerkökonomie. In Zimmermann, K.F. (ed.), Neue Entwicklungen in der Wirtschaftswissenschaft (pp. 277-319). 1st repr. Heidelberg: Physica-Verl.

Festa, P. (1998). "Click of death" strikes Iomega. CNET News. (Online).

Gehring, R.A. (2007). Sammelklage gegen Apple wegen DRM. Golem.de. (Online).

Goldfarb, A. (2003). Advertising, profits, switching costs, and the internet. In Sadeh, N. (ed.), ICEC 2003. Fifth International Conference on Electronic Commerce (pp. 266-275). New York, NY: ACM.

Gourville, J. T. (2004). Why Consumers Don't Buy: The Psychology of New Product Adoption. Case Study 9-504-056. Boston, MA: Harvard Business School. (Online).

Grant, R. M., & Nippa, M. (2006). Strategisches Management. Analyse, Entwicklung und Implementierung von Unternehmensstrategien. 5th ed. München: Pearson Studium (wi - wirtschaft).

Hass, B. H. (2007). Größenvorteile von Medienunternehmen: Eine kritische Würdigung der Anzeigen-Auflagen-Spirale. MedienWirtschaft, 4, Sonderheft, 70-78.

Haucap, J. (2003). Endogenous switching costs and exclusive systems applications. Review of Network Economics, 2(1), 29-35. (Online).

Haucap, J., & Uhde, A. (undated). Marktmacht bei ökonomischen Fachzeitschriften und mögliche Auswege. Ruhr-Universität Bochum, Fakultät für Wirtschaftswissenschaft, Lehrstuhl für Wettbewerbstheorie und -politik. (Online).

Heil, B. (1999). Online-Dienste, portal sites und elektronische Einkaufszentren. Wettbewerbsstrategien auf elektronischen Massenmärkten. Wiesbaden: Dt. Univ.-Verl. (Gabler Edition Wissenschaft).

Heitmann, M., Herrmann, A., & Stahl, F. (2006). Digitale Produkte richtig verkaufen. Harvard Business Manager, August, 8-12.

Klemperer, P. (1987). Markets with consumer switching costs. Quarterly Journal of Economics, 102, 375-394.

Klemperer, P. (1995). Competition when consumers have switching costs. The Review of Economic Studies, 62(4), 515-539.

Lieberman, M. B. (2005). Did First-Mover Advantage Survive the Dot-Com Crash. Los Angeles, CA: Anderson Graduate School of Management, UCLA. (Online).

Liebowitz, S.J., & Margolis, S. E. (1995). Path dependence, lock-in and history. Journal of Law, Economics and Organization, 11(1), 205-226.

Meisner, H. (2004). Einführung in die Internetökonomie. Arbeiten und Investieren in einer modernen Wirtschaft. Berlin: Lit-Verlag. (Internet und Wirtschaftspraxis, 3).

Messerschmitt, D.G. (2000). Understanding Networked Applications. A First Course. San Francisco, CA: Morgan Kaufmann (The Morgan Kaufmann Series in Networking).

Metge, J. (2008). Wechselkosten, Marktzutritt und strategisches Unternehmensverhalten. Frankfurt am Main: Lang (Europäische Hochschulschriften Reihe 5, Volks- und Betriebswirtschaft, 3310).

Nilssen, T. (1992). Two kinds of consumer switching costs. Rand Journal of Economics, 23, 579-589.

Peng, H., Lurie, N.H., & Mitra, S. (2009). Searching for experience on the web. An empirical examination of consumer behavior for search and experience goods. Journal of Marketing, 73(2).

Peter, S.I. (2001). Kundenbindung als Marketingziel. Identifikation und Analyse zentraler Determinanten. 2nd ed. Wiesbaden: Gabler (Neue betriebswirtschaftliche Forschung, 223).

Porter, M.E. (1980). Competitive Strategy. Techniques for aAalyzing Industries and Competitors. 52nd ed. New York, NY: Free Press.

Rams, W. (2001). Kundenbindung im deutschen Mobilfunkmarkt. Determinanten und Erfolgsfaktoren in einem dynamischen Marktumfeld. Wiesbaden: Dt. Univ.-Verl. (DUV Wirtschaftswissenschaft).

Shaffer, G., & Zhang, Z.J. (2000). Pay to switch or pay to stay - preference based price discriminationin markets with switching costs. Journal of Economics and Management, 9, 397-424.

Shapiro, C., & Varian, H.R. (2003). The information economy. In Hand, J. R.M., & Lev, B. (eds.), Intangible Assets. Values, Measures, and Risks (pp. 48-62). Oxford: Oxford Univ. Press (Oxford Management Readers).

Shapiro, C., & Varian, H.R. (1999). Information Rules. A Strategic Guide to the Network Economy. [repr.]. Boston, MA: Harvard Business School Press.

Staack, Y. (2004). Kundenbindung im eBusiness. Eine kausalanalytische Untersuchung der Determinanten, Dimensionen und Verhaltenskonsequenzen der Kundenbindung im Online-Shopping und Online-Brokerage. Frankfurt am Main: Lang (Informationstechnologie und Ökonomie, 23).

Stross, R. (2005). The Battle for Eardrums Begins with Podcasts. The New York Times, 07/03/2005. (Online).

Varian, H.R. (2003). Economics of Information Technology. Berkeley, CA: University of California. (Online).

Zerdick, A. et al. (ed.) (2001). Die Internet-Ökonomie. Strategien für die digitale Wirtschaft. 3rd ed. Berlin: Springer.

Part E

The "Illegal" Information Market: Piracy

Chapter 24

Possible Causes of Piracy

24.1   Piracy of Information Goods

The reproduction of information goods–legal or illegal–is relatively easy. The means of copying have existed for a long time. The "copy shops" of the Middle Ages were abbeys, where monks, using their specialist skills of reading and writing, copied and illustrated mainly the Bible. The invention of letterpress printing then made mass distribution possible for the first time. Today, contents that are available physically are technically easy to copy, e.g. by Xeroxing or recording on audio or video cassettes etc. This form of physical or analog reproduction has its limits, though, since every copy is of lower quality. Copying is much easier, and of higher quality, if the information good is available digitally. In that case, copying involves no loss of quality, which means that the original and the copy as well as any subsequent copies will be of equal quality. Data and quality loss, which are hardly perceptible by the individual, only occur if digital information goods are compressed for the purposes of copying. Information goods can be very easily reproduced in this way. There is no need for an elaborate "reverse engineering", since the consumed good itself is the "master", which can be copied any number of times, almost for free. Free usage of an information good can hardly be prevented by the author–we remember the public-goods problem–and this applies to both content and software offers.

We can distinguish between two different forms of illegal copying (Bundesverband Musikindustrie, 2007a). In traditional bootlegging, an existing information good is adopted, partly or wholly, and brought on the market in different external packaging than the original–e.g. under a fantasy label. In this form of illegal copying, the buyer has to be aware that he is purchasing an illegal product, due to

> purchase location, pricing or obvious differences in design, quality or features (McDonald & Roberts, 1994, 58).

This is mainly referred to as piracy, meaning the unlawful appropriation of intellectual property, manifested by the unauthorized making of copies (Castro et al.,

2008, 77 with further sources). Bootlegging and piracy will be used synonymously from now on.

Counterfeits, or ident-fakes, aim to reproduce the original good in every aspect, thus deceiving the customer as to its provenance and legal status (Staake & Fleisch, 2008, 17-18 with further sources).

Piracy is when information goods are commercially distributed and when they are illegally copied and used for private consumption.

	Physical Distribution	**Digital Distribution**
Commercial Bootlegs	Distribution of reproduced data carriers, e.g. • Cassettes • CDs • DVDs	• Illegal websites, e.g. AllOfMP3
		• Pay (FTP) Servers
Self Supply	Unauthorized, uncommer-cial production and distribu-tion of data carriers, e.g. • „ burning CDs"	• Usenet • Filehosting e.g. RapidShare
		• P2P/Filesharing platforms, e.g. eMule • Streams, e.g. YouTube

Figure 24.1: Distribution Forms of Piracy.

The forms of bootlegging bound to a medium are to be differentiated from the purely digital. The Federal Association of the Music Industry (Bundesverband Musikindustrie, 2007b) speaks of internet piracy, which appears in different forms:

> Apart from filesharing services (e.g. eDonkey, eMule, BearShare, Bit-Torrent), there is now a multitude of different forms of internet piracy. Thus, for instance, music files are "posted" in message boards and on blogs, and more or less professionally structured "release groups" ac-quire–often unreleased–songs and albums. A rapidly increasing form of internet piracy runs via so-called sharehosters, such as rapidshare.com. Here, music files are initially uploaded to a virtual hard drive on the in-ternet, after which the relevant download link is distributed via blogs and message boards.

For our further deliberations, a pirate copy will refer to any and all illegally produced copy, no matter whether physical or digital.

According to figures released by the Bundesverband Musikindustrie (2007b) illegal downloads account for a multitude of legally downloaded titles: in 2006, there were 27m legal, but 374m illegal music downloads.

For the German software industry, similar figures can be obtained from the Association of Software Providers, the Business Software Alliance (BSA), from the Association of Entertainment Software (VUD) for computer and video games, or, across the different industries, from the Society for Tracing Copyright Infringements (GVU). International statistics, also for books and films, are listed by the International Intellectual Property Alliance (IIPA). Particularly interesting here is the report ("Special 301") that must be compiled, according to U.S. Trade Law, concerning worldwide pirate activities in the software, music, film, gaming and book industries (IIPA, 2007).

Why is there piracy? What moves people to create bootleg copies?

A different distinction for answering this question is that between commercial copies and self-supply copies. For commercial copies, the motivation is clear, since there is a definite profiteering component. The copies are mainly produced as data carriers and sold to end customers. The International Federation of the Phonographic Industry describes this as physical piracy (IFPI, 2006, 4). Generally, this involves organized crime (OECD, 2008, 157 et seq.).

The case is different for self-supply. This term refers to the fact the end customer himself acquires the desired information goods illegally. Apart from physical private copying, self-supply increasingly moves to the digital realm, taking place on illegal websites (e.g. AllOfMP3.com), filesharing servies (e.g. P2P networks) or BitTorrent and FTP. The foundation of Napster, in 1999, marks a decisive turning point in the availability of digital goods, specifically of music, via P2P technology. In all generality, it can be noted that digital forms of distribution are gaining in importance. This goes for both legal (Bundesverband Musikindustrie, 2008, 14) and illegal offers (Dejean, 2008, 2), e.g. for music.

Since the motivation for commercial bootlegging is clear, we will now turn to the area of self-supply. There are manifold approaches to explaining the causes, most of them with empirical data backing them up. We will now address some central aspects.

24.2   Consumer Characteristics

The typical bootlegger of digital music can be relatively easily differentiated from the circle of people who buy or download music legally (Bhattacharjee et al., 2003). He is young and male, and his tendency toward piracy increases alongside the price of the music title and his available bandwidth. In this respect, it is not surprising that (male) students represent a large percentage of bootleggers. They have access to high-speed networks and significantly more time than money (Wade, 2004). Appropriate for this analysis is the observation that after the foundation of Napster, CD sales receded much more heavily in stores near universities than in other places (Fine, 2000).

This profile matches that of persons whose goal is to get ever more stimuli. Scientifically, the term "Optimum Stimulation Level" (OSL) (Raju, 1980) describes the tendency of every individual to seek his or her own ideal level of stimulation. If there are too few external stimuli, the person will want to intensify them, if there are too many, they will need to be reduced. The OSL correlates strongly with demographic variables like age, gender, education and training and employment status. As for pirates, the results here are:

> High-OSL consumers are relatively younger, more educated, better employed, and more likely to be male than low-OSL consumers (Sinha & Mandel, 2008, 2 with reference to Raju, 1980 and Zuckerman, 1994, 114).

High-OSL consumers, as empirically proven by Sinha and Mandel (2008), tend to turn to piracy. They are more likely to try out new artists and songs, and display a greater readiness to take risks, such as illegal downloads bring along with them.

24.3   Sense of Justice and Prices

We know about the unbalanced cost structure for information goods: high first-copy-costs are followed by very low reproduction costs. Appropriately, it has been shown that search costs, lowered by the internet, have made consumers more price-sensitive. However, as has been shown in a study by Lynch and Ariely (2000), this only holds for broadly available, easily comparable (mass) products, and not for very specific or individually manufactured products. Specifically for the mass product music, it can be empirically observed that the music industry's prices are regarded as too high (Deiss, 2006, 87-88, Buxmann et al., 2007). Similar statements are found with regard to digital games (Anderson, 2009, 72). It can be concluded that pirates regard the prices for all manner of digital goods as too high, and thus unfair, particularly in view of some of the rights holders' economic success. This imbalance gives bootleggers a justification for their illegal behavior (e.g. Gupta et al., 2004). This attitude is reinforced by offers of information goods that are free, e.g. Linux or Open Office from the Open Source community, or the manifold offers of free content on the internet, such as news, financial information, pictures and sometimes music.

Rising prices cannot be the reason for digital offers being deemed too expensive. Liebowitz (2003, 14) was able to use data from the U.S. music industry to prove that prices have stayed on almost the same level for more than 20 years. Similar results are drawn by Peitz and Waelbroeck (2006) in their study, according to which no clear pricing trends could be found for the world's five largest markets over the last few years.

Neither do per-capita income changes over time seem to be the cause of changes in music spending. A correlation is rather found in the level of an individual's income (Liebowitz, 2003, 15). The higher willingness to turn to piracy in younger people is partly motivated by their lower income. Younger users have less money than professionals, but much more free time. As a person's income increases, his willingness to buy legally increases in turn (Deiss, 2006, 95).

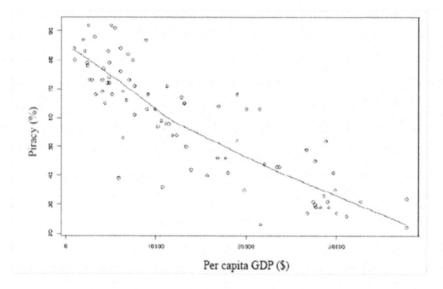

Figure 24.2: Per Capita Gross Domestic Product of Different Countries vs. Level of Software Piracy. Source: Varian, 2005, 125.

This pattern can be found not only on the individual but also on the national level. In general: who earns more downloads less. Varian (2005) establishes this correlation empirically and compares the Gross Domestic Product of different countries with their piracy quotas for software. It is made abundantly clear that as the per-capita GDP rises, piracy decreases. However–as an econometric study by Reinig and Plice (2010, 6) shows–the correlation decreases the more income increases. For an income spike from, say, $4,000 to $5,000, a sharper drop in piracy can be detected than for an increase from $24,000 to $25,000. Furthermore, two other crucial factors, besides the level of income, can be determined for software markets, which significantly influence the extent of software piracy in a country: the level of development of the IT industry and the extent of corruption in the respective country. It is shown that

> the relative size of a domestic software industry influences software piracy independent of income. [...] A one-percent increase in the relative

size of the IT market would imply that over 10 percent of all software would convert from unauthorized to authorized (Reinig & Plice, 2010, 6).

Corruption, on the other hand, only affects countries with an underdeveloped IT industry, as

a one-point increase in CPI [Corruption Perception Index, A/N] would result in a reduction in piracy of over four percent of total software in low IT countries (Reinig & Plice, 2010, 6).

Their conclusion is that corruption in countries with a low level of Information Technology should be fought and, in countries with a developed IT industry, the further growth of that industry encouraged. It can be assumed that these are also suitable approaches to industries for other information goods.

A similar impression is gleaned from observing GDP growth rates. The very pronounced reduction in growth after the dot-com bubble had burst was one of the principal reasons for the music industry's loss in revenue (from CD sales) (Peitz & Waelbroeck, 2006, 93). If we consider the fact that prior to this drop it was mainly young men, whose music needs are still very high, who were concerned, it stands to reason that there has been a shift toward illegality in this area.

In keeping with the previous results, Regner and Barria (2009, 399) observed, in an empirical study of voluntary willingness to pay for online music, that in countries with a low per-capita GDP people pay a lot less than in countries whose GDP is high. The result is a distribution that mirrors the piracy quota in Figure 24.2 exactly.

24.4   Morals and Social Norms

Pirates' moral views and the influences from their social surroundings concerning what is deemed normal and acceptable play an important role in answering the question of why people make illegal copies. As mentioned a number of times so far, piracy is largely a question of age. Liebowitz (2004) demonstrates, via a study of internet users in October 2002, that 41% of those aged 18-29, but only 21% of those aged 30-49 download illegally. This fact can very clearly linked to the ob-servation that young, male bootleggers have an underdeveloped set of morals (Levin et al., 2004; Hill, 2007, 11 with further sources). Their drive toward immediate gratification via digital goods eclipses the question of what is right and wrong. Concerning games, Anderson (2009, 72) writes that

anything at all standing between the impulse to play and playing in the game itself was seen as a legitimate signal to take the free route.

Added to this is the fact that until recently, the danger of being caught and convicted of illegal copying and downloading was relatively low. Whether the latest measures of rights holders to assert their rights more vigorously will achieve the desired results appears doubtful. For the film industry, Dördrechter (2007, 257) estimates that neither the previous PR campaigns and advertising initiatives nor the open threats ("Piracy is a crime") have managed to perceptibly change bootleggers' moral views. Following the Optimal Stimulus Theory addressed above, this increased pressure may even be counterproductive, as the risk of being caught increases the stimulus. As Sinha and Mandel demonstrate empirically on the example of students, this means that

> for consumers with high levels of optimum stimulation (and, thus, higher tolerance for risk), increasing the perceived risk might actually backfire by slightly increasing their likelihood to pirate (Sinha & Mandel, 2008, 12).

Appeals to people's sense of morals might thus work better for older groups of consumers.

Apart from individual attitudes to morality, the social environment plays an important role in people's readiness to illegally consume information goods. For film piracy, empirical studies by Dördrechter (2007, 253) reveal:

> By far the greatest positive influence on pirates' consumption of downloads and copies of films is wielded by the formative construct "social environment".

This results corresponds with other empirical studies in which the great significance of social environments, i.e. of groups norms, on the behavior in illegally acquiring software could be proven (Dördrechter, 2007, 253 and Hill, 2007, 11 with further references). In the relevant social circles, both the consumption of downloads and copies as well as the downloading and copying acts in themselves are regarded as common. Film pirates want to belong to the filesharing scene. They want to avoid incurring undesirable social sanctions for deviating from the group norm. For young male students, Sinha and Mandel (2008, 13) observe:

> If anything, digital piracy is the social norm among this segment of consumers.

The social environment in toto also influences people's sense of morals (e.g. Kini et al., 2004). In societies in which private ownership had long been suppressed, and the right to intellectual property only asserted weakly, there is little or no moral pressure to stifle piracy. Furthermore, in countries like China, where many companies are state-owned, people's sense of guilt regarding theft is underdeveloped–following the dominant ideology, what belongs to those companies also belongs to the people (Hill, 2007, 12).

Another reason for moral views that endorse piracy can be found when new laws, or changes to existing laws, are deemed unfair. The restriction of private copying via the prohibition of circumventing technical protective measures in German law from the year 2003 represents such a case. Copies for private consumption, hitherto legal, became pirate material in one fell swoop. It is understandable that this change was not countenanced by everyone. For the film industry Dördrechter (2007, 257) observes:

> In the eyes of the film pirates, the copying of DVDs does not result in any damage to the film industry, and what's more, the pirates claim the moral high ground. Film pirates view themselves as victims of the film industry, not the other way around.

24.5   Designing Products and Services

A very important reason for the illegal acquisition of information goods lies in the designing of the legal offers. If there were more attractive legal offers, this would significantly reduce the levels of piracy. Dördrechter (2007) was able to prove this empirically for the information good film. The practice of windowing, as demonstrated by the film industry, compels pirates to create their own exploitation windows. There is no possibility, so far, of buying or renting a film legally on DVD or VHS or to view it via Video-on-Demand (VoD) while it is still running in cinemas (Dördrechter, 2007, 254-255). In the case of music, it had for a long time only been possible to debundle the rigid CD offers, where the price for an entire album had been charged even if one only wanted to own a few songs. Only the increased elaboration of the legal offer made it possible to buy only the desired titles by an artist.

For music, Deiss (2006, 87-88) was able to demonstrate empirically that the attractiveness of filesharing services is so high especially because one has a significantly greater selection of music than in stores, is able to find even the rarest songs, can get introduced to new music and sample every music title.

The use of sharing services is apparently regarded as a more attractive alternative to legal acquisition, even though the illegal path, too, is not entirely effortless (Dördrechter, 2007, 254-255). Filesharing sites are repeatedly shut down due to police initiatives, and thus have to be continually relocated. Download speeds for new films are often relatively slow, because many users are accessing the same source file(s) at the same time. Also, quality control is elaborate because downloads and copies must be checked for viruses and their technical and contentual intactness. The film industry raises these costs deliberately by bringing so-called "decoys" into circulation before important film premieres. These are dummy files, which have the same title, file size and format as the original.

In conclusion, it can be said that filesharing services are used because they provide pronounced added value. They are free, have a large selection of music titles with corresponding sampling options and the acquisition of music is tied to relatively little effort.

24.6   Conclusion

- Bootlegging, or piracy, refers to the illegal acquisition of intellectual property by producing copies without the rights holders' consent.
- For digital information goods, the production of pirate copies is even possible with no loss of quality.
- The typical bootlegger of digital music is young and male and his tendency to bootleg rises in proportion with the price of the song and his available bandwidth. A large proportion of pirates are (male) students.
- Both on the individual and on the national level, it can be said: who earns more downloads less.
- The social environment has a strong influence on people's behavior in illegally acquiring information goods. This goes for the group level (pirates want to belong to the scene) and for the societal level (attitudes toward the value of intellectual property).
- A very important reason for the illegal acquisition of information goods lies in the design of the legal offers. If there were more attractive legal offers, this would significantly reduce piracy.

24.7   Bibliography

Anderson, C. (2009). Free. The Future of a Radical Price. New York, NY: Hyperion.

Bhattacharjee, S., Gopal, R. D., & Sanders, G. L. (2003). Digital music and online sharing: Software piracy 2.0. Communications of the ACM, 46(7), 107-111.

BSA - Business Software Alliance (2006). Pirateriezahlen. (Online).

Bundesverband Musikindustrie (ed.) (2008). Jahreswirtschaftsbericht 2008. (Online).

Bundesverband Musikindustrie (2007a). Raubkopien erkennen. (Online).

Bundesverband Musikindustrie (2007b). Internetpiraterie. (Online).

Buxmann, P., Pohl, G., Johnscher, P., & Strube, J. (2007). Cooperative pricing in digital value chains - the case of online-music. Journal of Electronic Commerce Research, 8(1), 32-40.

Castro, J.O. de; Balkin, D., & Sheperd, D.A. (2008). Can entrepreneurial firms benefit from product piracy. Journal of Business Venturing, 23(1), 75-90.

Deiss, B. (2006). Musik aus dem Internet - Filesharing in p2p-Tauschbörsen. München: GRIN.

Dejean, S. (2008). What Can We Learn from Empirical Studies About Piracy. Published by CESifo Economic Studies. Rennes. (Online).

Dördrechter, N. (2007). Piraterie in der Filmindustrie. Eine Analyse der Gründe für Filmpiraterie und deren Auswirkungen auf das Konsumverhalten. Wiesbaden: Dt. Univ.-Verlag.

Fine, M. (2000). SoundScan Study on Napster Use and Loss of Sales. Report by the Chief Executive Officer of SoundScan Engaged by the Plaintiffs in the Action. A & M Records Inc. et al. v. Napster Inc. (Online).

Gupta, P. B., Gould, S. J., & Pola, B. (2004). To pirate or not to pirate: a comparative study of the ethical versus other influences on the consumer's software aquisition mode decision. Journal of Business Ethics, 55, 255-274.

GVU - Gesellschaft zur Verfolgung von Urheberrechtsverletzungen (undated). (Online).

Hill, C.W.L. (2007). Digital piracy: Causes, consequences, and strategic responses. Asia Pacific Journal of Management, 24(1), 9-25.

IFPI (2006). Piracy-Report 2006. (Online).

IIPA - International Intellectual Property Alliance (2007). IIPA 2007 "Special 301" Recommendations. (Online).

Illing, G., & Peitz, M. (eds.) (2006). Industrial Organization and the Digital Economy. Cambridge, MA: MIT Press.

Kini, R. B., Ramakrishna, H. V., & Vijayaraman, V. (2004). Shaping moral intensity regarding software piracy. A comparison between Thailand and U.S. students. Journal of Business Ethics, 49, 91-104.

Levin, A.M., Dato-on, C.M., Rhee, K. (2004). Money for nothing and hits for free: The ethics of downloading music from peer-to-peer web sites. Journal of Marketing Theory and Practice, 12(1), 48-60.

Liebowitz, S.J. (2003). Will MP3 Downloads Annihilate the Record Industry? The Evidence so Far. Dallas,TX: School of Management, University of Texas at Dallas. (Online).

Liebowitz, S.J. (2004). File Sharing: Creative Destruction or just Plain Destuction? Dallas, TX: School of Management, University of Texas at Dallas. (Online).

Lynch, J. G., & Ariely, D. (2000). Wine online: Search costs affect competition on price, quality, and distribution. Marketing Science, 19(1), 83-103.

McDonald, G., & Roberts, C. (1994). Product piracy: the problem that will not go away. Journal of Product & Brand Management, 3(4), 55-65.

OECD (2008). Die wirtschaftlichen Folgen von Produkt- und Markenpiraterie. Paris: Organisation for Economic Co-operation and Development.

Peitz, M., & Waelbroeck, P. (2006). Digital music. In Illing, G., & Peitz, M. (eds.), Industrial Organization and the Digital Economy (pp. 71-144). Cambridge, MA: MIT Press.

Raju, P.S. (1980). Optimum stimulation level: Its relationship to personality, demographics, and exploratory behavior. Journal of Consumer Research, 7, 272-282.

Regner, T., & Barria, J.A. (2009). Do consumers pay voluntarily? The case of online music. Journal of Economic Behavior & Organization, 71, 395-406.

Reinig, B.A., & Plice R.K. (2010). Modeling software piracy in developed and emerging economies. Proceedings of the 43rd Hawaii International Conference on Systems Science.

Sinha, R. K., & Mandel, N. (2008). Preventing digital music piracy: The carrot or the stick. Journal of Marketing, 72, 1-15.

Staake, T., & Fleisch, E. (2008). Countering Counterfeit Trade. Illicit Market Insights, Best-Practice Strategies, and Management Toolbox. Berlin, Heidelberg: Springer.

Varian, H.R. (2005). Copying and copyright. Journal of Economic Perspectives, 19(2), 121-138.

VUD - Verband der Unterhaltungssoftware Deutschland e.V. (2007). Raubkopien. (Online).

Wade, J. (2004). The music industry's war on piracy. Risk Management, 51(2), 10-15.

Zuckerman, M. (1994). Behavioral Expressions and Biosocial Bases of Sensation Seeking. Cambridge: Cambridge Univ. Press.

Chapter 25

Economic Consequences of Piracy

25.1 Object of Consideration

Does piracy actually harm information providers? From industry representatives' point of view, this is established fact. Scientifically, the case is not so clear, though. The music market in particular has been investigated in a number of studies, which differ greatly in quality and expressiveness. Depending on which one you look at, you can find evidence for filesharing harming the music industry, having no effect on CD sales or even wielding positive influences. We will address these in more detail in the following. Other industries, such as those for software, film, games or books, have so far been investigated much less extensively, if at all, with regard to the effects of filesharing practice on sales figures, which is why we will mainly orient ourselves on the studies of the music industry. However, it can be assumed that the same principles apply to all information industries. Haller (2005, 182) sees structural similarities between the music and software industry, and Oberholzer & Strumpf (2009) correlate their metaanalysis of filesharing to all digital information goods, i.e. music, software, films, games and books.

In the following, we will thus initially observe, via simple microeconomic models, what consequences arise when piracy enters a market. Subsequently, the perspective will be broadened and the consequences of bootlegging are analyzed from dynamic viewpoints. As far as it is possible, the single arguments will be backed up by empirical analyses.

25.2 Consequences of Piracy from a Welfare-Theoretical Perspective

With the help of microeconomic models, initial (theoretical) insights can be gleaned into what happens when there are not only legal, but also illegal offers on a market. In order to conduct a before-after comparison, so-called comparative-static analyses are performed. One compares an initial situation (without piracy) with a second, changed situation, this time with piracy. The valuation standard in this kind of analysis is the welfare of the consumers. One situation is judged preferable as against another if it has a higher consumer surplus.

We will regard the market for a music title, as representative for all information goods. The provider is a quasi-monopolist in consequence of the title's uniqueness. Since there are, typically, similar titles to switch to, we have a hybrid situation, which is called monopolistic competition in microeconomics (e.g. Mankiw et al., 2008, 411 et seq.). Several or many "monopolists" compete with each other. This means that there are several providers on a market, e.g. for music or films, which make similar, but not identical and interchangeable offers, e.g. for music or films. For all further considerations, we can thus assume a monopoly situation, in which the provider seeks to maximize his profits according to the monopolistic profit maximization formula (marginal cost = marginal revenue). The existence of competition results in a shift of the demand curve. The individual provider is left, in case of increasing competition, only with a decreasing part of the total market (Linde, 2008, 67 et seq.).

Apart from regular competition, which will at first be blocked out in the following by the focus on a monopoly, two groupings are of interest when considering piracy or pirate markets: commercial providers of pirate copies on the one hand, and private individuals who self-supply with pirate copies on the other.

Self-supply, i.e. the production of (physical) private copies, has been extensively investigated by Lang (2005). He compares the changes to producer and consumer surplus for one provider and one sound carrier at two different points in time. At the first point, there is only the legal market, at the second, the consumers have CD burners and are able to create pirate copies themselves. The price for producing a private copy is set at the variable (marginal) cost. It is thus far below the monopolist's price. The demand curve for the original market (N_1) is turned inward in this model (N_2) and a black market is created, represented as demand for private copies (N_{PC}). Total demand is unchanged. As marginal cost is near zero, price changes are marginal and for simplicity's sake we will assume that the old price (p_1) is the same as the new one (p_2).

As can very clearly be seen, some dramatic welfare effects occur. The creation of a black market shifts part of the old consumer surplus ($C1-C_2-p_p$) to the private copiers (CS_1). The monopolist loses a significant share of his producer surplus ($x_1-x_2-C_2-C_1$), which is transformed into consumer surplus of the private copiers (CS_2). Due to the low price, or, respectively, the low marginal cost, there is an expansion of demand. Customers who had not been willing to buy for the market price now copy the information good. It is thus much more widely distributed than before, as the increase in copying eclipses the decrease in sales. This leads to a net welfare gain (CS_3).

From the provider's perspective, not all of these effects are problematic. Customers who would not have bought anyway can now possess the CD, but do not cause any fewer sales. Much more painful are the customers who copy instead of buying. They cause a decrease in producer surplus. This can become–in case of a preexisting price-sales function–problematic, if the producer surplus becomes smaller than the fixed costs for manufacturing the information good. In that case,

the provider loses money and it will become more rational for him to cease production of new copies.

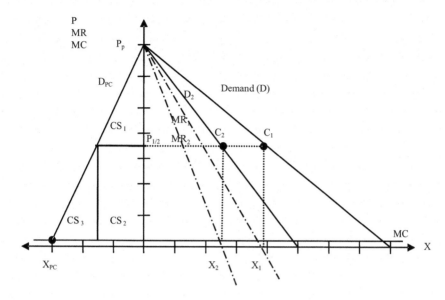

Figure 25.1: Effects of Private Copies on Net Welfare. Source: Following Lang, 2005, 636.

Hill (2007) performed a microeconomic analysis of the effect of the existence of
commercial pirates and legal protection of information goods on pricing and
market supply. An integrated perspective on the copying problem, which takes into consideration both commercial pirates and self-suppliers, can be found in Linde
(2008, 98 et seq.). His approach will be represented in the following.

The existence of pirate copies is principally to be regarded the same way as the
entry of competitors onto a market with a range of very similar or even identical
products. Since pirates have no development costs to shoulder, the progress of
their average-cost curve is significantly below that of the original provider's.
Commercial Pirates (AC_{CP}) will have to make higher investments for reproduction
than self-suppliers (AC_{SS}), which is why the cost curves progress differently. The
competing product puts pricing pressure on the original offer. The original provider can react to this by lowering prices. The result is–as already discussed above–a
redistribution from producer to consumer surplus and net welfare gains. The lowest price limit (LPL_m) lies, for the ex-monopolist, on a level where his average
costs remain just about covered. The black market causes a sort of price differentiation. Consumers who had previously been excluded from purchases and are
prepared for illegal actions, are now provided, or self-supply (p_{SS}), with the information good for a price right down to (p_{CP}). Net welfare increases. The greater the

price differences, and the lower moral qualms and (expected) quality deficits vis-à-vis the original product, the more people will defect to the black market.

The progresses of average costs depend on the kind of copying technology that is being used. If it is very difficult to acquire or use or if the costs are very high, average cost will be higher. Generally, cost behavior patterns in pirating CDs/DVDs are much higher than in using filesharing technology (OECD, 2008, 159). The effects on the legal offer just described are thus, again, much greater in the microeconomic analysis of the latter case.

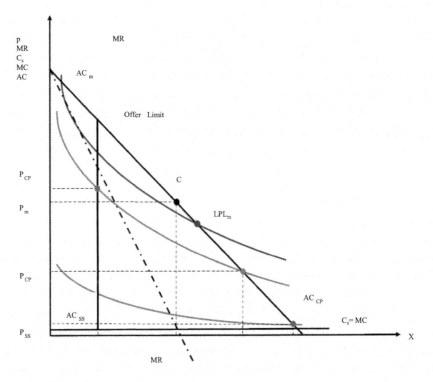

Figure 25.2: Effects of Commercial Piracy and Self-Supply on the Market Offer. Source: Following Linde, 2008, 103.

What will happen, then, if the original providers try to assert their exploitation rights more forcefully than they have so far? Firstly, measures to uncover illegal activities will incur costs for investigators, attorneys etc. The average cost curve (AC_m) shifts upward. The rising danger of being caught, however, also results in another cost progression for the pirates. Depending on the individual's assessment of the danger, the creation of illegal copies will be curtailed. This curtailment corresponds to a capacity limit, microeconomically speaking. Depending on the quantity at which it takes effect, the (commercial) offer of pirate copies can become unattractive. In case of a very low offer limit, the cost-covering price (p_{CP}) would lie above that of the monopolist (p_m). For the original provider, this would even harbor the opportunity of raising his price to cover for his increased costs.

The comparative-static analysis shows that the advent of black markets benefits the individual consumer as regards an existing offer of information goods. Consumer surplus is increased. This result is not surprising, as monopolies always undersupply the market for reasons of profit maximization. The granting of exploitation rights makes these monopoly profits possible, and infringement of these rights leads to net welfare gains from a static point of view. This does not take into consideration the question of how the existence of black markets–dynamically speaking–will affect the development of new information goods.

25.3   Consequences of Piracy from Dynamic Points of View

Let us now turn to the dynamic analysis, in which developments over the course of time are investigated, starting from a given situation. After the aforementioned problem of undersupply with new information goods, we will explore how the possibilities of getting to know new information goods via piracy (sampling) and the existence of direct and indirect network effects affect the original provider.

A prevailing argument against any kind of bootleg copy is that lowered profits will erode the motivation for creating any new information goods. The market is **undersupplied** with new intellectual property, such as music, films, games etc. (e.g. Hill, 2007, 17-18). This argument, which is, statically, absolutely correct, can be countered by citing the development of new releases. For the timespan between 1992 and 2003, the German music market suffered no notable regression (Lang, 2005, 638). Recently, Oberholzer and Strumpf (2009, 23-24) have proven that the number of new releases in the music and film industries has increased significantly. The number of new albums has risen, in the U.S.A., from 35,516 in the year 2000 to 79,695 in the year 2007. 25,159 of these were digital releases. In the film industry, there has been a worldwide increase from 3,807 in 2003 to 4,989 in 2007. Even in countries like South Korea, India or China, where illegal copies play a huge role on the market, the number of new releases increased heavily over the same period. The existence of bootlegs has apparently not impeded the creative energy of artists and publishers as far as quantity is concerned. Whether the quality of the products has decreased is an open, as yet uninvestigated question. Creative people–as several other studies suggest–do not necessarily require monetary incentives. Intrinsic motivation and the hope of hitting the jackpot and entering the charts, if only the one time, appear to be enough reason to create (Tschmuck, 2009a).

As we already know, information goods display obvious information asymmetries. For potential buyers, it is of great importance to glean an impression of the quality of the offer before purchasing. Piracy is a suitable means for doing so, as it allows them to get to know new information goods, to listen, view, read or play them–this practice is called **sampling**. The crucial question, for sampling, is economical: will it lead to a subsequent purchase of the product or will the sample suffice? Other than in sampling in stationary retail, where the information good must be purchased before it can be permanently used, illegal copies mean that the consumer already owns the good (as CD/DVD are already on his hard drive), which leads to the decision of whether to buy the original in addition. What effect will sampling haven then? Will it create an impetus to buy, or is it so substitutive that any purchases that would have been made are rendered obsolete by possession of the sample? Here, there are different studies for the music industry. Liebowitz (2003; 2006) is a prominent advocate of the statement that samples displace purchases, i.e. that the substitution effect prevails. His argumentation is relatively simple: if the copy is of equal quality as the original, and copying is free, the labels' profits will decrease because the free copy will be preferred to the original. For filesharing, he formulates:

> MP3 downloads are causing significant harm to the record industry
> (Liebowitz, 2003, 30).

As we mentioned in the previous chapter, however, it cannot be said in such a general way that a pirate copy replaces its original one-to-one. The illegally acquired titles must first be checked for quality, which can deviate noticeably from the original, if songs are incomplete, have a low bitrate or are virus-infested. Also, if a title is no longer available for purchase or if the original has special features, such as a booklet, a particular cover etc., the copy cannot replace it (Tschmuck, 2009b).

Peitz and Waelbroeck (2006, 908), among others, arrive at the opposite conclusion as concerns the effects of sampling:

> Sampling appears to be important in the market for recorded music–
> music is an experience good where horizontal product differentiation
> and taste heterogeneity are important. Due to sampling, music labels
> may actually gain from P2P networks (and other ways to listen to re-
> corded music for free) and use them to solve a two-sided asymmetric
> information problem between seller and buyers.

With the help of this model, the authors show that the providers of information goods generally profit from filesharing if consumer preferences are sufficiently heterogeneous. With regard to music, this means that if tastes are different enough, consumers will use filesharing to find titles that better suit their needs than in the absence of a black market. If, at the same time, the product variety of (music) providers is great enough, the possibility of sampling will lead to more sales. Profits rise

> because consumers can make more informed purchasing decisions be-
> cause of sampling and are willing to spend for the original although

they could consume the download for free (Peitz & Waelbroeck, 2006, 912).

The two studies represented above are based on theoretical models and arrive at the exact opposite conclusion.

What do empirical studies say about the relation between filesharing and sales figures? Oberholzer and Strumpf (2009) investigate this question via a metaanalysis of eleven studies of the music industry. Two of them state that filesharing has positive effects on music sales. In most cases, a negative effect is detected, which means that substitution effects prevail. They are estimated to amount to 20% in general (Oberholzer & Strumpf, 2009, 16). A significant portion of the studies arrives at a third result, namely that filesharing has no statistically significant effects on music sales. Tschmuck (2009c) classifies and investigates seventeen studies of filesharing, with similar results. Both investigations rate the quality of the different studies and conclude that filesharing is in no clearly detectable relation to sales figures. The same conclusion is also found in a current study of the U.S. Government Accountability Office, which notes that

> the net effect cannot be determined with any certainty (GAO, 2010, 28).

What can be determined relatively simply, though, is a redistribution effect created by filesharing. Blackburn (2004) compares album sales and downloads for very prominent and for unknown, seldom-charting artists. For the stars, the substitution effect prevails, and downloads partially replace album purchases. For the unknown artists, though, the sampling effect dominates and sales are increased. Ergo, there is a redistribution–for neutral overall effects–from superstars to less-known artists. Gopal et al. (2006) arrive at the same results regarding redistribution, but make out a positive overall effect of sampling.

> If there were no filesharing, the superstars would dominate the CD market and thus prevent a possible widening of diversity (Tschmuck, 2009d).

Another important influence quantity in relation to illegal copies is, again, represented by network effects. We remember that direct network effects are at play when the value of a(n information) good for the consumer is greater as a result of its wider prevalence than it would be on its own merits (basic value). Indirect network effects mean that the value of a good for the consumer is positively influenced by an attractive offer of complements.

Direct and indirect network effects are both ubiquitous for information goods, but they are not always equally pronounced (Linde, 2008, 42 et seq.). For a broader discussion of the correlation of network effects and illegal copying activities, consult Chapter 21 on Copy Protection Management. We will now investigate more closely how illegal copies affect the market development via **direct network effects**. Linde's (2008, 135-136) model shows very clearly that pirate copies can contribute decisively to the reaching of critical mass required for establishing oneself on the market.

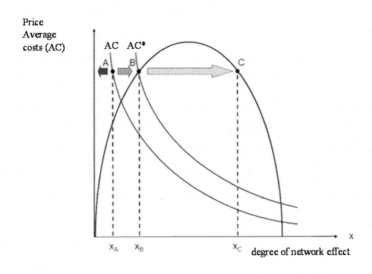

Figure 25.3: Effects of Illegal Copies on Market Development. Source: Following Linde, 2008, 136.

The model assumes a progression of the demand curve typical for information goods (Linde, 2008, 113 et seq.). High willingnesses to pay here only appear once the information good has reached a certain level of prevalence. If an information provider thus enters the market with a new product, selling it for price A due to the high first-copy-costs, too few units will most likely be sold in order to create network effects (x_A); it will flop. If, however, illegal copies are distributed, sales will increase. The market will be supplied with a legal offer of the volume x_A, and, in addition, with illegal copies (x_B-x_A). The total volume x_B is now enough in order to alert further, willing-to-pay customers. Critical mass has been reached and self-reinforcing network effects begin to work. The information good distributes itself further, because it has already reached a certain degree of prevalence. In the model, this means a jump to the equilibrium C with its corresponding volume x_C. Of disadvantage for the provider is the loss of sales that may result, which is represented by the shift of the average-cost curve to the right (AC*). The degression effect is only reached with a larger total sales volume of legal and illegal copies.

From the provider's point of view, pirate copies thus give the market development a significant push. This is precisely the effect that Andersen and Frenz (2007) confirmed in a study of Canadian users of sharing services. They observe that

> downloading the equivalent of approximately one CD increases purchasing by about half of a CD (Andersen & Frenz, 2007, 3).

Expressed differently, the factor of 0.44 means that at least one more album is sold for every three albums downloaded. Filesharing does lead to substitution effects, but they are overcompensated for by the market development effect.

In a study of the British music market, it has been found out that users of filesharing services count among the best customers of the music industry.

> Internet users who claim to never illegally download music spend an average of £44 per person on music per year, while those who do admit to illegal downloading spend £77, amounting to an estimated £200m in revenue per year (Demos, 2009).

These results beg the question: isn't the current behavior of the music industry counterproductive, scaring away its best customers as it does?

Further positive consequences of network effects–from the providers' point of view–resulting from a larger total distribution from sales and illegal copies consist of a higher Lock-In probability of customers and better chances of establishing a standard on the market (Castro et al., 2008, 85; Hill, 2007, 18-19). In the late 1990s, Bill Gates expressed a very pragmatic attitude toward this situation, contrasting short-term losses with long-term benefits created by network effects and Lock-In:

> 'Although about 3 million computers get sold every year in China, people don't pay for the software. Someday they will, though,' Gates told an audience at the University of Washington. 'And as long as they're going to steal it, we want them to steal ours. They'll get sort of addicted, and then we'll somehow figure out how to collect sometime in the next decade.' (Piller, 2006).

Staake and Fleisch report on the current situation, half a decade later, and the success of this strategy in the software industry:

> About 90% of all programs in the Chinese software market are not legitimately licensed (BBC, 2005). The vast majority of personal com-

puters use Microsoft Windows as an operating system, which, as a genuine product, is sold for a multiple of a Chinese white-collar worker's monthly average income. Needless to say, if no illicit copies were available, only a fraction of today's PC users in China would be familiar with Microsoft's product and would rather use open source software such as Red Flag Linux. Now, after the Chinese government required computers manufactured within the country's borders to have pre-installed authorized operating software systems when they leave the factory, Microsoft can build upon a large user base and use its strong market position to generate revenue. The stakes are huge as China has become the world's second-largest PC market, with more than 19 million PC shipments in 2005 (Gartner, 2006). In an interview with CNN, Bill Gates stressed the beneficial effects of software piracy on the development of Microsoft's market in China, mainly due to lock-in and barriers to entry for emerging legitimate competitors (Kirkpatrick, 2007).

Let us now focus on music again, and the **indirect network effects** that play an important role here. Music recorded on sound carriers is in a complementary relationship with other information goods, such as concerts, merchandising articles or ringtones. As Connolly and Krueger (2006) were able to demonstrate, concerts and merchandising have become an important source of revenue for artists. Concerts and new records are reciprocal complements: a CD calls back a concert, and music that listeners already know makes the concert more intense experience (Oberholzer & Strumpf, 2009, 20). From this perspective, however, filesharing could prove to be a double-edged sword. A greater distribution of (free) music could increase demand for concert tickets, but at the same time it is possible that concerts will no longer lead to the same volume of CD sales, if songs can be downloaded from the internet. This would decrease the impetus to go on tour. For this aspect, we can initially observe that ticket prices for concerts have risen over the past few years, and much more steeply than the price index has, and that this increase has been reinforced following the advent of filesharing (Krueger, 2005). Mortimer and Sorensen (2005, 25) demonstrate, in an empirical study of more than two thousand artists over a period of ten years, that in the time before and after Napster the number of CDs that had to be sold in order to generate $20 in concert revenue fell from 8.47 to 6.36. Filesharing provides artists with fans, who go to concerts without having to buy music. The artists, it can also be observed, have intensified their touring activities over the past few years since filesharing. Supply of and demand for concerts have increased with filesharing, and artists have earned more money.

Going beyond that, a higher distribution of music seems to also benefit sales of other information goods. Andersen and Frenz (2007, 34) demonstrate that people who are interested in entertainment goods (such as music) are also interested in DVDs, concerts, cinema/movies and video games.

Apart from the aforementioned concerts, many other goods appear to have a complementary character. Among them is, of course, the hardware necessary for playing music, i.e. the customary iPod or MP3-player. Oberholzer and Strumpf (2009, 21) have made the following rough calculation on this subject for the U.S. market: the much-discussed decrease in music sales lies at around 15% over the period between 1997 and 2007. If we add concert revenue, however, the music industry turns out instead to have grown by 5% over the same timespan. If we then add the revenue from iPod sales, the industry growth, over the period of ten years, is 66%.

This analysis is supported by a study of the Times for the British music market over the period between 2004 and 2008 (TimesOnline 2009). The results it arrives at is that CD sales have decreased, but artists' profits from live concerts have increased significantly. The total profits of the (British) music industry have even increased over the past few years. The crisis of the music industry thus seems to be less a crisis affecting the entire industry than a crisis of the big record labels, whose income is generated mainly via sales of sound carriers.

In conclusion, we can state that the negative effects of filesharing cannot be taken as solid fact. To the contrary, it is even possible that they are outweighed by positive effects. A discussion of the consequences of filesharing should thus not restrict itself to the substitution effect between illegal downloads and decreasing sales figures, but incorporate the wide area of direct and indirect network effects.

25.4   Conclusion

- The comparative-static analysis shows that the advent of black markets benefits the individual consumer as regards the existing offer of information goods. Consumer surplus rises.
- From a dynamic point of view, it is shown that the existence of pirate copies has not impeded the creative energy of artists and publishers in terms of output so far. Whether the quality of their work has suffered at the same time is an open, uninvestigated question.
- A popular theoretical line of argument on the effects of filesharing goes like this: when the copy is of the same quality as the original, and copying is free, the labels' profits will decrease because the free copy will be preferred to the original. Copies are not always a one-to-one substitute, though, e.g. with regard to quality or accessories. It can just as well be theoretically proven that providers profit from filesharing when the consumers' preferences are sufficiently heterogeneous.
- Filesharing creates redistribution effects from the superstars to lesser-known artists.

- Filesharing generally leads to substitution effects of originals by illegal copies. The market development effect that occurs simultaneously can overcompensate for this, however.
- The negative effects of filesharing cannot be regarded as proven fact. The opposite may even be true: that the positive effects outweigh the negative.

25.5   Bibliography

Andersen, B., & Frenz, M. (2007). The Impact of Music Downloads and P2P File-Sharing on the Purchase of Music: A Study for Industry Canada. London: University of London. (Online).

BBC News (2006). China to Tackle Software Piracy. BBC. (Online).

Blackburn, D. (2004). On-line Piracy and Recorded Music Sales. Harvard: Harvard University. (Online).

Castro, J.O. de, Balkin, D., & Sheperd, D. A. (2008). Can entrepreneurial firms benefit from product piracy. Journal of Business Venturing, 23(1), 75-90.

Connolly, M., & Krueger, A. (2006). Rockonomics: The economics of popular music. In Ginsburgh, V., & Throsby, D. (eds.), Handbook of the Economics of the Arts and Culture (pp. 667-720). Amsterdam.

Demos (2009). Illegal Downloaders are one of Music Industry's Biggest Customers. (Online).

Gartner Research (2006). Market trends: PCs, Asia/Pacific, 4Q05 and Year in Review. Document ID: G00138769. (Online).

GAO (2010). Intellectual Property. Observations on Efforts to Quantify the Economic Effects of Counterfeit and Pirated Goods. Report to Congressional Committees. Washington, DC: United States Government Accountability Office. (Online).

Gopal, R.D., Bhattacharjee, S., & Sanders, G.L. (2006). Do artists benefit from online music sharing. Journal of Business, 79(3), 1503-1533.

Haller, J. (2005). Urheberrechtsschutz in der Musikindustrie. Eine ökonomische Analyse. Lohmar: Eul-Verlag.

Hill, C.W.L. (2007). Digital piracy: Causes, consequences, and strategic responses. Asia Pacific Journal of Management, 24(1), 9-25.

Kirkpatrick, D. (2007). How Microsoft Conquered China. CNNMoney.com. (Online).

Krueger, A. (2005). The economics of real superstars: The market for concerts in the material world. Journal of Labor Economics, 23(1), 1-30.

Lang, C. (2005). Wohlfahrtsökonomische Analyse von privaten Tonträgerkopien. Wirtschaftswissenschaftliches Studium (WiSt), 11, 635-639.

Liebowitz, S.J. (2003). Will MP3 Downloads Annihilate the Record Industry? The Evidence so Far. Dallas, TX: University of Texas. (Online).

Liebowitz, S. J. (2006). File sharing: Creative destruction or just plain destruction. Journal of Law & Economics, 49(1), 1-28.

Linde, F. (2008): Ökonomie der Information. 2nd ed. Göttingen: Univ.-Verlag.

Mankiw, N.G., Taylor, M.P., Wagner, A., & Herrmann, M. (2008). Grundzüge der Volkswirtschaftslehre. 4th ed. Stuttgart: Schäffer-Poeschel.

Mortimer, J.H., & Sorensen, A. (2005). Supply Responses to Digital Distribution: Recorded Music and Live Performances. Harvard University. (Online).

Oberholzer-Gee, F., & Strumpf, K. (2009). File-Sharing and Copyright. Harvard: Business School. (Online).

OECD (2008). Die wirtschaftlichen Folgen von Produkt- und Markenpiraterie. Paris: Organisation for Economic Co-operation and Development.

Peitz, M., & Waelbroeck, P. (2006). Why the music industry may gain from free downloading–the role of sampling. International Journal of Industrial Organization, 24, 907-913.

Piller, C. (2006). How piracy opens doors for windows. Los Angeles Times, April 09, 2006. (Online).

Staake, T., & Fleisch, E. (2008). Countering Counterfeit Trade. Illicit Market Insights, Best-Practice Strategies, and Management Toolbox. Berlin, Heidelberg: Springer-Verlag.

TimesOnline (2009). Do Music Artists Fare Better in a World with Illegal File-Sharing. TimesOnline Labs. (Online).

Tschmuck, P. (2009a). Die Wirkungen des Musik-Filesharing - eine neue Studie. (Online).

Tschmuck, P. (2009b). Wie böse ist das File-Sharing?–Part 2. (Online).

Tschmuck, P. (2009c). Wie böse ist das File-Sharing?–Part 18. (Online).

Tschmuck, P. (2009d). Wie böse ist das File-Sharing?–Part 15. (Online).

Chapter 26

Strategic Starting Points for Dealing with Piracy

26.1 Strategic Action in View of Piracy

The previous two chapters provided some insight into the coexistence of legal and illegal offers on information markets. Crucial motives of (private) piracy have become clear. It has also transpired that bootleg copies cannot be condemned a priori, since self-supply with information goods, particularly through filesharing, can have positive effects on the legal markets. It must be considered how the existing offers might be changed in a way that is mutually beneficial, instead of using repressive measures against piracy and thus scaring away one's own clientele, the end customer.

In the following, we will again focus less on the commercial forms of piracy than on the self-supply aspect. As a further restriction, we will focus on the digital forms of piracy, since it is there that the decisive leverage for quick and worldwide distribution is found.

In the following sections, we will first consider how the different illegal offers should be dealt with, and discuss whether a further tightening of copyright law should be aimed at. Afterward, we will make some recommendations as to how a company can improve its existing (digital) information offer in order to increase its profits. Finally, we will discuss some approaches to developing new business models.

The following deliberations complement the chapters on information providers' competitive strategies. In those chapters, we focused on the strategic positioning in the competition for legal markets. Here, we will investigate how individual providers can survive against, or with, the black market. The variables known to us represent a useful set of instruments for this purpose.

26.2   Measures Against Illegal Offers

As an information provider facing piracy, one can, as a first measure, work toward stopping illegal offers. This form of defense, as can be clearly observed, is being used by the music and film industries. In many industrial countries, cooperation between associations and administrations in the fight against piracy has been intensified over the last few years. For Germany, the Federal Association for the Music Industry (2008, 3) observes that

> Germany [is] one of the few countries in which massive legal persecu-
> tion was able to at least contain the problem of online music theft.

This success is due, among other factors, to the fully automatized search for copyright infringements on the internet, and the subsequent filing of tens of thousands of suits with public prosecutors on the basis of this data (Heise Online, 2006).

As a further measure, the associations strive for a step-by-step sanctioning system against pirates, enforced by the internet providers, which will be applied in case of copyright infringements and leading, finally, to a complete shutdown of their internet connection.

Building upon the insight into causes and effects of piracy, we will rate some aspects of this repressive procedure.

How do moral appeals and a heightening of the pressure of prosecution affect the target group of filesharers? There are a few empirical studies that have tried to answer these questions. Surveys among Swedish and British filesharers revealed that there is definitely a prevailing interest in creative professionals (composers, lyricists, performers etc.) receiving a fair remuneration for their work. Thus, in the Swedish survey of more than 1,000 filesharers, 65% stated that it is a great disadvantage of filesharing services that artists are not paid for their music (STIM, 2009, 11). 74% of filesharers interviewed in the British survey would be interested in a legal filesharing service, and 90% of these proponents would like to see the artists be the main benficiaries of this system (BMR, 2008, 30-31). Consistently with these findings, Hennig-Thurau et al. (2007, 15) observe:

> Specifically, stressing the unethical element of appropriating copy-
> righted content without compensating the copyright owner in marketing
> campaigns could increase the moral costs of illegal file sharing and
> lower file-sharing activities.

A limiting factor, however, is the fact that for each respective target group, one must take into consideration that group's prevalent attitude toward piracy. Freestone and Mitchell (2004) determined, via an empirical study on ethical views on the internet (e-Ethics), that only around 5% of Generation Y (8-24 years old) think that the free downloading of music and films is wrong or unethical. Moral appeals are probably more effective for older target groups. A proof for this is the relatively high level of attention that this point enjoyed in the Swedish study mentioned above, where the average age of the respondents was relatively high (STIM, 2009, 6). In the British study, however–we can assume–it was lower. Here, only a little more than 10% of interviewees stated that they did not upload because they thought that artists should receive fair recompensation (BMR, 2008, 17). Moral views are generally less pronounced in younger people (Dördrechter, 2007, 275 with further sources), and it is to be assumed that they are not entirely aware of the correlation between downloading and not paying the artists. Educational work seems to be required here. Whether the German "Piracy is a crime" campaign, which is shown to paying customers in cinemas, is the right path appears doubtful (Dördrechter 2007, 276).

Likewise, it must be asked whether the criminal persecution of pirates creates the desired is as much of a deterrent as is aimed for. In the British filesharing study, only 15% of respondents stated that they do not upload because the risk of being caught is too high (BMR, 2008, 17). A survey of German film consumers explicitly concludes that

> the movie industry's initial reaction to the threat of movie file sharing—suing its own customers—appears to be misguided (Hennig-Thurau et al., 2007, 15).

An empirical study by LaRose and Kim (2007) investigates the intentions of music downloaders. They found out that apart from the expected (positive) effects of downloading (e.g. new stimuli, pleasant activity, social status), the individuals under investigation displayed an underdeveloped mechanism for self-regulation. This means that their self-control in utilizing media is inadequate. Following this insight, the music industry's measures of prosecuting and normative influencing are misguided, at least for the surveyed social group of U.S. college students, because they are foiled by the downloaders' personality structures.

Consumers' fear of being prosecuted is obviously no effective means of stopping piracy. Increasing the risk of being caught might even cause the opposite effect, since according to the Optimum Stimulation Level theory, it would only increase pirates' stimulus. For the film industry, Dördrechter (2007, 276) recommends tearing down the menacing façade. Instead, it would be better to make the actual damage caused by piracy transparent and to communicate in an educational manner. This insight should also be transferable to other industries.

It can additionally be discerned that there is less piracy in countries with great economic power (see Chapter 24). In such countries, copyright also tends to be relatively well protected. As can be shown, the relevant associations are even interested in tightening copyright further. Haller (2005, 305), in a thorough analysis of the existing theories and studies for Germanys, arrives at the conclusion that

> a further increase of copyright protection does not appear to be a sensible measure for overcoming the current crisis in the music industry.

A further raising of the protection level would increase providers' monopoly status even further and negatively affect welfare. The existence of network effects increases the severity of these consequences. German copyright in particular is already deemed to be one of the world's most restrictive (Haller, 2005, 294 with further sources) and should thus–from the perspective of the film industry, too (Dördrechter, 2007, 278)–not be tightened any further. The situation for countries without pronounced Intellectual Property Rights (e.g. China or India) is to be judged differently, be it in terms of laws themselves or in their execution. Here, a tightening of security measures seems generally advisable (Hill, 2007, 22-23; Reinig & Plice, 2010, 6).

From a more sociological perspective, Tschmuck, in his commentary on the British filesharing study (BMR, 2008) points out, rather formally, that filesharing is probably not to be regarded as a conscious property crime with the intention of harming someone, as is the case for traditional product piracy, but that filesharing is

> a novel form of social behavior clashing with very restrictive legal boundaries, which are being increasingly tightened. But this is precisely the wrong path. Legal frameworks should always take into account the reality of life, and not happily risk potentially criminalizing wide sections of the population. In this sense, legal boundaries must be broadened and file sharing [should] be accepted as legitimate social behavior (Tschmuck, 2009).

These deliberations are supported by the empirical study of Altschuller and Benbunan-Fich (2009), who were able to observe an ethical dilemma in U.S. students' dealing with illegal filesharing offers. This dilemma was made clear by the students' ambivalent attitude: there were clear deviations between what the respondents thought was right (e.g. not to download illegally) and what they would recommend others as correct behavior, namely to use illegal download offers and transfer them onto data carriers. They arrive at a similar conclusion as Tschmuck before them, which is that these

> inconsistencies support the notion that as technology evolves, it creates discrepancies between the way things are and the way the law expects them to be, leaving society in a muddle, trying to reconcile the two (Altschuller & Benbunan-Fich, 2009, 49).

It would thus presumably better to start with the time and effort of procuring pirate copies than to increase the legal pressure (of prosecution). The illegal acquisition of films, for instance, is directly tied to how difficult the process is. Factors such as retrieval, the download itself and particularly quality control play a decisive role in this context (Dördrechter, 2007, 254-255). The shutting down of known filesharing services increases the cost of retrieval. The flooding of filesharing services with bad copies would drive up the costs of quality control. Brodersen (2007, 233) here developed the idea of "Weak-Copy-Flooding". Information providers could "flood" filesharing services with low-quality copies of their information goods–possibly even in conjunction with advertising–even before their actual release dates. These copies would provide consumers with the option of gleaning an impression of the contents, but their quality would be worse than the originals'. At the same time, the large number of existing low-quality copies would make it harder for the service's users to identify the higher-quality illegal copies uploaded after the original's release. This procedure would increase the incentive to purchase without restricting positive network effects.

We will, very briefly, pick up the aspect of technical protective measures once more. To put it concisely: is Digital Rights Management (DRM) suited for stopping piracy? Generally speaking, this will probably never be the case, because

> every time a new copy protection technology (such as Macrovision) is developed, pirates quickly develop a counter-technology to defeat it (Cook & Wang, 2004, 569).

In connection with existing, or newly developed, illegal sharing networks, it is to be assumed that the transformed files will be widely distributed relatively quickly. DRM could perhaps cause a certain delay (Haber et al., 2003), but it will not manage to stop the distribution because it is enough if a fraction of users is able to upload the unprotected contents (Biddle et al., 2003). Dördrechter (2007, 278) even detects an adverse effect: not only does copy protection on DVDs not represent a real hurdle for pirates, but it is an additional stimulus for them, a sort of challenge. It must also be noted that the providers of cleaned-up files do not do so for profit, but strive instead to match the efforts of others (reciprocity) and gain renown in their peer group (Stryszowski & Scorpecci, 2009, 8). The costs incurred by the full implementation of DRM systems and the restrictions they place on legal consumption were already addressed in Chapter 21.

If we summarize the results collected so far, we will see that the principle of combating every instance of filesharing is untenable from a purely economical perspective. The study results listed in Chapter 25 demonstrate this for music, but similar effects must be assumed for the other industries, too. Bhattacharjee et al. have even found out, in an empirical and simulation-supported study of the music market, that the complete elimination of piracy would be downright counterproductive, since

> maximum profit outcomes occur in the presence of piracy (Bhattacharjee et al., 2006, 154).

This is because access to (illegal) sharing networks lowers search costs, after which the customers can make better purchasing decisions via sampling.

26.3   Improving Legal Offers

A very central starting point for information providers is an attractive offer that moves customers to buy the original product instead of downloading an illegal copy. Napster, in 1999, was the first and only (illegal) offer for downloading music from the internet. In 2001, iTunes entered the market as a legal alternative, and only in 2004 did the music industry come up with further offers for (legally) downloading music (Bundesverband Musikindustrie, 2004, 22). Legal offers have thus always been at a competitive disadvantage against their illegal counterparts from a chronological point of view. As we know from Chapter 17, on the Timing of Market Entry, the late mover's offer must be particularly persuasive. He must make the customer attractive offers in order to win their business. This leads us on to the question of what distinguishes legal offers from illegal ones.

A starting point for developing attractive download offers is the question of why filesharers prefer illegal services to legal ones. An online survey of the Swedish Collecting Society for Composers, Lyricists and Music Publishers, Svenska Tonsättares Internationella Musikbyrå (STIM), interviewing 1,123 Swedish filesharers, produced the results displayed in Table 26.1. The entries with the heighest percentages regard the legal aspect, which we will address in more detail in the following section, and the price. They are directly followed by the aspects of Extent of Offer, Usability, Quality of Content and Security.

Legal downloads cost money, usage of sharing services is possible without payment. As always, the customers want the price to represent a suitable relation between service and fee. Apparently, there are many consumers who regard the price of the legal offers as too high in relation to the service they provide. Let us first discuss the service aspects that arise from this survey and others.

Customers want a large music catalog, from which they can choose their product. Here it is also important–thus a study of the British collecting society (BMR, 2008, 13)–that rare and unpublished materials can also be found. Just like every website, usage should be simple and intuitive. In this regard, there is still room for improvement in many legal offers.

A great advantage of the legal offers is the quality of their content. The customer gets what is advertised, and in corresponding quality. Furthermore, the subject of security does not play a role in legal offers, as it is a given. In addition, adequate sampling options should be provided (BMR, 2008, 13) in order to prevent information asymmetries.

Form of Offer / Rating	Filesharing Sites	Legal Download Offers
Advantages	• Music is available for free (78.3%) • They are easy to use (58.7%) • Files can be stored anywhere (49.5%) • You can find anything you are looking for (48.5%)	• Purchases are legal (74.7%) • High sound quality (49.7%) • No danger of viruses (37.8%) • Easy navigation on the websites (23.9%)
Disadvantages	• They are illegal (66.2%) • The artists are not remunerated (65.0%) • Threat of viruses (60.9%) • Corrupt files (47.6%) • Files with wrong content (41.3%) • Incomplete files (40.3%) • Downloads take too long (22.2%)	• Titles are expensive (62.7%) • You do not find everything you want (61.4%) • Music is often DRM-potected (38.9%) • Formats on offer cannot be played on all end devices (38.8%)

Table 26.1: Comparison of Advantages and Disadvantages of Legal and Illegal Downloading Alternatives for Music. Source: STIM, 2009, 8 et seq.

Also empirically proven is the consumers' desire for additional offers.

> We found that all participants were less likely to pirate when the alternative, pay Web site offered features such as extensive music catalogs and the availability of extras, such as rare recordings, live concerts, and downloadable ringtones and videos (Sinha & Mandel, 2008, 12).

Here the wide area of complementary offers that can be made to customers opens up. Deiss (2006, 111-112) proves empirically that users of filesharing services go to concerts and listen to the radio more often.

Similar statements can be found with regard to the offer of films. Filesharers appreciate the flexible usage options of previewing (Dördrechter, 2007, 274-275). The film industry could significantly improve its offer via a better Video-on-Demand (VoD) system, which might offer the customer the possibility of previewing the first fifteen minutes of any movie, or even to select the scenes they wish to see. VoD could also make it possible to make films available earlier than they have been so far, as we discussed in Chapter 18 on Pricing (Figure 18.5). An attractive added-value offer could be peer-supported film ratings. Another advisable measure is to increase the attractiveness of moviegoing, preventing the substitution of visits to the cinema by digital offers. Here, the cinema industry is taking the first steps and is banking on luxury offers, which enhance the cinema experience via service offers such as ushers, good parking spaces, generous seating opportunities, good food and digital 3-D projections (Killing, 2009, 113-114).

Let us now look at the pricing side of things. What first recommendations might be tendered for pricing, in regard to the existence of illegal copies? The studies mentioned above have been very important in demonstrating the music, as offered legally, is regarded as too expensive. More than 70% of respondents in the British study stated, as their reason for illegal downloading: "It's free, save money" (BMR, 2008, 13). The same results can be found for the film industry (Dördrechter, 2007, 273). The costs for the original, be it in cinemas or on DVD, are regarded as too high by pirates. If providers are thus unable, or unwilling, to significantly improve their services, the first simple consequence to be taken might be the lowering of prices. There is much in favor of not doing so generally, but to open up the toolbox of pricing and introduce differentiated pricing models. An ideal strategy would appear to be Mixed Bundling, in which customers are offered either the entire repertoire, on a subscription basis, or single titles in online stores (Bhattacharjee et al., 2006). The "digital record store" Napster, now legalized (www.napster.com), offers such combined models, which thus represent more of an ongoing service than a one-off purchasing offer for a single product. For single titles, it also seems to be of advantage not to offer them at a flat price, as customers' preferences differ. With regard to piracy, Gopal et al. (2006, 1529) observe:

> Lower valued music items are pirated more than higher valued items [...] and consequently sales of those suffer. If a producer is aware of the true value of a song to consumers, he can set the price accordingly to maximize profits. For producers, the model shows that in the presence of online music sampling, uniform pricing for all music items is a suboptimal strategy.

Alternatively, the creation of legal music-sharing services might be of interest. In the Swedish study, almost nine out of ten users (86.2%) stated that they would be prepared to pay for such a service. More than half would thus be willing to pay between 50 and 150 Swedish Kroner (ca. €5-15) per month. Only 7.4% are unwilling to pay for filesharing (STIM 2009, 3 et seq.).

On the basis of an empirical study, Dördrechter (2007, 273-274) recommends that the film industry try to contain piracy by lowering admission prices in cinemas during the week and the prices for original DVDs.

Generally, the recommendation can only be to apply the manifold methods offered by the pricing of information goods in the first place (Linde, 2008). Bundling on its own already offers a multitude of variants, e.g. bundling sound carriers in combination with live offers, or selling cinema tickets and DVDs in one package. In the digital world, put simply, customers must be made attractive offers with high usability and appropriate prices, which make purchasing and direct usage as easy as possible. All that stands between the buying impulse and the buying decision is the potential danger of secession to the black market. This might be the reason why the existing offers still aren't balanced enough:

> The harsh reality for the studios is that for consumers to buy an official packaged media version of a film, they must be given more and pay less-a model that is being forced on other media markets (Starling & Roberts, 2003, 29).

Similar statements are made by Chiou et al. (2005, 170), concerning the music industry. There appears to be a need for creating

> easily searchable indexes of music items, fast download access to music items in different secure formats, provisions of posting consumer reviews on items, creation of fan club sites within the search portal, etc. Some of these items are now being made available on online music portals-however there is little evidence of an integrated offering of such strategies (Gopal et al., 2006, 1529).

26.4   Developing New Business Models

Apart from the measures that can be taken by information providers against piracy and to improve their own offer, there is also the option of "taking the bull by its horns". New, creative business models may provide them with possibilities for marketing their own offer in the digital world in new, and perhaps even better, ways. No matter what industry you look at, what is important is that the (legal) online offer has the quality that its target groups demand and an appropriate "ease of use". If that is accomplished, there will be good chances that the legal offers will oust their illegal competition (Stryszowski & Scorpecci, 2009, 12). We can only give some pointers as to the direction that such business models might take, where "business model" only means the rough summary of a for-profit enterprise (Knyphausen-Aufseß & Meinhardt, 2002). The central elements of such a model are the combination of product and market, the configuration of activities for creating added value and the revenue mechanism. Even without any changes to the product-market combination, ideas for altering preexisting business models can easily be developed. The different aspects of Price Differentiation, via Bundling, Versioning or Windowing, have been discussed in Chapter 18, and, partly, in the above section on improving offers.

At this point, we would like to introduce some seemingly radical solutions for pricing. Due to their known cost structures, information goods are eminently suited for being priced via the **pay-what-you-want** (PWYW) approach. Here the customer can either sample the product extensively, or even own it, and decides what it is worth only after sampling or consumption. Interestingly, a large number of customers is prepared to pay on a voluntary basis, which means that providers do not have to fear the their profits will inevitably decrease (Kim et al., 2009).

For small labels, and less-known artists, Regner and Barria (2009) found out that customers are even prepared to pay more than suggested by a price recommendation. Three central motives for the willingness to pay transpired in this situation: the customers felt the need of compensating for the openness they were granted in accessing music by paying accordingly (reciprocity), they could feel positive about themselves having contributed to a good cause, namely supporting the artists, and they did not need to have a guilty conscience due to having paid less than they should have. This approach gives rise to whole new possibilities of building business relationships and creating a relationship of trust between provider and customer.

A second line of thought goes in the direction of **offering information goods for free**. To put it simply: cost-free offers will substitute piracy if all the other parameters, such as usability, quality, freedom of use etc. are adequate as well. This variant must not be confused with a comprehensive sampling offer meant to lead to a purchasing decision. It actually means that music, software, films, books etc. should be offered for free. Of course, revenue must then be generated elsewhere. In this respect, it would seem advisable to only offer certain (lower-quality) versions for free and to make money from selling complements or advertising space. One example is the Chinese music market, serviced by Google (Schwan, 2008). Music from Chinese and international labels, among them EMI and Universal, can be searched via Google and then downloaded for free. Revenue is generated via ads.

Further potential for changes to preexisting business models of information providers lies in the restructuring of their value chains. The music industry could create greater pricing leverage for itself by changing the licensing structures. The predominant model of licensing payments per download could be replaced by blanket payments that depend upon the repertoire on offer, or percentage payments relating to the provider's profit. Bhattacharjee et al. (2006) determined that payment per download is the worst of the three variants for both retailers and customers. In order to lower the fees, and profit from possible revenue increases via lower prices, however, prices need to be redetermined throughout the entire value chain, i.e. incorporating artists, labels, retailers etc. (Strube et al., 2008, 200-201).

A step that would go far beyond this would be to expand the value chain. Music publishers, for instance, who have to realize that revenue from simple music sales is dropping, could try to make complementary offers. The music corporations are already thinking about fully supplying consumers, by not only assuming responsibility for sound carrier sales and the marketing of artists, but also offering concert tickets, MP3-players and merchandising articles (Postinett, 2008).

The increased revenue generated by the greater distribution of music due to piracy mostly goes to the artists themselves, not to their labels. In order to soften the pressure in the labels' repressive measures, and not to endanger the quality of new releases, artists might consider sharing some of their profits from touring with their labels. The stronger distribution of music should result in increased demand for sound carriers, live concerts and complements (Curien & Moreau, 2009, 111-112). Both sides in unison might manage to create a win-win situation.

A further variant would be the integration of filesharing into the value chain. A great danger for the music corporations lies in being circumvented by seeing artists self-marketing their work:

> [...] instead of fighting the file-sharing services, musicians would embrace the Kazaas of the world as a free promotion vehicle and distribution pipeline to an audience of millions (Lasica, 2005, 63).

One might even go further and grant consumers more extensive rights to the information goods they acquire. Why not allow users to integrate the music, film, text, game etc. into a creative process at their discretion and to create new works? This practice, often encountered in computer games, still seems unimaginable for music and film:

> Imagine buying the latest "Lord of the Rings" DVD and discovering that the cameras, lights, special effects and editing tools used in its making had been included at no extra charge. Or finding your favourite CD's crammed with virtual recording studios, along with implicit encouragement from the producer to remix the music, record your own material and post it all on the Internet (Marriott, 2003).

Social networks in particular represent an ideal breeding ground for the creation of new creative works, and the flexible rights found in the Creative Commons scene even provide an adequate legal framework.

In sum, the recommendations for information providers consists of making their own offers more attractive in order to allow for substitution effects in the reverse direction, i.e. to see legal offers displacing illegal ones. To attack filesharing services outright or to undermine them can only provide limited relief, namely only insofar as the desired network effects are not eliminated.

26.5   Conclusion

- Younger people generally have less pronounced sets of morals, and it is to be assumed that they are not totally aware of the correlation between downloading and failing to pay the artist. Educational work from the side of the information providers seems to be called for.
- The music industry's measures of criminal prosecution and normative influencing appear to be misguided, as they are undermined by the downloaders' personality structures.

- Dealing with illegal filesharing offers often means an ethical dilemma, in which there are clear deviations between what one thinks is right and what one would recommend others to do.
- In countries with great economic power, copyright is generally well protected. A further increase of copyright does not appear to make sense in these countries, because it would strengthen providers' monopoly status and create negative effects on welfare.
- A central approach to fight piracy is to make better legal offers. Apart from the advantage of legality, important roles are played by adequate prices, the extent of the offers, usability as well as quality and security.
- New, creative business models can provide possibilities for marketing one's own offer in the digital realm in new and perhaps even better ways. One option is innovative pricing via pay-what-you-want or free offers. Another variant would be to expand the value chain and integrate offers of complements, such as live events or playback devices.

26.6 Bibliography

Altschuller, S., & Benbunan-Fich, R. (2009). Is music downloading the new prohibition? What students reveal through an ethical dilemma. Ethics and Information Technology, 11(1), 49-56.

Bhattacharjee, S., Gopal, R.D., Lertwachara, K., & Marsden, J.R. (2006). Consumer search and retailer strategies in the presence of online music sharing. Journal of Management Information Systems, 23(1), 129-159.

Biddle, P., England, P., Peinado, M., & Willman, B. (2003). The darknet and the future of content protection. In Becker, E., Buhse, W., Günnewig, D., & Rump, N. (eds.), Digital Rights Management. Technological, Economic, Legal and Political Aspects (pp. 344-365). Berlin: Springer (Lecture Notes in Computer Science, 2770).

British Music Rights (BMR) (2008). Music Experience and Behaviour in Young People. Main Findings and Conclusions. University of Hertfordshire. (Online).

Brodersen, J. (2007). Illegale Selbstversorgung durch Tauschnetzwerke. In Linde, F. (ed.), Markttheoretische und wettbewerbsstrategische Aspekte des Managements von Informationsgütern (pp. 214-236). Köln (Kölner Arbeitspapiere zur Bibliotheks- und Informationswissenschaft, 53).

Bundesverband Musikindustrie (2004). Jahreswirtschaftsbericht 2004. Bundesverband Musikindustrie. (Online).

Bundesverband Musikindustrie (2008). Jahreswirtschaftsbericht 2008. Bundesverband Musikindustrie. (Online).

Chiou, J.S., Huang, C.Y., & Lee, H.H. (2005). The antecedents of music piracy attitudes and intentions. Journal of Business Ethics, 57(2), 161-174.

Cook, D.A., & Wang, W. (2004). Neutralizing the piracy of motion pictures: Re-engineering the industry's cupply chain. Technology in Society, 26(4), 567-583.

Curien, N., & Moreau, F. (2009). The music industry in the digital era. Toward new contracts. The Journal of Media Economics, 22(2), 102-113.

Deiss, B. (2006). Musik aus dem Internet - Filesharing in p2p-Tauschbörsen. München: GRIN.

Dördrechter, N. (2007). Piraterie in der Filmindustrie. Eine Analyse der Gründe für Filmpiraterie und deren Auswirkungen auf das Konsumverhalten. Wiesbaden: Dt. Univ.-Verlag.

Freestone, O., & Mitchell, V.W (2004). Generation Y attitudes towards e-ethics and internet-related misbehaviours. Journal of Business Ethics, 54, 121-128.

Gopal, R. D., Bhattacharjee, S., & Sanders, G. L. (2006). Do artists benefit from online music sharing. Journal of Business, 79(3), 1503-1533.

Haber, S., Horne, B., Pato, J., Sander, T., & Tarjan, R. E. (2003). If piracy is the problem, is DRM the answer. In Becker, E., Buhse, W., Günnewig, D., Rump, N. (eds.), Digital Rights Management. Technological, Economic, Legal and Political Aspects (pp. 224-233). Berlin: Springer (Lecture Notes in Computer Science, 2770).

Haller, J. (2005). Urheberrechtsschutz in der Musikindustrie. Eine ökonomische Analyse. Lohmar: Eul-Verlag.

Hennig-Thurau, T., Hennig, V., & Sattler, H. (2007). Consumer file sharing of motion pictures. Journal of Marketing, 71, 1-18.

Hill, C.W.L. (2007). Digital piracy: Causes, consequences, and strategic responses. Asia Pacific Journal of Management, 24(1), 9-25.

Killing, U. (2009). Neue Perspektiven. Wirtschaftswoche, 6, 02/02/2009, 113-114.

Kim, J.Y., Natter, M., & Spann, M. (2009). Pay what you want: A new participative pricing mechanism. Journal of Marketing, 73(1), 44-58.

Knyphausen-Aufseß, D. zu, & Meinnardt, Y. (2002). Revisiting Strategy: Ein Ansatz zur Systernatisierung von Geschäftsmodellen. In Bieger, T., Bickhoff, N., Caspers, R., Knyphausen-Aufseß, D. zu, & Reding, K. (eds.), Zukünftige Geschäftsmodelle. Konzept und Anwendung in der Netzökonomie (pp. 63-89). Berlin: Springer.

Heise Online (2006). Generalstaatsanwaltschaft klagt über ungebremste P2P-Strafanzeigen-Maschine. (Online).

LaRose, R., & Kim, J. (2007). Share, steal, or buy? A social cognitive perspective of music downloading. CyberPsychology & Behavior, 10(2), 267-277.

Lasica, J. D. (2005). Darknet. Hollywood's War Against the Digital Generation. Hoboken, NJ: Wiley.

Linde, F. (2008). Pricing-Strategien bei Informationsgütern. WISU, 2, 208-214.

Marriott, M. (2003). Games made for remaking. The New York Times, 4.12.2003. (Online).

Mercer Management Consulting (2003). Media Context: Media Strategies and Trends from Mercer Management Consulting. London.

Postinett, A. (2008). Wo die Musik spielt. Handelsblatt, 53, March 14/15/16, 2008, 12.

Regner, T., & Barria, J.A. (2009). Do consumers pay voluntarily? The case of online music. Journal of Economic Behavior & Organization, 71, 395-406.

Reinig, B. A., & Plice R.K. (2010). Modeling software piracy in developed and emerging economies. Proceedings of the 43rd Hawaii International Conference on Systems Science, January 5-8. Koloa, Kauai, Hawaii.

Schwan, B. (2008). Plattenindustrie verschenkt Musik. taz.de. (Online).

Sinha, R. K., & Mandel, N. (2008). Preventing digital music piracy: The carrot or the stick. Journal of Marketing, 72, 1-15.

Starling, A., & Roberts, J. (2003). The rise and rise of the DVD: Can the studios keep control. In Mercer Management Consulting (ed.), Media Context: Media Strategies and Trends from Mercer Management Consulting (pp. 24-32). London.

STIM (ed.) (2009). Pirates, file-sharers and music users. A survey of the conditions for new music services on the Internet. Studie im Auftrag der Svenska Tonsättares Internationella Musikbyrå (STIM). (Online).

Strube, J., Pohl, G., & Buxmann, P. (2008). Preisstrategien für Onlinemusik. In Gensch, G., Stöckler, E. M., & Tschmuck, P. (eds.), Musikrezeption, Musikdistribution und Musikproduktion. Der Wandel des Wertschöpfungsnetzwerks in der Musikwirtschaft (pp. 187-203). Wiesbaden: Gabler Verlag / GWV Fachverlage GmbH Wiesbaden (Springer-11775 [Dig. Serial]).

Stryszowski, P., & Scorpecci, D. (2009). Piracy of Digital Content. Paris: OECD. (Online).

Tschmuck, P. (2009). Neue britische Studie zum File-Sharing. (Online).

Glossary

A

Address information. Address databases usually offer information for marketing activities (e.g. mailing campaigns).

Adverse selection. If one side of the market (e.g. demand) is insufficiently informed about the quality of the offered goods prior to the completion of the contract, and if this information deficit cannot be made up via search activities, the result is adverse selection (via the quality assessments that have been made). The qualitatively good offers are displaced by the bad ones.

B

Banner advertising. A graphically oriented online advertisement that is offered in four basic forms: full banner, leaderboard, rectangle and skyscraper.

Blog. Site on the World Wide Web for publishing opinion-based documents. A blog consists of different single blog postings, which are arranged in descending chronological order.

Bundling. Two or more (information) goods are summed up under one offer and sold as a package, or set, for one (generally lower) total price. The key concern of bundling is to reduce the variance in customers' esteem, and hence their willingness to pay, for a product when compared with individual sales of the products.

Business information. All information that can be gathered about a company (company dossier, solvency, products and addresses).

C

Case (jurisdiction). Juridical decisions as an indicator of a "good law" (as part of primary legal information).

Censorship. An active prevention of the distribution of content, independently of the respective carrier.

Chicken-Egg Problem. In information goods, there is a chicken-egg problem in offering basic good and complement when both are offered by different companies. Basic good, i.e. hardware, providers desire a strong commitment on the part of software providers, i.e. complementors, in order to boost sales of the basic good. Complementors, on the other hand, expect high sales figures for the hardware (basic good) before they decide to commit to a more comprehensive complementary offer.

Collaborative service. Actual collaboration between members of a community in Web 2.0 with the goal of collaboratively working out a common information service (e.g. wikis, weblogs, microblogging, social networks, social bookmarking).

Company dossier. Key data including financial information about a company.

Compatibility. Also often called interoperability, compatibility means, in general, that different systems (products, individuals or organizations) are able to work together via a common interface.

Complementary goods. Complementary goods (complements) are add-on offers for a primary (or basic) good. This can mean additional products or even services. Generally, they provide a value through the joined usage of basic good and complement. The joined usage can also have negative effects, though. Merchandising offers that have been thematically aligned to an information good can be called quasi-complements. Complements create indirect network effects.

Computer criminality. Using the computer as a target of a criminal act. It encompasses malicious software or malware (i.e. viruses, Trojan Horses, worms and bots).

Consortium *see* Library consortium.

Content aggregator. Bundling the content of various different databases under one surface, using one retrieval system and marketing both their content as well as their search services.

Context-specific advertising. Online advertising that starts on the basis of a search request or a website and operates appropriate ads on exactly this basis.

Copyleft. No legal status, but a contract between software creator and user. Programs derived from the original software must be Copyleft-licensed as well.

Copyright law. Granting works legal protection as individual intellectual creations.

Creative Commons (CC). Information providers can use Creative Commons to define the degree of (legal) protection for the content themselves. The tiered licencing contracts allow content providers to no longer have to choose between complete ("all rights reserved") and no protection at all, but to make a differentiated decision as to what form their product's protection should assume.

Credence qualities. The quality features of a good that cannot be discovered by the customer, or only at great effort. He thus has to trust that the expected quality will be delivered.

Credit information. Databases with credit information enrich company dossiers by stating each respective firm's solvency.

Cyberbullying. Harming other people via internet (i.e. online mobbing).

Cyberharassment. Harassment via internet can assume the form of cyberstalking or cyberbullying, either in the workplace, at school or elsewhere.

Cyberinfrastructure. Global, Web-supported scientific cooperation.

Cyberstalking. Using the internet and its services to massively stalk and disturb other people.

D

Dark Web. Activities of terrorist groups on the internet.

Deep Web. Also called "Invisible Web"; digital information which cannot be found by Web search engines. Only the start pages of these information collections are accessible via the WWW. Important parts of the Deep Web are domain-specific databases and services of content aggregators.

De facto standard. A standard which develops out of market processes.

De jure standard. A standard which is determined via regulatory instances.

Design law. Register right, protecting design elements. Neither the novelty required nor the uniqueness are checked when a design is registered.

Deviant information behavior. Behavior, that does not conform to socially accepted values. It means both deviance (infringing on social norms) and delinquency (infringing on legal norms) when dealing with digital information. It includes problematic internet usage (excessive internet consumption), online harassment (cyberbullying, cyberstalking) and delinquent information behavior such as online fraud, computer criminality, and internet usage of terrorist groups (dark web).

Digital game. From the perspective of game research these games are distinguished into console games and PC games.

Digital divide. Social inequality concerning the use of information infrastructure and information content. In an information or knowledge society there is a gap that separates the information-rich from the information-poor (people, cities, countries, etc.), a gap between those who benefit from new technologies and those who do not.

Digital information services. In the early time of the information market: online databases, CD-ROMs, audiotex and videotex services; today all content services on the internet.

Digital Object Identifier (DOI). Each STM document, no matter whether it is a text, a fact etc., is uniquely labelled via an identifier. This facilitates interlinking between documents.

Digital Rights Management. In DRM, technical and legal components are used in unison in order to manage the rights to information goods by the rights holders. It is meant to preclude unauthorized access, thus preventing that goods which were originally private unintentionally become public.

Domain name law. Claims for domain names can be backed up by various norms (e.g. person, company or brand names, work titles or company labels).

Dominant standard. A standard is dominant if there is no close competitor (anymore) and if it maintains a very clear distance to alternative offers, with no reason to doubt that this will change anytime soon.

Downwards Compatibility. Products or devices that are downwards compatible are also able to execute applications from previous product generations.

E

E-Book. Digital books. Electronic versions of books to be consumed either on a normal computer or a specific device.

E-Commerce. Supply and sales of goods via networks (especially the internet).

E-Governance. Political and administrative activities supporting the development of a knowledge society as part of information politics.

E-Government. Public administrations work online with the public and collaborate with each other. The five steps are catalog, communication, transaction, integration and participation.

E-Mail advertising. Advertising via E-Mail requires, for legal reasons, the permission of the customers (permission-based marketing).

E-Science *see* Cyberinfrastructure.

Evidence-based STM. Looking for the best possible evidence for the solution to any given problem to close the knowledge gap between theory and practice in STM (science, technology, medicine).

Experience qualities. The quality characteristics of a good, which can only be assessed for free (via experience) after the product has been purchased.

F

Fair use. From an ethical perspective, morally adequate use of digital information and (for sellers) asking fair prices for information goods (i.e. different prices for citizens of developing countries and those of the First World, or for the economic elite and the socially underprivileged).

File-sharing service. In Web 2.0 prosumers share certain documents with the virtual community. Depending on the type of resource we distinguish services for videos, images, music and other media.

First-Copy-Cost Effect. In information goods, there are heavily decreasing average costs, because the proportional fixed costs of production (First-Copy-Costs) dominate the variable costs of reproduction. As production increases, average unit costs decrease exponentially.

Follow-the-free. A specific form of penetration pricing in digital information goods, where the products are given away for free.

G

Gambling. Virtual adaptations of games of chance known from the real world. Casino games and betting are the two main groups of online games of chance.

Game with a purpose. A digital game that is fun to play but serves another underlying purpose, e.g. tagging non-textual documents.

H

Host *see* Content aggregator.

I

I-Commerce. Distribution of digital information goods on the information market. I-Commerce is a part of e-commerce. In i-commerce, information goods are either sold or freely distributed (and then the attention of the customers becomes sold).

ICT Development Index (IDI). An index of the International Telecommunications Union (ITU) that covers the influence of information and communication technologies on a country's development.

ifo Economic Climate Index. Early indicator for the economic development of Germany. "Soft" indicator based on personal opinions and hence representing a mood variable.

Image sharing service. Platform for digital images in the Web 2.0 (Flickr), in which the registered prosumers can upload their content, choose their status, put them into photostreams and index them via tags.

Informational city. Prototypical city of the knowledge society. According to Castells, in an informational city the space of flows (capital, power and information) dominates the space of places. These cities can be glocally (i.e. locally and globally) aligned world cities and allocate headquarters of internationally active financial providers and of knowledge-intensive companies.

Information asymmetry. Information asymmetry is when information (e.g. about product quality or the provider's business intentions) are distributed unequally between the sides of supply and demand. If one side of the market is better informed than the other, options arise for exploiting this gradient strategically.

Information ethics. A specific area of ethics that applied to information production, storage, access and dissemination. It consists of ethical behavior of information professionals, protection of privacy, free access to knowledge and foundations of intellectual property.

Information good. An information good is everything that is, or could be, available in digital form and is presumed to be useful by economic agents. Information goods display a dual character, since they are always a combination of content and carrier medium.

Information infrastructure. Telephony as well as (broadband) networking and internet, and the usage of these technologies in private households, companies and government.

Information law. Law with respect to information. Traditional law applied to digital information (e. g., intellectual property rights and copyright) and new law dealing with digital information (e.g., in Germany the telemedia law). Law and thus information law is primarily nationally oriented.

Information market. Market of digital information goods, which are distributed via networks (especially the internet) and thus display significant network effects.

Information paradox. A statement going back to Arrow, asserting that the quality of an information good can only be assessed by making it publicly accessible, which leads to the customers receiving it for free. The statement is absolutely incorrect if put in this way, because information goods partly have search qualities, which means that their quality can be signalled in other ways than full disclosure, and the willingness to pay does not necessarily sink to zero once the information good has been transmitted. In a modified form, the information paradox reads: by disclosing (parts of) the information good prior to purchase, demand for the product may be satisfied so comprehensively that the customer's willingness to pay sinks to zero.

Information politics. Political activities on the internet. The WWW becomes a crucial element in election campaigns.

Information society. Society whose basic innovations are carried by the resource information (theory of the 5th Kondratieff) and whose members preferably use telematic devices of information and communication purposes. An information society is grounded by information and communication technology.

Information subculture. Defined by common interests Hackers, Crackers and Crashers form their own culture with own ethics and style.

Information substitutes. Signals that relate to the design of the provider's marketing policy as perceived by the customer. This form of signal serves as a substitute for inspection offers, i.e. access to the information good itself. Performance-related information substitutes serve to diminish insecurities with regard to a product's experience qualities. Information substitutes relating to all services are not meant to signal the quality of a specific product immediately, but point beyond the individual performance and signal that the provider is a provider of quality.

Information superhighway. Information infrastructure. In the U.S., there were in the 1990th programs for the construction of a national information infrastructure (NII) and for the global information infrastructure (GII). The programs were initiated by Al Gore. The political programs were goals for building the information society.

In-game advertising. A specific area of digital advertising. The player is not able to click away the ad.

Inspection offers. Making the information good, or parts thereof, available to customers in order to allow them to make a quality assessment.

Installed base. The installed base describes the number of users of a product or technology.

Intellectual property right. The right to one's intellectual property consists of commercial legal protection (technical protective rights: patents and utility models; non-technical protective rights: registered designs and trade marks) as well as copyright.

Internet TV. There are three options to integrate television and the World Wide Web: transmission of programs in real time, storage of TV programs and online access, creation of original programs for the internet.

Invisible Web *see* Deep Web.

J

Journal archive. Repository of all articles of a journal. There are two kinds: publisher-independent archives (e.g. JSTOR) and archives that are operated by publishing houses (e.g. Elsevier's ScienceDirect or SpringerLink).

Journal Impact Factor. Indicator for the evaluation of the importance of academic periodicals. The Impact Factor (first formulated by Garfield and Sher) takes into consideration both the number of publications in a journal as well as the number of these publications'citations.

K

Knowledge economy. According to Machlup, part of the economy which is based on intellectual activities, i.e., education, research and development, communication media, information machines, and information services (professional services such as law, engineering, accounts, medicine, finance, wholesaler, and government).

Knowledge society. A society that has all the aspects of an information society and in which information content (i.e. knowledge itself, as an additional basis) is available everywhere and anytime and in which life-long learning becomes necessary.

Knowledge worker. According to Machlup, Drucker and Porat, a worker who performs little manual, but "a lot of intellectual work" (Drucker). Knowledge work is accomplished in teams.

Knowledge infrastructure. Technical infrastructure in a knowledge society is joined by education, an adequate system of science and technology as well as a fully developed library system.

Kondratieff cycle. According to Nikolai Kondratieff, a long wave of business cycles (about 40 to 50 years) based on important technological innovations. Each Kondratieff cycle forms a typical network, e.g. shipping, rails, lines (electricity, gas), roads, internet.

L

Legal citation. Legal norms, cases, commentaries and specialist articles are interlinked via formal citations (tertiary legal information).

Legal information. Information on laws, regulations and judgments (primary legal information), law articles and commentaries (secondary legal information), and citation services (tertiary legal information).

Legal norm. Laws and regulations as primary legal information (for German law, e.g. legal norms of the European Union, Federal Law and laws of the 16 states).

Library consortium. In order to strengthen their negotiating power (licensing STM databases and literature), libraries join up and form consortiums, negotiating with publishers as a unit.

Lock-In. The binding of a customer to a product due to prohibitive switching costs.

M

Market data. Market and industry data can be found in information products such as market research reports, structure and industry information, stock market information and time series.

Media resonance analysis. Information compression of press articles concerning a topic (e.g., a company or a product name) over time.

Microblog. A very speedy medium for disseminating information in Web 2.0 (with the standard Twitter). The very short messages can be accessed via all kinds of mobile end devices.

MMORPG. Massively Multiplayer Online Role Playing Game. In these online video games, the players interact in a virtual world via their avatars.

Monitoring of companies. Searching for information of known companies (via the name of the company or its number in company databases).

M-commerce. Or mobile trade, which connects the online world with mobile telephony. E-Commerce with the use of mobile devices.

Moral hazard. Information asymmetries after the completion of the contract (e.g. via the programming of a software) bear a moral hazard, because the provider is able to exploit his scopes of action to his advantage.

Music service, commercial. Digital music (to be paid for) is offered by a content aggregator via WWW (iTunes has established itself as a standard).

Music sharing service. Platform for music in the Web 2.0 as well as an internet radio (Last.fm).

N

National license. License for a digital journal or a database for a whole nation, either for all citizens (e.g., in Iceland) or for all library users (partly at home, partly in the libraries; e.g., in Singapore).

Nearshoring. Shifting of internal activities to associated or foreign enterprises in neighboring countries.

Network. If the users are physically connected with each other, one speaks of real networks (e.g. telephone networks). If the users are not connected physically, but only logically, the networks are virtual (e.g. for all users of an iPhone).

Network Effects. One speaks of network effects when networks offer an additional value, the network effect value, via the number of their users (direct network effects) or the number of complements offered for a network good (indirect network effects).

Network goods. Network goods do not only provide a value via their qualities (basic value, original value) but also provide each user with an additional value that goes beyond the original one, called network effect value or derivative value.

New Economy. Conception of an economy with new "laws" based on "intellectual capital", which denotes the knowledge of a company. The notion of "intellectual capital" as an indicator for the company's value was misleading. Most of the market "success" of New Economy firms was not grounded in their intellectual capital, but in market-psychological circumstances caused by feelings of euphoria. Valuations of New Economy enterprises showed vast overestimations.

News information. Information products in news are press reports, press reviews and media resonance analyses.

O

Offshoring. Shifting of internal activities to associated or foreign enterprises in far-away countries.

Online advertising. Internet advertising has two goals: building up and maintaining a brand, on the other hand selling products via internet.

Online fraud. A deviant information behavior that refers to delinquency and can take the form of fraud on auction portals, Nigerian Letter Fraud, search engine click fraud and pishing (password fishing).

Online harassment. *see* Cyberharassment.

Online-host *see* Content aggregator.

Open Access. There are three approaches to grant customers free access to STM documents: The publisher carries the costs (golden road), the author pays for the publication (silver road) and authors or their institutions archive their documents themselves on their homepages (green road).

Outsourcing. Shifting of internal activities to foreign enterprises.

P

Patent family. All (more or less) content-identical applications and granted patents form a patent family, where the (chronologically) first patent is called the "basic patent".

Patent information. Patent and trademark offices of all major countries offer the totality of their documents for free usage available digitally.

Patent law. Patents are granted for inventions on all levels of technology, as long as they are new, based on an act of invention and are commercially applicable.

Peer review. Evaluation of manuscripts by assessors to decide any article's acceptability for publishing in a STM journal.

Piracy. The illegal appropriation of intellectual property by producing copies without any authorization by the rights holder.

Permission-based marketing *see* E-Mail advertising.

Population structure information. Comprehensive basic information on the population of single areas (e.g. household size, age of "heads" of household, their status, net income).

Preprint archive. Authors upload their manuscript directly after finishing it into an archive. ArXiv, focusing on high energy physics, offers free access to preprints as well as to the scripts of published articles.

Press report. Information on news via providers working with Topic Detection & Tracking (e.g., Google News), or via services using elaborate search tools (content aggregators).

Press review. Periodical compilation of press articles on any topic (e.g., on a company).

Privacy. The individual's privacy is threatened, in digital environment, by ongoing person-related information (e.g. name, age, gender) as well as digital traces. If people were at a disadvantage due to free access to "their" information, that information should not be freely available.

Problematic Internet Usage (PIU). Excessive and time-consuming internet consumption which correlates with the loneliness of the "patient".

Product information. Detailed representation of the products of a company.

Professional information ethics. Ethics regarding a certain profession, in our context information scientists and related jobs. Guidelines (laid down as "codes of ethics") regulate professional behavior by stipulating norms that information scientists should adhere to.

Prosumer. In web 2.0 services, the user acts both as producer of information and as its consumer.

Public good. The degree of a good's publicness can be determined, for information goods, via the two aspects 'principle of exclusion' and 'network effects'. If users can be excluded from consumption of the good, and if negative network effects are at hand, the good is private. If network effects are positive and there is no possibility of exclusion, it is a public good.

S

Sampling. This describes the possibility of getting to know new information goods, i.e. music, films, books, games etc., and listening to, watch, read or play them on a trial basis.

Scanning of companies. Searching for information of (unknown) companies via characteristics to spot new players on one's own market.

Search engine. Tool for searching and retrieving digital content. Development and maintenance of search engines is made by algorithmic means.

Search engine marketing. Providers of websites safeguard the visibility of their sites with the respective search engine market leader via search engine optimization (SEO) or content-specific advertising (sponsored search).

Search qualities. The quality features of a good that can be assessed prior to purchase via inspection.

Search engine optimization (SEO). The design of a website (text, entries in meta-tags, layout) in such a way that the algorithms of information linguistics and relevance ranking used in the search tool are able to correctly index the content of the site. There are on-site optimization (measures applied to one's own site) and off-site optimization (linking to one's own site in the context of the entire WWW).

Signaling. Companies can communicate with market participants via signals. Every company that is active on a market sends signals to the other parties via its behavior. Signaling provides the option of transmitting asymmetrically distributed information from the better-informed side of the market to its less-well-informed counterpart in order to provoke or prevent certain reactions. Signals always play a role when unobservable qualities or intentions are involved, and about which a credible statement must be made.

Social bookmarking service. In Web 2.0 prosumers' bookmarks are collected in one single platform. There are bookmarking in general (e.g., Delicious) and STM bookmarking services.

Social game. A digital game that is usually played via social networks (such as Facebook)–generally among friends.

Social network. User-specific personal profiles are recorded in Web 2.0 for communication with friends nurturing of social contacts; standard is Facebook.

Social software. Information services in which the prosumers form a virtual community. There are four classes: Sharing services, social bookmarking services, knowledge bases and social networks.

Software. Programs that can be run on hardware (generally a computer).

Software as a service (SaaS). Companies host application software and offer their services on a subscription basis.

Software development. Production of software. There are traditional specification-oriented models (cascade model and variants), risk-oriented models (e.g., the spiral model), scenario-oriented models (e.g., the simplified model), development-oriented models (e.g., the agile development model), and component-based development, which can be combined with one of the other models.

Sole provider. A sole provider creates a system offer, consisting of basic good and necessary complements, entirely under his own steam.

Sponsored links *see* Context-specific advertising.

Standard. A (communication) standard describes the totality of rules that represent the basis of interaction for people or machines. A standard creates compatibility.

Standardization. Standardization is a collective process of unifying interfaces, or protocols, in which a certain variant is chosen from a pool of possibilities and accepted, for a certain period of time, by a certain number of people.

Standards War. If several standards are in competition with each other and try to beat the respective others in order to become the dominant (industry) standard, one speaks of a Standards War.

Strategies of Standardization. Strategies of standardization relate to the competitors' access to a standard as well as its degree of compatibility with other products or systems.

STM bookmarking service. Big scientific publishers or independent institutions manage bookmarks of STM literature in Web 2.0 (e.g., BibSonomy, CiteULike or Connotea).

STM factual information. Information about facts (e.g. materials, gene sequences, inorganic and organic chemical structures and reactions). STM facts are intellectually extracted from publications and offered in domain-specific fact databases.

STM information. All documents and facts from science, technology and medicine.

STM information service. Bibliographical information services provide an overview about STM publications via their metadata. We distinguish between general scientific information services, discipline-specific information services and publisher databases.

STM market. There are three main groups of players: publishers, libraries and the scientists.

Stock market information. Information on prices of shares of listed companies.

Surface Web. Comprising all digital documents that are within the Web. Granting the access to the documents by search engines.

Switching costs. The costs that arise for the user of a product when switching providers. Switching costs contain all manner of impediments that make it harder, or even impossible, for a customer to switch from one provider to another.

System goods. System goods are in an immediate application relation with other products, which is taken into consideration by the customers prior to purchase.

T

Time series. Collections of numerical values, arranged according to time. Generally, economically oriented time series consider region, industry or product and an indicator (e.g., prices or market volumes).

Trademark law. Protection of brands, indications of sources and terms (company labels and work titles).

U

Underprovision Hypothesis. Decreasing profits from sales of information goods make the impetus to create new information goods ever smaller, and the market is undersupplied.

Upwards Compatibility. Products or devices that are upwards compatible are also able to process the applications of a more recent product generation.

V

Value net. The value net is a model for analyzing industries and market, in which four groupings of players that surround a company are represented: suppliers, customers, competitors and complementors. It is called value net because it is assumed that the different agents are not merely in a competitive relation but are able to also create values together. The value net is particularly relevant for information goods due to its explicit incorporation of complementors.

Versioning. Performance-oriented form of second-degree price differentiation. In versioning, the customer can choose from different variants that have been generated from a first-copy and which are available to him all at the same time.

Vickrey auction. Auction form used with context-specific advertising, in which the winner does not pay the sum of his own offer but that of the bidder closest to himself.

Video game. A story is told and the player is allowed to participate actively in the events they depict.

Video sharing service. A platform for videos in Web 2.0, in which the prosumers can upload content (e.g., YouTube).

Viral marketing. Advertising on the Web that banks on mouth-to-mouth propaganda. The user plays an active role in information diffusion.

Virtual world. Digital imitation of a world with landscapes, characters etc., following an own economy. Examples are "World of Warcraft" and "Second Life".

W

Web 2.0. Hyperonym of "social software", the corresponding technical basis and the information-legally significant aspect of open access. These services in the World Wide Web are predicated upon the active participation of broad masses of users.

Weblog *see* Blog.

Wiki. Collaborative construction of a knowledge base in Web 2.0. It collects entries on concepts and entities, which can be modified at any point (e.g. the domain-spanning internet encyclopedia, Wikipedia).

Windowing. In windowing (second-degree price differentiation), a finished information good, like a film or a book, is brought onto the market in different forms (cinema, DVD or hardcover, softcover) at different times (exploitation window). High-priced offers (e.g. films in the cinema) can be found at the beginning, low-priced or free offers (e.g. screenings in free TV) at the end of the exploitation chain. The basis of this is customers' willingness to pay, which is high at the beginning and low at the end.

Index of Names

Subject Index

CPSIA information can be obtained
at www.ICGtesting.com
Printed in the USA
LVOW01*2037250417
532155LV00010B/77/P

9 783110 236095